ABOUT
THE NEW YORKER
AND ME

A Sentimental Journal

Books by E. J. Kahn, Jr.

GEORGIA: FROM RABUN GAP TO TYBEE LIGHT

THE AMERICAN PEOPLE

THE CHINA HANDS

FRAUD

THE BOSTON UNDERGROUND GOURMET (with Joseph P. Kahn)

THE FIRST DECADE

HARVARD: THROUGH CHANGE AND THROUGH STORM

THE SEPARATED PEOPLE

A REPORTER IN MICRONESIA

THE WORLD OF SWOPE

THE STRAGGLERS

A REPORTER HERE AND THERE

THE BIG DRINK

THE MERRY PARTNERS

THE PECULIAR WAR

WHO, ME?

THE VOICE

MCNAIR: EDUCATOR OF AN ARMY

G.I. JUNGLE

THE ARMY LIFE

ABOUT
THE NEW YORKER
AND ME

A Sentimental Journal

E. J. Kahn, Jr.

G. P. PUTNAM'S SONS · NEW YORK

Library of Congress Cataloging in Publication Data

Kahn, Ely Jacques, 1916–
  About The New Yorker and Me.

  Includes index.
  1. Kahn, Ely Jacques, 1916–
2. Journalists—United States—Biography.
3. The New Yorker (New York, 1925–   )
I. Title.
PN4874.L25A32   1979   070′.92′4 [B]   78-11497
ISBN 0-399-12300-8

PRINTED IN THE UNITED STATES OF AMERICA

For Terry, Joey, Tony, David,
Lexy, Jaime, and Ian

January 1, 1977

I am one of those people who rarely watch news programs on television—though Ellie says my liking for televised sports is obsessive—and who never believe anything has actually happened until they see it on paper, preferably in the New York *Times*. Thus, in spite of the bang-up birthday party that Ellie gave me on December 4th, and in spite of all the flattering speeches there by my relatives and friends, I didn't really believe I had turned sixty until I read that in cold print the other day in *Harvard* magazine. It seemed like a good time of life, if perhaps a bit late, to start keeping a diary. When I see what I am thinking about in writing, I may be convinced it is true.

I started keeping a diary once before, in 1969, the painful, eventful year during which I was divorced from Jinny, married to Ellie, and separated from N. I stopped a month later, partly because Ellie said a diary, or journal, or whatever that was and this is, has to be something you can hide. I don't like secrets. In lieu of a diary, I was wont, in my first marital incarnation, to hold long private talks—rather, of course, monologues—with my Labrador retriever, Barge. A Labrador is an ideal vehicle for the repository of confidences, being large, warm, soft, patient, and taciturn. E. says one should use a diary the way one might, in other circumstances, use a Labrador retriever. She keeps her own diary, a conventional handwritten one, concealed beneath other unmentionables in a dresser drawer. I have read some of it. If I intended this to be an utterly secret diary, I would entrust to it my reaction to hers, but I have not even discussed that with Rainbow, our incumbent house pet, who is a cross between a Border collie and a Belgian shepherd.

Rainbow was given her name by Lexy, my younger stepson, when he was eleven, for no ascertainable reason, inasmuch as she, like Barge, and like New Zealand athletic teams, is all black. Sometimes when I am bemused or have drunk too much I call Rainbow "Barge." Sometimes, when it comes to that, I call Ellie "Jinny." I suppose after a twenty-four-year first marriage and a second one of only eight to date, that sort of thing is bound to happen occasionally.

Lexy, like most of my acquaintances, calls me Jack. There have been one or two who fancy "Jackie," and, since I use my initials professionally, there have been others—strangers seeking instant intimacy—who have guessed at "Ed," and, once, "Jay." The New York *Journal-American*, when *I* was about eleven, made it "John." I was up at the old Yankee Stadium one afternoon, hanging around with my autograph book during pre-game batting practice, when a photographer assigned to take a promotional picture for a Hearst project called the Just So Kids Club asked me if I'd mind his shooting me shaking hands with Lou Gehrig. Would I mind! It was one of those don't-wash-your-hand-for-a-week moments. When the photographer asked me my name, I said "Jack Kahn." That was too informal for the *Journal-American* caption writer, who was not only mistaken but inconsistent: He didn't call Gehrig "Louis."

The E. J. stands for "Ely Jacques." When I began writing, forty-odd years ago, and needed a byline, I elected to use the initials because my father, the architect, used "Ely Jacques Kahn" and I didn't want to poach on his nomenclatural preserve. The New York *Times* is worse than the *Journal-American* was. When Joey, my second son, got married, too, in 1969, I wrote out a wedding story, describing myself as "E. J. Kahn, Jr.," and had it hand-delivered to the society editor. The item was published as I'd sent it in, except that the *Times* changed me to "Elias J. Kahn, Jr." An exclusive. My oldest son, Ely Jacques Kahn III, has been known since birth as Terry. From the Latin *tertius;* I took four years of Latin and seven of Greek and was determined to have some permanent reminder of my classical upbringing. After my father died, at eighty-eight, in the summer of 1972, I could of course have dropped the "Jr.," but since I had been using it so long as a byline I elected not to, persuading myself that there were ample precedents—John D. Rockefeller, Jr., for instance, and my college classmate, Franklin D. Roosevelt, Jr. Terry accordingly kept his "III," except one summer when we were both listed in the Cape Cod telephone directory, he appearing first as an unadorned "E. J. Kahn" and I tagging along with my "Jr." Since of the two Kahns in the book the first one appeared to be the older, I got a good many of his calls, some of them quite bizarre. I also once got a letter from Harrod's, in London, addressed to Mr. E. G. Kahn. "We are writing to tell you we have received the tapestries," it went, "and they will be made into slippers as you requested." E. G. Kahn, whoever he was, was out of my class.

8

For my fifty-third birthday, when Lexy was seven, he painted me a picture. His brother David, then nine, gave me a photocopy of a school composition about butterflies. (For my sixtieth, he gave me a pornographic T-shirt; kids grow fast.) I gave each boy a dollar. Lexy threw himself into my lap, saying, "I never had a father before who gave me a dollar. I *love* you." Everybody knows love can be bought, off any sex at any age. My own father, who was eighty-five that December and had not long before had major surgery, paid me a birthday call, except that he came one day too early. It was his first visit to the duplex apartment E. and I live in, and he wanted to go upstairs and look around. My stepmother demurred, and I didn't encourage him, visualizing Ely tumbling down while I tried inexpertly to stem his fall. We pronounce Ely "*Ee*-lye," rather than the usual "Eely." He was supposed to have been named after the Old Testament elder, but the story goes that whoever filled out his birth certificate couldn't spell.

I have been a bear on spelling all my life, and whenever I have taught writing classes have tried—in vain, for the most part—to inculcate in my students a similar reverence for orthography. Twenty-five years or so ago, when I was living in Scarborough, up in Westchester County, I often worked at home. During a flu epidemic, there was a shortage both of teachers and substitute teachers at the Scarborough Country Day School, which my boys attended. Inasmuch as I was chairman of the board of trustees, the headmaster thought he could call on me for anything, and he phoned one morning and said he had absolutely nobody to take the fifth grade, and would I fill in? I drove over and asked the class what was on the agenda that morning. Spelling, they said. Splendid! I said, and what kinds of words were they supposed to spell? Vegetables, they said. We went through pea, bean, beet, and the like, without trauma, but when I worked my way up to artichoke and cauliflower they protested; they said those were *sixth*-grade words.

I next asked if they all read the daily papers. Oh yes, they chirped in unison. Fine, I said, everybody to the blackboard and write out a word you have all seen incessantly in the headlines—"Khrushchev." None of them got it right, but it occurred to me while they were trying, all muttering with indignation at my unfairness, that the school, although a private one, did receive some federal funds, and what might be the upshot if some McCarthy-minded parent stuck his head in the door at that moment and discerned what I was up to? Spell "Eisenhower," I quickly ordered. None of them got that right, either. I concluded that they probably watched the news on television.

Anyway, when my father arrived for my birthday, a day early, he brought a gift-wrapped bottle of Canadian Club—conceivably a present someone had given him on a prior anniversary. Or could it be, I wondered, that he really didn't know that I never drank whiskey? Did I know that little

9

about my own sons' tastes? Still, Dad remembered, which was better, that time around, than two-thirds of my three oldest sons did. If this were a secret diary, I would disclose which two among Terry, Joey, and Tony forgot.

Come to think of it, how much do I know about my father? Not long ago, I received a questionnaire from a woman who was writing a graduate thesis about him and his work and hoped I could fill some gaps in *her* knowledge. "Did Mr. Kahn play a musical instrument?" was one question. Not so far as I know, but can I be sure? "How significant was his interest in music?" I don't recall his ever saying anything emphatic *against* music, but on the positive side all I can think of is that one of his sisters sort of used to collect classical musicians, socially.

"How did the Depression affect the work of his firm?"

That one I can answer with assurance. "Disastrously." The firm shrank from more than one hundred employees to one—my father. But as to when he visited Frank Lloyd Wright at Taliesin West—why, I didn't know he had.

Since I am now sixty, I can tell by fifth-grade arithmetic that 1977 will mark the fortieth anniversary both of my graduating from Harvard and going to work for *The New Yorker*—rites of passage only a few days apart. (*The New Yorker* likes to have its "the" capitalized; that was the case long before the advent of *New York* magazine, which I have spent more time than I care to think about in the last several years explaining I am not connected with.) The magazine does not celebrate longevity, but the college has already begun preparations for the reunion of what we men of '37 call The Working Class. I forget the origin of the phrase; it probably had something to do with our being turned out into the world at the tail end of the Depression. *The New Yorker* paid me twenty-five dollars a week at the start, and I was glad to have it.

I never learned much at Harvard, academically, and never had much to do with the institution until I had been out of it twenty-five years. I went there too young, I suspect, having finished high school at sixteen. Or maybe I learned too much too soon. Recently, I came across a report card from Horace Mann High made out in my name, indisputably, and dated October, 1931. I got 97 in Greek and German, 96 in Math, and 94 in Latin, but in English—the only one of these subjects I have ever put to sustained use—a mere 88. Hmm.

I found the report card in an old baby book my mother assembled for me, nestling alongside a note from Harold Ross to St. Clair McKelway, written, I deduce, soon after I joined *The New Yorker*. "Kahn's piece on the Hotel Astor & the Cornell graduates pretty darned good," the editor was advising the managing editor. "I didn't have to do much to it in copy & it was a resourceful job of reporting I think." Nice to hear at any time, but what was the piece? And how did it get into my baby book?

I weighed seven pounds nine ounces at birth, my mother diligently noted for the record. She wrote further that I was born, at home, at 10:30 A.M., and that—this she put in, she said, for the benefit of my future wife—her labor pains began, at five-minute intervals, after dinner the previous evening. Her obstetrician, accordingly, slept at our apartment that night, but on examining Elsie in the morning said I wouldn't arrive until noon and went off on other business. When I crossed him up, my mother said, my father—now I *am* learning something about him—"displayed great calmness in spite of this unexpected adventure, and distinguished the occasion by giving ether, in ridiculously small doses, to himself and to me with equanimity and impartiality."

My second grandson was born at home, too, last year—in our Cape Cod house at Truro. Like most old Cape houses (ours dates back to about 1820), it had a borning room, to which the materfamilias would retire when her pains began; but when we bought the place, in 1953, we had the borning room converted into a bathroom. So Ian was delivered in what used to be the parlor—where doctors and preachers would sit during formal visits—and I guess we could legitimately call that a borning room now if we cared to. As my father had solely attended his son's birth, so did my son Tony lend a lone hand at his son's. This skipping of a generation while carrying along family traditions is positively Mendelian.

It was easy to get into Harvard in the fall of 1933; practically anyone could whose parents could, in those bleak days, afford the tuition, which was some ridiculously low figure like four hundred dollars. Harvard has figured importantly, though, in my last fifteen years. Terry and Joey both went there, and in addition to serving on my class committee and working on shows for the quinquennial reunions of 1962 and 1972 (there will no doubt be another Working Class Extravaganza this coming June), I was a director of the Associated Harvard Alumni for one three-year term, and I wrote a book about the university. The project began as a *New Yorker* series, and that was a break for me because Jinny and I were separated and I was able both to live and work in Cambridge during the 1967–1968 school year, with Terry and Joey on campus as an added attraction. I was granted library, squash-court, and faculty-club privileges (I never ordered the horsemeat that used to be a tradition of the club's menu), attended numerous classes in random disciplines, and probably learned a good deal more than I ever had as an undergraduate.

After buying a series of articles I wrote about Harvard, though, the magazine never ran them—in part, I suspect (one never knows for sure), because campuses were exploding all over the country and Bill Shawn, our editor, felt that I was mistaken in my general thesis that Harvard, then a third of a millennium old, would weather the storms that were rocking its particular serenity. I wasn't so certain about my thesis myself. The book version of my reportage had been set up in type when, in April, 1969, some disaffected students occupied University Hall and threw out the dean of students, who happened to be the First Marshal of our class, Bob Watson. I heard the news by radio while sitting in a dentist's chair. (If other people want to be kept electronically informed, that's all right with me.) I decided the book needed some revising, hopped out of the chair, grabbed a taxi, and took the Eastern shuttle to Boston. Jules Leaf had been looking after my teeth for nearly twenty-five years, and he knew I would be back sooner or later. Jules is an understanding man, though he keeps nagging at me for smoking too much.

I got even once. He turned up in Tokyo while I was on an assignment there, and he asked me to show him around town one night. We ended up at one of those enormous Japanese night clubs where one hires hostesses to dance with, and orders them by number, like Chinese food. My dentist, like me, was enchanted by the variety of choices on the *carte*. Trying to decide which of a couple of dozen beauties assembled behind us he would invite to our table, he leaned too far over backward and toppled to the floor. As he was going down, I noticed that, in the heat of the chase, he had lit two cigarettes and was holding one in each hand. "Jules, you're smoking too much," I said.

When I got off the shuttle, I took a taxi to the Harvard Yard, which was in a state of turmoil. There was some kind of secular protest meeting in progress at the Memorial Chapel, and as I approached its crowded steps the first familiar face I spotted was that of my son Terry, then finishing his senior year. "I knew you'd be coming, Dad," he said, handing me a sheaf of paper, "so I took some notes for you." I sensed then that he would probably become a journalist himself, and he did.

I still meet Harvard alumni who tell me how much they liked my book "Harvard," and some of them say they bought multiple copies to give to their fathers or uncles or whomever. The final sales figures, when the book eventually went out of print, did not exactly jibe with these hearty asseverations. I was not surprised. An author who has had more than a couple of books published—I am up to twenty, depending on how and what you count—can usually tell by publication day whether or not a book is going to take off. Somebody told me once that a girl arriving at a dance can glance around the room and know intuitively if the evening's going to be a success or failure. It is much the same with books. An author (I prefer "writer," but *The New Yorker* calls its writers "authors" and there are, after all, the Authors Guild and the Authors League of America to support its view) can walk by Brentano's or Scribner's and sense without slackening his pace that if he were to venture inside and ask a clerk for his book he would be met with a blank stare. In the case of "Harvard," I suspected the worst when, on publication day, I received a congratulatory telegram from my publisher, which had the ring of halfheartedness. (It was not even on yellow paper tucked in an envelope, but was a grey sheet recognizable as the handiwork of Western Union solely by its mistakes in spelling.) I could visualize somebody filling out a form at the publishing house: "I know it's sentimental but all of us at———wish you all success on publication day of your fine book '———.' " At least it wasn't a singing telegram.

A couple of hours later, I did wander into Brentano's, affecting the air of casualness that authors, writers, use on such occasions, and didn't find my book at all until I reached the education department, where a solitary copy was on display, dwarfed by a mountain of specimens of Dr. Haim Ginott's "Between Parent and Child." Brentano's doesn't think I write books for the general reader. It exhibited a biography I once wrote of Herbert Bayard Swope under "Business," and a book about South Africa under "Sociology."

According to a letterhead I saw just last week that has been printed in connection with the fortieth-reunion contribution of the Class of '37 to the Harvard College Fund, I am in charge of Special Gifts. That's odd, because in any fund drive the chairman of Special Gifts is supposed to be somebody who can match anybody else's pledge, and whereas we have by now a slew of chairmen of the board and presidents of banks and other large corporate entities, I am a non-salaried writer. I probably couldn't even match the classmate who is a maître d' at a gambling joint in Las Vegas. I think I got the title because I was only half listening when a classmate—now, like so many members of the Working Class, retired—phoned me on Cape Cod last summer just a couple of hours before E. and I were off to Europe with David and Lexy and asked me to help raise money. I said I had only a moment to talk and would be happy to do whatever he wanted me to. One should be careful about signing blank checks.

One of the purposes of that transatlantic jaunt was to give the boys a chance to travel on a ship, which for me has always been one of the noblest experiences imaginable. I was lucky in my childhood because my indulgent maternal grandparents twice took me by boat—in the nineteen twenties, there was no alternative—to Europe, and I have happy memories of shipboard life, notwithstanding that during a North Sea cruise a seagull once saw fit to relieve itself squarely on my head. When Terry, Joey, and Tony were young, Jinny and I once took them to Europe by ship, and because we thought they might never again have that chance, we laid it on big and travelled first class on the *Ile de France*. At the swimming pool bar one morning, while I was having a Bloody Mary, I was joined by another man in bathing trunks, and we fell into conversation. He was a delightful, witty chap, especially after our third drink, and when we parted I suggested that he reune with my wife and me for another round before dinner that night. When he arrived at the appointed bar, now of course fully dressed, he turned out to be wearing the splendid purple regalia of a monsignor of the Catholic Church.

Ellie and I couldn't find a boat to take us all to Europe last summer, but we did manage a one-week Greek-island cruise. She decided she wanted to buy a house on Santorini, which brings the number of places she wants to have houses in to about seven. It's too bad she isn't married to an authentic chairman of Special Gifts.

We are spending the New Year's holiday at West Cornwall, Connecticut, where E. is absolutely determined to buy a house someday. For the last five years, we have been renting here, to be close, in wintertime, to ski slopes. There is no skiing on Cape Cod, and anyway our Truro house is too long a drive away for weekend jaunts, and besides Tony and his Judy and their Ian are living in it. E. and David and Lexy like to ski, though I abandoned the sport years ago, out of fear and cowardice. Lexy, indeed, has been diffident about returning to the slopes ever since he broke *his* leg skiing in Vermont, on Christmas Eve a year ago. E. stayed with him that night at the hospital, and to cheer her up on that blighted holiday I brought her a bottle of wine. When I came back the following morning she seemed the more woebegone of the two of them; it had developed that the hospital, though equipped with first-rate orthopedic facilities, didn't have a corkscrew.

I had broken my leg skiing in Westchester County, way back in 1947, and had tried once or twice after that to take up the sport again, but every time I found myself poised to go down a hill I would chillingly anticipate being removed from it, in a splint, by a sled. When my tibia and fibula had snapped, I had asked to be taken to the Ossining, New York, hospital, since it was close to my Scarborough house, and I figured it would be easier for Jinny to visit me there and bring me presents. On arriving at the hospital, we discovered that there were no private rooms available and that the surgery that my leg required couldn't be done till the following morning. So I was trundled into a ward, with my unset leg in a basket, the toes sticking straight up. I couldn't sleep well, and was thus an interested spectator—the ward orderly was a sound sleeper—when an addled old man struggled out of the restraining bars around *his* bed and began to wander around the room. Standing next to me, he lost his balance, reached out for what he apparently thought was a bedpost, and seized my upthrust foot. My screams awakened even the orderly.

I spent three months in a cast, which was especially frustrating because at the time of my misadventure I had all but completed my research on a Profile I was doing for *The New Yorker* on Eleanor Roosevelt, and I wanted to start writing it. When I was finally able to get about the house on crutches, I phoned Mrs. Roosevelt's secretary and wondered if I could arrange one last interview. I was invited to lunch at Hyde Park. Jinny was teaching school and couldn't drive me, so I recruited my longtime friend, Bruce Bliven, Jr., and we set forth on a fierce winter day. The few steps leading up to Mrs. Roosevelt's front door were coated with ice, and the effort of negotiating them on my crutches was so intense that my hostess took one look at me and suggested that before her remaining guest arrived—Mrs. Roosevelt was always too busy to do only one thing at a time—I lie down on her living-room couch and catch my breath. I did, placing my crutches alongside me, and apologizing for my decrepitude, which, I was bound to confess, had been all my fault: I had crossed my skis, at the bottom of a beginner's slope, while travelling at a speed of perhaps two or three miles an hour. Mrs. Roosevelt began to explain that her other lunch guest was a distinguished leader of world Judaism—the septuagenarian former chief rabbi of Berlin, who had somehow miraculously survived an especially nasty concentration camp. She was at that point in her narrative when the chief rabbi was ushered in, looked at me, and, interrupting her eulogy of him, strode across, grabbed one of my hands in both of his, and exclaimed, "Ah, a real hero!"

We hung around the house at West Cornwall most of the day yesterday, waiting for a New Year's Eve party invitation (the Sandy Joneses always give a big one), and when none was forthcoming we took the kids to Bantam to see "Lawrence of Arabia," and toasted ourselves with champagne back at the house. A strange community, West Cornwall, very clubby, social sets within sets, the Van Doren clan dominating them all. We know most of the people in most of the sets—we have joined the little country club where they converge in summertime to swim and play tennis—but we don't seem to belong to any of them. We dined tonight at the C.s', who celebrated New Year's at the P.s', but we didn't feel too bad about that, because we didn't even know they were having a party. I told my downfall-of-the-British-Empire story, about how my London tailor lost my good tweed jacket, and on the way home Ellie chided me for doing so; she says it is a boring story. The trouble is she has heard it before. Driving back to our place, too, we saw four deer cross the road under a full bright moon. A nice way to start the new year.

January 2

At the dump this morning, Sandy Jones wishes me what seems like an excessively hearty Happy New Year. Guilt? He is depositing a vast trove of empties in the bottle bin. I toss in our solitary champagne bottle. Back at the house, I should be concentrating on the Profile I am writing about Cyrus Eaton—he was ninety-three last week, and the reasons for haste are obvious—but instead I pick up the "John McPhee Reader." McPhee is, in my envious view, the best non-fiction writer *The New Yorker* has. It was characteristic of the frailty of the supposedly non-fictional account of the magazine and its contributors written not long ago by Brendan Gill, who has been on West Forty-third Street about the same length of time as I have, that John is nowhere mentioned in the book. The "McPhee Reader" has a preface by William L. Howarth, a Princeton professor of English with whom John and Alan Williams and I once played squash doubles in New Jersey. I never could quite get the hang of that variation of the game, nor am I sure that I altogether grasp Howarth's analysis of McPhee's convoluted work habits. These seem to involve chopping up his research into fragments, tacking them to a bulletin board, and throwing darts at the impaled facts. John's squash is straightforward and first-rate.

I have never submitted my own professional modus operandi to an efficiency expert, and wouldn't dare. But one gets locked into one's ways of functioning. I bought an expensive tape recorder last year, thinking I would use it for notes, or even for interviews, but I haven't touched it once. I will probably go on for the rest of my life doing what I have always done—taking notes by hand, typing them up as soon afterward as possible (on out-of-town assignments that generally means arising at five or six and getting the previous day's accumulation out of the way before filling a few more notebooks), and, when it comes to actual writing, indexing the notes first, as one might index a book. Time-consuming, but for me it works. When I was teaching at Columbia, one of my students wanted to know how anybody could ever face up to the prospect of writing a whole long book. It was easy, I said offhand, and I still think the answer was a good one: You put yourself in the position of a person about to cross the Atlantic by rowboat. Rowing for three thousand miles is too awful to contemplate, but if you have a good pair of hands you ought to be able to knock off fifteen miles a day. So it is with a book: You do your fifteen miles a day, or the equivalent in words thereof, and after a couple of hundred days you've reached the other shore. McPhee is in better shape than I am; he could probably get there faster.

Back in New York from Cornwall, this evening, I try to catch up with almost a week's worth of the New York *Times*. In the December 30th crossword, one definition was "Cyrus's clan," and the answer was "Eatons." A reminder to me to go back to the oarlocks? Another *Times* had a sad obituary—the life story of a photographer who had been on the paper's staff for forty-nine years, and who just once in that awesome span travelled as far as Thule, Greenland, on a Sunday magazine assignment. A not very far-ranging journalist.

For the last few years, I have always turned to the obit page of the *Times* first—even before sports. If the average age of all the people who have died above the center fold of the page (lesser lights do not count in this reckoning) is higher than my age, I believe I am going to have a good day. Whenever Cyrus Eaton goes, I will be sorry to learn about it, but he will bring the average up nicely.

Ellie wants to buy an unfinished house in Cornwall, which we could then finish ourselves. I fear that in the end that would be no different from building a house from scratch, and I have done that once, in Scarborough, and once was enough. Even though my father designed it and had people from his firm supervising the job, it was a rough experience, and in eighteen years we never did get a sewage-disposal system that worked satisfactorily. Anyway, what would we buy a house *with*? At the C.s' the other night, the conversation dwelt for a while on the difficulty of living, these days, on eighty thousand a year. E. and I spent a good deal ourselves last year, and for what? Where can we cut down? Find a less expensive hotel for Rainbow to stay at when we travel?

Jimmy Carter will be inaugurated this month. It's interesting to reflect how strangely tranquil the period has been between Election Day and this moment. Nothing bad has happened, really. President Ford has all but disappeared from the news, much as the snow has vanished from the Colorado slopes toward which he is presumed to be heading. True, Elizabeth Taylor got remarried and a scandal has been brewing involving certain congressmen and South Korea, but some of the accused legislators will not be returning to Washington in any event; and, whatever may be revealed, it is going to surprise no one that President Park's government is capable of shenanigans and has a lot of money. The fact that the Reverend Moon has taken over the defunct Columbia University Club, right across Forty-third Street from *The New Yorker* offices, has scarcely ruffled our neighborhood, though I suppose if he were to take over Columbia University that might be something else again.

All in all, these past couple of months have been characterized by an eerie stillness, like the eye of a hurricane. The first hurricane I ever got caught in the eye of was on Cape Cod. Edmund Duffy and I were having a drink and we didn't know about eyes; we thought the storm was over, and went down to Ballston Beach to look at the surf, and barely made it back indoors safely.

January 3

A letter from Davies & Son, in London, today, about my missing tweed jacket, with a reference to "this awful mistake."

At an egg-nog party last week, I ran into my old friends the Bob Lows, who said that their eighteen-year-old son, Roger, has dropped out of school but that they were hard-pressed to complain about that, inasmuch as he is self-supporting. Roger makes his living at backgammon, and he will be leaving tomorrow for Nassau, to play in the Philip Morris World Championship Invitational Tournament. It is the equivalent of the Masters on the golf circuit. I am going, too, though Ellie, who is Scotch Presbyterian on her father's side, disapproves and refuses to accompany me to Paradise Island. George Gianis—S. George Gianis in the phone book—got me my invitation. "A man with your luck ought to be in the world championship,"

17

George had said not long before when I took sixty-four dollars off him by throwing an incredibly fortuitous double-six, and he had taken the appropriate steps. He will be there himself. George has played in big tournaments before—Monte Carlo, Biarritz, Abidjan, I forget which all glamorous arenas—but even with run-of-the-mill dice I can hold my own with him in the daily Harvard Club chouette game, which begins at noon and, although I am rarely on the premises in the evening, apparently goes on until whenever it is that the club closes. I went over at lunch today, for a last practice session, and lost sixty dollars in a dollar-a-point game. Roger Low, his parents told me, never plays for less than a nickel—that is, five dollars a point.

I started playing backgammon with my father when I was a kid, but never took up the game seriously until a couple of years ago. At the Harvard Club, the two point is known as the Gianis Point, because George never fails to make it when he throws an early six-four. A double-five used to be known as the Milton throw, because there was a lawyer named Milton (I know he was a lawyer because his checks had "Counsellor-at-Law" printed on them) who threw more double-fives than anyone else within modern memory. There was talk of proposing him for inclusion in the "Guinness Book of World Records." It developed after a couple of years that nobody had ever proposed him for membership in the Harvard Club, and that when he signed chits he signed the name and account number of his son-in-law. One day the club learned—conceivably by means of a phone call from Milton's daughter's aggrieved husband—that Milton was an imposter, and he was barred from the premises. That was too bad, because his checks never bounced, and because there were many times when in a chouette game we had desperate need of a man who could coax dice, even by talking to them, to produce a double-five.

It costs $150 to enter the Nassau competition, but George says there will be ample prize money—some of it from the proceeds of an auction pool—and several opportunities to dip into some of it: a first consolation tournament, a second consolation tournament, and a last chance. Moreover, one can always play for fun, or for money, on the side; and the very last chance for unlucky backgammon players will be provided right in the Britannia Beach Hotel, where the action is taking place, by its casino, which is open seventeen hours a day. My only problem is that the finals in all events will take place on January 9th, and I have to be in Athens, Greece, that day.

Well, I don't *have* to be, but the Greek Embassy in Washington phoned me last week and invited me to attend, as the home government's guest, a ceremony on the Acropolis, in the course of which the director general of UNESCO, M. Amadou-Mahtar M'Bow of Senegal, is going to call upon the nations and peoples of the earth to help save the Parthenon and its adjacent shrines from destruction. I thought it might make a nice Talk of the Town story, and Shawn concurred. *The New Yorker*, though, has a commendably strict policy against letting its reporters accept free transportation or lodging or anything of that sort; if a story is worth covering, the rationale goes, it is worth our paying our own way. But a round-trip to Greece for a Talk story? Out of the question. Shawn and I discussed this sticky ethical situation, and he finally agreed that in this one special instance we could break our own rule. After all, nothing the host government could say or do or spend could sway us for or against the Parthenon. The magazine has few firm editorial viewpoints, but it is unequivocally pro-Parthenon.

But who was to pay my way to the Bahamas? Certainly not *The New Yorker*, which does not normally underwrite its representatives' hanging around gambling dens with the international sporting set. (A whole planeload of European toffs is coming to Paradise Island, George has advised me, including some of the London crowd from the Clermont Club, where he has witnessed backgammon played for two hundred *pounds* a point.) Up to last week, I thought I had, like pros on the golf tour, a sponsor. Patrick Smith, my brother-in-law, was going to stake me to the trip in return for a cut of my winnings; he has more confidence in me than I have. But Ellie would have none of that. Fortunately, I persuaded *Sports Illustrated* to let me try a piece for that magazine about my adventure, so—how rare for a gambler!—I can't lose. Lexy is furious. If the arrangement with Patrick had materialized, I had promised the kid he could be my manager and have ten percent of whatever I netted; now, all family deals are off.

Patrick and Betty, even though he can no longer be my patron, are allowed to treat us all to a farewell dinner tonight at some Czechoslovakian restaurant the Smiths have discovered. I was born on Manhattan Island and have lived on it for much of my life, but I never discover any restaurants and soon forget the names of the ones that others have ferreted out and let me in on. E. complains, rightly, that I never take her out to dinner. I never know where to take her out to. Also, the cost of eating out, except on an expense account, is getting preposterous. A Harvard classmate from whom I was trying to wrangle a Special Gift took me to lunch at some run-of-the-mill fish place the other day, and the cheapest entrée on the menu was eleven dollars. I stopped having lunch at the Algonquin when the chef's salad went up to something like seven-ninety-five. I got nothing from that Working Classman, conceivably because he couldn't afford it after picking up the tab for lunch. A more likely explanation was that, as he sulkily complained, Harvard had turned down both his son and daughter and, worst of all, the Harvard University Press had turned down his book. As you sow, so shall you reap. I stopped giving money to Andover when Tony dropped out of it.

January 4

George, whose wife is scheduled to arrive for the finals, picks me up this morning and pays for the cab out to Kennedy. I think he feels guilty. He gave me a tip on an over-the-counter North-Sea oil-drilling stock last year, and because I happened to have some cash at the moment I bought a few shares. Then the rig sank. We reach the airport in time for me to have a shoeshine, at which point I perceive that in my eagerness to join the international sporting set I have donned a pair of non-matching brown shoes. (I remember then that I have also forgotten to pack my sneakers; George had said there would be planty of time for tennis.) While I am visiting, and hastily leaving, the shoeshine stand, George is buying flight insurance; I have never purchased any, and indeed have never travelled before with anybody who did. What does he know that I don't?

Our plane is filled with backgammon players, many of them familiar to George, all unknown to me. They are uniformly pale—indoor types to a man, and woman. A young fellow introduces himself to me; he is the Lows' self-supporting dropout son. He has been doing so well at backgammon lately, he confides to me, that he is treating his brother to a trip to Nassau. Also his brother's girl. George, whose best performance at backgammon, he told me in the taxi, was during a Racquet-and-Tennis-Club chouette session when he won thirty-two hundred dollars in a single game, points out a woman seated up ahead, who, he says with awe, is reputed to have once lost a million dollars in a single evening. She could evidently afford it; plenty of jewelry left. George engages another passenger in chitchat, asking her, "What are you now—roulette or backgammon?" "Twenty-one," she replies. "I used to be roulette, but I couldn't sleep at night." I hope by the time I leave for Athens I will have learned the lingo. A fellow with whom I play occasionally in New York engages me in chitchat. "It's a new step for you— to leave the Harvard Club," he says.

There are half a dozen backgammon games in progress on the plane. Young Low, he tells me, has earned back his own air fare long before we touch down. "Some of the strongest players in the world are on this plane," he says. "If it goes down, backgammon will be set back ten years." Not George's widow, though, presumably. George asks me, while he and I play a couple of desultory games on my portable board, what I am into these days, and have I traded much in commodity futures. He himself has been selling cotton short. He points to a cluster of young men in a chummy chouette game near the galley, and warns me against taking them on, because they cheat. Each other, too? I wonder. "Oh, yes," says George. In the taxi transporting us to Paradise Island (previously known as Hog Island) he asks me if I believe in psychokinesis. I am obliged to admit that I don't know what it is. "Well, backgammon players are usually thinking about double-sixes or double-ones," George says. "So when they are shooting craps the chances are that these numbers will come up more often than according to the law of averages." I do not remind him of the last time he counselled me on investments.

When I pay my $150 entry fee at the tournament registration desk, the receipt I get has me down as "Khan." I have been taken for the Pakistani branch of the family before. Jinny and I went to Europe in 1949 at about the same time that, with much hullaballoo, Aly Khan married Rita Hayworth and honeymooned with her in Europe. Rita's hair was red then, and so was Jinny's. When we checked in at a Paris hotel, and routinely handed over our passports to the concierge, he glanced at the "Ely Kahn" on mine, and at my wife's tresses, and until our imposture was detected we were treated with more deference than I've ever enjoyed before or since.

Whenever I travel, I always buy all the local papers I can get my hands on, provided they are in a language I can comprehend. I pick up a copy of the Nassau *Guardian* in the Britannia Beach Hotel gift shop. There is nothing in it about the backgammon tournament, but the sports page has a three-column headline about a local *checkers* group preparing to take part in a championship to be held in Atlanta next *summer*. The backgammon players who have already arrived are scattered around the swimming pool, playing for nickels and dimes. Nobody takes time off to go into the water. Real addicts, like me, but then everybody has quirks. E., for instance, is an ice-cream addict: Her idea of heaven would be to find herself alone in a Baskin-Robbins shop and to consume the entire stock. At poolside, I see an elderly gentleman who is addressed as Ozzie. Could it be—yes, here comes a page seeking out "Mr. Jacoby." Oswald Jacoby in the flesh! He is in bathing trunks; plenty of flesh. I don't have the nerve to introduce myself to him. It was the same damnable diffidence that kept me estranged from Marilyn Monroe. I was writing a musical comedy with Joshua Logan in the mid-nineteen fifties, working with him one morning at his place in Connecticut, when he was summoned to the phone. "That's Marilyn," he said a moment later. "She wants to come over for lunch, but we don't want to be interrupted, do we?" Like a fool, I agreed; after all, Josh and I were supposed to be collaborating. The musical-comedy project foundered not long afterward, and I never did meet Marilyn Monroe.

Before dinner, during which the players in the championship flight are to be auctioned off, there is a cocktail party. I meet, seriatim, a hypnotist from Boston (I make a mental note to keep my eyes off his if we chance to compete), a woman who is covering the event for the German edition of *Playboy* (it once ran a story of mine that originated in the American *Playboy* —a piece of fiction about a man raffling off his wife, which I thought was funny but Jinny didn't), and a chap just off a plane from Acapulco, where yet another backgammon tournament is evidently under way. "Some little Mexican kid beat me in the first round," he is grumbling. During dinner, Barclay Cooke, who practically invented backgammon and at whose table I am privileged to be seated, makes a speech in which he enjoins the male contestants to wear shirts, pants, and shoes while playing in the tournament, and not to get into fights. Cooke is one of twenty-one seeded players who will be sold off separately in the auction. The rest of us, numbering some hundred and fifty, are grouped into fields. Cooke fetches $2,500. The field I am in goes, flatteringly, for $5,200, conceivably because the auctioneer, even more flatteringly, says, "E. J. Kahn's a newcomer but I understand he knows the game."

I have told the tournament director I can't be around for the finals if I get that far, and he said I didn't have to worry about that eventuality, but George is not so sure. "If you're the only one in your field left in the running, and you take off," he warns me, "with the kind of money up for grabs here, there'll be a contract out for you. Your life will be worthless." I realize what he means when it is announced that the total prize money, including the auction pool, will come to $191,795.00. If I leave while I am still in contention, I will be forfeiting a chance to win $56,000. The Harvard Class of '37 might never forgive me, either. In the casino, before turning in, I keep betting on the number of E.'s birthday at roulette and win back my air fare.

January 5

A lovely, warm, sunny day. New York, we have heard, is experiencing a dreadful cold spell. I stroll from the Britannia Beach over to the Ocean Club, where George is more luxuriously encamped, passing a Paradise Island Hotel laundry hamper on which someone has scrawled, "How long will you live in sin? Jesus is passing your way right now. Will you let him in?" Is backgammon a sin, and have I doomed myself to perdition? I find Jacoby and Cooke over there, and make bold to join them, hoping to pick up some pointers. But they are talking baseball exclusively, wondering if Wally Schang ever played center field. Ozzie, as I am quick to address him, gives a practically pitch-by-pitch account of the final inning of the 1911 World Series, which he witnessed. Back at the Britannia Beach, I find the pairings posted in the Grand Ballroom. I have drawn a bye in the first round, which automatically makes me, as I see it, one of the one hundred and twenty-eight best backgammon players on earth. I watch young Low, who has no bye, play his first-round match. He wins it, but there are no handshakes afterward; his opponent made an incorrect move and wanted to change it, but Roger, quite justifiably, refused, inasmuch as the other chap had already picked up his dice. I finally get to play in the second round, against a woman. It is a nineteen-point game, and I am ahead most of the way—6–1, 10–4, 13–9. She beats me, 19–18. Sixty-five years from now, will I remember the fateful five-four she threw—the only roll of the dice that could save her—as well as Ozzie Jacoby recalls the 1911 World Series?

Probably better; he was only a spectator. George, who was watching us, tells me that my conqueror is only a fair player.

At roulette, I play E.'s birthday number again, and lose the equivalent of two air fares, which makes it easy for me to resist temptation as I depart through the gauntlet of hookers waiting outside the casino. Their fee, it is said, is a flat hundred dollars, with no bargaining, and they belong to a union that enforces their pay scale. Unlike George, and most of my fellow players at Nassau, I do not normally carry hundred-dollar bills (or ones, in the local jargon), and it would be just my luck to latch onto a non-union whore and have another contract out on me. Moreover, the papers have been talking about a savage new strain of gonorrhea imported from the Philippines, and whenever I think about the Philippines I feel uncomfortable. I was doing some research out there fifteen years ago or so and needed the assistance of the Philippine Constabulary, the national police force. I had written the general in command of it that I was coming to Manila, and when I got there I phoned him. He invited me to join him that evening for dinner. When he picked me up at my hotel, he was in mufti, exhibiting no sign of his high rank save a jewel-encrusted swagger stick. We started off down Dewey Boulevard in his unmarked car at about ninety miles an hour, and were soon flagged down by a marked police car. Its occupants approached us from both sides, with guns drawn, at which point the general airily waved his swagger stick, and his pursuers melted away into the darkness. Did I like Chinese food? he inquired when we were under way again. Oh, yes, I said. We pulled into the courtyard of an unmarked establishment, and a gate clanged shut behind us. The place didn't resemble any Chinese restaurant I had seen, and indeed it wasn't. It was a brothel, to which the general, with hospitality that J. Edgar Hoover would probably never have indulged in, had seen fit to bring his honored guest for a pre-prandial appetizer.

January 6

I read in the *International Backgammon News* this morning that the woman who beat me won the ladies' tournament at Monte Carlo. So much for George and his opinions. The overall winner there was Joe Dwek, an Englishman whom George not long ago proposed for non-resident membership in our Harvard Club, and to whom I was introduced last night. Joe would probably find our lunchtime games too tame; he is a professional and wrote "Backgammon for Profit," a reputedly autobiographical work. When Dwek won at Monaco, according to the *I. B. News*, "for perhaps the first time, the august walls of the Monte Carlo casino reverberated to a Harvard 'Rah.' " Sounds as though it was written by a Yale man.

Going down to breakfast, I am joined in the elevator by a disheveled young lady in an evening dress. She seems to have lost her shoes somewhere. I am minded to say that she and I are in somewhat similar predicaments, but she does not appear to be the kind of woman with whom E. would encourage me to strike up an acquaintance. In the Grand Ballroom I am pleased to discover that in the First Consolation I have drawn another bye. So I join a friendly three-dollar chouette game with George and a couple of friends of his, and take them for $114. They have kept the stakes low at my behest; I should have gone along with their original proposal of a quarter game; I could have made the equivalent of a round-trip to Athens.

I win my first match in the First Consolation, thus advancing to the third round, but come a cropper—it took another five-four, a seventeen-to-one shot, for God's sake, to destroy me—against the editor of the *I.B.N.*; no disgrace for an amateur to lose to a pro. He doesn't deserve to win even with the five-four; earlier, he took a truly terrible double of mine, and lucked out. Well, at least I beat somebody, which is more than George has done.

January 7

The Second Consolation won't begin until tomorrow, it has been announced, so that means I am hors de combat, inasmuch as I have to leave then to fly back to Kennedy and connect with Olympic Airways in time to get to Athens and save the Parthenon. I bought some sneakers, figuring I'd spend the day playing tennis with George, but he jilted me for the reigning queen of the hour, a young woman who beat the young man who beat Paul Magriel, or X-22, as this computer-minded giant of backgammon likes to be known. I saw Magriel playing "22" at roulette last night. I had switched to craps, investing heavily, with psychokinetically disastrous results, on boxcars and snake eyes. Magriel is the author of the just-published "Backgammon," which the au courant here are already hailing as a classic in its genre. Twenty dollars. I bought a copy, needing change from a hundred-dollar bill I had picked up over at the Ocean Club from George's friends at lunchtime. Could there be something psychokinetic about everybody's beating me by throwing five-fours? I have always been short in stature, but not that short. I am five-*six*, damn it, or, as Dr. Bishop's otherwise nice nurse, Laura, keeps reminding me during my annual checkup, actually five-five and three-quarters.

January 8

"Delta is ready when you are," goes the current advertising slogan for that airline. To make my Athens flight, I have to go from Nassau to Miami and thence to New York. I think I have plenty of time, but Delta is an hour late leaving Florida, and then spends half an hour circling Kennedy in one of those holding patterns, with the result that I touch down ten minutes before my Olympic flight is scheduled to depart from another area of that sprawling airport. Fortunately, Olympic's 747, appropriately named—considering my mission—the Olympic Zeus, is itself an hour and a half behind schedule. None of that matters once we are airborne, for this is a nonstop, ten-hour flight to Athens. There is no wine aboard, and the meat is inedible. I feel new respect for *The New Yorker*'s anti-free-loading policy, for here am I, a non-paying guest, hardly in a position to complain. Aristotle Onassis would never have stood for it. The man sitting alongside me has a complaint, too, of which I am the principal recipient. His luggage has been mislaid at Boston or Hartford or some intermediate stagecoach stop. I try to make him feel better by telling him how I once had all my luggage mislaid by the United States Army, while I was flying from Kwajalein to Majuro, in the Marshall Islands. I didn't recover it for ten days. Pete Coleman, an affable Samoan who was then district administrator for the Marshalls and later became deputy high commissioner of the Trust Territory of the Pacific Islands, lent me some clothes and a toothbrush. He also put me up in the house of an American teacher who was off on home leave. In the bathroom my first morning, I reached for the toothbrush and was surprised to see it move, apparently of its own accord. Closer inquiry revealed a cockroach exactly the same dimensions as the toothbrush. The cockroach had evidently fallen in love with my only possession and was trying to carry it off to its lair.

Growing boys are entomologically inclined, and all five of my sons, at one time or another, have begged me to tell them insect stories. Their favorite is the one about the termites in Panama. As a soldier, I lived there for nearly a year during the Second World War, and lived very comfortably, since I was working for, and sharing the spacious quarters of, the major general commanding the American ground forces there. Some time in 1943, DDT was unveiled, and since the war was on the armed forces naturally had first dibs on it. They wanted to destroy malarial mosquitoes with it. Inasmuch as Panama was rich in mosquitoes, the army experimentally sent some DDT down there—a single bomb of the then scarce stuff. Since there was only one DDT bomb, it was naturally delivered to the highest-ranking officer. Our general brought it home from the office one evening when we were entertaining a stateside brigadier general down on one of those inspection trips without which many generals would hardly have a raison d'être. While we were having cocktails before dinner (one of my military duties was to make the martinis), the host-general noticed a termite crawling across one of the wooden beams that supported our living-room ceiling. He instructed me to test the newfangled bug-killer on that bug. An order is an order. I squirted a stream of spray upward, and the termite (I had duly earned my marksmanship medal in infantry basic training) fell to the floor. So did half a dozen others. My barrage had a side effect: Several dozen other termites emerged overhead. "Get them!" commanded the two-star general. "Over here!" barked the one-star general, furiously brushing at his bestarred shoulders. Within minutes, as I strove manfully to cope with the enemy's apparently unlimited reinforcements, thousands of termites were raining down upon us. The floor was an inch deep in termites. There were termites in the infuriated generals' hair, worse still, termites in their tumblers. Perhaps never before or since has the effectiveness of DDT been so uniquely demonstrated. The generals agreed not to court-martial me after I made them another drink in another room.

My seatmate on the plane is also concerned about whether or not he will be able to see the Super Bowl, which is being played tomorrow. He says he understands it will be transmitted live, by satellite, to Turkey, but he has some doubts about Greece. I try to make him feel better by saying there will be other Super Bowls, but there is only one Parthenon. I had sort of hoped to see the Super Bowl myself.

Today is N.'s birthday.

January 9

This is the second time in seven months that I have been in Athens. I had lunch with S. J. Perelman at the Century a couple of months ago, and Sid, who is over seventy, wondered why it was that younger writers don't seem to want to travel as much as he and I do. There are some at the magazine who rarely appear to venture beyond the eighteenth-floor soft-drink machine. Perelman and I had a fine time engaging in reciprocal name-dropping—place-name-dropping, that was. He has been to more places than I have, but then he is older, and he has never been to Kapingamarangi. I learned on arriving in Athens that there would indeed be no Super Bowl on Greek television; I learned also that Rupert Murdoch had bought both *New York* and the New York *Post*. There will be people around *The New Yorker* looking for jobs for sure. The UNESCO ceremony at the summit of the Acropolis has been scheduled for tomorrow morning, and I am glad I am scheduled to fly back home two days hence.

When we were in Athens late last June, a European heat wave was in full swing, and after visiting the Acropolis and the National Museum, David and Lexy, sensibly enough, refused to do anything else except go to the beach. We had five days left before our island cruise began. Then it occurred to me that I was due in Montreal the following month to cover the summer Olympics, a pleasant stint I have performed starting with the Tokyo Games in 1964, so we rented a car and drove to Olympia and back. We returned to Athens just two hours before the *M. V. Orion* was scheduled to sail from Piraeus. Our hired Fiat hadn't been able to hold all our luggage, so we had cached some of it at our hotel, and there wasn't much time to collect it, dispose of the car, and get aboard ship. When our bags were distributed between our cabins, Ellie realized that her big blue one, containing almost all her clothes, was missing. Shades of Majuro!

The gangplank was slated to go up in twenty-eight minutes. We had an assistant purser phone the hotel in Athens and, in his most urgent Greek, instruct the desk clerk to send an emissary to the dock, by taxi, with the big blue bag we'd left behind. Twenty-seven and a half minutes later, a bellhop, as if approaching Marathon, raced along our pier, clutching a blue suitcase, while the by-now alerted passengers and crew cheered him on. Only it was the wrong blue suitcase. The one the bellhop had may have belonged to my airplane seatmate, waiting at the Athens airport to board a charter flight to Istanbul to catch a rerun of the Super Bowl. Eventually we got E.'s bag back. She said it was amazing how little clothing a woman could get along with if she really had to.

This time, in Athens, the Greek government is putting me up at the elegant, old Grand Bretagne, on Constitution Square. (Room only, no meals or drinks, Shawn may be relieved to hear, and a smallish room at that.) There is a cocktail party for the international press at the hotel this evening. I find Professor Emily Vermeule, the distinguished Harvard classicist, among the other American junketeers. I chat with M. M'Bow, the UNESCO director general. This is his very first trip ever to Athens, though he has taught Greek history at the University of Dakar, in his native Senegal. Recalling from my one and only visit to Dakar, six years ago, that Senegal is a one-crop country, and that that crop is peanuts, I ask how he feels about Jimmy Carter's election. "For peanuts, I think that's very good," the director general says.

I have a drink with the Greek minister of culture, Constantine Trypanos, who taught Greek literature and language for thirty-two years at Oxford and the University of Chicago. He returned to Greece only after its colonels' government was deposed. (The relationship between culture and politics is an edgy one. My friend Talat Halman, who teaches Turkish literature at Princeton, was a few years back designated Turkey's first minister of culture ever, and departed for Ankara with the zeal of a whirling dervish. Six months later, the government he was a part of had been deposed, and he was back at Old Nassau.) I ask Minister Trypanos whether, in view of the interest UNESCO is about to whoop up over the Parthenon, there is any chance of Greece's getting back the Elgin Marbles. "I wish we could," he says, but adds that if they do the treasure will not be replaced *in situ*. "It's the sculptured parts that get the most damage from pollution," he says. The Acropolis, he goes on, is being ruined, ironically, by those who love it most: Some of the pollution has been attributable to the exhausts of tourist buses, and its stone walkways have been worn thin by tourists' feet, six million of these, now, every year.

I go to bed early and have a strange dream about playing backgammon with Bill Shawn on a Greek-islands cruise ship; he keeps throwing five-fours and winning all my money but he says afterward not to worry, that I can put it on my expense account.

January 10

A cold, grey morning, with fewer than two hundred people assembled on top of the Acropolis, in a drizzle of rain, for the big ceremony. M. M'Bow's speech was clearly prepared ahead, for he alludes in it to "incomparable Attic light," and the light today would compare unfavorably with that in the Lascaux Caves. Three diplomats from the People's Republic of China are among the spectators, conceivably laying the groundwork for a UNESCO-sponsored campaign to restore the Great Wall. M. M'Bow appeals to the conscience of the world to save the spot where we are standing, and specifically includes schoolchildren among those global groups from whom UNESCO hopes to obtain support. There is a delegation present of thirty girls from the Presbyterian Ladies College, of Melbourne, Australia, and I ask one of them, who says they are on hand this historic morning purely by chance, whether she and her comrades plan to respond to the director general's impassioned appeal. "I guess we'll support it," she replies, "but we don't know what we're supporting, exactly."

I dine with Steve and Cokie Roberts, at a fine Greek restaurant with a Turkish cuisine, the name of which I promptly forget. Cokie is the daughter of the late Congressman Hale Boggs, of Louisiana, who disappeared while in a plane over Alaska, and of the incumbent Congresswoman Lindy Boggs, his widow. Steve is the resident New York *Times* correspondent. I make a point of looking up the area *Times* men when I am abroad; they are usually knowledgeable and hospitable. I have never met Steve before (he was in Turkey or somewhere last summer), but he and I have a common bond; we were both, though at different times, directors of the Associated Harvard Alumni.

Steve says he started in at the *Times* in the Washington bureau, as a legman for James Reston. That is illuminating, and disillusioning; it had never occurred to me before that Reston had a legman. I have learned in many conversations with *Times* people, afar and at home, that the trick is always to refer to the luminaries of the paper by their nicknames—Scotty and Abe and Artie and Jimmy and so on, and *never* mention a surname. When Steve throws in "Cy" he is astonished to learn something himself— that C. L. Sulzberger is, or was, my stepbrother. Cy's mother and my father, both now dead, were married for twenty-five years. I was best man at their wedding, and the bride was given away by her first husband's brother, Arthur Hays Sulzberger, then the biggest *Times* man of them all. When I *really* want to impress somebody from the *Times*, I allude casually and familiarly to his widow. I once badgered a *Times* editor who had nothing to do with circulation to expedite home delivery of the paper to an apartment of mine, informing him that if he didn't I would take up his remissness—I never would have, of course—with my friend Iphigene. I got the paper the next morning.

My father told me that the ceremony, an afternoon one at the bride's apartment, was going to be simple, and that I should wear whatever I happened to have on. I had spent the day on some grubby Talk of the Town assignment—walking through the new Lincoln Tunnel, possibly—and was accordingly quite rumpled; Arthur Hays Sulzberger, however, turned up attired in full morning-coat regalia, like a new ambassador presenting his credentials to a queen. Not that I could have matched him in any event; I've never owned a morning coat. I have never worked for the *Times*, either, but I've written enough pieces for various sections of it to feel a professional kinship, too, and on at least one occasion have been taken for a member of its staff. "You and your Henry Raymont!" a woman once said to me accusingly at a cocktail party. I was puzzled, because Raymont had not long before interviewed me for a story about a book of mine, a feature that never ran, and I thought at first she was alluding to that. It turned out, though, that she thought I worked for the *Times* (*The New Yorker* is not as widely read as some of us like to believe it is), and that she was mad at Raymont for a story of his, one that had run, about her ex-husband.

Back at the Grand Bretagne for a nightcap on my expense account—to change the subject from the *Times* long enough to justify the outlay, I ask the Robertses if they like the Parthenon—Steve points out the table across the lounge where Cy always sits when he is in Athens. (Cy's lovely late wife, Marina, was Greek.) We get to talking about internal censorship at publications. Steve says he once was told to clear an obituary of Bernard Gimbel with the *Times* executive in charge of department-store advertising, who had assessed the obit as satisfactory with the one exception that it had neglected to characterize the subject as "Mr. New York." I've never been aware of that sort of thing at *The New Yorker*, and indeed for many years there was an unstated policy that editorial and business people were to have nothing to do with each other. Not that fraternization does not exist, at least on my non-policy-making level. I was once invited to join the business-office crowd for a weekend at some posh country club. Later my hosts gave me a clock proclaiming me Tennis Champion of the weekend, an honor I was unaware I had attained. The brass tablet affixed to the clock had "Champion" spelled without the "i." The editorial department would have caught that. Though we have no censorship on the editorial side, we are not encouraged to write much about sex or toilets, or to use four-letter words. Good taste is supposed to be what counts. Once, when I was a novice Talk reporter, I was assigned to cover an autopsy on a seal up at the Bronx Zoo, but my piece never got into print; too gruesome for our unspelled-out standards of taste. The magazine is very nice when it rejects something; in that instance, I remember being complimented on the vividness of my descriptive writing.

January 11

My watch has jet lag. My plane back to New York is scheduled to leave the Athens airport at 12:15 P.M., and I plan to be out there at 11:15. I sleep late and dawdle around my room, typing notes, until it is, I think, 9:30, at which time I decide to take a short constitutional around Constitution Square. The clock in the lobby says it is eleven. I race upstairs, set a new record for packing (two minutes, eight seconds), and manage to check out and get to the airport by 11:45. By the time I have gone through all the formalities there, it is too late to buy E. any duty-free perfume. At least I have a Philip Morris Backgammon beach towel from Paradise Island as a homecoming gift. My Greek odyssey is so quick that the plane going back shows the same film as the plane coming over. I save *The New Yorker* $2.50 right there. To divert myself otherwise in flight, I dip into the "Oxford Book of Literary Anecdotes." Not all the anecdotes are humorous; there is one about how Thomas Carlyle lost the only copy of the first volume of his history because he lent it to John Stuart Mill, and Mill's cleaning woman threw it into a fire.

I have never lost a manuscript, but have had a few nightmares about the possibility. A *New Yorker* editor did once leave an envelope containing a proof of an article of mine, a sort of scoop, at a theatre. I found this out the next day when I received a phone call from an editor at, of all places, the *Daily News*. He had picked up the envelope and read my name at the end of the galleys. I said I would send a messenger straight over to retrieve it. Apparently the *News* man never bothered to read the piece itself; if he had, some of his confrères might have welcomed being made privy to the information in it.

We have the same problem in our household that John Stuart Mill had. Our cleaning woman is always throwing valuable things away, or so David and Lexy maintain—magazine coupons, third-class mail, dried insects, anything she can lay her disposing hands on. She has also acquired the reputation—fairly or unfairly, I cannot judge—of being a plant killer, or philodendronicide. I find it hard to throw any book away myself, even the kind that publishers send hoping for a plug, with titles like "How to Brew Beer in Your Kitchen Sink."

January 12

Too tired to do anything else but write up my excursion to Greece, I stop by the Harvard Club briefly to test my newly honed skills at backgammon. I get slaughtered.

I go to bed early, suffering from compound jet lag. Wake up, see by the clock that it is 10:30, think I have overslept, shower, begin getting dressed, and only then perceive that it is dark out and that I have slept merely one hour.

January 13

The mystery of my missing jacket has been solved! Twenty years ago, I had Davies make me one, of Harris tweed, that I dearly loved. But I wore it so often and so hard that even the leather elbow patches I had had put on it a decade ago were frayed. Last summer, I toted the heavy garment all through the European heat wave, and spent most of the few hours I had in London, when we finally got there, in solemn Hanover Street consultation with Davies & Son. It was agreed the jacket was made of fine material, the kind you really couldn't get any more, and that with the application of considerable hunks of leather to the cuffs, lapel edges, and elbows, the lovable old thing could be salvaged. I asked Davies to get it back to me by October, when the weather would be turning cool enough for me to put it on again. Around the 25th of October, I'd remembered that the jacket hadn't arrived, and had written Davies. A crestfallen reply from London, on a letterhead practically the whole top half of which was covered with royal crests and "By Appointment to's": They had forgotten all about the job, and would get right onto it and ship the jacket pronto.

In early December, still without jacket and beginning to shiver slightly, I had written again, this time receiving a cabled reply: The jacket had been mailed to such and such an address in New Rochelle and a letter was following. I have never lived in New Rochelle. Then the "this awful mistake" letter arrived, but it did not explain to whom in New Rochelle the package had been mailed. So I wrote a "Dear Occupant" letter to that address, and finally today had a phone call from a man there who said he had received a couple of notifications from the New Rochelle post office about some postage-due parcel but had thrown them away.

The caller also said something about my having met his father several years ago. It turned out that his father had bought the New Rochelle house from a Kahn, now long dead, whom I have never heard of. I have no male Kahn relatives I am aware of, except my sons, my father having been the only son of an only son. I am often asked if I am related to, among others,

Otto H. Kahn, but, alas, I am not. I did once have a chance to buy a beautiful old vintage Rolls-Royce that had belonged to non-cousin Otto, with a magnificent "K" emblazoned on its door, but I begged off because the seller was asking seven hundred dollars. I must have been out of my mind.

Anyway, I phoned the New Rochelle post office and learned that the package from London was still there, with accrued storage charges on it of $9.95. I sent the New Rochelle postmaster a check and should have the jacket any day now. I could use it today. It is cold.

We go to dinner, I wearing a medium-weight Davies fabric, to the James T. Flexners. It turns out, unknown to E. and me, to be Jim's birthday. Among the guests is Marion Hargrove's ex-wife. I haven't thought about Hargrove for years. She says (how can she know?) that I am much happier than he is—that after the enormous success of his "See Here, Private Hargrove" in 1942 he has had no comparable good fortune. Neither have I. His book came out at just about the same time as my first book, "The Army Life," and both were accounts of our experiences in basic training. We were stationed together for a while, though unacquainted, at Fort Bragg, North Carolina. I had begun writing pieces for *The New Yorker*, under the heading The Army Life, as soon as I was drafted, in July, 1941. They all appeared with Roman-numeralled subtitles, and there were XXXIX of them in toto. My book got good enough reviews, but Hargrove's got all the sales.

Before Pearl Harbor, I had no trouble writing the pieces, because we soldiers, once we had completed basic training, had weekends off from noon Saturday to Sunday evening. At Fort Bragg, I would leave camp at noon on Saturday, check into a hotel at Fayetteville, and stay there, writing, until I had to report back in. I was taking the elevator down to the lobby on the evening of December 7, 1941, when the operator asked me how come I wasn't back in camp. I said I didn't have to be in until eight o'clock, or whatever the prescribed hour was. "Haven't you heard the news?" he asked. I hadn't heard any news all day. "Well, you better get back there fast," he said, "because all soldiers are supposed to be at their posts." That was how I learned about Pearl Harbor.

January 14

A Friday, and our regular tennis morning at the Wall Street Racquet Club. One of the advantages of being essentially a free-lance writer is that you can play tennis whenever you feel like it without having to justify yourself to anyone. There are disadvantages, too: Since time is your most precious asset and you can't afford to waste much of it, you frequently find yourself working—even as a civilian—on Saturdays and Sundays. I have tried to arrange my life so that I can do large hunks of writing—books, for instance, or multipart *New Yorker* Profiles—in the summertime. This means, of course, that I have to organize myself and my time so I have an appropriate accumulation of research when mid-June rolls around.

When Terry, Joey, and Tony were growing up, Jinny and I would shepherd them to Cape Cod the day after school ended, and stay at Truro until the day before it resumed in the fall. During those three months, I would attempt to work seven days a week, but, as a rule, only from early morning till lunch. Then it was time for Bloody Marys, sandwiches, tennis, swimming, cocktails, and the customary other summer-holiday diversions. There was only one hitch to this regimen. My sons never thought I worked at all. I would go off to my study at seven-thirty or eight in the morning and remain there for four or five hours, and return to the house at just about the time they were waking up. They would come down to the kitchen for breakfast and find their father there, a drink in his hand, talking about in what non-income-producing fashion he proposed to fritter away the rest of that day; and they must have got the impression that being a writer was the easiest thing in the world. They have all gone into writing since then, and they know better now.

Actually, they learned better as children. About eighteen years ago, when Terry was twelve, Joey ten, and Tony seven, Jinny and I decided to imbue them with a sense of responsibility by starting up a small weekly mimeographed newspaper. The Cape Cod National Seashore, run by the National Park Service, had just been established, with our house blessedly spang in the middle of it, so we called the paper *Park Here*. (Regular contributors to *The New Yorker* know that that journal frowns upon puns, but it does not care what they do extracurricularly.) The boys were titularly in charge of *Park Here*, which we produced on an ancient mimeograph machine that Tommy Kane, the Truro town clerk, kindly let us borrow from his office. We charged a nickel a copy and attained a circulation of one hundred and twenty-five, with subscribers as far off as Hong Kong. I wrote a Leonard-Lyons-like gossip column and generally cut the stencils, and Jinny had charge of hand-cranking.

We came out on Friday morning. It was an established rule that any house guest who was staying with us on a Thursday night had to contribute something to the paper; after a while, visitors took to trying to arrive on Friday and leave on Wednesday, but we caught on. Arthur Kober, who was a professional writer and didn't mind singing for his supper (anyway, he sometimes stayed with us for weeks at a stretch) once contributed a memorable piece on getting lost in the Wellfleet woods. We had a tennis column and a Little League column and a shellfishing column (written by a retired Regular Army officer who had endeared himself to me because he had been General MacArthur's provost marshal general in Japan during the Occupation and didn't like his boss any more than I did), and we published every Friday for ten times a summer, four consecutive summers, and never missed a deadline.

That last took some doing, because what with one thing or another to distract the young editors, they sometimes didn't get around to start writing any copy until Thursday afternoon or evening, and it would often be three or four o'clock Friday morning, with the editors asleep on the floor of my office, before Jinny and I and whomever we could corral to give us a hand (since we lived on South Pamet Road, we also had a North Pamet Road correspondent) had finished our press run and delivered a bundle of copies to the general store in Truro, which was our sole outlet for newsstand sales. We gave the store owners a penny a copy for displaying *Park Here* alongside the Boston papers, the Provincetown *Advocate,* and the New York *Times.* When our boys decided, after four years, that they had learned all they had to about responsibility from *that* venture, we offered *Park Here* to a number of other Truro families with young children, but nobody wanted to carry on, probably because most of the people we approached had seen the bleary-eyed shape that Jinny and I were usually in every summer Friday.

At the tennis court, I am jovially hailed by a fellow whom for an instant I don't recognize. It is Sidney Simon, without his beard. Renée is with him, and she pronounces herself outraged at his self-depilation, in which he engaged after a strenuous New Year's Eve. She says he looks like his cousin the druggist, and that if he doesn't grow his whiskers back at once she is going to leave him. Ellie says Sidney looks younger than he used to (he is younger than I am, but his beard was white), but also less sexy. I tried to grow a beard once soon after I married E., conceivably in the hope that it would make me sexier, but abandoned the experiment when she said, after due contemplation and reflection, that it made me look like an unfrocked rabbi.

January 15

A Saturday: I intended to spend the whole morning at my typewriter, but end up devoting a good part of it to Skipper's friendly neighborhood Mobil station. This is about the fifth time we have had a flat tire on the same wheel of our station wagon, and if anyone can solve the mystery it is Skipper, who never touches a car himself, but, instead, confines himself to diagnosis. Befitting that role, he habitually wears a clean white surgeon's smock and drapes a stethoscope around his neck. Skipper examines our sick wheel, and, without dirtying a hand on it, isolates its disease: defective rim. If I will wait fifteen minutes, he will send an orderly around the corner for a new rim, and have me on my way.

While I am hanging around the service station, a tall young man whose Volkswagen won't start reminds me that he used to play tennis on my Truro court when he was a kid. He grew up into teaching, but abandoned that, as inadequately remunerative, for the house-maintenance business, which, while intellectually unrewarding, helps him support Skipper. I tell the lapsed academic that we all have our troubles: Tony phoned from the Cape late last night to inform me that during a freak winter storm the weight of accumulated ice on the wild grape vines that have grown on our tennis-court fence caused the whole fence to collapse. And the vines never even produce grapes.

After an hour and a half, Skipper informs me unapologetically that his tire-rim emissary seems to have disappeared, conceivably in search of a platinum hip socket, and perhaps I should come back tomorrow. My car has been reclassified from out-patient to in-patient status.

We have lunch at a dreadfully expensive Chinese restaurant with Joanandolivia, as all my sons have in turn called their two incurably indulgent maiden aunts. Joan and Olivia are very apologetic for having recommended the costly chopstick house (what is its name again?) but they are trapped; we only agreed to go to the place with them if they would agree to let us, for once, pick up the tab. Then they treat us (we were trapped, too) to an off-Broadway matinée revival of "The Vagabond King," which I saw many years ago, with Dennis King. Lexy seems bored by it, but "Only a Rose" puts me in tears. I can, and do, cry over almost anything, including bad television dramas. Ellie wonders if my undisciplined emotional outburst may not have something to do with Judy Holliday. E. is posthumously jealous. To the best of my recollection, Judy never had anything to do with "The Vagabond King"; if there was any woman in my life who had a strong influence on me at the time I first saw that show, it was probably my German nurse, Bertha.

Ellie and I rush from the theatre to the Cathedral of St. John the Divine, in one of whose outbuildings Stewart Mott is giving a mediaeval party for four hundred or so of his most non-intimate friends. Mediaeval costumes (Stewart has got himself up as some kind of king), mediaeval entertainment (jugglers, acrobats), mediaeval food and drink (parsley-bred trenchers, blancmange, Nomblys de Roo, pommes dorrées, gingered carp, Troycream, mulled wine), and after the tongue-twisting feast a fine performance of "The Book of Daniel" in the probably never-to-be-finished cathedral itself. A strange crowd at the dinner. Gerry Piel, my classmate who publishes the *Scientific American*, is here. Also George Gianis, just back from Nassau, where he didn't win in any of the consolations but, he tells me, made a killing in a dime-a-point chouette game. Somebody in my field got far enough along after I left, George reassures me, so that my life is no longer endangered, at least not from that source.

E. and I sit at a table with Betty Friedan, who says that she is into something far bigger than feminism, but can't reveal any details yet. Betty says we would be amazed at the number of angry letters she got not long ago from feckless former female disciples when she gave the *Times* her recipe for homemade chicken soup. Stewart's mother is at another table, and seeing her reminds me of the night I spent at the Mott home in Flint, Michigan, a few years ago, when I was doing a Profile on Stewart. His celebrated father, the General Motors man, Charles S. Mott, was still alive, aged ninety-five, and at dinner the old man was talking about how he had barely survived some medical emergency; Stewart kept nagging at him to say how it felt almost to die. After dinner, Mott *père* excused himself to fetch us some cigars, and when he returned, as if to emphasize his *joie de vivre*, he was sporting a fright wig and a false nose. Stewart and I share the same birth date. He turned thirty-nine this past December 4th, and in his remarks to his mulled guests he muses on what he calls his dotage. How in the world will he ever describe his state of life if, like his father, he reaches ninety-seven?

January 16

Today is Joey's birthday—his twenty-eighth. I remember to phone him. I call at 11 A.M., and Hillary and he are still in bed. Ah, youth! Still, we older men do not do too badly, in spite of what our sons may think. A couple of years ago, when Terry was editing the Provincetown *Advocate*, out on the tip of the Cape, Sidney Simon passed along to him—for background, not publication—a gossipy story he'd heard about a prominent regional figure, who had been spotted checking into an off-Cape hospital under an assumed name to have a case of syphilis attended to. Terry had roared with glee on hearing the sordid tale, but had then said to Sidney, "Wait a minute, it can't be true." Why not? Sidney had demanded. "Because ———'s at least fifty-five and couldn't *get* syphilis," my son reputedly said. We are going to Sidney's for dinner tomorrow night, and there is obviously nothing wrong with *him* sexually; at nearly sixty, he has one child aged two and another of three months.

At a cross–Central Park brunch we are delighted to find Edmund and Mariann Clubb, whom Ellie and I grew fond of when I was writing "The China Hands." Edmund tries to clarify for us the latest political upheavals in the People's Republic, which he still follows closely though he hasn't been back to Peking since, as consul general, he lowered the American flag there in 1950. I tell him about the Christmas card we got last month from Ma Hai-teh, the expatriate American physician who has been living in China for more than forty years and is often credited with having eradicated all venereal diseases *there*, and whom E. and I got to know in Peking in 1973; in his seasonal conveyance of good wishes, Dr. Ma could not resist taking a swipe at the Gang of Four and describing Chiang Ch'ing and her associates as four boils on the Chinese body politic.

Christopher Rand's son Peter is also at the brunch, and I tell him about my first meeting with his father. Chris and I had both been writing for *The New Yorker* for some time, but we never knew each other until I arrived in

Tokyo in the winter of 1951, to cover the Korean War for the magazine. Harold Ross, whose life would end later that same year, hadn't really wanted to send anybody over there, because he wasn't convinced that it was a genuine war, but he finally agreed to let me go. I had never been in Japan or Korea before, and knew nobody in that part of the world, but Bill Shawn gave me a letter of introduction to Rand.

Chris was out when I arrived at the old Foreign Correspondents Club in Tokyo, and I left the note at the reception desk. Then I fell mortally ill. I always used to get sick—psychosomatic hypochondria, I guess it was—as soon as I reached my first stop on an overseas assignment. I had rapped imploringly at death's door two years earlier in Wiesbaden, Germany, on landing there preparatory to covering the Berlin Airlift for *The New Yorker*. Now, in Japan, tossing on my bed, my choices loomed starkly and unattractively clear: Die on this wretched pallet or take the first plane home tomorrow. But how could I explain to Ross, whom I had badgered into sending me off to Asia as a gung-ho war correspondent, that I was back without even having set foot on Korean soil? I concluded that the face-saving alternative was to stay and perish. Having made that decision, I drifted into a fitful final sleep.

I was aroused at five in the morning by an otherworldly apparition: an unknown figure with a shaved head (Rand was a Buddhist) clad from neck to toes in a glistening poncho (it had been raining out). The ghost said cheerfully that he had just come in and had found my note. I groaned and said it didn't matter any longer. He asked what the matter was. I explained that I was either dead or dying, and that the distinction was, in the circumstances, trifling. My spectral visitor said he had a fresh bottle of Scotch in his room next door, and why didn't I try to make it that far and help him open it; if I was going to die, he pointed out reasonably, I might as well die drunk. I hate Scotch, but this was an emergency. By the time Chris and I had killed the bottle I was alive again, and as soon as I sobered up I went to Korea and stayed there the better part of three months.

I guess I was the last *New Yorker* person to see Chris Rand alive. He was living in Mexico in 1968, the year the summer Olympics were held in Mexico City. I went down there the preceding winter to do a pre-Olympics piece for *Holiday*. I was a bit miffed, on being reunited with Rand, to discover that he was doing a pre-Olympics piece for *The New Yorker*. The Olympic Games were supposed to be *my* beat. But I couldn't very well complain too much, because I was prowling that beat at the moment on another magazine's behalf.

New Yorker writers like to carve out territories for themselves. Bob Shaplen and I once informally divided the continent of Asia between us, but then he went to live in Hong Kong and gradually embarked on an anschluss of my allotted territories. I did manage once to sneak a "Letter from Bangkok" into the magazine while his back was turned. Shaplen was enraged. "You don't know anything about Thailand," he said, not altogether untruthfully. "How long were you there, anyway?"

"Two and a half days, Bob, two and a half days," I replied.

That made him even madder. Actually, I had been there for four days, but I considered the minutiae of my work habits to be none of his business.

I spent a little longer than that in Mexico, in part because Chris and I drove to Cuernevaca for a long, non-competitive weekend. He was delightful company, and seemed thoroughly cheerful, and when I heard several months later that he had jumped off the roof of a building in Mexico City, I couldn't have been more surprised. Or saddened.

There is a psychiatrist at the brunch who has diagnosed an ailment *he* is suffering from as a pinched vertebral nerve. He says he only feels relatively comfortable when he is sitting down with a patient. I wonder how he can give his patients his full attention when he is hurting. I have only tried psychoanalysis once myself, and not in length or depth, but it was an interesting enough experience, though I never could train myself properly to remember dreams. The only one that ever made an impact on me was a recurrent nightmare I had twenty years or so ago, when we were living in Scarborough, just after our Labrador bitch Cleopatra disappeared.

People used to steal good female dogs, and breed them illicitly. We had bred Cleo licitly and lovingly, to a splendidly pedigreed stud named Black Cargo. Thus the name of her son Barge—Royal Barge of Holbrook, as he was listed in the annals of the American Kennel Club. (We lived on Holbrook Road.) For six months after Cleo vanished from our and her home—I am crying as I write this, just as if I were watching "Dragnet"—I would leap out of bed in the middle of nearly every night, hearing her scratch at our front door. But when I rushed downstairs and flung it expectantly open she was never there. E. is much higher on psychoanalysis than I am, even though a one-time analyst of hers, a male Freudian, jumped out of a window himself. She finally settled with a female Jungian. Not long before this suicide, E. and I had been invited to dine at the home of still another psychiatrist, and to her fascination she found her analyst and his wife among the other guests. It is supposed to be bad social form to sup with one's shrink. E. didn't mention her relationship with the doctor when we were all introduced, but I have a nasty streak in me, I guess, and halfway through the evening I engaged his wife in chitchat and let drop the fact that *my* wife was *his* patient. The woman literally shrieked, as if she had seen a mouse.

January 17

I finished my backgammon piece today and sent it off to *Sports Illustrated*. It turned out to be as much about S. George Gianis as about me, but I didn't know how George would feel about having his real name used, so I called him "Stravros," for his "S." I have no idea what the S. actually stands for. Stavros, maybe.

South Africa has been so much in the news lately that I think I'll try to get Shawn to send me back there. That is unarguably my territory, in *The New Yorker* context, but I'm not sure Bill is particularly eager for me to go—I have a hunch he does not consider political writing my forte—and anyway I'm not sure South Africa will *let* me back. I tried vainly for a visa two years ago, when I was working on a biography of Charlie Engelhard that Jane E. commissioned me to write. I applied for the visa then in February, and said I wanted to leave on April 1st. Inasmuch as my main purpose in wanting to go that time was to talk to Harry Oppenheimer and other friends of Charlie's, it never occurred to me for a minute that I'd be turned down. My 1969 book about South Africa, after all, had been a good deal less antagonistic than most of the stuff that American journalists have written about the place. So I booked myself on a plane leaving New York at 10:30 P.M. on April 1st, reserved a room at the Carlton in Johannesburg, and wrote all my friends and acquaintances that I was on my way. At 10:30 A.M. on April 1st I had a call from the South African Consulate General in New York. No visa. No explanation, either. A not very funny April Fool's prank.

My own hunch was and is that I was turned down because of *The New Yorker*'s policy of refusing to accept any advertising for South African Airways or any South African tourist organization. The rationale, Shawn once explained to me, is that we wouldn't want to accept any ads for any places that any of our readers might feel uncomfortable in. Black readers, he meant. But I can't visualize many black readers of the magazine who don't know what's going on in South Africa. Moreover, as I have told Bill, if we are going to apply political criteria to advertising acceptability, we should be consistent: We run ads extolling the glories of travel in Taiwan, Poland, South Korea, and the Soviet Union, each in its own way as dictatorial as South Africa. There was one issue in which the lead item in Notes and Comments was a long diatribe against having anything to do with dictatorships, and singling out as an example of an especially bad one the Philippines; the same issue carried a full-page ad for Philippine Air Lines.

I finally went to London two years ago and saw Harry Oppenheimer there. When I was in Joburg in 1966, working on a Profile of Engelhard, Harry was out of town one night, and Jane and Charlie asked me to accompany them to Bridget Oppenheimer's for supper and a round of bridge. We were at the card table, into the second or third deal—both women had been at a wedding reception and were ablaze with diamonds and rubies and whatnot from two of the world's grandest privately owned collections of jewels—when it suddenly occurred to me that I had no idea what the stakes were. For all I knew, the Engelhards and Oppenheimers routinely played for two hundred rands a point. It was too late to make inquiries. Fortunately, I ended up ahead. Unfortunately, it was a tenth-of-a-rand-a-point game.

I turned fifty during that trip, and some friends in Cape Town were nice enough to give me a birthday party, which lasted late. The next morning, I picked up the phone in my room at the Mount Nelson to call my hostess and thank her for the bash. When the switchboard operator came on and asked me for the number, I discovered to my dismay that I couldn't talk. My God, I thought, the human voice was designed to last only half a century, and they never told me!

Shawn never ran my Profile of Engelhard. He said if he did people would interpret this as a pro-apartheid editorial gesture on behalf of *The New Yorker*. I tried to point out to him that if the magazine had any editorial position, surely that had been expressed by my already published three-part series on South Africa, but he is an authoritarian editor (also, of course, one of the greatest on earth), and that sort of argument gets an author-writer nowhere. So there I was—*The New Yorker* regarding me as excessively pro-South Africa, and South Africa regarding me, evidently, as excessively anti. I was on the horns of the kind of dilemma on which self-professed liberals so frequently find themselves ludicrously impaled.

I would also like to go back to China. Huang Hua, who had E. and me to dinner in New York while he was the People's Republic's ambassador to the U.N., is now foreign minister, and Peking might thus be more receptive to a request for a second visa than Pretoria. But I know Shawn will not pay my way to China. He didn't the first time. Anyway, Edmund Clubb told me at the brunch that *The New Yorker* has bought a book on China by Orville Schell, which should take care of *that* territory for some time to come. These days, I usually hear about what the magazine is up to from outsiders. There was a time many years ago when I pretty well knew what pieces were lying around in type, waiting to be run, because I would wander regularly into the nineteenth-floor make-up room to chat with Carmine Peppe, Frank Grisaitis, and Joe Carroll, its perennial gifted custodians, with whom before the Second World War I also often played poker. About twenty-five years ago, though, Leonard Lyons kept running items in his column about pieces *The New Yorker* was going to print, and inasmuch as it was known I was a friend of his, I was accused by a senior editor, while visiting the make-up room one afternoon, of having been the source of the intelligence. I haven't set foot in Make-up since. Life is full of ironies; it so happened that I never leaked anything to Leonard at all.

We dine tonight in the Village, at the Sidney Simons'. I lived in an apartment in their house for six months between marriages. When I moved in, it was like going abroad on assignment; I had scarcely unpacked when I took to my bachelor bed with a raging fever. Ellie came down and brought me some hot chicken soup and I miraculously recovered. The *pièce de résistance* at the Simons' tonight is some kind of pasta, made, while we all look on, by another guest. In such circumstances, one is expected to praise the chef's chef-d'oeuvre as incomparable; my ornery inclination is usually to resist. This time, I not only refuse seconds, but pointedly leave part of my first serving on my plate. When people react thus to one of my own clam pies, I am deeply offended. Dick Miller is still another guest, but he has a valid excuse for leaving his plate uncleaned; he is rushing off to play a nightclub gig with Woody Allen.

Dick reminds me during dinner of the evening he and I spent last year at some midtown club where the incomparable Bobby Hackett, who died not long ago, was the musical *pièce de résistance*. It had been Dick's lifelong ambition to play piano accompaniment to Hackett's trumpet, and tonight Dick apprises me of a mournful postscript to our night on the town: It seems that after I left the establishment, Hackett invited Dick to join him for a set, but by then Dick had had too much to drink, and his fingers couldn't find the right keys. Sic transit dreams of gloria.

After dinner, E. and I move along to another nightclub, the Village Gate. I rarely go to nightclubs any more, having had more than my fill of them when I wrote *The New Yorker*'s after-dark column, Tables for Two, for a couple of years before the Second World War. When I was covering that beat, I often stayed up till three or four in the morning three or four nights a week, in what I kidded myself into believing was the line of duty. On being drafted into the Army, I was amazed that I could pass the physical. The only story about my nearly four decades at *The New Yorker* that Brendan Gill deemed worthy of inclusion in his "Here at *The New Yorker*" related to my having expressed surprise once in those wild-oat-sowing days that not everybody threw up, as I allegedly did, every morning. Brendan swears I said it, nearly forty years ago, and his memory may be better than mine; but I recall vaguely having seen the story printed in an old joke book by Joe Miller or one of his stripe.

I fancied myself back then in love with nearly every girl singer I was supposed to comment about with critical detachment. One of my favorite haunts was the Village Vanguard, where I lavished praise—in this instance, deserved by any judgmental criteria—on the five young people who called their songs-and-sketches act The Revuers. Judy Holliday, who was then Judith Tuvim, was one of them, and she would often let me escort her home after her last show. Betty Comden and Adolph Green, who went on to achieve well-earned celebrity as co-authors and co-performers, were two of the others. Everybody has forgotten the names of the other two Revuers, but I do remember *that*: Al Hammer and John Frank.

Tonight, the upstairs part of the Village Gate, not to be confused with the ⁷anguard, has been taken over by Daphne Hellman for her annual private party. Daphne goes far back in my life, too. She used to give marvelous elegant lunches at her town house in the East Sixties, when she was married to Harry Bull, the editor of *Town & Country*. My finger bowl would be only inches away from Ludwig Bemelmans' or Lucius Beebe's. (But this polished hostess of yore, who also gave house parties in Cuba, was only a slip of a girl at the time, younger than my three older sons are today!) Daphne would go slumming periodically and lug her harp up to the third-floor apartment I shared just off the Bowery with Bruce Bliven and Dave Lindsay, and would join a band we had in its weekly Thursday-night performances.

We picked Thursday because that was when most of *The New Yorker* went ιo press, and its editorial staff could relax to the extent that people who have to put out a publication fifty-two times a year ever can. (The staff of *Park Here* always particularly relished Friday evenings; the following Thursday seemed aeons away.) Bill Shawn was our pianist. Gus Lobrano, one of the magazine's principal fiction editors, played the guitar. When Larry Adler was around, he played the harmonica. I played the drums, not only amateurishly but badly amateurishly. Various nightclub artists sometimes joined us. Harold Ross once stopped by, conceivably out of curiosity about how many of his employees diverted themselves after hours, and he was handed a trombone and invited to join in. He demurred, and never returned.

January 18

I decide not to go to the office today but to stay at home and concentrate on my Cyrus Eaton Profile. I rarely get any calls at home during the daytime, but this morning there are three in quick order. 1) Somebody hangs up when a man answers. 2) Monica McCall phones. Her agency has finally received the check from Eli Lilly and Company that was due me, on my book, the first of this month; all the human beings out in Indianapolis, it seems, have forgotten about me, and the computer that is supposed to remind them (it is thoroughly reliable, I know, when it comes to alerting them that they are running low on capsule gelatin) has neglected to flash my name. 3) A male voice says, "Mr. Kahn, this is Dan. Willie is having his seventieth this year." I don't recognize the voice right off; it is that of Dan Lang, with whom I chat from time to time in a *New Yorker* corridor or elevator, but whom I haven't spoken to on the phone for ages. "Willie" turns out to be Bill Shawn, and Dan thinks he and I should organize something— perhaps a ceremonial inscribed tray from Tiffany—in celebration of our leader's birthday next August.

I remind Dan that we did something of the sort once, with less than altogether desirable results. In the nineteen forties, while Harold Ross was still alive and in robust command of the magazine, Shawn, then its managing editor, decided to quit editing and indulge his lifelong ambition to be a writer. Sandy Vanderbilt, a *Herald Tribune* alumnus, who had come to *The New Yorker* in 1938 as a long-fact writer but had switched to editing, had been designated Shawn's successor. (Sandy Vanderbilt occasionally played the trombone in our band, but he wasn't much better at it than Ross might have been if he'd tried.) So Lang and I and a few other contributors got together and ordered a huge sterling-silver tray from Tiffany, and gathered signatures to be engraved on it from all the non-fiction writers—Janet Flanner in Paris, Mollie Panter-Downes in London, everybody everywhere; and eventually the finished offering was presented to the presumptive retiree at his apartment. A few days later, Vanderbilt hurt himself in an accident and couldn't take over. Shawn resumed his duties, and never did get much chance to write. I have no idea what he and Cecille have done with the silver salver.

Vanderbilt's full name was Sanderson Vanderbilt, easily the most patrician identification on the *New Yorker* staff. He was not related, so far as he knew, to any of the rich Vanderbilts. His office adjoined mine for a spell, and while we rarely had lunch together (often drinks afterward, though), we talked a lot about lunch. It was a running gag between us that he, in keeping with his glittering appellation, went to the Colony Restaurant every day at noon. It was also a known fact that Sandy rarely went out to lunch, instead having a neighborhood short-order counter send in, unvaryingly, a chopped-egg-on-wholewheat sandwich and a chocolate malted. I never went to the Colony for lunch, either, but I occasionally dated Dolly de Milhau, who often did, and who, further, was acquainted with bona-fide top-drawer Vanderbilts. She introduced me to Alfred Gwynne.

Somebody mentioned to Dolly and me at the Stork Club one night, when I was making my Tables for Two rounds, that no practical joke was worth playing if it cost more than five dollars. (We are dealing here in 1940 dollars.) That gave Dolly and me an idea. I arranged with the switchboard operator at *The New Yorker* to intercept the delivery of Sandy's daily sandwich, and—for five dollars!—Dolly arranged for the Colony to send to the magazine a fully uniformed waiter, bearing an egg-salad-on-wholewheat and a split of champagne. When the exquisitely caparisoned servitor arrived, and the switchboard told Sandy his lunch was on hand, and he said to send it on in, the waiter entered his office, greeted him like a regular patron, spread a snowy tablecloth on his desk, laid out a gleaming place setting, removed the sandwich from a polished serving dish, and uncorked the champagne. That terminated our badinage about lunching at the Colony.

January 19

My London jacket has arrived from New Rochelle. It looks beautiful—leather cuffs, leather piping, new leather elbow patches. It is a tweed jacket slowly turning into a leather one. I wear it to the Harvard Club at noon today, not to play backgammon but to have lunch with John Swope, who is in from Beverly Hills for a while because Dorothy is starring in "Night of the Iguana." I am amazed that John does not have a camera with him. We used to play squash together; as in his annual Christmas-card photo he always rigs up a time exposure so that he can get into the picture himself, so once he placed a camera in a corner of a squash court and snapped both of us in action. He always used to beat me at squash; so do most other people.

I have known John for a long time, but Dorothy McGuire even longer. Bruce Bliven used to date her when she played the title role in "Claudia" on Broadway. Occasionally I would go backstage with him when he picked her up after a performance. I did not know then that Jinny was her understudy. In the long run of that play, the star never faltered, the understudy never had her golden chance to go on. When later I met and married Jinny, and the Swopes chanced to come and live next door to us in Scarborough, the social relationship between the star—by then also a movie star—and her erstwhile standby was at first sticky. I couldn't blame Jinny for never quite having forgiven Dorothy for not having got laryngitis at least once.

Today, John is exhibiting symptoms of frustration, too. He has brought to New York with him a huge collection of the splendid photographs he has taken all over the world (D. and he are off on a three-and-a-half-month global tour as soon as "Iguana" closes), forty years' worth of sensitive work; and he has been told by all the art-gallery people he has shown them to that they would make a marvelous book, and by all the publishers he has shown them to that some gallery ought to grab them for a marvelous one-man show. He and I talk, as we always do when we get together, of the harrowing time I had, now fifteen years ago, when I wrote my biography of his uncle, Herbert Bayard Swope.

I had known Herbert, Jr.—Ottie, everybody called him—from the time we both attended Horace Mann High, and through him had met his dashing editor father. I saw a good deal of Ottie when we were both just out of college. We used to have lunch in a group that included, from time to time, Alfred Vanderbilt, Martin Gabel, Robert Paul Smith, Paul Douglas (the actor, not the senator), and Oscar Levant. Gabel and I decided at one of these get-togethers to fly down to Washington and watch Joe Louis put up his heavyweight title for grabs by Buddy Baer, Max's kid brother. Flying to Washington was not, before the war, the cinch that it is now; these days, when I have to go to Washington I usually take the shuttle down in the morning and back in the afternoon. My recollection is that Martin and I spent the better part of two days traveling by DC-3 to see the big fight, which was probably an uneconomic allocation of our time, though not of Louis'; he knocked Baer out long before the first round was over. If I'd been prophetic, I could have charged off the long day's journey as a business expense, because many years later I wrote a Profile of the indestructible DC-3.

Soon after Jinny and I were married, in 1945, we were invited to spend a weekend at the senior Swopes' opulent Long Island ménage at Sands Point. Herbert, Sr., had been beguiled at the notion of having a WAC officer as a house guest. In 1948, I wrote a supposedly humorous casual for *The New Yorker* entitled "What Is Herbert Bayard Swope?", but Ottie's mother did not find it amusing; Maggie wouldn't talk to me for several years. Then after Herbert died, in 1958, she forgave me and we signed an agreement for me to write his biography. I devoted two years to it—the most time I have ever spent on a single project. It took nearly half that time for me to go through Swope's accumulated correspondence, which filled one hundred filing cabinets.

At the outset of my research, Maggie enjoined me not to make the same kind of mistakes that had been made by a despicable Princeton student, who, in a thesis about Herbert, had falsely stated, she wanted me to be clearly aware, that she and Herbert had been the witnesses, in the summer of 1909, when the notorious gambler Arnold Rothstein got married at Saratoga Springs, during the racing season, to the showgirl Carolyn Green. Why, sputtered Maggie, Herbert had never been anywhere that intimate with Rothstein, despite all the base allegations to the contrary that certain ill-mannered people had so often circulated; and, moreover, how *could* anything of the sort have happened, inasmuch as she was only twelve at the time?

I had naturally believed her and had swiftly promised not to visit on her husband's memory any such comparable indignities. As I got deeper and deeper into my research, I kept running into trouble: Certain dates didn't jibe with what Maggie was telling me in our many interviews. Then one day I stumbled on something. When Herbert was courting Maggie, he called her "Pearl," and in memos he scribbled to himself he would allude to her by the Greek letter "pi." Here, in his own handwriting, in a note indisputably scrawled in 1909, was a reference to his going out somewhere with " π ." Dating a girl of twelve? Barely conceivable in 1962; unimaginable in the Edwardian era.

A few weeks later, I went up to Saratoga to have lunch with Frank Sullivan, who had worked for Swope on the New York *World*. I told Frank of my puzzlement, and after lunch he suggested that we stroll over to the town hall, where the regional vital statistics were on file. The clerk there—a character right out of a movie, with a green eyeshade and thick rubber bands around his shirtsleeves—knew Frank, as did just about everybody around, and after they had suitably analyzed the weather for the day, week, and month, at Sullivan's request he pulled down a huge ledger, blew the dust off it, and turned to the date I was curious about—August 12, 1909. There were the names of the bride and bridegroom: Carolyn Greenwald and Arnold Rothstein. There, in an adjoining column, were the names of their witnesses: Margaret Powell and Herbert Swope. It is easy to forgive a lady for fudging her age, but not so easy in the case of a biographer pursuing comprehensible chronologies.

Bernard Baruch, a longtime friend of Swope's, granted me a couple of audiences, but he, too, was something less than totally candid. For a while, the two men had a joint brokerage account, little if any of the initial capital for which was furnished by the junior partner. In one of my interviews with the celebrated advisor-to-presidents, I asked Baruch how long they had had that account. The old man fixed his bright blue eyes squarely on mine and said, unblinkingly, "We *never* had a joint account." I was momentarily stumped for a suitable follow-up question; I had copies of brokers' statements bearing both their names back on my office desk.

As I got further into my biography, things went from bad to worse. The book was under contract to Simon and Schuster, and Max Schuster professed to have an especially keen interest in it, because his wife was a close friend of Maggie's, and because he himself had delivered a panegyric at the unveiling of a memorial to Swope at the Columbia School of Journalism. Simon and Schuster had published my very first book, so I had known Max for a long time, but at, when possible, arm's length; he had the disconcerting habit, while treating an author to lunch, of spraying parts of his own lunch across the table. When I turned in my manuscript, Max showed it, without my knowledge, to the Swopes, and they hit the ceiling—in their case, since they lived very grandly, a high one. (Just how indignant they were I didn't immediately know, because by that time I was, only coincidentally, aboard a tramp steamer heading across the Pacific from Nukuoro to Kapingamarangi.) One of the things that made them sore was that I had had the audacity to repeat the preposterous old canard about Arnold Rothstein's nuptials.

There were other cavils—hundreds of them, in a line-by-line outraged annotation that Ottie ultimately provided. He and his mother tried to have publication stopped, and when I returned to the States there were all sorts of tense negotiating sessions involving agents and lawyers and publishers and Swopes and me. At one point, Ottie, with whom I was still more or less on speaking terms, invited me to join him for lunch—not at a restaurant, as in days of yore, but at his office. The purpose was for us to confer; i.e., argue, eventually snarl. He sent out for sandwiches. The Swopes were never notable for the lavish distribution of hard cash, and when the delivery man arrived with two paper bags, Ottie said, "Do you take Diners Club?"

I did reluctantly consent to delete a few incidents that seemed to upset the family most grievously, although the accuracy of my recounting of them was not challenged. (I hadn't even put *in* some of the facets of Swope's challenging personality that had rattled me the most, and to show that I am truly Mr. Nice Guy I'm not putting them in here, either.) Next, the spitting Schuster, possibly under uxorial pressure, began to waver and waffle; he finally published the book more or less as originally written, but he also did something I never heard of a publisher doing before: He inserted at the front of the volume the text of his own laudatory memorial oration, the effect of which was to suggest that Herbert Bayard Swope was a far greater man than the author had indicated.

After the book came out, Ottie and his mother never spoke to me again. He and I have since been at the same parties once or twice. No contact. About a year ago, I was shopping in a Lexington Avenue supermarket when out of the corner of my eye I noticed that Ottie was moving into the checkout line directly behind me. He can't be certain that *I* have seen *him*, I thought to myself; but he damn well knows I'm in front of him. Let him make the first move. No move.

But, as John Swope reminds me today when I tell him of this incident, or non-incident, I was not at publication time persona non grata among *all* Swopes. Shortly after the poor battered book did appear, with the minimum of advertising and promotion that Simon and Schuster could muster, John's older twin brothers, Gerry and David (also friends of mine and sons of Herbert's older brother Gerard, the General Electric man), celebrated their sixtieth birthday with a dinner dance. The guest list was large, but the hosts felt that there wouldn't be room enough on it, in the strained circumstances, for both their first cousin Ottie and for Ottie's father's biographer. I regarded it as a kind of moral verdict in my favor that they chose me.

January 20

President Carter is inaugurated today. I forget to watch on television, being preoccupied with Cyrus Eaton, in whose reveries the most recent chief of state who is apt to loom up is Herbert Hoover. As I am going out to lunch, somebody on the eighteenth floor (probably Andy Logan; she is the office source of all important intelligence) mentions en passant that we now have a new president. I wish him well.

I muse on the presidents whom—to stretch a point—I have known. The first was Calvin Coolidge. My grandparents took me to the White House during his tenancy, and in those days there were times when anybody could shake the president's hand. I shook his, taciturnly. The only time I've been to a party at the White House was during the Lyndon Johnson administration. LBJ was never close-mouthed. He wandered into the Green Room or Blue Room or Red Room or whatever chamber it was into which a young Marine officer ushered Jinny and me, grabbed her in an enveloping Texas bear hug, and said, "Hiya, honey." Jinny said afterward that she had not minded his familiarity but it seemed a bit much considering that they had not yet been introduced.

Last year Ellie and I took David and Lexy to the White House, and got the special congressional tour courtesy of Mike Mansfield, with whom I had become acquainted through the Engelhards. Mike once told me that Charlie E. was his best friend. An odd couple, the hedonistic precious-metals tycoon and the austere professorial senator from Montana. When I once asked Mansfield what on earth the two of them talked about when they were alone together, he said they didn't much; they engaged in mutually satisfying silent communion. While I am name-dropping, I might add that in addition to sharing the Engelhards' massive hospitality with the senator, I once spent a congenial weekend at their Far Hills, New Jersey, pad with, among other house guests, the Duke and the Duchess of Windsor. That gave me the opportunity to be included, in some stray footnote, in the "Guinness Book of World Records": I may be the only person on earth who ever danced simultaneously with the Duke and the Duchess. I was seated next to her at dinner on Saturday night, and when the orchestra began playing dance music, it seemed only civil to propose a turn around the floor. We hadn't been out there long when I felt a tap on my shoulder. It was the Duke, cutting in. The Duchess tried to shoo him away, saying, in a manner that endeared her to me forever, that she was *enjoying* dancing with this young man. But His Royal Highness was adamant. He insisted on dancing with her then and there. In that case, said the Duchess, he would have to dance *à trois*. So we did.

Senator Mansfield had invited E. and me and the boys to stop by his office in the Capitol after our White House inspection, and he spent half an hour with us in his majority leader's chambers. He apologized for the absence of a proper chandelier. Jackie Kennedy had borrowed it once for the White House, he said, and he had never been able to get it back. In a government predicated on the balance of power, something seemed to be atilt. Mike asked the boys what their hobbies were, and when it came out that Lexy was a magician (he does kids' birthday-party shows, twenty dollars an engagement, and has his own printed business cards), he invited a demonstration. Lexy did some simple sleight of hand. Then, to the astonishment and admiration of us all, the senator reciprocated with a skillful trick—it involved palming dollar bills or some such—of his own.

Mike Mansfield had the reputation of not talking much to anyone at any time. When he announced last year that he was going to retire as majority leader of the Senate, I thought it might be interesting to have a chat with him—if he would talk—about his long career in Washington, and he invited me to stop by his Capitol office one morning. To my surprise, he rattled on engagingly for three and a half hours. I wrote a long *New Yorker* piece based on this unique demonstration of loquaciousness, but before it could be scheduled Mike had left Washington and gone to Tokyo as our ambassador. Too bad. He may never talk at such length again—certainly not to me. It has been suggested more than once, not altogether seriously, that Shawn could bring out a second magazine composed of contributions he has seen fit to buy but hasn't had space enough to run.

Kennedy was the president I knew best. We had a nodding acquaintance. I had spent an evening with him and John Hersey just after the war, when Hersey did a *New Yorker* piece on Kennedy's PT-boat heroics. After his election, I read somewhere that, while in New York, the president had decided spontaneously to go to a hit musical comedy, and that got me to wondering how such patronage was arranged. I never did the story, because the Secret Service said, sensibly enough, that it wasn't going to disclose to me any of its methods of operation; but before I was thus stymied I went down to the White House to talk to the president's personal secretary, Evelyn Lincoln, whose office adjoined the Oval Office. While I was chatting with her, Kennedy walked in, and I reintroduced myself. He at once told me how much he'd liked a piece I'd had in the magazine a few weeks earlier—about the 32nd Infantry Division, the Wisconsin National Guard outfit, which he had not long before called up to active duty because of a crisis in Berlin, and which I had gone out to visit, at Fort Lewis, Washington, because the Red Arrow Division had been my old outfit, twenty years previous, in Australia and New Guinea. Then, to my delight, the president proceeded to quote, practically verbatim, the whole last paragraph of the article. I had heard that he was an omnivorous and retentive reader, but still and all it was a heady experience.

Tonight Ellie and I go to an Off-Off-Broadway production of Edward Harrigan's "Mulligan Guards Ball." It is the first time I have ever seen a Harrigan play, though I am familiar with his work, having read most of it when I wrote "The Merry Partners," about Harrigan and his fellow performer Tony Hart. I find that I am quoted, or paraphrased, on the theatre program. There is a famous scene in this evening's play in which a ceiling collapses and the dancing members of a Negro social club fall through it on top of the members of an Irish social club who are holding a dance below. I have often wondered how this could be staged on Broadway, let alone off-off. Tonight, the producers more or less evade the issue: They handle it with a lot of noise and a blackout.

I got interested in Harrigan and Hart through Joshua Logan, on whom I did a *New Yorker* Profile in the mid-fifties. Josh's wife, Nedda, was Harrigan's daughter, and it seemed that no one had ever done a book about the old theatrical team, though for twenty years or so, at the end of the nineteenth century, Harrigan and Hart were authentic luminaries of the American stage. The abortive musical comedy Josh and I worked on was based on my book. Random House published that one, and the editor in charge of it was the late Saxe Commins, one of the luminaries of *his* craft. It was said of Saxe that people like Theodore Dreiser and William Faulkner could hardly write a line without his constant counselling.

I have known many of the celebrated writers of my time—John Hersey, for instance, John Steinbeck, John Cheever, John O'Hara, John Updike. (I am name-dropping again, but only one first name.) Cheever and I once had a long-running backgammon competition. We kept the cumulative score, to show we were not boobs, on a flyleaf of Hersey's "A Bell for Adano." One of our wives lent the book to a third party to *read*, for God's sake, and we never played much together after that. The only time I met Faulkner was in

Saxe Commins' office, where the Mississippian was wont to write while visiting New York. This could be inconvenient for Commins, whose office was a tiny one, and it proved especially harrowing on the day in question, for Saxe had asked me to stop by and, with his counselling, select the illustrations for "The Merry Partners."

Most of these came from Nedda Logan's memorabilia of her father, and most of her memorabilia were large, framed, heavy, and, as delivered to Saxe's cubicle, stoutly packaged. When I arrived at ten-thirty or so one morning, they occupied every inch of Saxe's cramped premises save for a corner where Faulkner, a quart bottle of beer at his side, was pecking away at a typewriter. He scarcely turned his head when we were introduced. Saxe said that it was all right for us to go about our business, that Bill wouldn't be bothered, but I found it unsettling to be unpacking and moving around picture frames while the great man was trying to concentrate on what for all I knew would earn him a Nobel Prize.

After a couple of hours, Saxe suggested that he and I take a breather and go out to lunch. Faulkner did not seem to be included in the invitation. Perhaps he didn't eat lunch, although when we returned I noticed that he had a fresh quart of beer at hand. An hour or so later, we had concluded our selections, and then came the job of rewrapping our rejects. The editor and I were deep into that when, for the first time all day, Faulkner opened his mouth. He drawled, "Anything Ah can dew to hay-elp?" By then, my nerves had been worn pretty thin by the whole incongruous scene, and I replied, almost testily, "As a matter of fact, we could use a piece of string."

"Here," said Faulkner, handing me one instantaneously. To this day, I cannot fathom where that piece of string came from; maybe, like Lexy's, his avocation was magic.

January 21

A Friday, and thus our tennis morning. For several years, E. and I have been part of a group, a dozen strong, that rents two adjacent indoor courts for two hours once a week—men on one court, women on the other, spur-of-the-moment mixed doubles when there is a shortage of one sex and a surplus of the other. We usually take the car down the East Side Drive to our Wall Street bubble, but Skipper is not yet satisfied with its condition; I gather from what I can make of his laconic telephone prognosis that it has been moved to intensive care.

On Park Avenue, outside our apartment, tardy as usual, we try to hail a cab. One we think we have flagged down is captured by a fellow who emerges from his apartment building just to our south, with a little girl—taking his daughter to school, no doubt, in the best Upper East Side upper-class tradition. One sees them on and around Park Avenue every morning—the WASPy young men, bankers or lawyers, headed with their precious darlings toward Chapin or Brearley, or wherever. I suppose I am envious of them. Three sons, two stepsons, two grandsons; there are no female limbs on my extended family tree. There is hardly any point in my ever sitting down, family-wise-speaking; I have no use for a lap.

The taxi-hijacker, to our astonishment, commands his driver to halt at our canopy and offers to share his precious vehicle with us. This is very unusual for upper Park Avenue. So is our benefactor; he is black. He is also elegantly dressed. He would be better dressed than I am even if I were not in tennis clothes. He is taking his daughter, he says, to her kindergarten class at—I do not catch the whole name—some Episcopal church. We exchange introductions. The five-year-old at once addresses me as "Jack." So, with my blessing, does my six-year-old grandson, Jaime. So also does our sixteen-year-old mother's helper, though with mixed feelings on my part, inasmuch as she always respectfully addresses Ellie as "Mrs." Our Sir Galahad mentions an appointment his daughter has for an interview at Spence. He confides to us, in her presence but, he clearly believes, over her head, that in his view the only trouble with our neighborhood is that it has too many k-i-d-s. I had always thought that the principal drawback was the presence of too many D-a-l-t-o-n-S-c-h-o-o-l kids.

I don't know many American blacks, socially. I vividly recall a pre-war nightclub excursion to Harlem ("pre-war" to me means pre-Second-World-War)—in the days when one could visit Harlem at just about any hour with impunity—during which, before my popping naive eyes, minimally skirted waitresses, or whatever they were, snuggled up against the tables and deftly removed tips without using their hands; but that certainly didn't constitute a social relationship. I have written Profiles on blacks (Walter White, the longtime head of the N.A.A.C.P., for instance) and have, like most New York journalists, a few black friends, but I am in no position to lecture South Africans or American Southerners or anyone else on the merits of all-out social integration. We did once, years ago, have a Fresh Air Fund kid stay with us at Truro for a few weeks, and the kid was black. It was, all in all, a disaster; our guest got plenty of fresh air, but he could never quite get the hang of what was private property.

At the office, a call from a woman at *Esquire,* proposing that I do a tennis piece for them, a sort of *Consumer Reports* article in which I would test and assess various automatic ball-return machines. But today's paper says that *Esquire* is going to have a new editor, and when I ask the woman if she expects still to be there next week, she can offer me no assurances.

It is different at *The New Yorker.* Practically nobody ever leaves the place. I can think offhand of only one writer, for instance, who in the last forty years has vacated the premises involuntarily. And while the magazine has an extraordinary and laudable tolerance for eccentricity among its contributors, he was uniquely deranged. The last time I saw him (I was glad he did not spot me), he was shambling disheveledly up and down the aisle of a Madison

Avenue bus, haranguing the passengers in tongues of Babel. Even so, when he died, a dozen years after his last wavering stroll through our forgiving corridors, in the headline over his obituary, the *Times* called him "New Yorker Writer." Having been at the magazine for nearly forty years does not, accordingly, make me in the least unusual; I can also think offhand of a dozen members of the current staff who were on the scene when I arrived. But it is true, I guess, though I haven't counted, that by sheer survival I have probably written as many words for the magazine as anyone still alive. That and a token will get me a ride on the Madison Avenue bus.

The New Yorker does not mind if its staff writers take on assignments for other journals. For one thing, it could hardly object, inasmuch as most of us, though we are eligible for hospital insurance and for a modest institutional pension plan, are unsalaried, and are paid by the piece, much as if we were making neckties in a ghetto tenement. We are paid well, when we produce, but our piecework is intricate and time-consuming. Moreover, there are so many staff writers around by now that it is getting harder and harder to have one's output squeezed into the magazine. In a discussion a few of us were having one day not long ago about dreams, somebody wondered what Bill Shawn dreams about, and somebody else suggested that his most recurrent nightmare probably involves his thinking that it is time for the magazine to go to press and that he has nothing to put into it. That, the suggestor went on, was as logical an explanation as any for the fact the magazine keeps so many writers in its stable—around forty, I estimate—and so large a bank of unpublished pieces, many of which go down the drain because there simply isn't room to print them before they become hopelessly outdated. We run about seventy-five long-fact pieces a year, and probably one-third of these are bought from outsiders. That leaves fifty a year to be divided among forty writers. A discouraging state of affairs.

Thus it is essential for some *New Yorker* staff writers, if they want to live on a more than modest scale, to seek other sources of income. I am especially leery of taking on this proffered assignment from *Esquire*, though, because of what happened the last time I did. On that occasion, ten years ago or so, a male editor there said he wanted to discuss an idea they had, and could we meet for a drink? We did, at the Harvard Club (I grandly picking up the tab for his invitation), and it turned out they wanted a piece with some such title as "Whatever Has Happened to Arthur Schlesinger, Jr.?" I said I'd be happy to do it; I had known Arthur for many years, knew what had happened to him (in addition to writing, lecturing, and pontificating, he was a Distinguished Professor at the City University of New York, with a handsome office just across Forty-third Street from my own), and had occasionally played tennis with him, though his dexterity had never made him the human equivalent of even a semi-automatic ball-returning machine. Arthur was agreeable, too, especially when I promised not to dwell at undue length on his backhand. But when I turned the piece in, *Esquire* didn't accept it; they said I had made Arthur out to be likeable. But I *did* like him, I said.

That was too bad, they retorted, all at once rejecting both my article and my standards of judgment; they couldn't possibly consider running a piece on Arthur that made him sound like a nice guy. I probably should have suggested to the woman this morning that she offer the ball-return assignment to Schlesinger.

I have lunch at the Century with Gerry Piel, whom I want to talk to about Cyrus Eaton, a friend of his from way back. Before we get onto that, we discuss our forthcoming fortieth Harvard reunion. Gerry is in charge of the cultural portion of the program, and he solicits my views on that. I have mixed feelings about such high-minded fraternal diversions (though I suppose they are useful because they help convince wives that college reunions are not mere sustained mass drunks), having presided over one such solemn symposium at our thirty-fifth that was a semi-disaster: I assembled a panel of writers from the class, to discuss our peculiar way of life, and one of the participants whom I didn't know especially well, though I knew his professional credentials were quite in order, proved to be a colossal and unsquelchable bore.

We dine at Lilo's. Among my stepmother's other guests is a nice young woman who not long ago collaborated on an architectural book that mentioned my father. She and her co-author invited me then to talk to them about Ely at lunch at the Columbia University Faculty Club, and I said I'd be glad to have lunch with them, but not up there. For all I knew my name was posted at that club for being in arrears. I had joined it while teaching a course in non-fiction writing at Columbia (one of the most ego-building benefits of that stint was receiving mail grandly addressed to me as Professor, though technically my professorship, in striking contradistinction to Arthur Schlesinger's, was merely of the adjunct stripe) and the following year had received a bill for the renewal of my dues: five dollars per annum.

By the time I got around to notifying the club that inasmuch as I was no longer on the faculty it seemed inappropriate for me to belong to the Faculty Club, a month had gone by, and now I received a bill for $5.05—the extra nickel being a service charge slapped on me for my pokiness. I decided it would be easier to pay the whole amount than argue about it for the rest of my life. (I have spent more time than I care to think about over the last ten years trying to explain to Georg Jensen, Inc., and a host of collection agencies in its employ, that I do not and never have owed it forty-odd dollars; Jensen has never answered any of my letters, but its computer keeps sending me bills.) By the time I had remitted my $5.05, another month had gone by, and now Columbia sent me a bill, by first-class mail, in the amount of $0.05. I wrote back explaining that if we kept on exchanging first-class-mail communications *in re* this trifling sum, it would be a sad waste of both our limited resources, but as an instance of good faith, and also as an experimental thrust into man's now eternal duel with the computer, I enclosed a check for $0.04. Interestingly, that was the last I ever heard of that matter; for the past few years, whoever audits Columbia University's books may have been stumped by an inexplicable one-cent discrepancy on its balance sheet.

So I had asked the architectural writers instead to be my guests at the Harvard Club. They probed my memory about my father for an hour and a half and finally declared they had no further questions. As we rose to go our separate ways, the young woman's collaborator said he did after all have one more question: Inasmuch as they were comparative novices at reporting and as I had been engaged in that calling for most of my adult life, if I had been interviewing them instead of their interviewing me, what would I have done that they had not?

"I'd have taken some notes," I said.

Neither of them had written down a word I'd uttered.

Another guest at Lilo's dinner is a lady who keeps throwing Yiddish phrases at me and seems offended when I don't comprehend. I am Jewish—my mother's family came from Germany, my father's from Alsace-Lorraine—but I know fewer words of Yiddish than of Spanish, and my Spanish is confined to *"Hasta la vista."* There are, of course, many different degrees of Jewishness. My only visit to Israel occurred in 1967, just after the Six-Day War. I was shown around one rigidly Orthodox settlement by a black-frocked and -hatted Hassidic rabbi, who, while courteous and informative, could not refrain from chiding me once or twice for my having lapsed so patently from the faith of our mutual forefathers. The following day, I stopped for lunch at a roadside restaurant between Tel Aviv and Haifa, and there encountered an American man clad, like me, in sports shirt and shorts. A few moments' conversation revealed that we both hailed from Westchester, I from Scarborough and he from Scarsdale, on the other side of the county. He asked me what I did for a living, and I told him, and asked what he did. He was the rabbi of a reform synagogue, he said. I said that it must be a particularly exciting experience for a rabbi to be in Israel. "When I'm in Israel, I don't tell them I'm a rabbi," he said.

I never attended any kind of synagogue when I was growing up, and never really thought much about being a Jew until my freshman year at college. I tried out then for the editorial staff of the *Harvard Crimson*, and seemed to be doing as well as any of the other candidates. Toward the end of the demanding competition, the managing editor invited me out for a cup of coffee after the paper had gone to press—a most unusual gesture for one so highly placed to make toward a mere aspirant to glory. He complimented me at some length on my performance over the preceding several weeks, and said I had certainly earned appointment to the staff, but . . .

I waited. He was trying to figure out how to phrase his caveat. "I'm sorry to have to tell you that we've already filled our quota for this term," he finally said. I was so innocent that I didn't realize for a couple of minutes what he was talking about. I never got to see the second story of the *Crimson* building, admittance to which was by long tradition restricted to full-fledged members of the staff, until many years later, when I was the guest speaker at the paper's annual banquet. By then there were no more quotas, and the editors who invited me up were probably under the impression that I had been one of their ilk all along. I like to think that I do not much harbor grudges.

The first piece of writing I ever sold was about anti-Semitism. It was a short story, published in *Coronet*, that was really truth rather thinly—perhaps too thinly—disguised as fiction. It was an account of a vacation I'd spent at a Maine summer colony where the parents of my college roommate, Bob Wolf, owned a cottage. The colony, whose permanent occupants were almost all German Jews, also had a few bungalows that were rentable to transients. While I was there, a young Jewish couple drove up on their honeymoon and took a vacant bungalow. My story was about what happened to them, or, rather, did not happen: They were cruelly snubbed, for the reason—once more, in my naiveté I did not immediately grasp it—that they were Russian Jews. Bob's mother, like Ottie Swope's, didn't talk to me for quite some time afterward. But by then I had become a bona-fide reporter and comforted myself by remembering that Harold Ross had once told me in reference to something or other—I think, to the fact that he and Westbrook Pegler were not on speaking terms—that a forthright journalist can't afford to have any friends.

None of my three sons is Jewish, in a technical sense, because their mother isn't Jewish. But inasmuch as their name is Kahn, they will always, for better or worse, be regarded as Jews: In many parts of our society, a Jew can very simply be defined as somebody somebody else thinks is a Jew. When I was engaged to Jinny, back in 1944, she took me up to New Hampshire to meet her parents for the first time, and while I was unpacking I overheard her mother telling her in an anguished whisper that she'd inadvertently made the most awful mistake: She had ham planned for dinner and now what would she serve Jack instead? Our son Terry, whose religious upbringing was as sketchy as mine (Jinny and I did once send him to a Presbyterian Sunday School, but mainly because his friends went there), is the only member of the family, as far as I know, who has ever avowedly embraced Judaism, and his motivation made his devoutness moot. At Andover, all students were required to attend some kind of chapel service every Sunday morning, and when Terry learned that the Jewish rite began one hour later than any of the others, he elected to go to that one so he could have an extra hour's sleep. Ellie isn't Jewish, either, and indeed has given me a pair of plaid pants in the authentic tartan of her Munro clan. They go very nicely with my reconstituted tweed jacket. I have promised her—jokingly, of course—that if we ever bust up she gets the pants.

January 22

Another Saturday. I spend most of the day at the apartment, working on my Eaton piece. The innards of tomorrow's Sunday *Times*—book review, magazine, travel, business, those sections—are now delivered to our door at 2 P.M. Saturday. This is disturbing, because it means I have to stop and do the crossword puzzles. I cannot be confronted with a crossword without filling it in. It is an addiction as unshakable as chocolate candy, though less fattening. More time-consuming, however, especially every third Sunday when the *Times* has its two diagramless puzzles, which take longer than the others. The standard variety I can handle, ordinarily, with dispatch.

When I lived in Westchester, and took the commuter train to the city most weekdays, if I didn't have a gin-rummy opponent aboard I would often ride with three neighbors, each equipped—it was as automatic as shoes and socks—with that morning's *Times*. Nobody was allowed to peek at the crossword until the train began moving out of the 125th Street station. It then took, barring some mishap or foulup, exactly eleven minutes until the wheels stopped rolling at Grand Central Terminal. During that stretch, the four of us competed to see who could complete the puzzle first. (Not to finish it at all was considered thoroughly infra dig.) My recollection is that I always won. If the Philip Morris Company ever puts on a world's invitational crossword-puzzle championship competition at Nassau or some equally fetching oasis, I would like to be invited to that.

I think I might do well. Bel Kaufman once told me at a Saturday-night party that she was a speedy crossword solver, and we agreed to a race the following morning, conducted under the honor system. Neither of us was to glance at the Sunday *Times* puzzle page, cross our hearts and hope to die, until Bel phoned me. Then we would start in, and she would call back when she had finished the regular puzzle. It was one of the Sundays when the *Times* also had an acrostic puzzle. I had knocked off both by the time she phoned back to announce triumphantly that she'd finished the first one. I know this sounds like bragging, but facts are facts.

The new format of the daily *Times*, with all its sections on home and living and eating and whatnot, is disturbing. It is hard to find sports or obits or the crossword puzzle now without consulting the index. I always used to be able to turn to the various features of the paper by instinct, or rote. To have to look at the index is as unsettling to me as to have to ask directions while driving. The new New York *Post* is coming out now, under Rupert Murdoch's stewardship, and I wonder what effect if any that will have on the *Times*. More sex?

Even before Dolly Schiff sold out to the omnivorous Australian, strange things were happening on the New York newspaper scene. The *Daily News* was edging over in the direction of the *Times* (its crosswords no longer contained two-letter words), and the *Times* was edging over—relatively speaking—in the direction of the *News*, playing up all kinds of raffish stories that it might a few years back have handled more discreetly or entirely omitted. I suggested to Shawn that I try to do a Wayward Press department on this concurrent drift of both morning papers, but he demurred: He said he thought it was a wonderful idea but that he didn't want to revive the department. And indeed the magazine has not run any Wayward Press pieces since Joe Liebling died, in 1964. Most people think that A. J. Liebling did them exclusively, but I turned out a dozen of them while he was alive. Careless readers no doubt attributed mine to him because of the similarity in our initials. I wish that a few of his had been attributed to me.

I suppose my most memorable Wayward Press was a piece about Larry Adler and Paul Draper. The harmonica player and the dancer were both close friends—Larry was one of my very closest—at the time they got into trouble by instituting a libel suit against a woman who had caused an appearance of theirs to be cancelled in Greenwich, Connecticut, by accusing them of being pro-Communist. She had levelled the charge in 1949, a time when it was no allegation to be taken lightly, and when they turned to the courts for relief (they didn't get it; they got a hung jury), the right-wing press—the Hearst papers and their columnists, the *News* and some of its columnists, and such random other defenders of freedom and liberty as Igor Cassini, a.k.a. Cholly Knickerbocker—climbed all over them, in a nasty manner that I felt demanded a response. The case came to court early in 1950, and Shawn approved my writing an article about how the press was treating it. When I turned in my piece—advocacy journalism if ever there was any—a few *New Yorker* people were worried about it, because McCarthyism was beginning to flower and no one could be certain what estranging effect our printing it might have on some of our subscribers and, worse yet, some of our advertisers. Carmine Peppe, our chief make-up man, was worried, too, but for a different reason: The article contained thirty-eight footnotes. As a sop to editorial apprehensions, I agreed to a thirty-ninth—a declaration on my part that I was not and had never been a Communist.

Harold Ross, whose personal politics tended toward the conservative side, never saw the piece until it was in type and was scheduled to go—assuming that Carmine could magically wrestle all the footnotes into the appropriate columns—to press. Ross' reaction epitomized to me his greatness both as a man and as an editor. He ran into me in a nineteenth-floor corridor, rubbed his hand over his face in a characteristic gesture, and said, "God damn it, Kahn, why did you have to go and write that God damn piece? Now I've God damn got to run it." I received a few vicious letters from defenders of the detractors I had allegedly defamed, but if running the God damn piece lost the magazine any friends or any money, nobody ever told me.

The Harold Ross I remember was not the irascible, inconsiderate editor I have read about in various reminiscences about *The New Yorker*. Ross (I never called him anything to his face but "Mr. Ross") did not hire me personally in 1937, at which time the magazine he created was twelve years old. I was offered a job as a Talk of the Town reporter by St. Clair McKelway, Bill Shawn's predecessor as managing editor. I had no idea, when I reported for duty one Monday morning, what Ross looked like. (Once seen, he was unforgettable, with his mobile face the component features of which sometimes seemed to have been assembled by a kid playing with Silly Putty.) On my first day, with nothing much else to do, I busied myself learning the location of the nearest water cooler and the nearest men's room, the two basic balancing essentials, I had reasoned, of any office routine.

I was in the latter, urged on there by the former, when a commanding male figure entered, and took his stance in the adjoining urinal with an air of such authority that I knew intuitively it had to be the great Ross himself. Moreover, the stranger had a vaguely Gallic look and a bushy black sort of French-like mustache, and had I not read that during the First World War Ross had been in Paris, getting out the *Stars and Stripes* for the A.E.F.? My hunch was further confirmed when the dignitary alongside me said, buttoning his fly, "You're the new Talk reporter, aren't you?"

I said yes, sir, I was.

"We had another Talk reporter here named Kahn not long ago," he went on, rinsing his hands. "Had to fire him—" he was opening the door— "because he couldn't get his facts straight."

The door closed behind him. I was shaken, and remained so until I discovered three days later that the author of that particular genitourinary tract was Freddie Packard, the head of the fact-checking department.

When I did meet the real Ross (who, I wish someone had told me sooner, had his own private lavatory), he couldn't have been kinder or more helpful. Initially, my job was covering assignments and writing up straightforward, unembellished reports on them, to be rendered into *New Yorker* prose by Russell Maloney, at that time the Talk department's principal, indeed only, rewrite man. Maloney was a facile writer and an even more admirable typist; he would give me carbon copies of his rewrites of my reportage, and there was never a word, or even a letter, Xed out. (I can type fast enough—two thousand words an hour, if pressed—but I doubt whether I have ever managed a single flawless paragraph.) After a few months I was allowed to do Talk "originals"—that was, to report a story and write the theoretically final version of it too—and it was then that I began seeing a good deal of Ross. He handled Talk copy himself, with tender loving care, and he would often take a story of mine that he regarded as imperfect and put it through his own typewriter. Sometimes when he did he would walk the length of the nineteenth floor from his office to my cubbyhole to show me how he had changed my stuff and to ask me if I minded.

Did I mind! Here I was receiving a lesson in my chosen craft from one of its foremost practitioners, and he was apologizing for sharing his expertise with me! When I was further promoted, in 1938, to writing long fact pieces, I received the usual number of queries on Ross' galley proof: "Who he?" "What this mean?" "Don't get," and so on—the legendary Ross annotations that have sometimes been cited as evidence of his asperity. To me, they were more tutorial than tart. Ross had an unquenchable thirst for clarity, and to slake it one simply had to learn to write better.

Ross had one other memorable trait: When you wrote something that he particularly liked, he would stick a piece of paper in his typewriter (*his* typing was freeflowing and full of X's and strikeovers) and peck out a note of commendation. He had plenty of secretarial help and could easily have dictated these billets-doux, but he sensed accurately how much more they would mean to the recipients when they were patently handcrafted. Once in my mailbox at Scarborough—a small enough town so that the postmaster knew where everybody was employed—I found an envelope (containing a press release or some such throwaway contents) that bore no name but was addressed, pre-zip-code, merely to "The Editor, *The New Yorker*, Scarborough, N.Y." The envelope was dispatched by first-class mail, which set its sender back—this was 1949—exactly three cents. I passed the envelope, via cost-free interoffice messenger service, on to Ross, along with a note to the effect that I hoped he didn't think I was trying to usurp his position. In due course, I received a typed reply:

Mr. Kahn:
    Attached noted, finally. (It got under a large pile of stuff.)
    I construe this as God's doing and am willing to let you take over at any time, on four days notice. I've been waiting for this word. Come in any time and I will explain the office to you.

                                         Ross

I don't save many things, but I have had that note, so characteristic of its author, tacked to my office bulletin board ever since.

I never saw much of Ross socially. He was a whole war older than me, for one thing, and there was no reason why I should have. When toward the end of my war I became engaged to Jinny, though, and he heard the news, he asked us both to have a celebratory drink with him at "21"; he had no sons and I think he felt paternalistic, in the best sense of the word, toward his younger male writers.

With some trepidation, we invited him to attend our wedding. It was a modest, wartime ceremony, with only two attendants. Jinny's friend Mary B. Winslow, like her then an officer in the Women's Army Corps, was maid of honor; Bill Shawn, then one of my closest friends, was best man. The four of us, facing a judge who was presiding, had our backs turned to our audience while the formalities were conducted. It must have been the first time Shawn had ever turned his back to Ross. Then we did an aboutface and formed a receiving line.

As our families and friends came by, mumbling the conventional pleasantries, I hardly listened. I was waiting to hear what uniquely phrased sentiments Ross would see fit to convey. Soon he came shuffling along, smiling his familiar gap-toothed smile, extending his elastic hand for the familiar, limp, seemingly boneless shake. But the supposedly terrible-tempered Harold Ross could at times be as shy as a schoolgirl, and this time his diffidence overcame his tongue. He didn't say anything at all to the bride and bridegroom en passant, instead directing his remarks exclusively to the best man. "Jesus Christ, Shawn," Ross said, "you're getting bald."

The day Ross died, nearly seven years later, was the saddest in the history of *The New Yorker*, and when I cried in public that time I was not alone.

January 24

Lunch with Dick Clurman at the Century. I haven't used the club much in the five years I've belonged, but it's nice to have the option, and I once suggested to Cranston Jones that his house committee institute a backgammon area; that would divert some patronage—some of mine, at any rate—from the Harvard Club a block away. *The New Yorker* is an island in a sea of clubs—Century, Harvard, Yale, Princeton, New York Yacht, Coffee House, and, until they folded, Columbia and Lambs. There may be still others I never heard of. Dick, with three distinctive notches on his gun—chief of correspondents for *Time-Life*, John Lindsay's commissioner of Parks and Cultural Affairs, and chairman of the New York City Center—is now a public-affairs consultant for various private clients, the sort of thing Herbert Swope used to do after *he* gave up being an editor. Dick is on retainer from, *inter alios*, the Bronfman family, and he wants to discuss my doing a book, with their cooperation, on the recent Samuel Bronfman case, in which Sam's two alleged kidnappers were convicted merely of extortion. We talk of possible financial arrangements: No money straight to me from the Bronfmans, but they would probably underwrite a $100,000 advance from a publisher. The sum sounds attractive, and God knows would come in handy. The family would in any event reimburse me for my time if after preliminary research I concluded that Sam had not been totally in the clear in the whole murky business. But the root problem seems to me to be: How could I or anybody else prove that he was *not*, as charged, a homosexual?

Clurman says that after I had looked into that, my conclusion would necessarily have to be judgmental: Surely I would be prepared to state in writing, Dick says, that neither he nor I was a homosexual, but I couldn't *prove* that, either. One witness I could have summoned to bolster my contentions about myself is dead. He was a Greek tutor at Harvard who in my sophomore year took me to an elegant dinner at the Ritz in Boston, got me plastered, escorted me back to Eliot House, put me to bed, and tried to crawl in alongside me. Fortunately, my roommate came back to our suite at that crucial moment and saved me from a fate worse than stupor. The tutor later left Harvard, went to a smaller institution, and while on the faculty there committed suicide—conceivably because of some other undergraduate dalliance interruptus.

Clurman and I leave the Bronfman matter unresolved, and anyway I am more interested in a new train of thought: Can there be any significant connection between teaching the classics and homosexuality, or have my own experiences been coincidental? When I was in high school, one of the very finest members of the faculty was the head of the Latin department. He also coached a football team, and I was his quarterback one season. I caught pneumonia playing in the rain, and—this was before antibiotics— was bedded down at home, seriously ill, for quite a spell. When I had turned the corner, my teacher-coach came to call on me, was ushered into my room, and leaned over my supine body, to express, I thought, his sympathy for my plight. It was the first time a man had ever kissed me square on the mouth, and I sat bolt upright for the first time in three weeks. My mother happened to enter the room at that moment and pronounced herself delighted that the distinguished visitor had so noticeably hastened my recovery.

This has been a record day for me, of sorts—two meals at the Century. I seem to be using the place more than I think I do. E. and I dine there tonight with the Kenneth Wilsons, who've invited us to go with them afterward to an Alex Haley lecture at Lincoln Center. The Haley lecture is in the acoustically refurbished Avery Fisher Hall, and it is our first time there since Cyril Harris did the place over. I can hear very well, but this is perhaps not much of a test, inasmuch as we are in the fifth row. I probably should be listening to the speaker more carefully than I am—I have neither read "Roots" nor seen any of the segments of the television version, and feel like a cultural pariah—but Haley's remarks, which are largely auto-biographical, keep triggering mnemonic impulses in my brain, and I am off and running on a track of reveries. For instance, he says something about having been stationed in the Southwest Pacific during the war, as a Coast Guard enlisted man, and about having been called upon, because he was known to be a literary fellow, to write flowery letters to his commanding officers' girl friends back home. "Your hair is like the moonlight," Haley recalls having penned in his role of passionate amanuensis.

"Your breasts are like skinned coconuts, your eyes shine like a Papuan moon." I once wrote those words, from a New Guinea jungle command post, to a lady I had never laid eyes on. She was the wife of a Regular Army colonel, who was chief of staff of the 32nd Infantry Division, and who, though quite capable of composing his own letters, felt that his formidable military responsibilities had a higher priority. So he delegated to me the task of corresponding with his wife, and he even provided the V-mail forms. Unfortunately, he was too busy also to tell me much about his inamorata, so when I began writing home on his behalf I stuck pretty much to weather and scenery, sans, at the outset, any relevant metaphors.

After three or four exchanges of letters, the colonel said that his wife was complaining that he didn't seem affectionate enough, and he instructed me to enliven our half of the correspondence. Like Haley, I was only an enlisted man, and what the chief of staff said went. But I did point out to him that if he expected me to make love to his wife by V-mail, I ought at least to see what she wrote to us. He judged that to be eminently reasonable, and showed me her last letter, which had something in it about wishing his arms were around her. I shot back a testimonial to her legs that would have made Betty Grable blush, and her response to that was so downright bawdy that the colonel split his next ration of medical-alcohol-and-coconut-juice with me half and half. He moved on to another job soon afterward, and I don't know who stood in for him at mail call.

Now Alex Haley is saying, if I hear him correctly (and the acoustics are faultless), that in the course of his research for "Roots" he once spent $31,000 on air fare over a single ten-day stretch. I do not believe him; I don't think you can spend $3,100 daily on air fare even if you never touch the ground. That is the sort of statement which, if committed to paper by a writer, would spur into action *The New Yorker*'s redoubtable checking department, which operates on the not altogether unsound premise that no factual writer's facts are to be accepted at face value until they have been independently verified by somebody with more devotion to accuracy than any sloppy author could be expected to possess.

When I was contributing pieces to the magazine from New Guinea in the fall of 1942, however, the checkers once went too far in their quest for the pure revealed truth. I had sent back an installment in my Army Life series about Japanese night bombers causing us G.I.s to take refuge in slit trenches, and had made some high-flown literary comment about the beautiful synchronization between Japs and mosquitoes. During the war, it was quite permissible to call Japanese "Japs." In this instance, I'd have been better off using "Nips." By the time my cabled copy reached West Forty-third Street, "JAPS" had become "WAPS." The stenographer assigned to type out the piece for the editor who would be handling it, seeing that meaningless word in a sentence that also alluded to mosquitoes, understandably rendered "waps" as "wasps."

So now there was synchronization between wasps and mosquitoes. Fine. But what were these wasps that Kahn had suddenly introduced into his text without a smidgen of explanation? The checkers charged like cavalry to the rescue. They called up some entomological wizard at the Museum of Natural History and ascertained that there was, or could be, or once had been—the *New Yorker*'s keenly perceptive reporter in New Guinea had evidently rediscovered an insect species that science had previously believed to be extinct—a mud-dwelling wasp in that part of the world that might be found at the bottom of a slit trench. Forthwith a couple of sentences were inserted into the piece, clarifying for Ross' edification and to his satisfaction the mysterious wasps and their native habitat. The Japanese got off scot-free.

Now Alex Haley is in Brisbane, Australia. I had thought he was going to put me in mind of Africa. I spent several weeks in Brisbane, after I left New Guinea, disguised as a civilian war correspondent. I had got to that part of the world in the first place courtesy of E. F. Harding, major general, U.S.A., commander of the 32nd Division. He was a Regular Army soldier (West Point '09), and a rare one. He loved literature, and in recognition of his uncommon bent he had been awarded a pre-war tour of duty as editor of the *Infantry Journal*. When I got to Fort Bragg, he was a brigadier general and assistant commander of the 9th Infantry Division. He had read some of my stuff in *The New Yorker*, and he got me transferred to division headquarters, in public relations. Then, when he received his second star and his own division, he arranged for me to be transferred to that. I wrote a *New Yorker* Profile about him, but, for security reasons, couldn't identify his outfit or say where it was.

I was General Harding's secretary then, ignorance of shorthand notwithstanding. He wrote his own letters. Not long ago, though, I picked up a copy of a book, "Bloody Buna," which dealt with the New Guinea campaign in which the general and the colonel and I, with markedly different degrees of responsibility, were all involved; and I read in it, with genuine surprise, that I was then apparently leading a double life as a ghostwriter. The book—which did not allude to my wartime masquerade as a John Alden—stated flatly that from time to time I wrote General Harding's diary. If only I had settled in some nation with a high illiteracy rate, I could probably have made a nice living as an amanuensis.

The 32nd Division sailed from San Francisco to Adelaide in the spring of 1942 (the Japanese naval force assigned to sink us was diverted, happily, by the Battle of the Coral Sea), and went into battle on the northeast coast of Papua in October. Douglas MacArthur, for reasons I thought absurd, next decided that General Harding was too slow in going about the business of capturing the Japanese stronghold at Buna, but General MacArthur had more clout than I had; he had Harding relieved of his command. When General Harding was shipped back to Brisbane, for reassignment, he took me along, as aide, friend, and drowning-one's-sorrows drinking companion. The only trouble was that the hotel he was given quarters in wouldn't admit anybody below the rank of lieutenant colonel, and the best I could offer was a set of sergeant's stripes. The general and I agreed that we didn't want me sent to an infantry replacement depot; I might have got shipped out of there before either of us could do anything about it.

So for six heady wartime weeks I stayed at a large private home that had been rented by the fulltime war correspondents in the area, a fashionable gathering-place since it harbored the best food, drink, and Red Cross girls to be had for several thousand miles around. To make myself more socially acceptable when the dinner guests at Ashton Hall included military eminences of the stripe of the four-star Marine General Alexander Vandergrift, I removed my stripes from my sleeves. Inasmuch as all the other correspondents wore uniforms without insignia of rank, I was then outwardly indistinguishable from anyone else on the premises, and when a general or admiral who happened to be seated next to me at the table would inquire what publication I represented I would reply, quite truthfully, *"The New Yorker."* I was also by then a correspondent for *Yank*, the Army weekly whose contributors were exclusively enlisted personnel, but in Brisbane I rarely mentioned that accreditation.

The only problem that arose was when I came down with a violent case of malaria that I had contracted in New Guinea. I didn't want to go to an army hospital, because I'd have had to give a recognized military unit affiliation when I was admitted and when I was dismissed. I think it was Jack Turcott of the New York *Daily News* who came up with the solution. There was a Medical Corps lieutenant who used to hang around Ashton Hall a good deal; he considered the food, drink, and company far more stimulating than that furnished by *his* military unit. The doctor was informed that while his regular visits were still welcome, they were now conditional on his taking on a private patient. He agreed, and every morning and evening he would attend to my fever or chills, as the case might be, with suitable medication and bedside solace. None of us knew until he had restored me to health that the whole episode had been, for him, largely experimental; he was a research psychiatrist.

General Harding's initials stood for "Edwin Forrest." Named by his Ohio parents after a great interpreter of Hamlet, he could quote that play practically verbatim, and it was one of the few remaining prides of his life—following his unfair relief at Buna—that he had seen almost every major production of "Hamlet" staged in America in his lifetime. The general and I remained friends after the war, indeed until his death (he was one of my oldest son's godfathers—the other, because I believe in balance, having been a corporal); and one of the few peacetime kindnesses I was able to extend to him, in partial repayment of his many wartime kindnesses to me (by removing me from New Guinea, he may have saved my life), was to wangle a single matinee ticket for Richard Burton's "Hamlet" when Terry's godfather came east in 1964 to attend his fifty-fifth West Point reunion.

January 25

Toots Shor and Eli Lilly died yesterday. I was far from being a regular patron of Shor's old saloon, even while making my Tables for Two rounds, because I could never discern in him any of the lovable traits that others so assiduously chronicled. The only time I was ever treated with civility, let alone courtesy, at Shor's, was when I had dinner there one night with Frank Sinatra while I was doing a Profile on the singer. It was not the ideal setting in which to conduct an interview—the sidewalk outside littered with squealing bobby-soxers, and, inside, Sinatra surrounded by his usual retinue of flunkeys: press agents, gofers, and the omnipresent Mafia-type sidekick who functioned more or less as a bodyguard. On top of everything else—almost literally on top of Sinatra—was the fat, ugly Shor, hopping around that single glittering patron like a toad hoping to be changed into a prince.

Shor was seventy-three when he died, but today's obituary-page average is just a shade under seventy-seven. It promises to be a very good day. Eli Lilly brought the average up, having reached ninety-one. But I know that it was his ambition, and intention, to get to one hundred, and there was a doctor in Indianapolis whose sole professional responsibility was rumored to be to keep the pharmaceutical patriarch alive that long.

My maternal grandfather's goal was a relatively modest ninety, but Grandpa missed out by a couple of months. A year and a half before he died, Mima and he celebrated their sixty-second wedding anniversary. They were living in Elmsford, not far from our Westchester place, so Jinny and I invited them to dinner at Tappan Hill, one of the fancier restaurants in the vicinity. We made all the arrangements in advance—cocktails on the terrace overlooking the Hudson, this wine with the oysters when we were seated inside, that wine with the steak, and so forth and so on. At 6 P.M., just as Jinny and I were dressing, her parents called. They had driven down from New Hampshire to see us, and were an hour away. I do not like to be dropped in on unexpectedly, even by close kin. There was nothing to be done, though, but to call Tappan Hill and report that our party of four would now be a party of six.

Harold and Ruth Rice were dedicated Christian Scientists and thus did not drink, but neither my grandfather nor I let their austere presence dampen our spirits, or consumption thereof. When the dinner was over, and Grandpa was about to climb in his waiting automobile, he didn't notice a curb, tripped, and fell. He picked himself up spryly, and when I inquired worriedly the next morning whether he had hurt himself, Mima assured me that he had only a slight bruise to show for the tumble. He died a year and a half later, of stomach cancer, but my New Hampshire in-laws, without exactly saying so outright, always sort of gave me the feeling that they believed I had hastened, if not engineered, his demise, by getting him drunk at Tappan Hill.

I spent a lot of time in Indianapolis in 1974 and 1975, and didn't enjoy a moment of it. Eli Lilly and Company was going to celebrate its centennial year concurrently with the nation's bicentennial, and I had been offered a fairly handsome fee to write a history of the drug company to be privately published and distributed solely among Lilly employees and shareholders. I had done that sort of thing once before. In 1959, I had written a series of pieces for *The New Yorker* on the Coca-Cola Company, which later became the book "The Big Drink."

The genesis of that series was peculiar. Ordinarily, *New Yorker* writers think up their own subjects; we have an idea department at the magazine, but the ideas it concocts rarely work out as well as ideas that people conjure up themselves. At that time, though, I was stumped for a long-range undertaking, and Bill Shawn was aware of my predicament. We chanced to meet in an editorial corridor one afternoon, he walking in one direction, I in the other. As we drew abreast, Shawn said, without breaking stride, "Coca-Cola?" and I, also without halting, said "Yes." That one-second exchange was the only discussion we had of the project until I turned in my manuscript several months later.

In the spring of 1969, a decade after my initiation into the corporate world of Coca-Cola, I had a phone call from Atlanta from a member of the Harvard Working Class who had worked himself well up since 1937—J. Paul Austin, the chairman of the board of Coca-Cola. Paul said he had something he wanted to talk to me about, and could we get together when he was next in New York? A few days later, we met and he explained what was on his mind. The patriarch of the Coca-Cola Company, Robert Winship Woodruff, had his eightieth birthday coming up in December, and his associates at the company wanted to give him a special present. Having already bestowed on their leader a surfeit of sterling-silver trays, Steuben glass, replicas of George Washington's sword, and whatever, they had hit on the notion of surprising him with a short biography of himself. Since there wasn't much time to get a book written and produced before the end of the year, and since I knew Woodruff and knew a good deal about the company, would I take on the chore?

I agreed, and in the course of negotiating the terms of our contract my agent, Monica McCall, came up with a novel twist. Normally, the one thing a writer insists on, especially if he is dealing with living people (viz., the Swopes), is complete editorial control over the contents of his book. A commissioned book is something else again, however, so Monica had stipulated that the Coca-Cola Company was to have complete editorial control. I was protected by a clause of her devising that said that in the event the company insisted on changes that were unacceptable to me, I would have the right to remove my name from the printed work. There were no problems; indeed, after I turned in my manuscript Paul Austin suggested—not demanded—merely the deletion of a single anecdote, and I was happy to accede.

So when Eli Lilly and Company approached me in 1974 I had a precedent to go by. To this day, I do not know why I was approached in the first place. I had a phone call, out of the blue, from a Lilly public relations man. He said he had come to New York from the firm's headquarters in Indiana and would like to see me. He stopped by my office and explained that the company was looking for an outsider to write a centennial history—somebody with a fresh point of view toward the pharmaceutical industry. I said I had that, all right: I knew nothing about the business, had never been to Indianapolis, and hardly ever took even an aspirin tablet. (Christian Science had nothing to do with this; I just never got into the habit of taking sleeping pills or much of any other kind of medication.)

In due course, we signed a contract, along the lines of the Coca-Cola one, and I set forth on the first of many trips to Indianapolis. I made about sixteen of these altogether, as well as a few visits to other Lilly outposts, interviewing active and retired company executives (among them, old Mr. Eli himself, now designated honorary chairman of the board, and also his grandnephew Eli II, a route salesman in New England); and trying to keep my eyes open as I pored over reams of printed matter enshrined in the company's well-tended archives. I was given an office at headquarters, next to that of the company's full-time historian, Gene McCormick, who may have viewed my presence on his scene with mixed feelings (though Gene never said so and was most helpful); *he* was working on a company history, too, though it was understood all around that his, a full-blown, heavily-footnoted one, would probably never be published but, if he ever completed it, simply added to the bulging archives. And at that the prospect of his ever finishing was dim: He was on a treadmill moving backwards, taking a bit more than a year to chronicle each year gone by.

While in Indianapolis, I stayed at the Columbia Club, a not very hard club to get into; all one had to do was have a connection with Eli Lilly and Company, which occupied a dominant position in town not unlike that of Coca-Cola in Atlanta. I was beginning to have a wide acquaintance among big frogs in small ponds. I spent a good deal of time loitering in the Columbia Club, eating dinner every evening there alone. (I could have tried some of the city's restaurants, but I hate solitary dining.) The whole experience was baffling: Here I was a trusted employee, so to speak, of the big company, with ready access during office hours to all its top brass, and thus the antithesis of a nosy investigative reporter; and yet during the dozens of nights I spent in Indianapolis, I was never once asked out socially, for a meal, for a drink, for *anything*, by anyone connected with Lilly.

I had never before been treated like a social outcast, and hope never to be again. When I told Ellie about this, after my seventh or eighth invitationless trip to the Midwest, she concluded that it must be company policy not to mix its business with my pleasure, and I laughed at the notions her silly lovable little head could come up with; and yet, she may have been right, because the policy, if there was a policy, seemed to be nationwide. At one point, I went to Arizona to interview some retired chieftains of the Lilly tribe. One of them lived a couple of hours from Tucson, out in the desert, and after I'd driven to his ranch, getting lost once or twice on a hot dry morning, he never even offered me a glass of water. Very peculiar.

The icing on this particular cake (never was a figure of speech less appropriate) was provided on that same reportorial excursion. The following day, I drove from Tucson to Phoenix, a distance of some hundred and fifty miles, for a morning interview with another retired Lilly bigwig. The company had bought Elizabeth Arden a couple of years before, and had thus come into proprietorship of the high-class and high-priced ladies' health resort at Phoenix, the Maine Chance Farm, which Mamie Eisenhower and her set used as a physiotherapeutic retreat.

It so happened that the public relations man who'd initiated my whole association with Lilly had just recently been put in charge of Maine Chance, so I phoned him from Tucson, said I'd be finished with my interview in Phoenix around noon, and, inasmuch as I wanted to have a squint at the Farm anyway in connection with my research, why didn't I drive over and have lunch with him? He said that would be fine.

I arrived at Maine Chance just before twelve, and hungry, having had a very early breakfast back in Tucson. We talked for about an hour in his managerial office. Then he suggested a stroll around the grounds. We strolled for forty-five minutes, in the course of which he pointed out the dining hall where his patrons were lunching, and invited me to sample the fruits of a tangerine tree. I helped myself to two tangerines; they were small and stringy. Then we returned to his office and he wondered if I had any more questions. The only one I had I didn't ask: I was wondering when and where he was going to have lunch.

I myself had a hamburger at a diner down the road.

Ellie and I are slated to fly to Anchorage, Alaska, early tomorrow morning. At eleven-thirty tonight, she remembers that she has a manuscript she has to get in the mail to some magazine, and I am happy to be able to offer to drive her downtown to the one main post office I know is open; we have just retrieved our car from Skipper, after its long hospitalization. I am about to drop her off at our apartment, a few minutes after midnight, before returning the car to the garage, when we hear a funny hissing noise. Just as I draw up at our canopy, the same old tire runs out of air. I have never had any idea what makes an automobile run, but at least I have learned how to change a tire. I find it as good a way of keeping in shape as taking pills.

January 26

Kathie Field, who is going to fly to Anchorage with us, comes to the apartment for breakfast, and I apologize to her for my hands, which are not quite yet scrubbed clean after my late-night session of pneumatic calisthenics. Tires seem to be my bane wherever I go. Ellie's French is almost letter-perfect, but mine is woeful. Before I had her around to get me out of sticky Gallic situations, I flew to France from England one time, and was met at the airport by a friend who, in the course of driving me into Paris, stopped for gas. I chanced to remark how delightful it had been across the Channel to have barmaids say "God bless, lovey," as one reached for one's glass, and I wondered what the equivalent phrase, if any, was in French. My companion happened at that instant to glance at one of his wheels, and his response—addressed, as I learned only later, not to me but to the service-station attendant—was *"Gonflez nos pneus!"* Our next stop was at a café, for an aperitif. I raised my glass, smiled at my friend, and said, to his understandable bewilderment, *"Gonflez nos pneus!"*

At breakfast, we read in the *Times* of the frigid weather that has bedevilled the whole eastern part of the country, down to and including Florida. It has been colder in Miami than in Anchorage. I have been invited up there to take part in a weekend seminar on journalism being conducted by the University of Alaska. I—for air fare and the usual modest honorarium—am to represent magazines, although magazines do not know this. Technically, because Shawn is also unaware that I am going to Alaska, I can hardly claim even to be representing what I sometimes boldly call *my* magazine. Ben Bradlee, of the Washington *Post*, will represent newspapers, and Don Oliver, of NBC, the electronic media.

Ellie is going along. Aside from a brief visit to the transit lounge of the Anchorage air terminal, she has never been to Alaska, under any climatic conditions, and she is eager to see the place. Also, she has made the necessary advance arrangements. It is crucial for essentially freelance writers like her and me to have reasonable justification for deducting most of our travel expenses, if we hope to travel at all, from our income taxes. Greece last summer was a cinch; E. writes about art and I was anticipating the erosion of the Parthenon.

Now, to make the cost of Ellie's trip a legitimate business expense, she has got *Ms.* magazine to assign her to do a piece about Kay Fanning, her roommate at Smith and the editor and publisher of the Anchorage *Daily News*, one of the city's two dailies. E.'s expenses won't be extravagant in any event, because this time both of us are going to room with Kay, who has been running the *News* ever since the death of her husband, Larry Fanning. The paper won a Pulitzer Prize last year for an exposé of some Teamsters Union shenanigans. Kathie is Kay's daughter by her first marriage, to

Marshall Field IV. Kathie, Ellie, and I start off by taxi to the airport and have travelled exactly four blocks when we have a flat tire. I am not in the least surprised. A flat on a plane, though, is something I do not care to speculate about.

It has been eighteen years since my last trip to Alaska. I spent several weeks there in the winter of 1959, just after statehood, writing about the transition for *The New Yorker*. That was a conventionally cold winter, with the temperature in Fairbanks hitting minus fifty-six one day; somebody jostled my elbow then while I was drinking hot coffee at a dog-sled race, and the spilled coffee froze before it hit the ground. That is minus fifty-six *Fahrenheit*. I do not know what it is, Centigrade or Celsius. I sold *The New Yorker* an article on the nation's snail-like conversion to the metric system a few years back, but it was one of those pieces that, after being duly set up in type, never ran and eventually died; it is characteristic of the feebleness of my memory that although I did a reasonably faithful job of research, I still can't handle the metric system and doubt whether I would ever be comfortable with it. That is no argument against it, however; there are many changes, existing or planned, that I am not comfortable with, notable among them the American League's designated hitter.

The farthest north I got in Alaska in 1959 was Kotzebue, up on the Bering Strait, where I shared quarters, in the only hostel available (it was the second story of a general store), with some Texans who had gone there to hunt polar bears. They couldn't understand why anyone would be in Kotzebue for any other reason. I couldn't understand why anyone would be anywhere for *their* reason. I had flown in from Nome, on a scheduled airline flight; the flight consisted of a single-engine plane, a pilot, and me. The trip took longer than the schedule called for, because as we were approaching Kotzebue my pilot was informed by radio that a Texan had got himself lost on the ice chasing a bear, and we were asked to search for him. Never found him; but then Texans are surely more expendable than polar bears. The only other time I ever found myself on so small-scaled a scheduled flight was when I was the lone passenger on a single-engine aircraft belonging to Southwest African Airways, bound from Windhoek to Swakopmund. As we were crossing the bleak and seemingly limitless Namib Desert, the pilot, a playful Afrikaner, decided to chase ostriches, which meant that he kept swooping down to within fifty or sixty feet of the ground, which meant that I had an excellent close-up view not merely of flustered ostriches but of scattered bleached bones, species unknown. I left my fear of flying in the Namib Desert.

Now we are on a nearly empty Boeing 747 with a crew almost as numerous as the passengers, bound for Anchorage via Seattle. Ellie is relaxed, though airplanes used to terrify her, as unmanned elevators still do.

I cannot recall precisely where it was that she lost *her* fear of flying, but the catalyst was probably either Nigeria Airways, between Lagos and Kaduna, or Garuda Airlines, on the Bali-Singapore run. At Seattle we "deplane" after—this is a new one to me—the aircraft is "groomed." I have been copy-editing my Eaton manuscript en route. I would love to be able to edit aeronautical jargon—better yet, to be able to turn it on or off; it seems to me that the only time a pilot ever employs his loudspeaker system is to advise me of the weather at a distant destination at the precise moment when I have managed to go to sleep. I wish airlines would let passengers define what they consider their convenience and comfort. The Eaton manuscript has kept me awake for quite a spell, because there are a lot of words in it. The most often voiced complaint I hear about *New Yorker* pieces is that they are too long. My attitude toward that is, I suspect, just about the same as that of any other writer for the magazine: I think that everybody's pieces are too long except my own.

I wonder how much Alaska has changed since 1959. When I was there then, the whole state was (except for dimensions) like a small town. Everybody seemed to know everybody else. Things cannot be too much different now; in a book about the state by Tay Thomas that I brought along to help me refresh my memories, I note that the author, whose husband, Lowell T., Jr., is now lieutenant governor, observes that the population of Soldotna "has mushroomed to around one thousand residents." Only an Alaskan writer, perhaps, would use that verb in that context; Alaskan terminology is as distinctive as, and more colorful than, the airlines'. It is illustrative of the small-townness of Alaskan life that Kay has told us that two nights hence we are going to have dinner with Tay and that tonight Jay (Governor Hammond, an outdoorsy type Ellie and I met in New York last year), will be flying up to Anchorage from Juneau to dine with us.

Only in Alaska—or, come to think of it, Burundi. When we were on our trans-Africa junket, about halfway between Dakar and Dar es Salaam, we had a few hours' layover at Bujumbura, and the United States ambassador to Burundi, Tom, came to the airport in person to greet us and show us around; having anybody visit Burundi, however briefly, was a big event for him. We endeavored to repay the compliment by buying about a two-year supply of Burundi coffee beans.

The last time E. and I flew into Anchorage was in the spring of 1973, en route to the People's Republic of China. I had several times been around the edges of China, and indeed while on the offshore island of Macao had been, if I were a better swimmer than I am, within swimming distance. But I had never had a chance to visit the mainland, and when that opportunity arose E. and I were both quick to grab it. By coincidence, both of us were engaged at that time in research for books about China. Ellie, whose exposure to Chinese art and history dated back to her childhood (her brother Don

Munro is a full-fledged Sinologist), was working on one about the American missionary movement in China; mine was about the American Foreign Service officers, a few of them missionary sons, who had been assigned to China not long before the Communist takeover in 1949 and who, back in the days when McCarthyism was in vogue, had been pilloried for "losing China." So we had a special interest in seeing the country we were both spending so much time thinking about.

The *deus ex machina* who got us there was Max Granich—"Manny" to his friends—a longtime American Communist. His brother was Mike Gold, the *New Masses* writer; his wife was Grace Maul, a close associate of Earl Browder. Manny had a summer place in Truro, and we had met him once at a Cape Cod cocktail party, conceivably one at our house. (I am forever running into people whom I take for strangers, and who then remind me how much they enjoyed my quondam hospitality.) Although we knew Granich only slightly, we knew a good deal about him. A man in his upper seventies, with a startling physical resemblance to Ho Chi Minh, Manny had been an ardent radical, if not a revolutionary, for almost as long as his Vietnamese lookalike. Granich had worked as an engineer in the Soviet Union in the nineteen twenties, and in the mid-thirties had edited a left-wing English-language journal in Shanghai. In the fall of 1971, he and his wife had been among the first Americans to be welcomed to the P.R.C. after the Ping-Pong players had broken the visa barrier. The Graniches were in Peking at the same time that two other old-China-hand acquaintances of ours, the John S. Services, were returning to the capital for their first visit in more than twenty-five years. Jack Service had known Mao Tse-tung and Chou En-lai quite well in the pre-war days, and he and his wife were invited to a reception that Prime Minister Chou gave for the sixty or seventy foreign visitors in Peking. Jack had told me how impressed he had been, when the guests were about to have their picture taken with their host, by Chou's insistence that the Graniches sit in the places of honor on either side of him.

Granich had been invited then, by the Chinese People's Association for Friendly Relations with Foreign Countries, to return as the leader of a sixteen-person tour group. By the time the necessary arrangements had been concluded, his wife had died, so he had recruited fifteen others. At the last minute, one couple had had to pull out. On learning this, Ellie and I volunteered to take their places, and Manny seemed pleased: He evidently had a deal with Japan Air Lines according to which he would receive free round-trip passage between New York and Hong Kong, provided that he furnish fifteen full-fare-paying bodies. We enabled him to stick to his half of that capitalistic bargain. Ellie and I knew a number of people who had been trying for more than a year to obtain Chinese visas, without success; indeed, we had written to Peking ourselves, some six months previous, and hadn't had even an acknowledgment of our letter. So we asked Granich if, when we reached Hong Kong, we could be absolutely certain of being admitted to the P.R.C. He said yes, we could. Thus assured, we procured a scarce copy of the invaluable "Nagel's Guide to China," and took the customary shots.

It turned out that my doctor of many years' standing, Louis Faugeres Bishop, numbered among his other patients David Bruce, who had not long before been appointed chief of the American Liaison Office in Peking. I was well aware that Dr. Bishop was an uncommon physician, quite apart from his professional prowess; he is the only doctor I ever heard of who sometimes treats his patients to lunch. (He is the only individual on earth, moreover, I would wager, who ever favored a reporter with a usable anecdote at the same time he was fingering his prostate.) So I was not surprised when, along with a cholera booster, Louis gave me a gracious letter of introduction to Ambassador Bruce.

Ellie and I hadn't known whom we were going to China with until the Granich group assembled at the Kennedy Airport. We perceived at once that most of them, like our leader, were fairly well along in years, and it didn't take long for us to realize that most were decidedly to one extreme of the ideological spectrum; Manny sometimes referred to them en masse as "lefties." On the way to Anchorage (some of our fellow travellers did Tai Chi Chuan exercises in the aisles of the plane), one of them, a physician from Connecticut, referred to himself as "the Red Doctor of Hartford." He saw red at Anchorage, when the passengers on our flight were confined to the transit lounge. Ellie and I assumed that this was because we had already gone through an airport security check and Japan Air Lines didn't want to have to repeat the tedious procedure; the doctor and a couple of other members of our party, contrarily, grumbled that we were being barred from access to the rest of the terminal and its environs because of the repressive nature of the imperialistic American government. The doc's specialty was ophthalmology, but considering the average age of our group, it was comforting to have in it someone who had gone through medical school; indeed, even before we reached China, one woman in our party collapsed in a Hong Kong restaurant. Our doctor stretched her out on the floor and called for cold towels. A Chinese Communist tourist official who was escorting us said that in the P.R.C. they would have sat her up and applied *hot* towels. It was our first clash of cultures.

When we all finally made it, more or less whole and hale, across the border, we spent part of one morning in Peking touring the five-hundred-bed Chao Yang (Rising Sun) Hospital. (The day before, both the Red Doctor of Hartford and Ambassador Bruce, who on most subjects would not, I suspected, see eye to eye, had called my attention to a newspaper story about an eighty-three-year-old Chinese man who, blind for ten years, had had a cataract operation, and whose first words, on regaining his vision, had been, "My sight has been restored in my old age thanks to the wise leadership of Chairman Mao and the Chinese Communist party.") At the hospital, we were escorted into a room all of whose eight beds were occupied by women recovering from abdominal surgery. Our ophthalmologist surprised me by asking, through an interpreter, to be allowed to scrutinize the incisions; the parts of the women's bodies of which he was forthwith vouchsafed an avid glimpse seemed far from eye territory. He then inquired how long the women would be kept in the hospital to convalesce. Ten days, he was informed. "Tell them that in the United States they'd be out in *seven* days," the Red Doctor said to the interpreter. "The reason is that *our* hospitals are anxious to save money, so there'll be extra money for Nixon to have to drop bombs on Vietnamese." The interpreter, nonplussed, had not bothered to translate that Hartfordian war communiqué.

Kay Fanning, who would make an estimable ambassador to Burundi, is waiting for us at the Anchorage airport. The local temperature is thirty-six. Very warm for January, and this day practically the warmest place in the whole United States. The proprietor of a local skating rink has had to import some kind of synthetic surface he can spread and use in lieu of ice. Kay has already met Ben Bradlee's plane, and has the "All the President's Men" man in tow. We learn at once that Kay is in a crisis situation, involving her formidable journalistic competition. It seems that Bob and Evangeline Atwood, the proprietors of the Anchorage *Times*, which Kay is about to sue for abrogation of contract or restraint of trade or some such, have invited Ben to dine with them the day after tomorrow, and that Ben has refused to go unless they ask her, too, and that they have capitulated. So the lamb will sup with the lions, while E. and I eat at the Lowell Thomases'. As for Bradlee, he has a problem of his own: He hasn't even left the Anchorage airport, but he is already fretting about how he is going to get back down east in time to attend a New York ceremony at which Jason Robards will receive an award for portraying him in the movie version of the Bernstein-Woodward opus.

Kay explains her troubles. It seems that she made a participation agreement with the Atwoods' *Times* in 1974 under the terms of which the *Times* agreed to handle the *Daily News'* advertising and circulation and she agreed to discontinue Sunday publication. But the Sunday paper had been her most profitable, and now she is hurting, and has had to cut her staff from twenty-one to twelve; she has lost, *inter alios*, two of the three reporters who won her the Pulitzer Prize. "I got less publicity for the Pulitzer than for going broke," she tells us. She hands me a copy of the latest issue of the *News*, which contains a mention of our imminent conference on journalism. I note that I am identified as being associated with "The New York Magazine." What can I say? She is our hostess.

By the time we join Governor Hammond for dinner, at the spacious home of some transplanted Texans, it is close to midnight, New York time. I am seated next to an urbane Eskimo born and raised in Kotzebue, and we discuss other Texans and their polar bears. The Texan my pilot and I were looking for in 1959, I am glad to be informed, was eventually spotted, retrieved, and repatriated. The menu includes both Alaska salmon and grits. Did Alaskans eat grits in 1959, or, for that matter, before Election Day last year? The Eskimo was mentioned not long ago in a *New Yorker* piece of John McPhee's, about relocating the Alaskan state capital, and he tells me a story I hadn't heard about our redoubtable checking department. A checker called him long distance to ask if McPhee was correct in stating that the color of a Chevy pickup truck the Alaskan had been riding in on a certain day was green. The callee had said he hadn't the faintest recollection. "Well, could you tell us who would know?" the checker had persisted.

Governor Hammond is mum, at least in my presence, about the shifting of the capital, but he does request that I send him a back issue of the magazine in which *he* was mentioned. I am embarrassed to have to confess that I have no recollection of that citation myself, but I promise to institute a search as soon as I return to my office. Our hosts' daughter, apparently having been tipped off that I am an imported intellectual, asks me to help her with her homework. She needs an authoritative answer to a question her philosophy instructor has posed: What is reality? I am bone tired, and tell her to say that reality is whatever the teacher is supposed to have taught her it is by the end of the course. The girl seems satisfied with my response; I see no future for her as a *New Yorker* checker.

When we get back to Kay's house, on this January night in Alaska, there is a dark brown puddle oozing across her kitchen floor—chocolate ice cream that has somehow melted, for God's sake, *inside* her freezer.

January 27

I awake at 4 A.M.—9 A.M., of course, New York time, 3 P.M. in Athens. So it goes. We have to get up early anyway, because today it has been arranged for us to fly, courtesy of BP Alaska (British Petroleum), to Prudhoe Bay, the fountainhead of the Alaska Pipeline, where more seasonable temperatures are guaranteed to prevail. Up on the North Slope, there are only four recognized categories of winter temperature—"Cold," "Very Cold," "Bitter Cold," and "Exposed Flesh Freezes." As we take off in our executive jet, our escort for the outing, a debonair Englishman who has done tours of petroleum duty in Iran and other fountainheads kinder to exposed flesh, draws our attention to the spot where a Japan Air Lines plane crashed the other day, killing all hands aboard as well as its cargo—a load of Tokyo-bound beef cattle. The pilot is alleged to have been an American who, conceivably regarding his mission as ludicrous, was blind drunk when he tried to take off. We fly right alongside Mount McKinley on the way north, with two-thirds of its twenty thousand feet gleaming snow white above the clouds. We land at Prudhoe Bay at 11 A.M., as dawn is breaking. The weather prediction is three hours of daylight. We have come at a good time of year; from November to January, there was a fifty-six-day stretch without any sunrise at all. Even up here, though, the temperatures have been abnormal; instead of their usual minus forty to fifty degrees, the inhabitants have been basking, relatively speaking, at around minus twenty. Exposed flesh can take that, especially when fitted out, as ours promptly is, with parkas and mukluks. E. scores a first for the family: She walks on the Arctic Ocean.

Prudhoe isn't as close to the North Pole as Point Barrow, to be sure, but it's as far north as anyone has ever harvested oil. Nine billion six hundred million barrels of the precious stuff are lying under our feet, and they are scheduled to start flowing through the eight-hundred-mile pipeline in July. We know on arrival that we'll be staying more than the three hours of daylight, because our plane has to turn right around and fly two litter cases to the Anchorage hospital. Back injuries, from slipping on ice. The first thing I notice, on leaving the airstrip, is a tree. A tree in the tundra! I didn't think it was botanically possible. It isn't; on getting closer, we perceive that it is a leftover Christmas tree that somebody has stuck in the ice.

There was nothing at Prudhoe, before oil was struck in 1963, except tundra in summer and snow and ice in winter. Now we find a bustling community scattered over two hundred square miles. It cost four billion dollars to build. Incredible place, with dozens of structures—power station, refinery, pump houses, waste-disposal plants, drilling rigs, and more such going up all the time. In addition to construction men, who work a nine-week stint, seven days a week, and then get a week off (good pay: a chambermaid earns a hundred dollars a day), there is a permanent staff of a thousand, who alternate seven-day shifts and then are flown to Fairbanks, Anchorage, or Barrow to spend a week with their families.

They live well up on the North Slope, in two motel-like hostels, run, on behalf of eleven participating oil companies, by BP and ARCO (Atlantic Richfield). The BP hostel has three million-gallon water tanks and an indoor swimming pool. The pool is a hedge against fire. The ARCO digs boast one twenty-thousand-square-foot unit that contains a theatre, basketball court, billiard room, and small running track, thirty-two laps to the mile. The unit weighs twelve hundred tons and was barged in last summer with everything in place—theatre seats, carpeting, light fixtures, the works. What people can do these days with enough money and technology! Both residences have saunas. ARCO has two, one for women and one for men. BP's is unisex. Both have fresh food flown in daily, weather permitting, and in-house bakers. Nobody comes to Prudhoe by sea, except for six summer weeks when the ice drifts offshore. (In 1970, a seventy-ship convoy brought in one hundred and eighty-seven thousand tons of stuff, including one hundred and sixty-eight miles' worth of four-foot-diameter pipe made in Japan, for the pipeline. Maybe the ill-fated beef cattle were a partial quid pro quo.) We are told that it costs two hundred and sixty-five dollars a day to house, feed, and sauna-bath every individual on the scene. No alcoholic beverages of any kind allowed. If you get drunk and fall down outdoors, at minus fifty, you've soon had it.

No firearms, either, aside from those issued to security guards. The whole area is a game reserve. The guards need guns to cope with the cute Arctic foxes that come around begging for food. The poor critters are all rabid. We don't see any, or any caribou, but the pipeline people have these much in mind. For two years, aerial photos were made of herd migrations, and the pipeline snaking down to Valdez has dips in it, or ramps over it, at points where the big animals like to cross. At Prudhoe, there is evidence also of rare human behavior. Diesel engines are kept running nine months a year; otherwise, they couldn't be started up in the cold. Many car engines, similarly, are hardly ever switched off. The BP people truck up gasoline for theirs, but ARCO refines some crude auto fuel from the oil on the spot—gas so low-grade in quality, however, that the local joke is to call it ARCO Superknock. Just before it gets dark, we walk out to the head of the pipeline itself and, for good luck, pat the side of a length of Transalaska pipe. It feels cold.

Back in Anchorage, Kay takes us on a tour of her editorial premises. A young woman reporter leads me to a cage and asks me, proudly, "How many newsrooms have a pet snake?" The Panama *American* newsroom had one once, briefly, uncaged. I was doing public relations work down there during the war, for the Infantry, and we were engaged, for lack of anything else more contributory to the war effort, in a battle with the Coast Artillery, to see which branch of the ground forces could wangle the most space in the local press. I was trying to promote the notion that my constituents were fierce jungle fighters, and I chanced one day to attend a lecture by an itinerant herpetologist who, while talking, fancied draping a pet boa constrictor around his neck. After he was finished, I asked him how constrictive his boa was and whether anyone could wear it with impunity. He let me try it on, and though it felt a bit slimy, the pressure it exerted was gentle.

So I asked further if I could borrow it for a couple of hours, and when he acquiesced, I commandeered a jeep and driver, clad myself in jungle togs, and left the Canal Zone for Panama City. I thought it might divert the editor of the *American* to see at first hand how casually the Infantry hobnobbed with boa constrictors. I had neglected to take into consideration the volatility of the Latin American temperament. I never got as far as the editor's sanctum; as soon as I entered the newspaper's outer office, with the snake wrapped around me, all the women present reacted so uncontrollably that I was forced to retreat, as they crawled under desks, leapt toward windows, and exhibited other shrieking symptoms of mass hysteria. Score one for the Coast Artillery.

*   *   *

We dine at an Anchorage restaurant that Kay recommends. She is worried because I have said it is my treat, and she fears that when I see the prices on the menu I'll react as if confronted by a rabid python. But I come from New York, and am shockproof to restaurants, and while the Alaskan tab is as formidable as any back home, the king crab tastes infinitely better.

January 28

Kay is up and off early. She is flying to Fairbanks this morning, hoping to sustain her ailing paper by floating a loan from some Eskimos who, under the Native Lands Settlement Act, have got more cash than they purportedly know what to do with. Today, I sing for my supper. Bradlee, Oliver, and I are supposed to have one joint three-hour meeting to discuss journalism and answer questions, and then each of us is to devote another three hours to his special field. The way the schedule has been set up, our joint appearance is this morning, and my solo this afternoon. I know now what actors mean when they complain about matinee days. Still, I get tomorrow off.

The morning goes by easily enough; many of the questions addressed to the panel relate less to the practice of journalism in general than to the Washington *Post*'s coverage of Watergate in particular. Bradlee is asked, no doubt for the umpteenth time, to reveal the identity of Deep Throat, and he gives what sounds like a response he has uttered umpteen times before: If he knew, he wouldn't tell.

I am joined in the afternoon by two indigenes—a retired male editor of *Alaska* magazine and a female author of travel books. The moderator of this session is a University of Alaska professor who is a musical-comedy buff. He tells me that he once set two of Brendan Gill's poems to music, and sent the finished product to Brendan, but that the lyricist never let him know if he'd listened to their combined effort. Most of the questions put to me have to do with how one goes about selling pieces, or stories, or poems, or travel books, to *The New Yorker*. The simple answer, the truthful answer, is that everything sent in there gets read, and that without the discovery of new talent through unsolicited contributions from outsiders the magazine probably wouldn't have lasted fifty-two years.

I am not in a very good mood, because the moderator has seen fit to introduce me, unsolicitedly, by reading aloud the worn-out old throwing-up-in-the-morning story that Gill used in "Here at *The New Yorker*." The moderator apparently believes, mistakenly, that contributors to the magazine *liked* that book. (He also refers mistakenly to the incumbent editor of *The New Yorker*, an error that has been made countless times before, as "Ted Shawn.") Gill's opus was timed to come out in February, 1975, concurrently with the fiftieth anniversary of Ross' founding of the magazine, and it contained, as a sort of postlogue, a charming, reflective, reminiscent essay on Ross by Shawn. It was the first time that the second editor of *The New Yorker* had gone on record about his predecessor, and whatever his reasons were for making Brendan a gift of that memoir, there were some of us who were glad to see the real Ross described in the book along with Gill's skewed recollections of the man.

The publication-day party for "Here at *The New Yorker*" was held at the Gramercy Park town house of the press agent Benjamin Sonnenberg, a residence so overwhelmingly and intricately furnished that one gets the impression its contents are moved around with jeweler's implements. I had known Ben for years, from way back in the days when he and his Hilda and their then small children occupied a summer cottage on the estate of a Connecticut couple, the Rudkins, who had fallen on hard times during the Depression. Ben had persuaded me to write a Talk piece about Mrs. Rudkin, who was helping make ends meet by baking bread and selling it, loaf by loaf, under the name of her country place, Pepperidge Farm. Margaret Rudkin couldn't afford to pay any money for publicity services; all she could offer Ben was, when she incorporated, a fat loaf of common stock. Later, Ben had bought a summer home of his own in Provincetown, right next to Truro. I acquired my Cape Cod house at about the same time, and I happened to be driving past Ben's new place one afternoon when I noticed a pile of furniture on the sidewalk. I stopped and asked what was going on, and Ben said it was junk he was throwing away. I loaded my station wagon with it, and, twenty-five years later, am still using some of it.

Anyway, when Ellie and I were invited to the Sonnenberg party for "Here at *The New Yorker*," I wanted to go, although by then I had read the book and thought Gill gave a distorted picture of Harold Ross and some of the other people connected with the magazine. (Among the illustrations there was a reproduction of just one caricature out of the many hundreds that had been used in half a century to complement Profiles; curiously, the subject of this drawing, by Saul Steinberg, was Ben Sonnenberg, whose Profile hadn't been written by Gill but by Geoffrey Hellman.) Still, the publication party promised to be the principal social function for the editorial staff in commemoration of *The New Yorker*'s fiftieth birthday, and that made it eminently worth attending. The twenty-fifth birthday party, back in 1950, had been a bang-up affair that many of us still nostalgically recalled. The magazine had taken over the ballroom of the old Ritz-Carlton Hotel, on Madison Avenue, for a dinner dance, and invited everyone who had ever contributed anything to its pages. Ross decreed that there would be one exception to this rule; inasmuch as his magazine was called *The New Yorker*, he had asked to share the festivities with the rest of us the mayor of New York City, his friend Bill O'Dwyer. It was a great party, although toward the end of it two longtime staff writers got into a fist fight and, as far as I know, have not spoken since.

But there was nothing similar on tap for 1975—the magazine's contributors, and their spouses, could no longer be fitted into the most commodious of ballrooms—and so the Sonnenberg do would have to do. The invitation we got said the affair would run from 6 to 8 P.M. I was working in Indianapolis that week, and arranged to catch a 5 P.M. plane out of there. I reached our apartment at 7:10, dropped my luggage, picked up Ellie, grabbed a cab, and arrived at Sonnenberg's overstuffed jewel box at 7:35—at about the time, I reckoned, judging from other cocktail parties, that the celebration would be at its height. After climbing four flights of stairs to the party scene, I was surprised not to see any bar or any food. There were some waiters and waitresses circulating with trays of champagne, though, and I gratefully grabbed a glass and, while paying my respects to the host and to the guest of honor, wolfed it down. It was domestic, but thirst-quenching. At 7:45, I looked around for a servitor with a tray, but couldn't spot any. At 7:50, the staff reappeared, but only to collect ashtrays. At 7:55, the lights were flicked, as if to herald the playing of "Goodnight Sweetheart" at a dance. At 8:00 on the dot, the lights were turned off, and the guests felt their way gingerly back down the stairs and out onto the street. Strangest party I ever went to in somebody's residence. Maybe, unknown to the guests, we were the victims of a strike deadline imposed by a caterers' union. I wonder if Sonnenberg would have had the lights turned off if the mayor had been there.

Back at Kay's, before dinner, I share the last of my vodka (as a Christian Scientist, she does not keep liquor in her house) with the sports editor of the *Daily News*, who has stopped by for some after-class journalistic chitchat. He is twenty-one, and began working for newspapers at sixteen. So did I, I tell him, although I was actually only fifteen. I was shanghaied into journalism. An English teacher at Horace Mann, Al Baruth, was the faculty advisor for the weekly school newspaper, and he waylaid me in a corridor one day in my junior year and told me that I had to try out for the *Record* because he didn't have anybody else around who seemed likely to be able to take it over the following year. I suspected, probably unfairly, that my response might affect my grade in English. I was flattered, in any event, by his opinion of my unproved worth, and did join the staff. The following year—largely, of course, because of the lack of any competition—I became the editor.

After graduating, and obtaining a driver's license, junior grade, I further pursued my new-found calling by obtaining a summer job on the Tarrytown *Daily News*. I got it through an uncle, who knew somebody who knew the publisher, and there was not much competition for that job, either. There was no remuneration involved. It was stipulated in advance that I would work for ten weeks, six days a week, for nothing. My reward was to be Experience. We spent our summers then at Elmsford, only a few miles from Tarrytown, and I would drive to work each day in a beautiful old high-rise Buick convertible that belonged to my grandparents. They had confidence in my ability to handle it because once while I was at its wheel my sister Olivia had inadvertently run a picnic fork through my hand and I hadn't gone off the road.

I received a lot of newspaper experience that summer, being assigned to fill in, seriatim, for the salaried members of the staff as they went on vacation. Only while the mentor of the society page was on holiday did I falter badly. When I took down on the phone the names of the members of a family named Siska who attended a wedding, I put them all in print as "Fifka." Once or twice I got to write the lead story of the day, as heady an experience as a tyro journalist could ask for. I was also the summer drama critic, and would propel my stately Buick over to the Westchester Playhouse in Mount Kisco and write devastating analyses of the inadequacies of Broadway stars on the straw-hat circuit. Come to think of it, I must have been a drama critic long before Brendan Gill became one. Years later, I was invited to cover the New York theatre for the *New Republic*, but I begged off; I had already squandered my lifetime supply of critical bile.

At the end of my ten-week stint, the managing editor of the paper called me in and said that, while it had been clearly understood among all parties concerned that I was to work for nothing, he was on the whole so pleased with my summer performance that he and his associates wanted to pay me something notwithstanding. He handed me an envelope, and as soon as I was out of his sight, I ripped it expectantly open. It contained a ten-dollar bill. One dollar a week. Still, that was the first money I had ever truly earned. I don't know how much the man who pressed it upon me was earning at the time, but his lot eventually improved, too; he went on to the *Wall Street Journal*.

While Kay and Ben Bradlee are edgily dining at the Atwoods', Ellie and I borrow our hostess' Volkswagen and drive over to the Lowell Thomases'. They live on a road with a pine tree growing right in the middle of it; we learn on arriving that according to Alaskan etiquette one is at liberty to drive on either side of the hazard. The lieutenant governor is absent. He has flown up north—piloting his own plane, of course; this is Alaska—to witness some military maneuvers. I have often wondered what lieutenant governors do to earn their keep; now I have an insight. Tay Thomas says that not long ago her husband had to make a hairy emergency landing at a place called Tatitlek, and while he was sitting in his cockpit, trying to restore his breathing to normal, some local residents ran up to the side of his plane and said, "You going to Cordova? Please mail these letters for us."

Looking for something to read before I go to sleep, I find the bookshelves in our room have two biographies of Henry Luce. Each recounts a confrontation, at Harold Ross' apartment, between the editors of *The New Yorker* and *Time*—a meeting to discuss the imminent publication in the former of Wolcott Gibbs' celebrated Profile of Luce. Ross was attended on the occasion by St. Clair McKelway, his managing editor; and Luce by Ralph Ingersoll, who had once been managing editor of *The New Yorker* but had switched camps. Both books say that McKelway and Ingersoll almost came to blows in the course of the evening—a rare instance of duelists' seconds standing *in loco* principals.

I cannot visualize McKelway fighting anybody; he hardly ever even raised his voice. He was the man who actually hired me for *The New Yorker*, and he was habitually so softspoken that if he hadn't given me the good news by mail I might never have realized there was any news at all. I was in understandable awe of McKelway when I joined the magazine; he was my immediate boss; he had edited a newspaper in Bangkok; he was a much-married man about town. To a kid just out of college, he seemed nearly immortal—a person who could never conceivably harbor the same doubts about the quality of his work that afflicted me every time I turned in a piece. I was therefore astonished when, twenty years or so later, by which time Mac had long since stopped editing and was writing long fact pieces himself, he once told me that never *never* in his career as a writer had he felt certain, on handing in a finished manuscript, that *The New Yorker* was going to buy it. That had always been (and still is) my worried state of mind, but until Mac's confession it had not occurred to me that my insecurity was not unique.

The one time I ever talked to Luce at any length—at a dinner party given by the Dick Clurmans—he had only nice things to say about Ross. But that was long after both Ross and Gibbs were dead. *De mortuis nil nisi . . .* I never met Ralph Ingersoll until a couple of years ago, by which time he had gone through his *PM* phase and his autobiographical phase and was a semi-retired publisher of a chain of small-town newspapers. I got to know him, finally, because he spends his summers at Cornwall. Over the years, though, I kept hearing a lot about him; he roomed at Yale, between World Wars, with my doctor, Louis Bishop. Louis is an eminent cardiologist, and I became a patient of his nearly thirty years ago when Jinny was pregnant and her obstetrician wanted to have her heart checked out by an expert. As soon as she went to Dr. Bishop, I got jealous: Here she was carrying the child and having her heart looked at, too; why did nobody pay any attention to *me?*

I developed what seemed to me to be a near-fatal heart murmur, and made an appointment to go see Dr. Bishop myself. He found absolutely nothing wrong, but I kept going back to him annually for checkups; he had won my heart forever by something he did soon after we first became acquainted. My eighty-six-year-old grandmother fell ill one summer Sunday in her Central Park West apartment, and by the time I drove in from Westchester a young doctor who lived in the building had been summoned and had diagnosed her trouble as a heart attack. The members of the family who were gathered on the scene felt, as did I, that a confirming diagnosis by a specialist would be desirable, but on a sunny Sunday afternoon in August?

Impossible. I didn't know Dr. Bishop at all well then, but I said I'd phone him. His answering service said that the doctor was on Long Island, playing golf at Piping Rock. I left a message, explaining the situation, and figured that would be the end of that. A few minutes later Dr. Bishop called. He would drive right in, he said, as soon as he changed his golf shoes. He did drive in, and after he had examined Mima he said she had indeed had a heart attack, complimented the younger physician on the steps he had taken, and went back to Long Island. Dr. Bishop has been working on his memoirs lately, and he may not have considered that incident singular enough to warrant inclusion, but to me it was memorable—possibly the last time, for all I know, that any doctor made that kind of house call to benefit a total stranger—so I record it here.

January 29

The *Daily News* has a piece about me today, written by Kay's city-room snake charmer, who says that my leather elbow patches bespeak urbanity. (What might she not have said had she noticed my cuffs!) She flatters me further by putting me in the Harvard class of '39, thus knocking a couple of years off my age. The story is accompanied by a candid photograph of me holding a lighted cigarette. That is ridiculous, because, as I have told Ellie many times, I have stopped smoking. Kay suggests that we all convene somewhere for lunch, but she isn't yet sure where. This being a Saturday, most downtown Anchorage restaurants aren't open; on weekends, Alaskans head for the country. I hope we find a place; it is going to be Bradlee's treat.

In mid-morning, I have been asked to tape a television program with the musical-comedy aficionado who presided over yesterday's session. We are supposed to talk about magazine writing, but when he discovers that I know Josh Logan and Abe Burrows and Comden & Green and have even met Richard Rodgers, he is beside himself. They are all gods he has worshipped only in his dreams. He wants to know what musical comedy I liked best of all. I tell him it was "Fifty Million Frenchmen." William Gaxton, Victor Moore, Helen Broderick, I forget who all else. It is a show, 1929 vintage, with which the emcee is not intimately familiar. I favor him, on camera, with a couple of gravelly bars of "You Do Something to Me." It is a break that, as a frustrated actor, I have been seeking for many years. Who knows—maybe some producer with a Lionel Stander–type role to cast will see the show and track me down!

When it comes out further that I was also acquainted with the Zeus of my inquisitor's Olympus, Frank Loesser, he practically swoons. I got to know Loesser in 1944, when I was attached to something called the Special Information Section of Headquarters, Army Ground Forces. In Panama, promoting the jungle-fighting prowess of General Harding's troops, I had written and helped produce a short movie and had hand-carried it back to the States to try to persuade the War Department to adopt it as an official training film for soldiers destined for the tropics. In Washington, I ran into an Army colonel who'd been delegated by General George Marshall to organize a team of military journalists to publicize the Infantry, which in the view of the chief of staff had up to then been far too little appreciated by the general public, considering that these foot soldiers did the most dangerous work and incurred the heaviest casualties. The Marine Corps, which had shrewdly deployed journalists in *its* ranks as combat correspondents, was getting acclaim disproportionate, in the Army's view, to its comparatively puny size. So journalists already in the Army were summoned from all over to Washington, D.C., and assembled at the Army War College. Their big moment, they—we—were told, would come whenever D Day came in Europe. We would be there, covering the event, and properly extolling its Infantry heroes. I was delighted with this battle plan. I had experienced (safely behind the front lines, though I once did bravely fire my rifle at a strafing Zero) some of the action in the Pacific, and now I would get to see the other half of the war.

That particular Marshall Plan was, alas, never carried out, possibly because the civilian press got wind of it and regarded us as potentially competitive (we didn't thus view ourselves; we were competing only with the United States Marines); possibly because, with so many other more consequential things on his mind, the chief of staff forgot all about us. Some members of our specialized task force were eventually dispatched to the Pacific to do precisely the reverse of what they'd been recruited for—to serve as censors. The rest of us sat around Washington churning out press releases for hometown papers and speeches for generals, and swapping yawns. In time, it occurred to somebody that Washington was not the ideal spot from which to mount a public relations campaign; that if we couldn't help the Infantry on the Normandy coast we could at least establish a beachhead in New York, where all the important media people were based. Forthwith a small party of Special Information Section skirmishers headed north, under the command of a lieutenant colonel, Edward Hope Coffey, who had been a balloonist during the First World War and—a skill more relevant to our Second World War mission—the author between wars, under the pen name Edward Hope, of numerous works of fiction, among them "She Loves Me Not." Hope Coffey, as we called him, asked to have me assigned to his raiding party, and I was glad to get out of Washington.

In New York, we were tapped for all sorts of bizarre missions, though I suppose a fulltime press agent like Ben Sonnenberg would not have considered them strange. It was decided at one point, for instance, to promote the color Infantry blue (look at the success, we reasoned, of Navy blue), and I paid a solemn call on Mainbocher and persuaded him, out of patriotism for his adopted country, to make something in Infantry blue; and then I persuaded *Vogue* to run a photograph of the celebrated couturier's output. Let the Marines match that! The idea was that women who were both fashion-conscious and supportive of their fighting menfolk would rush to wear the color associated with them. Our Infantry blue campaign was not, all things considered, a rousing success; as far as I know, not a single wife, widow, mother, daughter, sister, aunt, girl friend, or casual bedmate of any Infantryman ever once walked into a store and asked to be shown something in Infantry blue. And if she had, the sales clerk probably wouldn't have known what she was talking about.

We also embarked on a shoulder-patch promotion campaign. Every Infantry division had its own shoulder insignia, and we wanted the general public to know what these were and what they represented. The end result of this effort, we felt, would be when some footsoldier on leave, standing lonely at a bar, would be approached by a civilian who would say, looking at his upper arm, "Ah, I see that you're from that splendid outfit, the Eighty-eighth Infantry Division, which made that spectacular assault by bicycle on San Martino! Would you permit me to buy you a drink?" The syndicated columnist Henry McLemore had by this time joined our little task force, and he and I collaborated on a book, "Fighting Divisions," which was published by the Infantry Journal Press; we included an illustrated capsule history of every division—Marine divisions naturally excluded—in existence. The main hitch in this endeavor was that by the time Henry and I did the book there were so many Infantry divisions extant that not even the co-authors of "Fighting Divisions" could keep them straight.

Then we decided the Infantry needed a song. The Marines had their "Halls of Montezuma," the Air Force its "Wild Blue Yonder," but we had nothing. It seemed unfair. We cast a covetous eye on Frank Loesser, a private assigned to the Signal Corps. He had already written "Praise the Lord and Pass the Ammunition," but for our purposes that otherwise estimable song was worthless, inasmuch as its lyrics didn't contain the word "infantry." When we first approached Frank about joining our crusade, he was not overly enthusiastic. Then we learned that he was a night person, and not altogether happy in his present assignment because, like soldiers in most non-combat areas, he had to stand reveille every morning. We told him if he defected to us he could stay at home, work at his own pace, and sleep as late as he liked. All he had to do to get all that was write a new national anthem. We had him. (We could probably have got him *ordered* to be transferred to our section, but Hope Coffey didn't believe that was the way to inspire a creative artist to do his best.) Frank said he would like to try a ballad about an Infantry hero, and we furnished him with a list of the names of all the footsoldiers who up to then had been awarded the Medal of Honor. Quite a few of these men were of European extraction and had formidable Polish or Czechoslovakian surnames that couldn't imaginably be rhymed with anything—at least not in English. But at the bottom of the roster Frank found a name that was perfect, and not long afterward I was invited to his apartment on Central Park South, late one evening, and treated to my first hearing of "The Ballad of Rodger Young."

This recital of the events that led up to the composition of that still stirring song does not jibe, I am aware, with a version I published back then in the *Saturday Evening Post*. (The *Post* was very good about plugging the Infantry.) To have told how "Rodger Young" actually came into being would, it seemed to me, have made us all out as crass and manipulative; so I invented a yarn—Sonnenberg might have done it better, but I was only an amateur—about how my friend Larry Adler, while on a USO swing around the Pacific with Jack Benny, had on New Georgia heard about a heroic sergeant who had died in battle there, and how Larry had told Frank about him on his return to the States and how Frank had been moved by the account to write his ballad. The facts were more or less accurate: Larry had been to New Georgia; Rodger Young had died a hero there; Frank Loesser had found his story affecting. In the *Saturday Evening Post*, I had merely sort of added some connectives to the facts. "Rodger Young" never became quite the hit we had hoped it would—it may have been too good to be popular—but at least we tried.

Colonel Coffey's New York liaison office opened up shop in mid-1944, and by then it had been decided by my military superiors that inasmuch as I was engaged full-time in public relations work for the Infantry, it would be inappropriate for me to write about the Infantry in *The New Yorker* and use my own name. When, accordingly, I turned in a Profile about a Regular Army enlisted man, and searched around for a suitable alias, I decided to borrow the name of a friend who I thought would be less likely than anyone else I knew on earth ever to have any legitimate connection with the magazine. I signed the piece "George Woodward."

George Woodward loomed on the horizon—my horizon, that is—around 1939. He was a buddy of Gene Kinkead, of the *New Yorker* staff, with whom I played poker and tennis. (It was one of Kinkead's chores at the magazine, for a while, to reject minor submissions, by means of a form letter that was unsigned but bore in the lower lefthand corner his initials. Because these were "E.F.K.," I was occasionally accused by aspiring contributors of having broken their hearts. On the other hand, I was also occasionally given credit for some of Gene's published light verse.) I don't recall how Kinkead got to know Woodward; it may have dated back to the time when Gene was a men's apparel buyer for a department store—the kind of crucible in which, in the old days, members of *The New Yorker*'s editorial staff frequently seemed to have been forged.

In any event, at the time that Kinkead brought Woodward around to one of our off-Bowery musical evenings, George was an advertising salesman for a short-lived women's fashion magazine called *You*. It was not a taxing occupation: The magazine carried little advertising, and one possible reason was that George was not much interested in selling any. It was never quite clear to anybody what he lived on, but there was a touch of authentic glamour to him; why, he had been divorced. He seemed to have only one suit, a grey-flannel pin-stripe double-breasted number; and yet, even after he had slept in it all night on somebody's couch, he and it would arise the following morning in tiptop shape, if in his case somewhat hung-over.

What especially endeared George to me was his behavior at our Thursday jazz sessions. Different individuals regularly comported themselves according to their lights. There were some who got morosely drunk and complained (not without justification) about the noise. Kinkead would now and then plant himself firmly in front of our third-story window, facing inward, presumably to thwart any attempts to jump out. (One night, when Joe Liebling brought down some marijuana—then a rarity—that he'd obtained in Harlem, Gene scarcely left his post.) In the case of Woodward, he could be counted on to be gallantly attentive to those women who, for lack of pulchritude or luck, can always be found standing around at parties hoping someone will talk to them. He was the benign hunter of the lonely heart. He was also a tennis addict, and we would sometimes play in Brooklyn with a girl he had discovered who was, in a way, *sui generis:* She was a platinum blonde Italian. We lost all track of Maria, alas, during the war years.

George became acquainted with many *New Yorker* people, and he was often to be found on the editorial premises, stopping by on the off chance that somebody would like to step outside and join him for a drink. His was so visible a presence that when during the war the magazine put out a mimeographed news sheet for those staff members who were in the armed forces, his name went on the mailing list. I did not know any of this until later, because I had been drafted early on. George, for his part, had been rejected by the Army on some such ground as irremediable physical deterioration. But then he had gone around to the Navy and had got himself commissioned, and because he was a doddering old man of thirty or so had been dubbed a lieutenant, junior grade, right off the bat. He looked even more dashing in his uniform, it seemed to be generally agreed, than in his mothballed chalkstripes.

Soon after joining the Navy, Lieutenant Woodward was shipped to London, and the officer who received him, upon looking at his curriculum vitae and perceiving that George had hardly ever even paddled a canoe, let alone had any basic nautical training, told him to stand by and await a duty assignment: There were no available slots of sufficient inconsequentiality to risk putting Woodward in one of them. But then things began to happen. In peacetime, the Navy had had a lovely large office on the ground floor of the American Embassy, on Grosvenor Square. Now it seemed that the embassy wanted the space back, and besides, the Navy was informed, it couldn't need the room much because there was hardly ever anybody there. The Navy was not disposed to budge. It had to appear to be using the chamber, and yet at the same time it didn't want to waste on it any manpower that could in some way help it perform its wartime functions. The solution to this dilemma was found in the person of Lieutenant (j.g.) Woodward, who was instructed to occupy the premises, never to close the door to the corridor, and, whenever he heard the click-clack of feet approaching his enclave, to pick up both telephones on his desk and talk into them importantly.

At about that time Anthony J. Drexel Biddle was assigned by President Roosevelt to serve as ambassador to the governments-in-exile of all the Nazi-occupied countries of Europe. Among the ambassador's perquisites were a military and a naval aide. As Mr. Biddle had strolled up and down the embassy corridors, where he was also berthed, he had noticed a trim young naval officer through an open door—a fellow who, judging from all the time he spent talking on the phone, must be well versed in the intricacies of wartime diplomacy. The ambassador asked if there was any chance he could have that lieutenant for his naval aide. The Navy shrugged and gave him Woodward.

There were many cocktail parties in London, and the ambassador was invited to all the best of them. Experienced as he was, Tony Biddle couldn't be everywhere at once, so he took to sending Woodward around as his surrogate, and going to parties was something George *had* had basic training in. Many of these affairs were also attended by Admiral Harold Stark, the four-star commander of all American naval forces in European waters. After seeing Woodward time and time again hobnobbing with the elite of British society, the admiral inquired who this young naval officer was, who was on such cozy terms with every platinum blonde in Mayfair, and most of the brunettes, too. Tony Biddle's aide, he was informed. "Well, I'm the ranking naval personage in this theatre," the admiral reputedly exclaimed, "and if this social lion is going to be anybody's aide, he's going to be *my* aide!" Which Woodward thereupon became.

All this, as I say, I got secondhand after the war was over and George had scaled still greater heights—ending his naval career, I believe, as a member of a highly specialized psychological-warfare group at SHAEF headquarters, possibly because a covetous General Eisenhower had pulled rank on Admiral Stark. By then, unknowing of any of this, I had signed George's name to a *New Yorker* Profile; and he had been getting the little mimeographed newsletter from West Forty-third Street; and I guess everybody just sort of assumed that he had been working for the magazine when hostilities commenced. (So, evidently, did I: My sisters not long ago showed me a letter I wrote to them, in June, 1942, from Adelaide, Australia, in which I said, "I got a long, newsy letter from George Woodward, full of chatter about the *New Yorker* staff . . . It is probably significant that his is the only letter I've yet received from anybody there.") *The New Yorker*, like many other institutions, conscientiously tried to find post-war jobs for all its people who had served in the armed forces. In the case of George Woodward, this wasn't easy, because nobody could recall exactly what it was he had been doing at the magazine before the war. So a new job was created for him, and for the next twenty-five years or so he presided happily over the magazine's European office, which, to his great good fortune and that also of those of us who periodically passed through London on assignment, was only a short walk from the Connaught Hotel bar.

Kay has found a downtown restaurant that's open, and at lunch Ben Bradlee, who seems to be playing host to more young admiring journalists than I thought there were in the whole state of Alaska, tells me that Evangeline Atwood, dowager duchess of the Anchorage *Times,* who sat in on the seminar I conducted yesterday afternoon, thought it had been inappropriate, in view of the fact that some members of my audience were college students, for me to tell a certain story about how books can come into being—the case in point being a book that I had dismissed as a lousy idea when the publisher who was *my* host at lunch broached it during the first and again the second round of drinks; but which, halfway through a third Bloody Mary, I had acclaimed as inspirational. (I did eventually write that book, and it had a modestly respectable sale and got agreeably reviewed.) But I had told the same story last year to a high-school audience, when I was a writer-in-residence at Western Reserve Academy, in Hudson, Ohio; and neither the resident students nor any of the faculty shielding them from unsavory outside influences had registered any objections. Perhaps Bradlee and I have discovered some fundamental tolerance gap between Alaska and the lower forty-eight.

In the afternoon, Kay's daughter Kathie drives Ellie and me down Cook Inlet, past the lovely snow-capped mountains of Chugach State Park. No moose, going or coming back, following which we find ourselves at a furrier's. I want to buy E. a bona-fide Alaskan parka as a souvenir of our northwest caper, and my generosity is almost unbounded when the proprietor of the establishment says he will knock two hundred dollars off the price of an $895 lynx or wolf or whatever if I will give him an autograph to add to his collection. He already has a Hubert Humphrey. Ellie spoils my fun by spurning my gift, whatever the cost, on the prosaic ground that there isn't a parka in the joint that fits her. I suppose I should be grateful to her for saving me $695. On the other hand, how do I know how long it will be again, if ever, before someone appraises my signature at two hundred dollars cash?

Cocktails and dinner at the home of John Lindauer, the chancellor of the University of Alaska. I have a drink with Evangeline Atwood, who doesn't seem the least bit put out with me, and who also demonstrates that she has a long memory. She wants to know why, in my piece about her state a generation ago, I called Alaskans "ethnocentrics," and what the word means, anyway. I think I know, but I cannot be positive, and there doesn't seem to be a dictionary within reach. Bob Atwood springs to my rescue by saying that the next time I'm in Anchorage I must join him for lunch, which is not the same as dinner but, for me, a big social step forward. And that may come to pass, because before the evening is out our host, John (this is Alaska, the First-Name State), has invited me to return to his university, summer after next, and teach a course that lasts longer than a weekend. I am not sure how much wine he has had, and to give him a chance to renege gracefully if he changes his mind in the morning, I say the prospect is inviting and I hope he can furnish me with some particulars, at his convenience, in writing.

At dinner, I also meet an eighty-six-year-old lady who came to Alaska when she was seventeen, as a schoolteacher, and whose memory eclipses that even of Evangeline. The new acquaintance recalls pieces I did for *The New Yorker*, in 1941 and 1942, signed "Pvt. E. J. Kahn, Jr." She remembers further that I got promoted ultimately to chief warrant officer and got married—here she beckons Ellie to join the reminiscent conversation—to a first lieutenant in the Women's Army Corps. Only she has the wrong wife. Ellie was just finishing high school when the war ended. Before she and I got married, she had met Jinny once or twice, and five or six months after E. and I were wed, she went and had tea with Jinny. It somehow seemed appropriate in our day and age. My mother and father didn't speak to each other—not within my hearing, anyhow—for about the last ten years of their marriage; but Jinny and I had not parted in that fashion, and I couldn't conceive of having a totally standoffish relationship with my ex-wife. After all, she is the mother of our sons. And there were bound to be rites of passage—graduations, weddings, yes, even funerals—where Jinny's and Ellie's paths would cross (my mother and my father were in the same room for the first time in nearly ten years when Jinny and I got married); and so it seemed civilized for them to meet. They chose to have tea without me present, and they apparently got on all right with each other, as I had suspected they would. Afterward, each complimented the other to me. Ellie concluded that—as others have of course been quick to tell me—she and Jinny look alike. E. said that, come to think of it, I look like Alfred. That hadn't occurred to me, and I went at once into David's room and stared at his father's photograph. I failed to detect any resemblance between Alfred Frankfurter and either Norman Mailer or Max Lerner, whom I *am* supposed to look like.

My mother looked uncannily like Janet Flanner, as they both agreed when I finally introduced them. Before that, during the war, I was dating a young woman who knew a lot of *New Yorker* people and had met Flanner. The girl was riding on a New York Central train one day, and chanced to sit next to somebody she recognized instantly as Janet. They chatted for an hour or so about the magazine and Shawn and me, topics with which both of them were thoroughly conversant. It was not until several weeks later that it developed the young woman's seatmate had been my mother.

It would have interested my mother—who died, young, at sixty, when my son Tony was only six months old—to know that her lookalike ultimately became her grandson's godmother. The boy's most memorable encounter with Janet occurred, appropriately, at Versailles, when that gracious lady came out from Paris to have lunch with us and brought along a godparental gift characteristic of her unerring taste: a pocketknife consisting of an old French coin sliced in half, with a blade deftly inserted in the middle. Kids lose most things, but when I last checked Tony still had that treasured keepsake.

On failing to buy a parka this afternoon, E. and I invest heavily in some frozen Alaska king crab, which we will take back on the plane with us tomorrow morning. It is guaranteed to stay frozen for eighteen hours; we are scheduled to reach our Manhattan freezer in twenty-four. Unfortunately, the package it is in won't fit inside Kay's freezer compartment, which in any event doesn't seem even to be able to cope with chocolate ice cream. I take the package outside and lay it on top of a garbage can, hoping 1) that this January night in Alaska will be sensibly frigid and 2) that I will retrieve our precious shellfish in the morning before the garbage men come around.

January 30

We arise at dawn to make an early-morning flight east. I am proud to remember the crab in the garbage pit, and am so preoccupied with self-congratulation that I omit to take along some reindeer sausage that I had bought and managed to fit into Kay's refrigerator. It is like leaving coals in Newcastle.

Our plane, in from Asia, is nearly empty again. A youngish stewardess stops by, chats, and on learning what I do for a living, says she is fond of *The New Yorker*. It is important for airplane passengers to keep up the morale of the crew, so I give her a rough copy I have been carrying around. (There are no jagged edges on a rough copy; it is the hot-off-the-press early edition of *The New Yorker* that we privileged mortals who work there generally get on Tuesday, at least one whole day ahead of our breathlessly waiting subscribers.) The stewardess has been on this job for nine months, and she says the older girls are very cliquey. She will have a twenty-five-hour layover in New York, and she expects to spend it—to my astonishment, considering what I have heard about her ilk—alone. She has already done the Museum of Modern Art, "A Chorus Line," and Central Park; this time, she is thinking of tackling Greenwich Village. Although seemingly a trifle primmer than most airline stewardesses, basically she is no different from the rest of them: When proffered a five-dollar bill at drink-serving time, she has no change.

January 31

Lexy was asleep when we got home, late last night—the king crab, happily, still rock hard—and so it was at breakfast that we first heard about the Bar Mitzvah party he attended Saturday night. His report was predictably laconic. "All we did was sit down and dance," he said. When I was thirteen, we danced standing up. I don't remember going then to a single Bar Mitzvah of any of my contemporaries; either they were all Gentiles or, like me, Jews of ill repute. I have since been invited to and attended a number of Bar Mitzvahs, though, courtesy of sons and stepsons. When Terry was thirteen, one of his classmates, from Hartsdale, had a truly memorable coming of manhood, with food that stretched from one end of a terrace to the other. So nearly did the paterfamilias; even before moving in on his own groaning board, he weighed, by my conservative estimate, three hundred and twenty-seven. I had a fine time at that party by introducing myself all around as "a cousin, once removed." Nobody asked me what my name was or from which side of the honoree's clan I was that far detached. I gained two and a half pounds.

On ceremonial occasions, in any event, Jews probably don't eat any more than Italians, but they seem to cater to their own appetites with irrepressible enthusiasm. Some years back, I drove one icy winter day from Westchester to upstate New York, for the wedding of an old friend, which was followed by a reception at one of the two principal country clubs. One of these was, in the usual practice of the time, Jewish, and the other non-Jewish. All of the country clubs that my family belonged to while I was growing up were exclusively Jewish. At one time or another my father was a member of three of the better Jewish country clubs of Westchester County—Sunningdale, Quaker Ridge, and Fairview—but he never made it into what was generally acknowledged to be the *best*, the Century C.C. Whether he wanted to or not I have no idea.

There were only a handful of guests at the wedding ceremony, which had its odd aspects. Conceivably because it was the bride's first marriage, ritualism was rampant; the proceedings included even the trampling of a goblet. The bridegroom, however, a singularly non-religious man who was embarking on his third matrimonial trip, stepped on the glass with the air of a man who was less concerned about complying with tradition than slashing his shoes. The bride's mother, who wanted to offer the witnesses a glass of champagne before they went on to the country club, had, not irrationally, bought a case of *fin champagne* at her local liquor store; and while the bridegroom was checking his soles for scratch marks an old family retainer passed around champagne glasses filled to the brim with brandy.

By the time we got to the country club, at around 8 P.M., the reception was already under way. Those of us who had travelled to the scene from downstate, and who hadn't eaten since breakfast, were delighted to see a large buffet table. It was totally surrounded by a ring of local folk who, not having been to the wedding, had probably already supped at home. Now they were having postprandial snacks—huge plateloads of them. After a while, I noticed that the best man looked as though he needed some food in a hurry. The poor chap, being a magazine editor, did not habitually travel much, and he had found the long day's excursion taxing; moreover, he had been called upon to propose and execute several toasts in hundred-proof *fin champagne.* So I hauled him up from a chair into which he had slumped, dragged him to the buffet table, and tried to figure out a way of getting him into the line of the indigenes who were circling it. Finally I spotted a man who would surely let me through: He was, judging from the condition of his plate and his chin, certainly on his second and perhaps his third visit to the buffet; and, weighing enough to rate a second glance even in Hartsdale, he was not in danger of perishing if he let somebody else into line. I tapped this behemoth on the shoulder, explained that I had the best man in tow and that because of his devotion to the bridal couple he hadn't had a bite to eat all day, and could the gentleman consider letting the best man cut in? The fat man gave the matter due consideration—not protracted but not instantaneous, either; it was a question he had to weigh the pros and cons of—and he finally let the best man into the line. Behind him.

Robert Paul Smith's obituary is in the *Times* this morning. He seems to have written very little since his "Where Did You Go? Out. What Did You Do? Nothing." But that appeared in 1951—more than twenty-five years ago. I know about writing blocks, although I have never suffered from one for more than a few days at a stretch; but what does a writer do with his time for a quarter of a century? There was a Profile of Ralph Ellison in *The New Yorker* not long ago that gave his work habits in some detail. Ellison spent, according to that piece, seven hours a day writing—and that was exclusive of writing letters and such. Seven hours a day writing, and nothing of consequence published since 1953! Is another writer supposed to believe that? I don't average seven hours a day although I can go on for more than twenty-four, nonstop, if I have a deadline. If I really sat at a typewriter for seven hours a day and produced nothing publishable for, say, seven years, I think I would give up writing for some such more rewarding pursuit as life insurance. Somebody in Alaska asked me what J. D. Salinger was up to these days. Shawn may know, because I suppose whatever Jerry writes again will first appear in *The New Yorker*, but I certainly don't. If Ellison hadn't preempted the title, Salinger could write an autobiography and call it "The Invisible Man."

We pick up Rainbow at Pet Lodge. Her bill, for the Alaska weekend, comes to $77.76. My first reaction is to check it to see what she has run up in room-service and long-distance charges. But I can't find any. Twelve dollars a day plus tax seems like a lot to pay to put a dog in a cage, but her coat does look passably shiny. I will have to check with Cy Corenthal and see if keeping our dog alive, while we are professionally obliged to be out of town, is a tax-deductible business expense. I know what he will say. He will say No. Then it will be on my overburdened conscience to decide whether Rainbow, already spayed without her knowledge or consent, next becomes an unwitting party to tax avoidance or tax evasion, or is allowed to slumber unmolested and uncontested in non-deductibility.

At the office, Bruce Bliven tells me that the halls have been buzzing with talk of the imminent sale of *The New Yorker* to the Washington *Post*. I had heard the rumor myself, and so had Ben Bradlee. He said there was logic to it. The magazine rib of the *Post*'s corporate umbrella has apparently been earning more profits—principally from *Newsweek*—than the rest of that business; and the people on the magazine side, Ben said, want those profits to be spent on acquiring more magazines, rather than used to support newspapers, radio stations, television channels, and the like. But Bradlee had never specifically heard *what* other magazines the *Post*'s magazine people were flirting with. *The New Yorker* has been rumored sold before. CBS was once supposed to buy us. Instead, it bought the New York Yankees. That was a bad mistake. Look at the comparable statistics ever afterward for Mel Stottlemyre and Roger Angell.

A phone call from a Los Angeles *Times* man in Austin, Texas. He is doing a story on the failure of Governor Briscoe to reappoint Lady Bird Johnson to the Board of Regents of the University of Texas. The *Times* man remembered a Talk piece in *The New Yorker* last fall, and has learned that I wrote it; it was an account of a conference at the Smithsonian Institution, which I was invited to attend, and to cover, by Wilton Dillon. Elspeth Rostow (Mrs. Walt W.), a University of Texas dean, was also at the Washington affair, and she and I had had a reunion of sorts at a cocktail party. We were both alumni of Claremont Avenue, where we grew up, in the then safe environs of Columbia University.

Elspeth had told me during cocktails that Lady Bird probably wouldn't be reappointed to the regents because the governor had thought she was too radical; and this ideological judgment had struck me as so ludicrous that I had put it in my piece. Now, the L.A. *Times* man has called Elspeth and she has denied telling me that. The reporter wants to know if I have my notes. I say that I threw them away when the piece came out; my office is cluttered enough as it is. Anyway, I tell him, I am not sure I wrote down what Mrs. Rostow said exactly while she was saying it, because we were drinking and chatting, and I probably had a glass in one hand and a cigarette in the other. Oh, no, the reporter said; Mrs. Rostow had specifically told him that I was taking notes while I was talking to her. In that case, I said rather stuffily, I stand by my story.

The little piece on the Smithsonian gathering had other repercussions.

The Librarian of Congress denounced the Talk item, in a letter to the president of the august American Studies Associations, as superficial and inaccurate. A copy of the waspish letter was sent to Wilton Dillon at the Smithsonian, and he sent a copy of the copy to me. I do not mind being accused of superficiality, but inaccuracy is something else again, and so I told off both Daniel J. Boorstin and Allen Davis, privately, and they proceeded to get mad at *Wilton*, for God's sake, and to demand a formal apology from him, in writing. I thought for a while I was going to have to accept, or instigate, a challenge to a duel with one or both of these irate intellectual eminences; but I finally figured out a way to bring the whole silly business to a halt. I wrote Davis a one-word letter. The letter went, "Relax."

I guess with respect to the governor and Lady Bird I had what all reporters aspire to and what few *New Yorker* reporters attain—a more or less bona-fide scoop.

I also had an inter-office phone call today from Mary D. Rudd Kierstead, of the fiction-reading department. Mary D. says she has a crucially important question to ask me: "What is the countess' surname?" The countess? Surname? What in the world has got into the head of this normally sane young woman? Mary D. reminds me that I passed on to fiction a six- or seven-hundred-page manuscript that some publishing acquaintance had dumped on me—the memoirs of a European noblewoman, with no title page attached. I tell Mary D. that I vaguely recall, from a phone conversation with the publisher, that the lady's name was either "Sternberg" or, more likely in the circumstances, "von Sternberg." Mary D. groans. "Are you *sure*?" she asks. "I was hoping the name was from 'A' to 'K.' " Now I am convinced she is totally addled, and I ask what she means. The explanation is beautifully simple. Mary D. reads unsolicited man-uscripts from authors whose surnames begin L-to-Z, and somebody else gets the start of the alphabet. People often ask me how *The New Yorker* operates, and now, by chance, after almost forty years, I have found out. Brendan Gill didn't have any revelation as breathtaking as this in *his* book.

February 1

Ellie advises me that the Alaskan who escorted us to Prudhoe Bay—well, the Englishman, to be technical about it—is in New York and that to reciprocate for his hospitality we are having him to dinner tomorrow night. Because his wife runs a repertory theatre in Anchorage, E. has also invited Joan Davidson, until recently the chairman of the New York State Council on the Arts. As for tonight, we are going to a meeting at the Lotos Club, which will be devoted to complaints by female authors about the way male critics review their books.

I will join this distaff picket line any day. Most of the reviews of books of mine that have pained me have been penned by men. The majority of these harsh critiques have appeared in the Sunday *Times* Book Review, which, of course, is the one place above all where a writer hopes to be well received. I have had terrible luck with the Sunday *Times*. When I was in South Africa in 1966, for instance, I received a nice letter from a congressman, who thought I would be interested to know that he had been asked by the Book Review to take on a forthcoming work of mine on Micronesia (he was a member of the House committee that dealt with the Department of the Interior, which supervised that region), and that he had liked the book enormously. Now, that was the kind of news a writer loves to hear. No waiting around wondering what the Sunday *Times* will say, or indeed whether it will say anything at all; instead, I knew in advance that the review was all set and that it was a rave. I was thus understandably perplexed when, week after week, I failed to find it in print. After several months, I asked a friend at the *Times* to make discreet inquiries. He reported back that the review had come in, all right, but that the editors had decided not to use it because it was so atrociously written. They never did reassign the book to anybody else, so it never got mentioned. The congressman whose prose style did not meet the *Times*' not demonstrably high standards of acceptability ended up as a judge.

When in due course I wrote a book about South Africa, the *Times* assigned it to Joseph Lelyveld, who was a full-time reporter on the paper (he had been its correspondent in Johannesburg) and could thus hardly be rejected on grounds of technical inadequacy. I wished when I read what he had to say that he could have been. Some six years later, when "The China Hands" was about to be published, James C. Thomson, Jr., a China Hand himself of high repute and scholarship, wrote to John Leonard, then the editor of the Book Review, and suggested that he review it. I think Jim felt guilty. He had read my book in manuscript, and then in reviewing a book of Edmund Clubb's—the Sunday *Times* gave it page-one treatment—had inadvertently cribbed a fragment of my still unpublished manuscript. I had forgiven Jim that trespass when I learned that he proposed reviewing my book, too—for had not he, like the luckless congressman before him, already told me in advance how much he admired it? Jim never had a reply from Leonard, who was succeeded as editor of the book section, at about that time, by Harvey Shapiro. By then Joseph Lelyveld had long since quit Johannesburg and had done a tour of duty in Hong Kong, and instead of Thomson "The China Hands" went to him. Lelyveld can have nothing against me personally, since we have never met; but he sure isn't fond of my work. I met Harvey Shapiro at a party not long after that review came out and said to him, "You son of a bitch, you just cost me ten thousand dollars," which I reckoned was about what the difference between a good and a lukewarm Sunday *Times* notice was worth. Shapiro did not even take a swing at me; maybe he had already become inured to that kind of criticism.

I have had somewhat better luck with the daily *Times*, but its reviewers probably can't make or break a book. They can surprise the hell out of a writer, though. I was in the locker room of the Yale Club one day, after playing squash with Pete Spelman, the public relations man for the non-editorial side of *The New Yorker* (see—we do mingle), when a total stranger accosted me and said, "You may want to know that I'm reviewing your book for the *Times*." I was glad to hear that, naturally, but asked him how on earth he knew who I was. "I recognized you from your picture," he said. That might have been a reasonable response in most circumstances, but at the moment I was stark naked. Reviewers for the daily *Times*, though, can be as exasperating as those who toil for the Sunday paper. When my book on Herbert Bayard Swope finally came out, after his family tried to have it suppressed because of its alleged derogation of him, the daily *Times* reviewer said it was a biography that could better be described as hagiography. Saints alive!

The lady writers' organization that is putting on the feminist pep rally at the Lotos tonight calls itself Women's Ink. Any men who tried to get away with something like that would be, and should be, suppressed. And as Ellie and I, late as usual, slide into some uncomfortable folding chairs to try to catch up with an ongoing dialogue, whom do we see up on the dais but Harvey Shapiro himself! Am I just imagining this, or does he flick a nod of recognition my way? If so, that may mean that he has forgotten our abrasive last encounter. Good! One should not push the Sunday *Times* Book Review too hard. A little jab, perhaps, every now and then, but no shoving.

Much of this particular literary evening to which E. has dragged me is devoted to a discussion of the last part (the sex part, to make the book sell) of "Lovers and Tyrants," the "novel" on which Francine DuPlessix Gray is currently riding the crest of bestsellerdom. The audience is asked for expressions of its views, and I am tempted to—but do not—relate how one of Francine's poodles, which she had just certified as gentle, tried despite the barrier of a screen door between it and me to take my right arm off at the shoulder; but I do not think one should tell off an author for omitting to call off her, or his, dogs. I also refrain from saying how bad a book I think "Lovers and Tyrants" is (surely Aristotle would agree with me that it is really not a novel at all, but a pastiche, *cum* sex), because my low view of it could conceivably, if anybody wanted to take the trouble to do enough research, be attributed to my attitude toward poodles. Or theirs toward me. I was once frustratingly detained from arriving on time to celebrate Robert Jay Lifton's receiving the National Book Award because someone had parked a Lifton poodle on the steps of our duplex and there seemed to be no way of my getting upstairs to put on a clean shirt without having the rest of my attire ripped to shreds.

All in all, this is the kind of evening, full of inane, fatuous talk by people who like to torture captive audiences, that I despise; and I was just about to get really sore at Ellie for exposing me to it when she remarked that she thought it was one of the most boring experiences she had ever had. What a marvelous woman! What keen critical discernment! What a companion with whom to grope hand in hand through the labyrinth of life! As we are leaving, she does say, though, that in view of my purported appraisal of the evening's divertissement, the eruptive applause I conferred on Harvey Shapiro's contribution to it was perhaps a bit much.

February 2

Sports Illustrated is out with my backgammon piece in it. George Gianis has read it by noon, and has only one exception to take—why did I call him "Stravros" instead of "George"? This is what comes from bending over backwards to protect one's friends' feelings. I had thought he might be offended at what I said about him; instead he is offended that I said it anonymously. What is that old journalistic dictum, anyway—something to the effect that it doesn't matter what you say as long as you spell the name right? I skip the lunchtime backgammon game today, not because I wish to avoid compliments or insults (how arrogant, to think these would be on anybody's mind besides my own!), but because Paul Killiam wants to discuss the program of a Harvard '37 dinner to be held at the club in April, a sort of warmup for the fortieth reunion in June. Paul and I and Mark Dall, inevitably, will have to furnish the text of the after-dinner entertainment.

Mark and Mike Stone, the dinner chairman, join Paul and me in the big central Grill Room, and Paul has hardly begun to extract papers (old jokes, mainly, from prior reunions) from his briefcase when Rocco, the maître d', tells us we cannot conduct business there. An excellent rule—one that every club should have and many do. But it is a rule violated daily at the Harvard Club by insurance men, brokers, bankers, and journalists; except in the case of the journalists, it is hard to walk through the Grill Room some days without hearing muted talk, with documentation, of making and saving millions. And we are not exactly conducting business: We are discussing a program for an affair that, directly or indirectly, is being staged to raise money for Harvard. But Rocco is unyielding, so we pack up and move into the dining room, where—logic being only a small part of a liberal education—there seems to be no objection to our spreading out papers, save from a waiter trying to find space to plunk down a salad bowl.

Joan Davidson thinks we invited her to our Alaskan dinner because she used to live up there; if Ellie and I ever knew that, we had forgotten it. Dinner is a latish one. The Burton Benjamins are coming, and Bud has to hang around CBS until the Cronkite news show, which he produces, gets safely into the air waves. Bud says Walter and he are going to South Africa, first time for both, and would I have lunch next week and talk about places and sources? Of course I will, but at the same time I am consumed with envy; I asked Shawn last week to consider sending me back to South Africa, and he hasn't yet given me his verdict.

February 3

At my sister Olivia's tonight, Ellie tells the group a story she hasn't yet told me—her first encounter, at 1095 Park, with our fellow apartment-dweller Mikhail Baryshnikov. They met in the elevator, while both were on their way to walk dogs, and E. hadn't seen enough pictures of the dancer's face to recognize him; nor had she been informed that he'd moved into the building. Anyway, sensing that this stranger had some difficulty with English, E. had said to him, like Tarzan's Jane, "Me Ellie Kahn." To which he had rejoined, as she understood it, "Me valet." That seemed reasonable enough, on upper Park Avenue; it was not until she *did* see a photograph of him in the *Times* a couple of months later that she realized what he had said was "Me ballet."

Olivia's guests tonight are mostly in publishing, and with Bill Koshland among them, it's natural enough that we get to talking about Alfred Knopf. Susan Sheehan has been working on Knopf's biography, and I am waiting for her to come around and interview me. I want to tell her the story about how I blew my one and only chance to meet H. L. Mencken, whose love of language and scorn of stuffiness combined to make him one of my true heroes when I was growing up. I got to know Alfred in 1947, shortly after I had broken my leg by idiotically crossing my skis on practically level ground. While I was moping around in my cast, I read in the papers that Alfred had broken *his* leg skiing while riding a rope tow *uphill*. Here clearly was a skier even more inept, if one could credit the published accounts, than was I. I felt better at once—like a vaudeville-house patron with a headache who feels relatively less anguished on watching a comedian take a banana-peel pratfall.

I wrote Mr. Knopf a note of commiseration (I had enough tact not to mention in it the psychotherapeutic effect his spill had had on me) from one maimed athlete to another; and soon afterward he invited Jinny and me to drive across Westchester County to Purchase and dine with him. Knopf's reputation as a gourmet was well upheld by the food and wines he served us. But he rarely had any other guests, and after we had agreeably partaken of his hospitality three or four times (he would not let us reciprocate; he must have guessed that our cuisine could not compete), we sort of ran out of things to talk about. So when I was at home one day with some kind of imagined illness and the phone rang and Jinny took the call and came to my bedside and said it was Alfred on the phone and that he wondered if at the last minute she and I could come to dinner, I groaned, buried my head under my pillow, and told her to tell him I was so sick that the likelihood of my ever taking any further nourishment of any kind at any time was remote, if not non-existent.

Jinny shrugged, went back to the phone, and then returned. "He said it was too bad we couldn't come," she reported, "because there were going to be just the four of us—you, me, Alfred, and H. L. Mencken."

I leapt out of bed. "Call him back," I said. "I feel perfect."

She refused, and not without reason. As an actress, she said, she had further dramatized my already poignant description of my condition to the point where she was in tears, and while it might be complimentary to her professionalism to confess instantly that she had been play-acting, it would hardly speak well of her real-life integrity, let alone mine. It didn't matter; by the time she had finished explaining why she really couldn't phone back to say I had miraculously recovered, the thought of not getting to dine with Mencken had actually made me sick.

February 4

Another Friday, and thus another tennis morning. I can't remember when I first played tennis. I don't recall ever having had a lesson when I was young. At forty, I applied to a Cape Cod pro for some help with my serve. My serve and my overhead, I have been told by observers, are both hit in a curious, sidewise, straight-armed fashion—highly unusual, visually ludicrous. I myself am unaware of any eccentricity. I feel about my serve the way people who snore feel about their snoring. However whimsical or irritating my serve may be to others, it doesn't bother me. I once tried to change it on my own, and my shoulder began to ache, so I reverted to my normal unorthodoxy. The people I play with most of the time were disappointed, and said so. I gathered they would rather have had me crippled than different.

The pro was kinder. When I showed up for my one and only lesson, he told me to demonstrate my serve. I did, and asked what he could do to alter it. "At your age, it's hopeless," he said. He proposed that we play gin rummy for the rest of our hour, and said graciously that he wouldn't charge me for the lesson unless he lost at gin.

My form would probably be acceptable if I'd taken lessons when I was young. My sons have good form. I delivered each of them into the hands of a pro at eight, and I am quite pleased with the way they have turned out. One summer, for instance, Joey, then eighteen, went to England and neglected to put in an appearance at a welcoming party a British hostess had thoughtfully arranged for him. He didn't show up because, after checking in at his hotel and dumping his luggage, he headed straight for Wimbledon. Terry was in Europe then, too, and in his first letter home he said that he was in a kind of a jam; he hadn't yet been able to figure out a way of strapping his racquet to a motorcycle on which he was planning to tour the continent. Two months after that, Tony, then fifteen, went off to boarding school. It was his first extended absence from home, and I was naturally concerned about how he would adjust to the new experience. I found his first letter reassuring. He said he had met a classmate who was the son of another court-owner—albeit only a New Jersey one. "I had to take this language-aptitude test," my son wrote, "so we only had time to play one set."

In a way, it's odd that my childhood was so tennisless. Our Claremont Avenue apartment was only a block and a half away from one of the outdoor tennis establishments that used to decorate New York City. I would go there faithfully in the wintertime, when the courts were flooded, to skate, but I never went near the place the rest of the year. Ice skating! What a wasted youth!

I didn't really get interested in tennis until I was out of college and at work. Some friends at the office needed a fourth for an afternoon game, and they couldn't recruit anyone else. They figured I was better than nobody, and I figured that anything was better than the office. We often played at another outdoor establishment, this one at Park Avenue and Fortieth Street. I used to feel a twinge of melancholy every time we settled up for the court, because during the Depression my grandfather had invested heavily in that particular site and had lost his shirt when a mortgage was foreclosed. I hated to be pouring more money into real estate that had already absorbed so much of the family fortune.

In 1939, I was a bachelor, and with my savings I bought a Plymouth convertible. It was the first convertible marketed with an automatic top. It was *that* long ago. Probably because I had transportation, *The New Yorker* invited me that summer to write its tennis column. I was flattered, and overjoyed, inasmuch as it gave me something to do weekends and there were lots of girls at Forest Hills and Longwood and Southampton and the other haunts I frequented, with my top down.

Unfortunately, I was shy. Not long ago, I looked over some of the stuff I wrote back then, and I was astonished to find how much space I had devoted to a young blonde player on the tournament circuit named Virginia Wolfenden. She never made much of a dent in the national rankings, but she must have made a big impression on me. I kept writing about her all the time. But I have no recollection of ever having mustered the nerve actually to speak to her. I could have interviewed her reportorially, it now occurs to me, but it doesn't seem to have occurred to me when it might have mattered.

People like Alice Marble and Bobby Riggs were very big in tennis when I was covering the sport. So was Ladislav Hecht, who, after Hitler moved into Czechoslovakia, came to the United States. Hecht, too, spends his summers at Truro, and a dozen years ago or so, when he must have been around fifty himself, I ran into him at the post office and invited him over to play on my court. He stopped by, just once, but he never came back. Thirty years after his heyday, he was still simply too good for the rest of us.

As I began to love tennis, thanks in large part to Virginia Wolfenden, I began to hate my Plymouth convertible. It kept breaking down. Since I had bought it brand new, I thought it only fair that its manufacturer replace it with a car that functioned. My anguished pleas got as high in the automotive industry hierarchy as Walter P. Chrysler's son-in-law, but I didn't get a substitute. Instead, the Chrysler service people would keep picking up the car and ostensibly fixing it. One of its peculiarities was that its brakes would lock, without warning, usually while I was out on a highway. I may be the only tennis writer who ever was towed into Newport.

I mention the car because its capriciousness got me into an embarrassing tennis situation. As a reporter who was as ignorant of the game's history as of its tactics, I made a practice, while covering tournaments, of trying to position myself as close as possible to Allison Danzig, of the New York *Times*, who knew more about tennis than practically anybody. He was very helpful. He always knew what Wayne Sabin and John Doeg had done in Australia three years before, and I gratefully let his omniscience rub off on me.

Toward the end of the 1939 tournament season, I drove to Longwood, outside Boston, for the national doubles. The car behaved irreproachably. When the last match ended on the last day, and Danzig remarked that he had to take right off for Boston to catch a train for New York, I sensed an opportunity to repay him for his many kindnesses, and offered to drive him back. He said he had to be in New York by eleven o'clock that night at the absolute latest, and I assured him that we had plenty of time.

The brakes locked somewhere outside Worcester. We abandoned the car, took a taxi to Boston, and caught an eight o'clock train, which got us to New York at one. I can't remember what, if anything, we talked about during the trip, but the conversation must have been strained. I should have hung around Longwood and tried to strike up an acquaintance and thus avoid going down into tennis history as a man who's afraid of Virginia Wolfenden.

February 6

After a whole weekend of typing, the Eaton manuscript is finished, at last. I suppose I could have saved time (though not money) by having somebody else type the final version, but where could I find anyone whom I could rely on to change, in rapid transit, a passable "perhaps" to a preferable "possibly"? I celebrate the completion of my stenographic marathon by going over to the Hendon Chubbs' brunch—their word, not mine—where I encounter, among others, Dick Harris. Dick says that he cannot write. He has diagnosed his own predicament as having nothing to do with writer's block but having been brought on by sheer laziness. I admire that kind of honesty in a writer, even a non-writing writer.

Ellie leaves the Chubbs' ahead of me, to keep her regular Sunday mixed-doubles rendezvous, a Sabbath assignation the details of which have never been made clear to me, although I know that the males involved are John Chancellor and Jimmy Greenfield. Ellie assures me, flatteringly, that I would be welcome to join the game except that I am too good for them; but I feel like a poor journalistic relation, someone who is likely to lose face in the course of a match by not being interrupted by an urgent phone call from NBC or the *Times*. I consider that I am even with her for the day, though, in one narrow respect, when later we go to Max Lerner's for cocktails and Walter Cronkite approaches me and says he hears I am having lunch with Bud Benjamin tomorrow and may he come along?

I always feel a bit strange in Max's presence because people say we look alike. There must be something to it. Joey was at the St. Louis airport not long ago, with Jaime, and Joe looked across a waiting area and said, "Hey, look, there's Grandpa Jack!" On closer scrutiny, it was Lerner. If my own son thinks I look like Max, who am I to say him nay? Arthur and Alexandra Schlesinger are at the party; somebody asks me if she isn't Nancy Kissinger. We are all reasonable facsimiles.

Ved Mehta is at the Lerners', too, and E. and I offer to drop him off on the way home. There has been a blizzard, and when we let him out we steer him around a snow bank. He would no doubt have skirted it without us. God knows how, but he would have. For a totally blind man, Ved gets around more nimbly than many of us with twenty-twenty vision. No cane, no seeing-eye dog, no holding on to anybody else's arm—I used to be firm about "anybody's else," but when Ted Bernstein gave up the battle I capitulated, too—one of the most formidable demonstrations of overcoming a formidable handicap I have ever been privy to. Ved's friends sometimes joke, not in his presence, about his propensity for using visual images, but they do so lovingly, as well as perplexedly. For how does he do it? How, at dinner parties at his own apartment, does he manage to make everybody's drinks himself and get them all straight? How, at somebody else's home, does he remember, even though he hasn't been there for over a year, exactly where the bathroom is? The other morning, I spotted Ved striding up to buy a container of coffee at the portable stand in the lobby of our office building. That very day, the stand was relocated from where it had been for a couple of years to a new spot, fifty or sixty feet away. I wish I knew how Ved learned it had been moved.

February 7

Lexy oversleeps this morning. His excuse is that his mother and I kept him up too long attending his rehearsal of the magic show he is going to put on at school. As a result of his arising late, he can't walk the dog. I don't want to. So, guiltily, I let Rainbow use the terrace. The question is: Would we keep a dog in New York—any dog, let alone a large black mongrel—if we didn't have a terrace? Ancillary question: Would I be less reluctant to take the dog outside if I didn't have to get breakfast? When Women's Lib came to flower, Ellie pointed out that inasmuch as we are both writers, to whom time is the most precious asset, it seemed unfair for the kitchen to be her domain just because of an accident of sex. That sounded plausible enough, and we soon agreed on how various meals would be handled in our household. Lunch would be catch-as-catch-can, every man, woman, and child taking care of his or her self. (Dogs generally skip lunch, unless they beg extra hard.) Dinner would be E.'s responsibility. Breakfast would be mine. I wasn't aware when we made this pact of one big difference between men and women. Women are smarter. Women realize that while a family is in residence it almost always has breakfast at home, but that people often go out for dinner.

E. swore when we were first married that among the things she would and would not do, a major Would Not would be having a dog in the city. I swore I would have only a Labrador retriever. So as in the case of the kitchen we compromised, which is the secret of success in any relationship, and we acquired a miniature dachshund. That did not work out especially well, because Jelly Bean was too fragile to withstand the wear and tear of being handled by two small boys. Out of compassion for the little dog's feelings, we gave him to a mature friend, which failed dramatically to improve Jelly Bean's lot; the friend inadvertently ran over him with her car. Rainbow, though a mongrel, is at least the size of a Labrador retriever, and, like most Labradors, she is all-black. Why, then, her multi-colored name? Why not indulge the imaginative whim of the eleven-year-old apprentice magician who brought her home? Why use adult criteria and question the nomenclatural judgment of a child when, after all, one sheeplike lets the same child's undeveloped tastes lead one time and time again to Howard Johnson's? Why isn't "Rainbow" every bit as good a name for a dog as "Jelly Bean"?

Barge was all-black, too, and unlike poor mixed-bred Rainbow, was a member in good, purebred standing of the American Kennel Club. Our beloved Cleopatra gave birth to Royal Barge of Holbrook, at Scarborough, roughly twenty-five years ago, on what was also my birthday. There was a party planned for me that night (I always say I don't want any fuss, but like most men I sure love to have a fuss), and inasmuch as Larry Adler was to be among the guests, that meant we had to get the piano tuned. If you expect a musical genius to preside over the singing of "Happy Birthday," you had better damn well have your ivories shipshape. The piano tuner misunderstood the directions to our house, and didn't arrive until 8 P.M., concurrent with the first guests. He was still lying supine underneath the grand, with Larry instructing him from above, when Cleo began letting me know that she was going to have her puppies and to have them not in the elegant whelping room we had created for her downstairs but upstairs in the master bedroom. The first of her litter of nine emerged at 9 P.M. I had never before officiated as a veterinarian-obstetrician; but during the ensuing five hours I came to have new respect for both professions. (Also for the beautifully tidy way in which dogs dispose of afterbirths.) It was 2 A.M. before I got downstairs to greet those of my guests who were still around— the piano tuner, as I recall, among them—but most were kind enough, at one point or another in the evening, to come upstairs and give me a hand, although in truth Cleo did most of the really dirty work herself.

Barge, who helped Jinny and me raise our children, lived to be twelve. For the last year or so, he was not well. He had a heart attack and a stroke and from time to time could barely use his rear legs. When he went upstairs to bed (no self-respecting dog would sleep anywhere but in the master bedroom, and no self-respecting dog-owner would wish otherwise), I would have to carry his hindquarters. At Truro, one bitter-cold Thanksgiving weekend, he got outside one night, managed to propel himself to a favorite drainage ditch of his in a poison-ivy swamp, fell in, and couldn't climb out. Eventually we tracked him down by his barking, dragged him clear, got him back to the house, and scrubbed the mud off him and then off us. When it became apparent that for his own sake he had to be put away, I just couldn't be a party to it, and cravenly let Jinny drive him to Dr. Grossman's for the *coup de grâce*. To the bitter end, Barge was the best possible confidant and companion, and every bit as good a watchdog as Rainbow is today. Barge's terminal bark was, though, in a very literal sense, worse than his bite: Had an intruder violated our home, Barge would have roared at him but would have been unable to get to his feet and take any further punitive action. I was once going to write a short story about Barge's old age. The first sentence was to have been, "The burglar didn't know the dog was paralyzed." But I never could get beyond that without breaking down.

Practically everybody in Scarborough, I reflect at lunch today with Bud Benjamin and Walter Cronkite, had Labradors except the Benjamins, who, though normal in most other respects, were cat people. We knew our neighbors' dogs as well as their children, maybe better, and the dogs were certainly often easier to get along with. Bud and I were going to have lunch *à deux* at some modest establishment west of Ninth Avenue, but I am advised this morning in one of a flurry of phone calls that since Mr. Cronkite is joining us we will be meeting, instead, at the Copenhagen. The Copenhagen seems to be Where Walter Cronkite Eats. His picture is displayed just inside the front door, and at the table which I sense is reserved for him daily there is a bowl of fresh dill. While I am admiring these totems of flattery, Walter asks me, flatteringly, what I think he should say in a speech he is going to give at Stellenbosch, the big Afrikaner university near Cape Town. I suggest that he talk about the impact of television on news and what this is likely to mean in South Africa when television starts up there—as it is about to—and what the impact of that is likely to be on the relative isolation in which South Africans—especially the Afrikaners among them—live vis-à-vis the rest of the world.

Walter helps himself to some dill and wonders whether the taxicab drivers in South Africa are mostly white or mostly black, or both. After not having been there for ten years, I cannot for the life of me remember. I do remember, though, and hasten to tell my companions, that the name of the chief concierge at the Mount Nelson Hotel in Cape Town, where one assumes people like Bud and Walter will be staying, is, or was a decade ago, Louis. (Unexpressed flash of memory: Louis once handed me seven letters at a clip, all from N. "Someone must truly love you," he said. Unexpressed afterthought: Is it actually Louis, or is it Victor, or is Victor the Ritz in London? One should write these things *down*.) Walter says this is a truly useful bit of information, worth the whole lunch, the reason he wanted to come along to lunch to begin with; because even if Louis isn't at the hotel anymore, merely asking for Louis will give him a certain otherwise unobtainable cachet. I refrain from pointing out that merely being Walter Cronkite probably confers on a person as much cachet as anybody could require for most purposes. Walter peppers me with requests for even meatier intelligence about South Africa, and I am surprised as we chat to find how much I seem to myself to know about the place, even after this long-time gap. I have got to get back there and try to verify my own hypotheses.

February 8

I have lunch with Jack Raymond at the Overseas Press Club, which I have never joined, in part because it has always seemed to have more publicity men like Jack as members and officers (he is a past president) than foreign correspondents. He wants to discuss a client as a possible Profile subject, and by one of those outlandish coincidences it turns out that the fellow he has in mind is one I got okayed as a possible Profile subject last fall—Robert Anderson, the ARCO oil man. I had proposed him when he bought the London *Observer*; he seemed like a potentially interesting American counterpart of Rupert Murdoch; and then I had much heard his name again, of course, when I visited the ARCO installation up at Prudhoe Bay. What I hadn't known, until Jack enlightens me at lunch, is that there are *two* Robert Andersons. I had thought that the ARCO one had been President Eisenhower's Secretary of the Treasury, but Jack says no, that was Robert *B*. Anderson—" 'B' for 'Bad,' " Jack adds. That Anderson is not his client. The one who *is* is Robert *O*.—" 'O' for 'O.K.,' " Jack volunteers, to help me keep them straight and, reasonably enough, keep himself in good with the Robert Anderson hand that feeds him. I have stumbled upon a confusion of identities conceivably the equal, in our day and age, of Clare Luce, Claire Luce, and Ina Claire.

In the evening, Ellie and I take Lexy to see a one-man (Len Cariou) performance of an odd play by Peter Handke, "A Sorrow Beyond Dreams." Clive Barnes has raved about it—over-raved, in our view. But this is a hard show for me to watch dispassionately, inasmuch as it is all about a man reminiscing about his mother, who committed suicide by taking an overdose of pills. When my mother died unexpectedly in the middle of the night, and some sleeping pills were found in her medicine cabinet, the coroner got called in. The verdict was accidental death, from a sudden heart attack, but before that there had to be an autopsy at the morgue, and I seemed to be the only member of the family who was composed enough to go down there and make a formal identification. It is not the most pleasant way imaginable to take final leave of one's mother.

Elsie was just sixty when she died—exactly my age today. Before I get too depressed about that, let me remind myself that her parents both lived into their late eighties, my father's mother into her mid-nineties, and my father himself to eighty-eight. I was in Munich, covering the 1972 Summer Olympics, when he died, coincidentally with the murder of the Israeli athletes by Arab terrorists; death took no holiday that week. I debated briefly returning home, but inasmuch as there was to be no funeral service for Ely and as *The New Yorker* had nobody else at Munich (*Sports Illustrated* sends armies to the Games, with generals and non-coms and privates in the ranks and even camp followers), I decided after a number of transatlantic phone calls to stay at my post, in the old show-must-go-on tradition.

I like covering the Olympics, because it gives me a chance to write against deadlines. Also, it is fun for a couple of weeks to be an authentic sportswriter—to sit up in press boxes with men who have devoted their entire professional careers to covering sports and have been universally acknowledged as the titans of their trade; and to pretend to share their ambience and expertise. At Montreal, I spent the better part of an exceedingly agreeable day, at the rowing venue, in the company of Red Smith, and was beguiled as always by the witty, erudite running commentary with which he clarified and annotated the action unfolding before us. Indeed, I was tempted to use what he offhandedly told me in one of my dispatches. Something stayed my hand, and that was just as well; for Red's next column contained nearly verbatim what I had taken to be casual chitchat. My roommate at Montreal, by chance and good fortune, turned out to be another dean of American sportswriters—Furman Bisher, sports editor of the Atlanta *Journal*, columnist for *The Sporting News*, president emeritus of the Association of American Sportswriters and Sportscasters, possessor of I know not what all other attributes of eminence. Furman was the ideal roommate for a quadrennial sportswriter like myself (by contrast, I was assigned one at Mexico City, in 1968, who insisted on calling me "roomie"); he, like Red, seemed to know everything there could be to know about all sports; and he didn't complain about my snoring.

It is the writing under pressure, though, that I find most exhilarating about the Olympics. I love to write, like a newspaperman, ripping off copy in takes, filing it take by take, none of this first- and second-draft stuff, beating that clock is what counts. Writing all night in Tokyo, at the 1964 Games, sending my wife and driver back and forth to the cable office in my car with a *New Yorker* flag (purple and gold) flying from its fender, I forgot by the time I got to the end of my piece how I'd begun it; but the important thing to me was that I had made my deadline. It was possible then to get copy to the Tokyo cable office by 5 A.M. Monday, New York time, and appear in the rough copy twenty-four hours after that. I had acquired the flag because my driver pointed out that every other correspondent on the scene—Associated Press, Reuter's, Agence France Presse, *Sports Illustrated*, NBC and the rest—had one on *his* car, and my chauffeur would irretrievably lose face if we didn't follow suit. It so happened, also, that his brother-in-law *made* fender pennants, overnight. The only remaining detail was: What were *The New Yorker*'s colors? I said that as far as I knew it didn't have any, and that Shawn, generous as he was about expense accounts, would not relish, though he would probably pay for, a query *in re* that. The driver and I agreed that we would let his brother-in-law select something appropriate. Thus, purple and gold. I brought the flag back home and gave it to Bill Shawn, who had, after all, paid for it; but *The New Yorker* does not much go in for blowing its own horn or waving its own flag, and I haven't seen our royal colors since.

The New Yorker is in many ways a singular institution. Stoutly ignoring the vast technological leaps forward of the last thirteen years, the magazine has managed somehow to *increase* the time it takes to get copy into print. During the Montreal Olympics of 1976, I was advised that the absolute bona fide going-to-press time for my copy (as opposed to the fake deadlines that editors are forever trying to fob off on writers they do not trust) would be 6:42 P.M., Friday. To give the editor who was handling me that week, Bill Whitworth, a break (not to mention the checkers), I telegraphed most of my copy on Wednesday. But because I wanted, in my hotshot-journalist fashion, to have the latest possible legitimate dateline—Friday, under the new order of things—I telephoned in additions. On the last Friday of the competitions, Lasse Viren, the extraordinary long-distance runner from Finland whom so many sportswriters spent so much time accusing of having consumed his own stored blood to make him run faster (I preferred to go along with his own explanation: reindeer milk), crossed the 5,000-metre finish line at 6:03 P.M. I ran down from the press box of the big stadium to the basement press center, grabbed one of the few phones that didn't appear to have been commandeered to transmit hosannahs to Helsinki, and, since that was the only way one *could* use those phones, put in a collect call to my office in New York. There was a night operator at the *New Yorker* switchboard who evidently hadn't been briefed on the urgencies of "Front Page"-style journalism, and who refused to accept the first call I put through because I had been in too much of a hurry to say whom I wanted to talk to. If Roy Howard had been working for *The New Yorker*, he might never have scored his scoop on the World War I armistice.

It was 6:15, after starting all over again and finally reaching New York via—it seemed to me, staring anxiously at my watch and envying the jabbering writers who were dictating to *their* offices—Helsinki, Leningrad, Tashkent, Pyongyang, and Ottawa, before I got through to Whitworth. Instantly I yelled at him, "Can 'after six o'clock' be, in our style, 'early this evening,' or does it have to be 'late this afternoon'?" Whitworth was probably relieved to hear from me, because it meant he could lock up The Sporting Scene for that week and go on to something more interesting, like dinner, but his first understandable reaction was to ask me not to shout; there was nothing wrong with his ear or the connection, at least not at his end, and I was, after all, merely in Montreal. He added that he didn't care what phrase I used in whatever it was I was about to give him as long as it did not run over five lines of type and could be delivered to make-up within the next six minutes. "All right, then," I snarled hoarsely, shoving an imaginary Fedora to the back of my head, "give me a 'Friday' dateline and take this down: 'Early this evening, Lasse Viren, the phenomenal Finn who . . .' "

Ellie properly tries to cut me down to size when I carry on in this fashion by calling me "Boy Reporter." She hopes that I will outgrow whatever my addiction is. I am in no hurry to. At the time of the 1988 Summer Olympics, wherever they are held, I will be only about the same age that Red Smith was at Montreal.

February 9

Ellie and I go to Town to watch Lexy's magic show. Lexy is worried that his flash powder won't explode; I am worried that it will. It does, pleasing him; and it doesn't injure anyone, pleasing me. While we are waiting for the performance to start, Mrs. Stanton, the chairman of the Town School board of trustees, mentions a speech she gave at a Phillips Exeter meeting not long ago on trustee-headmaster relationships. She tells me these are something special. I know. I was chairman of the Scarborough School board for several years, lost one headmaster, hired another, fought with both. We also lost a building, by fire, during my incumbency, and had to raise $300,000 for a replacement. I was a volunteer fireman at the time, but the old building was made of wood, and even if we'd had some professional laddies on the scene it couldn't have made much difference. I passed out from smoke inhalation. Very infra dig comportment for the chairman of the board while on school property. Still, not as bad as the normal behavior of one trustee, who invariably came to our meetings cockeyed drunk, and who once bewilderingly delayed our stately proceedings with an impassioned, if rambling, protest against a mild resolution having to do with somebody's wish to *enhance* the dining room. The addled board member was under the misapprehension that the rest of us wanted to commit the institution to spend a sum of money we would not even specify to provide the dining room with a brand-new and quite unnecessary *entrance*.

There was one year—the year after the fire, I guess—when I was so involved with school affairs that I put in a solid forty-hour week grappling with them. When it came to raising the money for the new building, the chairman of the board, like a Special Gifts chairman, was naturally expected to play a leadership role. Accordingly, I got a number of people to make substantial pledges by making a larger one myself than I could afford. Among those who responded swiftly and generously to my entreaties was our treasurer, an accountant by profession and to all appearances a successful one; he rode the club car on the commuter train. He made an exceedingly handsome pledge, in the amount of something like five thousand dollars, and his ringing announcement of his intention rightly won him the praise and admiration of all concerned. When, later, he declined to pay as much as a penny on his pledge, he welshed much more quietly; which may explain how some people make the grade as accountants and treasurers and others do not.

One of the school parents from whom we hoped to extract a tidy sum was a fellow with a castle and a Rolls-Royce, for whom a five-thousand-dollar contribution would probably have been mere lagniappe—equivalent, perhaps, on a relative scale, to the tip we gave the waiter when several of us trustees took that particular prospect to a lunch that was supposed to soften him up. We never got a cent out of him, either, but then he never promised us anything. In fact, there was something about his attitude that persuaded us we might find it costly ever even to approach him again. Soon afterward, his kid was thrown out of school. Trustees of independent schools all sooner or later conclude that headmasters, however much they may differ in other respects, are well-nigh indistinguishable when it comes to bouncing those students whose parents are most capable of rescuing the school from impoverishment. But the trustees are not always privy to all motivating circumstances. Some years later, I read about that father we'd treated to lunch; he was alleged to be the former head of a bank through which the Mafia had been channeling heroin money en route to Switzerland. We all know that children shouldn't be held accountable for their parents' sins (though that chap's offspring sure seemed to enjoy being driven to school in the Rolls-Royce), but maybe the headmaster knew what he was doing when he decided to have no more trafficking with that family.

February 10

This is a special time of the year—the only time when the fliers that people hand you on the street are just about evenly divided between come-ons for massage parlors and income-tax-form-filling parlors. Should I be proud or ashamed that I have never availed myself of either handy service?

I have been sitting around *The New Yorker* for two and a half days waiting to talk to Shawn about South Africa. But he has a cold. When Shawn has a cold, our world stops. I cannot afford to sit around forever, so I arrange to go to Atlanta next week. I have been meaning to do a Profile of the state of Georgia for some months. I phoned Shawn the day after the Democrats nominated Carter (I had no trouble reaching Bill; he was feeling fine), and he agreed with me that if Carter won the election a piece about his home state would be appropriate. Maybe I can knock one off in time to go to South Africa in the late spring.

We are due at Rita Gam's at seven. Rita is to her elevator at 1095 Park Avenue what Baryshnikov is to ours. I have many things in common with her besides our shared address. One of her ex-husbands is Tom Guinzburg, who runs the Viking Press, and who can thus more or less accurately be called the publisher of "The China Hands." Tom came to 1095 Park a couple of years ago, but not to Rita's elevator; rather, to ours, to attend a party Ellie gave me on publication day. He did not bring Jackie Onassis, although, she being one of his employees and this being a business engagement, I suppose he could have ordered her to come along. It would have served Tom right if he had had some embarrassing confrontation with you know who in the lobby; E. only gave me the pub-day party when it became evident that Viking wasn't going to give me one itself, though such gatherings were presumably not against its principles: We had read about a bash at some fancy restaurant a few days earlier to herald Tom's launching of the memoirs of an Italian woman who, if I remember correctly, was, could have been, or had once met an Agnelli. The most memorable publication-day party Ellie and I ever gave, I suppose, was in honor of Nora Sayre, whose publishers, like mine, had taken no such celebratory step themselves; what made the occasion memorable was that Abbie Hoffman, who had not long before brought out his archly entitled memoirs, "Steal This Book," turned up and stole Nora's book.

Tom Guinzburg didn't stay at our party long, nor did he ever mention my book to me. I have no idea whether he has ever read it; writers know that publishers are too busy conglomerating nowadays to have time to read; but it would have been nice if at least he had said something pleasant about, say, the dust jacket. No, come to think of it, not the dust jacket; that was where there was to be found a photograph of me that Ellie had snapped at the Great Wall of China but for which Viking had neglected to give her credit. It must be tough to be a publisher. You practically kill yourself day and night trying to make writers happy, and all you get for it is a lot of unwarranted, uninformed abuse. It would serve them right if you just shut up shop and forced them really to go to work like other people and try to earn a living.

Rita and I have had a continuing cozy relationship—one that existed long before we ever met—through crossword puzzles. With the possible exception of Ira (Gershwin) and Oona (O'Neill Chaplin), I would venture a guess that Rita Gam has turned up in more crossword puzzles than any other living human being, though to be sure she sometimes does have to share top billing—e.g., definition for a four-letter word: "Gam or Hayworth." I have been in puzzles once or twice myself (e.g., five-letter word—"Otto and E.J."), but Rita Gam has got to be *sui generis*, and it can also be said of her record that she leaves Hayworth floundering in her wake, because puzzle-makers use her two ways: Their definition for a desired "gam" is almost never "school of whales." Rita G. was once thinking of writing a book herself; I suggested that the most logical person to solicit a jacket blurb from would be the crossword editor of the *Times*. I used to mail her the puzzles I did that featured her, but out of consideration for my responsibilities to my own family I quit when first-class postage went up to thirteen cents.

I am fond of nearly all word games, and I have found them invaluable in drawing the sting from long automobile trips with small children. I once conducted a coast-to-coast spelling bee for Terry, Joey, and Tony—six weeks, nine thousand miles, and at the end of it not a soul in the car who would ever again, I hoped,* misspell "accommodation," or not get "all right" right. When Lexy was six, and we were playing "Who am I?" between New York and Truro, somewhere around Providence he came up with a character we were supposed to guess—dead man, name begins with "G," the manner of whose dying would, if revealed, instantly give away his identity. Even after some extremely broad hints that, Lexy said scornfully, *any*body should have been able readily to grasp, the rest of us remained stumped, and near Fall River we begged him to tell us who this baffling "G" could be. It was Jesus.

---

* Dear Diary: It will be noted, I hope, that I did not use "hopefully."

Among all verbal time-wasters, though, crossword puzzles and their next of kin (acrostics, et al.) are my favorites, although I have learned that— unlike Rita—one cannot expect them often to allude to oneself. (The only time a book of mine was ever used in a *Saturday Review* Double-crostic, I happened to be out of town, so I never enjoyed the thrill of seeing my own name and prose unfold before me.) Crossword puzzles can also, among other things, teach humility; I feel properly put in my place when the definition for "Kahn" is "Writer Roger ———." When Larry Adler comes across "Harmonica player Larry ———," for a five-letter word, he can fill in his own surname without much risk; but as a rule prudence should accompany pride every step of the way through a crossword. The innocent victim of the most shattering crossword-puzzle experience I ever heard of was my good old friend Arthur Kober, a man of many talents, conspicuous among which was kindness. His was a nature so generous that some of his intimates sometimes suspected that he went out of his way to lose to them at gin rummy. (Kober's parlor tricks included turning newsprint back into trees and tossing off what appeared to be genuine freehand James Thurber drawings; Arthur would sign these with an authentic-looking "Thurber," explaining, if asked, that he could hardly be accused of forgery inasmuch as the "thur" and the "ber" constituted the major segments of his own name. I once urged the curator of the Thurber collection at Ohio State to beseech for his archives an original Kober Thurber, but I fear he did nothing about it before Arthur died.)

Anyway, Arthur was once cruising easily through a crossword while staying with us at Truro or St. Jean de Luz or somewhere (he was a perennial, perpetual, and always welcome house guest), when he was delighted to encounter the definition "Playwright Arthur ———." The called-for word had five letters, and the first two of these, Arthur perceived, he had already written in as part of other words. And guess what these first two letters were! A "k" and an "o"! The greatest Thurber-faker of the twentieth century happily inserted a "b-e-r." But then he found himself in trouble. The rest of the puzzle simply wouldn't fit together for him. He appealed to me for guidance. It thus became my unhappy duty to have to inform him, as gently as possible, that the dramatist whom the composer of that dastardly puzzle had actually had in mind was Arthur Kopit. For a sensitive man already afflicted with a massive case of writer's block, this bit of truth was near-traumatic.

I thought we were going to have dinner at Rita's, but she is apt to be vague about this sort of thing; we are expected only for cocktails. The star of the west wing of 1095 Park utters a loud aside to Ellie, exits, later reenters, stage left, with an omelet, which I don't particularly want but which, clearly having been overheard grumbling about the unfairness of my lot in life, I feel constrained to consume, in its entirety, while the other guests look on, a few of them with undisguised envy. They are an odd lot. There is one guy who, if I understand him correctly, has a foundation grant to teach teachers how to conduct field trips in Central Park. E. seeks to interject some mild comment about the park into a monologue he is delivering that would put most teachers, let alone their charges, to sleep, and he turns on her and says, "Darling, you're full of shit." I swallow my eggy cud, put down my fork, turn on *him*, and tell him severely that he does not know my wife well enough to address either of those key words to her. Am I being a knight, or a knight errant? E. does not faint tremblingly into my arms; I sense that she thinks she can quite satisfactorily dispose of this punk park pedagogue without my intervention. I guess I sound like a prude.

But, perhaps through my long association with *The New Yorker* (and despite four years in the Army in the uninhibited company of people like Eddie Krajewski, whose favorite phrase was that he had as many of this or that as Carter had of little fucking liver pills), I am sometimes squeamish about the words I and others use in the presence of women, whom I still think of occasionally as ladies. I remember vividly a dinner at the Robert Jay Liftons' in New Haven, a decade or so ago, on a Saturday night after a Harvard-Yale game. (Bob would, I suppose, call it the Yale-Harvard game.) The conversation got onto the subject of the use of four-letter words in literature, and a Harvard professor's wife said (this was ten years ago) that she was not yet reconciled to "fuck," and that led our host to discourse eloquently on what he called "the motherfucker section" of a piece of his that had recently come out in the *Atlantic;* and that led Harold Taylor, who always seems to turn up on occasions like this, to chime in with some learned observations on the sociological impact on humankind of the word "cocksucker." I found all this somewhat embarrassing, though it was on the loftiest imaginable level, and I tried to get into the act by suggesting—I could barely get the word out—that "motherfucker" was really merely a mild Oedipal twist to the old phrase "son of a bitch," but I was too late; by then everybody else was discussing heatedly why, so late in the fourth quarter, Yale hadn't passed on third down.

There! I have got all the words—well, most of them, anyway—on paper. This diary could sell!

February 11

I dreamt last night, vividly, that I ran into Shawn somewhere, and he didn't mention any of the things I have been wanting to talk to him about all week. I dream about Shawn more than I do about women.

The morning paper says Kay Fanning is suing Bob Atwood for sixteen and a half million dollars. The journalistic fur must really be flying in Alaska.

Ved Mehta has posted a letter on the eighteenth-floor bulletin board, for all who pass to see. It is a copy of a communication he sent to the Sunday *Times Book Review*, complaining that the person who recently reviewed Ved's new book on Gandhi was racist for having said that Ved could not write objectively about his subject because he is an Indian. May an Englishman not write dispassionately about Churchill, Ved demands of the *Times*, nor a Frenchman about Napoleon, nor an American about Washington? Ved is right, of course. The *Times* has got to be put in its place periodically. I once took epistolary issue with its Sunday magazine for running a piece in which it was implied that I was a rapist, but it never occurred to me to tack a copy of my demurrer to the bulletin board. Most of the messages there are routine: official ones to the effect that the office will be closed on New Year's Day and that the minutes of the last meeting between the employees' committee and Mr. Shawn are available for inspection (one of these days I must inspect some); and unofficial ones telling of houses for rent, apartments wanted, and cats to be given away to qualified, responsible ailurophiles.

So Ved's letter is at least a change of pace—a change, however, less startling than one or two bulletin-board displays we have had in the last ten or twenty years, when writers in the throes of emotional upheavals have signified their distress by tacking up all kinds of aberrational memorabilia. Since the eighteenth floor is inhabited largely by creative people—though a singular aspect of the realm is that one rarely hears a typewriter in action—it is inevitable that we have our share of eccentrics, if no more of these, perhaps, than might be found among a similar-sized group of insurance salesmen.

Once while I was off travelling, a lady fiction writer who was having her troubles converted my office into her lodgings. *The New Yorker* knew she was there but didn't know what to do about her and decided to do nothing until just before my scheduled return. I came back early and found my room full of clothing, hot plates, and caches of food (she was out grocery-shopping), which didn't work out especially well because I had no refrigeration facilities. Also, she had ripped apart her bed—my couch, that was—with some sharp implement. The magazine got her out and tidied up the premises and reupholstered the couch, which had been in pretty bad shape to begin with, so actually I came out ahead on the deal. For some months afterward, however, I had to be careful about reaching into the shelves where I keep caches of research, because that, I discovered, was where she had elected to stow the shattered remnants of her glass peanut-butter jars. I don't know why she did that; she could just as easily have tossed them onto the roof of the Princeton Club.

I had lunch there today with Courtlandt Nicoll—my first time next door in nearly a year, which reminds me that I must nudge Shawn about running my piece on the troubles Princeton has been having with some dissident alumni; the article is now nearly a year old. Courtie, who was responsible more than a decade ago for my meeting Charlie Engelhard, now wants to discuss a literary project involving another friend-and-client, who turns out to be Jay Rutherford, whom I got to know when he was an assistant to Angier Biddle Duke during Angie's stint as LBJ's chief of protocol. I enjoy writing about people like Engelhard and Duke; during the research, one eats well. (They have elderly white waitresses at the Princeton Club; it is in that single respect like dining at one of the better Rockefellers'.) It seems that Jay used to work for the *Daily Mirror* in the thirties, and now he wants to write a book about that tabloid and its heyday, and what do I think of the idea? Not much. I am not sure Jay could write a book. Well, would I like to write it from his research? Sorry, no dice.

I stop at the bank to cash in some leftover drachmas, twelve hundred and fifty of them. I think I am doing very well to get two cents apiece. With twenty-five dollars' worth of practically found money in my pocket, I push on to a florist's to order a dozen Valentine's Day roses for Ellie. Valentine's Day is a holiday I can hardly forget, because Jinny and I got married on February 14th; if one is going to marry more than once, one should probably pick another date. The roses cost forty dollars. Three dollars and something per rose! I hope E. doesn't drop one.

Back at the office, I learn that Bill Shawn, who is one of the few people to have attended both my weddings, has recovered and is accessible. Bill is the only person at the magazine with whom I can discuss my work for it— nobody else is empowered to make any decisions—but over the last ten years or so I probably haven't talked to him for more than a total of ten hours, which, considering that he works seven days a week and I have no idea how many hours a day, has not represented a large hunk of his editorial time. The demands on his time are so intense and persistent, though, that I hate to impose on him except when absolutely necessary, as is the case today; nobody else at *The New Yorker* can authorize me to go to South Africa on its behalf.

I used to see a great deal more of Bill at the office and more socially, too, but when our paths cross at parties nowadays it is apt to be not at his and Cecille's place nor at ours but at one of my sisters' apartments. And I used to spend time with him, back in the days when he was Ross' deputy, going over pieces of mine. Shawn was fun to work with. I did a Profile on Al Capp once that ran in two parts. The subtitle for the first part was "Ooff!! (Sob!) Eep!! (Gulp!) Zowie!!!" When we were getting Part II ready to go to press, we decided to differentiate its subtitle from Part I's by appending one more exclamation point to each Cappism. It was doubtful whether any of our readers—or, indeed, anyone else at the magazine—would spot this nuance; but conceiving it pleased both Shawn and me; and I suppose that we bothered with it at all is indicative of the painstaking care with which words in *The New Yorker* are strung together.

Anybody who has had Shawn handle his copy knows Bill's brilliance as an editor; and by now I guess the public at large is familiar with many of his extracurricular quirks—the distaste for self-service elevators, the austere eating and drinking habits, the many layers of clothing, the excessively well-mannered shyness, and all the rest. His guise of timidity fools many people, but not those around the magazine, who know how unbending he can be about something once he has made up his mind. Thus, his quondam nickname: The Iron Mouse. What sometimes bugs some of us at *The New Yorker* is Shawn's seeming inability or refusal to delegate any authority. Ross had Shawn. Shawn—though he has had and has his share of able assistants, unsung heroes of American magazine journalism like Bob Bingham and Bill Knapp—has never had a Shawn.

Now, Bill is approaching seventy, and while he sometimes appears to be indestructible, he obviously cannot run the magazine forever. But who in the world—densely populated as the world is today—can succeed him? Among the many candidates whose names have, in trial, ballooned, my own long-shot favorite is Jim Stevenson, cartoonist and writer all neatly wrapped in a single bundle. The only hitch is that Jim lives in the country and has a flock of children. For an editor of any magazine to be successful, the magazine has got to be the editor's first love. (DeWitt Wallace solved that problem by having his wife as co-editor of the *Reader's Digest.*) It is hard to visualize Stevenson or anyone else giving as much of his life to an institution as Bill Shawn has to *The New Yorker.* I may not be as close to Shawn as I used to be, but I am reminded now and then of his extraordinary sensitivity and thoughtfulness. For my sixtieth birthday, for instance, he dug up and presented to me, with an accompanying note that touched me deeply, a copy of the April 3, 1937, *New Yorker*—the very first issue in which my byline ever appeared. It was appended to a casual about an African chief from the Gold Coast—now Ghana—whom my sister Joan and I met in Edinburgh when we were young, and who sort of promised to send us a diamond when he got home. But he must have lost our address.

Writers and editors, by the very nature of their work, are bound to have a love-hate relationship. In the case of editors at book publishing houses, the proportion between love and hate is, as a rule, determined solely by sales. With magazine editors, the relationship is much more subtle and complex. Shawn is a Grand Master at moving writers across his editorial chessboard. I mean today to demand of him right off when, if ever, he proposes to run a couple of pieces of mine that have been in type for a year or so, gathering dust, mildew, and other harbingers of rot; but Bill, at his tactical best, disarms me by saying at once that he plans to run my pieces on Cyrus Eaton shortly. Good; the old man is ninety-three. It is not until nine minutes later, after I have taken my leave, feeling guilty for having usurped so much of Shawn's day, that I stop and think: Did he say he was going to run Eaton "soon" or "very soon"?

The difference can be crucial, as we who have worked for Bill for all these years are well aware. There are *New Yorker* contributors who believe that the magazine is akin to the Bible and that its editor thus, ipso facto, must be analogous to God. I am inclined to disagree, on the ground that while *The New Yorker* is probably the best weekly magazine that has ever been published, it is still, after all, only a publication put together by human beings that comes out fifty-two times a year. However, just as there are Talmudic scholars who devote their lives to exegeses of the Old Testament, so perhaps should *The New Yorker* have someone on the premises analyzing and interpreting what Shawn says. When he tells you that a Profile, say, "looks good" or is "very interesting," you know, if you have been around long enough, that what he means is that after some hesitation he has decided to buy the damned piece but that the chances of his ever actually running it are minimal. I once tried to be a pseudo-Talmudic scholar of sorts myself and, as a favor to Bob Shaplen, who had only been on the *New Yorker* staff for twenty-five years or so and was thus rightly considered a neophyte, I compiled a kind of glossary of Shawn terms. I didn't keep a carbon, but my recollection is that it went something like this:

WHAT SHAWN SAYS	WHAT SHAWN MEANS
Good	Dubious
Very Good	Marginal
Great	Passable
One of your very best	B+
Extraordinary	A-
"We're going to run this in the next issue	"I'll be revising the schedule soon and plan to keep you in mind
—this month"	—this year, if all goes well"
—very soon"	—some time, probably, but don't count on it"
—soon."	—never."

But the main purpose of my calling on Shawn today is to confer about Africa. He is not a world traveller. Geography, beyond Manhattan Island, has never been his forte. To him Africa would appear to be a truly dark continent. A couple of weeks before Idi Amin's early-1971 coup d'état, for instance, Ellie and I and the young boys had been in Uganda. We'd been lucky enough to take a boat up the Albert Nile—its waters chock full of hippopotamuses, its banks on both sides lined with open-mouthed croco- diles—for a glimpse of Murchison Falls. I had been on my way to Victoria

Falls, at the Zambia-Rhodesia border, for a comparison study, when I learned that Amin had taken over. Boy Reporter got moving. I had previously agreed to meet Ellie and the kids—who had elected to stay in Dar es Salaam while I went on my own to Lusaka—back at the Norfolk Hotel in Nairobi, in time to spend one night there before we all took off together for Addis Ababa.

Now, converging one evening back in Kenya, they from Tanzania, I from Zambia, I informed E. that I was not going with her to Ethiopia but would instead attempt to return to Uganda in the morning. I spent a good part of the night on the phone to the American Embassy in Nairobi; ultimately I learned that there would be a flight to the Entebbe airport at 5 A.M. What a break for *The New Yorker*!, Boy Reporter thought. A first-hand timely on-the-spot account of what it was like in Uganda immediately before and immediately after a characteristic African coup d'état! But I would wait to let Shawn know what I was up to until I was sure I could get back into Kampala, the Ugandan capital. I didn't know then, of course, that "characteristic" was hardly an apposite word for Idi Amin, though soon after reaching Kampala and attending a meeting he was holding with the heads of all the religious bodies in Uganda I had an inkling of what *his* character was like. Amin had assembled a dozen or more theological patriarchs, each clad in his heavy ceremonial robes, at noon on a hot day; had had them escorted to an unshaded second-floor veranda of his house, which he was then also using as an office; and had kept them waiting there, almost literally melting in their embroidered brocades, for forty-five minutes—at which point he strode out, immaculate in crisp khaki shorts, and haltingly read a pious declaration somebody had run up for him about his love of religious freedom.

Anyway, I sent Shawn a cable from Kampala saying I would be at the Addis Ababa Hilton two days later and would be prepared to file instantly at any length he requested. On reaching Ethiopia, loaded with what I construed to be hot-stuff notes, I was astonished to find a cablegram from Bill saying that he was sorry but there was no room in the next issue for the piece I had proposed; and *he* didn't propose my writing anything about the coup for a later issue. I was puzzled—all the more so when I finally got back to the States, examined that next issue, and found in it a piece by Calvin Trillin, about the importance of earnestly eating french-fried potatoes or some such, which in my biased view had none of the hallmarks of irreplaceability. About five years elapsed before, in a fit of mild lingering pique, I chanced to mention to Shawn my disappointment at his erstwhile rejection of my potential scoop. He said he couldn't believe he'd done what I recalled he had. I urged him to refer to his files. He found my cable from Kampala and his reply, all right; he was reminded on rereading them that at the time he thought I was proposing going *to* Kampala and he wanted to head me off so I wouldn't risk getting hurt. In any event, Boy Reporter struck out.

Today, I have what strikes me as a new and persuasive argument for Shawn's sending me back to South Africa. It is calculated to appeal to his battered sense of editorial pride. Why shouldn't whatever *The New Yorker* knows about that nation be used to *The New Yorker*'s advantage, I ask, rather than be presented on a platter—with just a touch of fresh dill—to Walter Cronkite? (I am embellishing here; I did not mention the dill to Shawn. In the old days, I might have.) Bill listens thoughtfully, and in response artfully threatens my knight with his bishop: He does so by asking me what, assuming I could influence events, I would like to see happen in South Africa. It is the first time he has ever solicited such a political judgment from me, and I am taken aback, but I slide a pawn in his bishop's path: I improvise eloquently for four and a half minutes, probably my longest speech ever in Bill's company, talking about the necessity of doing away with the homelands concept and of providing bona fide representation in Parliament for non-Europeans (which is what ex-British colonies call non-whites), and, perhaps most important of all, conferring some dignity upon those millions of South Africans who do not now have it and who under the present scheme of things can hardly even aspire to it. Bill finally says well, yes, he will send me there, if I can get a visa; and I am so euphoric that I dance out of his office without remembering to ask him about the present status of my piece about Princeton University, which, he promised me nearly a year ago, would be published very, very soon.

There is a party in progress downstairs—a farewell to Rick Hertzberg, who is going to Washington as a Carter speechwriter. Jan Groth, our eighteenth-floor combination-receptionist-and-den-mother, has doubtless arranged the fête; the tradition is that if you attend these mid-corridor affairs (the alternatives are being taken as surly or pretending Shawn is sending you off on an urgent reportorial mission) you are supposed to kick in a dollar or so to help defray expenses. I suspect that Jan sometimes fails to break even, but she has a generous nature; without it, she could never, over all these years, have retained both her job and her sanity. Rick looks happy and expectant, but then he hasn't begun *his* job yet. Shawn puts in a brief appearance; he didn't always used to attend these happenings, but ever since there was a threat to unionize the editorial side of the magazine last fall, he has been more visible: One of the organizers' arguments was that top management was too unapproachable.

I am always amazed, at these gatherings, to perceive how many members of the staff there are whom I don't know; there are people I have seen often in elevators and corridors, and I probably have heard their names, but I cannot put body and name together. This does not upset me; it has long been the practice at the magazine not to introduce anybody to anybody else. Eventually, one learns who's who. Today, for instance, I nod cordially to Ed Koren, whom I have never formally met but whose identity I deduced a couple of years ago; and he gives me a no less genial greeting. I wonder if he knows who I am. Andy Logan, who *does* make a point of getting acquainted with all hands, tells me that she once used one of these gala occasions to approach Howard Moss, pin him up against a wall, and complain to our poetry editor (if that is his title; there are few formal titles at the magazine and, inasmuch as there is no masthead, no real need for any) of the lack of light verse in the magazine for the last decade or so. Andy is not alone in her nostalgia for the works of such as Ogden Nash and Phyllis McGinley. I would not want to hurt Howard's feelings at a party by telling him so, but I have practically stopped reading all *New Yorker* poetry. Much of it is plain too heavy.

David arrives home from St. Paul's in the evening. He has broken his finger in a wrestling match. It is the first time he has ever broken anything, and he will be sixteen in a couple of weeks. He has been fortunate. Terry, Joey, and Tony were forever breaking things when they were growing up. Kids always hurt themselves at inconvenient times, as when (long-range) you are going on a foreign journey, or (short-range) you are going to see the hit show you sent in for tickets to six months ago. Once, though, a child's injury turned out for me, if not necessarily for him, to be fun. I was fooling around with Terry one evening in the early nineteen fifties when I dropped him, and his chin caught the edge of a piano bench. We called Dr. Reed, and our unflappable pediatrician said it didn't sound fatal but did sound as though a couple of stitches would help, and he would meet us at the hospital. I wrapped a towel around Terry's head, and we took off, my forgetting until we hit a roadblock that this was a practice alert evening prescribed by Governor Nelson Rockefeller as part of his idiotic civil-defense program. Our interceptor was a man with a helmet, an arm badge, and a gruff manner. He demanded to know what I was doing out gallivanting at a moment when no traffic except emergency traffic was tolerable.

"I have an authentic emergency," I said, pointing to poor swaddled Terry. "I'm taking him to the hospital."

The man in the helmet was beside himself with joy at our having enlivened his soporific tour of duty. Within moments, at his beck, a police car materialized at the scene, and the cop at the wheel told me to follow him. Then he set off, siren screeching, lights flashing, south on old Route 9, and I fought gamely to keep my escort within sight. I had once or twice driven at seventy miles an hour or so, when I didn't espy any cops in my rear-view mirror, along that winding, two-lane thoroughfare, but ninety-*three*? I've never had more fun at the wheel of a car. Bzoom! Vroom!

The most uncomfortable misadventure of my own childhood was a broken collarbone that I suffered early in the third quarter of a high-school football game. A physics teacher, who was also a scoutmaster and was therefore deemed, wrongly, to know all about physical injuries and their prevention and cure, examined me on the sidelines when I came off groaning, pronounced that I had merely had the wind knocked out of me, and ordered me to get back in there and fight like a man, which I contritely did, though not without twinges. If the X-ray hadn't been invented, Mr. Payne might never have been second-guessed.

February 12

We drive to Cornwall, leaving early, because the Dick Waterses are coming from Newton to spend the weekend, and we told them we'd be in Connecticut last night. We beat them to the scene, but have barely walked in the door when the phone rings: It is a woman who hopes we will buy an unfinished house she and her husband have been building. Ellie thinks God is telling us something. As soon as Dick and Juliet and the girls arrive, we go to God's house. The husband of the woman who phoned is there, instructing a mason working on a chimney, and when I extend my right hand in greeting, the prospective seller awkwardly extends his left. He says that the asking price for the house, as is (it is an old barn in what seems to me an early stage of rehabilitation), is $73,000, and that if I am prepared to do a lot of the remaining work myself, I could finish it for perhaps another $3,000. I point to a bent nail lying on the ground and say, truthfully, that that is what happens when I try to use hand tools.

I do not learn until later that this jest cannot have struck the prospective seller as especially funny: The reason he extended his left hand was that he mangled his right one with a power saw, and that is why the place is on the market to begin with. Dick Waters and I calculate roughly that the house, completely furnished, would set E. and me back $150,000, not counting storm windows, which I am now having installed in Truro; besides, Ellie doesn't like the location of the kitchen and dining room, and to switch these around could cost another pretty penny.

I don't want to build another house. We lived in the Scarborough one for something like sixteen years, and we never did get the sewage-disposal system functioning properly. Erma Bombeck has written "The Grass Is Always Greener over the Septic Tank." Over *our* septic tank, the grass was not only lush but moist; when we were playing baseball or touch football and our system was malfunctioning at its peak, we had to declare certain areas of the arena of combat temporarily off limits. I suppose over the years we made wealthy men of Brown & Dubray. Brown & Dubray were among the local plumbers we all but kept on retainer.

But this weekend I am certainly on my way to acquiring a new house, should we ever decide to get one. I play Dick Waters backgammon for his maximum stakes—five cents a point—and I win twenty cents. Dick makes money, too. He is a wheeler-dealer type, engaged in mysterious business transactions, and he tells me today that he got a nice finder's fee from Wally

Bowman and some unidentified third party for having brought them together on a deal that, unfortunately, didn't work out. I don't know what the eligibility rules are for finder's fees, but I cannot refrain from remarking that it was I who brought Dick and Wally *Bowman* together. That seems to cut no ice. Twenty cents is all I get out of him, and I have to work for that.

The Hendon Chubbs and Patrick Smiths come over for dinner. Nita C. wants to be introduced as Nita Colgate. Almost as soon as she passed her bars, a couple of years ago, she gave up both bras and her married name. Seeing her reminds me to tell Ellie of a gracious liberationist gesture I have made on her behalf. Inasmuch as her professional name is "Eleanor Munro," I have changed her listing in my *Who's Who* entry from "Eleanor M. Frankfurter" to "Eleanor Munro Frankfurter." She is not as pleased as I'd hoped she'd be; she thinks I should have dropped the "Frankfurter." I say that would be unfair to her sons, who have been having enough nomenclatural confusion as it is. David, for instance, has been "David T. Frankfurter" at one school, "David T. M. Frankfurter" at another, "David Kahn" at summer camps, and on the roster of some Scottish society in which his maternal grandmother has enrolled him, "David Munro." His grandmother's nickname is "Nanoo," which struck me as preposterous the first time I heard it. Then I reflected that my maternal grandmother was known as "Mima," which probably struck everybody outside of our family as ridiculous. *Chacun à son grandmère.*

February 14

Everybody except me went skiing yesterday. Lexy, I was happy to see, in the group—the crashed pilot returning unfazed to the cockpit.

Today we arise at 5 A.M. to drive to New York. It is Valentine's Day, but in the dark and in the confusion of moving we forget that. E.'s first words to me are "Did you *really* throw out *all* the boxes?" She is quite angry, but I cannot for the life of me tell why: I haven't thrown out *any* boxes, and wasn't even aware that there were boxes of consequential disposability. I am leaving for Georgia today, but first we have an important ceremony to attend: the raising, on the Town School roof, of that academy's first official flag in its sixty or so years of existence. Lexy designed it, having been declared the winner in a schoolwide competition. He and Mr. Birge hoist it together. There is, disappointingly, no music—no ruffles or flourishes or anything of that sort. Nor does either of the two chief participants in the early-morning drama make a speech. The headmaster probably doesn't care, since part of his job is making speeches, and he may welcome an opportunity to keep mum; but I suspect that Lexy has a few pertinent remarks all prepared and, like as not, has rehearsed them.

Anyway, the two of them solemnly raise the flag, a very bright and colorful one, to the top of its staff, and when it gets there it hangs limply in the still air. Mr. Birge thereupon asks all the children present to puff, and they do, and immediately a gust of wind comes up and the flag unfolds to its full dimensions. I suppose it is the mark—or the luck—of a successful headmaster to be able to pull off something like this. Afterward, Lexy autographs paper replicas of the big cloth flag that are being sold, at five dollars per, for the benefit of some worthy scholarship fund or other.

Now there are two bright objects flanking the East River Drive to distract motorists and thus conceivably reduce the population of this overcrowded city: the purple-red-and-yellow bridge at 104th Street, designed by Bill Conklin and Jim Rossant, about which I did a Talk piece not long ago; and Lexy's multi-colored flag, about which I would like to do a *New Yorker* story but would have to disqualify myself under the doctrine of conflict of interest.

And so I head straight for the airport and Atlanta. It is always somewhat unsettling to start off on a new big project of this sort. There are no predeterminable limits one can put on the amount of research one plans to do. Where do you begin with a subject like Georgia? Prehistorically? What do you concentrate on? History? Politics? Race? I have resolved to steer as clear as possible of both Jimmy Carter and Plains, and, whatever happens, of the president's sibling Billy. But how, for instance, should I handle Atlanta—the biggest city in the state and the dominant metropolis of the entire Southeast? It has got to figure importantly in any account of Georgia, and yet *The New Yorker* ran a whole piece on the state capital just a few years ago.

Well, before too long, I will have worked out some course of action. More likely, judging from past experience, I will never come up with any fixed agenda, though I may have a tentative itinerary; I will probably merely accumulate notes until, at some unforeseeable moment, an inexplicable inaudible bell will signal me that research time is over and writing time— organizing time, more accurately—is at hand. It is easier to catch the signal when one is gathering material on an individual; then the time to stop, usually, is when one finds oneself telling people about the subject instead of asking questions about him. One thing I do know; I want to get the piece over and done with—research, writing, everything—by this spring. I don't want to do the definitive history of Georgia; I have done no reading yet about the place, but surely many heavy histories of it already exist; I merely want to give magazine readers who know as little about the place as I now do an inkling of what it is all about and how it got that way.

Fortunately, I am not starting in exactly from scratch. I have been to Atlanta before—several times, indeed, mostly in connection with writing about the Coca-Cola Company. Some of the Coke people I got to know are dead or retired. Franklin Garrett, the company's longtime historian, is still around, though, these days as head of the Atlanta Historical Society, and obviously he can be a useful source. And there are other familiar Coca-Cola faces still on the company scene: Wilbur Kurtz, Jr., for one, who has become the Coke archivist; and, of course, Paul Austin, the chairman of the board and my college classmate. (Any classmate of mine who is in business and isn't by now at least the executive vice-president of something must be accounted a disappointment, if not an outright failure.) All one needs in any community is a person or two to begin with.

In Atlanta, moreover, I am further fortunate because it is the hometown of Furman Bisher, my roommate at the Montreal Olympics last summer, and because it is one of the few places where *The New Yorker* maintains a regional office. (Advertising, rather than editorial, but I do not mind fraternizing.) The fellow in charge, John F. Crawford, happens to be an old friend, whose home I have often visited on past trips south. I have already arranged to dine tonight with Jack and Mary Lee. Twenty years or so ago, I might have hesitated to make such a date my first night away from home, out of my awareness of the probability that, beginning a longterm reportorial stint of this nature, I would be too sick to sup. It is nice to have exorcised at least one of one's habitual demons.

Moreover, I don't have to cope, on this assignment, with the recurrent vexation of how to spend my weekends when I am working out of town; I have decided to spend them at home and, in a manner of speaking, commute to Georgia. The cost of a day in a first-class hotel is not much different nowadays from that of a couple of hours in an economy seat on an airplane. In the mid-sixties, when *The New Yorker* was rolling in money, its operatives were authorized first-class air travel, and that could work out very nicely for a married writer on a farflung assignment; he could turn in his first-class ticket for two economy seats and take his wife along at precious little extra cost. That gilded era ended, alas, at about the time that *Life* and *Look* went down the drain and all other magazines began to feel the pinch of television competition for advertising dollars.

Atlanta must really be bulging. The only hotel in which Jack Crawford could get me a room (and knowing hotel people is his business) is the Hilton. Still, I have no cause for complaint; thanks, I suppose, to Jack, I find awaiting me a gift basket from the management full of liquor—gin, rum, Scotch, brandy. I guess I should offer to pay for it or declare it on my income tax or some such, but I do not consider myself susceptible to petty bribery, and besides there is no vodka, the only hard liquor I normally drink, in the assortment.

Soon after checking in, I phone Furman Bisher at the *Journal*, and he invites me to have lunch with him tomorrow at the Capital City Club. The Capital City is, of course, one of the social citadels of Atlanta from which, because of their restrictive membership policies, some of Jimmy Carter's cronies felt obliged to resign when he nominated them for their Washington jobs. Furman wants to be sure I know about the Capital City's recent notoriety. (The New York *Times* has lately infuriated Atlanta club men by writing about their exclusive fraternal retreats.) "That's where they don't allow Jews and Negroes," the sports editor says, laughing. He knows I am Jewish. He does not know that—through my Coca-Cola connections—I have been a guest at the Capital City Club several times before, and also, when it comes to that, at the Piedmont Driving Club, with which the bedevilled Carterites have also prudently elected to sever connections.

I think this whole business of expecting private clubs to abide by the provisions of civil-rights statutes is ridiculous; if this sort of thing were carried to extremes, it could end up that nobody would be allowed to give a party in his own home without inviting a certain percentage of blacks, Chicanos, American Indians, and so on. I have had lunch, without feeling uncomfortable, at clubs—the Racquet and Tennis, the Brook, the Links—to which I probably could not be admitted to membership; and I belong to one—the Century—which does not admit women and discriminates against, among others, people in trade; such elitism does not bother me, though it infuriates Ellie, whenever she stops to think about it, that a club purportedly established to serve the social needs of artists and writers excludes female artists and writers.

At least we have women in the Harvard Club now, and I suppose I can claim a share of the credit for that. When I was a director of the Associated Harvard Alumni, from 1969 to 1972, I was named chairman of an A.H.A. Committee on—*its* name inevitably provoked snide laughter—Harvard-Radcliffe Relations. Graduates of Radcliffe were by then being awarded Harvard College degrees, and our committee felt that all Radcliffe alumnae, past, present, and future, should be entitled to the same social rights and privileges as their male counterparts. Accordingly, we proposed to the A.H.A. board, which went along with us, that all Harvard Clubs anywhere on earth be asked to let in qualified women on the same basis as men. There were only two clubs with clubhouses, those of Boston and New York; and it was to the sexual integration of their august premises, therefore, that our ukase was primarily addressed. Given the generally accepted view of Harvard men residing in those two cities, one might have thought that the Boston Club would have been the stuffier when it came to implementing our decision; but its members voted unblinkingly to take in women. The first time the proposition came up for consideration in New York, though, it was defeated, chiefly by diehard old codgers, long past their athletic prime, who grumbled about females running around loose in the men's locker room upstairs adjoining the squash courts. The pro-Radcliffe constituency in the club thereupon rallied behind our president that year, Rod Perkins, and in a second balloting got the by-laws suitably amended to squeeze our sisters in. The surprising thing was how few women leapt at the opportunity; by belonging to the Radcliffe Club, they already had access to a good portion of the Harvard Club, at a modest dues rate; and they were disinclined to rock that particular boat. Equal rights was one thing, equal dues another.

After drinks at the Crawfords' with the George Goodwins—he a former journalist turned public relations man—we adjourn for dinner to a restaurant the name of which, inevitably, I forget to make a note of. I do jot down the names of several recommended potential sources around the state, most of whom, I know from past experience, I will never get around to looking up. George offers to take me, tomorrow evening—one thing easily leads to another on trips like this—to a monthly dinner meeting at the Piedmont Country Club of a men's group called the Inquiry Club. I am touching restricted bases fast. Jack, not to be outdone, offers to take me on a tour of North Georgia, where, he assures me, I will find people markedly different from—it is going to be hard to stick to my guns—the Billy Carters of Plains. George also says that he once met Bill Shawn, urged him to come to Georgia, and told him that when he did he would take him to see Stone Mountain. Upon which, George says, Bill said to him, "I can't bear to look at exposed granite." I find that hard to believe; it just doesn't sound like Shawn; but I can hardly deny it flatly. I have never discussed granite with Bill, exposed or veiled.

We break up early, for which I am grateful, since I arose before daylight in Cornwall this morning. I drop off to sleep almost as soon as I hit my Hilton pillow and am awakened at 11:30 P.M. by a long-distance phone call from a reporter from the *Daily Princetonian*. He has heard that my piece on Princeton is dead and he would like to pick my brains for a piece *he* is doing. I tell him I am sorry, but as far as I know my article is still scheduled to run, some time or other. Then I have a hard time getting back to sleep, engaging instead in an impassioned dialogue with Bill Shawn (I come out well ahead in the exchange) as to why he should run my Princeton piece next week. Oh well, I reflect self-comfortingly as I toss and twist, at least I can sleep late in the morning, because aside from lunch I haven't yet got myself tied up with a mess of appointments.

February 15

Ellie wakes me by phone at seven-thirty. She wants to be sure she catches me before I go out. She found my Valentine roses awaiting her when she got home, and is appropriately thankful. Flowers do make a difference, especially when you forget to send them. I read the Atlanta *Constitution* and search for local news on my television set—two always quick, easy, and useful ways of adapting oneself to an unfamiliar environment. Much of the TV news is devoted to welfare mothers, chiefly black, who are picketing the state capital, singing "We Shall Overcome," and carrying placards accusing Georgia of being the forty-seventh ranking state in welfare grants. I learn also that they plan to picket the Governor's Annual Prayer Breakfast, to be held here at the Hilton tomorrow morning. Sounds like something worth looking in on, if I can wangle an invitation.

I spend most of the morning on the phone, trying to set up appointments. Four or five a day is my usual goal. I have a mixture of luck, good and bad. Furman Bisher calls at eleven to postpone our lunch date till tomorrow, but then at noon a businessman—one of a half dozen potential sources whose secretaries were supposed to ring me back—phones to wonder if perchance I am free to lunch with him at twelve-fifteen. When I descend to the lobby, the hotel—indeed, as I soon notice, the whole town—seems to have been taken over by conventioneers from the paper-and-pulp industry, clad in loud, ill-cut checks and plaids, men whose faces (I deplore my own prejudices, but there they are) seem curiously to resemble their products. My businessman lunch date, who is in office supplies, does not. He went to Princeton. Still, he has some of the ineradicable hallmarks of a true Southerner; he refers to his father's father as "my granddaddy."

After lunch, I stroll over to the new giant Omni complex to pay my respects to the state's Department of Commerce and Trade, from which I hope, not in vain, to secure a batch of statistical material about commerce, trade, and ancillary matters. Atlantans, I have already perceived, are inordinately proud of how their city has grown in the last decade or so. And it has, as I observed yesterday, riding in from the airport. The airport itself is a gaudy, newish one, named after the late William B. Hartsfield, the perennial mayor of Atlanta, who used to give eminent visitors to his bailiwick gilded Coca-Cola bottles, in lieu of the keys to the city other chief magistrates were wont to distribute. A Coca-Cola bottler once gave me such a glittering receptacle, *sous cloche*. I was sure Ellie would not want it around the house, but, with the lovable, unpredictable perversity of women, she said she thought it would look nice in the front hall, and there it stands.

On the way to the city from the airport, one passes close by the new Atlanta Stadium, where the Braves and the Falcons ineptly cavort, and then soon gets glimpses of the clusters of high-rise buildings. Some are the creations of John Portman, the local-boy-who-made-good architect who achieved renown by, among other dubious innovations, creating huge hotel lobbies with all-glass elevators rising and falling inside them. But Atlanta hasn't changed all that much more than many other population centers. Its skyline isn't notably more prepossessing than that of, say, Hartford, Connecticut. Even so, an out-of-towner revisiting the southern capital for the first time in a number of years cannot help but be struck by its metamorphosis. It is only the city one lives in to whose growth one is comparatively impervious. The twin World Trade Center towers of New York have had no impact on my consciousness that I am aware of; I have never been inside either of them, let alone soared to one of their summits, and have no urge to explore the view of Manhattan from their heights. It cannot be a much more exhilarating sight than what one sees from a descending airplane on a clear night, and God knows I have had that experience often enough.

The guest of honor at the Inquiry Club dinner tonight is Philip Alston, the Atlanta lawyer who was one of Jimmy Carter's early boosters for the presidency, and who says that when Carter was elected governor of the state in 1970, after failing to win that job four years earlier, "It surprised Atlanta, but it didn't surprise him, because he had a sense of what Georgia was all about." That is what I hope to ascertain in the weeks ahead. Alston refers to Andrew Young, en passant, as "representative of the change that's taken place in our part of the world"; but he does not allude to the admissions requirements of the club where we are now comfortably seated over our cigars, nor suggest that this part of the world has changed sufficiently to give our incumbent seat-holder at the United Nations a shot at a seat in this room.

The speaker surprises me, relatively ignorant as I still am about this part of the world, by saying further that the white power structure of Georgia was reluctant to support Carter's presidential campaign at the outset, and cites one example: In a poll taken at a Rotary Club meeting, eighty-two percent of the votes went against the presumably favorite son. Alston says further that he was the only member of the board of governors of the Commerce Club, a downtown lunch spot of relatively low-keyed exclusivity, who came out for Carter at a session of that gubernatorial group; his lonely stand was noted by the servitors at that establishment, he adds cheerfully, as a result of which, when he returned for lunch the following day and everybody else present was served chicken, he was pointedly proffered a T-bone steak.*

February 16

I betake myself to Coca-Cola headquarters to call on Wilbur Kurtz, the resident archivist, and I realize again how hard it is going to be to play down Jimmy Carter in any contemporary piece about Georgia; I have hardly seated myself in Wilbur's sanctum, a museum of ancient Coca-Cola artifacts, when he tells me that Jimmy was a collector of antique bottles himself. As governor, he invited Kurtz over one afternoon to chew the rag about their mutual hobby, and told the Coca-Cola man that he hoped to find some first-rate specimens of ancient glassware in the bed of one of his favorite fishing streams. Most people who go fishing and come up with

* Alston was subsequently named by President Carter to be ambassador to Australia, where steak is routine breakfast fare.

bottles are outraged; I have been made privy to a new dimension of the presidential character. Kurtz's favorite Coke-Carter story is one that he says has been published somewhere but is new to me: It seems that after Jimmy was accepted by the Naval Academy, it looked for a while as though he might not make Annapolis after all because his feet were flat. So Miss Lillian spent a summer, in the best maternal tradition, rolling his feet over Coca-Cola bottles.

I remember how many photographs the company used to have around of President Eisenhower drinking Coke (I remember, too, from reading much correspondence between Robert Woodruff and Dwight D. Eisenhower, when I was last in Atlanta, how many gifts that president used to accept from high-placed corporation executives without, apparently, the batting of a single holier-than-thou eyelash), and I inquire if there are any pictures around of President Carter in a similar refreshing pose; astonishingly, the archives do not seem to contain a single one of the Georgian president with the legendary bottle close either to his head or his feet. Kurtz does offer to show me one of Lyndon Johnson swilling Fresca, but that is ancient history.

As I am leaving, to go over to the Capital City Club for my deferred lunch with Furman Bisher, an odd thing happens. Some months ago, when Joey was in Atlanta, my son stopped by the Coca-Cola Company to pay his respects to the chairman of the board, and was passed along by Paul Austin to Archivist Kurtz. Wilbur asked Joey to ask me if I knew where there might be any extra copies of my long-since-remaindered Coca-Cola history, "The Big Drink"; and I wrote Kurtz that I had only a couple of copies left myself and had no idea where additional ones might be found. Now, as I am taking my leave of Wilbur, he mentions casually that he has four hundred copies of "The Big Drink" stashed in a warehouse, and that if ever I am in need of one I should just let him know. Are Georgians going to turn out to be no less inscrutable than, say, Chinese?

The Atlanta establishment is ensconced at the Capital City—Furman points out former governor Carl Sanders, now practicing law, and other indigenous bigwigs—and the food is top-quality, too. One reason, my host tells me, is that the Capital City Club not long ago lured away the manager of the Standard Club, Atlanta's principal Jewish social haven. We talk about Jimmy Carter, inescapably. Furman recalls a time he went dove-hunting with Governor Carter, who proved to be a crackerjack shot. The state limit was twelve birds per gun, and Carter's companions had to keep stuffing his birds into other men's bags, because the commissioner of game was also in the party and they didn't want their chief executive caught in an arithmetical impropriety. "Practically every time Jimmy fired he brought down a bird," Furman says. "I shot my ass off, and got only four. Bert Lance was with us, too, and he got none."

At the Piedmont Driving Club last night, somebody suggested I drop in on an authentic local character—Ben Fortson, a septuagenarian who has been secretary of the state of Georgia for thirty years or more, and whose accessibility to reporters, or anyone else, is supposedly unrivalled. It seems that the secretary sits right inside the door of his ground-floor Capitol building office and practically drags people in to chew the fat with. Somebody else warned me that Good Ol' Ben would, given the chance, talk my ear off. That is all right with me; one can pick up a lot from listening, even to a putative windbag, and one can always make a getaway if one is on somebody else's premises. The danger with interviewees is to invite a tiresome one to your own office, or club, or, worse still, residence. Ushering him off your own turf, especially if he doesn't readily take to hints, can be awkward and time-consuming.

But no bores one meets in the line of work (and there are few of these actually; why would a journalist seek out someone to begin with except in the hope of some enlightenment or entertainment?) can compete for sheer irritability with those who book themselves on airplanes, for no other reason, I sometimes think, than to annoy the hapless wretches fated to sit alongside them. As a writer with no special field of expertise, I am theoretically interested in everything, but I have never been able to bring myself to be interested in anything recounted to me—as a rule, at appalling length— by any in-flight seatmate.

The most satisfying travelling companions I ever had on a long journey were a mother and daughter who occupied the other two-thirds of a three-abreast setup on an overnight flight from New York to Dakar. They were part of a two-hundred-person tour group, all of whom, when my two softspoken ladies proudly disclosed their identity, proved to be Jehovah's Witnesses en route to an African encampment. Not in Cameroon, I gathered; according to my seatmates, a couple of Witnesses had not long before been eaten there. The adjacent pair's undisguised disapproval of that kind of conspicuous consumption seemed, a moment later, not notably different from their reaction toward my indicating to a passing stewardess that I proposed to consume two vodkas, more or less in tandem. With so many teetotalers aboard, the service afforded those of us who by now had twin destinations—Dakar and damnation—was superb. As further inducement to a good subsonic night's rest, my mother and daughter, having evidently decided there was no chance in my case of conversion through conversation, but not having given up the fight altogether, nudged me nicely into sleep by singing hymns until I drifted off.

Ben Fortson is clearly a God-fearing soul himself. I haven't been inside his office, which, festooned as nearly every inch of it is with flags and banners and plaques, vaguely resembles my notion of a Civil War museum, for more than a few minutes when a soberly dressed young man pops in to remind the secretary of state that he is supposed to deliver the invocation at the governor's prayer breakfast tomorrow morning, and to be sure to try to keep it down to two minutes. After Mr. Ben has given the appropriate assurances, all but stamping them with the state seal, I seize the opportunity to remark that I have heard about this reverent annual ritual, and wonder if I could somehow wangle an invitation to the breakfast, even if only as a witness. (I can always avail myself of room service beforehand.) Mr. Ben says I should simply betake myself to the Hilton ballroom at the appointed hour, and if I am halted say that I am his personal guest. I sense from the authoritative ring of his voice that any other credentials would be superfluous.

I walk back to the Hilton. One thing that keeps Atlanta from being a truly major city is that it is possible to get around practically any part of its downtown area—from, say, any bank or government office to any big hotel—on foot. This convenience precludes my talking to many indigenous cab drivers. Too bad, in a way, because as the whole world knows (or ought to) cab drivers are the principal sources of all information elicited by all journalists in all cities on earth other than their hometowns. At home, though, cab drivers are regarded by journalists (or ought to be) as in the main ignorant, bigoted, and obsessed with the reputations they have somehow undeservedly acquired of being lowfalutin' philosophers. I am speaking here largely of the old-school New York taxi men, those in their fifties and sixties, to whom, to use their own vernacular, I am allergic. The younger generation of cabbies, those with the longer hair, do not nearly as much, thank God, engage in chitchat. One suspects, not without reason, that they aren't yet up to talking much because they are still trying to learn how to drive.

February 17

The Fifteenth Annual Governor's Prayer Breakfast is scheduled for 8:30 A.M., but long before the doors to the second-floor ballroom swing open, there are hundreds of early birds milling around the antechambers. Hungry for spiritual or temporal sustenance? More likely, for a nicely balanced blend of both; as any elected governor knows, politics is the art of successful compromise. When entrée is sanctioned, I espy Secretary of State Fortson at a table up forward (there is no dais), but I do not have to solicit his intercession or even throw his name around; if there are tickets of admission, they are neither examined nor collected. Presumably, no one in his or her right mind would go to excesses, at so odd an hour, to crash *any* affair—even as prestigious a one as this, which, I learn in due course from the printed program at my place, has been underwritten by the Georgia Business & Industry Association, whose president is also the president of the Georgia chapter of the National Alliance of Businessmen. The G.B.I.A., I am further informed in a commendable burst of printed candor, is registered as a business lobbyist with the state legislature. Georgians tell it to you square.

Inasmuch as the legislature is currently in session over yonder at the Capitol, it is a safe bet that the ballroom is aswarm with solons. There are no assigned seats. I head for the last empty chair at a table already occupied by a four-star general and a nun, a parlay that seems worth taking a chance on, but am outraced by a portly chap who I would guess is either a used-car dealer or a small-town banker—quite possibly, both. I end up alongside a young woman who turns out to be in public relations for the Department of Corrections and Offender Rehabilitation, an engagingly fancy name for the agency that runs the state's jails. She and I pause in the ritual act of swapping business cards to bow our heads (I sneak a glance at my watch en route) for Mr. Ben's invocation; I clock him at, praiseworthily, one minute and forty-eight seconds.

Governor George Busbee, the nominal host, arises. "A workhorse, not a showhorse," was one of the slogans he used when he defeated Bert Lance for the Democratic nomination in 1974; but Busbee looks quite spruce and presentable; if he can spare the time from his work I will try to go around and see him. *His* remarks, too, are brief; he says principally that he prays daily for virtuous pride. An unimpeachable point of view. My tablemate brings me back to the real world by saying that the recent increase in Atlanta's homicide rate may well be attributable to the frustrations of rural folk unable to find urban employment. She will mail me some statistics. We both sit back to enjoy a few nifty hymns provided by a choir from the Westminster School. The ensemble has one black member, but I have not been here long enough to know whether or not this constitutes tokenism. There are relatively few blacks in the room. One of these, though, a woman representative in the state legislature, reads the 15th Psalm. Her black-female-lower-house-New-Testament rendition exquisitely offsets the recital of Isaiah No. 35 by a white male state senator. After a numbing speech by the president of Mercer University that I find it hard to concentrate on (are grits soporific?), I shake off my cobwebs and leap embarrassedly to my feet as all hands begin singing the "Battle Hymn of the Republic." Then, at 9:35, everybody troops out to go to work—a number of women, and even a few men, including one priest, clutching to their breasts, as souvenirs, the bowls of tulips that have graced our tables.

I have a lunch date with Joe Cumming, the *Newsweek* bureau chief, whom I met at the Inquiry dinner. He is, more formally, Joseph B. Cumming IV, and his family rates very high, I have heard, in Augusta. His great-great-grandfather was, in 1798, that city's first intendant—i.e., mayor. I am breaking corn bread with a man with firmly implanted roots. We talk much about Georgia politics; it is a topic on which Joe, both by heredity and environment, is an expert. He urges me to look up, *inter alios*, Charles L. Gowen, an attorney, originally from coastal Brunswick, on whose unsuccessful campaign for governor Joe worked in 1954. Gowen is now out of politics and a senior partner in King & Spalding, the big Atlanta law firm, with longstanding Coca-Cola connections familiar to me, of which Attorney General Griffin Bell was until recently also a principal functionary. Joe says that Gowen is a special kind of clean-cut-looking Georgian who, like Jimmy Carter, can seem equally at ease playing golf or shooting rabbits. Joe is exceedingly generous with names of people in Augusta for me to seek out when I get over there—among them his sister and his father, a retired lawyer, now in his eighties, who used to be head of the Georgia Historical Commission, and who has probably forgotten more Georgia history than I could ever hope to assimilate.

In the best Southern-hospitality tradition, Joe invites me, further, to join him for drinks this afternoon at the home of a physician I also met the other night—John Kizer, who has made a name for himself in enlightened Georgia circles as a debunker of naturopaths. The Cummings and the Kizers are kinfolk, in a broad manner of speaking. Joe C. has ascertained, by what arcane research I cannot fathom, that he is Miriam K.'s twelfth cousin. I never before met anybody who claimed to have even an eleventh cousin, but then I have only been South this trip for a couple of days. One of the four members of this very extended family mentions John Cheever, and when I say that, though not related, he has been a friend of mine practically forever, I am importuned for gossipy tidbits about him; then, to my chagrin, it turns out that the cousins are better acquainted with the really important aspects of his career than I am; they can and do all but recite chunks of his work.

Miriam Kizer has a mild complaint to register with me, now that we are on the subject of literature, about the modus operandi of northern magazines. She had her kitchen redecorated not long ago, and then had a call from a woman representing *Good Housekeeping*, who had talked to the Kizers' architect and thought the refurbished room might be worth a pictorial feature. A date was set, and Miriam spent the better part of a day scrubbing and polishing her entire house, and then the woman arrived, walked toward the kitchen without comment, looked fleetingly at the new room, said "Very interesting," and, within three and a half minutes of her arrival, was back in her taxi, which she had instructed to wait. On behalf of all magazines above the Mason-Dixon Line, even ones that, like *The New Yorker*, do not editorially use photographs, I apologize profusely; whereupon my hosts, as they would probably, being hospitable Southerners, have done anyway, offer me another drink. I gladly accept.

Joe and Emily persuade me, without difficulty, to accompany them back to their house for a potluck dinner. Joe fondly recalls a convivial meeting he once had with Conrad Aiken—for many years Savannah's reigning man of letters—in the course of which the two of them vied spiritedly in exchanging bad limericks. How delightful a way to spend an evening with an eminent poet! I can hardly wait for Joe to subside to tell of my one and only encounter with another literary lion. It took place in 1967, on Martha's

Vineyard, where my Harvard class was celebrating its thirtieth reunion, at an inn we were under the impression we had exclusive occupancy of that weekend. We were just sitting down to dinner when a classmate's wife—her husband was a man of distinction; he had been captain of the swimming team our senior year—tapped me on the shoulder and said an outsider, Thornton Wilder, Yale '20, was sitting alone at the bar downstairs and desirous of company, and inasmuch as I was, to her knowledge, the only Harvard writer available, why didn't I join him, and her, for an intercollegiate drink?

Peggy Connolly was attractive, and I was flattered, and at once left the group I was with and joined the Great Man, who welcomed us warmly and ordered a round of martinis. This meeting occurred soon after the publication of A. E. Hotchner's controversial memoir on Hemingway, in which the author was criticized for, among other things, having professed to be able to recall in minute detail lengthy colloquies with his Papa the mornings after protracted drinking bouts. Here was my chance to do for Wilder what Hotch had done for Hem! All that stuck with me the next morning, alas, about a conversation—a Wilder monologue, more precisely—that lasted some five hours was that I never got to dinner; that Wilder quaffed, before he took a surprisingly steady leave of Peggy and me, a staggering number of dry martinis; and that I couldn't remember a single blessed word he said.

February 18

I am heading back to New York for the weekend. Anticipation is what I like to think of as my most shining virtue; and so, knowing I will at some time or other be calling or writing Atlantans for appointments from New York, but not remembering whether or not *The New Yorker* boasts an Atlanta phone book (I know it has London and Paris, but they are more in what the magazine thinks of as its orbit), I painstakingly copy out addresses and numbers from the directory in my hotel room. Then I discover that it will fit in my suitcase. It is a much more useful keepsake of my stay, in any circumstances, than a towel or a Gideon Bible. (There was a time when every Hilton hotel room also had in it a biography of Conrad the Founder, presumably free for the swiping, but that practice has stopped. God knows why; it is hard to imagine anybody's *buying* a book on Conrad Hilton.) The only thing that worries me about my misdemeanor is that I have heard this Hilton is now owned by a syndicate from Kuwait. If I am caught stealing, will the proprietors, in keeping with what I believe to be their traditional practice at home, cut my hand off?

Before my plane leaves, I have time to see a showing of a Georgia documentary film that George Goodwin has arranged for me, in John

Portman's Peachtree Tower offices. Like Portman, my father designed the building (2 Park Avenue) that he worked in for most of his career, but Ely's digs were never this grand, not even during boom times. I worked in my father's office one summer, following my freshman year at college, just after Ely, who had little else to keep him gainfully occupied during the Depression, was happy to accept a Carnegie Foundation grant that enabled him to go around the world.

All creative people were grateful then for small favors. When my father wangled a modest decorative commission for Isamu Noguchi, the sculptor at once invited his benefactor, in reciprocation, to sit for a handsome bronze bust. Later, Ely supplanted the head as a display object with a, to me, vastly inferior clay portrait by Jo Davidson, done at a time when Davidson was a celebrity and Noguchi had pretty much drifted out of my father's life. So I asked for the Noguchi and got it. Isamu told me years afterward, while we were dining in Osaka, that Ely and he once nearly collaborated on a war memorial at Appomattox. But they couldn't agree on the basic design: The sculptor wanted forty-eight tall gravestones, with a brooding tall figure, his arms clasped behind him, walking among them; the architect thought a war memorial should be more cheerful and needed at least a couple of angels toward that end.

At least two books emerged from my father's office. One was Ayn Rand's "Fountainhead." She did her architectural research there. The other was a book about Ely's global trip, "Design in Art and Industry." I worked on it with him during that college vacation. I have been pleased to find it listed in the card catalogues of several prep-school libraries. In the course of trying to help five boys decide in which direction to escape from home, I have visited quite a few boarding-school campuses. One is always taken on a tour, usually with a student escort, who, it goes without saying, is not a malcontent. (At Taft School one time, our guide was Horace Taft, a descendant of the founder, which seemed a bit much.) The tour always embraces the library, and I always urged the boys *I* had escorted to the scene to make a furtive check of the card file to see how many, if any, of our family's books reposited there. I made a point of discouraging matriculation at any institution that did not harbor at least two of mine. My advice, sensibly, was in the main ignored. I must say, though, that when David chose to enter St. Paul's, I was delighted. Five.

My father was exceedingly proud of his book, and equally proud of the buildings he designed, though the sad truth is that, having partners as (when times were good) he did, it was never quite clear to his family exactly which buildings were his creations and which belonged to somebody else. After Ely's death, Ellie and I went to a fund-raising dinner on the Upper East Side of Manhattan at what had been a municipal asphalt plant, a structure which, though no longer used for its original purpose—the idea of the party was to convert the rundown place into a community center—had been highly acclaimed as an example of a utilitarian building of considerable aesthetic charm. For the last three decades or so of my father's life, his firm was called Kahn & Jacobs, and Bob Jacobs was at the dinner, claiming, near as I could make out, exclusive credit for the design of this building—for which, when Ely was alive, *he* claimed exclusive credit. Ellie and I were outraged at what we took to be Bob's unwarranted usurpation of Ely's work of art. But then, a few weeks later, I was seated, by chance, at a Harvard fund-raising affair, alongside a retired architect who had also been with Kahn & Jacobs when the asphalt plant went up, and who said flatly that it should be credited not to Kahn but to Jacobs. What was I to make of all this? As a writer, I am lucky. Though like most members of my tribe I have been valiantly helped on many occasions by creative editors, I still know pretty much what is my handiwork and what is not.

Arriving in New York City, I drop my bags at 1095 Park and go straight down to the office. Pat Crow, a creative editor, tells me that in my relatively brief absence my Princeton piece has been both scheduled and unscheduled. At least Shawn has made a gesture. The trouble with this kind of gesture, though, is that once Bill has scheduled a piece at all he may not feel constrained to have to schedule it again for another couple of years.

February 22

I am back in Atlanta, after a quiet Connecticut weekend, staying, this time, at a hotel far from the center of town, the Sonesta. Jack Crawford says I am lucky to have a bed this side of Macon. The Sonesta isn't within walking distance of anywhere; at last I will have ample opportunities to expose myself to the wit and wisdom of Georgia taxi drivers. One of them asks me right off: Why do I suppose cabbies have such tough hides? "To protect them against their passengers' bad jokes?" I wonder. "No," he says, nearly convulsing himself out of his traffic lane with his own laughter, "taxidermy."

Considering the amount of snow we had way north in West Cornwall, I am probably also lucky not to be still in residence up there. I spent most of the weekend catching up on back magazines. We seem to get an awful lot of them, with the exception of those I care about—the ones with the lapsed subscriptions. Computer-initiated resubscription notices are so relentless nowadays, not to mention incomprehensible, that I find myself either resubscribing to the same magazine three or four times within a twelve-month stretch (thus, I suppose, entitling me to receive it until whichever one of us dies first), or neglecting to resubscribe at all. Then it is apt to be six or eight months before I become aware that I haven't been reading that particular journal—perhaps an indication that I could probably have got along quite nicely without it from the outset.

We are still, however, receiving *Publishers Weekly*, a state of affairs that I regarded, upon perusing the latest issue, with mixed feelings. The current *PW* devotes quite a number of pages to an exhaustive listing of all the prizes given in 1976 to all books in just about every category imaginable. I am crushed—well, bruised, anyway—to observe that the granting last year to "The China Hands" of the Sidney Hillman Foundation Award for the best book in the civil-rights field (I received a handsome scroll, $750 in cash, a free lunch at the late and not much lamented Hotel Commodore, and a chance to sit next to and chat with Jacob Potofsky, the dean emeritus of the Amalgamated Clothing Workers) is nowhere mentioned. This sort of lacuna is not recommended for anyone suffering from incipient paranoia.

I return to John Portman's Atlanta turf today, this time to talk to the great architect himself. He is rather stiff and pretentious at the start ("I'm trying to build a city, not just a building; to merchandize the city from the standpoint of all the things—shopping, food, entertainment, work—that the people in it are interested in; and to orchestrate this with, say, a Scandinavian restaurant, a Jewish delicatessen, and a hot dog stand. . . . The base root of what I'm doing designwise [sic] is to create a more human environment. . . . In the South, people are most concerned with people"), but then he becomes aware that my father was an architect, too, one of the revered generation before Portman's, and he thaws, and we stop talking about contemporary affairs and reminisce about—these are mere names to Portman, but I got to meet them all when I was growing up—Raymond Hood, Ralph Walker, and, yes, Frank Lloyd Wright.

Wright came to dinner at 25 Claremont Avenue one night when I was ten or so, and the only thing I can remember about him was his flowing black cape. What was he doing there? I don't recall a gathering. I recall merely Dad and Wright and me. My mother was probably out with her lover, but where were my sisters? (They may have been right there; memory can be conveniently obliterative.) Had the two architects run into one another at some professional cocktail party—no, this was during Prohibition—and had Wright confessed to being at loose ends for the evening and had my father graciously (no doubt breathlessly, too; he would not keep this coup to himself) asked him up to 25 Claremont for potluck? Portman proves helpful to me about Georgia, but when it comes to architectural history I am afraid that I cannot convey to him much solid fact about his precursors that he does not already know. And the relationship, or lack thereof, of my father and mother is, to orchestrate this encounter, totally irrelevant.

I have a lunch date with Millard Farmer, a civil-rights lawyer who's a friend of Joey's; it is nice to have sons old enough to direct their father to sources of potential information. Afterward, I betake myself to the Atlanta

Historical Society, which occupies a handsome building in the northwest environs of the city, where most lofty Coca-Cola executives and other local V.I.P.s, among them the governor, reside. Franklin Garrett, who presides pontifically over the society, has not altogether forgotten whence he sprang to this eminence; he has Coca-Cola ashtrays on his desk. He tells me, incidentally, that a gift of $1,000,000 from Robert Woodruff made possible the construction of the society's new headquarters; in keeping with the anonymity that Woodruff frequently made a condition of his largess, the building is named after somebody else. Franklin tells me that he is coming along as nicely as possible, everything considered, with his own historical chef-d'oeuvre. In 1930, he conceived the notion of compiling a necrology of all white males, twenty-one and over, who ever lived in what are now Fulton and DeKalb counties—the environs of Atlanta—from ancient Indian times to date. He has probably spent as much time cruising around neighborhood cemeteries as most gravediggers, and in two fat published volumes has, in the last forty-seven years, got himself necrologically all the way to 1952. I ask him if in view of changing Southern attitudes about race he wishes he had included black male adults. "Blacks were not so much in the public eye when I began as they are now," he says. "I'll be fortunate if I ever finish with the whites. I'll leave the black necrology to some black historian."

Franklin escorts me to his library, to show me shelf upon shelf of books on Georgia history that I am welcome to browse through, or even to read if I choose. At the only table occupied by a scholar, surrounded by heaps of books and newspaper clippings, I espy an old friend. He is Harold H. Martin, for many years a columnist for the Atlanta *Constitution* and also a feature writer for the *Saturday Evening Post*. We got to know each other covering wars in the Pacific. Now Harold is doing research on a biography, to be published by the Historical Society, on Atlanta's longtime mayor Hartsfield. Harold is Southern gentlemanliness personified. He invites me out to his home, just a short drive away, for a drink. En route, he remarks casually that we are about the same age. He is sixty-six. I hope he is joking. Do I look to other people as old as Harold Martin looks to me? Maybe Delta Airlines stuck me in first class on the way down here (though I had only an economy ticket) because it thought I wouldn't be able to make it any farther back in the plane.

At an age when anybody who has written as much for two capitalistic institutions as Harold Martin has could be expected to be enjoying a well-earned and decently pensioned retirement, he is still hard at work. He has to be, he tells me ruefully: He got no pension from the *Constitution* because it considered him an employee of the *Post* and paid him by the column, as if he were a county correspondent on space rates; and he got no pension from the *Post* because it folded, although he did get back what he himself had paid into its retirement fund, plus a princely two-percent interest on his own money. So he has been writing commissioned histories to make a living—the one on Hartsfield; one on the state of Georgia, for some bicentennial project; one on Robert Woodruff (an archival one, probably never to be published), for the Coca-Cola Company. Harold tells me about still another—a book on the Alaska pipeline that was offered to him because the company involved thought he had written "The Big Drink." Harold now apologizes for not having referred the pipeline people to me; instead, he turned them over to a writer who he knew was strapped because that man, too, had been on the staff of the *Saturday Evening Post*.

Perhaps feeling contrite, Harold generously offers to let me read a carbon copy of the text of his not-yet-published history of Georgia. I accept eagerly, and then after a moment's introspection withdraw my acceptance. I fear that I might inadvertently crib something of his, and if I did and if what I wrote about Georgia was printed ahead of his work, my gaffe would be not only embarrassing but unforgivable.

On our way to his house, Harold stops off at the site of a reconstructed old farm, complete with slave house, which dates, he says with awe, all the way back to 1840. I am enough of a Northern gentleman to refrain from mentioning that our Cape Cod house is a good deal older, and never contained any slave quarters. Come to think of it, my study at Truro, into which when I am sweatily toiling I sometimes feel as though I had been involuntarily incarcerated, is about the same size as these slave quarters. But the slaves occupied their identical space when they were *not* working. I shouldn't make jocular comparisons about this sort of thing. The slave cabin now serves as a gift shop. In the farmhouse kitchen, a woman guide tells us we should have come by at a time when real cooking was in process. Harold says yes, he has seen this taking place, he well remembers the old black woman who did the culinary honors. "It's a white woman now," says our guide. It is hard even for a Southerner to keep up with all the changes in the new South. But some of these by which the Martin family has been confronted intimately have not bothered Harold a whit. He tells me that when Atlanta schools were finally integrated he asked his then teenage son, "How do you feel about going to school with blacks?" The son replied, "Gee, Dad, that's swell; they're damn good football players."

The bad evenings on out-of-town trips like this are the evenings alone. A woman said to me once, when I lamented my lot in away-from-home life, "Why don't you go out to a theatre and meet some cultivated people?" I said that in fifty or so years of going to the theatre in New York, I had never once, so far as I knew, made a friend of a cultivated stranger, and had little expectation of faring better on the road. So it will be another of those one-too-many-martinis-followed-by-a-shrimp-cocktail-and-steak evenings. To-night, I vary the pattern; I have a crabmeat cocktail. Most hotels, though they profess to cater to the travelling businessman (nobody ever caters to journalists unless they are giving large wedding receptions), encourage their unaccompanied guests to waste their time and possibly get into trouble by keeping their restaurant lights so low that the solitary diner, unless gifted with infrared eyesight, cannot read.

The grim alternative is eavesdropping. Tonight, my ears are amply rewarded for their straining. I have, only a few feet to my left, a woman, recently divorced, dining with her lawyer, for whom she is, I infer, on the make. She is overweight, overdressed, overmascaraed—and on top of all that a blonde beehive. She is trying to apprise her companion of her cultural elitism. She keeps too busy reading, she says, to fritter away her time watching television. He nods commendingly, and asks what books have especially impressed her lately. After what I am tempted to whisper to her escort seems suspiciously long hesitation, she comes up with "I'm O.K., You're O.K." and "Jonathan Livingston Seagull."

Next, she orders some hideous-sounding drink, the principal ingredients of which, if I overhear her correctly, are Southern Comfort, Crème de Cacao, and Seven-Up. The waiter can't understand her much better than I, or maybe he refuses to believe her; he has her repeat what she wants three times. Then, trying perhaps to make her companion seethe with jealousy, she tells him about some bounder who tried to pick her up on a bus. She naturally rebuffed him, but then on Valentine's Day the scoundrel sent her a whole half-ounce of genuine French perfume. Her dinner date, who has—in pure self-defense, if you ask me—ordered another extra-dry martini, wonders drily how this cad obtained her address, in view of her having spurned his advances. She says she has no idea, and that the perfume was worth sixty dollars. Probably closer to thirty, says the lawyer, who by now seems ready to beseech the jury, namely, me, to invoke the death sentence. The woman says that naturally she hasn't yet acknowledged receipt of the gift. The lawyer reflects aloud that Valentine's Day was not much more than a week ago, and that she still has time to do the polite thing. I do not think she will get any further with her counsellor than she apparently got with her ex-husband, for whom I feel immense sympathy.

February 23

I have an appointment this morning with the governor of Georgia, George Dekle Busbee. No big deal, I suppose; there are forty-nine others like him, scattered from Maine to Hawaii. But still and all, if there is anything we have learned in the last couple of years, it is not to take governors of Georgia lightly. On Busbee's desk are prominently displayed (facing the visitor) some words once uttered by his father, a mule trader: "Anybody can tear a house down, but it takes a man to build one." The governor, more prosaically a lawyer, is not quite fifty and has been in politics most of his adult life, having first been elected to the legislature twenty-one years ago. His hometown is Albany, not far from Plains, but he has spent only a few nights there since he took gubernatorial office, in 1974 (Bert Lance was his chief rival), having elected to devote as much time as he could to boosting Georgia all around the world. He has a hunch that he travels more than any other governor extant. The governor is pleased to cite one modest example of how his peregrinations have paid off: In wintertime Georgia's coastal resorts, sometimes called the Golden Islands, now harbor more Canadian tourists than they do natives.

As for Americans rooted in colder climes, he is resentful of Northerners suggesting that the South is causing unemployment up there by enticing industries away with unfair gimmicks. Governor Busbee tells me sternly that it isn't devices like tax breaks that make industries migrate, but, rather, Georgia's devotion both to old-fashioned work ethic and newfangled environmental standards of the highest quality. Like his father, he is given to apothegms. "When you're swimming upstream you don't have the same enthusiasm you have as when you're swimming downstream," he says. What makes Georgians sanguine about their state's prospects, he adds, not to my surprise, is that they are happily aware that they're moving with the current.

I drift with the urban tide to Henry Grady Square, over which the celebrated editor presides in brooding bronze; the headquarters of the *Constitution* he used to edit are a block away, and I am paying my respects now to Hal Gulliver, its incumbent editor and chief columnist. Gulliver has an old "Henry Grady Square" street sign in his office, as if to remind himself of his links to an honored journalistic past; and he reminds me of another link—Ralph McGill, the *Constitution* writer of whom it was said, Gulliver says, that he had guts when it took guts to have guts. Gulliver is just back from a trip to Washington, where, as he recounted in his column the other day, he had lunch with President Carter. It was spontaneous. Actually, the writer had a date with Bert Lance. When Carter heard that the Atlantan, a respected journalist when the chief executive was a mere state legislator, was at the White House, the president horned in. "He's very pushy," Gulliver tells me, with an affectionate smile. What surprises me about this incident is that Mr. Carter evidently had no lunch date in the first place.

Lunch is a less disagreeable meal to eat alone than dinner. One can always have a sandwich at one's desk and pretend one is busy, which is harder to do after sundown. My reluctance to eat lunch alone and my unwillingness to spend the time it takes to arrange to have lunch with somebody may well have been what inspired me to take up backgammon in the middle of the day. You can hold a drink in one hand and a dice cup in the other; the only danger, naturally, stems from emptying the wrong receptable onto the playing surface. This happens more often than one might think. The president of the United States would hardly dare spend *his* lunch hour rolling dice; someone would surely leak it to the gossipy press. Anyway, Hal Gulliver's experience would seem to indicate that Mr. Carter has the lunch problem neatly solved; he can assume control of anybody's lunch within range; he is the commander-in-chief of warmed courses no less than of armed forces.

I have no lunch problems of my own today. By easy prearrangement, and without usurpation from higher authority, I stroll to a nearby restaurant (I am learning my way around Atlanta; I only have to ask directions twice) and there join Robert Hanie, an articulate conservationist and a fifth-generation north-Georgia man. We spend a few vivid, graphic minutes with one of his great-grandfathers, taking mules to a slaughterhouse at Vicksburg. It is perhaps not the ideal conversational preamble to ordering a meal, but I have had worse experiences.

Some years back, I had a lunch date with a physician friend who was attached to the Massachusetts General Hospital, in Boston. He and I had agreed to eat in the cafeteria there, on the theory that he was busier than I was. Almost everybody on earth thinks his or her time is more valuable than a writer's, this in spite of the fact that time is often a writer's only manageable asset. It is a topsy-turvy world, and it was a somewhat skewed lunch, too, from my non-medical point of view. The doctor, who shall be nameless because I would hate to have to stop playing tennis with his wife, met me at his office and then, at noon, suggested that we head for the cafeteria, explaining that it got crowded if one waited too long. But we had not been long on our way when, passing a door with a sign on it that went something like "Keep Out; Restricted Area; Absolutely No Unauthorized Persons Admitted," he pushed open the door and escorted me into a Hogarthian or Goyan scene: a half dozen or so dogs, participating in I have no doubt praiseworthy vivisectional endeavors, lying trussed on their experimental pallets. I walked through this torture chamber—torture to me, I hastily make clear, because I believe research on four-legged animals furthers the well-being of humankind—as quickly as I could; a few of the dogs seemed to have only two or three legs left.

We pressed on gamely toward the cafeteria, but—wait! Here was an unmarked door. My knowledgeable escort flung *it* open, and now we were in a viewing room, looking down through a glass floor on an operating table, upon which lay an inert figure, covered with a sheet from the chest down, with a surgeon alongside brandishing a knife that, from my angle, seemed adequate to bisect a St. Bernard. We had not been there fifteen seconds when the surgeon raised his scimitar and slashed that supine body's throat from ear to ear, throwing upward a stream of blood that, save for my protective glass partition, seemed likely to incarnadine my soles. "Beautiful thyroidectomical incision," remarked my doctor friend as I was stupidly examining the bottom of one shoe. "Well, now let's go eat." The cafeteria was indeed our next stop; but a fruit salad was all I could bring myself to order.

Robert Hanie was, he says, the first Southerner to join the Peace Corps. He was dispatched to the foot of Mount Kilimanjaro. We interrupt his program long enough for me to get in edgewise that I have been to its foot also; he is kind and does not ask me how much higher (no higher) I have ascended. I have been no farther up Fuji, I might as well confess here and now, than *its* foothills, and I believe that the only sensible way to approach the summit of any hill is by machine, preferably an airplane. How well and how mortifyingly do I recall a time when John Cheever, accompanying me on what he called a stroll up a New Hampshire mountain that seemed to me as demanding as the Himalayas, assented to my panting plea for a rest after we had climbed perhaps two thousand feet, and then literally stood over my recumbent body—he smoking a cigarette!, I gasping for breath! And this was *years* ago, for God's sake!—and asked me worriedly if I wanted to turn back. Of *course* I wanted to. Didn't this singularly sensitive analyst of contemporary life understand *any*thing? I hadn't even wanted to set *forth*. But, naturally, according to the peculiar code of behavior by which some of us attempt to live, I didn't express my true feelings, and as soon as I had recaptured what remained of my breath, John pressed out his cigarette and we both pressed on. I have always abhorred anything that entails going uphill on foot.

My conservationist companion, after returning home from the rugged slopes of Kilimanjaro, concentrated on saving the Georgia coastline from the clutches of various would-be developers. He was especially happy, he tells me, to be able to halt the planned construction of some proposed river dams. It turns out that his father was a civil engineer who built dams. I have had generation-gap clashes of my own. In a recent conflict over whether or not there should be a nude beach on the coastline of Cape Cod, my three sons and I have been dug in on opposite sides of the argument. I sided with most of the other local property owners, who felt that Truro wasn't big enough to accommodate comfortably all the people who seemed to want to get bitten there, on sensitive spots, by sand fleas. My sons do not pay taxes on land, so they are not much concerned, nor need they be, with the protection of private property; they sure do love enjoying the use of it, though.

Dining alone again tonight, I realize that I'll probably spend eight of the first thirteen weeks of this year outside New York, where in theory I live. Why do I do it? E. says my gadding about is compulsive. I say it is a way of earning a living. But it is not an easy way. Still, think of how much worse it was before hotels put television sets in every room.

February 24

The *Constitution* says this morning that President Carter has a meeting scheduled, to discuss Cuba, with Rep. Jonathan B. Bingham, Dem., N.Y., who has just been down there conferring with Castro. It is hard to believe that Jack Bingham is now one of the senior members of the House. He and June were living in Scarborough when we moved out there in 1947. They had a private tennis court, on which I learned, the hard way, that I play better with my glasses on than off. June, a woman with a doughty forehand, was my instructor. She lashed a drive at me while I was at the net, and it caught me flush in the eye. The doctor to whom I repaired for repairs suggested that I might enjoy tennis more, and live longer, if I played with glasses on and thus give myself a sporting chance to observe a ball in oncoming and potentially eye-gouging flight.

Jack Bingham's congressional district is in the Bronx, but when he first aspired to the House he tried to unseat Vito Marcantonio, the fiery radical from upper Manhattan. Inasmuch as the Binghams were living in Westchester, they had to establish some sort of residence in New York City to make his candidacy legitimate; the story around Scarborough was that June, volunteering to find a suitable *pied à terre*, missed the confines of Marcantonio's congressional district by several blocks. By the time the Binghams got their geography squared away, it didn't much matter; Marcantonio helped sweep aside his rival suburban upstart by derisively chanting, *"Jonathan Brewster Bingham of Groton."*

Jack went on from that prep school to become part of the famous Yale class of 1936, whose ranks included John Hersey, Brendan Gill, and August Heckscher. (Harvard '36 had David Rockefeller, to be sure, but not much more.) Still another Yale '36 man was a lawyer from Connecticut who must have done fairly well after graduation; he rode around in a Rolls-Royce with his first name on his license plates. I never knew him well, but, to my surprise, I was invited in the mid-sixties to his fiftieth birthday party, a stag affair in a private dining room at the Century. There were a couple of dozen guests, seated around a large circular table. When we reached the coffee-and-cigars stage, Gill, who was acting as master of ceremonies on his classmate's behalf, proposed that each of us in turn say a few apposite words about the honoree. The ensuing consternation was profound. It turned out that many of the others present knew the birthday boy even less well than I did, and thus were hard put to recite any suitable recollection. I discovered only later how this had come about; the lawyer had not long before been divorced, and nearly all his authentic oldtime friends, the ones who could have waxed anecdotal about him had they been at the Century, had sided in the split-up with his ex-wife.

I don't recall that Jack Bingham attended that uneasy anniversary do at the Century; he was in Congress by then, and no doubt had loftier things on his mind than the celebration of uncelebrated classmates' rites of passage. June Bingham, for her part, was beginning to make a name for herself as a non-fiction writer, but there had been a time, back in the Scarborough days, when she was a fledgling dramatist. I once acted in a play she wrote. I remember nothing about my part save that I was a Yale man; and to make sure the audience didn't forget that, June pinned to my chest a large blue "Y." In truth, it didn't seem to make me feel any different. Jonathan's role called on him to play the violin or viola. He, too, was outfitted with the appropriate prop. But he had no labels affixed to him; presumably the audience—almost exclusively members of June's family—knew he had matriculated in New Haven.

I envy Jack Bingham his trip to Cuba. I haven't been there since 1940, when Daphne—then Bull, later Hellman and Shih—rented a house and invited me down. In a Havana brothel I saw my first live sex show. I don't imagine Congressman Bingham saw one. I don't imagine there are any left to see. Pity.

Jack Crawford is going to take me around north Georgia today—a two-hundred-and-fifty-mile skim over its hilly surface. I am certain the trip is going to be fruitful when, even before we have left the outskirts of Atlanta, I notice a directional sign advising passing motorists that they are approaching Spout Springs Road, which leads to Flowery Branch. Our first stop is at the headquarters of the Georgia Mountains Planning and Development Commission, just outside Gainesville, where we are received by its director, Sam Dayton. He used to be Samuel, but like many others of his generation, he says, he switched formally to informality. I gather he is about Jimmy Carter's age. Sam is full of data about his region, and as we are leaving also imparts to us his version of the difference between north Georgia and the rest of the state. "People up here believe in trying something before saying it's bad," he says, "instead of, after the fashion of south Georgians, saying it's bad and not trying it."

Jack has us set for lunch with a woman from nearby Clarksville, Amilee Graves, the publisher of the weekly *Tri-County Advertiser*. The counties are White, Hall, and Habersham. We are going to eat at a White County place she recommends called—I have not yet passed my course in Elementary Understanding of Southern Accents and think at first she has said "Manor House"—the Manna House. White County happens to be a dry one, so there is no nonsense about drinks before lunch. Mrs. Graves says we should not feel too sorry for the indigenes; the distillation of corn whiskey occupies a good deal of the time of many of them. Corn whiskey from Georgia! The first Georgian I ever knew was a Smith College girl, in the nineteen thirties, whose indulgent parents kept her plentifully supplied, at Northampton, with home brew. It was pale and potent and, because of its remote origins, romantic; and now, forty-odd years later (the Smith girl who then generously dispensed the contraband was, when last heard of, contentedly married to a judge), I have found my way to the source of this nostalgic nectar. Latter-day Smith girls are much tamer. Ellie went to Northampton, too, and not long ago she received a fund-raising appeal from the Smith College Club of New York, which disclosed excitedly that it had just realized $3,600 from the sale of 4,800 bags of Georgia pecans. If it had had the gumption to peddle 4,800 quarts of Georgia moonshine, this might have netted a good deal more, and would also have been less fattening.

The Manna House has estimable food (we do not sample its current best-seller, a Jimmy Carter Sundae that has in it both peanuts and peanut butter, and costs sixty-five cents), but gives the impression of being the kind of place that might not go along even if the rest of White County went wet. Incorporated into the restaurant are both a religious shrine and a Christian bookstore. Our waitress says she and her husband, a retired soldier, think north Georgia is far and away the grandest spot of any of the many they have lived in on earth; and because their move here is the last they ever expect to make, they are calling their home Checkmate Acres.

On the Chattahoochee River, we make a pit stop at Helen, which used to be a small town wholly dependent on a single textile factory. An enterprising young Scotsman persuaded the town fathers a few years back to convert Helen into an ersatz Bavarian village, with new façades on all its commercial buildings. On our way to a pub where, Jack promises me knowledgeably, we can get Löwenbräu on tap, we pass a Strudel Haus and a Wursthaus and a Matterhorn Restaurant and—Helen is a singular oasis in arid White County—a Bavarian Bottle Shop. The imaginative Scotsman who started this Bavarian boom was also a balloonist; he died when he ran into a power line soon after Helen endorsed his face-lifting scheme. But the gingerbready Helen of today may be more or less what he had in mind, however the natives of Helen may feel about the new order of things, and the proprietor of Kübler's Hayloft Pub, while drawing our Löwenbräus, assures us that *he* is much happier than he was in his pre-Bavarian life. He used to be a gifts and housewares buyer for a Florida department-store chain.

It is getting late. We are due at the Crawfords' for dinner, and so we give relatively short shrift to Dahlonega, where the discovery of gold in 1828 set off a rush of riotous proportions, and where, between 1838 and 1861, a federal mint stamped out more than six million dollars' worth of coins from local ore. I never knew about any of this before, and must learn more. Back in Atlanta, Jack makes me privy to the existence of something else I never heard of previously—a fat volume entitled "Coca-Cola Collectibles." I find to my astonishment and, I guess, delight, that my name is the very first one mentioned in the opening chapter. That makes me, I guess, a sort of Coca-Cola collectible myself, though I might be gravely disappointed if I were put up at auction as such.

At dinner, we get onto the subject of spring vacations. When one has kids at more than one school, it is inevitable that their vacations will not coincide. David and Lexy each have three weeks off this spring, but only one of these together, and Ellie wants us all to go somewhere warm. She was thinking about Mexico, or Guadeloupe. Why not Georgia? Jack suggests. The idea, so profound in its simplicity, had never occurred to me. Why not Georgia indeed! I can, as the saying goes, combine business with pleasure. But where in Georgia? The Golden Isles, assuredly, Jack and Mary Lee enjoin me. And I can do no worse than Sea Island, provided a cottage is obtainable there for a one-week rental. It would have to be a large one, I tell Jack, because E. has tentatively agreed to spend that week in the company of Jeannette Rohatyn and some of her brood. Jack says not to worry about size: At Sea Island, there are no cottages other than big ones. Would a six- or seven-bedroom house, he asks, suffice? I say we could probably make do with something like that.

February 25

I have been scrambling all day, trying to get done what I felt I had to get done to justify my spending the weekend in New York; I get to the Atlanta airport barely in time to catch Eastern's New York flight, and it naturally figures that the plane leaves forty-five minutes late. The stewardesses seem to spend an inordinate amount of time peddling drinks—so much that they do not start to serve dinner until after we have begun our descent toward La Guardia. That is all right with me, inasmuch as we are dining at the Frank MacShanes', but I should think some of the other passengers, especially the abstainers among them, would be furious. When I decline a proffered tray, the harassed stewardess tendering it, says, with a half smile, "I don't blame you."

It is Lyn MacShane's birthday, and Frank has put the whole meal together himself—shopping, preparation, cooking. I do not know about cleaning up afterward. I am sure that some of us husbands will be hearing about his *beau geste* later tonight, or tomorrow, or as long as we live. Among the husbands present is William Jay Smith, who, being from Louisiana, is interested to hear that I have just returned from the South. I am flabbergasted to hear that Bill, as suave and urbane a poet as I can conceive of, spent the first twenty years of his life residing on various military posts, as the son of a Regular Army enlisted man. I promise to send this shining example of upward mobility a copy of that Second World War Profile I wrote of a Regular Army sergeant.

February 26

With E.'s brother Don Munro in town from Ann Arbor over the weekend, there is a family dinner get-together at the Patrick Smiths'. I don my Munro tartan trousers. I sense that D.J.M. regards me as something of a sartorial imposter, maybe because he is the last living male Munro of this particular branch of the clan and doesn't have any such plaid pants himself. When he does indeed confess that he wished he had a pair, I promise to try to find him a swatch, so he can get off on the right tack. E. says when we get home that Don and Patrick and I were jointly guilty this evening of indulging in machismo talk, bragging about all the big male things we have been doing.

I haven't done anything today except type up some Georgia notes, a routine, pedestrian, asexual chore, which is in fact interrupted by a female. Rita Gam drops in to tell us that she is into transcendental meditation, to enable her to sleep, and has a new phone-answering service. She wonders if her recorded "Please leave a message" voice comes through adequately, and asks me to call her number and check it out. I do. She sounds a bit raggedy, but I can understand her, and I leave word that the system is A-O.K. Rita says that her T.M. training is costing her $125 for two lectures and four group sessions, and that she also stands on her head, at, I gather, no extra expense. I have a T.M. book at my bedside that Ellie gave me for my birthday, but I haven't opened it yet. I see no more need to than to essay handstands. Unless I absentmindedly drink coffee after dinner, I have no trouble sleeping. E. says she wishes I did; then I might snore less.

Rita and Ellie go for a walk after R. stops by, and indulge themselves, E. says on her return, in girl talk. That is a corollary, I suppose, of machismo talk. Machismette? The two of them somehow got onto the subject of a man R. left her husband for a quarter of a century ago, and it turned out that E. was dating him then, too. Neither of the girl-talkers seemed offended by the mutual revelations. The fellow in question had a large black poodle. He never married anyone. That is all I am allowed to know about him. Whatever you think about men, women are the greater teases.

February 27

I am in a snappish mood, having spent most of the day working on my income tax, and perhaps a lot of other people have been preoccupied with the same bleak task, for the crowd at Marjorie Iseman's cocktail party seems uncommonly querulous. (Lexy has been paid five dollars to tend the door. Joe and Trude Lash are leaving as Ellie and I arrive, and when Trude learns that Lex belongs to us, she says that her son, at some undisclosed age, used to charge his friends a nickel to peek at his mother's surgical scar. What kind of operation? I inquire nosily. Abdominal, she says. So Lyndon Johnson was not unique! But at least he didn't charge the White House press a fee for their looksee.) In the general atmosphere of crankiness, both the R.'s are asserting vehemently that Jews are not entirely welcome on Martha's Vineyard, which surprises me and would, I think, no less surprise Lillian Hellman, Art Buchwald, Dan Lang, and some others. When another guest, who identifies herself as Budd Schulberg's sister, overhears Ellie introduce me to somebody as "E. J." rather than "Jack," *she* gets angry about *that*. I have no idea why, until I remember later that her father, the movie producer, was known as "B. P." There is probably some simple psycho-historical explanation for her aversion to initials. On our arrival home, all it takes is for E. to say "Is *somebody* going to do the dishes?" to make me explode. I am the only one who has done a goddamn thing in the kitchen all day long and who, when it comes to that, has walked the goddamn dog, four times in fact, and with an unseen nod to our cocktail-party hostess and all her testy guests and the commissioner of internal revenue and the rest of my oppressors whoever and wherever they are I tell my beloved wife to get lost and I drag the poor bewildered dog back out into the street. Rainbow caps my woes by refusing to do anything.

February 28

A letter from an old Alaskan friend, a woman I met in Juneau eighteen years ago, enclosing an interview with me in an Anchorage paper and chiding me for having skipped the state capital this time around. "Do you still play tennis with your gloves on?" she asks. What in the world can she mean? Did I ever play tennis with her bemittened? Did I tell her some story about outlandish court behavior? I am sure she isn't making this up. But why is my memory so much worse than everybody else's? I write back—trying to make the best of this confounding situation—that I am now much more competitive than I ever used to be, and thus play exclusively with no holds barred and gloves off.

I agree to meet E., who has more or less forgiven me for what I said under stress last night, at one of those P.E.N. literary cocktail parties, at the Lotos Club. There are usually half a dozen guests of honor—men and women who've recently had books published. If you're one of these, you get a white carnation and one free drink, and people who haven't the foggiest notion what the title is of your latest opus congratulate you warmly on its appearance and wish you the same kind of success they trust you will wish them when carnations next in *their* lapels bloom. Many of those who regularly attend these rituals, though, are authors whose success has been minimal, and inasmuch as the drinks are not cheap, gossip often flows more freely than booze. A woman calls my attention to one author across the room who could buy a round for the whole crowd—his last novel has just had a six-figure movie sale, or paperback sale, I forget which, maybe both— and she says he has just invited his ex-wife to go on from here to dinner, to the clear distress of his ex-girl friend, that grossly overweight creature in green near the bar, and what do I think of that? Being unacquainted with either ex-ux or ex-ox, I beg off rendering an opinion.

March 1

The draw sheet has been posted for the annual Harvard Club backgammon tournament. I once got to the semi-finals. Ted Tuck, who is running the tournament this year, must read *Sports Illustrated:* I am seeded No. 8, and the No. 1 seed is "Stavros." George Gianis has, I see, already fallen by the wayside, and I join him on the sidelines early this afternoon, losing to a youthful Citibank bond salesman. After my congratulatory handshake, he tells me that he devotes forty or fifty hours a week to the game. I am tempted to report him to his bank, but he beat me fair and square (I can remember only one truly bad move that I made), and maybe he gets by on a modicum of sleep. Trying to shake off my defeat, I wander over to a Park Avenue law factory for an interview with Morris Abram, the attorney who probably more than any other individual was responsible for the defeat of the county-unit voting system that so long dominated Georgia politics. He says he has just had lunch with Dorothy Schiff. Evidently he told the *Post* publisher that he had a later engagement with me, for Morris says that Dolly told him to let me know what a true gentleman my father was: when once Ely spilled something on her at a dinner party, he sent her a handsome present afterward. This is all news to me. I had no idea Ely knew Dolly. Suddenly I remember a dinner party at Emmet Hughes' bachelor digs on Central Park West, when *I* was sitting next to Dolly Schiff and spilled something on her myself. Has she got us telescoped into one person? But I have no recollection, I am embarrassed to have to acknowledge (to myself, why bother Morris Abram with it?), of having sent the lady any token of my contrition, so I am forced to conclude that my father and I both committed the same sloppy social gaffe. I never inherited any of Ely's considerable gift of drawing, but there seems to have been a genetic transmittal of the capacity to dribble on Dorothy Schiff.

I was not working—i.e., taking notes—that evening, so the one reportorial trick I have learned over the years did not come into play. The trick is always to be sure, while you are interviewing somebody and eating at the same time, to try to occupy a seat that leaves your writing arm clear, so that while scribbling you won't inadvertently jab your elbow into the person alongside you and thus create, instead of a future literary message, an immediate cuisinary mess.

March 3

Many eminent scholars, one often hears, do their monumental research at the New York Public Library, which is certainly handy for *New Yorker* researchers, being only a block away from our office and being accessible, moreover, by walking through the graduate center of City University of New York, a scholarly aisle if ever there was one. Arthur Schlesinger stepped here. The purpose of my visit to the N.Y.P.L. yesterday was hardly calculated to qualify me for a Guggenheim; I wanted to avail myself of the Main Reading Room's collection of nationwide phone books, so I could write to Georgians outside of Atlanta—Dean Rusk, for instance, now at the University of Georgia, in Athens—and alert them to the likelihood of my being in their vicinity some time soon. My mission was not as easy to accomplish as I'd anticipated. Someone had played hob with the Georgia directories, putting them in the boxes they didn't belong in; the thin little book for Plains seemed to have vanished entirely. Maybe the Secret Service, which probably answers calls put in to the number listed down there for Jimmy Carter, removed the directory to simplify its labors. Stranger things than that have happened at the library. A couple of years ago, scraps of paper kept turning up all over its premises, reading "F.B.I. in Public Library." I was going to do a Talk of the Town piece on the mystery, and what (with, presumably, the aid of the F.B.I.) was being done to solve it, but I couldn't get any cooperation from the library, which declined to discuss its security measures, though one loose-lipped person over there did, before I abandoned my pursuit, mumble something about a hush-hush C.I.A. angle having to do with the institution's map collection.

Returning to my office, I found a letter from June Shaplen, in Hong Kong, thanking me for a just-arrived present for Kate. But it was supposed to have been a *Christmas* present, and the airmail postage I bestowed on Lord & Taylor to make certain it would reach my goddaughter in December came to almost as much as the cost of the gift itself. Now the big question is: Do I drop everything else and devote myself exclusively to straightening this out with the store? Because these situations cannot be lightly settled. I decide in the negative; much of my energy is already being channelled into negotiations with the large-type weekly edition of the New York *Times*, which I have been sending to my mother-in-law in Florida for several years. I had inadvertently sent the paper two subscription renewal checks, and when Lucile notified me that she was getting duplicate copies of each issue, I had written asking the *Times* please to send her only one and to allocate my extra check to an extension of her subscription. I am still waiting for an answer to my letter. Or perhaps it came yesterday: I received a bill from the *Times* for a renewal of one of the subscriptions.

June Shaplen says Bob is getting traumatic about his impending sixtieth birthday. He spends his time staring at a mirror, she reports, worrying about his greying eyebrows. I must look at mine sometime. Worst of all, his ten-year-old son took a set off him at tennis. I don't know why that has Shaplen perturbed. Anybody can beat him at tennis. *I* beat him last time out. I bet I could beat him with gloves on.

We ate dinner twice last night, first at home and then again, not wishing to seem ungrateful or impolite, at the Bert Taylors'. Lisa invited us back there after the opening of the Brighton Pavilion show at her Cooper-Hewitt Museum. Because I only picked at the Taylors' food, I drank, relatively speaking, too much of their champagne. The man seated next to me kept complaining how terribly old he was. Discreet inquiry revealed that he was two years ahead of me at Harvard.

Lunch at the Century today with Bill Knapp, who is putting my Cyrus Eaton Profile into type. John Brooks and Dick Rovere are at the members' bar, and within seconds the four of us are spiritedly into *New Yorker* Conversational Topic No. 1—Who Will Succeed Shawn? No new ground is ploughed, but many old furrows are reexplored for telltale seeds.

March 5

After tennis yesterday, I found a message at the office to call Lady Selina Hastings. When I call today, Selina, who is scheduled to marry Larry Adler if he can ever get his latest divorce squared away, asks me what I have been up to, and when I mention Georgia she says she expects to be going there next year with her mother. Apparently a bygone Countess of Huntington is warmly remembered down South for having been a patroness, not long after James Oglethorpe settled the area in 1732, of the dissident English theologians John and Charles Wesley. I promise Selina to keep my eyes and ears open, when I return to Georgia, for intelligence about her noble ancestor.

Inflation has hit Harvard Club backgammon. Nickel and even dime games (five or ten dollars a point), once unheard of in this normally low-keyed gambling den, have raised their ugly—to losers—head; until recently, a dollar a point was the going rate. Howard Reiling, who is eighty-seven, says he can remember when the lunch crowd played for a non-metaphorical dime—for, that was, ten cents a point. Well, that makes sense: It costs exactly ten times as much to ride the New York subways now as it did fifty years ago.

Last night, we took Joan and Olivia, and Lexy, to see the Comden and Green show, which for me, especially when they reprise their numbers from the Village Vanguard aeons ago, is practically a singalong. Betty and Adolph have become revisionist historians. In reminiscing about their pre-war existence as members of the Revuers, Adolph says there were three of them—Betty, himself, and Judy Holliday, whose Tuvim surname of that era has disappeared from his recital. Worse still, the other two Revuers, John Frank and Alvin Hammer, have been entirely eliminated from their tiny niche in theatrical history. In Brendan Gill's review of this Comden-Green collage he, too, alludes lovingly to the Vanguard, which he says didn't, while the Revuers were there, have a liquor license. For that to have been true, the management would have had to have got away with selling me an awful lot of illicit drinks. (And if the place was dry, what in the world was the seedy poet Maxwell Bodenheim doing there at two or three o'clock nearly every morning, trying to cadge a drink?) I am inclined to believe, rather, that *The New Yorker*'s incomparable checking department relied too heavily on some other revisionist historian for its verification of this particular fact.

I must ask Adolph some time, incidentally, if he remembers when I was co-host at his wedding reception. At the time that I was a steady patron of the Village Vanguard, I learned that Philip Wrenn, who was running the magazine's idea department, had joined the staff the same day I had, though not the same year. The coincidence struck us both as deserving of celebration nonetheless, and so for a couple of years, on whichever early June day it was, the two of us dined together in style. One year we went across the Hudson River to Ben Marden's Riviera and lost our shirts, my shirt anyway, in its casino. (Milton Berle can testify to this, if he cares to; he was at the same roulette table.) Another year, Phil and I were sitting in the Algonquin Hotel lobby, having a drink and trying to decide where to splurge, when Adolph Green walked in with a carnation in his lapel and a young woman on his arm. We hailed them, and learned that they had just got married and, in lieu of any other premeditated plans, were about to have a drink. That wouldn't do at all, Phil and I declared; newlyweds deserved a wedding reception, and since nobody else seemed ready to tender them one, we would, then and there. So we ordered some champagne and executed appropriate ceremonial toasts.

Today being a Saturday, E. has asked me, not unreasonably, to accompany her on a round of art galleries. I wangled a confession out of her that the main reason she wants me along is not that she is panting for my critical appraisals of the Mary Franks and Lee Krasners and other works we are going to ponder, but because she cannot stand riding alone in the self-service elevators with which Fifty-seventh Street abounds. The Betty Parsons Gallery has the scariest of all; the creaks and groans they emit in transit sometimes even frighten me, and I have been to the bottom of a ten-thousand-foot-deep diamond mine. Before we embark on our perilous cultural trek, we have a duty call to make—the annual Town School Fair.

Unlike most of the other parents, we haven't helped to put it on, so the least we can do is patronize it and buy some things we neither desire nor need. I do not feel guilty about our non-participation in the preparations; if one received merit badges for hours put in at private-school fund-raising events, I would be an eagle scout from all the Scarborough School book fairs and raffles and whatnots I got mixed up with while helping to raise my first batch of children.

After we survive the rise and fall of the Betty Parsons empire, it is time to dress and head for the Robert Jay Liftons' twenty-fifth wedding anniversary party. The first person we run into when we get to their apartment is the poet, R. M. It has been six months since Ellie saw her last. R. had phoned then and asked, agitatedly, if she could come to *our* apartment. On arriving, she had poured out such a tale of woe—involving her rejection by, in ascending order of anguish, her husband, her lover, and her publisher, let alone three months' arrears in rent—that E. impulsively lent her a thousand dollars. There had ensued neither a thank-you note nor a note of indebtedness. Now here R. is, elegantly accoutred and coiffed. She doesn't greet E. at all, but greets me, whom she scarcely knows, with a kiss full on the mouth. What does all this mean? It means non-reimbursement, E. and I later surmise, but can we persuade the I.R.S. that this sad transaction is a bad debt, come tax time next year, without an I.O.U. to substantiate its existence? Or does R. perchance think that even if it took Helen of Troy's whole face to launch a thousand ships, her lips alone can staunch a thousand bucks? Our accountant will surely say that a kiss is just a kiss.

The Liftons' apartment, once we manage to wend our way past our welcoming Circe, is jammed with editors, writers, and political scientists. One of these last urges me to go on a Greek-island cruise with him, which sounds agreeable enough until it turns out I am to be a paying guest; I beckon to R. M., introduce her to the skipper, and sail myself off toward the sunset. Herman Badillo arrives, late, in formal togs, having earlier attended some testimonial dinner. I would hate to be a politician and have to chop evenings into segments—so much for vote-getting, so much for fence-mending, so much, eventually, for plain socializing. Because of the special nature of this felicitous ocasion, there are many jests about marriage. Herman says that up in Riverdale, where he lives when not in Washington or on Cape Cod (one could hardly ask a congressman representing the South Bronx to *live* there), nobody ever gets married anymore except nuns, priests, and gays. I'll bet he wouldn't have said that at whatever gathering he came here from.

March 6

I met Jinny at a wartime cocktail party in New York given by a corporal who worked in an Army public relations office where she was a WAC first lieutenant. I, being a chief warrant officer at that moment, ranked just about halfway between the two of them, and when Jinny and I eventually announced our engagement there were the inevitable, and not inaccurate, jokes about my marrying above my station. Actually, warrant officers—junior grade as well as chief—generally considered themselves as inferior to no one much below a lieutenant general; there were so relatively few of us, and our rights and privileges were so rarely understood (we did have access to officers' clubs and we did rate salutes from *our* inferiors) that we could get away with a good deal. My courtship of Jinny did not begin auspiciously. Trying to impress her with my manliness-about-town, I led her on our first date to the "21" Club, which I had rarely patronized as a civilian. The guardian of its portals, unimpressed by the fact that she and I were both in uniform (or maybe acting on that fact) refused us entrée; I was obliged ignominiously to fall back on the Stork Club, where I was no more a regular patron than, as other warrant officers sometimes cuttingly reminded me, I was a Regular Army warrant officer.

Ellie and I met, twenty-five years later, at a dinner party on Cape Cod. A widow with two small sons, she had rented a house in Truro for the whole summer, and I didn't turn up there until August. Throughout July, I subsequently learned, various well-meaning mutual friends, knowing I was separated, planned to bring the young widow Frankfurter and me together, and I had barely reached the Cape when I received two invitations to dinner that first night. So did Ellie. Luckily, we both accepted the same one. What I did not know until just a few days ago was that there was another more or less single man at the house she and I turned up at, an eminent journalist who was also taken with E., and who not long after I had whispered to her that I would be honored if I could see her home had made the same gallant proposal. My luck held; she climbed into my car.

I first met N. when I was asked to be the master of ceremonies at a Truro fashion show, and she was one of the models.

Tonight, in New York, Ellie and I are having some people in for dinner. Among them is Jimmy Greenfield, who has just been named assistant managing editor of the *Times* and asks my opinion as to whether or not the paper should run a backgammon column to complement its bridge and chess departments. Digressing long enough only to tell him, now that my views on the state of contemporary journalism have been solicited by someone who can implement them, that I find the *Times'* crossword puzzles far too easy, I give an emphatic affirmative to the notion of a backgammon feature, and even recommend someone to conduct it—the youthful expert Paul Magriel, whom I encountered at Nassau during the World Championship and whose new book, "Backgammon," was favorably reviewed in the *Times* not long after that. Jim seems grateful, and I am pleased to reflect that humankind may derive an unexpected byproduct, a bonus, from this evening's assemblage.

March 9

After playing hookey from Georgia for a week, I returned to Atlanta the day before yesterday. Jack Crawford managed to get me into the seventy-story Peachtree Plaza Tower Hotel, only six floors short of the summit. This is the highest, while theoretically on the ground, that I have ever slept. When my room-service waiter brought me breakfast at six-thirty yesterday (I like to rise early and watch the religious hours, farm programs, and continuing-education lectures that hold television together until the "Today Show" bestirs itself), he told me that some of this establishment's upper-echelon guests get up early to watch the sunrise from on high. I can take a hint. I headed for the window and flung back the drapes. I could see nothing. I was in the middle of a cloud. I do not think room service was pulling my leg. The weather may have been fine down on kitchen level when he set forth.

I didn't learn much about Georgia yesterday, but a Delta Airlines executive with whom I had lunch at one of my clubs—the Commerce, this time—imparted to me what he asserted to be a universal truth: If you have the gout, chicken is O.K., but turkey is deadly. It must be dreadful to suffer from gout; one evidently has to be no less watchful of people who might step on a big toe than of the ingredients of a club sandwich. Never having had gout, I can concentrate, when ordering club sandwiches, on trying to obtain these without mayonnaise, an ambition usually as hard to realize as to grasp the end of a rainbow. Why is it so difficult to keep mayonnaise out of club sandwiches? My own hunch is that inasmuch as few persons in command of their senses would *ask* for mayonnaise on anything, mayonnaise manufacturers must be bribing sandwich-makers to smear the stuff on unsuspecting victims' bread. Al Capp once uttered what struck me as the last word on the subject. The cartoonist said that in his view all the mayonnaise on earth should be dumped into a huge vat, and all the people on earth who liked mayonnaise should be shoved into it.

Yesterday afternoon, over at Morehouse College, where so many of the black leaders of the country have received their higher education, I was waiting to talk to Hugh Gloster, its president, and picked up a community newsletter. There was an ad in it for one of the twelve candidates vying for Andrew Young's seat in Congress—a black state legislator who announced that he had a committee of fifty working on his behalf, including "drunks when they are sober." This is the furthest I have ever seen a politician go along the lines of appealing for the support of special-interest groups.

In New York last week, after my sojourn to the public library, I wrote a couple of dozen letters to various scattered Georgians telling them about my project and entreating their cooperation. On returning to my hotel from the Capitol this afternoon, I have my first response. It is from Dean Rusk. He evidently received my letter this morning, at once phoned me at *The New Yorker*, was referred to the Peachtree Plaza, and has left word here for me to call him pronto in Athens. When I do, he says he is going to be driving to Atlanta later today, and could we get together at the motor inn where he will be staying at nine-thirty? We could indeed. I have previously met the former secretary of state only at large public affairs, and I welcome this opportunity to talk to him one on one about Georgia or, for that matter, anything else.

When I reach his room, Rusk has just finished a sandwich; after proposing that we have a drink, he calls room service and says he wants to place another order. When, a few minutes later, it is delivered, the waiter tactfully remains out in the corridor and lets Rusk take the tray from him there; this servitor seems to be well-trained in the niceties of handling situations where one minute a room contains a single man and the next minute he has acquired a friend. Mr. Rusk and I have a long and, for me at least, delightful and rewarding talk. Neither of the subjects that might have caused some mutual awkwardness is raised. I do not mention Vietnam (though he alludes to it en passant), and he does not mention "The China Hands," in which book I subjected him to what seemed to me fairly harsh criticism. Of course this is not exactly a standoff: He knows that I know about the war in Vietnam, but I haven't the faintest idea if he has ever heard of my book.

March 10

My first appointment is at King & Spalding, the big Atlanta law firm, with Charles Gowen, who ran vainly for governor in 1954. Eight years after that, he moved from Brunswick, on the coast, to Atlanta, to fill a partnership gap caused by the appointment of Griffin Bell to the federal bench. I learned yesterday that we have got our cottage at Sea Island—only a seven-bedroom one, and thus no great shakes by local standards, but at least it has a rec room large enough to swing a catamaran in—and when I mention to Gowen that we'll be spending a week in the part of the state he comes from, he says we should be sure to look up the fellow who runs Sea Island, and has been prominent in littoral Georgia affairs for half a century—Alfred W. Jones, known up and down the coast as Bill.

At the headquarters of the C & S Bank, Georgia's biggest, with something like a hundred branches in and around Atlanta alone, I am greeted, with a big smile and a no less substantial hello, by Richard Kattel, the chairman of its board, who was born in New York but more or less atoned for that by matriculating at Emory University. "Georgia is a state that no matter where you are—even here in downtown Atlanta—you run into strangers who will smile at you and say hello," he says. Mr. Kattel discourses learnedly, and smilingly, on the intricacies of Georgia banking laws, old and new. Much of this, though—for instance, the role in the regional economy of what I believe he is describing as "multibank holding-company banking"—soars irretrievably over my head. I began not being able to comprehend financial lingo when I took Economics A at Harvard (the "A" was part of the course name, not my mark), and I have been drifting steadily downhill ever since, being by now, I suppose, perhaps the only living member of my generation who cannot differentiate offhand between a put and a call.

The remainder of the day is devoted to keeping up with the Joneses—two old acquaintances from Coca-Coladom. Both are extremely close to Robert W. Woodruff. Boisfeuillet Jones, who may well be the classiest-named Jones this side of Eugene O'Neill's Emperor, mans the spigot through which the gush of Woodruff's philanthropies mostly flow; Joe Jones, who more than makes up for his comparatively lacklustre Christian name by his unrivalled access to the venerable Santa Claus, has been R.W.W.'s right-hand man (also left hand, right foot, left foot) almost as far back as anyone can remember. He is much closer to Mr. Woodruff, who never had any children, than are many sons to their fathers. In the annual report of the Coca-Cola Company and other such documents, "J. W. Jones" is listed as merely one of a number of corporate vice-presidents. People acquainted with the inner workings of the company know better.

A local television station is doing a series on the various contestants in the forthcoming special congressional election. This evening's featured candidate is a black minister, Clennin King, the same one who several months ago made a much-publicized attempt to integrate Jimmy Carter's church in Plains. The reverend is shown at the state capitol, calling on Secretary of State Fortson ("I haven't seen you in a long time," says Mr. Ben; "What y'all here for?") and at a shopping center in a white residential area. Mr. King explains, on camera, that he won't campaign in black areas, though he says he gets along equally well with black street dudes and white rednecks. At the shopping center, he accosts a white woman and tells her, perhaps to her total confusion, "It may not look like it, but I'm a white person on the inside, and for your own sake vote black."

I have reached that stage of life where, after three or four days' intensive research, I've had about all I can stand at a stretch. Also, I noticed in my bathroom mirror this evening (hotel mirrors are huge and reveal all) that my bottom is sagging. Overweight, or overage? Whatever the reason, I am dismayed, because E. complimented me not long ago on its attractiveness. Can one apply to a plastic surgeon for an asslift?

March 11

I slept poorly, because I couldn't remember George Brockway's surname. For a couple of hours, I thought it was Braziller. I had the first two letters right at that. But why should I have been thinking about either of these publishers? True, George Brockway (W. W. Norton) has put out three of my books, but he and I never had much to do with one another at the time, and I can't understand what impelled him to turn up unidentifiably in the middle of an Atlanta night and rob me of my rest. Not long after another cloud-shrouded breakfast, I have a phone call from Macon, in reply to a letter I'd sent to a potential source there. The voice is that of a youngish man. When I ask him how he spells his name, he says, "H-y-l-a-n-d—like your ex-mayor, except of course for the 'd.' " How does this youthful Georgian know about John F. Hylan, who presided bumblingly over New York City half a century ago? "Oh, I know all about Red Mike," the man from Macon says. "Because of the similarity in their names, my grandfather was once shot at by mistake."

I'll be heading back to New York this afternoon, thank God, for the weekend, and then plan to turn right around and drive back to Georgia. E. and I finally solved the problem of how to cope with the boys' non-matching school vacations. We will sandwich parts of each around Sea Island. I am to take off with David Monday morning, spend a week with him driving around parts of Georgia I haven't yet inspected, and join Ellie and Lexy at our cottage, where of course it will be handy to have our own car. After our week there en famille, I aim to spend a third week, this time in Lexy's company, looking around still other unexplored sections of the state. This will entail a lot of driving, but I find that relaxing, if there is nobody in the car telling me to slow down.

I have consecrated most of today to reading, at the Atlanta Historical Society. The evening, back in New York, is consecrated to a gourmet dinner at Helen Frankenthaler's house. Helen hand-paints her menus; some unscrupulous art dealer could probably make a fortune by rifling her garbage. She does not have to worry about her guests; they are all high-minded, virtuous types like the Tom Wickers and ourselves. I hold forth, at what I hope is not excessive length, on the drifts of political currents in Georgia today. I am pleased, listening to myself orate, at how much I have already absorbed. And I haven't even yet touched down in Plains.

March 13

Newsweek has a cover story on John Cheever. That should gratify the magazine's Atlanta bureau chief and John's other fans in Georgia. The Cheevers spent ten years in Scarborough in the rented house we passed on to them after we built our own. I believe that I spent longer than John did, though, as a volunteer fireman. He enlisted in the Scarborough Fire Company first, but then he quit shortly after recruiting me. He had been chosen secretary of the outfit, on the sensible premise that a professional writer would be adept at taking minutes of meetings; and he after a while figured, cleverly, that the only way he could shuck that responsibility was to find another writer to take his place. I thought fleetingly that I was being urged to become a volunteer because I showed promise of rescuing women and children from blazing infernos. The real reason was that I had a typewriter and could spell. On John's retirement from active service, I was elected secretary by acclamation, although most of the men who voted me in as yet scarcely knew my name.

I have to get my Atlanta notes typed up this weekend while I can still read them—and, of course, before I return to Georgia and scribble down still more—and E. is sore at me for devoting so much time to work when I have been so much away from home. But the household's agenda does not seem to depend heavily on my availability. E. has her regular Sunday tennis tryst, and Lexy is off to an all-day magic show at the Hotel Diplomat, on West Forty-third Street, roughly halfway between my office and Times Square. He wants to know if I have ever heard of the establishment.

Who my age has not? There was a time, thirty years ago or so, when the Diplomat was just about the only hotel in town that would harbor meetings of extreme left-wing groups, and so many of these accordingly convened there that by merely sticking one's nose into the lobby one ran the risk of being branded a Commie for the rest of one's life. It wouldn't astonish me to hear that there were excessively cautious New Yorkers who would walk only on the north side of Forty-third Street, because the Diplomat was on the south. But Lexy is of a different era, and in his view the hotel is not a dangerous place to be seen in, but, rather, a likely haven from the present-day horrors of the sidewalks of New York that lead to it.

March 14

David and I hit the road, heading south. He is nervous as we approach Baltimore, and not without cause. The last time he drove over this stretch in this same Plymouth station wagon, it broke down. Ellie was at the helm; I was in Arizona and was going to fly east and meet her and the kids in Florida. The car collapsed because we had kept getting repeated warning signals from our oil-gauge light but the mechanics at the main Chrysler-Plymouth service center in New York had kept assuring us it was nothing serious. It was. Evidently no oil had been circulating through the engine for twenty-five thousand miles or thereabouts, and the engine was, E. was told when she got towed into a Maryland garage, a total ruin. (Thirty-odd years ago, I had a similar experience with an older Plymouth, and I had taken an oath, practically in blood, that I would never again purchase a Chrysler product as long as I lived. Shows how much you can rely on a man's word.) Anyway, E. had left the station wagon where it foundered, had ordered a new engine, rented a Hertz car, and proceeded on her way, favoring me, as I later pieced together the unfolding drama, with muttered imprecations all the way to South Carolina. I accompanied the family back north. When we stopped in Maryland to dispose of the rented car and retrieve our own, we were so glad to put the whole sordid business behind us that we neglected to remove Lexy's typewriter from Hertz's trunk, and we never saw it again.

As David and I now drive through Virginia and North Carolina, both of which contain a good many dry counties, it is easy to tell from the billboards heralding the advent of Holiday Inns and Howard Johnsons that, while children under eighteen may be lodged for free (David, blessedly, is sixteen), you aren't going to be able to buy or beg a drink before dinner. "Lounge" is the telltale word, its absence the tipoff. I have been caught unawares in the South before. On one trip, Ellie and I ended up two nights running in loungeless motels, which she deemed crisis enough to warrant dipping into her elevator vodka. Her elevator vodka is the little bottle she always carries in her purse, which is going to save her from dying of fright someday when she gets stuck between floors in a self-service lift.

Some of these motel billboards also pledge special discounts for A.A.R.P. members. I have an authentic membership card in my pocket from the American Association of Retired Persons, which one can join at age fifty-five and in which I enrolled a couple of years ago when I was thinking of writing a book about so-called senior citizens; so I guess I am eligible for the special old-timers' room rate. But will I avail myself of this right? Not on my life, at however advanced a stage it may be. For one thing, my pride would never let me. For another, if David found out I was doing it, he might seriously injure himself laughing.

We finally put up for the night at Rocky Mount, North Carolina. The next big town is Fayetteville, and I certainly don't want to stop *there*. It is too close to Fort Bragg, and for all I know some M.P. will loom up and order me back to my barracks. Besides it was in a Fayetteville hotel that I learned about Pearl Harbor; any community that purveys that kind of news is worth steering clear of. Rocky Mount has no cocktail lounge, but I have an answer to that: a half gallon of vodka, for our Sea Island larder, but, as I'm sure E. would concur, available in emergencies.

After dinner, David and I stroll over to an amusement center—bowling alleys and pool tables. The establishment is integrated, naturally, but the diversions aren't; all the whites in the place are bowling, all the blacks are shooting pool. I used to bowl at lunch sometimes, in my early days at *The New Yorker*, with Gus Lobrano, Andy White, Jim Geraghty, and a few others. If people bowl at lunch anymore, it is news to me. I was never any good at bowling. I have never in my life rung up a 200 game. I did once hit 198, but that was a fluke. It is an indication of my singular ineptness at certain sports that I suspect my average lifetime score would be lower for ten frames of bowling than for eighteen holes of golf. That in itself might constitute a competitive record of sorts, in a class with the most consecutive strikeouts or the highest earned-run average.

March 15

Across the South Carolina border, we see signs pointing to Spartanburg. These make me uneasy, too, because it was there, at Camp Croft, that I received my basic infantry training in the summer of 1941, and being able to think dispassionately about basic training is about as easy as drinking your orange juice when you have reason to believe someone has laced it with castor oil. I got one home leave during my thirteen weight-reducing weeks at Croft. A barracksmate of mine was a licensed pilot, and because he had confidence in small aircraft, we rented one along with *its* pilot, to ferry us up north. The plane could hold three passengers, so to reduce the per-capita cost, we persuaded another embryonic footsoldier to come along. That was a tactical error, because whatever he saved us in disbursement he more than outmatched in discomfort; he began vomiting almost as soon as our wheels were up and kept at it so assiduously it was as if our platoon sergeant had ordered him to.

Then it developed that our pilot, as we were hovering in the vicinity of Philadelphia, with the sun sinking fast, had never flown north of Richmond and had no idea how to get to the Newark Airport, our hoped-for destination. We guided him there ourselves by spotting Route 1 beneath us and instructing him to follow those cars. He landed on the wrong runway in the wrong direction, and was enveloped by irate airport security people as soon as he stilled his prop. Sunday evening, on the way back, he ran out of gas somewhere in North Carolina and had to make an emergency landing in a pasture. Luckily, we were able to engage a taxi, and by driving all night, at some hideous extra expense, we got back to camp before reveille.

When, a few weeks later, my mother proposed that she take a train down to South Carolina and visit *me*, I was on the whole much relieved. I was able to get an overnight pass Saturday, and booked two adjoining rooms in a Spartanburg hotel. In the middle of the night, I was awakened. There was a woman sitting on the edge of my bed. How sweet, I thought, raising my head from my pillow—mother coming in, just like old times, to make sure I am properly tucked in! Then I became aware that the body bending over mine was not being solicitous but was soliciting. I got that hooker out of there as fast as I could. After all, what would my mother have thought if she'd tiptoed in to smooth my covers?

Reminiscing—selectively—with David about the good old Army days, we plod on south, and reach Augusta in mid-afternoon. We are already set to have dinner with Joe Cumming's sister Nancy and her husband, Hugh Connolly, who is in real estate. Hugh is a native of Pontiac, Michigan, but has adjusted. Nancy and he live in a house that is only seven years old. Since it stands on land, however, that has been occupied by the Cumming family for seven generations, they talked their architect into making it look older. Nancy's father, the present patriarch of the clan, is in the hospital, but his wife graciously comes over from her house next door to greet us, and we are all but smothered in Southern hospitality. A nice way to start this kind of trip.

The Connollys say they are going to stick around during the Masters golf tournament this year. Like many of their Augusta neighbors, they used to rent their home that frenetic week and flee to Florida. (The local radio stations are already announcing that there is a critical shortage of housing available during the tournament, and will anybody who has a spare room to let please call such and such a number?) For a couple of years, their golf-buff tenant was an undertaker from Texas; it was a joke in the Connolly circle that he used to bring along empty caskets and rent *them*.

Nancy and Hugh make me promise that *The New Yorker* will not do to Augusta what the *Reader's Digest* has just done: Its current issue has an article about Georgia, and Augusta doesn't even appear on the accompanying map. (Neither does Macon, and I have no doubt some Maconian booster will complain of the oversight when we get over there.) I make the promise with my fingers crossed; we may very well not run any map at all, and if we do I will surely have minimal cartographic input.

March 16

Wyche Fowler, white, and John Lewis, black, came in first and second in yesterday's congressional election. Now there'll be a runoff. I leave David in charge of receiving further local news in our room at the Executive House (a hostelry that not long ago, in keeping with the New Georgia, all at once sheltered both the D.A.R. and the Harlem Globetrotters) and set forth on my appointed rounds. We have allotted ourselves a mere two nights in Augusta, and I have a full agenda. Far and away the most interesting person on it today is the octogenarian lawyer Roy V. Harris, a genuine old-school Southern segregationist—his fire now somewhat banked but still warm— who for twenty-seven years, from 1947 to 1974, put out the Augusta

Courier, which to many local rednecks was all but required weekly reading. Mr. Roy, who has been up to his own neck in Georgia politics since 1916, is gracious, and informative, but he admits to being depressed about the prospects of the nation. He is convinced, he tells me, that the United States has already reached that decaying stage of civilization that Demosthenes predicted the Periclean Greeks would arrive at—the Americans have become high-salaried paupers at the close of a Golden Age. The fact that Jimmy Carter, whom Mr. Roy of course knows, is in the White House does not strike him as being at all ameliorative of our precarious condition.

David and I have been invited to dine at Waynesboro, some thirty miles south of Augusta, at the home of Joe and Lennie Dolinsky. Joe runs a furniture business there, and they live in a house that could have been transported from Scarsdale. It is separated by a six-foot fence from the markedly less elegant homes of their immediate neighbors. Enisled there in what I hope it is not supercilious of me to call the sticks, the Dolinskys seem hungry for news of the faraway North—even news brought to them by a Northerner who has spent a good part of this winter concentrating upon the South, and has come to inquire into their lives in their part of the Georgia world. Waynesboro, they say, is a highly conservative community, more so even than Augusta, where the John Birch Society still flourishes and the Ku Klux Klan appears unhooded on television; but Waynesboro is not what it was several years back. A few miles outside that town, for instance, is the only extant black boarding school in the state, Boggs Academy. About ten years ago, the Dolinskys say, a white preacher lost his job because he had the temerity to ask the Boggs choir to sing in a public square. Today, by sharp contrast, a black sits on the Waynesboro public school board.

March 17

On our way out of Augusta, with Macon our destination for tonight, we stop for a talk with a black lawyer, John Ruffin. I was eager to see him as an antidote, so to speak, to Roy Harris, and Ruffin proved to be praiseworthily accessible. He invited me to come by for a chat on very short notice. Attorney Ruffin, Morehouse '57, Howard Law '60, began practicing in a turbulent era, and he was much more involved, at the start of his professional career, in civil-rights litigation. Today, his militancy is comparable to Roy Harris' bigotry—smouldering but subdued. "If I were a militant," Ruffin tells David and me, probably only half-seriously, though it makes David's ears prick with real interest, "I'd set off bombs simultaneously at the two main anti-intellectual strongholds in Augusta—the newspaper office and the courthouse."

During our drive west through the center of the state—flat, clayey, by all outward appearances far from prosperous—we pause at Sandersville. With a big courthouse squatting in the middle of its central square, it is typical of many a Georgian county seat. This is Washington County—named after George, not Booker T.—which dates back to 1784, when it was established to provide landholdings for Revolutionary War veterans. The big red Victorian courthouse is Sandersville's third. The loss of the first one can't be blamed on William Tecumseh Sherman. It was a victim of what, as historical markers scattered around Courthouse Square accommodatingly inform the transient curious, the indigenes call The Great Fire of March 24, 1855, which was survived by a mere five town buildings. The pyrotechnical Civil War general did, though, account for the demise of the second, short-lived hall of justice.

David and I cannot dally unduly. We have a lunch date farther west, at Milledgeville, with Professor Emeritus James C. Bonner, who since he has retired from Georgia College there has been working on a history of Milledgeville, a mid-nineteenth-century capital of the state. Bonner is the kind of academician one doesn't often encounter up our way. When we pick him up at his home and admire its brick façade, he remarks shyly that he laid all the courses himself. Professor John Kenneth Galbraith lives in a Cambridge, Massachusetts, house with, I judge, many more bricks, but one can hardly visualize him, despite his enormously long reach, wielding a trowel on Francis Avenue. Bonner is a sort of pro-Sherman historian, in the sense that he believes the Union commander has been accused of more arson than he was a party to—if not pro-Sherman, then at least not anti-Sherman. At lunch, after a learned and welcome lecture on just which 1864 Milledgeville structures Sherman's men did or did not set the torch to, Professor Bonner laments that the Georgia Historical Commission, of which he used to be an officer, is no longer autonomous and is suffering from the burdens of bureaucracy. "I wouldn't know where to go to get something done," he says over his iced tea. "I wouldn't know where to go to get an historical tablet replaced that's been knocked down." I am glad to be able to report that the ones at Sandersville need give him no concern.

We have no more time today for roadside briefings; I have an afternoon appointment in Macon with Phil Walden, the head of Capricorn Records. He is a would-be rock singer who couldn't sing, but who liked to hang around musicians anyway and was booking bands for fraternity dances while he was still a sophomore at Mercer University, Macon's own. Walden made an early and profitable connection with the Allman brothers, still other hometown boys who made it big in the pop-music field. When Jimmy Carter began running for president, and was low on funds, Walden arranged for the Allmans to give seven benefit concerts for him. (Also, Walden tells me, somewhat bafflingly, the brothers were helpful in introducing the candidate to young Americans at a time when Carter was suffering from a bad identity crisis.) For his pains, Walden was bedevilled by a right-wing group called the Liberty Lobby, which evidently hoped to prove that he was selling drugs and using the proceeds therefrom to further swell the Carter campaign coffers. Preposterous, Walden tells me; how could anyone harbor suspicions of a man who, like himself, distributes five hundred turkeys to the needy every Christmas?

Some Macon Chamber of Commerce people capture David and me and bear us off to dinner at a local restaurant practically smothered in Atmosphere. They are kindly folk, staunch Macon boosters one and all, and they serve up a rich feast for both body and mind. Do I know, for instance, that Macon's own Sidney Lanier is one of merely three American poets to have been honored with a postage stamp, or that the Cincinnati Reds' Pete Rose got his start with the Macon Peaches, in the Sally League? Am I aware that just a few miles outside of Macon is located the world's largest manufacturer of school bus bodies? If David can assimilate even half of all this, he has surely got himself a term paper for St. Paul's.

We are not to get the impression, however, that Macon is unimpeachably peachy. The incumbent mayor of the city, our hosts unanimously agree, is an improvement over his unpredictable predecessor, a fellow known as Machine Gun Ronnie (his campaign buttons featured a machine gun), who rode around town in a red-white-and-blue armored personnel carrier, who once imposed a municipal curfew because he feared Macon was going to be burned to the ground by outside agitators, and who refused to declare Martin Luther King, Jr., Day a local holiday because, he argued, King had never done anything for Macon. One last disclosure, the denouement of which is definitely out of the mainstream of conventional chamber-of-commerce intelligence: Macon's Wesleyan College, attended by, among others, China's Soong Sisters, may be one of the country's preeminent academies for young females, but its swimming pool has acquired the nickname, among some of Macon's loutish young males, of the Bay of Pigs. That last adolescent scurrility, alas, may be all that David retains from this variedly instructive day in middle Georgia.

March 18

Our first engagement today is for lunch, at Oxford, about an hour and a half north of Macon, if I analyze the road map correctly. We are supposed to meet up there with William B. Williford, a squire of Covington, adjoining Oxford, where he lives in one of the stateliest antebellum homes, presides over his own printing press, and is the author of, among other regional books, a history of Americus, in which Sumter County seat he was raised. It used to annoy him as a boy, Williford told me when we first met in Atlanta a couple of weeks ago, that he was kin to just about everyone in Americus. "I couldn't go out into the street without some old lady calling my grand-

mother right afterward and saying, 'Billy passed me and didn't say hello,' "
he said.

Bill Williford is a member of the Board of Councillors, the governing
body of Oxford College, whence sprang Emory University. Because the
councillors are having one of their quarterly meetings today, he has
suggested that David and I meet him, at noon, outside one of the campus
buildings. Williford is standing there when we pull up, his arms graciously
laden with Georgia history books that he has brought for me. He says we
have a few minutes to spare before proceeding on to lunch, so he shows us
around the institution, which was founded by the Methodist Church in
1836. Its principal building, a huge Victorian pile, boasts a bell in its clock
tower that was a gift from Victoria Regina herself. Today, the trees in the
main campus quad are garlanded with toilet paper; the students have been
celebrating the onset of their spring holiday. I hope David doesn't take any
such ideas with him back to Concord, New Hampshire.

Now, says our escort, if we will be good enough, it is time to eat. To my
amazement—and perhaps even more to that of blue-jeaned, uncombed
David—we learn we are to partake of a sumptuous fried-chicken-ham-and-
fixin's buffet in the company of the entire august Board of Councillors and
the college's chief administrators. What's more, we are not being sneaked in
to a side table. We are flatteringly introduced to the assemblage, while
David tries desperately to comb his hair with the flat of one hand, as visiting
northern V.I.P.s. After a reception like this, an honorary degree would be a
letdown. The director of development of the college tells me that he has a
summer place at North Truro, on the Bay, and that while we have never
met before he has watched me go sea-clamming. An elderly lady councillor
excuses herself, goes out to her car, brings back the current issue of *The New
Yorker*, and asks me to autograph its cover for her. Nobody has ever asked
me to autograph the magazine before. I once did receive, though, a page
from it signed by every one of the Gae Foster girls who put on the stage
show at the old Roxy Theatre. It was the lead page of a Reporter at Large
comparing them, hugely favorably, with the far more touted Rockettes of
the Radio City Music Hall. Not only were the girls at the Roxy estimable
precision dancers; they danced, precisely, while on unicycles and large
rubber balls. I was madly in love with them, but collectively, not
individually.

I was doing research on them, in the fall of 1940, when I wrote to my
sister Olivia, then a student at Bryn Mawr. It was the day the Gae Foster
Girls began to rehearse on two-dimensional, unsupported ladders. "I sat
high up in a box above the balcony with Gae Foster and various assistants of
hers," I wrote, "and we all watched in a cold sweat as the girls went through
their routine. Only a few fell, too. I feel, after four months backstage, or a
large part of it backstage, that I've had just as much part in shaping that
show [come, come, now, Kahn] as any of the producers, and I am just as

proud of them as Mother is, say, about your passing your German exam."

Four months backstage! I really over-researched that one. I probably would have done the article faster had it been about trained dogs.

Lunch is so tastily protracted (David manages to overcome his diffidence long enough to sample each dessert) that if we are to reach Madison at a decent hour late this afternoon—I have been told that it is a lovely old town, with more antebellum houses even than Covington, and we shall sleep there—we have to get moving. Madison isn't far from where we are, but I have elected to travel in exactly the opposite direction first—westward, toward Atlanta—so David may have a look at Stone Mountain. Why hold him responsible? I have never looked at it myself. So we wend our way toward that great granite monument, and are properly fascinated. After gazing at the sculptures on its face, we drop in at an information center and listen to a recorded spiel. The finished monument was dedicated on May 11, 1970, we hear, by "the vice-president of the United States." No further identification. We pick up a souvenir booklet, which contains several pictures taken on dedication day. Here is one of Senator Talmadge, and another of Secretary of State Fortson, both suitably labelled and identified. Here is another, of the exterior of a helicopter, flying past General Lee astride Traveller, carrying "the vice-presidential party." Thus has Spiro Agnew been virtually eliminated from at least one repository of Southern history.

The Holiday Inn at Madison is in a dry county, but it has a "club," to which registered guests automatically accede to membership, and in which they may buy drinks just as if it were an ordinary cocktail lounge. A beehive-blonde is at the bar when I arrive. She leaves a few minutes later, and the bartender, a fellow whose age I would estimate at thirty, shakes his head in wonderment and says she is "five-oh old," as if it had never occurred to him a woman of fifty could get in and out of a place like his without assistance. I refrain from remarking that some of the women I consider most fetching are in the immediate neighborhood of five-oh. David joins me at that point, rather unnecessarily bringing his mother into the conversation, and while he is trying his skill at an electronic shooting game, I reflect that if one raises children by precept and example, this week, so far, has been mainly exemplary. I have been going, under I hope his observant eye, at a fairly good clip—averaging a couple of hundred miles a day behind the wheel, making essential phone calls to arrange appointments in this town and the next one, keeping the appointments, taking notes and then typing them, and performing all the ritual acts associated with one-night journalistic stands. But I may have to stress precept from here on, because example doesn't seem to have been very effective. I have been taking showers twice daily. In five days, he, to the best of my knowledge, has taken one.

March 19

A retired Air Force colonel, Dan Hicky, and his wife have offered to show us around Madison this morning. We are expecting them at eight-thirty. At seven-fifty-five, David and I are about to go to our Holiday Inn dining room for breakfast and a look at whatever newspapers we can corral, when the phone rings: The Hickys are here and perhaps we would care to join them for breakfast. I must say that the older I get the more churlish I become when other people change my plans, even when they are ostensibly doing me a favor. David is feeling churlish, too, and for the same sort of reason: I made him take a shower.

The colonel, who was a pilot and left the service in 1971, after thirty-one years, to become a Holiday Inn representative (no wonder the toast is warm!), politely asks David what *he* plans to become (a neurosurgeon—which means that he probably won't be self-supporting for another fifteen years), and then says that he has a son at Annapolis who would like to fly except that he is color blind. So he is going into submarines. Can the lad's parents not be aware that the sky would seem to be the limit for male Georgians who graduate from the United States Naval Academy and then enter the submarine service?

Madison has forty-odd antebellum homes extant, most of these with distinctive outside chimneys, and many of them inhabited by elderly women. Early in the nineteenth century, it seems, there were so many widows in town that a compassionate gentleman earmarked his estate for the education of fatherless Madison children. That made the place attractive for widows to settle in, and a tradition began. A contemporary widow whom we drop in on is Colonel Dan's eighty-six-year-old mother, the author of a regional history book, who tells me that she is working on a different kind of manuscript—an account of a recent stay of hers in a hospital. She says she hopes it will be a big seller because she has thought up what she believes to be the kind of title that appeals to present-day book-buyers: "Ladies in Bed." I agree. Paperback—movie sale—I can see it all. If I could think of a hot title like that I would drop Georgia like a hot peanut. We discuss how fortunate Madison was to be spared when Sherman marched to the sea. There were some tense moments, the elder Mrs. Hicky says, as when a Union cavalryman rode his charger through the hallway we are now standing in and with his sword speared a roast off the family dining table; but the only civilian casualty was an overexcited young woman who fell off a balcony when the Yanks came strutting through.

Among the other homes we inspect on our grand tour is one called Boxwood House—its shutters are always closed, so the original drapes won't fade—with a handsome boxwood garden out front. On learning that one of David's hobbies is horticulture, the Hickys urge him to take a boxwood cutting home with him. He does so, with appropriate thanks, but I wonder what will come of this, because his specialty is growing plants exclusively from seeds. He does unbelievable things with, or from, seeds. From seeds that I can barely detect with a naked eye he has grown watermelons and pumpkins that I can barely *lift*. For a couple of years, the pride of my *New Yorker* office was a lush coleus plant that David coddled from a seed. It was one of the showiest plants our austere premises ever boasted. (Janet Flanner and I once gave Shawn a tubbed tree, a willow, I think, which had promise, but did not thrive; either Bill was too busy to water it or it succumbed to effluvia from the Princeton Club kitchen.) When I went to Cape Cod for the summer I would let Bruce Bliven, down the hall, keep the coleus in his office and water it; on my returning in September and reclaiming it, Bruce would look nearly as griefstricken as a foster mother obliged to yield up a child she had come to love more than one of her own.

The death of my coleus—may Robert W. Woodruff and J. Paul Austin forgive me—taught me something about the properties of Tab, which like Coca-Cola I had always assumed to be ninety-nine per cent water. I used to water my coleus faithfully (following, naturally, David's precise instructions pertaining to time, quantity, etc., etc.). One Friday afternoon when I had to leave my office in a hurry I remembered that I had neglected to give the plant its weekend sustenance. There was no time to get to the water cooler and back. There was on my desk, though, an only half-consumed can of Tab. I flung its contents onto the coleus and took my callous leave of it. On Monday, the poor dear thing was limp and livid. By Wednesday, my office smelled so badly that messengers refused to enter it to deliver mail or proofs or anything else. On Friday, I threw the plant mournfully away, pot, dish, and all. I wonder what Tab contains. Ellie drinks it the way Marv Throneberry drinks Lite beer. I used to have both my coleus and her. I am probably lucky to have either of them left. Bruce thinks I am a murderer.

Tonight, Savannah. We have been here before, but only for a few hours' detour on one of our motor trips north. Now, en route to Sea Island, we are to stay a couple of nights, and how nice to perceive that we will be spending them in a large tenth-floor corner room of the DeSoto Hilton, with a panoramic view of what is surely one of the most attractive cities to look at in the nation! The management has welcomed us with a toothsome basket of fruit, though *sans* fruit knife. David is not much of a one for unpacking—I unpack everything every night, but he says that is stupid, I just have to repack in the morning—but now, with prestidigitation that his brother Lexy the Magician might envy, he plucks from somewhere a wicked-looking dirk that, were he in different circumstances, could get him arrested on sight, and he proceeds deftly to carve a pineapple. He should make a damned fine neurosurgeon.

Along with our fruit, we have a message to call a couple who, we have already heard, have done much to keep Savannah as handsome as it is— Emma and Lee Adler. Lee is a moving force in Historic Savannah, a group which, a decade or so ago, imported a crew of architects from Virginia. They made an inventory of two thousand downtown buildings and concluded that eleven hundred of these deserved preserving, whereupon the National Park Service pronounced two and a half square miles of the city a National Historic District, not subject to casual demolition. I phone the Adlers, and they most hospitably invite D. and me to be their guests this pleasant, almost-spring evening at a testimonial dinner being held in the Grand Ballroom of our very own hotel in honor of the retiring head of the local branch of the National Association for the Advancement of Colored People.

I know kids. David would be for declining, for having a hamburger from room service, and for watching "Charlie's Angels" or whatever. Since I have the phone in my hand and am bigger than he is, I heartily accept for both of us. David, now obliged to change his clothes, hurls his bluejeans partly toward the TV, but I have anticipated that and have neatly ducked behind a Gideon Bible, a stoutly bound shield the presence of which during hotel-room confrontations has perhaps been sorely underrated. When David calms down and spruces up, I dispatch him to the lobby for an evening paper, from which we determine that tonight's honoree is Westley W. Law, a black postman, who it seems has been a tower of strength in Savannah's civil-rights battles, and ordeals, for the last couple of decades.

We are lucky to have arrived in time for the celebration. I am reminded of my initial arrival in Bangkok, in 1964, on the very eve of the Royal Barge Festival, when the king's sleek slim dazzlingly colorful vessels (His Majesty's personal craft, a two-hundred-year-old barge, was golden, with a swan-necked dragon-headed prow, seven nine-tiered umbrellas, and gilt-tipped oars) are removed from their boathouses—this happens only once a year—and are paraded along the Chao Phya River. Some Thai acquaintances congratulated me warmly at the time on my perspicacity, for having arranged to turn up at so momentous a moment. But the truth was that I had never heard of the glorious Royal Barge Festival until I stumbled unwittingly upon it.

The DeSoto's ballroom is not filled to capacity, but from the viewpoint of a white Northerner who is all for integration and hopes it can somehow come about, it is comfortably and compatibly crowded. About two-thirds black, one-third white, by my not always reliable counting eye. Most of the white men present are in business suits, most of the blacks in black tie. (David and I, not having brought along evening clothes and having no option, are statistically irrelevant.) Some of the black women, for their fashionable part, have on white gloves that reach nearly to their shoulders, and enough feathers to choke a cat.

There is a near-interminable invocation, in the course of which Mr. Law is compared to both Moses and Joshua; and then, as various guests are introduced (one of them a hundred and three years old), numerous standing ovations. Then come the tributes and testimonials. Lee Adler, a stockbroker who is a scion of a department-store family, reads a truncated version of one of these, following which the guest of honor says, "You'll notice that he cut the resolution, but they don't cut prices at Adler's." Mr. Law is essaying a joke, of course, but his remark seems in questionable taste. Somebody mentions that the honoree has never had an automobile of his own, and when the time comes to present him with a retirement gift, I wonder what make of car it will be. Instead, to my disappointment (conceivably also to his) he gets a free weekend in New York City. There are so many politicians to be introduced, and so many congratulatory messages from absentees to be read—from Bert Lance, from Herman Talmadge, from Jimmy Carter, from the mayor of Savannah, who has proclaimed today Westley W. Law Day—that it is 11:25 P.M. before Mr. Law gets a chance to speak himself ("If there're any more fights to be fought, we're ready to take them on, too"), by which time some of the guests have begun drifting out, and I have whispered to David to be sure to nudge me sharply if, in drifting off to sleep, I start to snore. We who stay to the end are rewarded, though, at midnight, when the whole assemblage arises and, hand in hand, black and white, friend and stranger, joins, touchingly, in singing "We Shall Overcome."

March 20

The Adlers have adopted us. Very agreeable. This being a Sunday, the stock market is closed, and when Lee picks us up the program he has outlined for us is dizzying—sightseeing, tennis, country-club lunch, it is hard to keep track. Lee says as we set forth that he can make enough money in two or three days each week to indulge himself the rest of the time in his avocations and hobbies, and in that respect he compares himself to writers in general and specifically to me. But if that is true, what am I doing here in Savannah, working, on a Sunday?

At the Law testimonial dinner last night, we met, among others, the banker Malcolm Bell, chairman of the Savannah Bank and Trust Company. He is the president also of the Georgia Historical Society, and when he learned that I was anxious to visit it, he said that although it is normally closed on the Sabbath, he'd be glad to open it up for me himself. So Lee drives us over to a stately old building, put up in 1873 by Margaret Telfair Hodgson in memory of her husband. Inside the main entrance, just above the door, she had it unequivocally carved that there was to be no feasting, drinking, smoking, or amusements of any kind within these walls. Inasmuch as the men and women who keep the institution going nowadays need to have fund-raising affairs there from time to time, the stern century-old injunction poses them a problem. They have resolved it to the satisfaction of their own consciences, Malcolm tells us, by trying to keep their eyes averted from the prohibitive proscription.

David and I wander around—having a whole institution to ourselves is exhilarating—inspecting various relics and portraits. He is fascinated by the actual bullet that felled Count Casimir Pulaski during the Revolutionary War; I by a painting of John Elliott Ward, a Savannahan who was the first United States ambassador to China; and by another of Selina Hastings, Countess of Huntington, the ancestor Larry Adler's fiancée was telling me about the other day; and by a likeness, moreover, of General Sherman, here included because, I read, he "spared Savannah." But there is something about the printed information attending the general that bothers me. He is said to have spared Savannah in 1865. That cannot be right. I suggest to Malcolm that surely this soldierly absolution took place in December, 1864, and as I say this I realize in a flash that if I know enough to correct the Georgia Historical Society, I am far down the road on my historical research. Malcolm does not immediately show the white flag. He goes to a high shelf across the spacious room to check up on General Sherman and me.

Suddenly there is a dreadful crash. A great tomb of tomes has engulfed the chairman of the board of the biggest bank in town and the head of the sovereign state of Georgia's biggest memorial to its past. We all scramble to pull Malcolm free and to restore the precious volumes to their perches; in the excitement all hands drop the investigation, which is fine with me, because I don't want to seem uppity or smartalecky or know-it-ally. And I am happy to perceive that Malcolm is apparently not only not wounded but not offended at my having questioned the Historical Society's history in the first place; it might have been different had I found a mistake at his bank. Indeed, he is so far from being angry that he invites us all over to his house later for a pre-lunch drink.

Lee Adler is still very much involved—it is his principal avocation—in rehabilitating old Savannah homes, and he drives David and me through some of the areas of the city, once slums, in which entire blocks of buildings, many of them earlier abandoned, have been restored to handsome and usable shape. Emma Adler joins us for drinks at the Bells', and then Emma and Lee take David and me to lunch at their country club, which differs from the northern variety in that it has on its grounds both Confederate military bunkers and ordinary golf-course bunkers. After lunch, we embark on a long drive—to Fort Pulaski (containing twenty-five million bricks, but nonetheless readily breached by Union artillery during the Civil War), to Tybee Beach (reserved, in the Jim Crow days, for whites only), to Thunderbolt (home port of a shrimp-boat fleet), to Isle of Hope (large summer cottages and larger oaks), to Vernonburg (where the Adlers have their summer place, equipped with the biggest collection of fishing rods David has ever laid eyes on), and eventually to a Chinese restaurant.

Driving us back to our hotel, Emma asks David what he likes most for breakfast. Pancakes and syrup, naturally, what else?

March 21

When I come out of the shower, the message light is flashing in our room. I call down to the front desk. The message, anonymous, is "Jar on counter." The mystery remains unsolved until we check out. Then we find that the Adlers, in one last burst of Southern hospitality, have brought around some homemade corn syrup for David's delectation.

Spring begins today. It is comfortably warm in Savannah. Ellie and I spent the first spring of our marriage in Japan. We had gone to Asia in part for me to cover the World's Fair at Osaka for *The New Yorker*. It was E.'s first trip to the Far East, and she logically relied on my judgment as to what clothes she should bring along. I assured her the weather would be balmy. She damn near froze to death. The night of March 21st was the worst. We were staying at an inn in Kyoto. We drove over to Nara to attend a traditional start-of-spring temple festival. The ceremonies did not get under way until midnight, and by the time they ended, even though we were wearing just about everything we had, we were congealed. But the Japanese have their own lovely ways of coping with human frailty. When we returned to our inn, even though it was 4 A.M., we found a steaming hot connubial bath awaiting us.

Next stop: Sea Island. Ellie and Lexy and the Rohatyn crew, who are flying from New York to Jacksonville, aren't due to arrive until this afternoon, so I have arranged for David and me to have lunch at Sea Island with its doyen, Alfred W. ("Bill") Jones. This trim, vigorous, seventy-five-year-old patriarch leads us to a lavish buffet at the Beach Club; for a moment I fear David's eyes will pop out irreparably. A native of Dayton, Ohio, Bill Jones first came to these parts in 1923, to visit his older cousin, Howard Coffin, a Hudson Motor Company executive who acquired vast land holdings in southern Georgia, including Sea Island, where, in 1928, he built The Cloister, still one of the splashier hostelries along the coast. (As cottage renters, we will be allowed to sign chits at its buffet lunches and other amenities.) The Cloister and the rest of Sea Island almost went under during the Depression, Jones tells us (he has been mainly in charge since 1933, when Coffin moved to New York), but it came back strongly, so much so that today it can accommodate four hundred and fifty people in the main hotel and ancillary guest houses, and an additional fifteen hundred or so in its three hundred roomy cottages. Jones tells us that the Sea Island Company, of which he is chairman of the board, has so little need to sell any more of its unimproved acreage that its whole real-estate business is attended to by a single retired Navy captain. "We don't sell real estate," Jones says. "Sometimes we let people buy it."

Ellie and her group—counting cousins, we are a party of nine, three adults and six children—arrive on schedule. By then, David and I have moved into our spacious cottage, which looks out over a vast salt marsh. (We are in Glynn County; it was this landscape that inspired Sidney Lanier's "The Marshes of Glynn.") The house seems, in the phrase I have heard somewhere, exquisitely appointed. It has two ice-making machines. But when I prepare to open a bottle of wine before dinner, there is no corkscrew. Fortunately, the house next door has one, though the man who kindly lets me borrow it says—can there be a shortage of corkscrews in this enclave of splendor?—would I please be sure to bring it back as soon as possible.

March 23

Sea Island is a lovely seashore spot for a spring vacation if you don't mind not going into the sea. It was chilly and breezy yesterday, though the kids did swim in the pool. I took some reading matter Bill Jones had given me to poolside, foolishly put it on a table, and a gust of wind scattered it all over the place. But several fellow vacationers sprang to my rescue, and only a few sheets of paper landed in the water. People are the same the world over. When once a briefcase of mine burst open at the Scarborough railroad station, with an express train due to roar through at any instant and blow anything that wasn't staked down into the Hudson River, the alacrity with which my fellow commuters dived upon my spilled homework was heartwarming.

All writers who carry briefcases have had nightmarish experiences, some, may they rest in peace, having lost entire finished manuscripts. *My* number-one horror story was not that bad, but was scary. It occurred in New York City, on a windless winter evening. I habitually tote one briefcase to and from my office, even if I have nothing special to transport. (If schoolkids can have a security blanket, why can't I have my briefcase?) I was working on two books at the time, and, planning to go to West Cornwall for the weekend and not knowing which project I'd want to devote myself to, I carried home both sets of research. That called for two briefcases, and inasmuch as each one, filled to capacity, was quite heavy, I took a taxi uptown. I was supposed to pick up our car at its garage, so we could make a fast getaway to the country, and I told the cab driver to let me off at the northeast corner of Park Avenue and Eighty-seventh Street. Our garage is on that cross street— a westbound one, of course—between Park and

Lexington. I paid off the cabbie, picked up my briefcase, and got out. He drove off, and then I remembered I'd begun with *two* briefcases. He didn't hear me yell after him, but I watched him turn right on Eighty-eighth Street. What would he do next? I knew what his only choices were—to continue east across Eighty-eighth, or to turn south on Lexington. If he took the first option, I was a goner. If he took the second, perhaps I could—now I began to run eastward, as fast as the remaining heavy briefcase would let me—cut him off. It was dark, and when I reached Lexington I saw, to my dismay, the lights of four unoccupied taxis bearing down on me. I stepped out in front of the closest one. Four-to-one odds. He squealed to a halt. My briefcase was on the back seat.

When, at the Beach Club pool, I have my papers more or less reassembled, I decide not to take any further chances with the wind but, rather, to stuff them for safekeeping inside a reticule Jeannette Rohatyn has brought to the scene. Her bag is stolen a few hours later. (Whoever swiped it may be chagrined to find that the portable backgammon set I put inside it has one piece missing.) Is somebody trying to tell me that this is supposed to be a holiday and to cut out this interminable research?

Today, lightheartedly abstaining from taking notes, I accompany the rest of the household to Waycross, our departure point for a plunge (with a boat bottom beneath us) into the Okefenokee Swamp. The truth is that I can't take notes. I have difficulty managing the paraphernalia of my trade unless I am wearing a suit coat, with appropriate built-in niches for pens, notebooks, and the like. This morning I put on the bush jacket I bought several years ago in anticipation of crocodile-watching in Uganda (Okefenokee has alligators), and my pen has somehow slipped out of it. I suppose I could try to write in blood, but Okefenokee alligators, as we are told almost as soon as we arrive, go mostly for dogs. A woman tourist once tied her pet poodle to her car door while she was looking around, the Okefenokee story goes (I warrant we are not the first to hear it), and an elderly alligator named Oscar, a sort of local house pet, shuffled up and swallowed the dog whole.

We are introduced, from a prudent distance, to Oscar, who looks as though he would need help to open his jaws, and in the next few hours, as we travel around this strange, spooky, silent place, we spot a gratifying number of other alligators, and of turtles, and a marvelous variety of vegetation—cypress, moss, lily pads, and much more, all from time to time magically reflected on the mirror-like surface of the waters our helmsman steers us through. (No birds, though; the chilly weather has sent them sensibly into hiding.) Our guide is a young man of twenty-five who has been working here since he was fifteen. He went to college for a couple of years, but dropped out. He didn't want to graduate, because if he had a degree somebody might have made him take a white-collar desk job. He would rather spend his days outdoors, gliding through the swamp.

We dine tonight at a seafood restaurant on St. Simons Island, which lies between Sea Island and the mainland. The tables, ingeniously, have big holes in their middles, so you can sweep your shells or gurry or whatever right out of sight. I work the hardest of any of our group, having ordered roasted oysters and been favored with two heaping platters' worth, unshucked.

March 25

Some mail arrives, forwarded from the office. A note from Bud Trillin, at the magazine, who has been in Texas; he encloses the unannotated business card of George Carmack, associate editor of the San Antonio *Express and News*. George Carmack! Major Carmack, suh, executive officer of the Special Information Section of Headquarters, Army Ground Forces, where so many of us wasted nearly a year in uniform, singing, largely unheard, the praises of the Infantry. The major sat right inside the door of our area, like a house-mother, doing nothing beyond trying to figure out things for the rest of us to do, while *his* superior, Colonel Waine Archer, was usually over at the Pentagon, trying to get authorization for all of us to do something more stimulating than whatever we were up to, or not up to.

So much for the remote past. The mail that deals—I hope—with the fairly immediate future is more interesting. Shawn has had a note from the private secretary to Dr. the Honorable C. P. Mulder, minister of information in Pretoria, saying that the matter of my visa is receiving attention—first word we've had from the laconic South African government since I filed my application. And I myself have a note from Helen Suzman, M.P., who is more sanguine about my prospects of being admitted than I am, and who is urging me not to come over in mid-May, because she will then be in the United States. I would hate to miss Helen in Johannesburg or Cape Town, but if Doctor the Honorable decides to let me in solely during May, I will certainly try not to inconvenience him.

These have been two ego-building days. Ellie, Jeannette and I, leaving the kids to their own devices (tennis, golf, bicycling, swimming, skeet shooting, horseback riding, and the right to buy snacks and sweets at several locations simply by signing a slip of paper with our house number), have been shepherded all over the map by none other than Bill Jones himself. He cannot have done this for too many other people; otherwise, how could he be alive? As some elderly golfers like to shoot their own age, or better, so does the three-score-and-fifteen Bill Jones evidently enjoy equating his years with miles per hour. Moreover, he crosses double yellow lines on blind curves, just as if he owned the area; maybe the secret of his success, or survival, come to think of it, is that in large part he does. It has never occurred to me before that "right of way" could be a translation for *"droit du seigneur.*" Our two excursions, though—those portions of them, at any rate, when his passengers' eyes were open—have been both enjoyable and enlightening. And we are here to tell about it. Also, back in time each day for some tennis.

First there was the kind of house tour of Sea Island that one associates with Hollywood or Beverly Hills: There on your left is the home of the late senator Walter George, on your right Philip Alston's, where Jimmy stayed after his nomination; that lot is where John Portman is planning to build his own home, which will have to conform, naturally, with Sea Island Company regulations; the two-hundred-thousand-dollar house being erected yonder on a two-hundred-thousand-dollar lot—what perfect symmetry!— will be occupied by the chairman of Exxon; the president of Singer Sewing Machines preceded him in residence; this place belongs to Bert Lance, who will probably not be able to use it much now that he has gone to Washington; and that one to a Nunnally, if you have ever heard of the Coca-Cola Nunnallys. I have. The house *we* are renting, it develops, is, at the moment, a sort of black-sheep establishment; it was built for an Atlantan who got badly hurt when that city's real-estate boom went sour; technically, a bank controls the place right now, and the reason we were able to rent it for so short a spell, Mr. Jones said, is that the bank, against the Atlantan's wishes, *made* him rent it, so our money could be applied to his indebtedness.

There were a toy manufacturer and a brain surgeon and I forget how many corporate executive vice-presidents among the fraternity of cottage-owners, but there did not appear to be any writers. Perhaps not now, Mr. Jones said, but he played a trump card that made me feel much better: *There* is the house that Eugene O'Neill dwelt in, for six years back in the thirties, when he was doing some of his most productive work.

We crossed the causeway to St. Simons Island. Bill Jones may sell choice oceanfront property for around a quarter of a million a building lot, but he also has a powerful sense of aesthetics; at his insistence, there are no intrusive road signs all the way from Sea Island to Brunswick, which lies across a toll bridge from St. Simons. Jones was on the Brunswick school board, he told us, back in 1930; he and his cousin Howard Coffin had long since begun developing the islands, The Cloister was operating, and Jones found to his dismay that the history books used in his district, texts that had been written up North, characterized the entire Georgian coast south of Savannah as a low-lying malaria-infested area that was both uninhabitable and uninhabited. It took him several years, but eventually he got the offending volumes replaced by ones with descriptions he could recognize.

One of our several stops on St. Simons was at the Musgrove Plantation, where Jimmy Carter rested up just after his election. The big estate, formerly one of the homes of Richard J. Reynolds, is now the Georgia home of a grandson of the cigarette man, Smith Bagley. He and his wife, Vicky, who also have a house in Georgetown, are reputedly going to be the chief

Washington social lions of the Carter administration. At the moment, they are in residence here, and Smith Bagley, who welcomed us affably (any friend of Bill Jones etc., etc.), showed us around. He and his wife, he said, didn't stay here themselves when the president-elect was their guest. No room at their own inn. As a sort of bread-and-butter present, Carter—more accurately, the Secret Service—left behind a battery of outdoor floodlights, which go on automatically after dark; not being an Indian giver, the Secret Service, no matter who is living at Musgrove, foots the electric bill.

Now, Bagley went on, some government agency is planning to build a helicopter pad on the marsh out there—across which Mr. Carter trod one day on foot to fish; Bagley himself, because of snakes and alligators, would never dream of trudging across that particular expanse. Inside his main house, he called our attention to a huge alligator, over a fireplace, which, he said, somebody once shot in that self-same marsh. After we had thanked him and moved on, Bill Jones, who had kept politely silent, spoke up, politely but firmly. That alligator over the mantel wasn't bagged in that bog at all, he said, but in a nearby stream, and he could say so with authority; it was he, fifty years or so ago, who shot it. Our knowledgeable chauffeur-interpreter-mentor delivered us safely back to Sea Island in time for our tennis-court reservation. This is, after all, supposed to be a vacation.

Today our tour resumes, and in modest reciprocation for all Bill Jones' attentiveness, we are providing a picnic lunch. We are going by boat—the only way possible—to Sapelo Island, which is off limits to ordinary tourists. The whole island once belonged to Jones' cousin Coffin, and part of it is now a National Estuarine Sanctuary. Aboard the little ferry to Sapelo, Jones tells us that the island is widely regarded as one of the world's most estimable spots for untrammelled estuarine research. He is not at all sure, by the way, that the Secret Service will, with impunity, be able to plant a helicopter pad on the Bagleys' marshland. The state of Georgia, for the last six years, has regarded all marshes within its bounds as precious assets, and has frowned on tinkering with them; why, when the Sea Island Company wanted to dig up a mere forty-foot-square patch of marsh to improve a ladies' tee on its golf course, it required seven months and the permission of six state agencies to accomplish the deed. It is a warmish day, and I am thirsty, and I ask Mr. Jones if it is okay to have a beer from our picnic basket. Of course, he says. I have barely had time for a swig when the captain of our little ship strides up and rips the bottle out of my hand. Verboten. In this one small respect, at least, Bill Jones is not after all either omniscient or omnipotent.

We have our picnic, unchallenged, inside the old mansion on the south end of Sapelo—a spacious residence set in a grove of live oaks which, at this time of year, are garlanded their full majestic length with purple wisteria. Bill Jones shows us the room where President Coolidge slept. Our driver was, in 1928, also Coolidge's driver; he remembers the president as being very voluble when he was being taken around Sapelo. During Coolidge's stay as Coffin's guest, a telephone line was run over from the mainland. When Jimmy Carter goes to St. Simons Island, Smith Bagley told us yesterday, two hundred extra lines are installed. We live in an inflationary era.

Sea Island is not only well-scrubbed, -polished, and -clipped, but also super-organized. There is something going on for all ages at all times— almost like a cruise ship but, blessedly, without a cruise director. (Everybody despises cruise directors, but the last time we encountered one, while we were doing the Greek Islands, the thought fleetingly occurred to me: Look what *he* has to put up with. If I could ever become successfully radicalized by either the political right or left, such dreary middle-of-the-road thoughts would never cross my mind, and I might be a lot better off. But then—here goes the doubting liberal mind again—would I?) Today is a Friday, and Friday night is Family Night, with an outdoor plantation supper—considering the amount of fried chicken I have consumed in the last couple of months, it is a good thing that the poultry industry is so big in Georgia—held down the road, past the cottage area. The swells from The Cloister are transported to the site by a little train. The Smith Bagleys have come over, *en famille*, from St. Simons. Bonfires and torches abound. After peach pie, there are old spirituals rendered by old black men, some of them probably as old as Bill Jones. Later, The Cloister crowd, if I have the right night, will have bingo when it gets back aboard ship.

March 27

This is our second day in a row of little more than pure sybaritic loafing. To cap it all, and since this is our last Sea Island night, we put on our best clothes and betake ourselves to The Cloister for the regular Sunday-night buffet. Still another reason for this self-indulgence is that tomorrow is Ellie's birthday, and we will be in different states, she and David in Florida, Lexy and I somewhere else in Georgia. E. will not consent to go to the hotel, though, until I take an oath steeped in solemnity that I will not undertake to do anything underhanded about a birthday cake. I cannot imagine why she feels this way. She has been agreeably surprised by flaming baked goods and serenading strangers in Kowloon, in Lech, and in North Conway, New Hampshire; is it my fault that we never seem to be at home on her birthday and thus cannot fittingly observe it without creating a scene? But tonight I defer to her wishes. Next year we will get even and encourage the people staying wherever we are to join us in singing "Happy Birthday" twice.

Tomorrow it is Lexy's turn to accompany me on the road for a week. I tell him to stuff himself, though if we receive treatment at all comparable to what we got when David was with me, he might better fast tonight. Dressed up as we have tried to be, our wardrobes are put to shame by the folks around us—everybody in Madras and Lilly Pulitzer prints. This is WASP America at its handsomest, decent, clean-cut, and honest-looking people one and all, not to mention rich; but unless one were a golf nut it is hard to visualize having any *fun* with many of them. Had I ordered a birthday cake, they might not have greeted it with gusto. They fall somewhere in between the sort of crowd you would like to rub elbows with and keep at arm's length.

March 28

Lexy and I have a longish drive—most of the way across the state—to our goal, Americus; but the time goes fast, not because there is anything especially interesting to see (although it behooves me, reportorially, to look), but because we have that special treat city folk can, probably snobbishly, enjoy while riding along rural roads: listening to small-town radio stations. One can get near-mesmerized (the driver of the vehicle must be careful not to let himself go too far) by the country-music-makers and the fundamentalist preachers; both types cry incessantly and despairingly of the misfortunes of humankind, but at least the singers don't keep nagging at their auditors to send a contribution to this or that post office box to assuage their grief. For big-city people like Lexy and me it is good to hear announcements that begin, "If you need to have your cotton ginned," or, on passing through Jessup, to listen to the solemn death notices intoned over its airwaves— accounts of demises that include not only the names of all the relatives (and families around here run to depth) but also of all the pallbearers, active and honorary. Pallbearing in New York, except in egregious instances, is an anonymous burden.

Somewhere along the line we tune in on an item of state news: A woman who has written a book on how to take advantage of Georgia's no-fault divorce law was arrested at three o'clock this morning on the charge of practicing law without a license. Georgia is the only state in the union that prescribes capital punishment for rape; the accredited members of the Georgia bar may think she deserves something worse. But to drag a writer from a bed on this kind of technicality? Can King & Spalding and the other big Atlanta legal factories regard her as *that* dangerous competition? The executive board of P.E.N. has been urged to lend whatever strength we possess to the defense of Larry Flynt, the publisher of *Hustler*, whom I guess we are supporting as a matter of high principle. I would just as soon devote our energies and resources to defending this woman, whoever she is; the chances are that even if she keeps out of jail her probably unillustrated book will net her less than any single one of Flynt's crotch shots.

Small-world Department: As we are passing through Albany, we hear a commercial. "Keep a salesman out of jail, buy a Buick today," it goes. It seems that Huckabee Buick has decreed that any of its salesmen who fails to make a sale today will be locked up by a deputy sheriff and have to stay in custody until five cars are sold. Lexy, shaking his head in wonderment at the commercial mores of southwest Georgia, looks out the window: We are abreast of Huckabee Buick. Personally, I would not care (what a way for a civil libertarian to talk, but this is all part of the liberal dilemma) if all car salesmen were locked up and the keys thrown away. My non-favorite of the species is the one who sold us our last Plymouth. A couple of times a year, he sends us—and I suppose the rest of his patrons; the letter is mass-produced—a missive that always starts off the same way and that, by way of demonstrating his chumminess with us, is in what purports to be his own hand. "I am writting you," it starts. If he is "writting" to many writers, that may cost him at least five used cars a year.

We know we are closing in on Carter Country when at Dawson we pass a National Peanut Research Factory. And soon we are driving through Plains itself. I refuse to slow down. I have made a commitment to myself not to get caught in a tourist trap. But as I press stubbornly on toward Americus, I sense that Lexy is disappointed. And what will he say if there is a post-holiday show-and-tell at his school, and a teacher asks him about his visit to Plains? "Jack wouldn't stop long enough to let me look at it." How will that teacher look at *me* come the next Parents' Evening? Here it is Ellie's birthday, and just because it is my foot that controls the accelerator and the brake I am refusing her son an opportunity to imprint on his memory a birthplace that, while conceivably of less permanent historical importance than Bethlehem, is certainly as consequential as, say, Abilene, Kansas. I should be ashamed of myself.

But I do not turn around. We have an after-dinner engagement in Americus with Stephen Gurr, a professor of history at Georgia South-western College, which is still another outpost of the farflung state university; and I want us first to get checked in and cleaned up and fed. We select the Best Western Motel, where some of the White House press corps put up when the Carters are in hometown residence. (There are no beds for rent in Plains, nine miles away.) When the journalists from Washington are here en masse, I have heard, a press room with special phone lines is set up at the Best Western. When a single representative of *The New Yorker* (which hasn't the faintest notion that he is here) arrives and reaches for the phone in his room to start trying to make appointments for the morrow, he finds to his dismay that outgoing calls can be placed solely by going through the lobby switchboard. Are southwestern Georgians unaware that, for the travelling man, direct dialing may be the greatest invention since the self-starter?

In the light of all that has been printed about integrating churches at

Plains, it is interesting for us to hear, at the Gurrs' after dinner, what the professor has to say about presumably more sophisticated—because so much larger—Americus. "I'd be shocked to see a black person in my church," he says. "I wouldn't be shocked anywhere else except my country club." There is much talk about a controversial school-bond issue, which is to be voted upon any day now. The Georgia Southwestern academic crowd is for it; the John Birchers and other conservatives agin. My putting in a couple of cents' worth of commentary is not altogether appreciated. "We are really getting tired of Northerners coming down here," Professor Gurr says, with a smile, not censoriously but matter-of-factly, "and trying to put us at ease by saying they have problems in South Boston, too." To show further that he means nothing personal, he invites Lexy and me to visit his Coca-Cola Room, an upstairs chamber, or shrine, entirely furnished with bottles, glasses, advertising posters, and other artifacts pertaining to the sainted beverage. Lexy, *aet.* fourteen, says these collectibles look very ancient to him. They are, indeed, the professor replies; it has been his unbending policy not to add anything to his trove of later origin than 1942, the year he was born. That is indeed a time of yore; why, J. Paul Austin and I had been out of college scarcely long enough to celebrate our fifth reunion.

Before we go to sleep, I promise Lexy I'll take him on a guided tour of Plains.

March 30

My first interview yesterday was with an ex-mayor of Americus, J. Frank Myers, who is now practicing law. If I stay in Georgia long enough, I'll learn what all these preliminary "J.'s" stand for. Myers was born in Plains, he tells me; Miss Lillian was the attending nurse, and the doctor who delivered him was the same one who delivered Jimmy. The attorney's life has been much intertwined with the Carter family. He ran for state senate against (and lost to) the president's father; he handles the legal affairs today of the Carter peanut warehouses, and also of Brother Billy. He says that Americus has done little, so far, to capitalize on the notoriety of Plains. "We're numb," he tells me. "We don't seem to understand the significance of what's happened to us."

Back in our car, Lexy and I rode out to Andersonville, the grim Civil War cemetery now under the jurisdiction of the National Park Service; we visited Koinonia Farm, the "Experiment in Christian Living" that had such a hard time of it in the fifties because many white neighbors believed it to be an experiment in interracial living and thus not to be condoned; and we returned to Americus for cocktails with Mary Ann Thomas, who served for a while on a bi-racial committee that Frank Myers, when he was mayor in the early nineteen sixties, instituted in an effort to keep simmering racial tensions from boiling over. Mrs. Thomas wondered if there might not be more serious tensions up *our* way, nowadays, than here in relatively tranquil Americus. Like many other Georgians, she went to New York last summer for the Democratic National Convention. She was in a fancy Upper East Side delicatessen one morning, and was asked by the chap serving her, because of her accent, where she hailed from. When she said "Georgia," another customer, well-dressed and to all outward appearances a gentleman, turned on her savagely, called her a Communist, and added "Carter shits peanuts." She was taken aback and understandably affronted. On behalf of Governor Carey, Mayor Beame, Lexy, and myself, I apologized and begged her forgiveness for the scoundrel's misbehavior. One would like to hope that he was a transient from, say, South Carolina.

The word in Plains this morning is that Billy is out of town. He is demonstrably the Number One Attraction, and his absence is a clear blow to a number of people around me, including Lexy, though I can take it in stride. We board a Carter Country Tour, in a Volkswagen Microbus. Two-fifty a person for a half-hour ride, and a taped commentary fairly well synchronized with the vehicle's course. Our invisible guide points out to us the Baptist church, the peanut warehouse, Cousin Hugh Carter's place, where he grows worms; and some property belonging to Miss Lillian; but inasmuch as there is a barricade across the road leading to the president's house, we get merely a distant glimpse of that. Lexy feels cheated. I try to mollify him, even though it will no doubt spoil his appetite for lunch, with a chocolate peanut-butter ice-cream cone from the Back Porch Café. I have read a lot of nasty things about Plains and tourists, so I probably should note that nobody charged us anything to park in a vacant lot.

In Lumpkin, after a quick trudge around Westville, a restoration—à la Williamsburg or Old Sturbridge—of an 1850 community, we stop for a sandwich at a quick-lunch stand. A black farmhand pulls up on a tractor, asks where we have come from, and when we say "Westville" remarks that we must have a lot of money, to have gone there. (It cost $3.50 for the two of us.) Where are we from? he wonders. New York, I say. He says he knew we were from out of town because I looked nervous. I have never felt more relaxed in my life. He says there is a witch's place in the town square that can probably cure me of whatever it is that ails me. I begin to feel nervous.

We get to the Callaway Gardens barely in time to find a vacant room at its huge Holiday Inn; the place is crowded because it is azalea time and—what site could be better?—the Georgia Horticultural Society is in convention. After checking in, we drive through the gardens, but it is raining so hard that we can't leave the car to stroll along any of the azalea trails. No matter; there are ample roadside azaleas visible between swipes of the windshield wipers. We take refuge inside a greenhouse, where we can enjoy the flora and stay dry. Lexy has his camera with him, gets ready to take a picture while I am several yards away, and signals to me with his free hand. I think—how nice!—that he wants a souvenir color photo of me against a handsome Easter background of banked daisies and lilies, but he waves me impatiently off; it seems he wants me to get behind a door so I won't spoil his shot. His focus is sharper than a serpent's tooth.

We have no plans tonight; no horticultural connections. After a buffet dinner—there is but one kind of buffet in Georgia, and by now I well know its constituent parts: ham, yam, fried chicken, catfish and/or shrimp—we retire to our room. Lexy is overjoyed. At last, for him, an evening of unalloyed TV pleasure. No journeys down dark uncharted streets to professors' or divorcees' homes to sit mutely and politely while Jack drones on interminably asking these people how they think Georgia differs from other places or whether or not Oglethorpe invented Coca-Cola or whatever it is he is constantly gabbing about, but a chance, finally, to watch "Happy Days" or "Good Times" or whatever is on the delicious electronic menu this rare night. The rain gets worse. A thunderstorm is brewing. Lightning strikes what feels like a few feet away. The television set goes dark. So do all the rest of the lights as far as one can see. When they come back on, a half hour or so later, the telly doesn't.

March 31

E. has often told me, in loving jest, I like to think, that my snoring is worse than thunder. This morning I ask Lexy, than whom no one has ever been in a better position to judge, which is truly the more intolerable. Heredity scores another triumph over environment: He votes for snoring.

While I am licking that wound, I pull out a road map, to figure out this day's itinerary. I want to end up at Athens, the hub of higher education in the state, by nightfall. I had planned en route to visit Franklin D. Roosevelt's Georgia cottage, and my finger traces the way to Warm Springs. My eye simultaneously crosses the nearby Georgia-Alabama border, and it is arrested by a place name. Gadsden. *Gadsden.* But that is where the Nadlers, Lexy's maternal ancestors, came from! It is only a couple of hundred miles from where we are right now. "Roots" is on the best-seller lists. Who am I to deny Lexy, so recently a proven champion of heredity, a chance to dig into his own origins? Anyway, if we go to Alabama (he can read about Warm Springs some day when he gets older) and come back, it will give *me* a chance to ascertain how it feels to enter Georgia from a neighboring deep-South state. That could be very important for a conscientious investigative reporter.

This Callaway Gardens motel, as Woodward and Bernstein would surely appreciate, *does* have direct dialing, and in a trice I am connected with Sarasota, where Ellie is spending a few days with her mother, and I ask E.

to ask Lucile Nadler Munro just where it was in Gadsden that Jacques Nadler built his furniture store and the house she was raised in. Fourth Avenue and Chestnut Street for the store, comes the prompt nostalgic response, one block over, down Fifth, for the house, a two-story brick residence. We can't miss it.

LaGrange, Georgia, is on our way to Alabama. *It* is the home town of J. Paul Austin. I espy no historical plaques. Maybe these are among the ones that have fallen down and have not been replaced. But there do seem to be more Coca-Cola signs, and fewer ones for Pepsi, Royal Crown, and that lot, than in most of the Georgia hamlets we have traversed. A Gulf station brazenly displays signs for *both* Coke and Pepsi—thereby declaring itself, I infer, a no-man's land in the all-out soft-drink war. When I muse on this, aloud, Lexy asserts, flatly and shockingly, that in his opinion Pepsi tastes better than Coke. Luckily, we are close to the Alabama border and can probably get across it if anybody has overheard him and has mustered a posse in pursuit. But who *teaches* our children these subversive beliefs?

The Bugg Furniture Company is located at Fourth and Chestnut, in downtown Gadsden. High on the façade of its building, carved irremovably in stone, we make out "Nadler 1903." Lexy has his camera at the ready again, and this time he does not object to personalizing pictures. I lie supine on the sidewalk, aim up, and hope I have got him and his ancestor's lofty chiselled imprimatur in the same frame. I have contrived cleverly to arrive in Gadsden at one-thirty, just after what I assume to be the Alabama business lunch hour, but nobody has told me that Alabama and Georgia, conceivably just to spite interstate investigative reporters and their retinues, are in different time zones.

Thus it is twelve-thirty in Gadsden, and the only operative visible on the Bugg premises, when we saunter genealogically inside, is a salesman. He is trying to persuade a pregnant young woman with her hair in curlers to grab, while it is still available, a three-piece dinette set, for $189.95. A real bargain. I clear my throat, ask for Mr. Bugg, and announce sonorously that the young man at my side is none other than a great-grandson of the very self-same Mr. Nadler who founded this enterprise, and whose name is carved topside. The salesman says to me, curtly, that Mr. Bugg is out to lunch and says to Miss Curlers of 1977, at greater length and with more passion, that if one searched the ends of the earth for a better buy in three-piece dinette sets, one would assuredly search in vain. He makes the set sound so good that I am tempted to bid on it myself.

Lexy takes some indoor shots (his flash attachment unfortunately failing him in the clutch) for his grandmother, and we slink out and head for Fifth Avenue, where we soon come upon a two-story brick house that seems perfectly to fit our telephoned description. He uses up the remaining film on the exterior of that. Then, as we are driving down the avenue, looking for a suitable place for a U-turn, we come upon another two-story brick affair.

There is a man sitting on its porch. We ask him if we were correct in assuming that the building behind us was the old Nadler residence. No, he says, *this* is it, and he is the present owner, and how in the world did we know the name "Nadler"? I introduce Lexy to *him*. They shake hands very formally. The owner offers to show us inside. The establishment has changed. It has been chopped up into one- and two-room apartments for singles—elderly men who, I gather from a sign in the downstairs hallway, cannot altogether be trusted. The sign says that there is to be positively no consumption of alcoholic beverages on the premises. There is no need to tell Lucile all this.

We make it to Athens, after a dogged day's drive, in time to keep a dinner engagement with Richard Harwell, the University of Georgia's curator of rare books, its authority on Margaret Mitchell and Erskine Caldwell, and the author of a scholarly treatise on the mint julep. He introduces us to Greer's, a restaurant in an old Athenian home, where I am just as glad that nobody proposes we drink mint juleps. Harwell says the university is a splendid place—with one exception. It has a good campus, a good faculty, and a good library. Lexy wonders what else a first-rate academic institution could possibly need. Good students, he is told crisply. Like many other Georgians we have met, the erudite Harwell is an unapologetic sports fan. He says that when the Bulldogs played the Alabama eleven here last fall, twenty thousand people who couldn't get into the sixty-thousand-capacity stadium clung to a bridge and to a railroad trestle in order to have at least some glimpse of the storied contest.

Our motel is full of cowgirls, who seem to have galloped in from Texas. There is a rodeo in town. Lexy implores me to take him to it tomorrow night. But tomorrow, I remind him, we have a dinner date with a history professor. Lexy groans and says that he thought this trip was supposed to be a *vacation* from education. I promise we will do something special for lunch. Lexy bets me a thousand dollars lunch will turn out to be with somebody like an art teacher.

April 1

I am lucky. I have contrived, on exceedingly short notice, to set up a lunch date with the distinguished painter Lamar Dodd, who largely organized and for many years, until his recent retirement, presided over the university's Department of Fine Arts. Lexy says I owe him a grand. I say that on April Fool's Day foolish bets don't count. Dodd and his wife, Mary, take us for lunch to the university's Center for Continuing Education, where he is warmly and respectfully greeted by waitresses and customers alike, and where, before we depart, Lexy is thoroughly appeased by the most

extravagant slab of strawberry ice cream cake he has ever confronted.*
Professor Dodd thinks that the students at the U. of Ga. are quite
intellectually presentable; one cannot judge from where we sit, because this
center is largely for adult-education programs—seminars, our host tells us,
in everything from hair-dressing to tombstone-carving.

Lexy and I take a drive in the afternoon, so I can have a look, before I
finish my research, at the city of Washington; we return to Athens for
dinner with Phinizy Spalding and his wife. Our host's name is a
combination of two historic Georgia surnames, and it is fitting that he is a
professor of history, an expert on James Oglethorpe, and the editor of the
Georgia Historical Quarterly. The Spaldings live not far from Milledge Road,
the main Athens residential thoroughfare in times past, lined on both sides
with sprawling Greek-revival mansions. (Many of these now belong to
Greek-letter fraternities.) We dine at a restaurant occupying part of the
city's no-longer-used railroad station. The one-time white waiting room is
now the eating area, the one-time colored waiting room the bar. A neatly
integrated establishment.

April 3

We are back in New York, after an easy two-day drive. It could have been
quicker, but just as I had taken pains to look at what is often considered the
southernmost landmark of the big state, the lighthouse at Tybee Island
(actually, it is considerably north of the Florida border, being just south of
Savannah), so I did feel impelled to look at, and drive through, Rabun Gap,
Tybee Light's north-Georgia counterpart. We didn't get to see much. We
shot the gap in a heavy fog. On the other side of it, on US #40 in North
Carolina, we were flagged down by a state trooper. I was caught a year ago
at almost exactly the same spot. But this time, like last, I was let off with a
warning. When Ellie hears this, she will be furious. I generally drive faster
than she does, but she always gets tickets, I only get warnings. I have tried
to explain to her that the trick (except on US #40 in North Carolina) is
never to look ahead of you when you drive but to concentrate on your rear-
and side-view mirrors. Yesterday's trooper described my fleet chariot on his
cautionary notice as a 1972 Plymouth. That made *me* furious. I know our

---

* My ignorance prevents Lexy from having a chance two days in a row to muse on
his roots. It turns out when we get back home, and I mention our lunch with Dodd
to Ellie, that Lexy's maternal grandfather, the aesthetician Thomas Munro, was one
of the artist's close friends.

wagon is well along in years, but it is a *1973* model, damn it. I am getting oversensitive about age.

Adults and children react differently to the same circumstances and experiences. At a Holiday Inn last night in Hendersonville, North Carolina, I was upset because the diehard guests at a wedding reception made too much noise and kept me awake. Lexy, who says I am a fine one to be complaining about noise keeping me from sleeping considering that the noise I make when I *am* sleeping is a far louder cause of insomnia, is upset because he put a quarter in a mechanical-game machine in the motel lobby, and the contraption didn't work, and because he then put another quarter in a bed-vibrating machine in our room, and that contraption *did* work. He wanted it to stop, so he could fall off to sleep before the terminal nuptial celebrants stopped and I began to snore.

We reach New York this evening in time for me to go with E. to dinner at the Phil Hamburgers'. A predominantly *New Yorker* crowd—the Bill Maxwells and Geoffrey Hellmans being among the other guests. Geoffrey, who doesn't look well, says with the kind of authority I wish I could muster that all speculation about Shawn's successor is immaterial because Bill— who like Geoffrey is approaching three score and ten—will be presiding over the editorial scene for a long while to come. Everybody present seems to be time-conscious. Anna Hamburger asks me if I don't agree that a writer can only write three hours a day. I disagree, but not, in my reply to her, as emphatically as I would like to; I do not wish to rock any boats in case Phil has convinced her that one hundred and eighty minutes is as long as any wife can reasonably expect any writing husband to stick to his last, keep his nose to the grindstone, and stare prayerfully at his typewriter. Quite apart from whether a writer *can* write three hours a day is whether many of those at *The New Yorker* do so. Most of the staff writers have offices, either at the magazine like Hellman and Hamburger, on the twentieth floor, or, like me, on the eighteenth. (Shawn, on the nineteenth, is the sandwich meat between those of us who thus try to earn our bread.) I don't get up to the twentieth floor often, except when I need a check in a hurry from editorial accounting, which is also berthed there, but if that level at all resembles ours, then three hours a day may be an overgenerous estimate of its average productivity.

April 4

After being away from New York, one weekend excepted, for nearly a month, I have a lot to catch up with at home. My sister Joan reports that Tony and Judy got married last week. I must be old-fashioned: I think that when one of my sons takes that step I should hear the news first from him. True, this wedding is not a cataclysmic event; their baby was a year old last month. Still, it is the kind of family tidings that I would prefer not to learn at second hand. During my absence, Joan and Olivia have made one of their reticular pilgrimages to Tucson, to visit Jaime. My older grandson is fine, they inform me, but they disapprove of his maternal grandmother's new boy friend. I cannot see that this is really any of their business. But then to be a great-maiden-aunt can't be easy; everybody is always trying to keep you from running things.

Ellie has more news. She is about to sign a contract for a book about women artists. There is to be some kind of a tie-in with a series on public-service television. Because her deadline is next fall, she will have to work straight through (no three-hour-a-day business here), and accordingly, instead of renting the Truro house for a month, we'll be able to occupy it all summer ourselves. I must arrange to have the tennis court curried into shape.

April 6

Played squash yesterday with Bob Bingham, who now sometimes uses the grand title of executive editor of *The New Yorker*. If I am going to be beaten, as I was, it somehow feels better to lose to somebody so highly placed. At lunch afterward, I was complaining, as writers always do to editors when they have their ear, about the difficulty of getting finished pieces into the magazine. Bob said that *The New Yorker* is fundamentally no different from any other institution. I was in the Army, wasn't I? Well, then, don't I know that it is the squeaky wheel that gets greased?

I had planned, on returning to the office, to sit right down and start in on the long and tedious task of indexing and organizing my stack of Georgia notes. Instead, I wrote a squeaky memo to Shawn. I knew he wouldn't answer it directly; he is singularly averse to committing himself to anything in writing; but I had a few things to get off my chest. (One that I left there was that I took a dim view of his running a piece by Trillin about Georgia while I was doing research on and in Georgia.) I did, though, remind him, for one thing, that he had had a Talk of the Town piece of mine lying around in type now for five or six months, on the venerable Chinese statesman and diplomat Wellington Koo, and that Koo had been eighty-eight when I wrote it. I took Ellie along when I had tea with the old man, something I don't normally do on interviews. But she is much interested in Chinese history, and it would have been mean of me to deny her a chance to meet someone who was foreign minister of China when Mao Tse-tung was an obscure librarian.

There was a lot of office gossip to catch up on, moreover—nearly enough to make it impossible for me to think Georgia at all, and more than enough to satiate Bob Shaplen, whose latest letter from Hong Kong chided me for

191

not having transmitted more juicy tidbits when I wrote him last. Edith Oliver, who is widely conceded to have the nineteenth-floor gossip concession, said that both Ved Mehta and Dick Harris have been awarded Guggenheim fellowships, apparently to help sustain them while they are working on long pieces that will, she and I imagine, ultimately appear in *The New Yorker*. It seems odd to me that a foundation should pay toward the production of something that the magazine will pay for, too; but I suppose if anybody made me a comparable offer, I would jump at it. Andy Logan, who has the eighteenth-floor concession (the twentieth is too far removed for me to know who has the franchise there; Gill, most likely), told me that somebody had told her that somebody else had overheard somebody say at a Doubleday bookstore that the next editor of *The New Yorker* was going to be Burt Bernstein. How about that, Shaplen!

At breakfast this morning, E. says I am trying to commit suicide by smoking, and I promise once again to stop. I hold out for three hours. Not bad. When page proofs of the Talk section for next week's issue are distributed, who should step forth to greet me but Wellington Koo! Few squeaks can have been so swiftly lubricated. Shawn must be to grease jobs what Midas is to mufflers. The checkers have brought the piece up to date. Koo is now eighty-nine. I plan to get down to work on my Georgia notes as soon as I have gone over my Koo proof and have written to Shaplen, or certainly right after lunch.

John Cushman's office is in the same building as mine, and when the literary agent and I meet on the sidewalk this afternoon, both of us looking for a taxi, it develops—Who says New York doesn't have any attributes of a small town?—that we have the same destination: a cocktail party Lois and Rolf Myller are giving uptown for a visiting English historian. John is his agent. When we arrive, Cushman introduces me to the guest of honor as "Jack Kahn," and Aaron Asher, who is standing alongside me, reprimands him and says he should have used my full byline.

We all have our troubles. Ever since Alfred Frankfurter died, Ellie has been getting Social Security checks for her children. The other day, she received a computerized communication, relating thereto, from the Internal Revenue Service; it was addressed to "David Frankilfermer Minor, Eleanor M. Kalu Guar." This morning, I noticed a bill, on Ellie's dresser, from her analyst, who spells her name "Monroe." A dollar a minute and she can't even get her patient's byline straight! Or does the analyst not know that Eleanor Munro is a writer? If she doesn't, what then do the two of them talk about? Me? Self-flattery will get me nowhere. I retained a lawyer once, to help me clear the title to a piece of property, and after several months he phoned one day and said he had things well in hand, but there were one or two matters he had to ask me about and could I drop by his office? I did, and waited breathlessly for his first question. "Tell me, Mr. Kahn," it went, "how do you spell your name?"

I leave the cocktail party early, because I have to pick up E. and take her to dinner at the Harry Kahns'. No relation. When we arrive, we find Harry and Margery, and Marjorie Iseman, at the dining room table. We were supposed to come *next* Wednesday. Margery K. says we haven't missed much anyway; she and Harry and their cook are all on a crash diet and, collectively, have lost seventy pounds in the last several weeks. Marjorie I. reflects that if they keep up this pace, in no time at all they will have caused the disappearance of the equivalent of a whole person. The mix-up of dates gives E. and me a chance to do something we often have talked about—to wander around the Upper East Side and stumble across a jewel of a restaurant that we can forever after treasure as our very own discovery. We come upon a place that looks attractive, and we go in and sit down and have dinner and get up and walk out and agree that this particular jewel is made of paste.

April 8

At lunch yesterday with S. L., he brought his son along. S. said morosely that he and his wife have sort of gone to war, and that the son is living with them temporarily to act as a buffer. I told S. that the colony of Georgia was set up, in 1733, to serve as a buffer between South Carolina and the warlike Spanish of St. Augustine, and that that eventually worked out pretty well for all concerned, but the parallel did not seem to cheer him up. I must get cracking on my Georgia piece.

This is our next-to-last Friday-morning tennis session before the winter season ends. Because of Georgia, I haven't played recently. Damn Georgia! Why couldn't we have elected a president from a smaller and newer and simpler state? Iowa, for instance. I bet if I were doing Iowa I'd have the piece half organized by now. E. and I take Lexy down to the Village Gate tonight for Elizabeth Swados' "Nightclub Cantata"—eight lively young people, with piano and percussion, acting out poems set to her music, a bit repetitious but on the whole engaging. ("Lively . . . Engaging"—Kahn, *Journal.*) We buy eight-dollar seats, but they are poorly located, so I pay an additional four-fifty and exchange them for nine-fifty seats, in which section we are joined, as soon as the lights dim, by all the other people who have bought eight-dollar seats. There is a lesson here, but I don't know quite what it is.

April 11

I have spent three days mostly in bed, with what I have diagnosed as the flu, although someone with more objectivity might call it not writing. I got in some reading. One of my sister Joan's Dick Francis mysteries. He is one of the few of her authors whom I consistently enjoy. Jack Dempsey's autobiography, a bore. John Gardner's "October Light," a delight—and, since it is a novel within a novel, two delights for the price of one. Being sick can bring one unexpected rewards. I got to watch the last two rounds of the Masters, at Augusta, on the color TV set in our bedroom, with no interruptions and no remonstrances. Ellie says, "Men are always at their nicest when they're sick. It's because they get doted on." She is undoubtedly correct. Women often get doted on, though, as their spouses vowed to do at the outset, both in sickness and in health.

April 12

I arise from my bier because there is a rehearsal, this afternoon, for the show we are putting on at the Harvard Club tonight during the pre-fortieth-reunion dinner. Taking special care of myself, I don a vest for the trip downtown, and feel uncomfortably warm all day. Ellie makes me take a thermometer with me, but I don't dare check my temperature, lest it turn out that I have one. Late in the afternoon, after sweating through the rehearsal, I see by a headline in the *Post* that the outside temperature has risen to eighty-nine—the highest on record for this day ever. I feel better at once.

E., who has precious little use for these old-grad get-togethers, sportingly comes to the dinner notwithstanding, and she is introduced to the faithful who materialize for these nostalgic affairs—Charlie Thieriot and Phil Straus, Herb Jaques up from Boca Grande, Rusty Crawford from the Bowery (the Savings Bank), but not Paul Austin from Atlanta; Gibby Gibson from Akron, Jim Honeywell, Dick Axten, and Bill Bentinck-Smith down from Boston (but not Harry Kahn from upper Park Avenue), and so on and so on. G. C., who brought his third wife to our last reunion, confides that he has since remarried. I ask if his fourth is coming tonight. No, he says, she has a concussion. Sounds as though he may be getting ready for his fifth. Floyd Haskell, the only member of the Working Class who has worked himself into the United States Senate (D., Colo.), asks what I am up to these days, and when I mention that I am trying, with little success so far, to get a visa for South Africa, he offers to help. I cannot remember offhand which committees he sits on, but it can't hurt to have a U.S. senator in one's corner. I will remind him.

Paul Killiam, as always, is directing and starring in the class show, which tonight is supposed to be a "roast" of Bob Watson, our First Marshal, who announced his retirement as of this spring as director of athletics at Harvard. The high spot of the show is the presentation to Watson—this part is on the level, and has required quite some doing—of varsity letters from all the seven Ivy League institutions save Harvard. (Bob earned his "H" as an undergraduate—football and crew.) It isn't until we are all assembled at the club tonight that it occurs to anybody that no individual, probably, has ever before received all eight Ivy League letters. Archer Trench phones the *Times* sports desk, but can arouse no enthusiasm. While we are at cocktails, a young man in the room, a friend of the piano player Killiam has hired for the entertainment, discloses that *he* works for the *Times*, and we try to give him the exclusive story. He says sorry, he is an op.-ed.-page man himself, and therefore naturally can do nothing in sports. The hell with it; I will write Red Smith about it one of these days.

April 13

Patrick Smith is an uncommon brother-in-law. He shares his mail with me. As a music critic, he is on lists I could never hope to make. Today, for instance, I receive his forwarded invitation to attend the gala opening of the Jack Kahn Piano and Organ Showrooms. This makes three outside Jack Kahns who have thrust themselves upon my consciousness. No. 1 was an amateur golfer in Westchester County, who, when I was a kid, was good enough to get his name, in small type, in the sports pages. No. 2 was a restaurateur in Sarasota, Florida, in whose establishment I once pointedly threw *my* name around, hoping, no doubt, for a free drink or some such; unfortunately, he was off the premises that night. And now, a triumvirate. Could these other Jacks all be the same Kahn? Hardly likely. Did they start off life as John Jacks, or Jacques Jacks, or something else? Could they be related to the toy people? When Terry, Joey, and Tony were young, they liked to go down to the Scarborough railroad station now and then, and stand on the footbridge that spanned the tracks, and watch trains roll past under their feet. One day what did their wondering eyes—not to mention mine—perceive but two freight cars bearing on their sides the legend "E. J. Kahn Toy Co., Chicago, Ill." It was not easy to convince them that they were growing up in a world of extraordinary coincidences.

My sons' mother and I have one of our periodic lunches. Jinny is going to quit her job this fall as head of the Off Off Broadway Alliance (which I have never been able to bring myself to call "Ooba"), sell her apartment, and move to New England, preferably Boston. She says she can't afford to live in New York any longer. Neither can I, but I don't know where else to go. Jinny also complains of being in too high a tax bracket. That strikes me as paradoxical, and in any event she picked a bad day to raise this issue: I have to go see our tax man this afternoon, and this morning I mailed off my monthly alimony check. When and if she does unload her co-op, she wants my sisters and me to take back my mother's books, which have been shelved there since we split up. There are hundreds and hundreds, maybe thousands. Where in the world will we put them? Ellie and I have already built two now-crowded sets of shelves since I moved into 1095 Park. We are running out of blank walls, and one does like to have space enough to display a few pictures. Joan keeps talking about buying some old lady's apartment as soon as the incumbent dies, but that will turn out to be the kind of old lady who outlives everyone on the block.

When, after lunch, Ellie phones and asks me to accompany her down to the World Trade Center, to look at a big Frankenthaler painting that Helen is displaying there, I volunteer heroically—one might even say eagerly—to stop what I am doing and go along. After all, I have never been to the Trade Center. One should savor every new experience that life puts forth. Would I want it to be said that I was a person so narrowly focused on Georgia that I rejected the World Trade Center, let alone Frankenthaler, out of hand? I sweep my research into a corner and head for the street. Helen is on the scene herself, this exceedingly hot spring day, supervising the installation of her piece, which measures thirty-one by sixteen feet and which I last gawked at a decade ago when I covered Expo 67, in Montreal.

It is sister Joan's birthday; the obligatory party this evening is at Olivia's. Edith Oliver is there, of course; also the Shawns. I mention to Bill that I am keeping a journal this year, and that it has in it some reminiscences about *The New Yorker*. Do I see, or merely imagine, a flicker of dismay cross his face? On the other hand, that fleeting reaction may have been relief: Here is one work-in-progress, he can be thinking to himself, that I won't have to worry about not serializing in the magazine without hurting the author's feelings.

Joan says, as she has before, that she has submitted a letter of resignation to Harper & Row, after all these many years, because—I forget what the reason is this time. Once I ran into her boss, Win Knowlton, not long after she'd told me she was quitting. Win said that he had received so many letters of resignation from her that he no longer bothered to read them. I myself decide about once a year to sever all connections with *The New Yorker*. I cannot exactly resign, since I am not exactly employed, but I could give up my office and my perks, and have written Shawn quite a few letters proposing to do just that forthwith and so forth. But I have never delivered any of them. He might read one, and take me up on it. I have learned—for the most part—never to mail a letter written in heat until it has cooled overnight. Then it almost invariably sounds stupid.

April 14

The morning *Times* discloses some of the details of President Carter's proposed energy program. Ellie's sister Cynthia is staying with us for a couple of days, having flown in from Cleveland for a psychologists' symposium. At breakfast, Cynnie notices that we have a Cuisinart in our kitchen and says, to my ear rather accusingly, that in this time of national crisis we shouldn't be indulging ourselves in a contraption that consumes so much energy. I haven't yet had enough coffee to dilute my short temper and cannot resist the rejoinder that we could save far more energy than this little machine eats up if people like me didn't have to turn on electric lights early so they could get out of bed early so they could go to work early and earn enough money to provide enough tax revenue for the government to underwrite practically nonstop assemblies, week in and week out, of itinerant social scientists.

Ellie's sororal rejoinder to my rejoinder is that by charging *The New Yorker* for part of our stay at Sea Island I am, in a manner of speaking, using Cynnie's tax money to underwrite my family's skeet shooting. And indeed, when I reach the office, Sheila McGrath comes by to ask about something on my Sea Island bill, which I have attached to one of my Georgia expense vouchers, which she finds it hard to believe I should be reimbursed for— "teenage dance." After I have managed to explain to Sheila's satisfaction that the portion of our charges there that I allocated to myself and to the magazine does *not* include that terpsichorean item, she sits down and muses upon expense accounts in general. Sheila says that much of the history of *The New Yorker* could be written from the photocopies she has stashed away of zany expense accounts writers have submitted, though she does not, unfortunately, offer to open her files to me.

There was one meticulous woman writer, Sheila says, now retired, who years ago would in her accounts specify every nickel she shelled out for every subway ride. When once the woman asked to be repaid two dollars and forty-five cents she had spent on transportation, she felt it incumbent on her to append a lengthy explanation of the unusual outlay. She had got off the Staten Island ferry and, as she was walking toward the subway, had been propositioned, and in her panic had leapt into a taxicab. Sheila reflects that anybody who could have taken that particular writer for a hooker must have been nearly as weird a character as some of those now active in our midst.

Today's papers tell of a "rap-store" proprietor who has been arrested because an ex-hooker, a real one, entered his premises, ostensibly applying for a conversationalist's job, with a tape recorder in her purse. She was accordingly later able to furnish the district attorney's office with a vivid account of all the peculiar activities employment there would have entailed her to engage in. Times have changed.

On the way to work, incidentally, Cynnie and I took the subway together, and she wanted to know if I always wore a jacket and shirt and tie. Why, of course, I said; they are my city uniform. She says her husband, John, never wears a suit coat in Cleveland; he did buy a sports jacket, once, but he looked unfamiliar to her in it, so he put it away. I didn't know Cleveland was that much more informal than New York. Cyrus Eaton

197

wears a necktie on his farm out there. But he is almost seventy years older than John, and I guess customs change.

Shawn sticks his head in my doorway to say, in further response to my shrill memo, that he hopes to run my Princeton piece next month. He doesn't mention another matter I raised—the possibility of my making a return trip to Micronesia one of these months, or years. Having been there twice already, I try to keep up with what's going on, and quite a bit has been: the separation from the rest of the Trust Territory of the Pacific Islands, for instance, of the Northern Marianas; and, more recently, some talk of establishing, in the Palau District of the Western Carolines, a multibillion-dollar oil-storage facility on the big and largely unsettled island of Babelthuap. I haven't nosed around those parts for seven years; I would like to get back before my sources forget me, or die. (One of them is, or was at the time he visited us at Truro, the only Yapese ever to swim in Cape Cod Bay—and what a swimmer!) If ever any *New Yorker* writer had a part of the globe that he could claim to be his very own exclusive staked-out territory, Micronesia is *mine*. I am tempted to remind Bill of my query now, but he looks busy and I have to rush off downtown for a P.E.N. executive board meeting.

Much of the session is devoted to a discussion of a writers-in-prison program, to which, I am astounded to learn, we devote something like one-ninth of our entire annual budget. And this, mind you, isn't to help, à la Amnesty International, imprisoned writers. It is to help prisoners who think they'd like to take up writing. Well, I suppose that is a respectable step up from murder or rape. Bel Kaufman is sitting next to me. We both doodle. She cannot resist whispering, after a sidelong glance, that her doodling is far superior to mine. She is absolutely correct, no question about it, but why does she have to rub it in? I think she is trying to get even for the time I put her in her place in a crossword-puzzle race.

April 15

Bob Blinken set up a lunch at the Harvard Club today for Irwin Shaw and me. It has got to be ten or fifteen years since I last saw Irwin. He has put on weight. So, he may have noticed, have I. He is also in a state of understandable euphoria; he plans to write the last sentences of a 175,000-word novel—a sequel to his "Rich Man, Poor Man"—this very afternoon. There is no television money to be made from it, Irwin says, because ABC owns all the TV rights to his "Rich Man" characters. Still, his paperback sales have been phenomenal since the television series became such a big hit. There is much talk of Klosters, where Bob skis and where Irwin has been living, most of the time, for a quarter of a century. I can't identify half the people under discussion; the closest I've been to Klosters is Lech, but that is in the *Austrian* Alps. I used to ski a lot with Irwin, before he became an emigré, but that was, prosaically, in New England.

One great thing about Irwin Shaw has always been that even when he isn't finishing a book he seems so exuberant; he is an unapologetic hedonist, and I suspect that his affability and jollity have had as much as anything else to do with the fact that solemn critics are forever putting him down as a mere storyteller not to be alluded to in any profound discussion of serious literature. Irwin's attitude has always seemed to me to be: Let them wear hair shirts; cashmere's more comfortable. Irwin spends a great deal of time laughing, the ability to engage in which (hyenas obviously aside) is surely one of the important differences between human beings and lesser animals. Most of the literary critics I know, and I guess I have bumped into the majority of them by now, seem to go out of their way to practice looking glum, laughter being in their view perhaps incontrovertible evidence of frivolity.

Irwin tells me, solemn for an instant, that Al Capp is seriously ill, and that Al's family wants somebody to do a biography of him while there's still time. Irwin has been approached, and begged off; but, he wonders, inasmuch as I did Capp's Profile for *The New Yorker* years ago, would I be interested? Apparently there is a big deal already set with a publisher. Yes, I would be interested; I am not as hedonistic as Irwin, but I enjoy spending money whenever I can lay my hands on it. And Capp might be interesting to write about at length, depending on how he and I get on nowadays. We didn't get on at all well for a while after my *New Yorker* stuff on him came out. But that was long ago, and Capp certainly has had a life worth exploring—the liberal in the McCarthy days who turned conservative in the campus-upheaval days, an authentic American iconoclast, in some ways not unlike Mencken. I never found him a particularly attractive person, however. No matter; one doesn't have to be fond of one's subjects. Irwin says he will tell the family to get in touch with me.

A theatrical evening tonight—a Town School benefit performance of the revival of "The King and I," once again starring Yul Brynner. Our school group, parents and children together, are served box lunches in the theatre lobby, but the kids somehow quiet down before the rest of the audience turns up—a suave black-tie gang transported by chartered buses from a cocktail party—the Sam Reeds escorting Charlie Baskerville, for instance— who bought *their* tickets on behalf of the Madison Avenue Boys Club.

The first time I saw "The King and I," Brynner was playing opposite Gertrude Lawrence, and I am nostalgically partial to what my hazy memory tells me about that 1951 production. During the entr'acte, Ellie and I wonder how old Brynner is now. Lexy figures he is about forty-five, which would make the actor fifteen years younger than me, and, I suspect, probably even more years than that younger than himself. When in the final scene the old King of Siam lies down and dies, I cry a little. At home, later,

Ellie says that when she asked me at the theatre why I was so touched, I did not respond satisfactorily, and that my failure to do so was clear evidence of my uncommunicativeness. But, as I try to explain to her, unsatisfactorily, I cry at all *kinds* of things, good and bad, often when I am really not touched at all. I have no rational explanation for it. So what could I have communicated? That I was sorry Gertrude Lawrence couldn't be around tonight to watch Yul Brynner die? She would probably have been too old, alas, to play her old-time part.

April 16

The *Times* says that Andrew Young has stated in answer to a question that the government of South Africa is illegitimate. That is nonsense, of course; according to its own disagreeable laws, it is thoroughly up and up. Ambassador Young's analysis, moreover, is not likely to prove helpful to other Americans, wherever and whoever they are, whose visas are pending. Happily, I cannot be accused of being Young's buddy; he hasn't even answered a letter about Georgia I wrote him weeks ago.

April 17

There have been temporary defections from Ellie's Sunday-tennis ranks, and I am invited to go along, *vice* Jimmy Greenfield, and play mixed doubles with her against John Chancellor and some female substitute John has recruited in lieu of *his* regular court inamorata. One thing, though: I am not to hit the ball hard. John is newish at the game, E. says, definitely a cut beneath me, and whatever my curious motivation may be in the yelling, racquet-flinging set-tos that seem to give me so much incomprehensible pleasure, *this* tennis is supposed to be for *fun*. To my surprise, the first time E. has the serve, Chancellor returns the balls to me at net like rockets. I think E. is slightly surprised, too, and a bit irritated. She really belts her third serve to him. I walk back to her half of the court and remind her to take it easy; this is supposed to be *fun*.

April 18

E. says at breakfast that her friend P. told her that at a dinner party the other night George Steiner said he was going to Chicago, and somebody asked if he knew Harold Rosenberg, and when he said he didn't, the third party said he'd give George a note so the two critics could get acquainted. Oh, no, P. says George said: It was Mr. Shawn's fixed policy that no two

New Yorker contributors could get together unless he personally authorized such communion. If people who write for the magazine actually go around talking like this in public, no wonder so much of the public thinks we are crazy, and poor maligned Shawn the nuttiest of the lot. I suppose Bob Bingham and I should request permission (retroactively) to play squash.

In the morning office mail, a free copy of the palindromically titled "Look Ma, I Am Kool," a collection of short humor pieces edited (could this be the source of the bookshop rumor?) by Burton Bernstein. These, as Burt observes in his proem, are what we call "casuals" around the magazine, for want of any better term for a genre that can embrace fiction, non-fiction, and hybrids. Burt explains that the contributors to his anthology are the younger set. I don't make that set—nor, for that matter, the older set. As a casual writer, I have fallen between two stools—a casual casualty, you could say. If only my name were Eros, I could be palindromically sore.

Al Capp's sister Madaleine calls. She and her older brother, Elliott Caplin, have arranged a "whopping" package deal *in re* his biography, and would I have lunch with them Wednesday at the Yale Club and talk about it? I will be there. I phone Monica McCall at once to tell her of our incipient good fortune, but she receives the news, as I suppose any sensible literary agent would and should, with something less than glee. She says that without having any specific figures at her fingertips to prove it, she would guess that eighty-five per cent of all negotiations that begin with a whoop end up with a whisper, or just plain silence. But she urges me to go to lunch anyway; she hears that the Yale Club food isn't half bad.

Our friend Talat Halman, who was briefly Turkish minister of culture, is giving a lecture tomorrow at the United Nations, and the Turkish ambassador to the U.N. is kicking off the event with a cocktail party this afternoon at his Gracie Square apartment. Many Turks there, and myriad hors d'oeuvres, most of these made of one ingredient stuffed inside another. My sisters are among the infidel guests, and E. and I go with them afterward for a bite of something plainer at Martell's, where, as usual, I get into an argument with Joan. Tonight she is taking the affirmative in the debate, "Resolved: That it is a grandfather's ultimate responsibility, rather than a father's, to bring up the latter's children." It had never occurred to me before that there were two sides to this one, but then Joan's whole life has been grandparentally oriented. She is also mad at me for having raised my children in the suburbs—principally, I would retort if we were debating that topic, because she lives in the city and doesn't know how to drive. A bad end to the evening, not improved any by our learning, a moment before our departure, that Joan was under the misapprehension that she was paying her first visit to Maxwell's Plum.

April 19

I learn from Bob Bingham that a young woman candidate Bill Knapp and I have put up for the Harvard Club ran into some snags in her interviews with the admissions committee, which are customarily pro forma, and that she has been asked, unprecedentedly, to meet two more of its members. When I report this dismaying intelligence to Ellie, she is enraged; I can see a branch of the Female Writers Self-Protective Association being organized and meeting at our home, the way her C.R. group used to. Come to think of it, some of those consciousness raisers would probably also be members of the F.W.S.-P.A. To change the subject, I take E. to Talat Halman's lecture. He is witty, but professorial, and he begins talking at six-thirty and is still going strong—only up to the seventeenth century—when we tiptoe out at eight-fifteen. When do Turks eat?

April 20

Inasmuch as I may be in South Africa later this spring, I go to Dr. Bishop's today for my annual checkup. I am appalled to hear that he is retiring. Today is his seventy-sixth birthday, he tells me, and while he feels fine, and loves to practice medicine, he is no longer up to handling sick people—to visiting each hospitalized patient, as has been his wont, at least twice daily. He doesn't think it's fair for a doctor to see only people in good health. So Louis is going to quit and take some drama and writing courses (his autobiography is due to be published next month) at the New School. Maybe he is getting on at that: I have to remind him to look at my prostate. I wouldn't dream of skipping that part of the exam, because he said last year that my prostate was beautiful. He pronounces it still exemplary, and adds that the path to a healthy prostate is a healthy sex life. I lower my eyes modestly. Louis does find some slight vascular constriction in one leg, but it is nothing serious, although I should give up smoking. I begin that symbolically, at the office, by throwing away two of the five cartons I bought at rockbottom prices while David and I were in North Carolina. When I stop smoking, I will probably put on weight, and in view of the false economy I have practiced in buying the cigarettes that I jettisoned, I guess I could call myself penny foolish, poundwise.

So I will have to find a new doctor. Louis has been mine for nearly thirty years. And Jules Leaf has been my dentist for even longer; *he* cannot be getting any younger. I hope I can dig up somebody in each category who is around forty, and who can reasonably be expected not to retire before I expire.

April 20

Elliott Caplin once asked his brother Al Capp, I am told over a quite passable omelet at the Yale Club, whether he thought Nixon knew what was going on at the White House. Al's response was that he once went there for a prayer breakfast (this must have been in his latter-life conservative incarnation), and while waiting for the president to arrive, desperate for some coffee, summoned a butler, and asked for a cup—one lump of sugar, please, milk, not cream. A couple of years later, Al continued, he was sitting in the Oval Office chewing the fat with the president, Charles Colson, and H. R. Haldeman. Nixon said it was refreshment time and he knew what Chuck wanted—Scotch on the rocks or whatever, and he knew what Bob wanted, and then he turned to Al and said he knew what *he* wanted—coffee, one lump, milk, not cream. Capp told his brother he guessed he would have to say that Nixon knew what was going on at the White House.

This tidbit anecdote whets my appetite. I haven't written anything about Capp for thirty years, and there will be much new larksome fertile ground to plough. Also, some mud. Al, now sixty-eight, is old, fat, suffering from emphysema, and barely able to stand up on his one good leg, his brother and sister inform me. (They know that I know he has had a wooden leg since childhood.) His faithful comic-strip assistant, Andy Amato, has just retired after a forty-year collaboration. The Boston *Globe*, in which "L'il Abner" first appeared, in 1934, has recently dropped it, because young Winship can't stand Al's ultraconservative politics. In the old days, when papers didn't run the strip, usually temporarily because they regarded some episode in it ultraradical, they would get thousands of indignant letters from worshippers of Moonbeam McSwine and her Dogpatch coterie. This time, there was scarcely a peep of protest.

The siblings are sad. True, Al may in recent years have lost some of his global esteem, and at home in Cambridge, where he has long been officially domiciled, the friendship of J. K. Galbraith; but let us not forget the heady days when it became known that Queen Elizabeth had been a Capp fan as she was growing up, and John Steinbeck declared that Al deserved the Nobel Prize for Literature. ("Get to work on that," Capp had told Elliott.) In any event, severed friendships, I am told, have never bothered Brother Al. He thrives, they say over coffee, on hate. The cartoonist Bud Fisher was his No. 1 anathema for many years, and Al wishes he could resurrect him, so he could have somebody around to hate that much again. Probably the person he hates most now is Jack Anderson, because it was the columnist who broke that story about that trouble with that coed in Wisconsin. Naturally, though, we would not want to include any of Al's such extracurricular activities in this book.

But, I interject, as the temperature in the Yale Club rapidly cools, how could anyone write an honest story of Al Capp without alluding to his widely known sexual escapades? Any writer who tried to get away with that would probably not only end up in Jack Anderson's bad graces but would be laughed out of town by every book reviewer this side of Eau Claire. We change the subject; it is time to discuss the whopping golden deal, which on examination seems about as firmly set as quicksilver. Elliott says he hopes I won't be offended, but the same people who bought Al's friend Nixon's memoirs offered a quarter of a million for a Capp biography written by Jimmy Breslin. Breslin can't do it; apparently, he is too busy trying to shoot down the Concorde, and although Elliott and Madaleine personally consider me a far better writer than Jimmy, let's face it, I am not—how should they put it?—not as hot a literary property as Breslin is. So the best they will probably be able to work out for a Capp-Kahn package will bring me something in low six figures. Can I live with that?

I could, but naturally I do not say so; such delicate matters are for one's agent to negotiate. I also do not say that if they are looking for a really hot literary package, what about Al Capp and Xaviera Hollander?

I have a further meeting involving money this afternoon at the office of a lawyer handling a family estate. The stockbroker involved has been asked to come by to go over its portfolio, and he remarks that Jeane Dixon has said something about the fine prospects of some company or other; maybe we should switch into that. He is kidding, of course, but only half-kidding, in my view; so I suggest to the lawyer, half-kiddingly, that perhaps we should consider switching to an investment advisor without an astrological bent. I get home in time to hear an attractive young woman try to convince Ellie and me that Lexy would like nothing better this coming summer than to attend a camp in which the children pretend to be American Indians.

Tonight we are *really* invited to the Harry Kahns'. Harry's huge success as a broker does not hang, I daresay, on signs of the zodiac. The A. H. Raskins are there. The longtime labor reporter has retired from the *Times*, of whose Newspaper Guild unit he was an early member. Now that Abe is back at the paper not as an employee but on a contract basis, the Guild wants him to rejoin, but he doesn't want to and doesn't think he has to. So there may be some pickets outside the *Times*—just about when Abe's biography of David Dubinsky is published. Aside from his own union, Raskin still clearly has friends in the labor movement; he has to leave the dinner table to take an urgent phone call from the coast. Harry Bridges. I should think David Dubinsky would be easier to write about than Al Capp.

After dinner, we all listen to the president's speech to Congress on energy, and I get an inkling of what makes Harry tick. When Mr. Carter says something about the possibility of conserving energy by installing more gas and electric meters to measure consumption, our host sits up attentively.

First thing tomorrow morning, he tells us, he is going to look into the stocks of companies that manufacture meters.

April 21

Burton and Aline Benjamin come to dinner, Bud bringing along a list of people he and Cronkite saw in South Africa and whom I might find useful. The prime minister's name is not on the roster. They got to see Mr. Vorster, but it was not an altogether amiable session, and to identify oneself as a friend of theirs would be undiplomatic. Bud says that Harry Oppenheimer—to whom I just wrote a letter about my visa—has been in town; the Cronkites and Benjamins dined with Harry and Bridget, on top of the World Trade Center. (I never got higher than the mezzanine the other day.) In Scarborough, I used to see Bud and Aline a couple of times a week, at the minimum. Now we only get together a couple of times a year, and we have much catching up to do. I had not known, for instance, that he is about to go to a hospital for an operation: his prostate. I hope it turns out to be as healthy as mine has been certified to be. I inquire, naturally, about the Reimans' health. They are fine. Good. Don R. once saved my life. Saw me choking, speechless, on a hunk of steak and whacked me on the back. He is strong-armed; a man of lesser clout might not have set me free.

April 22

In many respects, *The New Yorker* belies its reputation for institutional eccentricity. We have some writers and editors around who could pass for bankers and who, as they walk toward the New York Yacht Club on West Forty-fourth Street, could not unreasonably be expected by passersby to continue on inside. And yet we do have our authentic oddities. Jan Groth is surely one. She is finishing her Ph.D. dissertation in English. She has taught that subject at a high academic level. (She also writes an elegant Italian script.) But in twenty years or so she has never risen at the magazine—possibly of her own volition, though I doubt it—beyond being the eighteenth-floor receptionist, which is where she started off. We who spend many daylight hours there, mind you, are delighted with her permanence. She takes our messages when we are away from our desks, as we often are; she has learned to recognize the voices of our wives and children. As in our absences she comforts our friends, so when the occasion demands does she protect us against our enemies.

This year, Jan cannot be at her post on Fridays, because she is conducting a seminar in English composition at Vassar. She has invited me to make an appearance at today's session, and I am happy to oblige her. I have missed teaching on my own, ever since I got a taste of it at Columbia, and it is nice to be back, however fleetingly, in the world of academe. I am to be the last in a long line of *New Yorker* people to be a guest on Jan's weekly talk show. She has already played hostess, she told me, to Michael Arlen, Burt Bernstein, Bob Bingham, Paul Brodeur, Dick Harris, and Bud Trillin. (She enumerated them to me in alphabetical order, which I considered further evidence of her consummate tact.) Michael Arlen arrived, much as I suppose his father-namesake might have a generation earlier, in a chauffeured limousine.

When I was living in Westchester County, I would now and then act out a similar role in front of a class John Cheever's wife, Mary, taught at Briarcliff College, a two-year institution for young ladies, many of them with a strong social bent. After I moved back to the city, Mary was good enough to ask me again. The date she picked was a Monday morning in November. The class met at nine. Nobody turned up—not a single student. The explanation seemed to be that all the girls had gone to Dartmouth for a football weekend and had been either unwilling or unable to escape. This morning, driving myself up to Poughkeepsie in my own somewhat weathered station wagon, I am glad to be able to reflect that it is not the start of a fall week and that Vassar has gone coeducational. Still, it is a lovely, warm, spring day, and if I were a student and had the choice of lying on the grass or listening to one more person descant on the quirks of *The New Yorker*'s checking department . . .

The attendance in Jan's classroom is heartening. I count a dozen noses, of both sexes. I am flattered, until I learn that this is the last meeting of the course, and that at the end of today's sitting the students will get a chance to grade the teacher. It used to be the other way around, of course, but I am aware that there have been radical innovations on many a campus since the turbulent days of 1969. In Jan's case it doesn't much matter what kind of marks she gets, because she has already been informed that there is no room for her in the college budget next year. Still, she would understandably like to depart with honors. I am probably not much help to her; I raise doubts among her students. They have evidently been told by all their previous emissaries from *The New Yorker* that it is the holy of holies; my view of the place is more earthly. Students don't like to be confused. When they are, they are apt to blame it on their teacher. Jan may suffer for my apostasy.

Jan has invited me to lunch, on her college expense account, at the nearby Culinary Institute of America. It is known for short, inevitably, as the C.I.A. *Its* students prepare and serve gourmet meals as part of their curriculum. We stop first for an iced-tea apéritif at the Vassar Commons, where a couple of her students join us. One is a young man named Nadler. I ask him if he is related to the furniture-store Nadlers of Gadsden, Alabama.

No, his Nadlers are from Brooklyn. He didn't know there were any Nadlers in Alabama, or, for that matter, any place south of the New York City limits. At the C.I.A., which occupies a big Hudson River site that used to be a Jesuit seminary, we are ushered ceremoniously into the Escoffier Room. The waiters and busboys (some of them girls) on duty—their trays laden with as imposing an assortment of wine glasses as I have ever seen—are all of student age. The only attendant who appears to be over twenty-five is the maître d'—their teacher. There are no prices on the haut-cuisine menu. I perceive that Jan is nervous, and I suspect that the expense account with which Vassar has endowed her was created with a Burger King in mind. So I hastily offer to treat her—little enough recompense for all the courtesies she has extended to me over all the years. She seems much relieved and orders pheasant pâté as a starter. There are at least six waiters and waitresses for every patron on the scene, but the service is dreadful; this particular class, we discover, has just been transferred from Advanced Gravies and Sauces, or whatever, to what the syllabus may describe as Elementary Dining Room Etiquette. The student whose turn it is today to be the sommelier, for instance, proffers me a wine list with a beautiful bow, but then when my attention is momentarily diverted, he removes it before I have a chance to scan it. When we finally get to dessert and Jan asks for some grapes from the fruit bowl, an apprentice does something I have never seen a servitor of any age or experience do before. He plucks each grape from its bunch and washes it individually. It takes him about ten minutes to provide Jan with ten grapes. What takes the students longest of all is the preparation of our bill, but, considering its robust size, that may be because the C.I.A. does not also instruct them in higher mathematics.

During lunch, and afterward while I am driving Jan back to New York, I mention to her my surprise at having been omitted from all of Burt Bernstein's categories of humorists. Jan is surprised that I consider myself a humorist. (Maybe this is my root problem.) But I do, and John McPhee, who has been in Alaska since Ellie and I were there in January, says that when *he* arrived somebody who'd heard me talk in Anchorage repeated to him something funny I had said about dentists. There!

"Annie" is a smash hit on Broadway, and Jan and I talk about what a marvelous break that is for Tom Meehan, who wrote the book for the show. He used to be one of the eighteenth-floor chickens whom Jan mother-henned. I would love to be the author of a smash-hit musical comedy. Considering what "Little Orphan Annie" hath musically wrought, it is too bad that "L'il Abner" has already been converted to the stage. That limits the spinoffs from my Capp biography. But what about a TV series, like "Roots" or "Rich Man, Poor Man"? Of *course;* that is why they went after Irwin Shaw in the first place! I am going to be rich, though perhaps not rich enough to eat regularly at the C.I.A.

April 23

I must be nearly ready to start writing about Georgia. I awake this morning with an opening sentence in my head. Fiction writers often contrive situations in which a male protagonist wakes up and finds a beautiful woman alongside him. He has no idea how she got there, but his reaction is one of boundless gratitude; and what he does in gratification of that gratitude is often what makes the work of fiction sell. A writer of non-fiction is no less anxious than the fiction writer to capitalize on heaven-sent bounty, even though he may have been dealt no more than a simple declarative clause. He leaps from his pallet to make use of the gift while it is still fresh—that is, to get it down on paper before he mislays a word of it. In his eagerness and joy, he hopes just as much as his fictional counterpart to find adequate lead in his pencil.

It is Saturday, and Ellie and I take Lexy to the bubble under the Queensboro Bridge to hit tennis balls for an hour. Two middle-aged couples (I'd have called them elderly not too long ago) have the court adjoining ours. Husbands and wives, exceptionally poor players one and all. I try, as I often do in such circumstances, to figure out what they are. The men look like doctors, and to be able to afford to play here regularly would probably have to be doctors. They strike me, judged by mannerisms, tones of voice, general demeanor, and attitude toward their women, as a cut below surgeons and a cut above veterinarians. That leaves psychiatrists and dentists. But these two males are so loud-mouthed and over-dressed and so inept at the net that I infer further that they are socially inferior to dentists. Ergo, they must be psychiatrists. I never do find out, but when I discuss my hypothesis on the way home, Lexy says that he has had a phone call from the mother of a kid for whose birthday party Lex has been hired to do a magic show. The mother is a psychologist, and she has proposed that Lexy and she go over his repertoire beforehand to make sure he has nothing in his bag of tricks that might upset her child's apparently delicate psyche. Lexy wonders what he should do. My suggestion is unfit for any mother's ears, including, as I am sharply advised, Lexy's own mother's.

Lexy was nearly mugged yesterday, he confides, by a gang with ten-speed bikes. He escaped them by ducking into a museum, which apparently has strict rules about bicycles. He was less lucky last year, when he had a whole bag of tricks ripped off him while he was sitting, at midday, on the front steps of the Metropolitan Museum. A couple of evenings later, I took him over to a West Side precinct where the police department keeps its mug-shot library, and we spent a couple of hours looking over photographs, hoping to flush the perpetrator, who Lexy recalled distinctly was in his early twenties, of medium height and weight, Spanish origin, dark-skinned.

Before we were through, Lexy had confidently identified five men as his robber. The sergeant in charge of the files told me he was perfectly willing to have all five tracked down and questioned, just to give them a good scare, but that it seemed unwarranted to have all of them brought in, inasmuch as at least four were patently innocent.

While he was at it, the sergeant asked Lexy how old he thought *he* was. Twenty-eight, said Lexy assuredly. After a while, the sergeant took me aside and said that in view of the fact that the mug shots we'd scrutinized were all of men (following Lexy's guidance) in their early twenties, and in view of the fact that he, the sergeant, was forty-three, perhaps we had been looking at the wrong files from the outset. Never having been mugged myself, it is grossly unfair of me to make light, like this, of Lexy's traumatic experience. One can easily replace stolen bags of tricks, but while Lexy's favorite magic shop, Louis Tannen's, has for sale a thousand ingenious ways to confound the mind, it stocks nothing that can restore a child's confidence in his surroundings.

This afternoon all three of us—safety in numbers—drive down to Soho to see various shows Ellie wants to look at; now that she is going to write a book about art, she feels understandably duty-bound to keep up with as many late developments as she can. Lexy espies some discarded scrap wood in the gutter, which he says is precisely what he has been searching for in connection with some project or other. When his mother and I agree under pressure that we wouldn't wish to curb his creativity, would we, and when we further grudgingly concede that this trove of trash is probably no longer anybody else's prized property but is up for grabs, he pounces on it. How lucky the lad is that his family travels by grubby old station wagon rather than spotless limousine!

We stop in at a cheese store (has anyone ever passed one by?) and, remembering that we are going to William Jay Smith's birthday party tonight and don't yet have a present, we buy him a handsome nutcracker. I also select two large walnuts to go with it, but E. thinks *two* nuts seems vaguely dirty, so we settle for one. When we get home, she suggests further that I write a poem to go with the gift. I protest: To offer an eminent poet some doggerel is like carrying ashes to Newcastle. But she wins me over, and when, later at the Smiths', Bill's birthday cake is carried into a room full of writers, and no one steps forth to say a few appropriate words, Ellie calls on me to read my verses. She wins me over again, and I receive a reward: Bill Smith dubs me "The Poet of Park Avenue." He can do so without self-abasement; he lives on York. I spend much of the rest of the evening talking to Ralph Ellison, who seems a bit stiff to start with but warms up when I remind him that we last saw one another at the Century. Much of the dialogue, unsurprisingly, is about race relations, although I do also vaguely recall a digressive discussion about whether or not alligators have teats.

April 24

We spend much of the day preparing for a large dinner party we are giving for Lee Falk and his recent bride, Elizabeth. A lot of Cape Cod people are coming—the Xavier Gonzalezes, Dick Millers, Herman Badillos, Sidney Simons, Palmer Williamses, et al. Irwin Shaw calls and asks if he may bring along a beautiful girl. E. says yes, of course, but unhappily; she is afraid we already have more guests than forks. We are serving the frozen Alaska king crab we toted back from Anchorage in January, and it is consumed with gusto, though with not much more gusto than, periodically during the evening, I find myself being bitten on the shoulder by Irwin's date, whose beauty is moot but whose inebriety spectacular, and who appears to have less appetite for shellfish than for human flesh. After she has fallen down a couple of times, Irwin hauls her away. I expect E. to be enraged at this performance, but instead she says she pities the poor thing.

Lee Falk, who as the creator of "The Phantom" and "Mandrake" has much in common with Al Capp, and who also has known Al for years, is interested to hear of my possible involvement with him, but wonders how I will handle his—ah—Lee is a thorough gentleman—extracurricular activities.

April 25

Yesterday was Sunday, so I begin this week with a hangover. I trust this does not adversely affect chest X-rays, because as part of my annual physical I am to have one at 8:45 A.M. Instead of marching through Georgia, I shuffle through it all day, ending up at the Timothy Seldeses', where Lee S. is giving a party to celebrate Walter Annenberg's withdrawal of his offer to put up a big communications center as an annex of the Metropolitan Museum. The room is full of people we have met and vaguely recognize, among them a young woman who reminds me that we dined together at the Smiths' two nights ago. I knew I had seen her somewhere.

April 27

A call from Senator Haskell's office. They are trying to do something about my visa through the American Embassy in South Africa. I tell the chap who phones that I appreciate their efforts all the more because I have no connections with Colorado. He says not to be silly, he is from New York himself.

In the mail, something I have always yearned for. A press pass to the Yankee Stadium! Only it reads, "Roger Kahn, *The New Yorker.*" I send it, ruefully, up to Roger Angell, who reports back that he already has *his* press pass, and suggests that I keep this one. I am tempted to, but we both know that it belongs to Roger K., who keeps publishing baseball books at the same time that Roger A. does. Each has one coming out soon. I have been taken for Roger Kahn before, though never by the New York Yankees: People who hear I am a writer for *The New Yorker* tell me either 1) how much they enjoyed Brendan Gill's book, my feelings toward which are analogous to those of Roger Angell to Roger Kahn's coverage of the national pastime; or 2) how much they enjoyed my book "The Boys of Summer."

I have had some good luck writing about baseball, some bad. Back in 1938, when the Brooklyn Dodgers played their very first night game at Ebbets Field, I covered the innovative event for the Talk of the Town. The evening turned out to be far more historic than anyone could have anticipated: Johnny Vandermeer pitched his second successive no-hitter. Many years later, I thought it would be interesting to accompany a ball player on the winter banquet circuit for a couple of days, and the Yankees arranged for me to tag along with Joe Pepitone, who was once, honest, star enough to be invited to banquets. I wrote a piece and it got into page proof—was scheduled, that is, to run—and then it disappeared. So, in due course, did Joe Pepitone.

The best idea I had for a *New Yorker* baseball piece came to me in the winter of 1976, when at a dinner party I met Peter Seitz, the arbitrator whose decision made a lot of players free agents, and enabled the Yankees to catch, for one, Catfish Hunter. Hunter was scheduled to pitch the opening game at the newly refurbished Yankee Stadium, and I thought it would be fun to go to the game with Seitz and write a Talk piece on the arbitrator's reactions to the sport he had done so much to restructure. Shawn liked the idea, and Seitz was agreeable. He even changed his schedule so he would be in New York on the big April day. I had the magazine get me a couple of tickets, in the grandstand. (I didn't want to be anywhere near the press box, where Roger Kahn or somebody like that might catch a glimpse of my guest and make use of his presence before I could myself.) But at the last minute Shawn decided that whatever I wrote might conflict with a long piece Angell had in the works, so I had to disinvite Seitz. I took Patrick Smith to the game instead, and did not offer to reimburse the magazine for the cost of the seats. I wouldn't have gone myself if I hadn't been planning to go on business; I fell out of love with the Yankees years ago.

The original Yankee Stadium opened in 1923, and it was not long afterward that I became one of its habitués, a loyalty that was in part economic. My father, though he had nothing to do with the ball park, designed a number of buildings—breweries, residences—for Colonel Jacob Ruppert. I was too young to express my vicarious thanks by drinking beer, but I could and did betake myself frequently up to the Bronx to root hard for Babe Ruth, Lou Gehrig, and the other gods in my striped-suit pantheon. Ruth in right field, Bob Meusel in left, and the incomparable Earle Combs between them—was there ever such an outfield to worship before or since? Oh, I know all about Mickey Mantle and Joe DiMaggio (I once even saw DiMag hit three triples in a single game!), but Earle Combs, the Silver Fox, will always be my all-time all-star Yankee centerfielder. I said as much, when Combs died in 1976, in a eulogy that ran in *Sports Illustrated*, and I was rewarded with a touching note from his widow; she said nobody had ever written nicer things about her husband. *New Yorker* pieces do not, as a rule, elicit that kind of mind-boggling response. But Combs was merely my favorite *outfielder*. On a more or less direct line, defensively, between the Silver Fox and home plate, stood Tony Lazzeri, and I guess Push 'Em Up Tony was my own true baseball love.

I used to get to the stadium an hour or two before game time, so I could cruise the edges of the field with my leather-bound autograph album and enshrine in it the lefthanded signature of, say, Herb Pennock or the dextral one of Waite Hoyt. One of the most disheartening setbacks of my youth occurred when Connie Mack's Philadelphia A's came to town for a series. I already had Mr. Mack and George Earnshaw and others of his teammates in my collection, but I had never been able to corral Lefty Grove. Finally one day Mr. Grove responded to my beckoning summons as I leaned out of a front-row box. I offered him a clean page of my precious book and held out a pen. To my astonishment, he reached into his pocket, pulled forth an ink pad and a stamp, and in that fashion imprinted his name. I was outraged. What would this bastard version of an autograph do to the value of my book? It was not until years later that I forgave him, upon my reading somewhere that poor Robert Moses Grove, though one of the very few thirty-game winners in history, was illiterate. How wrenching it must have been for him to admit this to fans more perceptive than I was! He could have simply ignored their requests for his signature, and left them thinking him merely uppity or surly, instead of so sorely handicapped. I wonder how much that star-studded book would be worth today. No matter; I have no idea where it is.

An old friend of E.'s, in town for a couple of days from the Midwest, comes to dinner tonight with her husband, and he opens our eyes and ears to a world that we rarely come in contact with. He is pro-Nixon, always was and still is, thinks his man was to most presidents what I used to think Tony Lazzeri was to most second basemen, would vote for him again, etc., etc. We fight the Battle of Watergate all evening, and our guest, though outnumbered, is not outshouted nor, in his steadfast view, outscored. It is a truly refreshing experience to run into someone like this, although, like a close ball game, hard on the larynx.

April 28

Dr. Bishop has the results of my various tests, including the chest X-ray, nothing wrong there, and says when I stop by that I should be fine for another year, although I shouldn't smoke. Yes, I can play singles, if I choose; yes, I can play squash. My cardiologist is a firm believer in the efficacy of violent exercise. When I wondered once if there wasn't a possibility I might die on a squash court, he shrugged and said, "What better way to go?" He used to be a ranking player himself, but he gave the sport up; I keep forgetting to ask him why, and at what age he made that big decision.

The Georgia piece is going very slowly. The trouble is, I don't have a deadline. If Shawn would only tell me he has to have it in two weeks! I wouldn't really mind, this once, his not saying what he means or not meaning what he says. I don't even have an *imaginary* deadline, which can sometimes be just as prodding as a real one. Where did the old self-discipline go?

Dinner tonight at the Dan Roses'. A literary evening, in the main—Ved Mehta, the MacShanes, Ruth Prawer Jhabvala, and, last but never least, George Steiner, who is over here on one of his periodic visits from England. George always has lunch with Shawn and always tells everyone he has had lunch with Shawn. I do not ask him if he asked Bill if he would be permitted to have lunch with Harold Rosenberg. George's principal Shawn gossip tonight is that Bill's son Wallace's latest play has got him into some kind of obscenity scrape in London. There is a discussion of why, considering the father's strict—some say prudish—editorial code, the son has veered so far in the opposite direction. The consensus is that this is a perfectly normal case of generational revolt. George has lately been credited with having launched the rumor, in London, that Brendan Gill was going to succeed Shawn père. When I ask him about this, he says, "The Irish dramatist [I guess he means Brendan] wrote in the *Observer* that he was going to be the next editor of *The New Yorker*." Brendan *himself* wrote that? I ask unbelievingly. Well, George says, retreating like Napoleon from Moscow, somebody else wrote it and quoted Gill to that effect. Always mysterious, Steiner then compliments me on my piece about Formosa. He says it made him numb. The next time I am in Cambridge—Cambridge, England, of course—he wants to introduce me to the Sinologist Joseph Needham. I accept the invitation, but in bewilderment. Whom does George Steiner think he has been talking to all along? I haven't written a piece on Formosa.

Ruth Jhabvala has written the movie script for "Roseland." The last time her research took her to the dance palace, she tells us, a stranger invited her to dance, explaining that she had a nose that reminded him of his ex-wife's.

Ved Mehta has heard that Bill Knapp and I have encountered snags, trying to get our young woman into the Harvard Club. Ellie wants to know what this is all about, and when I tell her of our temporary setback, she is certain it is somehow all my fault. By the time we get home, she is talking about grounds for divorce. And it was I who pushed so hard to get women into the damned club in the first place! I retreat to the living-room couch, where I toss and turn sleeplessly (the couch has a gap in its middle) until E. comes down and says we can be married again. Hell hath no fury like a woman who thinks another woman hath been scorned.

April 29

For the first time in a couple of months, we spend a weekend in Cornwall. Tom and Marie Whiteside hitch a ride as far as Pawling, where they generally leave their car during the week. Not a bad idea: Our garage bill is up to ninety dollars a month, and seems unlikely ever to decelerate. Tom brims with glum talk of how Shawn is holding pieces of his that ought long since to have been published; why, there are two Whitesides on the bank right now. I can't imagine what Tom is moaning about; I have five there. Tom is doing a piece now on the radio and television experiences of authors on promotional tours. Out of the goodness of my heart, I present him with an anecdote, but he does not seem enthralled, conceivably because it involves me. It also involves the "Today Show," which is reputed to be the *sine qua non* of spots to be seen and heard on. I appeared on it when my book on the 1970 census, "The American People," came out, in 1974. Arriving at the NBC studios in Rockefeller Center at the appointed hour, which was something like 6:45 A.M., I found myself unable to find a seat in the waiting room. The place was full of cats.

I have no use for cats. I am unapologetic. Some of my best friends hate cats. If there is anything worse than cats, though, it is people who exhibit cats. This week was International Cat Show Week, or some such, and champion cats were to be featured on "Today" this day along with me. While I was reflecting grimly on various cats I have lived with—there was once, God help me, a litter of ten—Barbara Walters threaded her way bravely through the feline pack and told me that when I went on she and Frank McGee (who was to die of cancer just a few weeks later) were going to ask me a lot of short, snappy questions about census findings, and would I please answer no less swiftly and concisely. I said I understood the scheme, but I did not tell her, naturally, that I was a bit worried. I had written the book nearly a year before, and hadn't looked at it since, and my working mind had long since passed on to other areas of inquiry. Anyway, when I was summoned on camera, Ms. Walters held up a copy of the book and very flatteringly suggested that everybody watching the program buy it. (The

"Today Show" is purported to send people flocking to bookstores. Judging from the sales figures my publishers later furnished me, as soon as Ms. Walters' audience switched off their television sets they all rushed out and bought cats.) Then she explained that she and her co-host were going to fling questions at me, and that I would fling back knowledgeable responses.

Now, then, would Mr. Kahn please tell the world what was America's favorite recreation. I knew the answer was in my book somewhere. But where? Was it baseball? Bowling? Squash racquets? How long would this dead air continue while I was wrestling with my memory? What was going to be *my* favorite recreation from now on? Suicide? Cat-breeding? I had noticed that—invisible to the millions watching the program and hanging on for my reply—the permanent members of our panel had in front of them copious notes to glance at. Now Frank McGee, after what seemed to me hours and may have been five precious seconds, sensed my difficulty, looked downward, the angel, and answered in my stead: "Picnicking." Of course! Any fool would know that. The ice was broken, and from then on I hurled answers back as fast as questions were thrown, although when it came to citing the percentage of non-white eighteen-year-olds who had completed high school in Tulsa, Oklahoma, or whatever it was I was being asked, I may have cheated a little and just invented the statistics.

Since Tom Whiteside does not seem to think much of the fact that his old buddy and chauffeur once nearly committed hara kiri on network television, live, I forbear from helping him further with his research. So I do not tell him about my second chatty appearance on a morning talk show originating in Boston, when the master of ceremonies, exuding bonhomie, walked over off-camera and said, "We've met somewhere before, haven't we?"

"Yes," I said, "on this show last year."

On another trip to Boston to publicize another book, I was escorted around town by my publisher's regional salesman, who had set up autographing appearances at a couple of bookstores. When we arrived at the first, exactly at the prearranged hour, the proprietor was out to lunch and the deputy she had left in charge had never heard of me or my book. Things seemed better organized at the next store. I was met at the door and ushered, with murmurs expressing appreciation of the trouble I'd gone to to get there, toward a card table with a dazzling heap of copies of "The China Hands" on top of it. There were five people already waiting for me, holding books they had plucked from the pile, so I slipped quickly into a chair behind the table, asked each his or her name, and grandly scrawled an inscription. One young man gave me the name of his uncle, who he believed had once, as a Marine, been stationed in or near China. The only thing that puzzled me was that none of the five looked like the sort of person who would normally shell out $12.95 for a treatise on the diplomatic history of the Second World War. Perhaps a more reasonable explanation of their presence was simply that they were long-standing fans of mine who had seized this opportunity to view their idol in the flesh. With a smug flourish, I polished off the fifth inscription, and then, because for the moment there appeared to be no one else waiting for my imprimatur, I rose to stretch my legs, walked around the table, and, at the front of it, saw a little placard that had escaped my glance when I was escorted to my seat. It said that the first five people to enter the shop after twelve o'clock could have a copy of "The China Hands" for free. A little humility is good for writers, and for everybody else. The important thing is to keep it from degenerating into humiliation.

May 1

Our car has Massachusetts plates, and the finicky Commonwealth requires semi-annual inspections. I decided yesterday, Cornwall being only a half hour's drive from the Conn.-Mass. border, to get my spring sticker. That's never easy on a Saturday morning, I have learned from bitter experience; the proprietors of service stations authorized to make inspections always seem to be busy repairing snowmobiles. So I was overjoyed, on reaching Sheffield, when the very first place I stopped at said it could inspect me right away. The fellow who did would not give me a sticker. My brake lights weren't working. Well, would he adjust them? Oh, no, he didn't have time, I could come back Monday if I wished. Eventually, in Great Barrington, I found an establishment that could and would both fix the lights and issue a sticker. On returning to Cornwall and getting out of the car, I discovered that the brake lights had been fixed too well. Once they went on, I couldn't turn them off without furiously pounding the brake pedal. If I forget to do that some day, my battery is doomed.

We return to the city early today because Ellie wants to take Lexy to the opening of Ned O'Gorman's latest day-care center in Harlem. Ned has guts. He has already been burned out of a couple of buildings, presumably by blacks who do not like the idea of a white man, no matter how noble his purpose, invading their turf. Ned merely finds another unused brownstone and relocates. When I drop E. and L. off at his new place, Rainbow barks furiously at every black person she sees. What is this about dogs, anyway? In southern Africa, some whites have dogs that are bred and/or trained to bark at—also bite—all non-white visitors, but why should that be true of mongrels in the U.S.A.? In Rainbow's defense, I must observe that she also seems to be aroused to anger by persons—regardless of color, sex, race, or religion—riding bicycles, and by all individuals wearing caps with brims. My old dog Barge used to react similarly to men in uniform. He would even growl at me when I decked myself out, for parades or funerals, in my formal volunteer fireman's suit. My hunch is that there would be no more jokes about dogs' biting postmen, and fewer lacerated mail carriers, if these long-suffering couriers were issued tam-o'-shanters.

While Ellie and Lexy are in Harlem, I read an advance copy of Roger Kahn's new baseball book, "A Season in the Sun." The title alone ought to irritate Roger Angell, being so close to "Season in the Sun," which Wolcott Gibbs used both for a series of *New Yorker* casuals and a play derived loosely therefrom. (The action took place on Fire Island, and a principal character was an editor out for the weekend who was manifestly based on Harold Ross.) In a prologue, Roger K. says, of baseball, "The game begins with sons and fathers, fathers and sons." He is so right. I was astonished, at the age of ten or eleven, to learn something really interesting about my own father. He knew, just like me, the batting averages of all the Yankees! I had never dreamed he was capable of anything like that. Of course, he had Colonel Ruppert for a client at the time, and may have deemed it prudent to keep himself informed.

Baseball looms large in my memories of raising Terry, Joey, and Tony. There were the endless practice sessions on the back lawn in Scarborough, with me hitting fungoes for the boys to catch, trying on the one hand to steer clear of the pond and on the other to avoid the squishy part of the lawn, where our malfunctioning sewage-disposal system had left its mark. (David and Lexy have grown up in the city, and are markedly, alas, less interested in baseball. When David was fourteen, I was pained to discover at Shea Stadium one afternoon that he did not know there were nine innings in the standard ball game. D. and L. don't care much about football, either, which means that when we are all at home on a fall Sunday afternoon and the television set is on there is nobody in the household with whom I can learnedly discuss O.J.'s cutbacks or the putative condition of Joe Willie's right knee.) And then there were Little Leagues, in not one but two communities—Westchester and Cape Cod.

James A. Farley, whom I got to know when I was writing about Coca-Cola, once cited an adage that he thought applicable to the patrons of Little League baseball: "No man is so tall as he who stoops to help a child." I have myself stooped to help a child win a Little League game, but I am not sure that the episode enhanced either my stature or my morality. Tony was going on eleven at the time I'm thinking of—a difficult age for a boy, and one not easy on the boy's parents, either. I have heard it said, for instance, that if a father can survive Little League baseball and his children's birthday parties, he can survive anything. I came to grips with both on a single day. The Little League game was scheduled for 6 P.M. (Half the fun of running a Little League is holding its games at times certain to inconvenience, if not infuriate, the largest possible number of players' parents.) The birthday party—an expedition to Playland—was scheduled immediately before the contest, a crucial one. My nefarious act was to conspire with my son to have as his principal party guests the pitcher and catcher of his opposing team, whom we stuffed with so much pizza, cotton candy, banana splits, and caramelled apples (following each treat with a ride on a roller coaster or comparable agitator) that when it came time to play ball they were equally awash in soda pop and ineptitude. Our team won the game handily, oblivious to cries of "Foul!" from a couple of mothers on the opposing side.

Today was the day I had planned, weather and visa permitting, to leave for South Africa.

May 3

The South African Consulate had no word for me yesterday morning, when I called to inquire, but a fellow on the South African desk of the State Department called me: Washington has been informed by our embassy in Pretoria that it has been informed that a decision will be rendered in the Kahn case later this week. How can it take the jury so long to reach a verdict? Particularly when I haven't been asked to testify in my own defense? I do not even know what I've been charged with. Or, come to think of it, am I the plaintiff? Going out to lunch, I shared an elevator with Emily Hahn. E. Hahn and E. Kahn—we sometimes get one another's mail and calls. I also get some calls intended for Ed Koren, one of the few cartoonists who has an office at *The New Yorker*. Until I can straighten out his wooers, they all beseech me to draw them pictures, for which they are prepared to pay handsomely indeed. I was tempted not long ago to accept a particularly attractive offer to do a cover for an accounting magazine with a huge circulation.

Apropos of I forget exactly what, Emily remarked *en descendant* that there is no word for "no" in Swahili; "not yet" is used instead. "Not yet" pretty well sums up what the Republic of South Africa is saying to me. Have I, through this accidental dialogue, stumbled upon a linguistic link between black Africa and Afrikanerdom?

Cynthia Lindsay phones. She is in town from California for a couple of days, staying at a friend's apartment, and she invites me to stop by for a drink this afternoon. I do. Jo Sullivan Loesser, now married to Jack Osborn, is there when I arrive. Jack is very big in croquet, and says that the first important tournament in seven years is going to be held in New York soon, and why don't I cover it? I say I'll be glad to if Ottie Swope isn't in it. He says that Ottie is now known exclusively as Herbert, and has a radio talk show in Palm Beach, where he is much in demand as an extra man at dinner parties—so popular that he probably won't be able to take time off to come north for the tournament. I reminisce with Jo about Frank Loesser; apparently, he never told her about the wartime genesis of "Rodger Young." I tell her. She wants to know if in a program she's giving of Frank's songs at the Players Club she can use the bit about his agreeing to write that ballad if we would let him sleep till noon. Of course she may. Cynnie Lindsay says the incident is fully covered in her Loesser book. I remind her that I've never received the copy she promised me.

Cynnie has just abandoned a biography she has partly written on a famous movie star. The star is now seventy-four, she says, and his conversation, even when being interviewed by a supposedly sympathetic biographer, runs to statements like "I hate niggers and I hate Jews." I tell Cynnie that that would make an eye-catching title for a biography of practically anybody. That literary project foundered partly, I gather, because her subject began also to hate *her*. It seems that she had been showing him her manuscript seriatim as she wrote it, and he had submitted it to a couple of anonymous critics who didn't think much of it; so he, too, had begun to have misgivings about the venture. I chide her for having showed him anything in the first place. As a professional, she should know enough not to let the subject of anything have a look at it before it's finished. Better yet, not before it's published. People who have a chance to look over their own remarks—even ones more attractive than her subject's—too often dislike what they see.

May 5

This business of waiting around for a visa is getting to be a strain. It's tough to work on a complicated, multipart piece when one doesn't know if one has a day to complete it before starting in on something else, or a week, or a month. It's sort of like sitting around during a war waiting for orders to ship out. I learn today that the South African handling visas at the consulate in New York is, if I have his name spelled correctly, Mr. Labuschagne. He is the person I dealt with when I tried to get a visa, vainly, two years ago. Why doesn't he get promoted to something else? I doubt that he has much, if anything, to say about my entry, but I judge by the tone of his voice that if he did and decreed in my favor, it would be to have me admitted no farther than the Jan Smuts Airport and then as a May Fool's joke, perhaps, have me put aboard the next return flight. I do not tell Brother Labuschagne what I have heard from Washington. I will deal with my government and let him deal with his.

Diana Michaelis, up from Washington, comes for dinner with her son David, up from Princeton. David is rooming with a kid who apparently made an atom bomb on his own, and who is bringing out a book about the feat. Because he knows so much, he has been accorded F.B.I. protection. David is doing the actual writing, and is to receive ten per cent of the take. I tell him he is being reamed. Diana is convinced that she is going to be Jimmy Carter's ambassador to Upper Volta, and urges us, since that was one of the countries we skipped on our swing across Africa, to visit her when she is in residence there. The Perle Mesta of Ouagadougou. I cannot fathom why Di thinks she is going to get the nod, though the competition for that post is probably not intense: She is not an Africanist, and to the best of my knowledge the president doesn't owe her anything. I wonder if it is easy to get an Upper Voltan visa.

May 6

Big headline in today's New York *Post:* "S. Africa May Bar Andy Young." Now, I can understand why they might be leery of letting *him* in; I hope they don't strike a bargain with Washington and agree to admit either Jimmy Carter's plenipotentiary or William Shawn's, but not both.

This evening, we go to see "Annie Hall." I am a sucker for anything Woody Allen does. His only poor joke is the one about not being able to make love during a party, because there are *New Yorker* editors in the other room. He probably threw that one in just to tease Roger Angell, his editor at the magazine. (I must tell Roger that I found a mistake in Roger Kahn's book. R. K. is writing about the Berkshires and Tanglewood and then goes straight into a summer camp he once attended. I know the camp in question. It is nowhere near the Berkshires, but at Sturbridge, which Kahn probably has confused in his mind with Stockbridge. He reminds me of a base runner who has forgotten how many men are out.) Ellie suggests that I find the character Woody Allen is portraying in "Annie Hall" appealing because he reminds me of myself, and I suppose that is basically true. But I do not recognize myself in Woody's frequent presentation of himself as a chap who is worried about his relationships with women but who (as the film audience can plainly see) is a great and inexhaustible stud. Indeed, in this movie, he has two women within, if I calculate my time sequence correctly, half an hour, in two different places, and under considerable emotional stress. I'll bet he doesn't do that in real life. I don't. I love his beautiful attacks on intellectual pretentiousness, epitomized here by his gag that *Dissent* and *Commentary* have merged into a new magazine called *Dysentery.* I suppose that is how one spells it; it is a verbal joke. Surely an in joke, too; for of the millions of people who go to Woody Allen films, how many have ever heard of either *Commentary* or *Dissent?* If *The New Yorker* were merged with *Hustler,* would the end product be called *The Nude Yorker?* Woody Allen handles this kind of material better than I do.

We have a cold supper at home, and watch a Channel 13 documentary about the role of women in a changing society. God help us if these real-life women, with all their solemnity, their appalling humorlessness, aren't exactly like the ones Woody Allen was caricaturing a few minutes ago.

May 7

Foreign Minister Botha of South Africa says that the trouble with Andrew Young is that he doesn't have any manners. What about the manners of a government that by this date has not seen fit to reply to a visa application that was filed in February for a first-of-May departure?

The *Times* has a photograph of Franklin D. Roosevelt, Jr., and his fourth bride at their wedding, he in foxhound regalia, she in virgin white, both on horseback. Separate horses. He is sixty-two, she twenty-seven. The basis for a good many jokes at our fortieth reunion next month has now been solidly established. There is nothing wrong about one of our classmates or anybody else marrying a twenty-seven-year-old. But how in the world do you get saddle soap off a wedding gown?

The book page of today's *Post* has an interview with a Harper & Row salesman about a book he has coming out—a Joan Kahn book—on a homicide trial in which he was a juror. The accused was acquitted, and the salesman felt sorry for him, and helped him put his life together again. And then, with the manuscript complete, the protagonist was arrested for another attempted murder. That can be jarring to an author. Bill Buckley went all out for Edgar Smith, the murderer who wrote his own *non mea culpa* book, who was with Buckley's help released from prison, and was then found guilty of rape and sentenced to life. I guess I have tended, professionally, to side with cops more than with robbers. I did a *New Yorker* Profile, for instance (one of those that withered on the bank), on David Durk, the New York policeman who first achieved celebrity by trying to recruit cops on college campuses. There was a nice scene in my unpublished piece about Durk and me visiting the Amherst campus, bumping into David Eisenhower (a student then renowned not as husband but merely grandson), and the one David trying to cajole the other into joining the force.

Later, I wrote a whole book, "Fraud," about the Postal Inspection Service, that comparatively unsung but highly effective federal law-inforcement agency. (The book didn't sell much; the service remains unsung, or at least unlistened to.) I wrote it largely to avoid rewriting "The American People." The idea for *that* one originated with Truman M. Talley, of Weybright and Talley. Mac Talley invited me to lunch at the St. Regis one day and over a Bloody Mary proposed that I do a book on the census. There are many subjects I am ignorant of; among these demography and sociology rate high, somewhere close to biochemistry and astrophysics. I laughed at Mac's ludicrous suggestion. He shrugged and ordered a second round and halfheartedly tried out a couple of other notions. None struck a vibrant chord. As he plied me with a third drink, he returned to his No. 1 idea, and I agreed heartily that a book written by me about the findings of the 1970 census would be just about the most memorable happening in the annals of English literature since the birth of Harold Robbins. Almost before I gathered my wits, I had signed a contract and spent the advance. Then I pulled myself together, went to see Bill Shawn, and explained to him that I wouldn't be doing anything for the magazine for a while because I had a book to write. On what? he asked politely. On the 1970 census, I said, feeling as abashed as a schoolboy who, reaching for a handkerchief, spills a packet of dirty postcards on his teacher's floor. Bill said that he hoped I would let him see the manuscript; perhaps *The New Yorker* could use some of it. I could no more imagine the magazine's running it than my writing it; I thought he was just reviving me with kindness.

Months later, after several trips to Suitland, Maryland, where the Bureau of the Census is entrenched, Mac Talley and I reconvened at the St. Regis, and I handed him a manila envelope containing my manuscript. He picked it up between thumb and forefinger, waved it and shook it, placed it unopened on the table, and said, "But this isn't a book. A book is twice as big." My jewel was deficient in carats. I told Mac I would undertake somehow to expand the work (I did not tell him that as of that moment I had absolutely nothing to say about the subject that was not already inside the manila envelope), and I returned, dejected, to my office. Then I remembered Shawn's courteous expression of interest. I rummaged around and found a scuffed carbon of my manuscript, and sent it up to him. To my amazement, Bill phoned a few days later to say that he liked the material very much and wanted to buy it—though of course it was too long for the magazine and while he planned to run it in two parts, it would still have to be cut some.

Even so, it took me a while to drag myself back to Suitland, so while I was waiting to get up a head of steam I wrote "Fraud." I had got interested in the Postal Inspection Service twenty years earlier, when I'd done an "Annals of Crime" piece for *The New Yorker* about a crooked accountant in Rochester, New York, who, after fleecing some of his clients, had absconded and, of all improbable things, joined the French Foreign Legion. He had been tracked down and brought back to justice by a young upstate postal inspector named Charles A. Miller. Charlie Miller and I became friends. He was a cop, he carried a gun, but he didn't look or act much like anybody's conception of a law-enforcement officer, and he was extraordinarily helpful to me in reporting a couple of other articles on crimes that had occurred up in his bailiwick. Now, in 1973, he was stationed in Washington, in charge of all mail-fraud investigations for his service, and I knew from past experience that if I wanted to write up some of its cases, I would have ready access to its files and to the memories of its inspectors, quite a few of whom, through Charlie, I had got to know. When I finished the book, the chief postal inspector, William J. Cotter, wrote a preface (I suspect Charlie may have been his amanuensis), and there was a publication-day party in Washington with the chief and Charlie and the rest of the inspectorial gang flatteringly in attendance. I dedicated "Fraud" to David and Lexy, hoping thereby to curb the gullibility of youth. That has not seemed to diminish to the slightest degree their zeal for responding to every direct-mail-win-a-million-dollars scheme that has come their trusting way.

After the book was published, it became public knowledge that over the years the Central Intelligence Agency had been opening first-class mail, which is a federal crime and which the C.I.A. could hardly have done to any extent without the Postal Inspection Service being aware of it. I knew, of course, that Bill Cotter had spent nineteen years with the C.I.A. before he became chief postal inspector, but I could not believe that any of my pals in the service had had a hand in whatever the C.I.A. was up to, and I thought I'd write something in the service's defense. Charlie Miller had by then retired, but the service still regarded him as its principal conduit to me. When I wrote to his successor about what I had in mind, it was Charlie who responded, and he begged me to drop the idea. Bill Cotter was at home with a heart condition, and unavailable for comment, and what had happened was that the C.I.A. had peeked at mail at the Kennedy Airport while the postal inspectors on duty there were out to lunch. I concluded that whatever defense I tried to make for my friends might not be very convincing to any jury, or even to me.

When I was a volunteer fireman, in Westchester, I was automatically exempt from jury duty. The theory was that by serving as volunteers we were already shouldering more than our fair load of civic responsibility. But when I moved back to New York City, I was no different from anyone else. Well, not exactly. I get summoned for jury duty every couple of years now, but as soon as my name is drawn and it is ascertained that I am a journalist and have written, *inter alia*, about crime, I am almost certain to be excused by an attorney for one side or the other. As a result, I spend two weeks sitting frustratedly in the impanelling chamber.

I am not sure, actually, that I *want* to be a juror. Jurors are not allowed to take notes. A lawyer once tried to explain to me the rationale behind this prohibition—it has something to do with the belief that a note-taking juror might exercise undue influence over his peers—but I find the argument unimpressive. Judges may take notes. Prosecutors may take notes. Defense attorneys and defendants may take notes. But jurors must rely on their memories, and I wouldn't trust mine any more than I would trust a person thrice convicted of perjury.

Still, I would rather serve than simply sit and wait, and once, when there was a chance of my being picked to help decide an obscene-films case, I neglected to disqualify myself, though I probably should have: Had I not, as a volunteer fireman, uncomplainingly sat through showings of blue movies at our annual banquets? (We were in little danger of running afoul of the law ourselves; our guests generally included all the police in the area.) But I was challenged before that case went to trial, by the district attorney, who, I sensed, took me for someone who would condone sinfulness incarnate. I certainly would have liked to see those films. They would have been a welcome relief, while consigned to jury duty, from doing crossword puzzles.

This evening, Ellie and I go to an off-off-Broadway theatre the chief advantage of which is that it is in a church on East Eighty-eighth Street and we can walk to it. (With taxi fares what they are these days, that is no small advantage.) The play has something to do with "The Arabian Nights," and there are two kinds of seats—three-dollar ones, entitling people to a cushion on the floor; and five-dollar ones, entitling older folks like me to a chair. My seat, unfortunately, is practically in the middle of the orchestra, which does not let my proximity deter it from playing with vigor. E. and I leave after the first act and on the way home stop at Elaine's for a brandy. We almost never go to Elaine's, and, not being a regular, I don't feel comfortable there, but at least tonight I look like a fashionable contemporary author—even, perhaps, a bit like Woody Allen. I haven't shaved all day and am tieless. If only I had thought to wear sneakers, we could probably move from the bar to one of those tables up forward like that one where Tom Guinzburg is presently enthroned. My publisher, who wafts no sign of recognition in our direction, is dining with two women, but neither appears to be Jackie Onassis, so why should we waste another precious moment of our time worrying about *him*?

May 8

At Sunday-night supper—after a whole day in, or with, Georgia—Bruce and Naomi Bliven say they have heard from a United Nations source via Phil Hamburger that some of the diplomats from the black African countries don't like Andrew Young because they are all (depending on whether they hail from francophone or anglophone nations) Sorbonne-St. Cyr or Oxford-Sandhurst types, and regard Young as a "country nigger." This third- or fourth-hand intelligence doesn't seem to jibe with what Hugh Gloster, the president of Morehouse College, told me in Atlanta; he said that one of the things that made Young an effective emissary to Africa was that he so often found fellow alumni of Howard U. in government bureaucracies over there, and that they were all part of a sort of old-boy network. Perhaps there is a little truth in both points of view.

Rita Gam asked us over this evening, too, and we said we'd stop by if we got home early enough. We reach her elevator landing just as her guests, Harold Taylor and Alastair Reid, are about to depart, but they go back in and we all have a drink together. Alastair, over from London for a few months and temporarily occupying some vacant cell at *The New Yorker*, says that the corridors he has been prowling there are abuzz with rumors anent Shawn's successor, and that his information is that Roger Angell is the heir apparent, or presumptive, I never can remember which is which. Alastair wonders if I think there is much truth to this rumor. I propose an experiment: I will float a rumor tomorrow morning to the effect that Bill has brought Alastair back from England to groom him to take over, and we will see how long it takes for the word to get back to Alastair himself.

May 9

Office hours at the editorial side of *The New Yorker*, as far as the nosy outside world is concerned, are from ten to six. In fact, many of the editors, most of the checkers, and even some of the writers often work until much later, especially on evenings when parts of the magazine are going to press. Bill Shawn, knowing he may be around for a longish stretch, often sensibly doesn't arrive until noon. But I am a morning person (I have little choice; Lexy's breakfast must be on the table by seven-thirty if he is going to be able both to eat it and get to school on time), and I usually get downtown early, sometimes by eight-thirty. This morning, I am rewarded. At nine-thirty, while I am snugly ensconced in my office, sipping coffee, and while most of the rest of the staff is presumably wending its way here, the sky darkens wickedly and the city is wracked by a violent hailstorm. When Tom Whiteside turns up around lunchtime, he says Cornwall had three inches of snow at dawn, and he is lucky to be back in the city at all. I ask him what, if anything, he has heard of the wild story that Alastair Reid has been tapped to succeed you know who as you know what.

Senator Haskell's office, which apparently also gets a jump on the working day, calls to say that a decision on my visa will be rendered tomorrow. I have a strong hunch that I am going to make it to South Africa this time around, notwithstanding Andy Young. So instead of writing about Georgia, I spend much of the day drawing up lists of things I have to do before I leave: bills to pay, people in Joburg and Cape Town to write to, traveller's checks, vaccination booster, notify my sisters, remind E. to keep after the people who are going to refurbish the Truro tennis court, tell Monica McCall to keep on top of Al Capp, and, most important of all, read through the South African stuff I have been piling up all these months.

Many weeks ago, my Harvard classmate Ethan Allen Dennison called. He said that in connection with our fortieth-anniversary gift to the college there was going to be a telethon (his word, not mine) originating at the Harvard Club on the evening of May 9th, and would I please help phone classmates who had so far not come across and urge them to make a contribution? I had said that I expected to be in South Africa by then but that if by any slim chance my departure was delayed, I would of course do what I could. Now Denny calls back; I am hooked. These unfeeling Afrikaners are stirring up trouble all over the world. I cross the street to the club at six, and the management has certainly made things agreeable for us telethonists: a waiter to ply us with free drinks, and a splendid collation to be washed down by them. It is a thankless kind of mission on which we are embarked; some of the people on our lists haven't given a penny to Harvard in forty years, and it is not likely that a phone call, even from Ethan Allen Dennison, Myron Kay Stone, Richard N. M. I. Lewisohn, or me, will spur them into affirmative action. I get Vic Theriot on the line. He used to play in our Eliot House band. He is retired, after thirty-one years with J. C. Penney, and is now in the real estate business in Greenwich, Connecticut. I say that must be a good place to be in that business. He says business is slow. He will give seventy-five dollars. I jolly him up to eighty. I get Carl Goullaud, my big fish of the evening's casting. He pledges a hundred and I nudge him up to a hundred and ten. We have been instructed that every penny counts. That's fifteen hundred pennies I have rung up by sheer perseverance. I get a classmate I never heard of who says he has just had an operation and he's broke and his mother-in-law is dying, and I am tempted for an instant to make a pledge to *him*.

By eight o'clock, I have been through my list of prospects. I ask to be excused, and say I am going to play a little backgammon, if there is a game in progress, before I go home. I am urged to contribute my winnings to the Harvard College Fund. Why not? Mike Stone says he will match whatever I win. Great! But what if I lose? he asks. Mike is a businessman and clearly a shrewd one. In that eventuality, I say grandly, I will shoulder the loss alone. I find a nickel game going on, sit in it for an hour, and end up thirty points plus—a hundred and fifty dollars. What with Mike's matching gift and *The New Yorker*'s matching-gift program for worthy educational institutions, I have earned Harvard four hundred and fifty bucks—far better than I did on the phone. I should have started playing sooner. At least I have the sense to quit while Harvard is ahead.

May 10

My Princeton piece is finally going to press, fifteen months after I wrote it (Shawn asks me plaintively to try to work in some recent fact, to give it a fresher look), and I am scrutinizing a proof of it this morning when Mr. Labuschagne calls from his midtown *laager*. "We have had word on your visa." Dramatic pause. "It has been disapproved." There is some further desultory talk: No, there was no reason given; we are both aware that Pretoria doesn't give reasons. I point out to him that this time Pretoria hasn't merely disapproved of me. It has turned down *The New Yorker*, which is something quite else again, and he may not have heard the last of this. I hang up, quivering with frustration, and the checking department pulls me back into the real world. It has been in touch with Evan Thomas about an anecdote I have in my Princeton piece about his renowned father, and Evan has denied its validity. "But he told it to me himself," I say. He did, at lunch one day a year and a half ago; here it is in my notes. The checking department is sorry, but if I have no independent source for the anecdote, and Evan denies it, would I not agree that it has to come out? I agree. It wasn't all that much of a story to begin with: It was simply (as their son told me at lunch) that Norman Thomas' wife's father disapproved of her marrying a Socialist until he learned it was a Princeton Socialist.

I go across the street and try to drown my sorrows in drink and backgammon.

May 11

Somebody at the garage forgot to kick the brake pedal last night and douse the lights. So the car battery is dead. Since I am not going to Africa, I guess I will have time to attend to it. By the time I reach the office, the State Department is after me. It has heard that Congressman Diggs is contemplating holding some committee hearings about South Africa. He is reported to have it in mind to propose that if South Africa won't let bona-fide American journalists in, perhaps the United States, reciprocally, should deny admittance to some of the representatives of *its* press. Should this come to pass, my State informant goes on, I may be a test case. Pat Crow and I wonder, when we meet in the hall a moment later, whether Shawn will be invited to testify, or worse yet, be subpoenaed. Pat guarantees me that before Mr. Shawn goes to Washington he will resign. How ironic that would be, inasmuch as Bill may not really care whether or not I get into South Africa and wasn't particularly eager for me to try to go there in the first place.

May 12

Our New England tennis-court reconditioner calls. We need new tapes. Do I want the cheap plastic kind that we have had all along or the guaranteed long-life ones, slightly wider? Decisions! Decisions! Decisions! I would hate to be president of the United States and have to make ultimate judgments like this every day. This question is a real poser. What if we sell the Truro house? Will we get any more for it because we have Grade-A Super-fine tapes? Hardly bloody likely: I put a whoppingly expensive all-new kitchen into our Scarborough house just before selling *that*, and there was no indication that this refurbishment, hand-wrought panelled ceiling notwithstanding, raised the purchase price a whit. And do I want my tennis-court tapes to outlive me? (Well, I certainly don't want them buried with me.) When I find, as I stall for time, that the *cheaper* variety of tennis-court tape now bears a ninety-dollar price tag, the whole business of owning a tennis court and keeping it up seems so preposterous that I tell my man to install the more expensive kind.

Town School is holding its annual Field Day this morning, on Randall's Island as usual. After getting my battery revved up with my jump cables, I head for the scene, stopping off en route at Skipper's vaunted Mobil station to get a full charge and to have the flawed brake lights examined. The customarily white-coated Skipper, who, as is also his wont, never touches a car himself, waves his stethoscope and commands someone in his crew to operate on my rear end; and upon my settling up with him for that, he waves me cheerily on my way. When I get to Randall's Island, dismount, and walk toward Lexy, he tells me I have forgotten to turn off my brake lights.

The municipal park on Randall's Island on which Town School kids have their outdoor recreation is a pig sty. It hasn't been cleaned up, one would guess from looking at it, since Mayor Beame was an eighth-grader. Still, in contrast to other public sports facilities around New York, there are tennis nets on the courts. So many vandals in New York have ripped off (literally) so many tennis-court nets that the word around town is that whereas it used to be difficult to find a public court to play on, now it is a cinch: All you need is your own net. Some years ago, at a garage sale in Truro, Malcolm Preston bought a used tennis net. Everybody thought he was out of his mind, inasmuch as the Prestons' property, a steep escarpment, is just about the only place around where it would be impossible to build a court. But Malcolm knew what he was doing. Harry Kahn has an all-weather count. When Harry and Margery Kahn close their house for the winter, and tuck their net away, Malcolm—with, naturally, their permission—unfurls his net and rigs it up till spring.

I leave Field Day early, because I have to stop back at Skipper's and apologize to him that my brake-light situation seems no better in spite of his having let me pay him for attending to it. On the occasion of last year's school outing to Randall's, I also proceeded directly to Skipper's; that time, somebody shoved a wire trash basket under the front of my car (on Randall's Island, trash baskets serve no other purpose), and I drove over it and busted the underbelly of my radiator. At least this year when I reenter Skipper's realm I am not wreathed in steam.

I heard the other day that some auto mechanics in New York are now getting twenty-five dollars an hour, which puts them almost exactly halfway between many freelance writers and most psychoanalysts.

When I eventually make it to the office, Bill Knapp says that the Harvard Club has asked him and me to withdraw our candidate's name. We resolve to decline to withdraw. There are times in life when one has to stand and fight. She seems to have put a few admissions-committee noses out of joint, and thus we wish we had a better cause to go to bat for, but no matter; we cannot falter; we are like the American Civil Liberties Union, Bill and I concur, defending the rights of the Ku Klux Klan.

Ellie has made a date for her and me to have a drink at the Algonquin—convenient as it is to both the *Times* and *The New Yorker*—with Nona Balakian. I hope that Nona will give us some heart-warming gossip about the Sunday Book Review—that, say, Harvey Shapiro is going to nominate me for the Nobel Prize—but instead she pumps *me* for news of the *Times*, as if I were somehow supposed to be a repository thereof. I think hard and tell her that there is talk of soon initiating a backgammon column in the daily, but under no circumstances to breathe a word of this to anyone, especially Harvey Shapiro.

May 13

The Algonquin Round Table flourished before my day, but I got to know many of its knights and ladies—in several instances, alas, after their prime. In 1943, when I was in the States between tours of duty in New Guinea and Panama, the Treasury Department borrowed me from the War Department to go on a bond-selling tour; there were not too many soldiers around who were both reasonably articulate and had actually been in a combat zone. I travelled around Pennsylvania for a few days in the engaging company of Ogden Nash and Dorothy Parker. We visited schools, mostly, and at each one each of us would give a more or less set spiel—laced, we hoped, with humor, and calculated in a low-key way to instill patriotic fervor in our auditors. After we had been to three or four institutions, we could tell pretty well when to expect our listeners to laugh; but this did not hold for parochial schools. The kids there would not laugh until a nun laughed. After the war, Dottie Parker took a fancy to Jinny and me. She kept asking us to visit her. She was not writing, not doing much of anything, really, just passing time. She was small, and wistful, often drunk, not infrequently in tears, and too world-weary to be witty. She was living at the New Weston Hotel then, less than half a mile from the Algonquin, but I don't think she spent much time, if any, at the hotel she helped make famous. When I first went to work at *The New Yorker*, before I belonged to any of the neighborhood clubs, I used to eat lunch at the Algonquin at least a couple of times a week, and it was not anybody at the magazine that introduced me to the place, curiously, but my mother. Elsie liked to drop in there, if for no more than a cup of coffee; the headwaiter in the Rose Room when I was in college—John, wasn't it?—knew and liked her and because of her was later deferential to me. So was his successor Thomas, and Raoul next door in the Oak Room, and Thomas' assistant Helen, who must have been one of the earliest female assistant headwaiters in town. They are all gone now (Helen works for *The New Yorker*), and I have only the same difficulty getting a table at the Algonquin as any shoe salesman from Boise or Butte who comes in off the street.

Nick the Greek is gone, too. Nicholas was a captain of waiters in the Rose Room, and I never paid much attention to him until I was having lunch there one day with S.L.A. Marshall, the distinguished military historian. Halfway through our meal, Slam Marshall summoned Nick to our table and told me that *here* was a man, considering how close *The New Yorker* had long been, spiritually as well as geographically, to the Algonquin, whom we should write about. General Marshall (he was only a brigadier in some state reserve, but he enjoyed being called "General," and why not?) paused for effect, and then revealed solemnly to me that Nick was one of the very few holders of the Victoria Cross in New York, and indubitably the only one on *The New Yorker* block. Slam knew I would be impressed. He knew that I had done much writing about soldiers, their heroism, and their decorations; he knew that I was aware that the Victoria Cross is awfully hard to get—harder than our own Medal of Honor—and is as often as not a posthumous award. And I reacted as Slam knew I would: I told Nick as we were leaving the Rose Room that I would like to interview him, when he got off duty some afternoon, for a Talk of the Town piece.

We made a date, and he came by my office, bringing along some newspaper clippings attesting to his special valor—I read how at great personal risk he had helped the British in Greece during the Nazi occupation—and, in two or three fascinating hours, telling me the story of his life. I wrote a piece about him, but as I was retyping it there were one or two discrepancies that puzzled me. I got the British Information Service on the phone, and they said they would check with London, where there was an up-to-date and accurate—and not very bulky—roster of all holders of the Victoria Cross. Word soon came back. My Nicholas was not on the list. Nick was an imposter. If my Talk piece had run, he would have had one more credential to thrust upon the next person who interviewed him. But I didn't feel too bad about the whole episode. After all, he had done me no harm, and if he could pull the wool over the eyes of a military historian of the epic stature of Brigadier General S.L.A. Marshall, why not try me?

These days, I hardly recognize any of the hotel's staff, though I always make a point of nodding to Mrs. Bodne, the owner's wife, as she sits in the lobby. She probably does not know who it is who is greeting her. Norman Mailer? Max Lerner? Some character actor in that new play that's having previews? A much-decorated hero of the Greek Resistance? More likely, I seem to her just another ship that passes in a busy night. My latter-day relationship with the Algonquin being what it is, how strange that, having left the place at six-forty-five yesterday evening, I am back, at eight-forty-five this morning. The occasion is a farewell breakfast, in the Oak Room (usually not open till lunch) for Julie Hayden, who is embarking on a leave of absence from *The New Yorker*. There are five tables set up, all round, though this isn't the room the original Round Table was in, and place cards have been laid out, and I am flattered that I am to sit next to Julie, and even more flattered that I am the only fact-piece writer who seems to have been invited. Most of the others are editors and checkers. There is a good deal of talk at our table about older members of the staff, prompted by the presence of two very senior editors with a total of something like a hundred years' *New Yorker* service between them. They have been assigned to tables at opposite ends of the room, apparently because in their case, someone at my table avers, familiarity has run strikingly true to form. And speaking of form, somebody else wonders, how old, anyway, is our surely most ancient writer, G.F.T. Ryall, the "Audax Minor" of our race-track column? It has been some years since I wrote my book on Herbert Bayard Swope, but it seems to me that while I was doing research for that I learned that Ryall was writing for the New York *World* in 1906, and that he had covered racing in his native England before *that*. He must be about as old as Cyrus Eaton.

One of the younger members of our group asks me when *I* joined the staff. In 1937, I say—and then realize with a start that my fortieth anniversary at the magazine came and went last month and I never even thought about it. Julie says she has been cooking, and that some asparagus soup came out too yellow, and to make it greener she wanted to add something blue, but she couldn't find any blueberry cordial, so she tried Angostura bitters, but that made the soup taste so terrible she had to throw it away. (I didn't think until later of recommending methalyne blue, which when we were kids we used to try to slip into people's food; it turned your urine blue and could scare the bejezus out of you if you didn't know what was going on.) Julie continues: She is writing a long non-fiction article about a garden. She takes her typewriter to it, sets it up on a bird bath, and works surrounded by her subject matter. I urge her to have somebody photograph her thus in action; it would make a perfect picture for the dust jacket of her next book. Bill Knapp, commuting from Connecticut, arrives at the breakfast late. Julie tells him about her bird bath. Bill says a picture of that would be ideal for a dust jacket.

May 15

A beautiful spring Sunday. Inspired by a front-page review of Roger Angell's new baseball book in the *Times*, I persuade Lexy—and to my surprise and delight, Ellie, too—to accompany me to Shea Stadium, where Tom Seaver is to pitch for the Mets against the L. A. Dodgers, who are running away with their division in the National League while the Mets sink ever deeper into the cellar of theirs. It is a splendid game—goes all the way to the twelfth inning before the Mets lose it, having wasted numerous glorious scoring opportunities. Men on second and third with nobody out in the twelfth, for example. In a way, though, it is good that the home team doesn't tie it up then, for I promised E. that I would leave at the end of that inning, no matter what; she was getting understandably restless. I made her in turn promise not to tell anybody if I departed before the game was over.

Poor Lexy! He does not know, at fourteen, which field is left! What do they teach kids at school these days, anyway?

May 16

A helicopter crashes on the roof of the Pan Am Building this afternoon. Five dead, one while walking along the street below. I can see the big building from my window, only three blocks away, but I don't hear the impact, and nobody in New York pays any attention to emergency-vehicle sirens any more. I am not ordinarily a fearful person, but these last couple of months, whenever I have been walking near the Pan Am Building and have seen or heard a 'copter fluttering overhead, I have carefully anticipated what evasive action I might be able to take—whether it would be quicker, for example, to duck into the Yale Club, or make a dash for the sheltered doorway of Feron's tennis shop.

My first helicopter ride was a trying one. In the winter of 1969, when I was separated but not yet divorced, Ellie and I were invited by Eileen and Arnold Maremont to spend a weekend with them in Jamaica. It was the first time that E. and I ever went off together anywhere. We took a taxi out to Kennedy Airport in a snowstorm that got worse and worse; by the time we reached the Pan Am terminal, our cab could barely move, and we were not surprised to learn that all flights, incoming and outgoing, were delayed. That was the great blizzard that paralyzed New York City and stranded people like us at airports for thirty-six hours. When it became apparent that we weren't going anywhere for quite a while, if ever, and that, according to radio reports, this was considered a major crisis, I queued up at a phone booth and, on reaching the head of the line, called Shawn and suggested that I write a piece about our predicament. He consented, and said he would hold space open for me in the next issue. *That's* the kind of scheduling I'm fondest of.

There was not much to eat or drink at Pan Am, after the first few hours, and no place to sleep but the floor, using luggage or laps as pillows; but a kind of convivial strangers-in-a-lifeboat togetherness prevailed. Inasmuch as by now I was playing a double role—both partaker of and reporter on the experience—I sought out an airport official to obtain what information there was to be had. He confided to me that a helicopter had just arrived with supplies, and that it would be returning shortly to Manhattan with a handful of passengers who needed urgently to return. I had to get some copy to my magazine fast, I said, and could he find room aboard for me and my friend? He said there were just two remaining places, but, to avoid a stampede among the hundred of others on the scene who didn't know about the 'copter, would I please keep this to myself and just proceed with my, ah, friend to such-and-such a gate.

Ellie and I were the last two passengers to get in the helicopter, and, being seated alongside its door, were also—as if part of some accounting system— the first two out. We landed at Wall Street and the East River. It was dark outside, and I started gingerly down the steps of the machine, with Ellie immediately behind me. We were still several feet from the ground when a blaze of light hit us in the face. We were being filmed by television cameras, because we were the first victims of the ordeal at Kennedy to return safely to the city. Fortunately, E.'s kids, whom she had told she was going to visit a girl friend over the weekend, did not watch the eleven o'clock news.

Unfortunately, Shawn did not buy the piece. Not because of my friend— she wasn't recognizable in it—but because he thought I had too frivolously treated what he regarded as a tragic occurrence. It didn't seem all that catastrophic to me. Some people got inconvenienced (Ellie and I far more than Bill or anyone else back on the mainland), but nobody got hurt; and the city, for a day or so, looked dazzlingly beautiful. Shawn's rejecting the piece turned out to be a break for John McCarten, who had left the staff, retired to Ireland, and sent back some "Irish Sketches"—the sort of timeless pieces that any prudent editor loves to have deposited in his bank. With my piece scheduled, but shelved, there was suddenly a hole in the magazine that had to be filled. One McCarten sketch must have been just the right length, so in it was dropped. I sold my account of the Kennedy caper to *Travel and Leisure*.

Big party at the Liftons' tonight. It is Bob's fifty-first birthday. Hardly an earth-shaking milestone, but any excuse for a party is better than none. Alice Mayhew, Bob's editor, who will be also handling Ellie's book for Simon and Schuster, is there, but she evidently would rather talk about baseball than women artists. How lucky for Ellie that she dragged Lexy and me to watch Tom Terrific pitch yesterday and can knowledgeably join in! It is always good for a writer to have a strong common interest with his editor. Her editor.

Fred Morton is present, too. We talk of Cape Cod. He has heard I have my own tennis court there. "I suppose you have a swimming pool, too," he says. Having written "The Rothschilds," he must be obsessed with wealth. When I was growing up, my mother's parents could probably have put in both a court and a pool at their Westchester place, but the best they ever produced was a wading pool—too big for goldfish, too small for grand-children. There never was much outdoor activity at Knolltop. At noon on

Sunday, though, everybody who was around for the weekend would travel about one hundred feet from the big house to a shady spot under some maple trees, and Emily the cook would come out from the kitchen and grill hot dogs. My father rarely attended these effete picnics, preferring golf. Often on Saturday nights he would bring back to our house, down the hill from the aval manse, the rest of his foursome, so they could spend the evening playing bridge. As some children become violin prodigies at an early age, so did I exhibit marked precocity as a bridge kibitzer. My father called his sporting set "The Vultures." I couldn't have been more surprised when, some years later, one of the vultures turned out to be my mother's lover and her second husband. It hadn't occurred to me that weekends at Elmsford could be so romantic.

I never played golf with my father, only with my grandfather Plaut. When he was seventy and I was twelve, we were about equal, each of us shooting, on a good day, in the neighborhood of 120. I have in my study in Truro a trophy that he acquired when he was younger, a desk receptacle for pencils. In the annual Governor's Cup tournament at his country club, he won the championship of the Fourth Sixteenth, which, come to think of it, may have been composed exclusively of men who had never broken 90. I did once score a birdie on a par-4 hole. This involved, as I reconstruct the feat, my ball's bouncing off a couple of trees and skipping like a stone across the surface of a pond, and then my being conceded a fourteen-foot putt. My grandfather was a generous man. When I was fifteen, he and I decided that golf was a game neither of us was ever likely to master, and we both gave it up forever. Nothing has ever made me less sorry. I do like to watch golf now on television, probably because of the large sums of money involved. I must ask Fred Morton, next time I see him, if he watches it, too.

Still another guest at the Liftons' is Anne Richardson Roiphe, who not long ago wrote a piece for the *Times* Sunday magazine about Sarah Lawrence College, which evoked loud outcries because she dwelt at length on campus homosexuality. Anne says that after the article came out she was awakened several times at two in the morning by women who identified themselves as lesbians and said, "I'm going to rape your daughter." Journalists have to put up with a lot, but this is about as nasty a reader reaction as any I've ever heard of.

May 18

Helen Suzman is in town from South Africa. She is over here to receive honorary degrees from Columbia and Smith. (She already has one from Harvard.) Helen is not surprised that I didn't get the visa. She talked to Dr. Connie Mulder, the minister of information and interior there, the other day, and he told her that "on the basis of information I have" he couldn't let me in. She and I will meet tomorrow and go into this at greater length. Jim Thomson, running the Nieman Foundation up in Cambridge, has heard the glum news, too. He has something like seventeen Nieman Fellows working on various South African publications now—one of them, Percy Qobosa, is the editor of the principal black paper, the *World*—and he has it in mind to let them know *The New Yorker* was turned down. He thinks they may wish to do something about it.

Lunch with Jack Crawford, up from Atlanta. He wants to know if my Georgia piece has been scheduled yet. Hah! I haven't even finished it. I do know where the light is at the end of that particular tunnel, but I haven't glimpsed it yet. We swap war stories, most of them reflecting poorly on high-ranking soldiers. Jack tells me one about how Omar Bradley, in combat garb, went to some hotel to report to Ike during the Battle of the Bulge, and how General Eisenhower, who was in the midst of an important bridge game when his subordinate arrived and didn't enjoy being disturbed, seemed less concerned about the dire situation his troops were in than that General Bradley was out of uniform. I tell Jack one about Douglas MacArthur. That general seldom visited the New Guinea front during the first two months his troops were fighting there, and when he did he always managed to fly back for a comfortable night's sleep at his headquarters. (He never spent a night in Korea, either, during the three months I covered his war *there*.) In the fall of 1942, MacArthur, who had lofty political aspirations, arrived suddenly one day at 32nd Division Headquarters. He had in tow Philip LaFollette, a former governor of Wisconsin, who the general presumably hoped could steer some votes his way at a nominating convention. When MacArthur arrived, everybody on the scene naturally scurried about to receive him in suitable style, and my General Harding, as Red Arrow commander, was naturally the first to throw his superior a crisp salute. MacArthur wasted no time stating his business, though to us witnesses it seemed as though he had neglected to apprise Major LaFollette of it beforehand. "Phil," he said sonorously, "I want you to meet Forrest Harding. He will lead you to your glory or to death." LaFollette, by comparison to whom most deskbound officers looked like Tarzan, gulped; one sensed that he would rather take his chances on swimming back to Australia, crocodiles or no crocodiles, than to fool around with those options. He didn't have to, ultimately; he was so inept that he became a censor.

Bill Knapp has made an appointment for us, at eleven tomorrow, in his office, with the chairman of the Harvard Club's admissions committee and its secretary, the latter a woman whom our candidate has allegedly offended. The woman works for *Time*. It is good to know that that magazine has employees with uncommon sensitivity.

May 19

One senses how far detached South Africa is from the rest of the world when one meets Helen Suzman—as cosmopolitan and travelled a citizen as that sad nation can boast—at the East River apartment of the Benjamin Buttenwiesers, where she is staying, and she looks south toward a tall building and asks what that is: It is the United Nations. Helen says she talked to Connie Mulder several times about my visa, and the first time he said that if she insisted on an immediate decision, she could have it then and there and it would be negative. She dropped the subject. She brought it up again last week in Cape Town; she sent him a note while Parliament was in session, and they chatted in a cloakroom. Mulder told her this time that his Ministry of Information had a thick dossier on me, and that if she could see it, which she didn't get to, she would understand why I was unacceptable.

I suddenly wonder—this has not occurred to me before—whether the ministry could have me confused with somebody else. Just as we Americans wrongly tend to think that all South African government officials named Botha are one and the same, so maybe do they think there is only a single suspect Kahn. There was, maybe still is, an American writer of about my age named Albert E. Kahn, whose views were far to the left and whose name could regularly be found on the rosters of front groups called, say, the Committee for Fair Play for William Z. Foster. If South Africa has a dossier on that Kahn, it is unquestionably thick, and if his dossier is in mine, then mine is thick. Helen says this is a beguiling possibility, and she will look into it when she gets home. She cannot understand what, if the dossier on me is exclusively about me, it can contain that is incriminating; why, she has always believed that, politically, I am somewhere to the right of *her*.

Over coffee, we talk about recent political developments in her South Africa. Instead of Helen's being the only member of the Progressive Party in Parliament, she now has eleven cohorts, which makes her working life more tolerable. Sir de Villiers Graaff, the longtime head of the United Party, the official opposition to the reigning Nationalists, is about to step down, and that could mean the demise of the U.P., and in that event her Progs could become The Opposition. The Nats of Hendrik Verwoerd and now John Vorster came into power in 1948. Mindful of the fact that the Labor Party in Israel, which attained its first majority that same year, has just been deposed, I point out to Helen that should the Progs one day take over the government, she might become prime minister. Never, says Helen, who, though like Golda Meir a grandmother, looks less grandmotherly; she wouldn't consider taking the post. But *if*, I persist, she somehow *did*, could I then have a visa? She promises me one.

We talk about Andrew Young, who not long ago denounced Helen as a paternalistic liberal (he later retracted), and she says she has no idea what Young has against her; that it can hardly be personal, because they have only met, and then briefly, at some Washington breakfast. In any event, she goes on, he is mistaken in continuing to draw parallels between what is going on in South Africa and what has gone on in the American South. What blacks over here have endured has been against the law, she reminds me; their sufferings in South Africa are embedded in its laws. A big difference, of course, and one that she thinks a statesman should be aware of.

I rush back to *The New Yorker* for the meeting Bill Knapp and I have with the Harvard Club admissions pair, a Mr. Banker and a Ms. Journalist. They are dead set against reconsidering our candidate's application, because she wouldn't take an elevator up to somebody's office and also spoke rudely to somebody's secretary on the phone. (Would it be possible to explain to nineteen million oppressed black South Africans—or, for that matter, to Helen Suzman and Andrew Young—why we are having this solemn conversation about the entrance of a single person into a social club?) The chairman of the admissions committee is greyish, fortyish, very stuffy; leaning back on the couch in Knapp's tidy office, Banker allows as how he is worried about how our girl would behave were she in the club. I say she has been to my home for dinner a couple of times and that her behavior was exemplary, a veritable Elsie Dinsmore.

Bill K. says that if a list were to be drawn up of the ten most bizarre idiosyncratics at *The New Yorker*, ours wouldn't even be on it; and that if our visitors want to make something big out of her aversion to riding in self-service elevators, they should be apprised that William Shawn feels the same way himself. So does my wife, I add; should this pair of guardians of the Harvard Club gates want to keep on our good side, they had better steer clear of the subject of self-service elevators. But the trouble is that they don't seem to care whether or not we are buddies. Banker wants us to withdraw our sponsorship, because if we don't he will probably be obliged to send us a formal letter of rejection. Tempers are running short; Knapp snaps that that would be fine, we are sponsoring a novelist, she can put the letter straight into some book.

We dine at the apartment of B. A., whose husband has abandoned her and moved to Pittsburgh, or Toledo, or one of those places. B. tells us at some length how each of two extra men she tried to get for dinner didn't show up at the last minute. It is hard to be newly single in New York, or so I say without, I must confess, ever having been to a singles bar. During the time, between marriages, when I was a bachelor, I was told by several well-meaning friends of both sexes that single men were in great demand and short supply, and that I would be deluged with dinner invitations. In six months, I got just one, and that, coming at 3 P.M. and involving a formal dinner the very same evening, gave me the impression that by the time my hostess called me, she had got awfully near the bottom of her own socially eligible barrel.

May 20

As soon as Bill Knapp comes in to work he asks me to stop by his office for a moment; he wants to show me something. A telegram from Banker to the effect that after sleeping on it he has changed his mind, and we are in? No. There is a ghastly smudge on Knapp's impeccable office wall, above his couch, just where The Chairman rested his head yesterday as he leaned back to make pontifical pronouncements. This banker greases his hair! People who use pomade should not be entrusted with other people's money and should certainly be ostracized from any gentlemen's and gentlewomen's club. Near as Bill and I can make out from a cursory inspection, the woman left no visible traces of her presence.

To dinner at my sister Joan's. The Talat Halmans are there. Patrick Smith called me this morning about my Princeton piece, which has finally come out in the magazine, and my brother-in-law, P '48 and the first Son of Old Nassau I've heard from, says there is a mistake in it. He says the *Princeton Alumni Weekly* is not, as I wrote, a weekly except during the football season. Now Talat, who is on the faculty there, more or less sides with me: He says the *Weekly* is, too, a weekly, except in the summertime, when it doesn't exist at all. The Halmans urge Ellie and me to take some tickets to a charity ball they are promoting. I am leery. The last time I got involved with one of those, it proved costly. I won a free table for ten, in a raffle, at one of those fifty-dollar-a-plate affairs; but by the time I had bought whiskey and wine for the guests I'd invited to share this bonanza with me, not to mention other more than incidental expenses, I ended up the evening practically a charity case myself. Also, at these big eleemosynary feasts, one is rarely served anything to eat before 11 P.M., if then; and unless one is Spanish or a member of the idle rich, that's a ridiculous hour for dinner.

May 21

Seattle Slew, the favorite, wins the Preakness today. Andy Young is in South Africa and has clearly won that race from me; I had thought that our odds were about equal.

It is Sidney Simon's sixtieth birthday, and E. and I take Rita Gam along to his party. Again, E. suggests that I compose a poem, and again, since nobody else seems willing, eager, or prepared to treat this landmark event as anything other than a routine Greenwich Village cocktail party, I climb on a table and declaim. Elise Asher, standing alongside Ellie in the throng, cannot see who is giving the recital but, hearing it, says it is the most terrible poem she has ever heard. All right, so her husband *did* win the Pulitzer Prize for poetry; had Stanley Kunitz himself been in the audience, I'm sure he would have given me at least an A for Effort.

We go on, with Diana Michaelis and Rita, to the Cherry Lane Theatre to see "I Was Sitting on My Patio This Guy Appeared I Thought I was Hallucinating." This is the latest avant-garde opus of Robert Wilson, who in the last few years has punished me through more long and numbing evenings—"Deaf Man Glance," "The Life and Death of Joseph Stalin," "Einstein on the Beach"—than any crimes I may have committed warrant. He is the first half of the evening, solo; Lucinda Childs the second. We are in the front row, practically on patio, and this play, which if it is a play by comparison to which I deserve the Nobel Prize in Poetry, is so deadening that within a few minutes Rita is sound asleep on my left, Diana dozing nicely on my right. I, surprisingly, maddeningly, am wide awake. I never wanted more to sleep through a theatrical evening. The only memorable line in the script, if there is a script, goes, apropos of nothing that takes place on the stage, "It doesn't make any sense."

May 22

We drive out to Scarborough, for lunch and tennis with the Benjamins. There is a large boat parked in the driveway of my ex-house. I have no desire to see what changes have been wrought inside. Not long after we sold the place, I foolishly peeked in through the window of what had been my study. When the house was built, I stipulated that the study was to be mine and mine alone. It was under no circumstances to be converted into a guest room or anything else—though if I chose to take a nap on its daybed that was my business. On revisiting it, I found that it had been converted into a maid's room, and for a servant of apparently epic religiosity; the chamber was aswarm with icons, crucifixes, and still other symbols of intense reverence that my Peeping Tom's eyes could not identify—perhaps partly because the whole area was bathed in an eerie crimson glow. Bud and Aline say the old neighborhood has changed in other respects, too. Somebody up the road killed himself and his three children not long ago. The worst we ever had was the suicide of a close friend, whose husband said he wanted a church service for her. The only problem was that she hadn't been a churchgoer. Some of us who were helping with the arrangements persuaded a local minister to officiate, but he said he would do so only if—inasmuch as he had never met the deceased—somebody would prepare appropriate remarks for him to deliver. At times like that, one wishes one were not known to be a writer. That was a tough assignment to fulfill.

May 23

Douglas Watt, in the Sunday *News*, dismisses the Wilson-Childs happening at the Cherry Lane as nonsense. A critic of rare good judgment. I myself, though, would have used "arrant nonsense."

I was wondering, trying to get to sleep last night, what the South Africans can have on me besides my having written a book about them and my being associated with a subversive weekly magazine. Do they know that Ellie and I, though not normally politically activist, went down to the District of Columbia in January, 1973, to march in protest on the eve of Nixon's second inauguration? At one point, strolling purposefully from the Lincoln Memorial toward the Washington Monument, we came into range of some newspaper photographers, and we obliged them with a hearty wave; only after their cameras clicked did E. and I become aware that the banner fluttering over our proud defiant heads read "Gay Activists Alliance." Good Lord, do you suppose the prudish Afrikaners have got hold of a print of that shot and deem me morally unfit to roam at will among them?

Mac Talley takes me to lunch at Doubles, a private club that I have no doubt I could get into, or even get somebody else into, if I tried hard enough. He is reorganizing his publishing house, and searching around for new financial backing. (As angels, this Doubles crowd looks unpromising; too high-fashion in dress, two high-pitched in voice.) Inasmuch as Mac cannot sign any contracts with authors until he finds some money, our exchanges of ideas have to be perfunctory. He is as always, however, a repository of odd and diverting bits of information. Today he tells—a conscientious reporter would seek corroboration—how the internal-combustion engine came into being. It was devised, he says, in order to find some profitable use for the gasoline that used to be dumped, as a supposedly worthless byproduct of kerosene, into the Gulf of Mexico.

Alastair Reid says, back at the office, that he has heard a rumor that Anthony Bailey, another staff writer resident in England, is going to be the next editor of *The New Yorker*.

May 24

The *Times* has an editorial this morning entitled "Should Homosexuals Be Teachers?" Its answer is a guarded "Yes." The reservation has to do with gays fooling around with their students. Nobody seems to object, editorially, or in any other way, to teachers fooling around heterosexually. I don't know if any statistics exist in this connection (I doubt very much whether the Bureau of the Census has any), but I would bet that the majority of second wives of university professors are women at least twenty-five years younger than their husbands who first met them in a classroom.

Ellie and I go to Cleveland today for a reunion of her family, the occasion being the first Thomas Munro Memorial Lecture at the Cleveland Museum of Art, where her father was a curator (as well as the founder of the American Society of Aesthetics) until his retirement. Mother Lucile is coming up from Sarasota, brother Don over from Ann Arbor, sister Betty will be travelling from New York with us, and other sister Cynthia, as the only member of the clan still resident in Cleveland, will have us all on her neck. At some point or other in the course of the celebration, we may all be called upon for nostalgic remarks, and I wonder if I should recount my first meeting with my father-in-law then presumptive. Ellie was staying with her parents in Florida, and I had been visiting the Maremonts—alone—in Jamaica, and inasmuch as E. and I were planning to get married, I thought it would be appropriate for me to stop by Sarasota on my way back north and be introduced to my future in-laws. Tom and Lucile seemed a bit cool when I arrived; only later did I learn that Ellie hadn't got around to telling them I was her husband-to-be, and so to them I was no different from a clutch of other escorts who had taken out their pretty widowed daughter.

I hadn't been at the Munro house long when we all drove over to a country club for their daily go at golf. They played golf in a fashion I deemed most peculiar. They didn't keep score. Ellie and I were to walk around the links with them, but we hadn't strode beyond the third tee when Tom remembered that he had forgotten his nitroglycerin. His nitroglycerin was his security blanket. I was instructed to drive him back home for his pills. He sat next to me on the front seat, pale, rigid, silent, and I was thinking: This man I scarcely know is going to have a fatal heart attack before I can get him to his medication, and I can't recall where his house is. I jolted him out of his trance, thus obtaining his navigational aid, by making some casual allusion, to his utter astonishment, to the effect that his daughter and I were planning to have a young Southern Baptist minister officiate at our nuptials. It was good that his heart was basically sound, for another thing I didn't then know was that he was a staunch practicing atheist.

I spent a good deal of time in Cleveland and its environs last year, when I was doing research on my Eaton Profile. (I also spent an agreeable four days as a writer-in-residence at Western Reserve Academy, in Hudson, Ohio, halfway between Cleveland and Akron.) When the Eatons were not hospitably putting me up in their farm's guest house, I stayed at a big brand new downtown hotel which, while comfortable enough, had its claustrophobic drawbacks; out-of-towners like me were warned by presumably knowledgeable indigenes not to venture beyond its portals after dark. Say what you will about New York, most of its midtown hotels are not yet fortresses. This time, Cynnie has booked us into the Alcazar, one of Cleveland's oldest hotels. It used to be *the* place. When Bob Bingham was growing up in Cleveland, he would go there during college vacations and listen to Willie "the Lion" Smith play piano in the bar. Now the establishment has been taken over by the Christian Science Church, as an old folks' home. The lobby is full of exceedingly senior citizens equipped with strollers and canes and wheelchairs, who cross it in slow and silent motion, as if they were characters in a play by Robert Wilson. They do not have to worry about danger in the streets outside; many of them look as though they could not make it as far as the street. It goes without saying that there is no longer any bar.

We all convene at Cynnie's for cocktails, and then proceed to the Chagrin Valley Hunt Club, where Sherman Lee, the incumbent director of the museum, is giving a dinner for all of us and a couple of dozen others. I am seated next to Mrs. R. Henry Norweb, one of Cleveland's grandes dames, patroness of the arts (she is a former president of the museum), a famous collector of coins (we will see some of hers when we tour the museum tomorrow), and, she tells me, the senior resident, in terms of continuing tenancy, of River House in New York. Here is proof indeed that Midwesterners are not parochial, but my dinner companion is perhaps not typical of her part of the country; her husband was in the foreign service, and when one is a diplomat the world shrinks.

Henry Norweb tells me after dinner, upon hearing that I am associated with *The New Yorker*, that when he was a member of the United States mission in Paris, during the First World War, the Army assigned James Thurber to him as a code clerk. Norweb says that to this day he has been unable to comprehend why the military would put a person with only one eye on a job like that. Did I know Thurber? he wants to know. Yes, but, unfortunately, only in the last few years of Jim's life, when both of his eyes were gone, and he had become a sort of dual personality—charming until some time in mid-evening, at which time a combination of drink and despair (by then *The New Yorker* had begun rejecting some of his casuals and they were coming out in odd magazines like the *Bermudan)* made him testy. He was spending much of his time, by then, in West Cornwall, but this was before Ellie and I got to know that community. I have difficulty trying to fit him into it.

There are many fine and gracious testimonials made to Tom Munro during the dinner, and the family is, of course, enormously pleased. No sons-in-law are called upon to speak, which is just as well. There has been some apprehension among the second-generation Munros in town about how long Lucile, once given the floor, might hold it; she is from Alabama, after all, and Southern ladies are notoriously loquacious. It is the unanimous opinion of her four children, conveyed to her in firm terms, that seven minutes is a suitable maximum for whatever she feels like saying; privately, they doubt if she can settle for fewer than sixty. How little do offspring know about their progenitors! I clock her: Her remarks about her late husband—quite touchingly expressed—consume precisely six minutes and fifty-three seconds.

Back at Cynnie's for a solid hour's worth of instant replay of the testimonial evening, *her* kids ask me for a bedtime story. They know my limited repertoire. Which will it be tonight—the icre-cream (sometimes lollipop) factory or the whale dentist? We are inland, not at the seashore. They opt for the ice-cream factory. All right, here we go: There was this terrible crisis one time in Cleveland when Kevin had a birthday party coming up and his mommy suddenly discovered that nowhere, *nowhere* in the city was any chocolate chip ice cream to be found. So the board of directors of the ice-cream factory was summoned into emergency session, and Chairman of the Board Kevin said to President John and the others, "Gentlemen, we have a crisis. . . ."

In the whale-dentist story, I am the whale dentist. The whales call me "Doc." We have a secret language. I can hear them calling me in it from hundreds of yards offshore. I carry a trombone in my rowboat. I use its slide to keep their mouths propped open while I work. . . .

Hey, what do you know! The kids are asleep!

May 25

The honor of delivering the first Thomas Munro Memorial Lecture has been conferred—along with, I suppose an adequate honorarium—on Robert Brustein, the dean of the Yale School of Drama, who never knew Thomas Munro. Dean Brustein's topic is, wait till I consult my notes, "Towards a Metaphorical Theatre: A Proposal for a Theatrical Aesthetic." The family is pleased that he got that "aesthetic" in; bound volumes of the "Journal of Esthetics," Thos. Munro, ed., stand prominently on Lucile's bookshelves. Otherwise, the speech is more or less a history of the modern theatre, from O'Neill to Arthur Miller and points between, and it sounds to me (I am probably being snide) like a speech that has been delivered before. What makes me suspect that is that the oration ends with a discussion of the works of Robert Wilson, and the most recent one cited is "Einstein on the Beach." Maybe Brustein figures nobody in Cleveland will know better.

May 26

Back at the office in New York, I find a few letters about my Princeton piece. A woman in Los Angeles writes that her favorite detail is my mentioning that in keeping dozens of people apprised of an interminable correspondence between the president of the university and a disgruntled alumnus, thirty-seven and one-half reams of paper were consumed. That piece was checked by Martin Baron, a tiger for accuracy, who will leave no fact unchallenged until he has chewed it to the bone. Not long before we went to press, he came deferentially into my office and said he had authenticated all but a few of my asseverations. But what still had him stumped, he said, were my figures on the quantity of paper. Would I mind telling him where I had got them, so he could reconfirm with my source? "I made them up," I said. Martin was shaken. *"You—made—them—up!"* He tottered away as if I had slugged him with an unabridged dictionary.

After work, I pick up Rainbow at *her* favorite hotel, the Pet Lodge. David is learning how to drive, and it occurs to me that a good way of finding out if a person is qualified for a license would be to put him into the driver's seat of an automobile during evening rush hour in Manhattan, and place alongside him a large dog that has just been sprung from incarceration in a kennel. It is easy enough to drive with one arm, but it requires two to keep a dog from loving you to death.

We are home in time to catch the closing night of "Bye Bye Birdie," which Brustein did not mention in his address; the Town School is presenting it, and Lexy is playing the juvenile. He has no songs, but he does get what so many actors aspire to—a chance to play a drunk scene. He handles it very realistically, indicating that he has not been unobservant in the course of growing up.

May 27

I should have been a public relations man. Red Smith's entire column in the *Times* today is about Bob Watson of Harvard and Booze's getting all those Ivy League letters. I didn't even know Red had got *my* letter. Red evidently phoned Booze—who has been a teetotaler for all his life—and picked up a lot of details, but nowhere does he write that Watson's classmates initiated the whole business. It's just as well that he doesn't. A good public relations man wouldn't want a plug for his client to sound contrived.

While Bob Bingham and I are catching our breath with the score in our running squash-racquets war two games apiece, he asks if I am a friend of John Cheever. I say yes. Bob wonders if I know why John no longer writes for *The New Yorker*; he has heard it was because he had a dispute with his editor, Bill Maxwell. I find that hard to believe; didn't John tell me that the only story he has had in the magazine in the last ten years was one he wrote as a sort of farewell present for Maxwell when Bill retired? Bob has also heard that the fiction people at *The New Yorker* were offered "The Falconer" before it came out in book form, but rejected it without even letting Shawn know. Would we ever have published it without considerable bowdlerizing? Bingham seems to think we might have. Now that he has got my mind way off on something else, he wins the fifth and final game scarcely without puffing.

Cheever—Labrador retrievers, wood fires, dry martinis, people we both knew in Scarborough romping as fictional characters through the Wapshot books and other chronicles. As he drifted into that Westchester community through me, so did I drift there via Julian Street, Jr. (Street, Sr., was the author and wine connoisseur who once wrote a disparaging magazine article about a city out west; the miffed town fathers gave the principal thoroughfare of their red-light district a new name—Julian Street.) Julian, Jr.— Pete to his friends—was married to Narcissa Vanderlip, and the Vanderlips had practically created Scarborough. It was Nar's sister Char's cottage on the family estate into which Jinny and I moved in 1946, initially for the summer, then year round. The Cheevers succeeded us there. The Streets lived up the hill, a mile or so away, in a house we almost bought until we decided instead to build our own. When I first arrived at Char's place, I did not think I would find the neighborhood congenial. I pulled in there, with a nearly newborn baby, in the late afternoon, and the slanting rays of the sun, as they hit the garage steps, brightly illuminated seven of the largest rats I had ever seen or heard of. The house was near the Hudson River, and I guess they were river rats. No more than a few rats at a time, though, ever penetrated the house itself. We were even nearer Route 9, the Albany Post Road—so close that trucks roaring down it in the night would shake our house, and presumably agitate the rats lurking outside it, too. During the great blizzard of 1948, when that road became impassable, we entertained nineteen overnight guests, most of them truckdrivers. Very congenial bunch.

It was Pete Street who, while working for the Treasury Department during the war, arranged for me to go on that war-bond tour with Dottie Parker and Ogden Nash. Later, the Streets moved to Paris for a while, and they were living there on April 1, 1949, when I had an April-in-Paris day, chestnut trees in full bloom and so forth, that was all the more memorable because it was totally unexpected. I had gone to Germany, to write a piece about the Berlin Airlift—*die Luftbrücke*, they called it over there, the air bridge—and was on an Air Transport Command night flight back to the States. We were supposed to refuel at dawn somewhere—Iceland, the Azores, it didn't matter because the passengers were all asleep—and so we were surprised, on being aroused by the pilot's voice, to hear that we had been turned back by headwinds and would be landing momentarily at Paris. We would not be taking off again till midnight. I rushed to an airport phone and called the Streets. In air travel, one loses one's sense of time. What on earth did Pete mean when he said groggily that Nar and he had been in bed?

Oh, it was 6 A.M. I apologized. Pete has the world's best manners. He said they'd be out to fetch me as soon as they could get dressed. We spent the whole day together. The weather was perfect. Paris was beautiful. We dined sumptuously at the Grand Vefour. We had lunch at a side-street café, where we got onto wines, a subject on which Pete is nearly as knowledge-able as his father was. I did a mean thing. I suggested that Pete's palate wasn't as sensitive as he thought. We had two carafes of *vin ordinaire* on the table, one *blanc*, one *rouge*, and I bet him that blindfolded he couldn't tell which was which. First time he took the test, he flunked it. I refused to let him try again. How's that for glaring abuse of hospitality?

May 28

Bruce Bliven, Sr., died this morning, in California, at eighty-seven. I could count almost unfailingly on a cheerful note from him whenever I had a signed piece in *The New Yorker;* and the mimeographed Christmas letter that Rosie and he sent out, which Harry Reasoner and Ann Landers and others have quoted from, will be missed equally by those of us who knew Big Bruce and those who merely received at holidaytime a secondhand reading of his wit and wisdom. It would be nice to hope that one could grow old so gracefully.

The thumb Lexy hurt playing baseball while we were in Cleveland (the school nurse told him it was a sprain and he should wiggle it) is still bothering him, so Ellie took him to the Lenox Hill Hospital for an X-ray. It is broken. He did "Bye Bye Birdie" notwithstanding. A real trouper.

Alfred Kazin's wife and daughter are giving him a birthday party this afternoon. Alfred is a man of immense dignity. He and Ann were on the Cape a couple of summers ago, renting an old house in Wellfleet with the usual extremely steep Cape Cod stairs. Alfred was upstairs taking a shower when he heard the phone ringing downstairs. He ran, slipped, tumbled, and dislocated his shoulder. The pain was fierce. Ann, responding to his yells, called the fire department emergency number, so the rescue squad could take him somewhere for emergency treatment. When help arrived, Alfred, though still where he landed, was less concerned about his own anguish than that a hook-and-ladder was chewing up his landlord's lawn and that all these strangers were coming to attend him while he had no pants on. He's sometimes a strange man, too. He asked me to have lunch with him a while ago; he proposed that I write a history, for *The New Yorker*, of City College, where he and so many other intellectuals of our time have received their higher education, tuition-free. I liked the idea, and was going to pursue it, but when C.C.N.Y. and its parent body, the City University of New York, got so hung up on finances, I tabled the notion. A few months later, at dinner at our apartment, Alfred bemoaned the fact that I had decided not to do a piece, after all, on Hunter College, where he teaches. But Hunter had never been mentioned during our lunch.

Ved Mehta is at the Kazins'. He is going back to India this summer, in connection with a book he's writing about his mother. He doubts whether it will be serialized in *The New Yorker;* he tells me that the magazine has already published, at length, everything he has to say about his native land. Another author, Cynthia Ozick, whom I have never met before, engages Ann Kazin and me in conversation. Ann is talking about a mutual friend of ours who has grown grotesquely stout, and I tell her and Ms. Ozick about an unhappy experience I had during the war. When my Army Life series was coming out in the magazine, I acquired quite a few pen pals, young women who, I guess, were doing their bit to bolster soldierly morale. There was one girl, in Detroit, whose letters I particularly appreciated, and we got into rather an intense correspondence. I kept asking her for a picture, but the snapshots she sent were either out of focus or were portraits of her cats.

Eventually, when I was stationed in New York, she wrote that she was coming east, and I suggested a date. For someone whose letters were so warm, even intimate, she was curiously standoffish, but she finally agreed to meet me at the Astor Bar. I realized as soon as I arrived why there had been no photographs and why she hadn't wanted us to get together. She weighed about three hundred pounds. And that—as I tell the two lady authors at the cocktail party—was the end of our relationship.

Ann clucks sympathetically. Ozick says I should feel guilty. Guilty? After thirty-four years? I feel guilty about certain women, but not about Laura Jean. Ozick has the bit in her teeth. She and Ellie and I all happen to depart in the same elevator, and to my wife's astonishment (What can this man of mine have been saying to this woman the moment my back was turned?) Ozick glares at me and says, "There's something wrong with your story. It has a grain of metaphysical discomfort. You're merciless." Whew!

E. says Ozick really is a good writer, no matter what. I feel no imperative urge to find out personally. The quality of my mercy, in respect to her, is strained.

We drive down to Soho for supper, at one of those small anonymous places, and I have the sardine platter. I love sardines, but I always forget to put them on the shopping list. I can never eat sardines without thinking of Ed Duffy, who invariably served them with drinks in Truro (we shared a lot of both), and of Arthur Kober, who until he was well along in years, by his own account, did not know that the name for sardines was "sardines." He had believed it was "skinnels and bunnels." That was because when Arthur was a boy in Harlem and his mother sent him to the corner grocery for some sardines she always adjured him to be sure they were skinless and boneless.

May 29

I have by now gone through two cartons of cigarettes purchased expensively a pack at a time (inasmuch as each is going to be my very definitely last pack) since I threw away the cartons of low-priced butts I bought in North Carolina.

May 30

Tony is twenty-five today. Of all my sons' birthdays, his is the one I am least likely to forget—not just because it falls on Memorial Day but because of the circumstances of his delivery. Like his two older brothers, he was a Caesarean baby. Dr. Halsted—Harbeck Halsted—brought them into the world. The obstetrician's first words to me after Tony was born, uttered as Dr. Halsted walked worriedly through the room where I was waiting, were, "It's a boy—fractured skull." This was not the kind of skull fracture inflicted by a blow. The foetus' soft head had pushed, *in utero*, against a knob on his mother's pelvic bone; and Tony emerged with a dent in one side of his skull, sort of like a dent in a Ping-Pong ball. There was nothing wrong with the infant, for the moment; the question was, what would happen as he grew, and his skull hardened? If the dent remained, there might be brain damage. Dr. Halsted consulted with several other physicians, and they all concurred that there were two options: Leave the child alone, and nature might make the dent pop out in due course; or, have the trouble surgically corrected. The neurosurgeons were for operating at once, the pediatricians for waiting. The decision was left to the parents. It was one that Jinny and I felt notably unqualified to make. Finally, we took Tony to Dr. Rusty McIntosh, the head of Babies Hospital. "If it were my child, I would do nothing," he said. Dr. McIntosh had something like half a dozen healthy children. We decided to follow his counsel. When Tony, aged six weeks, aroused us one morning, we perceived that there was no more hole in his head.

I was a volunteer fireman when Tony was young and impressionable. On Memorial Day every year, our company would dress up in our stiff blue serge uniforms, with our shiny silvery badges and peaked caps, and (after I had calmed down Barge, barking furiously at this hateful accoutrement) we would march in the annual Briarcliff Manor parade, behind police cars and our own big white engines. The firemen's kids were expected by their fathers to be among the onlookers who flanked our route. (Firemen's sons, however, now and then were permitted to climb aboard a real life-size engine.) For several years, Tony had the notion, which I did nothing to disabuse, that the Memorial Day parade was, like candles on a cake, something that was arranged in his natal honor. The longest stretch I ever spent on duty was one fall, at the height of the leaf-burning season, when our truck rushed from one out-of-control spot to another practically nonstop for twenty-three hours. The most unnerving moment I had was when, as I was carrying some hose into a residence, a blazing crossbeam fell square on top of my helmet. Hey, it suddenly occurred to me, this isn't all fun and games and drinking beer and dirty movies at the annual banquet. I have vast respect for firemen, though I could never have been a successful one, because of my aversion to ladders.

Ellie, Lexy, and I pay a condolence call on Naomi Bliven. Bruce, Jr., has flown to California to be with his mother. Among the other sympathizers at Naomi's are Cecille Shawn and a physician who lives in the Blivens' building. Espying Lexy's splinted thumb, the doctor calls him over and gives him a learned explanation of just how and where it got broken, illustrating his lecture by jabbing at the ailing member. Lexy flinches. I suggest to the doctor that inasmuch as Lexy has two thumbs and they are structurally similar, perhaps he could poke just as instructively at the hale one.

Cecille asks if I am going to South Africa. I infer that Bill is one husband who doesn't tell his wife everything. Maybe he has forgotten that I can't go. It would be quite possible, in the *New Yorker* scheme of things, for one of Shawn's reporters to go somewhere like South Africa, and return, without his being kept informed of the perambulations.

May 31

Lexy's birthday today. They come in clusters. He wants a good camera. Macy's is having a sale. When one is spending $249.95 on a camera for a fourteen-year-old, it is comforting to reflect that the price has been knocked down from $289.95. I had a Nikon once, way back—before Nikons were exported to the United States. I got it because I was having a drink at the bar of the Foreign Correspondents Club in Tokyo, during the Korean War, with David Douglas Duncan. I was on my way home, and David wanted to know if I was planning to buy a then scarce Nikon; he had access to the factory. It had never occurred to me that I should get one. I never carry a camera; it interferes with taking notes. The kind of money we were using was military scrip, and I had something like a hundred and fifty dollars' worth stuffed in a pocket. It didn't seem like real money, so I gave it to David. Then I forgot all about our conversation. When, six months later, I received a Nikon, and was complimented far and wide on my rare acquisition, I tried to make light of my shrewdness. A decade or so later, when Nikons were commonplace in the States, I was one of the few people around without one; some son had borrowed it along the way and it had disappeared.

Monica McCall phones. The Al Capp deal is dead. The publisher who was involved has told her that he is interested solely in a paperback, not a hardcover, and that he doesn't consider me a paperback author. Should I feel flattered?

Joey is in town. He is trying to earn a living as a freelance non-fiction writer. He is not finding it easy. I have trouble with it myself, and I have been doing it my entire adult life—a non-best-selling hardcover man all the way. I have it in mind to write a soft-core pornographic novel, and have jotted down a good many spicy notes for it, and some pillow talk that makes me blush. I really should get on with that and make a killing. The *Daily News* says that Pete Hamill has a blockbuster of a book coming out, all about incest. Why didn't I think of that first?

I have a number of rules about my work. One is never to look at a magazine piece after it's been published. If you do, you may notice changes that editors sneaked in at the last minute. Too often I break my rule. Today, for instance, when the current issue of *The New Yorker* is passed around, I read in it the Talk story that I did recently on a Central Park croquet tournament. I had written that a contestant "struck one ball with another from a distance we estimated at forty-two feet eight inches." That was supposed to be a joke, obviously. Well, not so obviously after all. Some literal-minded editor, without giving me a chance to debate the worth of my wit, has changed this to "estimated at well over forty feet." I am tempted to complain to Shawn about such editorial myopia. But I don't. With a new issue confronting him every seven days, it seems unfair to confront him with a flaw—or what I consider a flaw—in an old one that he can't do anything about.

June 1

My father, were he alive, would be celebrating his ninety-third birthday today. Ely was just about Cyrus Eaton's age. I wish I had known him better. I would hate to think that my sons feel no closer to me than I did to my father.

Bingham and I have a gallery at squash. John McPhee, who can beat either of us at half throttle, is having lunch with us and, arriving early, watches the tumultuous conclusion of our match. It is a standoff, because before we can finish our fifth and deciding game, there is an imperious rap at the door of our court; our half hour is over. So this session will go down in the record books as a tie, though in all honesty I should note that Bob was leading, 8–5, in the crucial game when I was saved by, so to speak, the doorbell. McPhee, who is not a member of the Harvard Club and has to be the guest of one or the other of us, tactfully refrains from critical analysis of our performance. After we have dressed and are eating, John and I exchange compliments, he alluding to my Princeton piece, I to his award from the National Institute of Arts and Letters. Another standoff—except that in cold figures he is $3,000 ahead.

McPhee and Bingham are into jogging. John says once you get past the first mile the rest is a snap. He has a book with a point chart for various forms of exercise. He says you need—provided you neither smoke nor drink—thirty points a week to stay in shape. Well, I say cheerfully, I play tennis doubles and squash at least once a week each; what is my score? John will give me five points for the squash. Even as much as three hours of doubles, he adds scornfully, is worth nothing. Zero. Zilch. I am amazed that I am alive at all.

McPhee, who spends Alaskan winters in pup tents, now graciously changes the subject to make me feel better. He brings up "the Kahn Rule," which he has always tried faithfully to observe. Does he mean the one about never looking at the magazine that I myself have just so maddeningly violated? No, no, he means what I told him when he first came to *The New Yorker*, in 1963. Oh, my God, I have forgotten what the Kahn Rule is. Could Einstein have forgotten $E=MC^2$? Jogger John jogs my eroded memory. The Kahn Rule is, in his phrasing thereof, "Always know what you're going to do next." Yes, yes, that is it all right: The worst thing that can happen to a freelance writer is not to have a new assignment to get down to work on as soon as he's finished a piece. I must tell that to Joey; a Kahn should be guided by the Kahn Rule before anybody else.

When I get back to the office, instead of finishing up Georgia, which I intend to turn in to Shawn next Monday, I will spend a few minutes arranging to go to Washington at dawn on Tuesday to do a Talk story on the two-dollar bill. McPhee wants to know if I don't lose sleep when I am finishing up a piece. I say I don't. He shakes his head, wonderingly. The light at the end of his tunnel apparently strikes his pillow as stabbingly as the rays of the rising sun. When I lose sleep, it is generally from worrying either about money or children, which in many instances comes to pretty much the same thing.

The importance of the Kahn Rule, which in deference to the writer who seems most aware of its existence should perhaps henceforth be known as the McPhee Rule, is that the greatest asset any of us has is time. Like oil, unlike trees, it is an unrestorable natural resource. Once squandered, we have lost it irretrievably. That we have embraced this precarious way of life is, of course, a matter of choice. We elect not to be salaried employees because we cherish our independence; for that independence we sacrifice security. We also sacrifice things like annual vacations with pay. Not long ago, I was having dinner with a tenured university professor who was complaining bitterly, as academics so often do, about how overworked he was. Why, he had three hours of classes a week and five graduate students' Ph.D. dissertations to supervise. Or he would have, he added, were he not on sabbatical. Was it not true, I asked him (knowing before I asked that it was), that he had a full year's paid sabbatical every seven years? He nodded. Well, I told him, I had been working for forty years with never even one week's paid vacation; by the criteria of his profession, I should have accumulated five and half years' worth of free rides.

June 2

I had a strange dream last night—that when we moved to Truro later this month, the surface of our clay tennis court was thickly carpeted with grass.

The *Times* carries an announcement by A. M. Rosenthal that it is going to run a weekly backgammon column, written by Paul Magriel. Am I entitled to a finder's fee?

Lunch with Joey at the Harvard Club. I introduce him to the McPhee Rule. Joey's application for membership has not yet been put to a vote, but he seems at home already. He wandered in unchallenged yesterday, looking for me, found George Gianis instead, and lost three dollars to George at backgammon. Maybe Joey can just use the establishment—could our woman, too?—without bothering to join up.

June 3

At home all day, fighting the battle of Georgia. We drive out to Scarborough in the evening to dine with Louis and Nina Engel, and I am pleased to see that a niche of honor in their living room—a sort of literary shrine—has been exclusively consecrated to books by John Cheever and me. Not even Louis' own "How to Buy Stocks," which may have sold more than all of both of ours together. John Cheever introduced me to the Engels, when they came to Westchester as newlyweds (with six children between them), after a romance that evidently was a *cause célèbre* on Long Island. Nina's ex-husband was so mad at her that afterward, when he had to correspond with her about their children, he refused to put her name on an envelope; he would simply write on it the number of her box at the Scarborough post office. When Nina's daughter got married, relatives from both sides of her family attended the ceremony. At the reception afterward, the bride's maternal kin gathered at one side of the room, her paternal kin at the other, and nobody crossed an imaginary dividing line. My mother and father found themselves in the same room for the first time in nine years at my first wedding, but at least they said hello to one another.

Louis has gone into politics since his retirement as a bigwig at Merrill Lynch, and very successfully; he is supervisor of the town of Ossining. While he was still on Wall Street, his connections often proved helpful to me when I was on one of my trips to the Far East; for instance, he furnished me with a letter of introduction from the head of Merrill Lynch (who had never met me) to the head of a big brokerage firm in Japan. The recipient forthwith arranged a lavish geisha party for me at a secluded inn. Having never been thus honored before, I inquired of a Tokyo acquaintance what would be expected and I was told, *inter alia,* that the host might be offended if, at the conclusion of all the eating and drinking and singing and playing of children's games that constitute such an evening, the principal guest did not select one of the geishas and retire with her to one of the *ryokan's* private chambers. I said that was not my life style.

My acquaintance said when in Rome do as the Romans do. I said we were not *in* Rome. He said if I wanted to insult one of the most important men in the Japanese financial community that was my business. I decided not to put on a show of bad manners. There were seven geishas in our party, and three of them, while as graceful and attentive as anyone could ask for, looked old enough to be grandmothers. There was really only one in the lot I found appealing, a youngish geisha, perhaps an apprentice, in a green kimono—a bit stout, but with a nice smile. All right, I said to myself, if the alternative is to impair relations between two now friendly countries, I will take the girl in the green kimono. I was sure that if the sordid culmination of this evening ever became known, my loved ones at home would understand that I had meant no wrong but was, rather, a victim of circumstances. When in due course the party was over and we all rose from our knees (I, not being Japanese, more awkwardly than the rest), I found myself being swiftly ushered by one of the men in our party out of the room, through a maze of corridors, to the place where I had parked my shoes, into my shoes, out the front door, and into the back seat of a waiting limousine. It all happened so fast that I never had a chance properly to thank my host or say goodbye. Just before the car pulled away, though, he gave me that opportunity. He appeared in the doorway I had exited from, and with one arm waved *sayonara.* His other arm was possessively wrapped around the waist of the girl in the green kimono.

When I went to Tokyo in 1964 to cover the Olympics, Louis introduced me to some people he knew himself: Don Knode, the American manager of Merrill Lynch's Tokyo office, and Don's wife, the former tennis star Dorothy Head. The night the United States crew won the gold medal in the main rowing event, the Knodes gave a party for the victors, and were good enough to invite me. Loafers are very practical in Japan: No tedious untying and tying of laces as one enters and leaves a social scene. There was no danger, I reminded myself chucklingly as I deposited mine in the Knodes' vestibule, of my shoes being confused with the no doubt huge ones of the towering oarsmen of the U.S. crew; I take a very small shoe. Size seven. My own sons cannot fit into my shoes—literally, I mean. I left the party early, retrieved the loafers, and returned to my hotel. The next morning, I noticed that although they fitted fine, they weren't mine. I phoned the Knodes, and Dorothy said yes, she knew there had been a mixup; I'd gone off in a crewman's shoes. A crewman? Size seven? No way. Yes, there was a way, Dorothy said; it was the coxswain. I was sort of sorry to have to give up strutting around in a gold medallist's shoes, but I phoned the Olympic Village, reached the cox, apologized profusely, and said I'd be right out there to make an exchange. When I arrived, I was surprised to find him quite angry about the whole incident, as if I'd tried to steal his shoes. His reaction was all the more puzzling in that his loafers, I had noticed by daylight, were old and scuffed, whereas mine were practically brand new.

When Louis Engel was a vice-president of Merrill Lynch, I used to go downtown now and then for a three-martini lunch with him and some of his Wall Street cronies. Louis retired from the firm a decade or so ago, and announced to all and sundry that he was going to fulfill a lifelong ambition by taking the Trans-Siberian railroad from Vladivostok to Moscow. Nina, to whom that proposition seemed less attractive, said she would meet him in Warsaw or Paris or wherever. Louis' associates at Merrill Lynch decided to mark his departure from their midst with a bang-up surprise lunch party at "21." Inasmuch as I was known to them as a sometime midday companion of the victim, and as I was one of his few fellow tipplers with a strategic midtown location, I was not only invited to the affair—if one can use "invited" when one is expected to contribute $100 toward defraying the expenses—but was entrusted with the heavy responsibility of getting Louis to the scene without his catching on. Once he had recovered from the surprise of the party itself, he was to be further startled by the emergence of a naked woman from a pie. One of the reasons why I agreed to take part in the deception was that I had never actually seen a naked woman disgorged from any baked goods, and I did not want to miss any more of life's rich experiences than possible.

I phoned Louis, proposed lunch, and said that inasmuch as I had ventured downtown so often to sample olives with him, why did he not, for a change, come uptown? We could meet at *The New Yorker* and then decide where to eat. When he arrived, I suggested that we stroll east on Forty-fourth Street and up Fifth Avenue; I had something confidential to tell him. It seemed that at a cocktail party a few days earlier I had met a stunning blonde named Gloria, fortyish, who happened to mention that she was going to take a westbound ride, alone, on the Trans-Siberian. "What an extraordinary coincidence!" I had said to her. "I have this handsome Wall Street friend who is planning just such a trip himself." Well, I went on to Louis, Gloria had said she would just love to get acquainted with this peripatetic paragon, but inasmuch as she was in the middle of some delicate divorce negotiations, she could not afford to be seen meeting any man in public, and why didn't I arrange for the two intrepid explorers to get together at, say, a private dining room at "21"?

I couldn't believe anyone would buy this preposterous story, but I also couldn't help notice that Louis' pace was quickening. By the time we reached Fifty-second Street and I had furnished a few more details about Gloria's remarkable attributes, I could barely keep up with him. I probably laid it all on a bit too thick. When we arrived at the restaurant, and were ushered into a salon where he was welcomed with loud acclamatory cries by his wife, his secretary, and a dozen or so convivial Merrill Lynchers, he almost seemed disappointed. The pie was of papier-mâché, but the girl emerging from it was real enough, and it turned out that her function was to serve as Louis' personal waitress—attentions which he seemed, understandably, to find embarrassing.

Another oddity, though for all I know it may be routine at businessmen's farewell parties, was that the roll at every place setting was in the shape of large male genitalia. I do not know to this day whether "21" bakes these objects on the premises or imports them from some specialty shop. Most of the men present not only refrained from mutilating their rolls but requested doggy bags so they could take them home to their wives. It was my impression that if I were to do any such thing, Ellie would throw me out. Shows how little men know about women. She said she would have liked to see such a roll, and she elicited from me a promise, which I had no intention of keeping, to return to "21" the next day and fetch her one.

June 6

John McPhee might be interested to know that because I have a self-imposed inflexible deadline of noon today to finish my Georgia piece, I scarcely slept last night and arose at 5 A.M. in order to get in three hours of typing before breakfast. I can do about two thousand words an hour, in full stride, which, considering that I never learned the touch system, is not bad. I meet my deadline, which enables me to have lunch, conscience crystal-clear, with Warren Munsell, who at eighty-eight is my oldest best friend. He has stood in partial *loco parentis* to me since I was twelve or so; I call him "Pop." I pick Pop up, en route to Sardi's, at the offices of the Actors Fund of America, over whose eleemosynary affairs he unflaggingly presides. (For many years before that, he was business manager of the Theatre Guild, and through his kindness I saw dozens of shows when I was a kid.) Warren says that the Actors Fund has been so gratifyingly endowed by its supporters that it had an $800,000 surplus last year. What an enviable organization to run! He says he carries money—his own pocket money, that is—in three places, so that if he is mugged he will, with luck, have enough cash left to take a cab home. I tell him truthfully that although I was born in New York City and have lived or worked in it all my life, I have never been mugged and have never seen anyone else mugged. The closest I ever came was one spring Sunday, on an otherwise deserted Upper East Side street, when a huge black man blocked my passage and, as I anticipated the worst, asked me if I could let him have a quarter for subway fare uptown. "But it costs fifty cents," I told him, adding that while I was short of change I did have a token.

He accepted it, said, "Thank you very much, sir," and proceeded on his way.

The building Warren lives in is going co-op, but he refuses to buy his apartment. If you were a single man of eighty-eight, he keeps telling the owners when they press him, would *you* buy a co-op? When he takes his vacation this fall, he is going to sail to Europe aboard the QE2 and revisit some of the First World War battlefields he fought on.

Back in the office, I find a note from John Brooks, attached to a clipping from the *Princeton Alumni Weekly*, which says of me, "He spent a week on campus last year researching the article and at least that much time again studying the accumulated literature." Are they kidding? I reply to John that as he well knows all long *New Yorker* fact pieces are reported in the morning and written the same afternoon. Robert Lewis Taylor allegedly once actually accomplished that, while doing a Profile of some circus performer. My own record for a Profile is three days—one for reporting, one for writing, one for retyping—but I would never let anyone know this. Shawn, in his intuitive way, may well have sensed it, though; the piece in question was one of those he bought but did not run.

New Yorker articles—my *New Yorker* articles, at any rate—do not as a rule elicit much mail, in part no doubt because we do not regularly run letters-to-the-editor. (Most of the unsolicited comments addressed to me about my principal workplace have to do with the alleged lateness of delivery of subscriptions.) We do have a department of amplification—in the old days it was called the Department of Amplification, Fuller Explanation, and Abuse—but it is as much used by staff writers explicating on their own previously published pieces as by outside readers. If I get a dozen letters complimenting (or castigating) me on any single piece, I figure that I have done pretty well.

Among the unsolicited responses I've had to my article about Princeton is a letter that came in today from Old Nassau alumna Abigail Bok, niece of Derek. I had mentioned her in connection with a pie-throwing incident on campus, her adversary being a man who in my version of the story towered over her. Miss Bok writes that I was wrong in this respect, because she is six feet tall. That will teach me to interview people over the telephone. I have no defense for my diminution of her stature, but I can and do reply to her that in an article about the Ivy League a writer could hardly mention any-one with the surname of "Bok" and refrain from saying that the person either was or wasn't related to the president of Harvard.

Ellie and I drop in at two museum openings tonight—an architectural one at the Cooper-Hewitt and an impressionist one at the Modern. The former is showing an exhibit entitled "200 Years of American Architectural Drawing," and I am pleased to observe that this includes a beautifully executed sketch, dated 1930, of an uncompromisingly phallic building designed by my father, though never constructed. On our way out, we bump into Ellie and Randolph Guggenheimer, respectively the city's commissioner of consumer affairs and the president of the board of directors of our own co-op. Randy, who, though my Ellie is on his board, evidently has her confused with the Cooper-Hewitt's president, Lisa Taylor, says to E., "You always have such a marvelous crowd here."

June 7

Having turned in Georgia yesterday to Bill Shawn, it behooves me, following the Kahn-McPhee Rule, to betake myself on the 8 A.M. shuttle to Washington today to do a Talk story on the two-dollar bill. It was launched last year, bicentennially, on April 13th, Thomas Jefferson's birthday, an historical fact I remember because that is also my sister Joan's birthday. Somebody gave Joan a two-dollar bill last April 13th; that is the only one I have ever seen, though the director of the Bureau of Printing and Engraving insists to me that there are lots of others in circulation. I ask him if I can watch some of them being printed, but alas, none are scheduled for today's press run. Having by lunchtime obtained from him all the information I think I will ever need about two-dollar bills, I decide to sample public opinion on the subject within the District of Columbia, so I phone my old friend Murray Goodwin, with whom I used to play gin rummy regularly on the commuter train when we both lived in Westchester, and ask him if he has any two-dollar bills on him. He hasn't, but he will be glad to meet me for lunch, which, I now having asked him the telltale question, I can legitimately put on my expense account.

We eat regally at the Madison Hotel. At the next table, a Korean is huddled with two men who might well be congressmen. Murray, with his great shock of snow-white hair, looks eminently legislatorial himself; whenever we have lunch in Washington, I address him loudly as "Senator," on the theory that that will get us better service. Should I report the men at the next table for potentially underhanded fraternization? Ellie saw a kid shoplifting at Bendel's last week and did nothing about it, and felt miserable afterward for her cravenness. I do nothing, either; my evidence of bribery is flimsy.

Murray's daughter Anna has an office job at another hotel around the corner. I have finished my day's work, and he says he is in no rush to get back to his, so he buys a deck of cards (they will no doubt turn up somewhere on *his* expense account) and Anna graciously permits us to convert a vacant room at her hotel into a gin-rummy parlor. She says we must vacate the premises by two-thirty. We ascend furtively to our chamber, not unmindful of the battle that Anita Bryant is currently waging in Miami against homosexuality. Come to think of it, for two grown men to play gin rummy in a hotel room in the middle of a weekday afternoon may be just as offensive to Miss Bryant's Christian ethic as sodomy. Worst of all, Murray triple-Schneiders me just before we are compelled to evacuate our den of iniquity. It would serve him right if I exposed him to the Washington hotel detectives' association as an advertising man fobbing himself off as a United States senator.

June 8

There are too many quid pro quos on earth. Because Phil Straus agreed to have lunch with me not long ago to discuss money for Harvard, I feel sort of morally bound to agree to his suggestion that I attend a fund-raising lunch, at the Yale Club, of the Center for Defense Information, an outfit in Washington run by a retired admiral and a retired general, and dedicated, praiseworthily, to a common-sense approach (in contrast to the usual Pentagon approach) to national security. Phil thinks there might be a piece about the center for us, and I profess to agree, but I know in my bones that this is the sort of story Shawn isn't particularly interested in my tackling. So when I get to the Yale Club and find that a seat has been reserved for me on the dais, right alongside the admiral in command, and hear myself introduced to the assemblage as an especially distinguished guest, I feel guilty and embarrassed, if not subversive.

Afterward, I was supposed to have a chat with the admiral, but I can only allot him a couple of minutes because the Town School's eighth graders are having their graduation exercises. I am pleased to see, on arriving, that the colorful flag Lexy designed for the school is on prominent display behind the stage; Headmaster Birge gives the banner a nice testimonial plug.

There are a lot of blacks in this assemblage. Town has evidently tried really hard to integrate, and E. says the black kids are good students, too. After the formal ceremonies, we all troop up to the roof for a punch-and-cookies reception, which is jarred when word comes up from street level that somebody has rifled a station wagon parked out front. The car turns out to belong to one of the black families; the stolen goods, fortunately, consisted merely of a laundry bag full of dirty clothes belonging to a child just home from boarding school. We hear all the time that most urban

258

crimes are committed not by blacks against whites but by blacks against blacks, and this incident adds further weight to that particular set of statistics: The perpetrators, who were seen as they drove off with their sketchy loot, were black.

Somebody jotted down the license number of the thieves' car. Will this information ever be put to good investigative use? Years ago, just before Christmas, I was delivering presents around New York, and as I parked my parcel-laden station wagon near my father's apartment, a car drove by slowly, its driver peering intently at the contents of mine. Some instinct prompted me, as I was carefully locking my car, to jot down *his* license number. When, only a few minutes later, I returned to my wagon, the back window had been smashed open and some of the packages removed. On reporting the break-in to the nearest police precinct, I said that I had absolutely no proof that any particular suspect was involved in the crime, but here was a license number that might be worth checking out. The detective assigned to my case thanked me and said he would certainly get onto that right away. That was the last I ever heard of the matter.

I have to go to the dentist's. A portion of one of my back teeth seems to have fallen off. Dr. Leaf suggests that I lost it in a drunken brawl. I tell Jules that I incurred the damage without being aware of it, and that I suspect—I always appear to be suspecting things—that I must have swallowed the missing fragment, and if I have, will that be injurious to my all-around health? Not at all, Jules says: Teeth are chock full of minerals and vitamins. It is a beguiling thought that if one ingested all one's teeth the result, however cosmetically deplorable, would be therapeutic.

Jules says this has been a long working day for him, with one major bridge job and two minors, along with random cleanings and fillings; he says he has generated $20,000 worth of income today, not even counting me. But he is worried: He has cut himself down to a three-day-a-week schedule, yet nonetheless is making too much money. He has asked his accountant to come by next week to go over his books and advise him whether he can afford to work at all. I offer commiserations, reflecting at the same time that, unless Shawn decides that he wants me to zero in on the Center for Defense Studies, this day will have elapsed without my generating any income at all.

Ellie and I go to an opening of a new show at the Whitney, where, as usual, we run into S.D. He is not with his wife, but with a young woman with whom, I whisper to E., he is living. Ellie is astonished, and wonders how I can know this. I do not know it, but I am sure of it. (I am right, it develops.) E. seems put out—probably, I suspect, because this is an area of human relations about which women are traditionally supposed to be more intuitive than men, and here I have gone and outplayed her at her own game.

259

June 9

John McPhee sticks his head, preceded by several inches of beard, into my office. He wants to report on a dialogue he had this morning on the subway. A stranger, evidently recognizing John from a cover photograph on a recent *Princeton Alumni Weekly*, accosted McPhee and said, "You know this fellow Kahn?"

John said he did.

"He an alumnus?"

John said yes, an alumnus of something.

"How did he come to write that piece about Princeton?"

John said he had no idea.

"How come *you* didn't write it?"

John said he hadn't because, for one thing, *that* idea had never occurred to him.

At that point, the train pulled into a station and the stranger abruptly disappeared.

In pouring rain, I head for the Tavern on the Green, where, in accordance with a promise I made to Lilo months ago, I am to address the annual lunch of the New York Chapter of the Women's Division of the American Friends of Technion, the Israeli scientific institution. If my stepmother weren't the president of the local branch, I certainly wouldn't have been invited and probably wouldn't have accepted. The members of the group had been informed in advance that their guest speaker would be "E. J. Khan, Jr.," and on their tables, I find upon arriving, is a printed slip apologizing for the misspelling of my (and their president's) surname.

I stopped en route for a fortifying drink, which was a sensible precaution, inasmuch as it develops these ladies, mostly elderly ones, don't imbibe at their bash. No wine, even. I told Lilo that I would speak about some of my reportorial travels, and I begin with Africa. When I reach Uganda and mention Idi Amin, his name evokes a murmur of hisses—his behavior at the Entebbe airport being much on the distaff Jewish mind. I discourse on how exemplary a foreign-aid program Israel had among some of the emerging African nations when I wandered among them seven years ago, and the audience beams. When I say that Israel's only friend on the African continent today appears to be the Republic of South Africa, the audience frowns. When I add, with attempted levity, that I am apparently persona non grata in South Africa, but that I hope that would not be held against me should I seek to revisit Israel, the women look puzzled, and wary: With what as yet unopened can of worms am I about to spoil their lunch? This audience that I thought I had firmly in my hands is about to slip away. I plunge recklessly into my story about the reform rabbi from Scarsdale who said, outside Haifa, "When I'm in Israel, I don't tell them I'm a rabbi." This proves to be the uncontested anecdotal dud of 1977. Lilo assures me afterward that my speech went over extremely well, that it was just what her ladies wanted, but I have my doubts.

June 10

According to the morning *Times*, Joseph Papp is withdrawing from his entrepreneurial affiliation with Lincoln Center. Maybe Robert Wilson will succeed him. And Herman Badillo has announced that he is once again running for mayor. This means, beyond a question, that there will be a fund-raising tennis brunch for Herman at Lee Falk's before summer is over. We will go, naturally, and will contribute our bit to the cause; it would be ungracious to partake of Lee's non-fund-raising tennis brunches time after time and then abstain from putting one's money where one's mouth has so often been filled.

This is my last day at the office before taking off for Truro. It has been more than twenty-five years since I have spent more than one or two days of any July or August in New York. The checking department, I learn, has received word to get started on my Cyrus Eaton Profile, which may mean that the piece will run before too long. I stop in to discuss this likelihood with Bill Knapp, who is editing the piece (Bill's wife Peggy was Eaton's wife Anne's college roommate, but at *The New Yorker* we are impervious to such potential petty conflicts of interest), and he shows me his just-received copy of the thirty-fifth anniversary report of the Harvard class of 1942. I note that Roger Angell '42 has in his autobiographical paragraph cited the title of his latest book; I must remember to do this, should I have a book in print at the time, when I compose my own next updated account of my life. Riffling the pages, I come across the entry for my backgammon rival S. George Gianis. It was that "S." that inspired me to call him "Stavros" in my *Sports Illustrated* piece about the Bahamas tournament. Now I realize for the first time what the initial stands for. Socrates. I wish I had known that sooner, though if I had dubbed George "Socrates" in my article some *S. I.* editor might have asked me to change that to something less far-fetched.

I go straight from the office, carrying two briefcases bulging with stuff I plan to work on over the summer, to a party at Daphne Hellman's, on East Sixty-first. Daphne urges me to hide them under a pile of topcoats. She neglected to lock her front door while entertaining a couple of nights ago, she explains, and some kids sneaked in and made off with the purses of the lady guests. The intruders were seen running down the street, but then vanished unapprehended. Everybody at tonight's gathering seems much relieved that the despoilers of the earlier soirée were indisputably Caucasian. To be informed that the burglars were white is the kind of shot in the arm that liberals need every now and then to sustain their much-stretched faith in the imperfectibility of *all* mankind.

June 11

My first child was born thirty years ago. Today is a Saturday, so I call Terry at home, at 11 A.M., to wish him a happy birthday. Rose says he is still in bed; he apparently began celebrating the crucial milestone last night. When he drags himself to the phone, I tell him that he is getting older and should be careful, in view of his advancing years, not to overdo things.

Shawn has had my Georgia piece for five days now, and hasn't called. This probably means he will not buy it. Why did I ever decide to take on Georgia, of all peculiar places, to begin with? I can see clearly now that I botched the project. What can I salvage from it when Bill finally calls to reject it? Maybe, though, he hasn't yet had a chance to read Georgia. Of *course* he has read it. What probably has happened, he just hasn't yet been able to contrive how to tell me in his usual gentle way that the piece, for all its glittering merit, didn't quite work out.

Terry, like Joey, hopes to make a go of it as a freelance non-fiction writer. Why do two of my sons have to try to accompany me down a road that is so grotesquely crooked and rutted?

This evening, Ellie tells me, we are scheduled to attend a modern-dance recital—Merle Marsicano's troupe, which is appearing on East Fourteenth Street, just west of Second Avenue. A dismal, repellent part of town; E. and I want to have a brandy during the intermission, but we don't dare enter either of the two bars on our side of the block, which seems to be populated, aside from us outlanders, exclusively by hookers, winos, crazies, and the like. Happily, there is a grocery next to the hall that sells orange pop.

I have had little to do with the modern dance since, back in the thirties, I dated for a while a lithe member of the Hanya Holm group. I was doing the nightclub column for *The New Yorker* then, and took Katie to the Bossert Marine Roof, over in Brooklyn, for some extracurricular dancing. I had asked her not long before to let me have a photograph of herself, and between sets she fished in her purse and pulled one out. It showed her naked to the waist. I was young, and innocent, and profoundly shocked. I wish I could remember what I did with the picture. I also wish now that I had learned what she looked like from the waist down. It would have been easy enough for someone not so abysmally unsophisticated to have found out.

Katie once suggested that we spend a weekend together. I picked her up in my car at her Village apartment, and as we stood there, her overnight bag neatly packed, she asked me where I thought we should go. I chickened out. I panicked. I phoned my grandmother up in Westchester and asked if I could bring a girl up for the weekend. My grandmother said her house was full. I said she *had* to take us in, that I was sure my cousin wouldn't mind sharing her room with this girl, and that I could sleep on a couch. My grandmother acquiesced, grudgingly, and that was where and how Katie and I spent our weekend. I didn't see much of her after that, clothed or unclothed, and I can't say on reflection that I blame her. No wonder that I have never since felt totally at ease in the presence of the modern dance.

After the performance, E. and I repair with other members of the audience to a party at the Marsicanos' loft, which is on Fifteenth Street but, comfortingly, far west of Second Avenue. Nick Marsicano tells me that while his wife is choreographing a new work she practices it for him here; and that sometimes when her mind can't remember all the movements she has planned, her body can, all by itself, almost automatically. I find myself at one point in an increasingly heated argument with a foundation executive who is singing the praises of Ezra Pound and arguing that the poet's pro-Fascism and anti-Semitism were of no account, considering how much he had done for so many other writers. "Not for the ones the Fascists killed," I hear myself loudly rejoining. Loudly enough, it appears, for E. to excuse herself from the conversation she is in and come over and drag me away.

June 12

No word from Shawn this morning. He probably phoned last night while we were out. Well, no news can't be bad news.

We pack the car and head for Truro. An agreeably light load: I can see behind me through the rear-view mirror, practically for the first time ever on a start-of-the-summer journey. We are travelling light because Ellie has left most of her research behind, since she will be commuting until August, gathering material for her forthcoming book on women artists; and because my accumulated research is a paltry two briefcases' worth. I don't really know what I'll do with my time this summer. Maybe I'll get down to work on my dirty novel. Should I try to make it hard-core porn or soft-core? Am I experienced enough by now—N. would certainly say I am—to write a credible account of a young man and his modern-dance girl friend romping through a weekend at a Long Island or New Jersey motel?

In the old days, when Jinny and I moved the family from Scarborough to Truro each summer, we usually had two cars, both jam-packed with children and dogs and, for a long time, a live-in maid, who for about ten years transported her belongings back and forth in the same purple department-store gift box. I forget which store, but it sure had sturdy receptacles. There was a time when we had his-and-her light-blue matching Chevrolets, very fancy: mine a station wagon, hers a convertible. It was not easy to raise children in the suburbs and not be a two-car family.

Our very first trip to Truro was in the summer of 1950. I had never been to Cape Cod before and had never heard of Truro. It was the Irwin Shaws who got us there. They said they were taking a house in Truro for the summer and why didn't we, too? Irwin put me in touch with an Outer Cape real estate agent, through whom I rented a house for the season, sight unseen. In due course, I reported to Irwin that our place was situated on something called South Pamet Road, and how close was that to theirs? "Oh, I forgot to tell you," he said. "We've changed our minds and are going to Europe." The Shaws stayed abroad permanently, but not, I am reasonably certain, out of guilt.

We were still a one-car family in 1950, Terry and Joey being too young (three and one and a half) to have to be transported to schools, Little League practices, and the demanding like. I was to drive to Truro, carrying cribs, playpens, and whatnot, and open up the house; my sister Olivia gallantly offered to come along and keep me company. Jinny and the boys and their nurse would take the train to Hyannis the following day. (There used to be both a day and a night passenger train from New York to Hyannis, and freights all the way from there to Provincetown; one laughs to think how quaintly the generations before us lived, not even able to do their own steering.) I managed without too much trouble to find South Pamet Road and the house of Arthur Joseph, everybody's favorite caretaker, who had the key to the Washburn house, which was to be ours for the season.

When I came upon the place, I was startled by its size; I had inadvertently rented one of the largest, if indeed not the largest, residences in Truro. Eight bedrooms and four baths, or some such. I had also arranged in advance for a diaper service to put us on its roster, and now, as I was about to unlock a door, I espied a note. "Your diaper can got delivered to me by mistake," it said. "Come by next door and have a drink." The note was signed "Amy Hamilton." Amy turned out to be the daughter of the Dr. Washburn whose threshold I was upon; four years later, I was to buy a house that he had earlier given Amy and her husband Stewart when they got married. Dr. Washburn, who once owned a whopping stretch of the ocean beach at Truro, had been the director of the Massachusetts General Hospital, in Boston; he was reputed to have ordered all young physicians serving their internships under him to sew up their pants pockets, because he didn't like to see them ambling around with their hands in their pockets.

Dismayed by the size of our summer house, I suggested to Olivia that we delay unpacking the car long enough to go next door and retrieve the missent diapers. Amy already had one drinking companion. He was Edmund Duffy, the eminent cartoonist for the Baltimore *Sun* and now the *Saturday Evening Post*—the only practitioner of his art, I believe, ever to win the Pulitzer Prize three times. I had never met Duff before, but we had many mutual friends in journalism, and it took us several martinis to run through them. By now, it was dinnertime. Amy and Duff said they were going over to the local restaurant—the only local restaurant—to eat, and why didn't Olivia and I tag along? A splendid suggestion! Forgetting about the diapers, we accompanied our new friends to the Blacksmith Shop, where I did remember at least that I had told Jinny I would call and let her know that we had safely arrived.

"What's all that noise?" she wanted to know when I reached her.

"This is the greatest spot on earth," I yelled. "Friendliest people you ever met." I'm afraid my voice was slightly slurred.

"What's our house like?" Jinny asked.

I had to confess that I had not yet stepped inside it.

But for the diaper service's gaffe, I might not have met Amy and Duff all summer. Between them, they knew practically everybody else worth knowing in Truro, so it did not take us long to feel at home in that thitherto totally alien territory.

Today, driving back to Truro for the umpteenth time, Ellie takes the wheel after lunch, and hasn't had it more than five minutes when she gets nabbed in a radar speed trap. Why is it always she who gets caught? I drive much faster than she does, all in all, and I haven't had a ticket (I do not count warnings) in twenty-five years. Anticipation may be the partial answer. I always assume there is a police car lurking around the next bend. Ellie's David has just turned sixteen, and he will be getting his license this summer. The only instruction I plan to give him (I do not believe in trying to teach one's own children to drive, and insisted that Terry and Joey, for instance, take lessons in Provincetown, which has some of the world's narrowest and most crowded thoroughfares) is to remember, when driving, to keep his eyes on his rear-view mirror almost as faithfully as on the road ahead.

Now here is something truly weird. I had that dream the other night about finding grass growing on my tennis court. As soon as we get to Truro, I check the court before unloading the car, and find it in fine shape. But as I am walking into the house, the phone rings. It is Sidney Simon, calling helpfully to fill us in on the latest local gossip. Sidney's *pièce de résistance* is our first tennis story of the summer. It seems that last fall Lee Falk, wearying of the trouble and expense involved in taking up *his* clay-court tapes at the end of the season and then having the court resurfaced and the tapes replaced in the spring, leapt at a tip from Kirk Wilkinson, whose Wellfleet court is an all-weather one but who is laudably concerned about the welfare of all court owners. Kirk proposed that Lee simply cover his court, over the winter, with a thick layer of salt hay, which he could peel off when the weather turned; his court would presumably then be in tiptop, playable shape. But Lee was only half listening to Kirk. Instead of *salt* hay, he dumped a couple of truckloads of ordinary hay on his court. Hay did what hay does. And now, Sidney tells me, cackling with laughter, Lee has the only grass court in Truro.

June 13

We have scarcely got the house organized when it is time to depart for the Chatham Bars Inn, half an hour's drive away, and the fortieth reunion of the Harvard Class of 1937. Ellie takes her typewriter along, though I cannot for the life of me figure when she expects to use it. I am one of the youngest members of the class, I reflect en route to the scene, and many of the crowd have already retired. There was a retired lieutenant general at our *last* reunion, five years ago. Ellie, of course, will be in the second-wife category. The first wives, I know from previous get-togethers, generally look older than their husbands. They tend to look like, well, *grandmothers.* Come to think of it, I am anticipating the Truro visit of my grandson Jaime (younger grandson Ian is already on the Cape), to whose eyes I may look grandparental myself.

When we reach Chatham, we learn that three hundred and eighty people have already registered—two hundred classmates, one hundred and seventy-nine spouses, and one classmate's widow. The youngest wife present, certainly a second, maybe a third, tells me when we are introduced that she has been a lifelong fan of mine. Her husband couldn't have picked a better woman. At the tennis courts, Ellie is surprised to run into Joe Iseman and *his* second wife. His ex, Marjorie, is one of E.'s best friends. The hotel courts are crowded; Ellie and I join up with Mogie and Nancy Lazarus and drive over to a nearby girls' camp where H '37 has been accorded playing privileges for the weekend. We split sets, and agree to resume tomorrow. At cocktails, I am greeted by C. G., who has flown in from London for the frolic. I tell Ellie sotto voce that he is the class nut. She upbraids me for my unkindness.

The after-dinner divertissement this first of two reunion nights is the Paul Killiam show, which this year will be largely a warmed-over potpourri of numbers—some of them written by me—presented at earlier reunions. Our biggest show was produced for the twenty-fifth reunion, fifteen years ago; Paul and I and the other participants labored over that one for six months. Children are permitted, nay, encouraged, to attend the twenty-fifth; but a couple of weeks before that get-together, Paul was informed that no offspring could attend the big show. There weren't enough seats for them in the theatre. Having knocked ourselves out for so long putting the production together, he and I were determined that *our* children would not be excluded, so we whipped up a new number to be acted out solely by our joint progeny. As members of the cast, they could hardly be denied admittance to the premises.

The show tonight includes—along with a couple of predictable jokes about Frank Roosevelt's latest marriage (the newlywed FDR, Jr.s, are not among us, presumably having better things to do with their time)—the projection of some still photos from our collective past. The Eliot House band, circa 1936, is flashed on the screen. The only veterans of that cacophonous ensemble who have made it to Chatham are Bill Cann, piano, and Kahn, drums. How young and innocent we look! How young and innocent I was!

Toward the end of the performance, somebody whom I can't see from my seat in back grabs emcee Killiam's microphone on stage, asks for Dr. Prout, and heads for an exit. Curt Prout, one of several notable physicians who have come up from our ranks (not long ago, he gave up a lucrative practice to work in a prison clinic), follows whoever it is out of the room. When I run into Curt later, he says that the fellow who summoned him so peremptorily was C. G., who asked—his wish was quickly granted—to have himself committed to a hospital, because otherwise he was going to have to kill his weekend roommate. He is rooming with Paul Killiam. I feel less abashed about having told Ellie that C. was the class nut. I remind Curt gratefully of the time fifteen years ago, at the twenty-fifth reunion in Cambridge, when he and another of our class medics, Perry Culver, held an impromptu consultation over my supine body at 3 A.M., near the bar of the Hasty Pudding Club. "He'll live," they declared, in what proved to be an astute diagnosis. What they did not realize at the moment of their examination—a rather cursory one, I recall—was that while I undoubtedly had had too much to drink, I was also in a state of shock. I had just been advised at the bar by John Ladd, a professor of philosophy at Brown and a fellow who would not jest about serious matters, that I was one of three members of the class who, twenty-five years after graduation, had been dubbed honorary members of Phi Beta Kappa.

June 14

After breakfast, when Ellie and I resume our tennis competition with the Lazaruses, E. tells Mogie that the best cure for a hangover is to take some Coricidin the night before. Why in eight years of marriage has she never imparted this secret to me? Conceivably because I practically never have hangovers; switching from Scotch to vodka twenty years ago was one of the sagest major decisions of my life. Anyway, how can anybody, man or woman, know the night before that he is going to be hungover the next morning? I never think ahead like that; I do not unfailingly practice the anticipation I so often preach. Given the circumstances of our rematch, it is perhaps no surprise that E. and I slaughter Mogie and Nancy. By the time we all foregather for Bloody Marys and a giant clambake, we can hardly remember who won, which is as it should be.

At lunch, Bob Bishop, the M.I.T. economics prof who used to be dean of students there, is asked by several of us prurient classmates to comment on the recent flap over two M.I.T. coeds having publicly graded male students' sexual prowess. Bob says the faculty is much relieved that the girls didn't rate *them*. It develops during lunch that the only class casualty so far, not counting psychiatric ones, is Burt Wolfson, who sprained an ankle this morning at tennis. Burt is a retired shoe manufacturer, so there has got to be a moral in this somewhere, if I could only think of one. If it had happened yesterday, Killiam could at least have got a joke out of it for his recitatif. Peggy Connolly, swimming captain John's wife, stops by to remind me (*vide supra*) of the evening she and I and Thornton Wilder spent *à trois* during our *thirtieth* reunion. She says—this is news to me—that she kept careful count and that Wilder, before he drove off into the dark, consumed precisely eleven dry martinis. Ellie wonders if she will have to keep on accompanying me to these reunions for the rest of her life. I assure her that inasmuch as they occur only at five-year intervals there won't be many more—*can't* be many more.

Reunion planners invariably put something uplifting on the agenda; this helps husbands justify the whole strange ritual to their wives and their consciences. I skipped a political symposium yesterday afternoon, though it had an impressively star-studded cast—Dick Lewisohn, former finance commissioner of New York City; and two incumbents, Federal Judge Eddie Gignoux and United States Senator Floyd Haskell. Three other classmates are booked to perform this afternoon in a scientific symposium—Chief O'Keefe of NASA, Pete Ahrens of Rockefeller University, and Dick Schultes, the Harvard professor who has spent about half his post-undergraduate life stalking hallucinogens in the Amazon jungles—and E. and I resolve to attend; had we tried to play tennis again right on top of the clambake Curt Prout would probably have had to send me to a hospital, or mortuary.

Dick Schultes is now, among other things, chief custodian of Harvard's celebrated collection of glass flowers. He tells us that when the university agreed to send some of these down to New York last year for a bicentennial display, he was so concerned about their fragility that he had a study made of various vehicles to determine which had the best springs. On learning that ambulances, generically, are less well sprung than hearses, he hired two funeral wagons to transport his precious cargo south.

At one of the Chatham Bars Inn bars, a few minutes after this elevating interlude, a classmate I have never laid eyes on before confounds the bartender, and every one else within earshot, by asking for a root-beer-and-rum.

After dinner tonight we have a dance. Brent Abel, a Harvard Overseer, confides to me that Mogie Lazarus has just been elected to that august body, which already boasts two other members of our class—Judge Ed Gignoux, and Gerry Piel—and I propose announcing the good news to the fraternal celebrants; but Mogie will not permit it. When the music stops, Ellie says she is tired and retreats to our room. I hang around a bar with Paul Killiam and Mark Dall and two unrelated Goodhues (Albie and Fag), and we have a long solemn discussion, Heaven knows why, about hippopotamuses, and then we sing some songs from past H '37 shows, and eventually we run out of steam. In our room, I find a note from Ellie on my pillow, scribbled on the back of our activities schedule. "I confess, it was fun," she has written. She hasn't yet removed her typewriter from its case.

June 15

We arise very early (I should have taken ten Coricidins last night) because Ellie has to go to New York to get to work and we have to pick up David at the Hyannis bus station. After I drop off his mother at the Boston airport, I am to drive him to Concord, New Hampshire, where we are to retrieve all the plants he has been nurturing throughout the winter in his St. Paul's dorm, and which he wishes to incorporate into a Truro garden. After a couple of days in never-never land, we are returning thumpingly to the real world. At breakfast, Ellie says that Joe Iseman's second wife was talking to her yesterday about E.'s rugs. When Ellie, newly widowed, abandoned her Fifth Avenue apartment for the smaller one we now inhabit, she sold some of her stuff, and Marjorie Iseman bought some rugs. Then when Marjorie and Joe split up and divided their property, Joe got the rugs. Now Joe's new wife tramps over them. E. reflects that this sort of thing happens all the time; the bed she and I sleep on in New York, she informs me, originally belonged to *her* first husband's second wife. "Things outlast people," Ellie remarks. I say that is it exactly: That is what college reunions are all about. Harvard outlasts people.

It is 6 P.M. before, exhausted, I return to Truro with David and a small horticultural jungle. This is going to be a strange summer, with my wife largely working in New York and, as so many Cape Cod husbands do, occasionally returning to Truro for weekends; and with me responsible for the children, the dog, the shopping, the cooking, the laundry, and other household chores. How much time I will have left for tennis and work is debatable.

June 16

I spend most of the day buying groceries, picking up slipcovers we left at the dry cleaner's in September, arranging about car insurance, and the dreary like. Also, we are at the height of the tick season, and Rainbow already has one of the nasty creatures lodged close to an eyeball. I can't get it off without running the risk of hurting her eye. Maybe the tick will decide to drift along to a more manageable perch. Tony, Judy, and Ian come by for dinner, and then they take David to "Annie Hall," at the Wellfleet Drive-in. Lexy and I do not go along. We have already seen the movie, and besides I have to do the dishes.

June 17

The Boston *Globe* has a feature story on the Provincetown *Advocate*, our Lower Cape weekly, and among the subscribers to it who are mentioned I am first. This is odd, because my subscription lapsed several months ago and I haven't done anything about renewing it. For a while, I got it for nothing. I owned ten per cent of the paper for a few years (an unrewarding investment), and accordingly got on the free list. Terry—through talent, rather than nepotism—edited the paper for a couple of years, and I was both proud of him and envious of him for having had such a journalistic opportunity. He would occasionally let me write for the *Advocate*, and I did, *inter alia*, some Art Buchwaldish columns (at least *I* thought they were in the Buchwald genre) involving a character I invented named "Snowberg." Snow is an old, WASP, Cape Cod name. Snowberg was supposed to represent the cross-fertilization of our part of the Cape by so many urban Jews, notorious among them the colonies of psychiatrists who flock to the beaches every August. I insisted to Terry that I be paid no more and no less per column than any of his other, unrelated feature writers, who, I was bemused to be informed, received ten dollars per contribution. At that they fared better than I did; when the paper changed ownership again, Terry still owed me for five pieces of mine he had run. I doubted whether the new owners were obliged to consider that fifty dollars a valid carry-over debt, and I never pressed them for remuneration. *The New Yorker* is much more honorable in its fiscal relations with its contributors, and pays better, too.

June 18

Ellie arrived yesterday (a day otherwise of mourning: the Mets traded Tom Seaver) and pronounced the house reasonably shipshape. She said Shawn hadn't called me in New York, at least not while she was at home.

Perhaps he tried to reach me here while I out rolling the tennis court.

At the post office this morning, I run into Bob Worthington, who wonders if he can come over to play tennis. Of course he can; it is refreshingly novel to have someone ask first. I tell Bob how surprised I was to find so many of my classmates still galloping around tennis courts, forty years out of college. Bob smiles indulgently and says that at his *fiftieth* Harvard reunion, four years ago, there was tennis galore.

Lexy is curious to know, apropos of I do not know what, whether his mother and I have invested in "Annie." The answer is, alas, negative. The only play I ever had a piece of was one by Arthur Kober and George Oppenheimer, a comedy that foundered after a couple of performances, my six hundred dollars sinking along with the rest of the frail craft. I was touched when Arthur left me five hundred dollars in his will—manna from heaven, as it were, to a mundane angel.

Palmer Williams and I ceremoniously open up our tennis court for the season. When I first got to Truro, nearly thirty years ago, the community had only two private courts. (Palmer's hair was not white then, nor mine grey.) One was surfaced with asphalt and the other with clay—or, rather, the ravaged remnants of clay. The Bob Shaplens and the Bud Benjamins jointly rented the clay-court house one summer. Every morning, while Bob dawdled over coffee and the newspapers, Bud could be found outside, coaxing the beat-up old court into playing shape. When he had it more or less presentable, Bob would come striding out in his whites and shoo Bud off. Somehow they remained friends, though in separate summer establishments.

The other court, the asphalt one, belonged to John and Tiny Worthington. She is called Tiny because she is remarkably tall. There were a few weeds poking up through cracks in that court's surface, but it was playable, and we beggars were in no position to be choosers. You just had to be careful about the rough spots, and the worst that could happen to you, if you tripped and fell, was the loss of some skin off an elbow or a knee. There was a time when you could tell the persistence of a Truro tennis player by his scabs.

The Worthingtons, who did not play tennis themselves and were thus never in our way, were and are a couple of unique tolerance and patience. They cannot have been partial to afternoon naps, for no one could have slept through the shrieks of elation and dismay that have traditionally characterized Truro tennis. John and Tiny had only a few mild requests to make of us who unflaggingly partook of their hospitality. We were not to go inside their house, unless somebody was so badly scraped he or she might die of loss of blood before anyone could get to the next nearest phone. We were, moreover, to park our cars carefully, inasmuch as the court was at the side of a two-lane road, and in case an emergency vehicle—an ambulance, say—had to get down the road, it would have been awkward to have its passage blocked by a car belonging to the very individual it had come to succor. The Worthingtons, finally, let it be known that they wanted their own parking lot left free for their own cars.

I guess I was responsible, in a way, for the construction of Truro's first post-war clay court. I had invited Lee Falk, who had recently joined the summer community, to play at the Worthingtons' court, toward which I had begun to adopt a proprietary attitude myself, but I forgot to tell him about the parking regulations. Lee innocently put his car, one day, where Tiny was wont to put hers, and when she came home and found her berth occupied she was quite put out. Lee, feeling that he had better find another place to play, built his own clay court. I felt so contrite about the whole episode that I took what seemed to be the only decent way out; I built a court myself. There was another reason. Terry, Joey, and Tony were growing up, and I wanted them to have a chance to play without, as so often happens, having to yield to adults. The only rule in effect on my court was that consanguinity conferred priority. All in all, this regulation worked out fairly well, except once when the brother of an ex-girl friend of one of my boys maintained that because he was sort of related he had more right to use the court than the friend of an actor who had taken the part of Jinny's husband in a summer-stock production.

One never knows who will turn up next for tennis. In the summer of 1967, both the New York *Times* and CBS saw fit to feature Truro tennis (the *Times* implied that it was I who gave the tennis brunches on which Lee Falk lavished so much time and money), and one day a stranger attracted by this publicity roared into our driveway on a motorcycle and said he was looking for a game. He was a seminary student, bent on priesthood. I thought a little moral uplift was what our court could stand (some of the language used on it was dreadful), and invited him to play. He turned up regularly for several years.

But after a couple of seasons of Truro tennis, he began to harbor doubts about his proposed vocation. He became a spiritual dropout. When I last saw him, he had left the seminary and was tooling around Provincetown with an attractive young woman clinging to the rear of his motorcycle. Once he forsook the celibate life, though, his tennis deteriorated. He began putting on weight, and his net game also went to pot. There seemed to be as little chance of his ending up at Wimbledon as at the Vatican. I hope he didn't become one of Hell's Angels.

June 19

At Ellie's suggestion, which may be too mild a word, I take Rainbow up to Eastham today for a tick bath. It is hard to explain to a dog, much as it used to be to a child being dosed with castor oil, that what is being done to one is being done for one's own good. From past experience, the immersion should prove effective just about as long as it takes for Rainbow to get back out of doors and reintroduce herself to the resident tick population. Still, ticks are easier to cope with than fleas. Last summer, we occupied the Truro house in late June, and then rented it for July while we went abroad. Our tenants had barely moved in when the weather turned uncommonly hot, and the high temperature inspired a cloud of fleas to emerge from wherever they had been lurking. The tenants fled, and we had to refund their rent, which we had been counting on to help get us through Europe. The fumigation bills were something else again. I suppose it costs about as much to harbor a dog these days, all ancillary things considered, as it did, forty years ago, to send a boy to college.

June 20

It is Monday morning, and I put my commuting wife on the 8 A.M. flight from Provincetown to Boston. Ellie used to be fearful of flying, especially on small planes like those of the Provincetown-Boston Airline, but she has pretty much got over that. Now that she is rid of those apprehensions, and that we have removed the stately old windmill outside our Truro house, which she was convinced was going to topple over some day onto her children, she is free to concentrate full-time on her fear of self-service elevators.

June 21

It is Judy's birthday, and she and Tony bring Ian over for a champagne dinner. Lexy has baked a cake. After supper, Tony and Judy have been asked out to continue celebrating with friends, and I am accordingly asked to babysit, until his parents return to collect him, for my fifteen-month-old grandson. Tony explains to me patiently how Pampers work. This is the first time that I have ever been entrusted with responsibility for taking care of a very young grandchild, and I reflect later, while complimenting myself on how well I have carried out the assignment (I have no opportunity to attempt to follow Tony's instructions about the Pampers, for Ian does not stir), that never once while Tony, Joey, and Terry were tiny did any of their grandparents on either side of their family tree look after them for as long as a part of an evening. How strange, all the more so in view of the fact that when my sisters and I were young, Joan, Olivia, and I spent so much time— albeit with nurses also in attendance—in grandparental custody. Come to think of it, Joan and Olivia never sat with their three young nephews, either, though they were around quite a bit. They were better with gifts than with croup.

June 22

Summer officially began yesterday.

Bud Stillman calls. He wonders if he can use the tennis court this morning. Of course; anybody can play in the morning as long as I am not expected to play with them. That will be no problem, Bud says; he is bringing along a partner—chap named Munroe. Ellie's maiden name lacks that final "e," but I suppose they all belong to the same ancient clan. I had forgotten that the Stillmans had bought a house in Truro, over on the bay side, and that I had sponsored their application for membership in our Pamet Harbor Yacht Club. This seems to be my year for putting people up for clubs, with signal lack of overall success, but the Stillmans, Bud advises me, made it into the Pamet establishment, which is less grandiose than its name implies, having no yachts and a harbor that is silting up. The place in New York where we play tennis during the winter has an equally high-class name—the Wall Street Racquet Club—but anybody can become eligible to use its facilities by walking in off the street and paying for a court.

When Bud and his Munroe arrive, I evacuate my study long enough to greet them, and when Lexy emerges from the house to find out what has made the dog bark, I introduce him as another authentic twig on the old Scottish tree. The Munroe with the "e" says proudly that he visited the chief of the clan in Scotland last October. Here is one of the greatest opportunities I have ever had for oneupmanship, and I do not let it slide by ungrasped: This young man here, I say with unmitigated smugness, visited the chief three months before *that*. In neither case can it have been a very splendid audience with the principal living wearer of the old tartan; Ellie told me after she took Lexy and David to pay their respects to the chief that the incumbent holder of the title seemed in such distressed circumstances that she slipped him a fiver for a couple of clannish postcards.

At the post office, I run into Colonel Chaplin. Long retired from the Army, the now also retired chief shellfish correspondent for *Park Here*, who must be close to eighty, tells me that he has had to give up tennis, finally, and also reading. He is going blind. He conveys this sad news with the calmness and resignation one would expect of a good old soldier.

Ellie phones from New York while I am preparing dinner. She is bringing Rita Gam with her weekend after next. E. cannot come until Saturday, but since Rita has to leave on Sunday, she would like to arrive, in advance of her hostess, on Friday afternoon. But, I point out to Ellie, the boys will be gone then and there will be nobody in the house save Rainbow and me. E. wants to know why that matters. I say it matters to me: Devoted a husband as I am, I prefer not to spend a night alone with the queen of crossword puzzles. Ellie agrees that Rita will have to wait until she can be chaperoned. I was once the laughing-stock of some of my Harvard classmates when, in my sophomore year, I invited a fifteen-year-old girl to Cambridge for a football weekend and her mother sent a chaperone along.

We are having fresh asparagus for dinner. I have never cooked that before—only the frozen kind. I am amazed at how easy it is; you simply look up "asparagus" in a cookbook. I am wiser about this sort of thing than I was in my youth. Just after graduating from college, when I shared a flat off the Bowery with my classmates Bruce Bliven and Dave Lindsay (neither Dave, now an invalid, nor Bruce, now a Harvardphobe, made the reunion), we had a maid who came in every morning to cook our breakfast. Those were the days! Ora couldn't make it one morning and I, awakening with a fierce hangover (I was drinking Scotch then), had desperate need of a cup of coffee. But I had grown up in a household with a live-in cook, and, at twenty-one, didn't know how to make a cup of coffee. I tried to extemporize. We had a coffee pot, but I didn't want to fool around with anything as complicated as that. So I filled a dishtowel with coffee, tied the loaded towel around the bottom of the hot-water spigot in our kitchen sink, placed a cup beneath the towel, and drank what dripped through. I have progressed. I hope before I am seventy to concoct an edible soufflé. I have got as far, culinarily, as achieving some small renown as the fashioner of sea-clam pies. The secret of my success is to lace the filling, copiously, with high-quality brandy. Enough of that basic ingredient, and everything else seems to fall into place.

June 23

I don't feel like playing tennis today, so I just plain don't. Palmer Williams says that one of the nicest things about a long vacation (if I am on vacation) is that one can indulge in the luxury of not playing tennis on any given day. He and I borrow Sidney Simon's staple gun and try to fix up the places on the courts where balls have been rolling through the fence into the poison ivy.

Nothing in the mail from Shawn today. That is par for his course; Bill has an aversion to putting things on paper. He may answer mail from outsiders (though more than once people have asked me what in the world you have to do to get a written reply from him to some query), but he rarely responds in kind to interoffice memoranda, preferring to use the phone or to material-ize—always apologetically, as if loath to distract a writer from his muse—in one's doorway.

Harold Ross was different. He loved to put things on paper, more often than not himself initiating the exchange, if any answer was called for, of messages. Not long ago, in the back of a desk drawer where I had stuffed, among other things, a reel of pornographic movie film, I found a note from Ross that was characteristic of its kind. (The film got there because I once subscribed to a book club that began reasonably clean and went dirty. Like most such clubs, this one would send out a notice of its forthcoming selection each month, and if you didn't almost instantly say you didn't want to receive the offering, you got it. I was out of town when the announcement arrived about the X-rated film, and thus couldn't turn it down; not having a projector that can accommodate it, I have never been able to turn it on, either.) Ross was commenting on a Profile I'd written in 1939—one of my first, about Brenda Frazier, in her debutante heyday. Walter Winchell, with his characteristic inaccuracy, also commented on that; he wrote in one of his columns that Brenda okayed the proofs, which she had not, and that the piece, a rather kindly one, proved that she "can take it."

Ross, who apparently didn't much read either gossip or society columns, didn't know how to spell the girl's name—he had it "Fraser" in his note to me—and he said that although he thought the Profile a bit too long he had been unable, after reading it with "vigilence"—again his spelling—to find very little soft, or semi-soft, stuff in it that warranted being cut. What I liked best about that particular Ross memo, though, was his taking the trouble to say, "After this one, you can definitely consider yourself out of the debutante stage as a writer."

St. Clair McKelway was a note man, too. Another piece I did about debutantes, this one for the Talk of the Town about some young ladies coming out on a hayride (I secretly wanted to date them all, but was too shy to ask), elicited from a reader in Haverford, Pennsylvania, an outraged letter to the editor saying that the smart-aleck who wrote it was a skunk and the editor who let it go into the magazine was a cheap cur. "Hi, Skunk!" McKelway addressed me in passing the diatribe along, and he signed himself "McK (Cheap cur)."

Today's mail does contain one unsolicited letter—from a physician in California. He writes:

This letter concerns the disproportionately high number of people (to my mind, at least), who, if they are known by their first two initials and last name, have the letter "J" as one of the initials. Since you are such a person, I am writing to ask if you (1) agree with the observation, and, if you do, (2) have you written about the phenomenon or know someone who has?

S. J. Perelman, J. D. Salinger and the late A. J. Liebling qualify, as do A. J. Foyt, girls known as B. J. whom we all knew in college, C. J. Reynolds, Arjay Miller, L. J. Reynolds, numerous cartoon tycoons who are called "J. P." by underlings, P. J. Clark's restaurant in New

York, C. J.'s restaurant near Madison (Wisconsin), J. D. Ploetz (a friend of my son), and others.

I would be interested in your comments.

I always answer my mail (unless both anonymous and abusive), but I hardly ever keep carbons of my letters, so when I get around to replying to this one I will have no record of what I aim to say: that I know of no writings, not even a doctoral dissertation, on the subject at hand; and that he is right about the "J. P."s (my grandfather Joseph Plaut was called that even by his wife) and the "B. J."s (Betty Jean Lifton, long out of college, has let it be known that henceforth she wishes to be called "B. J."). As for the remainder of the doc's hypothesis, I expect to tell him, how does he account for the prominence of A. E. Housman, A. M. Rosenthal, B. C. Forbes, B. P. Schulberg, C. P. Snow, C. Z. Guest . . . but I am not going to struggle through the entire alphabet to make my small dissenting point.

June 24

I stopped by Feron's tennis shop in New York, just before leaving for the Cape, and ordered a dozen cans of balls to be shipped to Truro. They haven't arrived yet, and I am embarrassed at having to sponge off my guests, though in truth, as Ellie pointed out to me over the weekend, if I am providing the court it will not hurt them unduly to provide the balls. She said she would phone Feron's notwithstanding, and now she reports that the shipment went out a few weeks ago. The balls were probably sent to the Harry Kahns. I used to be able to get mail addressed simply to "Kahn, Truro, Mass." but then Harry, old friend and college (non-reunion-goer) classmate, had to go and buy himself a house here, too. I sensed that there was going to be trouble when, not long after Harry and Margery moved in, they called to wonder if they could possibly have received by mistake something that might be intended for us—a rope-ladder fire escape with a card in it reading "Love, Joan." My older sister, who has no children, is forever worrying that I am going to let something dire happen to mine. Also, she cannot resist buying things. Someone once described her, not inaccurately, as a kleptomaniac who pays.

Next, Harry Kahn built a tennis court. In the spring of 1975, I received a letter from the mayor of some town in New Jersey, saying that his wife and he were avid tennis fans and were planning to spend the summer in Truro. Having read somewhere that I had a court (probably in *Sports Illustrated*, which ran a piece of mine about the tribulations of owning one), he wondered if they could come and play when the court wasn't in use. I wrote back that anybody courteous enough to make such a request in writing in advance was welcome to play at practically any time, and why didn't he give me a ring when he arrived? In due course he phoned, and I suggested that he stop by the following day. He said he'd be delighted to. I didn't see the mayor and his first lady, but figured they had come and gone while I was out shopping for calcium chloride or something else necessary to comply with a court's insatiable demands. The mayor phoned again a couple of days later, said they had enjoyed playing, and would it be all right if they came back again? Of course. This went on for a couple of weeks, without my ever laying eyes on my will-o'-the-wisp guests. The puzzle was solved when Margery Kahn called to say that she had found an expensive bottle of wine on her doorstep with a profuse note of thanks from someone she'd never heard of. The mayor had the right name but the wrong court. I told Margery to keep the wine, or, if she preferred, swap it for a fire escape.

Today is Friday, and all the commuters' wives, plus this husband, are getting ready to welcome their loved ones for the weekend. I wash my hair, sweep the kitchen floor, clean the terrace, pick some rambler roses from our split-rail fence, replace a missing fence rail, cut the grass, buy wine and swordfish, and wangle some fresh Wellfleet oysters from Joe Francis, who, because I am sort of family now (he is living with my daughter-in-law's sister) lets me have three and a half dozen for three dollars. When Ellie arrives, she can't comprehend how the house got so messed up in her brief absence, but she has had a tough week in New York and I know she will be all right as soon as Rainbow fetches her pipe and slippers.

June 25

Just as affirmative-action programs are designed to atone for some of the inequities whites have heaped upon blacks in past generations, so does the arrangement Ellie and I have to share household chores ease my conscience, I guess, for the way past generations of males have made females suffer. E. has some strong views about women that I am not sure, though, that I altogether share. It is her theory, for instance, that women haggle the way they do over splitting a restaurant check not because they are niggling about money but because they are *generous*. Unlike men, who, in her view, often pay restaurant tabs without scrutinizing them out of sheer laziness and stupidity, women take the pains they do to make certain they are cheating neither the establishment nor their companions. Some day I mean to ask E. to explain to me why it is that a woman getting out of a taxicab on a rainy day, when I am waiting to get into it, never has her money ready in advance, and can take up to three minutes, after bargaining with the driver over the size of the tip, to collect her change, put the change in her little change purse, put the little change purse into her bigger purse, and assess the entire interior of the vehicle for health and fire hazards before finally opening the door and getting the hell out.

Now, because my wife is working harder this summer than I am, we have signed a further compact: When Ellie is on the Cape for a weekend, women are to have tennis-court priority over men. This estimable libertarian concept may work in Truro, but it would never get off the ground in an old-fashioned community like West Cornwall, where we have recently spent part of a couple of summers. There, it is an unwritten rule at the Cream Hill Club (written, for all I know) that when men want to use the principal courts on weekends, women must yield.

We are dining this evening at the Dick Waterses' (in the new order of things, I am not quite sure who would be cooking if we stayed home), and I bring along some of our oysters and open them for hors d'oeuvres, disdaining a proffered glove and not cutting myself once, except for a single tiny nick that hardly bleeds at all. John Worthington, a squire, if not *the* squire, of the year-round Truro community (he used to be, among other noteworthy things, our first selectman), taught me how to open oysters. Tiny and he were over for drinks one day, and while John was in the living room he heard some dreadful noises emanating from the kitchen, where I was at the sink. He ran in to ask what was going on. Nothing untoward, I assured him; I was just opening some oysters. "With a *hammer*?" he exclaimed. John grabbed a knife and demonstrated the other, correct way of doing it. The fact that the tip of one of his fingers, as I couldn't help noticing, was missing was, as I later was much comforted to learn, coincidental.

After dinner, we play "Dictionary"—the game in which you have either to guess the real definition or invent a plausible one for obscure words. It was Tony Perkins, who in his young bachelor days often hid out in Truro when not acting, who introduced us to Dictionary. For the word "tinamou," the authentic meaning of which has left me as quickly as it arrived, Dick Waters comes up with "canned milk." Not bad at all.

June 26

A rainy Sunday, our first really bad day. I can tell from the size of the puddle in the driveway outside our bedroom window that the tennis court will be unplayable today and probably tomorrow, too. A lousy break for Ellie and Les Girls.

There is a picture on the front page of the *Times* of ex-president Ford leaning over somebody he has skulled with a golf ball. Why is it—to enounce a generalization that is probably quite rebuttable—that Republicans play golf and Democrats tennis? Businessmen golf, what's more, and intellectuals tennis. The answer, it seems to me, is that golf—not counting the graceful version exhibited on television by Jack Nicklaus and his ilk—is a far stuffier sport than tennis, and Republicans and businessmen, by and large, tend to be stuffier than their antitheses. I can rebut this myself. Governor Carey of New York is a Democrat and he plays golf. But then nobody ever pays any attention to Governor Carey.

E. and Rainbow and I go for a walk on Ballston Beach, a lovely spot regardless of the weather. Because of the rain, the seashore is practically deserted, save for a man and woman walking toward us out of the mist with two small boys. Who should it be but Tony Perkins and his family! Tony is pleased to learn we played his game last night. He says he has a new one— based on real and fake quotations from Bartlett's, and we agree that we must play it together some time. But Tony and his wife, Berry, who has never acted before, are in rehearsal, for a summer-stock production at Dennis of "The Voice of the Turtle." Tony is taking the Elliott Nugent role. He wonders if I have ever heard of Elliott Nugent. Yes, I saw him play the part, and when it comes to that, I well remember seeing Tony's father Osgood on Broadway. Tony flabbergasts me by saying that his father has been dead for forty years.

After Ellie takes off for New York in a car pool Palmer Williams has organized, I go to Provincetown for the opening of a new artists' co-op gallery. Sidney Simon is involved, also Budd Hopkins and Bob Motherwell. Jack Tworkov tells me he isn't, because he doesn't like groups shows. The gallery is on the site of what used to be Leo Manso's art school; Leo shows me the spots on the floor where his students once slopped. Many of the Cape people whose names I can't remember from one summer to the next are present, and we greet each other warmly, they no doubt trying to remember where they saw me last. Those who do know who I am inquire guardedly after my wife; one can never be certain how a long harsh winter may have affected domestic relations. When I say that she is working in New York, and hopes to be able to join me weekends, a few eyebrows are cautiously raised.

After cooking and cleaning up I go over to Dick Miller's to play poker and, predictably, to lose. Poker is not my game, as all the other participants are gleefully aware. The last time I played poker, though, I made a bundle. It was at Cornwall, in the course of a fund-raising evening for the local Democratic party (not a golfer in the bunch). There was a roulette table, and a craps table, and a poker table. Patsy Van Doren, the first selectman of that community, served as dealer, but did not play; she merely took ten per cent out of every pot, as stipulated in advance, for the evening's cause. The game started off modestly enough with raises of dimes and quarters and occasionally a dollar, but as the evening progressed (one could also benefit the Democrats by buying drinks), things got so out of hand that I found myself involved in raises of fifty and a hundred dollars on a single card. There was over a thousand dollars in one pot. Patsy, though a commendably impassive dealer, must have been delighted; her tithe netted the Democrats more funds that evening than all the other concessions combined. I was delighted, too, though on reflection petrified at what might have happened if I hadn't raked in fifty per cent of two of the last three giant high-low kitties.

June 27

No word from Shawn—this is most unlike him—but my tennis balls have arrived from Feron's, which is quite close geographically to *The New Yorker*. They had already travelled a long way before they left Forty-fourth Street. They were made in Taiwan. Somewhere en route from there to me, they have lost most of their bounce. Palmer Williams' tennis balls are from Korea, and much bouncier.

Ellie calls from a motel somewhere in upstate New York. She is on the road, doing research, and says motel life is dreary. How well I know! I can picture her eating alone in the dimly lit, fake English Tudor dining room of her hostelry, two martinis, a shrimp cocktail, a steak medium rare, and then falling asleep in her ascetic room without bothering to turn off the bad movie on the television.

David and Lexy want to take in a bad movie at the drive-in, but I am too bushed from cooking and washing up to transport them there. They console themselves with some of our old *Life* magazines, which date back to 1940 and were in the Truro house when I bought it in 1953. The boys—as my older boys did before them with the same now tattered *Lifes*—are reliving the Second World War. David is outraged, as he pores over one of our more recent issues, to come upon a kindly obituary of Senator Joe McCarthy. Last Sunday's *Times* said that kids in Scarsdale don't relate to analogies (if you don't relate nowadays you've had it) because they don't read newspapers. I have been reading newspapers regularly since I was ten, or maybe younger, but there was of course no television then for me to relate to. I guess our kids don't read papers much either, nowadays: Lexy asked me the other day who Andy Young was. But now, thanks to our cache of *Lifes*, Lexy has learned a good deal about Lord Halifax and the operations of the British Embassy in Washington at the start of the Second World War. In Scarsdale, his peers may not know that there was a Second World War.

June 29

At Schoonejongen's general store this morning, where those of us who have reserved newspapers troop ritually to pick them up, Sidney Simon tells me about a practical joke he was going to play on me. He got to Schoony's as soon as the papers were delivered. His dastardly scheme was to grab the *Times* and the *Globe* with my name on them, do the crossword puzzles in both, and return them to the reserved pile. Sidney knew how enraged I would be to find the squares filled in. But Ellie Schoonejongen, who evidently has a higher sense of ethics than she is universally credited with, would have none of his caper.

Ding Watson stops by to drop Tommy for his tennis lesson. She is off, she says, on a ten-hour round-trip drive to Putney, Vermont, to sign some papers, which she could have signed just as easily here in Truro had not her attorney up there neglected to mail them to her in time to meet a crucial deadline. I wish her Godspeed and suggest that she charge the lawyer fifty dollars an hour for her driving time. She has barely departed on her trek when Joey and Jaime arrive with Hillary, which means that—a rare occasion indeed—I will have both my grandsons for dinner. Jaime is six now, and marvelously articulate. Joey has just finished a magazine piece on an attorney who told him that he got paid a hundred and fifty dollars an hour for his advice, but when the lawyer learned that Joey planned to put that in print, he begged to have the dimensions of his fees reduced. David charges $2.50 an hour now for mowing lawns—$3.50 if he brings along his own (i.e., my) lawnmower. Martha, our cleaning woman, gets four dollars an hour, and Tony ten, when he is doing a garden job *cum*-Rototiller. I have never tried to figure out what my time is worth per hour. If Shawn doesn't like Georgia, it will be one of the highest minus numbers on record.

June 30

Today is our eighth wedding anniversary. I try to phone my absent working wife to congratulate her, but she isn't at the New York apartment, and I don't know where on the road she might be. I hope she will be pleased with the anniversary present I gave her yesterday. It isn't very romantic, but it's something she has been yearning for: I got the plumber to adjust the flush rate of the downstairs toilet. This morning I put David and Lexy on the 7:20 bus to Hyannis, where they are to catch the 8:30 bus to New York to keep separate doctors' appointments, one orthodontic and one orthopedic. Lexy is going to have his cast removed, and I give him one of my briefcases, so he can carry his X-rays without wrinkling them.

I have three briefcases now, and use them all, though two are terribly battered. My No. 1 briefcase is a beautiful leather Gucci job that Ellie gave me for my birthday. We ought to take it as a tax deduction, since never was there any object more unqualifiedly related to my work, but E. hasn't put it on the list of deductible things she makes out for our joint return, and it would seem churlish for me to bring up the subject.

At 9:45 A.M., David calls, collect, from Hyannis. Lexy and he have missed their bus to New York. They didn't have enough fare. They were only seven dollars shy, but the bus company wouldn't accept David's personal check, even though he presented his brand-new Commonwealth of

Massachusetts Registry of Motor Vehicles learner's permit by way of identification. I can think of no one in Hyannis whom I know well enough to ask to run over to the Greyhound terminal with seven dollars, and there is time, if I drive fast and traffic isn't bad, for me to get up there before the next bus departs, so I take off. There goes this work day.

Jaime, not yet quite reoriented to Truro, is loath to go to the beach with Hillary. She and I know he will have a good time once, and if, he gets there, so although I do not believe in lying to children, I propose that she tell him he *might* see a whale spout. That is not altogether a prevarication, because we have had whales off Ballston Beach. Many newcomers think that our neighborhood strand is called "Boston Beach," but the stretch was entitled after the Ball family, whose last resident name-bearer was S. Osborn Ball. Ozzie Ball, an amiable but eccentric lawyer, used to handle the caretaking chores himself for the old wooden summer bungalows his family had put up along the ocean, and which, though unarguably tumbledown, were much prized by the seasonal tenants who occupied them. N. used to stay in one. She is gone now and so are the shacks; the National Park Service tore them down when it acquired jurisdiction over the seashore.

Jaime is persuaded to go to the beach after all, and on returning says he had a good time, though, unaccountably, he saw no whales. Hillary returns minus one of her sandals, and there is some jocular talk about whether or not Joey should run back there and look for something so ridiculously easy to detect. When he was twelve or so, Joey exhibited such a flair for finding things other people had lost that we used to call him the human retriever. He could find a sandal blindfolded. Anyone visiting us could leave a watch or a pair of sunglasses on the beach with impunity; Joey would have it back for them in no time. His most remarkable feat consisted of retrieving the diamond from his mother's engagement ring six months after it had dropped out of its setting—irretrievably, as far as everybody around except Joey was concerned—one autumn day into a pile of leaves. Joey simply waited until the following spring, when the snow had melted, went out with a rake, scratched around a bit, and returned with the missing stone.

At tennis, Sidney Simon reports ruefully that he has been defeated in some litigation with a tenant he has been trying to evict from the Simon brownstone in Greenwich Village. The lessee evidently convinced an arbitrator that his landlord was not to be believed, being a man of patently loose morals: In proof of that, the tenant told the referee, Sidney was "a much-married man with too many children." Sidney has six children and has had just two wives—one for eighteen years and one for ten. I was once a tenant of Sidney's, for six months between my only two marriages, and the only complaints I had about my then landlord was that 1) if you slept too near the edge of the bed the bed tipped over and you landed on the floor and 2) the laundry service he recommended lost, irretrievably, a tennis sweater that N. had once hand-knit for me.

July 1

The Cape Cod Mosquito Control truck comes by, its crew parking as usual in our driveway before tramping down toward the Pamet River marshes to do whatever it does down there. (Miles Standish is reputed to have roamed more or less the same area late in 1620, looking vainly for food for the Mayflower passengers; at that time of year he shouldn't have been much bothered by mosquitoes.) The mosquito-control man, when he resurfaces and retrieves his truck, tells me that it looks like a good year, and he is gone before it occurs to me to ask him whether he means a good year for mosquitoes or for the rest of us.

I dine at Joan and Jerry Cohen's in celebration of our annual triple celebration—our anniversary, their anniversary, and Jerry's birthday. But without Ellie around to remind me, I forget to take along a gift, and I try to get myself off the hook by saying that if I have any luck when I go sea-clamming early tomorrow morning (the Truro Package Store's infallible tide calendar says that will be an ideal time), it is my intention—as, while I am talking, it so becomes—to present them with one of my homemade clam pies. The Jim Thomsons are on hand and Dick Neustadt, and so with the Harvard faculty triply represented, there is naturally much talk of Cambridge and of "Derek." Seth Cohen has been admitted to Harvard, but that comes as no surprise: The Boks used to babysit for the Cohens' dog. Jim says that his Nieman Foundation, having wangled out of Derek $100,000 of a Walter Lippmann bequest to Harvard for the purpose, is going to move to a new headquarters, on Francis Avenue. Jim has written to several South African journalists who are ex-Nieman Fellows about the status of my visa, but has not yet had any replies.

Professor Neustadt, longtime advisor to and expert on United States presidents, says Joe Califano has asked him to do a definitive survey on swine flu for the Department of Health, Education and Welfare. Dick Neustadt has a "Man at Work" sign at his driveway entrance in Wellfleet: It says that he toils until 5 P.M. and that absolutely nobody is to disturb him before that hour. Dick will be altering his inflexible regimen soon, he tells us, to head for Atlanta and get started on his swine-flu research. I cannot conceive of how a no-doubt handsomely reimbursed study of swine flu by a non-physician can benefit the taxpaying public at this peculiar stage of history, but I refrain from saying so; let him who has never boondoggled himself cast the first stone.

July 2

Joey has to take off today on a magazine assignment, but before that has to get a manuscript to the editor of an I.B.M. magazine in Atlanta. (Atlanta has been much on my mind in recent weeks; would that that were true of Shawn, too!) Joey's editor in Georgia is sending a taxi from Hyannis to Truro to pick up his piece and deliver it to Air New England, which will ferry it to New York to connect with an Atlanta flight. It has taken many interstate phone calls to firm up these arrangements, and I calculate offhand that it is costing I.B.M. at least one hundred dollars to receive Joey's copy. His manuscript is not especially long, and it seems to me that it would have been faster, easier, and cheaper, to put a stenographer on the phone in Georgia and let Joey dictate to her. (Or, as Ellie would be quick to point out to me were she here, to him.) But companies like I.B.M. are probably so reliant on computers nowadays that they don't have anybody around who can take dictation.

The taxi is due at our house at 8:30, but the sea clams are so abundant this morning that we have been out to the North Truro flats and collected a basketful and brought them back well before that. I reckon that I will finish cleaning them, if I don't dawdle, at just about the time that the manuscript reaches Atlanta. As usual, there was practically nobody else out sea-clamming this morning except the old standbys: Palmer and Barbara Williams, and Leo Salzman. Sea clams—the big ones, the kind whose shells serve nicely as ashtrays—are relatively simple to hunt; they all but sit up and beg to be captured, either in the water or just beneath the surface of the sand; the only danger, if you go after them with your hands instead of using a clam fork, is that they may close their hard viselike shells on your fingers. When Terry was a kid a clam once fastened itself around one of his and I had a hell of a time prying it off.

Ellie arrives with Rita Gam, and we have clam pie for dinner. We eat the pies I had earmarked for our household and also, before I can put a halt to the gourmandizing, the pie I had baked for the Jerry Cohens.

July 3

I decide to go clamming again. Rita asks if she may make some chowder. The clams I had newly designated for the Cohens go into it. I hope Rita does not duplicate the performance of a New York *Times* photographer who came to Truro to shoot some pictures to illustrate a Sunday magazine piece I'd done on the Provincetown fishing fleet. The photographer spent all day preparing a chowder, and when he pronounced it ready he poured it into a large glass bowl, which instantly cracked. Our kitchen floor was awash in soup. We caution Rita to use a sturdier receptacle, and when her concoction makes it successfully to the table, we gratefully christen it Clam Gam.

This being the Fourth of July weekend, there are a lot of parties scheduled. For many years, the big Truro social event was a Fourth of July cocktail party given by Gilbert Seldes, who occupied an out-building at Peggy (Mrs. Clarence) Day's place. Gilbert never sent out any invitations, and hundreds of freeloaders, most of them unknown to him, would converge upon his modest digs. After Gilbert died, we took over his party and tried to convert it into an invitational affair. But notwithstanding, so many people brought so many house guests that we sometimes had a crowd of two hundred and fifty, which was more or less manageable unless the weather turned bad and we had to try to squeeze the mob indoors. (The only saving grace about a party that size is that one invariably lays in too much liquor, with the happy result that one has to buy hardly any more for the rest of the summer.) One year, just after our very first guests, Paul and Nina Chavchavadze, had shown up, a mosquito-control helicopter showed up, too, swooped down, and unleashed a cloud of insecticide perilously near the tables outdoors where we had put the cocktail food. We had the honor then of having two members of the Russian nobility—Nina was one of the last of the authentic Romanovs—pressed into service to carry trays back indoors until the air cleared.

I had met the Chavchavadzes' son David, who, like his father, could probably have called himself "prince" any time he cared to, during the Second World War. This was in the winter of 1945, not long after Soviet and American forces had linked up triumphantly at the bridge at Torgau, on the Elbe River. It was a moment of rare euphoria in Soviet-American relations. The National Council of American-Soviet Friendship, one of the old Communist-front groups that used to decorate our ideological landscape, was putting on a big celebratory rally at Madison Square Garden. The Infantry public relations office to which I was assigned in New York was instructed by our headquarters in Washington to furnish the National Council with full cooperation. We went all out. We provided an American lieutenant general to speak, not altogether to his satisfaction, to the largely pro-Communist audience.

Then we had an even better notion: Why not add to the bill an American soldier of incontestably Russian origin? We asked Washington to find us one and deliver him to New York, where I was designated to compose a speech for him extolling the brave Red Army soldiers. In due course, Lieutenant David Chavchavadze reported in, for temporary duty, from Alaska. He did not quite know why he had been dispatched with high-priority travel orders to New York. When the princely White Russian learned that he was supposed to appear at a Stalinist rally, and when he read the text of what he was supposed to say, he balked. He was damned if he was going to utter *those* words before *those* people. We offered David a choice. He could do what the Army wanted him to do, or he could return at once, in bleak mid-winter, to Alaska. He delivered the speech.

Since David was more or less in my custody, though technically, of course, a lieutenant outranked a warrant officer, I proposed a further deal. Jinny and I were about to move from one apartment to another, and if he would give us a hand I would have new travel orders cut for him, so he could enjoy an extra week's leave in New York. Prince Chavchavadze proved to be a resolute moving man, and as, years later, I watched his blueblooded parents toting salami and cheese from our terrace to our kitchen, I could not help wondering if there was something genetic in this Czarist family's talent for servitude.

I was mad at the appearance of the mosquito-control helicopter for another reason: There is no better way to terminate an outdoor mid-summer Cape Cod cocktail party, we had learned from long experience, than to have the hangers-on dispersed, at sunset, by mosquitoes.

Among this weekend's parties is Lee Falk's first tennis brunch. Luke and Ruth Wilson are there—first time I've seen them since we went to China together in 1973. Ruth reminisces cheerfully about that trip, which surprises me, because my recollection is that she spent about half of our three weeks there in a People's Republic hospital. Kirk Wilkinson, who is persona grata at Lee's in spite of the grass-court debacle (at what additional cost I dare not contemplate, Lee has had his court ploughed up and suitably delawned), wants to know if I am acquainted with the *New Yorker* writer George Trow. I am not exactly acquainted with him, since nobody at *The New Yorker* is ever properly introduced to anybody else, but there is one thing about him that I know well and that baffles me. Trow has had the office directly adjoining mine for several years, and when, rarely, he is on the premises, he sometimes laughs into a telephone nonstop for twenty minutes at a stretch. He does not say anything; he just laughs, a loud, carrying, braying laugh that beats against our connecting wall like the ocean surf after a hurricane. Justin and Anne Kaplan are standing with Kirk and me while I describe this scene, no doubt exaggeratedly, and when I say that I cannot for the life of me imagine what Trow could be laughing at on the phone, Anne Bernays suggests that he may be connected with Dial-a-Joke.

There is another holiday party at the Pamet Harbor Yacht Club, which we joined so David and Lexy could Make Friends. David asks how long we plan to stay and then says he can't make a friend in half an hour. He and Lexy play Frisbie in the parking lot until we leave. Malcolm and Mary Alice Preston say that their daughter Mandy and her six-year-old son are coming back to Truro. Mandy has decided to return to college; she hopes a degree will bring her security. At the Falks', Judy Post, whose fiftieth birthday party we went to last year, revealed that she is entering law school; she wants independence. Security and independence are what everybody craves for; I have elected, over the years, to favor the latter over the former. Being unsalaried, I can spend whole summers on the Cape without asking anyone's by-your-leave. But my bank balance this morning, if my arithmetic is correct, was $4.54, and as soon as the bank slaps a two-dollar service charge on me for having less than five hundred dollars in my account, my working capital will be sliced in half.

July 4

Ellie and I are not giving a Fourth of July party this year. A few people may turn up anyway, out of habit. We switched our big seasonal shindig to the Labor Day weekend for a couple of years, but we have just about decided to forgo that one, too, because last year's was, for me, a disaster. I forgot to tell the police in advance that there would be a hundred or more cars parked on South Pamet Road (had I told them, I would have been able to hire an off-duty cop to handle traffic and parking), and as a result I spent most of the party up on the road, begging the local constabulary not to have my guests' cars towed away. Quite a few of them received parking tickets despite my remonstrances, but even if they had to pay the five- or fifteen-dollar fines or whatever their transgressions were assessed at, I figured that, considering all the food and liquor they consumed, they would have about broken even.

The Sidney Simons have attempted to fill the vacuum we have created by organizing a bring-your-own-food beach picnic tonight at Corn Hill, where there is a commodious parking lot. Corn Hill got its name because it was there that the Pilgrims, close to starvation after the Mayflower anchored in Provincetown harbor on November 11, 1620, found some corn that the indigenous Indians of the Pamet tribe had stashed. This would be news to the editors of *Time;* a paragraph in their current issue begins, "The *Mayflower's* destination was Virginia; instead, the boat pulled up at Plymouth, Mass." That the Pilgrims made their first landing at Plymouth Rock is one of the longest-lasting misconceptions in American history. Like other aficionados of Cape Cod, I have tried more than once in print to set this matter straight; but *The New Yorker* is not as widely used in schools as a whole slew of textbooks that perpetuate the Plymouth myth, and the Plymouth Chamber of Commerce has never much gone out of its way, understandably, to give Provincetown its due.

It is windy at Corn Hill tonight, and thus chilly, but as a result we picnickers do not have to cope with mosquitoes or any other bugs as we huddle around a bonfire—you need a permit, but our fire chief, Ray Joseph, is always agreeable about granting it—waiting for a glimpse of the fireworks unleashed in Provincetown, nine miles away. (Plymouth is too far off, across the bay, for us to view whatever pyrotechnics it may be engaged in.) At Corn Hill, a stranger tells me that he can remember when I was a chief warrant officer. I can remind myself of this, when in New York, every day; I still have in my *New Yorker* office a "CWO Kahn" emblem that used to decorate a military desk behind which I sat contriving ways to make the dowdy old Infantry more glamorous.

I didn't meet Sidney Simon until long after the war, but a few weeks ago, rummaging through an old filing cabinet, I came across a copy of a 1945 *Mademoiselle* in which a number of soldiers gave their views on the role of women in the post-war world. The feature was entitled G-Eye Slant On Working Wives. One of the G-Eyes was Captain Sidney Simon, war artist at MacArthur's headquarters; another was Chief Warrant Officer Kahn, flack at Army Ground Forces headquarters. Captain Simon said, "Young painters *have* to have wives willing to carry their share of expenses. And my wife wouldn't be content with just housework." CWO Kahn said, "Cooking? The suffering Gini goes through to prepare a meal doesn't justify the results. [I did not then seem to regard myself as an alternate cook.] Babies? I see no objection to mothers working. A child whose mother is home all day gets too dependent on her." I had no children then.

I might have ended up my wartime service as a captain myself had General Forrest Harding, under whose protective two-star wing I basked on three continents, had his way with the War Department. In New Guinea, commanding the 32nd Infantry Division, the general had had the authority to make me a warrant officer junior grade; and he was later able, on his own ukase, to promote me to chief. (Most chief warrant officers, by striking contrast to me, were grizzled old ex-master sergeants who had specialized for twenty years or more in Finance or Supply or some such.) In Panama, the general decided that inasmuch as I was holding an officer's job—I was his assistant G-2 and his principal public relations officer—I should be a lieutenant. He did not have the power to make me one. But he could and did convene a board of officers to test my qualifications and to submit a recommendation to the War Department that I be granted a direct commission. (The recommendation was ultimately turned down.)

Part of my examination consisted of a field exercise. I was put in charge of a platoon that was supposed to flush out an enemy force secreted in the jungle. My soldiers for the day, in full combat dress, assembled at a prescribed point and boarded a few trucks. I was to sit in the lead truck, alongside the driver, and I was handed a map with some markings on it and told to proceed with my men to the designated spot and then proceed as I saw fit. I had had only minimal experience at map-reading, and hadn't the foggiest notion where to tell the driver, a private first class, to go. Fortunately, he *could* read maps, and he got me to my destination.

We moved out into the jungle—I bravely in the lead—and suddenly we found ourselves in an enemy ambush. We were being fired on (the ammunition was blank, I was happy to perceive) from two sides. I knew what to do. I had to order the men behind me to hit the ground, fast. So I raised my hand in the approved fashion and brought it sharply down. It was my bad luck to bring it down along the length of a thorn tree. I was given a passing grade on this exam, but I did not much care; I was too preoccupied, over at the medics', having a clump of long black ugly thorns extracted, one by one, from my commanding palm.

July 5

Ellie is going to Boston and thence to Los Angeles today, to press on with her research. The first time I ever went to the West Coast was in the summer of 1938, when I flew out to Minneapolis to meet my college classmate Tom Dillon and to drive with him toward California. Tom never graduated from Harvard, and it was my fault. In our junior year, my longtime friend Warren Munsell, Jr., then a junior at Princeton, decided that instead of finishing up college he would take a trip around the world. I agreed to join him. After the arrangements were more or less set, my parents vetoed my participation in the joint venture; travel could wait, they decreed, until I got my degree. I didn't want to let Warren down, and felt it was incumbent on me to find a substitute. I found Tom Dillon. They set off together and stayed together until they reached Tahiti, which Tom found so beguiling that he waved Warren on his way across the Pacific and remained there, in some little grass-skirted shack or other, six sybaritic months. Many years later, I found myself ensconced on an even more remote Pacific outpost, the atoll of Kapingamarangi, which had no communications with the outside world, but I only stayed there a fortnight, and that was long enough; the average weight of the women over sixteen in that seeming Polynesian paradise was about two hundred and seventy-three pounds.

Dillon and I couldn't leave Minneapolis as soon as we had planned. Tom was a copywriter in the Minnesota outpost of Batten, Barton, Durstine & Osborn, and he couldn't start his vacation until he had turned in a set of singing commercials for Clark's Candy Bars. He said that if I would assist him it would expedite our departure, and so I did. The singing commercials were pronounced first-rate by his superiors. On balance, I have to think that I helped Tom's career more than I hurt it: While he never finished college, he did end up as chairman of the board of B.B.D.&O. International.

Before Ellie leaves, she asks me what I am going to be working on this week. I had better start writing *something* soon, I say, but it is hard to concentrate until I have heard from Shawn. I admit to being profoundly discouraged. (I am also baffled; Shawn's promptness in reporting on pieces is legendary.) She nods sympathetically, and an instant before boarding her plane hands me a slip of paper on which, encouragingly, she has typed out an excerpt from Emerson's "Nature"—". . . no man can write anything, who does not think that what he writes is for the time the history of the world; or do anything well, who does not esteem his work to be of importance. My work may be of none, but I must not think it of none, or I shall not do it with impunity."

July 7

E. phones from L. A. *Her* work is going well, and how is mine? Terrible; here I am supposed to be writing a novel all about sex, and I can't even get to first base. Any word from Bill about Georgia? Nope, and it has been more than four weeks now since I turned the confounded piece in. It is all Jimmy Carter's fault; if only he had lost, I wouldn't be in this fix. E. suggests, cheeringly, that I forget about work and spend a few days in New York with her next week. I agree, unhesitatingly; what a nice idea, to leave one's home to spend a holiday with one's wife!

July 9

Joey is back, and he and I decide to go to Walter Bingham's and watch the final round of the British Open—Nicklaus vs. Watson—on television. This is *Sports Illustrated* day for Joey and me; Bing's fellow writer there, Sarah Pileggi, is going to drive us over in her spectacular antique Daimler convertible, the car of cars in Truro this summer. For directional signals, it has little pop-out arrows that Jaime and his peers find enchanting. The golf match is on tape, and while waiting around for Sarah to fetch us, Joey and I have been begging everyone who comes by not to tell us, if they know, who won the title. Palmer Williams knows, but confines himself to telling us that we will find the contest very exciting. It is, Watson nosing out Nicklaus after a barrage of fantastic shots by both of them. A strange feeling— watching an event like this that one knows has been concluded several hours earlier, and making sure that one does not ascertain how it came out. We feel somewhat like the British colonialists who, receiving a whole month's worth of *London Times*es at a clip, insist on reading them, without peeking ahead, in chronological order.

Joey and I dine at the Lee Falks'. The Justin Kaplans are there, among others. Joe Kaplan insists that Louis Untermeyer, whose name somehow crops up in the conversation, has not yet turned ninety. I regard myself as something of an expert on nonagenarians and insist that he has. Lee doesn't have any reference book around that can settle the dispute, but when I get home I consult my 1950 edition of "Who's Who in America" and find my contention confirmed: the old poet was born on October 1, 1885, and I was right with almost two years to spare.

July 10

The Sunday *Times* has an article about the restoration of the great Buddhist temple of Borobodur. Ellie and I made a pilgrimage, at her behest, to that Indonesian shrine in 1970, after I covered the World's Fair in Osaka. We took the night train, an elegant one, from Jakarta to Jogjakarta, which in the view of the people who made up the railroad's schedule can evidently not have been considered a consequential stop; the train got to Jogjakarta at two-thirty in the morning. I wonder what happened to the huge hotel in which we were among the very few registered guests; it contained a casino, but back then hadn't yet been issued a gambling license, and it could not have long survived merely by accommodating travellers like us who believed there was something in Indonesia worth seeing between Java and Bali. Borobodur was amply worth a detour, surely one of the world's preeminent religious edifices, and remembering what state of decomposition it was in seven years ago, I am pleased to learn that it is going to be preserved.

We had also planned, on that trip, to visit Angkor Wat, and indeed had plane reservations from Bangkok to Phnom Penh. But the United States had just then made its discreditable incursions into Cambodia, and the travel agent who booked us into that country could give no guarantee that we'd be able to get out again. I am usually bolder than Ellie about embarking on adventures, but this time I cravenly hung back and struck Angkor Wat from our itinerary. The chances are that we may never get to see it. All subsequent developments in Cambodia notwithstanding, Ellie has never quite forgiven me for depriving her of that treat.

The Sunday *Globe*, for its part, has a nostalgic feature on Sinatra at Sixty. One of the illustrations shows a bit of the first page of the third installment of my 1946 *New Yorker* Profile on the singer. The series came out subsequently in a book entitled "The Voice." I didn't see how that book could fail to be a big seller. Sinatra's fans were numbered in the legions, and it was well known that they would practically claw each other's eyes out to be privy to the latest printed words about him. The sales figures for "The Voice" seemed to be irrefutable evidence that, while a few paragraphs about Frankie might cause the circulation of a movie magazine to soar, his disciples were not of a sort to stampede bookstores. Just recently, Earl Wilson has produced an unauthorized biography of Sinatra that has done quite nicely— in part, I suspect, because the singer sued the author. My book was no less authorized, and might have done much better if only Sinatra had had the decency to apply for an injunction against it. Maybe I wrote that one thirty years too soon.

With my wife away, I am being invited out to dinner a good deal, which is a tribute to Truro's neighborliness. My hosts tonight are the Harry Kahns. Harry and Margery have just been to Czechoslovakia. They had a great time, in spite of the fact that Harry discovered as they were leaving the country that he had some leftover money he wasn't supposed to have and that it was too late to spend. So he simply threw it away. His bringing up the subject of money prods me into confessing to Harry that I suspect, not having been billed by Feron's either for my deadened Taiwanese tennis balls or for a pair of sneakers I carried away from the store with me in June, that the merchandise has been charged to his account. Harry says grandly that he paid his Feron's bill without looking it over ("See!" Ellie would say; "that's men for you every time!"), and that he has had a very good year in the market, so I shouldn't give the trivial matter another thought. I feel like a poor relation.

Though unrelated, Harry and I have known one another since we went to the same summer camp—Camp Winnebago. That was back in the days when competitiveness among young teenagers was not decried. Winnebago's official camp colors were brown and green, and every camper became, immediately on reaching the Maine woods, either a Brown or a Green. There was fierce, summer-long rivalry (condoned, if not instigated, by Chief, our leader, and his wife, who liked to be addressed as Mrs. Chief), between the Browns and the Greens; curiously, neither Harry nor I can remember which of the two we were. Savage as were our efforts to outdo the wearers of the other colors in bird-watching and bed-making, the intramural enmity was nothing compared to the violent hatred that was instilled in all of us for the arch-fiend, Camp Kennebec, whose largely German-Jewish-New-York-City clientele was regarded by our largely German-Jewish-New-York-City clientele as the dregs of humanity. It was difficult, in July and August, to visualize surviving the winter ahead if a team one was on should be vanquished in its annual confrontation with Kennebec.

I was the third-string diver on the Winnebago swimming squad, a dubious honor, attained solely by being willing enough, or foolhardy enough, to do back flips. I was able to sleep fairly well in the week preceding the Kennebec contest, because each camp would be putting only two divers on display. Then the day before the big match, our second-string man came a cropper, hitting his chin on the diving board while practicing a jackknife. The accident was excusable: Our diving board was on a float, and if the wind was whipping up our lake, the float tended to rock. The wind had not abated when the Kennebec swimmers, looking enormous and mean, arrived on their bus. Diving was the final event of the meet, and as the various other events took place, the Winnebago counsellor who was keeping a running score told me that we couldn't lose; all I had to do to wrap up a victory for the Brown-and-Green was to execute a simple back dive, not even a flip, and we were a shoo-in. I walked to the end of the board, turned around, tried to balance myself for takeoff, and plopped sideways into the lake. In my mortification, I stayed under water as long as I could, but when I finally had to come up for air (though drowning seemed a not unattractive alternative), the air still pulsed with loud, triumphant, Kennebecan cheers.

July 11

Today's mind-tugging obituary in the *Times* belongs to Hoke Norris, the longtime book editor of the Chicago *Sun-Times*, who has died, at a mere sixty-three, in a veterans hospital. I always feel a special pang of pity for people who die in V.A. hospitals; the chances are they would not have died there if they could have afforded to die anywhere else. Hoke once invited me, fifteen years or so ago, to be one of the three writers featured at a mid-winter Book-and-Author lunch over which he presided in one of the big Chicago hotels—the Ambassador West, if I remember correctly. I could have, and should have, taken a train to Chicago the day before, but I was busy and figured that if I caught the 8 A.M. breakfast flight from La Guardia I could make the lunch in plenty of time. The weather wasn't especially bad when I set off from Scarborough, at six in the morning, to give myself ample time to park my car at the airport, and indeed at 7:50 I was sitting in a plane, ready for takeoff. That plane never budged; the pilot had been in a car accident, and no substitute seemed available.

I was too busy rushing around the airport trying to get myself rebooked to worry about breakfast. I finally got a substitute reservation, phoned Chicago, and told Hoke I'd be turning up, but I was not quite sure how soon. He told me not to worry, that he'd arrange for me to be the last of the three literary lions to speak, and that if I made it by about 1:45, Chicago time, that would be fine. My flight, it developed when we were airborne, was not a food-serving flight, and for one reason or another it did not reach Chicago until 1:15. I leapt into a taxi, hoarsely bade the driver to race with all possible speed to the Ambassador West, and tried to relax. The cab ran out of gas in a tunnel. It was 2:15 when I arrived at the hotel, noticing peripherally as I ran toward the Grand Ballroom that there were three stacks of books-to-be-autographed on tables in an anteroom—two stacks commendably depleted and one, mine, untouched. As I pushed at a swinging door to the ballroom, I was almost knocked down by a surge of six hundred exiting women.

By the time I got into the chamber, Hoke Norris was about the only person left inside it. He was sympathetic, and said I looked as though I needed a drink. I concurred. We repaired to a bar and had a couple of enjoyable conversational hours, at the end of which I allowed as how I ought to be heading toward the airport to return to New York. Hoke said this was a terrible time of day to try to fight Chicago traffic. He was certainly right; it took me nearly two hours to get there, with the result that I missed my return flight. The plane I ultimately boarded left at around 8 P.M., and turned out to be a non-dinner flight. I got back to Scarborough at 1 A.M., not having attended the lunch I'd gone there for and, indeed, not having eaten anything all day. I have never subsequently been invited to a Book-and-Author lunch anywhere, but I cannot let myself believe that this is because poor Hoke Norris spread the word among his confrères that I was undependable.

In the mail, a note from an Eli Lilly and Company person, passing along the first and, as far as I know, only review of my privately-published history of that outfit. Written by a professor at the University of Indiana, the critique is in the June, 1977, issue of the *Indiana Magazine of History*. The reviewer says, "The account is undocumented and laudatory rather than analytical, but it is most interesting and will be of some use until a full scale scholarly history of this important enterprise is available." Hmph.

I take off for New York and a reunion with Ellie. Judy Post, en route to a law class, boards a Provincetown-Boston DC-3 with me, and when she says something snooty about the aircraft that sounds like a book review by an Indiana savant, I assure her that the DC-3 is the most reliable plane ever devised and executed. I should know. I wrote a Profile all about the sturdy old DC-3 some years ago; why, I tell Judy, this indestructible old machine has been known to land safely on mountaintops. A few minutes later, we are told that we will have to take another plane because ours has magneto trouble. I don't recall even parenthetically alluding to magnetos in my article.

Arriving, eventually, in New York, I find two new portraits in our apartment—pictures of Ellie's mother's parents that E. has obtained in a recent redivision of her family's spoils. I say they would be great to fill a vacuum that has existed on our Truro walls since Jinny and I split up. She and I used to have hanging there portraits of six of our children's sixteen great-great-grandparents; but when Jinny and I were divorced and I got the house in our spoils division, she took with her, naturally, the two pictures from her side of the family. Now, I suggest to Ellie, David and Lexy can display two of *their* great-greats to complement the remaining four great-greats of their stepbrothers.

July 12

Summer in New York—a strange time. Torpor is the word for it. The *New Yorker* office, like the streets that surround it, is all but deserted. There is a pile of mail on my desk that was supposed to have been forwarded to me, but the old raincoat that I have kept there for emergencies has vanished. There is no word of any kind from Shawn.

Yes, there is. I sent him a memo this morning about an old piece of mine that I hope he is going to schedule soon, and right after lunch he knocks on my office door, which he doesn't have to do because I always leave it open. His appearance confirms, for a hideous instant, my very worst fears about Georgia. More often than not, when Bill has good news to convey, he conveys it by phone; and when the news is bad he delivers it in person. This latter takes guts; most people will go to any lengths to avoid rejective confrontations, and to tell a writer his work is unusable must be, for Bill, as painful an experience as it is for the tellee. So I have already put on my best it-doesn't-really-matter-there-will-be-other-days-and-other-pieces face when Bill tells me how much he liked Georgia, that he thought the articles were very funny, and that he expects to use them very soon. He has been trying to reach me, it turns out, for several weeks, on and off, but has missed me every time. Still, it has been five weeks and one day since I turned the Profile in, and while awaiting his reaction I have probably aged thirty-nine days.

Editors can stand a New York summer better than writers, it would appear from who's around and who isn't; more to the point, editors have to get the magazine out every single week, which precludes their lolling around beaches or mountains when the weather turns sultry. Not only is Bill Shawn on the premises, but also Bill Knapp, who on the heels of Shawn's nice acceptance speech favors me with some bleak non-acceptance intelligence: On reconsideration, the Harvard committee has again rejected our luckless candidate. Knapp adds, almost offhand, that my Georgia pieces were sent along some time ago, for editing, to Derek Morgan, who will be putting them into type any moment now. If I hadn't happened to come to New York, galley proofs would have been out and circulated around the office, and everybody at the magazine might have known before the writer did that Georgia was O.K.

Knapp says that he told Morgan, who has never handled anything of mine before, that Kahn is easy to edit. Is that good or bad? Edmund Wilson is reputed to have stipulated before agreeing to contribute to *The New Yorker* that his prose was sacrosanct and was not to be changed by so much as a comma. (I can believe that story even if it isn't true: Wilson-in-print could have stood some pruning, just as some muting might have made more tolerable the shrill stabbing voice of Wilson-in-person, which, whenever the great man approached to within about a hundred feet of where anybody else was trying to think, murdered cerebration.) Some of our writers, I know, even staff writers, have to be rewritten extensively. My copy used to be chopped up—I did not mind, I found most of the alterations to be improvements—much more than it is these days. If after forty years that weren't true, some heavy soul-searching would probably be in order. The only time, nearly twenty years ago, that I complained about an editor was when the one assigned to a reportorial piece of mine that I had deliberately written in a certain vein put the piece through his typewriter and completely changed its concept. I told Shawn that if he wanted to run the revised piece he could do so, but not with my name attached to it. The article was already in type, but Shawn—this is illustrative, I think, of what makes him the great editor he is—gave it in manuscript to a second editor, who put it through largely as I had written it in the first place.

July 13

Ellie is leaving for Europe, to interview more women artists, tomorrow evening, and she spent much of last night trying vainly to call Beverly Pepper in Rome. E. has to go out this morning and wants our phone covered in case Beverly calls back. So I rush off early to the office, where I have left all the papers I planned to wrestle with today, and rush back home with them to learn that E. has been trying to intercept me; she got through to Rome soon after I took off. I get back downtown to *The New Yorker*, the second time around, at ten forty-five, which is sooner than many members of the staff arrive on their first effort.

At lunchtime, during normal periods of the year, there is always a backgammon game in progress at the Harvard Club. Approaching the place today, I am hailed on the sidewalk by Bill Myrick, who knows where I am heading and instead of saying "Hello" or "Hi" says, no less affably, "No game." Where have all the players gone? Bereft, I go to the bar, which is deserted except for W. A., a backgammon kibitzer of long standing but a non-competitor aside from the one year he entered the club's annual tournament and knocked me out of it. I bear him no grudge; any time one loses at backgammon, it is wholly a matter of luck. W. is complaining about the difficulty of obtaining decent brands of liquor at any club bars any more; and he goes on to say I am a good guy, because I often eat and drink at the club. He feels, in that respect, that some special house charges ought to be levied against the likes of T., S., and H., who use the club's gaming facilities incessantly but never order anything and thus don't *support* the establishment. W. shifts to the finances of another club of his, a golf one in New Jersey, where he is glad to be able to inform me acceptable brands of booze are still available. W. mentions Chivas Regal, for one. "That's what all the Jews drink," he says. You learn something new every day.

Heading homeward, I step off the Madison Avenue bus at Eighty-ninth Street and am handed a tract by a young man. His literature is a plug not for a politician nor a Korean clergyman nor a massage parlor; it informs me, rather, that a real estate firm in Brooklyn stands ready to sell me waterfront properties ranging in price from $159,000 to $273,000. There cannot be many neighborhoods in which distributing such brochures is worth the trouble. I am flattered but uninterested; I have my own waterfront property in Truro, and I wish I were there right now, *sans* necktie. Tonight's New York *Post* carries an excerpt from a recent biography of Montgomery Clift. The actor spent one summer in Truro, I read, staying in, and doing his best to demolish, a house that Kevin McCarthy had rented there for the summer. No date is given. Can this have been the season that Kevin rented *my* house? I must check for old damage when I get back.

David has arrived in town, to see his dentist, so he joins his mother and me for dinner at a blessedly air-conditioned restaurant at Seventy-ninth and Third. I ask David how things are going at the Cape and who has been around the house since my departure. Ellie is only sort of half-listening to this dialogue until David says, "The lady with the Daimler came by again."

Wham! Bam! Bang!

"*Who—is—this—lady—with—this—Daimler?*"

I try to explain to E. that when Sarah Pileggi arrives in her ship of state, her husband, Nick, is as often as not sitting uxorially beside her, but all things considered it would have been better if David had limited his recital of *dramatis personae* to males with whom his mother was already acquainted. He will handle this sort of thing better as he gets older, especially if he has a wife.

David is grown-up enough, though, to perceive that a conversational switch is in order. He tells me that the Chase Manhattan Bank has sent him statements crediting him with three nest-egg accounts, whereas we well know he has only two. I say he must notify the bank to break one of his eggs, though I have better reason than most mortals to let the Chase stew—this mixed-menu metaphor would never get by at *The New Yorker*—in its own juice. Twice in the last few years the Chase has debited my checking account with large sums I had nothing to do with, and another time it deposited a substantial check of mine in somebody else's account and badgered me with overdrawn notices for a month before I could get it to acknowledge its error. I haven't yet taken any of this up with David Rockefeller, under whose aegis the Chase has often been accused of slipshod management, but I am tempted to sic my David onto the Chase's David if the bank doesn't soon shape up.

I knew David R. at Harvard—he was a year ahead of me, but we both lived in Eliot House—and that made it easier to get started when *The New Yorker* let me do a Profile on him in 1965. I haven't seen a great deal of Rockefeller since—we don't move in the same social (or, when it comes to that, fiscal) circles—but we run into one another now and then. Our most startling post-Profile confrontation occurred in the summer of 1973. Ellie and I were just finishing up our tour of China with our left-wing travelling companions, and we had acquired the reputation among them of being—would that the government of South Africa would concur!—hard-core reactionaries. One day, indeed, in the course of a mild ideological skirmish, one member of our group had turned on Ellie and, pointing a finger at her face, had denounced her in the strongest terms he could muster. "Miss Im-*per*-ialist!" he had screamed.

Anyway, as we were leaving the People's Republic, at the border post of Shumchun, sitting in an anteroom on some of the overstuffed, antimacassar-bedecked armchairs that are the hallmark of contemporary Chinese décor, I happened to glance through an open door toward a corridor that led to China, and was astonished to see David Rockefeller cross my field of vision. I leapt up, ran to the doorway, and hailed him. David and his wife, Peggy, were as startled to see Ellie and me as we were to see them, and for a couple of minutes the four of us stood in the corridor in animated chitchat. It was while we were thus engaged that the other members of our party were instructed to move along, and as they all trooped out of their waiting room, what to their wondering eyes should appear but the Kahns, those two who had kept denying that they were in the enemy camp, in intimate colloquy with the embodiment of capitalism! Our fellow travellers' worst suspicions were immediately and unshakably confirmed.

We leave the restaurant at nine or so and start walking home up Third Avenue. We are in no rush, so we stop off at a bookstore and browse. I am feeling benevolent, having heard from Shawn, and I offer to buy both D. and E. a book of their choice, any hardcover short of the coffee-table kind. While I am at it, having gone to Panama a year ago to do a *New Yorker* piece on the Canal, I decide to treat myself to David McCullough's "The Path Between the Seas." I lay a copy of it on the cashier's counter, and wait for Ellie and David to come along with their selections. Then the lights go out.

The proprietor is so anxious to lock up his premises that he will not tarry long enough for me to pay him for my book, so I leave it where it is. Third Avenue is dark. Near as we can make out, so is the rest of the city. We walk home edgily, and unaware, until we run into a cop, that we have been afflicted with a citywide blackout. Ernest, our apartment super, is scurrying around the lobby placing candles at strategic spots. He lends us two tapers to guide us on our sixteen-story hike up the back stairs.

We have an operable transistor radio, and snap it on. Everybody is comparing this disaster, reminiscently, with the blackout of 1965. I remember that one with more clarity than pride. I had had a midday motel rendezvous upstate with N., and I was on a New York Central train when the power failed. Only it wasn't my regular commuter train back from Grand Central to Scarborough. It was on a train that was taking me *to* Grand Central so I could catch my regular train home, and I was stuck north of White Plains. I played bridge for several hours with three strangers, by a dim light that was functioning at one end of one car, but I found it hard to concentrate on my cards. Eventually I got home, but I was more delayed than most of my suburban neighbors. I remember, too, how N., who was—still is, I imagine—exceptionally long-legged, would brush her teeth. Without straining, she could put one knee up on the edge of a sink and stick her lower leg out sideways on the adjoining counter top. I have never seen anyone of any sex perform that feat before or since.

July 14

When Ellie goes into the bathroom at 9 A.M. to wash her hair—preparatory to leaving for Rome this evening—there is no water. Oh well, the power will surely come back on long before she has to set off for the airport. David's dentist lives in Westchester, and his midtown office is on the twenty-eighth floor; we can forget about that appointment. I have left the manuscript I am supposed to be writing on my eighteenth-floor desk downtown. I can forget about that. On the radio, Mayor Beame is saying, "If the food is suspect, refrain from eating it." He has been with his police commissioner, and is beginning to talk in apprehend-the-perpetrator jargon. But the mayor is seventy and has been up all night, and it is cruel to fault his language. Now at least he can campaign for reelection against Con Edison instead of Mario Cuomo and Bella. I find a deck of cards and, for want of anything better to do, start playing solitaire. David scoffs at this puerility. What's the matter with playing solitaire? Mamie Eisenhower does it all the time, and nobody picks on her.

The phone rings. A woman in Florida, which is operating on all cylinders, wants me to go to Atlanta—Atlanta again!—over the Labor Day weekend and give a speech on current Chinese-American relations before the annual convention of the U.S.-China Peoples Friendship Association. I know this to be a somewhat Maoist-oriented group, and, although I don't think I can make the date in any event, I am bemused to be asked. Has the association not heard from the members of our 1973 safari about me and David Rockefeller? Anyway, I know little more about the status of contemporary relations, friendly or otherwise, between the two nations than what I read in the newspapers. The conventioneers would probably do better if they invited David R.

The blackout is still on at 5:15 P.M., when we all have to leave our powerless aerie—Ellie, hair lamentably unlathered, to head for Europe, David and I for Boston and Cape Cod. We grope our way down sixteen flights. I am due for dinner in Truro at the Justin Kaplans', and arrive very late, also unshaven and unwashed. Still, I am something of a folk hero—the first survivor of the New York paralysis to arrive in Truro with on-the-spot adventures to recount. The Kaplans and their other guests seem disappointed that I have no looting stories with which to edify them; I try to explain that there wasn't any looting on our stretch of Park Avenue; I sense that they feel I have let them down by not dwelling in more combustible environs. Knowing that Joe Kaplan has just reviewed David McCullough's Panama book for the *Saturday Review*, I do relate our experience, at the instant of the crime, in the bookstore. Joe says that McCullough is on Martha's Vineyard and may be coming to the Cape for a visit soon. Fine, I say; have him bring a copy along; I'll pay him the full $14.95 retail price for it, and he'll be doing me a favor at that, inasmuch as he'll be saving me the New York City sales tax.

July 15

At exactly 1:37 P.M., I am sitting in my Truro study typing some notes about the New York blackout when my desk light goes out. I make a couple of investigative phone calls around the community. There is no electric power anywhere. (It turns out that a truck hit a utility pole up in Orleans.) This is really too much. I look up for solace at a fading tintype of Judy Holliday, a souvenir of an evening she and I spent at the New York World's Fair in the summer of 1939. Judy is smiling. This is not my idea of a joke. Winchell said in his column later that year that she and I were "making the same shadow." I recall being offended at the time. Why should I have been offended? I should have been flattered.

My sisters are due in for the weekend, scheduled to arrive at the Hyannis airport at 4 P.M. Hyannis, being the other side of Orleans, has power. After picking up Joan and Olivia, I have to shop for dinner (we will be ten), but stupidly neglect to do so in Hyannis and find, on reaching Wellfleet en route home, that all the powerless food stores there are closed. I decide to cook some frozen clams, with which I had intended to make a pie for the Cohens, on our charcoal grill, and my briquettes are just beginning to glow when the lights come back on.

July 16

In the mail, an invitation to a Provincetown party honoring Norman Mailer, which at first glance I take to be a black-tie affair (I don't have dinner clothes on the Cape) but turns out to be a black-velvet one. It is a benefit for the Provincetown Museum of Fine Arts, where, for ten dollars per capita, black velvets will be served. For one hundred dollars, I can also go to a supper afterward at the Flagship Restaurant, with wine. Wine on top of black velvets doesn't sound appetizing. I throw the invitation away. Ellie and I once shelled out a hundred dollars to attend Norman's fiftieth birthday party at the Four Seasons, and the evening was a colossal bore.

I cannot help feeling akin to Norman, though, because I am often taken for him, along with Max Lerner and Jerome Wiesner, the president of M.I.T. I do not think I look much like Lerner, Mailer, or Wiesner, and when I was introduced to Norman's mother at that Technion lunch in New York last month, *she* didn't say I resembled her son. On the other hand, one of Norman's ex-wives, the one he stabbed, once told somebody at a cocktail party she and I both went to that she had carefully remained on the opposite side of the room from me until she realized I wasn't whom she had initially taken me for. Once at a cocktail party at my Truro house, Norman got into a belligerent argument with another guest, and when that guest finally decided to take a swing at his adversary, he aimed at and hit me. So I have firsthand, painful evidence that I certainly do look like Norman to drunks.

It is terribly hot on the Cape, but in New York, where the thermometer has hit ninety-eight, it must be worse. Leo Salzman comes by for some tennis but quits before even finishing one set. (Sarah Pileggi graciously volunteers to take his place, and I hope nobody sends word of this latest Daimler-lady monkey business to You Know Whom in Europe.) An exemplary, rare psychiatrist, Leo doesn't try to impose his climatological trepidations upon others. That cannot be said of all his professional colleagues. A couple of them were watching a tournament one day, some years back, sitting in the shade provided by a grape arbor that overlooks one side of our court. Originally, the arbor was only five and a half feet high, and at its summit there were projecting horizontal slats of wood that could deal the unwary a wicked blow.

On the day in question, the temperature was close to one hundred degrees. After the draw was made, one player's wife said he'd have to default, because of the heat. He acquiesced, and his partner, forced to default, too, made a nasty crack about henpecking. *His* wife in turn prevailed on a doctor in the audience, the eminent Freudian analyst Sandor Rado, to tell *my* wife that if the tournament were permitted to go on someone would surely succumb to sunstroke. To my dismay, Jinny was bamboozled by this quackery, despite my contention that Sandor, for all his lovable qualities, was merely a psychiatrist and probably knew less about sunstroke than an Eskimo. Notwithstanding, the competitors' wives caucused and cancelled the tournament, whereupon the competitors themselves swiftly uncancelled it.

Within hours, Truro had been transformed into a battlefield evocative of "Lysistrata." When we defiant men took to the court, our wives were mobilized alongside it, waiting tight-lipped for us—nay, it seemed, *hoping* for us—to keel over. The women had Dr. Rado in tow, presumably to render some kind of first aid to whichever faction needed it more. Several other psychiatrists had left the beach and come to the combat zone, possibly to gather research for a scholarly study of the sexual implications of mass hysteria. One of them suggested pleasantly that he hadn't done an autopsy since medical school but was willing to give it a try if any professional services of that nature seemed warranted.

Up to the last match, nobody dropped, though there was some weaving and tottering. My partner was Ansel Chaplin, a young Boston attorney in the bloom of health, and he carried me through three hard-paced sets before we lost. At the end, we were exhausted, but upright. (So were the winners.) As Ansel and I walked off the court, he strode briskly toward the grape arbor. He must have had sweat in his eyes, for he hit one of the horizontals head on and slumped down as though pole-axed.

The wives had been so busy fanning Sandor, who had complained on and off of dizziness, that they were not aware of what had happened to my luckless partner until they saw him stretched out on the ground. With mingled squeals of dread and triumph, they swooped upon him, nearly suffocating him. Dr. Rado was of no help. He began muttering about mouth-to-mouth resuscitation, when all the victim needed was some ice for a lump on his forehead. Some unreasonable Truro women believe to this day that Ansel was laid low by a combination of sun and stubbornness. He has a slight scar on his forehead, and they sometimes ask him sweetly if he suffers from chronic headaches, and they remind everybody else that if *their* advice had been heeded that blistering day he wouldn't have been permanently disfigured. They refuse to believe, though their husbands have tried more than once to set matters straight, that Ansel's cicatrix had nothing to do with his tennis mishap. What actually happened was that he decided to quit smoking, to improve his wind, and took up chewing gum as an oral substitute. In Boston one day, he ducked into a drugstore to buy a pack of gum, and, on emerging, was so intent on unwrapping a stick that he forgot to look where he was going and bumped into a no-parking sign.

Nevertheless, to placate the distaff part of our crowd, I had the grape arbor reconstructed, at a higher elevation. It no longer constitutes a hazard to the average tennis player, though I suppose it could give a basketball player trouble. I am sometimes asked if I have any advice for someone who is contemplating putting in a private tennis court and wants to keep out of trouble; I guess on reflection I would have to recommend not building it too close to a low-slung grape arbor.

July 17

I am sorry that I no longer subscribe to the Provincetown *Advocate*, for the copy I pay cash for at Schoony's this morning has two fascinating personals. One is an ad offering a hundred-dollar reward for information leading to the arrest and conviction "of the person who trespassed on my property, stole my neighbor's green paint and threw it on my collie dog"; and the other also promises a reward, amount unspecified, for the return of two lost stinger bees, both bearing magnesium markers, which "may be biologically harmful if subjected to beryllium."

There is a neighborhood softball game at the Truro Central School field this morning, all ages and sexes eligible to play, but while I am glad to go over and watch, I decline to participate. I always manage to injure myself in these informal contests, as, indeed, Bruce Fishberg does today within minutes of my arrival, limping off the field with what he self-diagnoses as a severely pulled leg ligament. The fourth finger of my right hand is permanently misshapen as the result of a parent-and-child game I did participate in years ago at Scarborough. I was in right field, the spot traditionally assigned, in such pickup games, to that individual known by past performances to be the most inept; and in attempting (and failing) to catch the only fly ball that came my way, I bent my finger back. When I returned to the bench after that half inning, I muttered something to the effect that I thought I had broken a finger, but anyone who had been responsible for two unearned runs that ruined his pitcher's shutout could hardly expect sympathy, let alone attention. So I played out the game clutching a beer can in my right hand, to keep the aching digit rigid; and both batting and fielding—the limitation had little effect on my prowess—left-handed and single-handed. After the game, I drove to the hospital to have the fracture X-rayed and splinted, but the finger never resumed its original shape. Wrong brand of beer, perhaps.

Today, resolutely committed to the role of spectator, I cannot even root for either side. I have a son pitching for the one team, a son catching for the other, and, scattered between both line-ups, a grandson, a stepson, and a daughter-in-law. There is one hideous moment when son Joey, covering home plate, goes down to tag son Tony, sliding in, and they collide with a bone-rattling crunch. Somehow they both arise whole from the dust, and I have been miraculously spared a further hospital run.

Feeling profoundly paternal, I move along to Provincetown to watch Terry in the singles final of a tennis tournament. I do this with some misgivings, because our father-and-son relationship has not always been halcyon on the courts. Once he and I were pitted against each other in the semis of a Lee Falk tournament. Terry was playing net, and I hit a ball as hard as I could at him. The ball dribbled back into my court, and he was awarded the point. I lodged a protest: He had returned the ball, I argued, not with his racquet but with his nose. The umpire was about to dismiss my ridiculous claim when Terry began bleeding profusely, and my team got the point after all, quite properly. Terry's aunts, Joan and Olivia, were in the audience and thought the decision cruel and unfair, but as I tried to point out to the assembled family afterward, rules are rules. Terry was the only member of our domestic group who agreed with me. I am diffident now about going to Provincetown to watch him, because my mere presence when he is in a tournament seems to be a jinx. He wins today, nonetheless, possibly because toward the end of his match I am called away from my spectator's seat to move my car so somebody can get out of a parking lot.

Terry first got blooded in tournament tennis—only figuratively, I am happy to say—during a Christmas holiday in Jamaica, fifteen years ago. I had persuaded him and his brothers and his mother to eschew skiing by obtaining accommodations for all of us at Round Hill, which had grass tennis courts. The boys had never played on grass, and as a further sop I had bought them a dozen cans of special grass-court balls, which, after I had finished paying the overweight charges on our luggage, may have been the costliest tennis balls ever purchased.

It is not supposed to rain in Jamaica at year's end. But that year it rained nearly every day, and the grass courts were so soggy Nadia Comaneci couldn't have bounced on them. In desperation, we took to hanging around the Montego Bay Racquet Club, which had all-weather, quick-drying courts and also had, as a resident pro, Donald Budge. I treated Tony to a half-hour Budge lesson, and asked his mentor to concentrate on the boy's backhand. I figured that anybody with even a trace of a Budge backhand was halfway up life's ladder. Four years later, the daughter of a friend of ours was sent by her parents, who had high aspirations for her, too, to a summer tennis camp Budge conducted. She wrote us a postcard saying, "Mr. Budge wants me to tell you that he remembers you as wonderful people and he sends his best." Imagine finding that good a backhand and that good a memory all in one package!

The Racquet Club put on a men's doubles tournament while we were there, and I entered with Terry, largely to give us something to do to get our minds off the weather. In the first round, we were matched against another family unit—a pair of local brothers named Yap. The Yap brothers were well known in Jamaican tennis circles, and deservedly; I have never before or since laid eyes on any two siblings who can hit a tennis ball as hard as they could, and as, alas, they did. They won the first set 6–0, with such dispatch that I, whose grunts on a tennis court have been known to awaken a child napping a hundred yards distant, was still breathing normally at its conclusion.

The second set pretty much followed the same pattern. The Yaps blasted off to a 5–0 lead. Then came a turning point. Somehow or other, Terry and I gained an advantage. There we were, one point away from avoiding the ignominy of a shutout. At that crucial moment, one Yap launched an errant missile that, had it been permitted to fly its full course, might have reached Cuba. Unfortunately, it was directed straight at Terry, who was standing four feet behind the baseline. In his youthful innocence, and also in self-defense, he blocked it with his racquet. He was not familiar with strict tournament protocol, but the umpire was, and correctly awarded the point to the Yaps. Deuce. They won the next two points, for another love set, and the match; and neither Terry nor I has had any stomach for Jamaican tennis ever since.

July 18

Another murderously hot day. After two sets of tennis, everybody collapses. I go into the ocean for the second day in a row—something I rarely do because it is too much trouble to find a parking space, even with a permit, at Ballston Beach.

The Cohens have me over for dinner again, and tactfully refrain from mentioning the clam pie I am abashedly aware I still owe them. Ann Kendall is there, down from Cambridge, hard at work these days trying to get the E.R.A. ratified; and so among others is Henry Brandon, about to go to Peking, for the London Sunday *Times*, with Cyrus Vance. Henry also hopes to get into North Korea, and Jerry, one of the few Americans who has crossed its border voluntarily in the last twenty-five years or so, briefs him, not very favorably, on conditions over there. I suggest to Jerry, who has also made several post-rapprochement trips to China, that he speak, *vice* me, at the Labor Day Atlanta gathering of the Friendship Association. Jerry says if he tried to address that audience he would probaby be hooted down; he had trouble enough last summer right here in Truro, where he talked about China before some local group and was annoyingly heckled by a left-leaning woman who went to the P.R.C. with Ellie and me. I apologize for her behavior.

July 19

A man I haven't seen in a decade comes by for tennis, and after he has, by my lights, misbehaved egregiously three times, I feel constrained to inform him sternly that on our court we do not question opponents' line calls. He is so chagrined that he subsequently declares to be good two shots by his opponents that were out by a foot. There has been no discernible change in the weather, so for the third straight day I go into the ocean—a modern midsummer record for me. Afterward, Palmer Williams refuses to play backgammon. He is two hundred and sixty dollars behind in our running score, and his wife has enjoined him to quit. While that doesn't seem to be an insuperable deficit for a CBS producer, or a backgammon player, Barbara W. clearly has a different view.

Joan Cohen phones to say she will pick me up to take me to Joan Wulsin's for dinner. This seems to be Joan Day, even though my sister Joan has gone back to New York. I had another call from someone who identified herself simply as "Joan," which in the circumstances was manifestly not revealing.

It was Joan Colebrook, who wants me to know that Flossie Hammond Phillips, Jack's current wife, has become an actress. Jack, says this Joan when I get her identified, went to see Flossie not long ago in a play with only two characters—a black man and a white woman. Most of the on-stage action took place in darkness, and when the lights finally came up, Jack, according to Joan, was taken aback to perceive that both actors were entirely naked. I wonder what Flossie's father, the distinguished Harvard Professor of Classics Emeritus Mason Hammond, might have thought of it all.

The Cohens and I are delivered to Joan Wulsin's in Ann Kendall's ancient seven-passenger fishtail Cadillac, but Ann hasn't even parked her car before she is upstaged by the flashier arrival of the Pileggis in their Daimler. Sarah says at dinner that she had to look something up for a *Sports Illustrated* piece in an ancient *New Yorker*, and came upon my Brenda Frazier Profile in the same issue. Joan Cohen has never heard of Brenda Frazier. Either that dates Joan C., or it dates me. I get delivered home in time to watch the last couple of innings of the All-Star Game, which, though perhaps more skillfully executed, is far less exciting than the game at the Truro school the other day. My sons are all of all-star age, if not, save in my eyes, ability.

July 20

The temperature reached one hundred and two in New York yesterday. It is close to that here. Our house must be entirely rid of fleas; otherwise this brutal heat would surely have flushed them into the open. Jim Thomson says at the post office that he is thinking of buying an air-conditioner, surely the first in Truro's history. It is too hot for me to drag myself to the ocean, so my string of consecutive bathing days will have to end at three. Joey is obviously made of sterner stuff—paternity notwithstanding—than I am. He goes down to Provincetown to play tennis with Ladislav Hecht, who must be made of steel: He was a member of the Czechoslovakian Davis Cup team a dozen years before Joey was conceived.

July 21

Lilo flies in from Hyannis for a few days' providential stay (it was a hundred and four in New York when she left), bringing along her granddaughter Elise. My stepmother has one of the better blackout stories to recount. She spent it with a near-total stranger, an elderly gentleman who had offered to escort her home from a Cooper-Hewitt exhibit and remained in her fourteenth-floor apartment—he had a game leg and couldn't walk down—for thirty hours. She has ambivalent feelings about her companion. When the power finally went on at 11:30 P.M., the second night of their enforced co-habitation, her guest, who had been sleeping in Lilo's spare room, suddenly materialized in the doorway of her bedroom. She asked stiffly what in the world he thought he was doing, marching into her chamber like that in the middle of the night. "But you have the television set in here," he replied. "Don't you like to watch Johnny Carson?"

Lilo says that her new friend may not be much of an acquisition; he is saving all his money so that in his terminal illness, if any, he will be able to afford private nurses around the clock, and as a result he has proved, ever since the blackout, too stingy to take her to a restaurant where dinner costs more than five dollars. I didn't know that any such place still existed in New York.

Five years ago, I was asked by Simon and Schuster to write a restaurant guide in its "Underground Gourmet" series, this one to cover Boston and its environs. I enlisted my son Joey, who was then living in Cambridge with his wife and baby, as a collaborator, the original idea being that he would do most of the research and I the writing. We decided arbitrarily that no restaurant that charged over four dollars for a full meal (drinks excluded) would be eligible for consideration, and I felt that Joey would be more tolerant of minor flaws in establishments in that price category than I might be. Also, he had a more tolerant stomach. In the course of his eating out, he often took Jaime along, and having a babe-in-arms in his party no doubt got him better service than he might otherwise have obtained. So in a way "The Boston Underground Gourmet" was a three-generation collaboration. Joey's research reports were so estimably written that most of them went straight into the book editorially untouched by me; that was evidence as good as any other I could think of that he had the makings of a successful non-fiction writer. Now, we have the same agent, and when a call comes in to Truro from Monica McCall's office it is more likely to be for him than for me. "The Boston Underground Gourmet" did not do particularly well in spite of Joey; the trouble is that inexpensive restaurants like the ones we wrote about often have a low survival rate.

July 22

The *Times* reports the deaths of Katharine Angell White and John Robert Powers, both at the age of eighty-four. Mrs. White—Mrs. E. B. White, of course—was a pioneer pillar of *The New Yorker*, one of the great fiction editors of her time; and it is ironic that two of the principal fiction writers she is credited today with having started on their redoubtable careers are Irwin Shaw and John Cheever, both of whom have drifted away from the magazine. (It is no less ironic, considering how many living *New Yorker* people feel about his views of its staff, that in the body of the obit there is a subhead that goes "Praise from Brendan Gill.") Irwin fell out with the magazine, in fact, or so he once told me, because of a disagreement over the handling of a story of his with Mrs. White's son and fiction-editor heir, Roger Angell. Mrs. White never handled any of my stuff personally. The casuals I used to submit to her department usually ended up in the custody of her co-fiction-editor Gus Lobrano. After Gus died, in 1956, I somehow lost the knack of being able to write short humorous pieces that his successors liked; the only comfort I could derive in my frustration was that Jim Thurber, late in his life, had the same problem.

John Robert Powers probably never knew Mrs. White. I got to know him because in 1940 I decided to do a Profile of one of the Powers Models who had made his name famous (he in turn made their faces, or bodies, famous), and he introduced me to a lovely one, the subject I finally chose. At Joan Wulsin's the other night, Joan Cohen, when she finally was apprised who Brenda Frazier was, asked me if I had ever dated the celebrated deb. No, but for a while I went out with the Powers Model—the only Profile subject in my experience, aside from a champion fox terrier, ever to sit in my lap.

A couple of years ago, David sang in the choir of the Church of the Heavenly Rest, and when Ellie and I dutifully went over there for services, and I looked at the program, I would see a familiar name—with, surprisingly, a "Miss" before it—among the flower-givers. Miss Powers and I were about the same age, and while the rest of the congregation busied itself, properly, with prayers and lamentations, I kept looking around for someone whom I might recognize from thirty-five years back. I spotted a couple of women, one of them white-haired, who could conceivably once have been Powers Models, but I didn't have the gumption to ask either of them if my hunch was right. Then David's voice changed, and we stopped going to the Church of the Heavenly Rest.

Nine tennis players show up today, so many that Sidney Simon says that Lee Falk will be furious at my giving a tennis brunch, albeit one without food. Among the arrivals are M. and S., whose now two-year-long affair, which began on the local courts, was for a while the scandal of the community, involving as it did the breakup of two homes with seven children between them. S. and M. haven't been much visible in these parts since then, but today they have come, so to speak, out of the closet. They are already acting like an old married couple: M. roundly criticizes S. when she misses a shot.

Lilo says at dinner that my father (whom she married in 1964) lost all his money in the Depression by entrusting it for investment, unwisely, to his then brother-in-law. She may be correct in that. My uncle Bobby, my mother's brother, was a starcrossed man. When he eventually committed suicide, it became my unhappy responsibility, no one else in the family being willing to assume it, to inform his doting parents—they did not read the *Daily News*—that their only son had blown himself up, rattling an area several blocks across, by turning on the gas in his oven.

July 23

Joey and Hillary depart this morning to attend the wedding, in Long Island, of Hillary's sister. I am left in charge of a household comprising a stepmother, a grandson, a stepson, and a stepmother's granddaughter, the relationship of whom to my son's girl's sister's new husband I will not attempt to define. Lilo says that the man she spent the blackout with told her he had absolutely no kin at all. How strange.

One of Ellie's woman artists phones. She is looking for E., who reached New York from Paris last night but cannot join us on the Cape immediately because she must first go to Sharon, Connecticut, there to replace, before Lexy enters a summer camp, the clothes he lost while boarding an airplane last week at Traverse City, Michigan.

I can keep the family's movements more or less straight because I have always been fairly good at geography. Part of this is attributable to my having been an indefatigable stamp collector back in the days when Bosnia-Herzegovina was a distinct philatelical entity; but the major credit probably should go to my Horace Mann schoolteacher Mr. Martin, who presided over a no-nonsense course called Geography. Would that geography were still its own distinct curricular entity; kids nowadays seem to have no grasp of where any place on earth actually is, and I wonder how they can keep up with the news. If indeed, of course, they try to. Mr. Martin had a map pointer with a bright-red tip, which he always let us infer, though I am not certain he ever came right out and said so, had been incarnadined with the blood of imbeciles who were unable to differentiate unhesitatingly between Upper Silesia and Outer Mongolia.

Ellie's telephone-artist friend, about whom I know more than she knows I know, wants to get in touch with E. at once because she is going on a cruise. I know with whom. I say, sneakily, that I hope she meets some interesting people aboard ship. "I go just for the fun of tuning out," she says. I had thought the modern phrase was "making out."

July 25

This is not expected to be a particularly good blueberry year—too dry or too wet this spring, I forget which, but whichever it was made the difference—yet I managed to snare a few yesterday for dinner. The bushes that fringe our property, their roots nourished by adjoining swamps, produce high-bush blueberries, in contrast to the low-bush berries that grow on the upland neighboring dunes. You have to do a lot of stooping to harvest the low-bush variety. To get at some of ours, I would have to carry a ladder out with me, and I don't like ladders. (I stipulated when I joined our volunteer fire company in Scarborough that I would not climb a ladder, except in a life-or-death situation; and happily, I never had to.) I almost always pick blueberries alone. It is a nice time to reflect, and also the same soil that is hospitable to high-bush berries attracts waist-high poison ivy, with the result that I am not overwhelmed by offers of assistance. So I am generally accompanied solely by Rainbow, who loves blueberries as much as I do—she eats the ones off the bottoms of the bushes, which obliges me to do a good deal of overhead reaching—and is apparently impervious to poison ivy. I am not, but it is somehow important to me to pick as many blueberries as I can every summer. I guess it is part of my living-off-the-land syndrome. My favorite summer meal is clam pie, with blueberries for dessert. This could, of course, be considered simply a manifestation of my skinflint syndrome.

Before I went blueberrying, I took Lilo to an art opening at a Provincetown gallery. There is an opening of some kind or other on the Lower Cape nearly every day, and for some patrons of the arts—patrons in the sense of enjoying free drinks, not necessarily causing stars to be affixed to any painting or sculpture—these affairs are the bedrock of their social life. At yesterday's show, Joe Kaplan and I agreed that the canvasses on display had a disappointingly slapdash look, as though the painter had knocked them all off in a single morning and had then gone to the beach. In the mimeographed catalogue for the exhibit, though, a writer well known to both Joe and me declared that the artist was transfigurative, subtle, serene, refined, and had a fruitful communion with trees. Ellie used to be a professional art critic, but she quit when she became convinced that too high a percentage of the stuff put into words about art nowadays is plain hogwash.

Today is the last day of Lilo's stay, and there is no chance to take her to the ocean for a farewell plunge; we have rain and high winds, a sort of mini-hurricane. But the storm has, blessedly, reduced the temperature. When I get back from the airport, I am pleasantly surprised to find that Barbara Williams has given Palmer permission to come over and try to reduce his backgammon debt. He doesn't manage to this evening, but he should be given credit for trying. It turns out, anent something or other that crops up during the between-games chatter, that Dr. Halsted, who delivered my three sons, was also Palmer's first wife's obstetrician. Tony comes by, and I apprise him of this coincidence, and he and I reminisce about his scary birth with the pre-natal skull fracture (Tony's memories, naturally, consisting of what his mother and I have told him), and the curious thing is that, although for the six weeks or so until the fracture cured itself I have never suffered more distress, now neither Tony nor I can recall which side of his head the dent was on.

July 26

Terry calls from Boston. He is going to do a piece for *The Real Paper* on Living Together. He wants me to write a two-to-three-hundred-word sidebar on how a parent feels about his children's extramarital domesticity. My feeling is that people should have last names. Terry had been living with Rose for a long time before I discovered the identity of the "R. Vella" who kept getting mail in my box. The other point I aim to make when I write my sidebar is that I am probably less concerned about young people shacking up than I would be if any of my children were daughters.

Terry also says that the anniversary present Ellie is giving me this year, and which she evidently commissioned him to obtain for her, should be arriving some time today. What in the world can it be? Something, he tells me, that I have long wanted, and have needed, too. Within the hour, a truck rolls up and disgorges, before my wondering eyes, a great big new (well, used, but new to me) tennis-court roller. Now, there is a woman who knows how to make a man happy! I call Palmer, and he comes over at once and we fill and baptize the machine. It works beautifully. Oh, this will make Lee Falk absolutely seethe with envy when he hears about it! Lee phones a few minutes later. He is giving a fund-raising party for Herman Badillo in August. I say that we will take two tickets, but I know that in the Democratic mayoral primary, if we get to New York for it, Ellie will vote for Ms. Abzug. I refrain from telling Lee myself about my marvelous new acquisition. He will hear about it soon enough from Sidney Simon, and I do not think it nice to gloat.

I have drinks with Jim and Diana Thomson. Jim confesses that ten years ago, when the Thomsons first came to Truro, they were in awe of me. I am flattered, but cannot imagine why. Jim explains that he had read a piece that Arthur Gelb wrote about the Lower Cape in the *Times*, a rather imaginative account of our summer scene in which Artie characterized me as the mayor of Truro, and mentioned among my other celebrated constituents Edmund Wilson, who lived in Wellfleet and whom, as it happened, I had never met.

David has asked to be allowed to prepare dinner tonight, and whips up what he describes as a gourmet meal, the *pièce de résistance* of which is a Brazilian beef dish embracing black coffee, garlic, and dry red wine. Among the ingredients required for his gourmet dessert are raspberries, gelatin, and framboise, lacking the latter of which he reluctantly agrees to substitute blackberry brandy. The gelatin, alas, neglects to gel, but even so we all concur that it was a noble effort for a sixteen-year-old, and it takes Joey and me only a couple of hours to clean up the kitchen afterward.

July 27

Terry's friend Ray Elman is under the impression that I can put a whammy on him whenever we meet on a tennis court, and I am beginning to believe this superstition myself. Ray is an infinitely better player than I am, and yet he simply cannot win when I am on the other side of the net. Today, for instance, Ray and Sarah Pileggi are leading Palmer and me 4–1 in the first set; then I cry "Whammy!" and we win the set, 7–5; in the second set, they have us 4–0, but after I point a finger at Ray (he construes this rightly to be a silent whammy), Palmer and I take five games in a row, and Ray stalks disgustedly off the court.

Terry used to have another friend, named Howie, an itinerant roofer, who owed me some money from backgammon and, in an attempt to recoup, challenged me to a singles match at tennis, double or nothing, two sets out of three. I don't much like to play singles, especially on a hot day against an opponent thirty years my junior, but I thought it only fair to give Howie a chance to get even. He won the first set 6–0, and was leading 3–0 in the second set when he hit his most powerful serve of the afternoon. I could barely get my racquet on it, and sent back a weak lob that, after it bounced, he was bound to murder. My service return arched up over the net and landed directly on top of a loose ball in his forecourt. Howie said we should play the point over. Not at all, I insisted; it was not my fault that he had left a ball on his side of the net. The point was *mine*. Convinced by the spectators that I was within my rights, Howie went into a total tailspin, and the final score was, in my favor, 0–6, 6–3, 6–0. Howie disappeared from the Cape soon afterward, all debts unpaid, and hasn't been seen since. Another good reason for clearing loose balls off your half of the playing surface is that you might step on one and break your leg.

Marian and Steve Schlesinger stop by to play. Steve wants to know what I know about the rumor that Jonathan Schell is going to be the next *New Yorker* editor. I tell him everything I know for certain, which is nothing. Marian says she is writing her memoirs, about Cambridge in the old days, and that she has been using my book about Harvard as a reference work. While I was living in Cambridge doing my research on "Harvard," I was invited to a party one night at the home of a Harvard professor of physics. I brought Marian along. She and I were the only people present who were not, directly or by marriage, connected with the Harvard physics department. I had heard a lot about the inbreeding and singlemindedness of university scientists, and on this occasion perceived startling evidence thereof: Although Marian's ex-husband, Arthur, Jr., and his father, Arthur, Sr., had been well-known members of the Harvard faculty over a span of thirty years or more, no one in the assemblage seemed ever to have heard the name "Schlesinger."

July 29

I had a dream last night about being in South Africa, at some place that dealt with visas. I was snooping around trying to find out who over there had put a whammy on me. While the Afrikaner in charge of the premises wasn't paying attention, I stole a look at a file card and saw the name "J. K. Galbraith." Why him? He has had nothing to do, so far as I knew, with South Africa. But of course he has been a long-time crony of Arthur Schlesinger, Jr.

What do dreams know that we don't? First thing this morning, Jim Thomson calls. He has heard, finally, from one of his South African Nieman Fellows, Tom Vusslo, the editor of the Afrikaans-language newspaper *Beeld*. Vusslo, whom I have never met awake or asleep, wishes to inform Jim that Pik Botha's Foreign Ministry recommended approval of my visa application, but that in Connie Mulder's Ministry of Information, which has the final say in these matters, "the cards are stacked against Kahn." Vusslo has gone so far on Jim's and my behalf as to discuss this situation personally with Mr. Botha, and Botha has suggested that I re-apply. So I will.

At dinner tonight, next door at the Manny Furers', I evolve a new theory about my turndown by Pretoria. The Harry Kahns are there. (So is a young Yale student who has a summer job devising a computer program to prevent NATO airplanes from bumping into each other while airborne, yet who is late because he couldn't figure out the bus schedule from Boston to Truro.) Harry, now a sturdy capitalist whose small talk often dwells on his various robust philanthropies, reveals that he has been very active in recent years as investment counsellor for the N.A.A.C.P., and that just after getting out of Harvard he worked in the Treasury Department under—shades of the days of Communist conspiracies in Washington!—Harry Dexter White and Frank Coe. Can the stack of cards the South Africans have on me include one about a Kahn, Harvard '37, who hobnobbed with these suspect characters and now pretends to be ideologically simon-pure? This seems as logical as anything else.

Frank Coe is one of a handful of Americans who moved to Communist China during the McCarthy era and has lived there ever since. Ellie and I met him in Peking in 1973. He seemed thoroughly domiciled, though curiously, he had not learned to speak Chinese in thirty-odd years there. Another Western expatriate we got to know in the P.R.C. was an Austrian woman who had lost a job with the U.N. because of alleged Communist leanings, had migrated to Peking, and had married a Chinese. Her two sons spoke only Chinese. She had a job as editor of the German-language edition of the *Peking Review*, and she did a rare thing for any person of any national origin in China today; she invited Ellie and me to her apartment for tea.

While we were there, she remarked that she missed seeing *The New Yorker*. I offered to send her a subscription, if it could get through. Why, of *course* it could, she said. As soon as we returned home, I entered a subscription in her name, and gave the matter no further thought. A few months later, I had an angry note from her. The magazine had run a short humorous fiction piece by Marshall Brickman, about Chinese restaurants in New York, in which, among other things, he had had some jocular things to say about Mao Tse-tung. No rational person could have taken the story for anything but a larksome flight of fancy, but our Peking tea hostess had been deeply offended by it; she regarded it as an insult to The Chairman, and she never wanted to lay eyes on *The New Yorker* again. I cancelled her subscription at once, but her letter had taken a while to reach me, and several succeeding issues must have gone out to her before my revocation order could take effect. I hoped there was nothing in any of them that could have got her in trouble with her superiors at the *Peking Review*.

July 30

Up at 4:30 A.M. to take Joan Wulsin sea-clamming, her first exposure to this eoan sport. I am going to make the Cohens a pie today if I do nothing else.

July 31

The usual Truro crowd turned up for dinner at the V. Henry Rothschilds' last night—Sidney Simons, Leo Salzmans, Dick Waterses. To balance my extra-manness, V. Henry and Jacqui imported a single woman from Provincetown, who said that life is not easy there for someone like herself, because she is straight and everybody assumes she is gay. Reverse discrimination rampant. She had something to do with the Provincetown Art Association, and I was so touched by her plight that I promised I would join it, provided that this did not entail my supporting social affairs designed to glorify Norman Mailer. She said she had just realized what it was that had been bothering her all evening: Had anybody ever told me that I looked uncannily like Norman?

Juliet Waters announced proudly that she had quit smoking two days ago. Dr. Salzman said she should have stopped long before that, and he then launched into so chilling a discourse on the various forms of death and other dire fates that lay in store for people stupid enough to persist in that malign manner of self-destruction that I handed my cigarettes to Renée Simon and vowed never to touch one again.

Driving to New York today, to collect Ellie and bring her and her amassed research back to Truro, I make the long trip without a single puff. The trick is to be alone and not to have any cigarettes on you.

August 1

We are to head back to the Cape today, but not until evening. Thus we can reasonably expect to receive our morning mail, which in our privileged quarter of Manhattan still usually arrives in the morning, though occasionally only after winning a neck-and-neck race with high noon. In this day's batch, emerging gratifyingly from a pile of junk, is a gift copy of "The Birth of a Specialty: The Diary of an American Cardiologist 1926-1972," by Louis Faugeres Bishop, Jr., M.D. I am as pleased by my doctor's flattering handwritten inscription as I hope Louis will be when he learns that I have now gone thirty-six hours without smoking. This memoir is a vanity-press book—that is, one that the good doctor has paid for to have published. That seems perfectly unobjectionable to me, provided a writer knows what he is plunging into and can afford the immersion. The potential evil of vanity-press books is twofold: 1) Publishers passing themselves off as conventional practitioners of their trade, and 2) Writers passing themselves off as practitioners of *theirs* whom a publisher has sought out.

An out-of-town nephew of mine, a would-be novelist, was once seduced by one of those newspaper ads: "Publisher's editorial director will be in town soliciting manuscripts . . ." etc., etc. The nephew sent me a copy of a contract that the travelling salesman had drawn up, for my perusal and, the young man hoped, approval. The gist of the proposed agreement—buried among long dazzling paragraphs about how the publisher would "try" to arrange network television appearances and coast-to-coast bookstore autographing parties—was that the publisher would have at least one hundred copies of the author's manuscript printed, and that the author would pay the publisher at least four thousand dollars. I replied with what I thought was sound avuncular advice that any reputable publishing house would pay *him* four thousand dollars if it liked his manuscript, and would order a somewhat more substantial first printing. I thought I was being helpful, and that I was saving the nephew—his doting father, actually—four thousand dollars; but while as far as I know my counsel was followed, it may not have been appreciated, because I never heard further from the budding author.

The Son of Sam has struck again. Ellie wonders why, in view of his notorious and lethal ubiquity, any two people would go out and park in a lovers' lane nowadays; we agree that as has so often been demonstrated in the past, passion usually prevails over prudence. That is what keeps vanity presses going as well as mad killers and their victims. One would hope that this latest late-night shooting would stiffen the will of those too few enlightened congressmen who are trying to persuade the president to push for the banning of handguns, but this is probably too much to expect of a chief executive from rural Georgia.

At loose ends, I decide to drop in unannounced at *The New Yorker.* I am pleasantly surprised to find that nobody is living in my office. The room would not be worth much as a bedchamber this summer in any event; my couch is covered from stem to stern with Georgia research. Of course, anyone determined enough to camp out on the premises could have tossed the stuff out onto the roof of the Princeton Club. I run into Roger Angell, who says that E. B. White objected to only one word in the magazine's graceful obituary to his mother. Andy White didn't particularly like Bill Shawn's characterization of Katharine as "majestic." (The obit was unsigned, but everybody knows who wrote it.) It is curious that Bill, who for so long wanted to be an author rather than an editor, has ended up writing more obituaries in his magazine than any other kind of copy. I wish that I could bring myself some day to ask him whether—as Alden Whitman did so often for the New York *Times*—he has ever prepared one in advance, as he might well have in the case of a woman of eighty-four whose health was poor. In Shawn's case, I doubt that he would even consider that possibility; he might think that he was putting a whammy on somebody.

The office mail is more interesting than most days, too. Here is a private communiqué from Foreign Minister Botha, in South Africa: "I have noted the contents of your letter and I will discuss the question of your visa with my colleague the minister of the interior." Maybe I'll get over there after all. This is the second time, to my knowledge, that travel plans of mine have been taken up on a cabinet level. The other occasion was in the winter of 1965, when I was meandering around Micronesia gathering material for a *New Yorker* series and, ultimately, a book. The Trust Territory of the Pacific Islands was divided into six administrative districts, and I naturally wanted to visit them all. There was no problem with Palau, Yap, Truk, Ponape, or the Marianas. The only way, though, to get to Majuro, the capital of the Marshall Islands, was—short of entrusting oneself to a sailing canoe—to fly in from Kwajalein.

The Trust Territory, technically a ward of the United Nations, was under the jurisdiction of the United States Department of the Interior; and I had credentials from that agency granting me free access to its enormous oceanic expanse. Kwajalein, however, was an enclave run by the Defense Department; that Second World War atoll battleground had been converted into a Nike missile base. I wasn't especially interested in Kwajalein. I just wanted to switch planes there in transit to Majuro. But the Army informed me that it wouldn't permit that. So I cabled word of my dilemma back to *The New Yorker,* and the magazine took up the matter with the Interior

Department, which passed the buck up to Secretary Stewart Udall, who felt that the controversy could be resolved only in a face-to-face confrontation with Secretary of Defense Louis Johnson. The first time the two of them happened to meet—I got this story second- or third-hand, so the details are imprecise—was at some ceremony they both attended with President Lyndon Johnson, who didn't not like to know what was going on at the summit of his government. So when Udall muttered something to his cabinet colleague—he thought sotto voce—about the pesky Kahn business that had come up, the president wanted to know what he was whispering about, and when LBJ had to be told, he said that it was absurd for two persons of their stature to have to concern themselves with something as trifling as that, and why for God's sake didn't they let this Kahn, whoever he was, fly in and out of Kwajalein and address themselves to matters of greater import to the Great Society?

The Army thereupon grudgingly let me pass through, though not without keeping me under close surveillance while I was at the Kwajalein airport. It would not let me into the lavatory without an escort. I got even. I picked up a copy of a military newspaper in the terminal, and from it borrowed more information about the hush-hush Nike base than I had ever seen in print before. The Army got even, too. It failed to put my luggage aboard my plane to Majuro.

Ellie doesn't seem especially happy about being on the Cape as a resident instead of commuter. I suspect this may be because, as I was transporting *her* luggage from elevator to car this morning, I dropped her electric typewriter.

August 2

I am awakened early by a dimly heard foghorn. Even one day's absence from Truro has made the familiar environmental sounds seem strange, and alerting. I would expect to be aroused in New York City by a foghorn—though not, naturally, by a siren. That it is foggy now down at the North Truro lighthouse does not mean it is going to be a bad day. One of the marvels—miracles, maybe—of our Cape Cod weather is how quickly it can change, like a soggy mess of eggs suddenly transformed into a soufflé. Now, since it is too soon to get up, I dip into Louis Bishop's autobiography. He has horrid things to say about smoking, but I already know how he feels about that. Even so, he did once hearteningly tell me that my lungs were in better shape than those of another patient of his—Floyd Patterson.

At the post office, I find, finally, the pornographic tennis shirt that David commissioned for me as a birthday present, seven months ago, from one of his favorite mail-order establishments. My gift is not at all as obscene as I—

and possibly he also—had hoped it would be. The front of the T-shirt merely bears a picture of a bare-breasted young woman swinging a racquet. And whoever picked the model can't know much about tennis: Any women with boobs that big would, at least while on the court, have to wear a bra.

We dine with Cyril and Ann Harris. He is much in vogue, what with having redone Lincoln Center and also having had Bruce Bliven recount his acoustical prowess again in *The New Yorker*. Cyril is asked tonight how often he is called in as a consultant on other acousticians' efforts. "I do not give second opinions," he says. Louis Bishop welcomes second opinions. Ellie points out afterward, astutely, that while the professional work of every man present was discussed and admired, never in the course of this long and glaringly male-chauvinist evening did anyone present think to allude to the fact that our hostess is enjoying a good year herself: A book Ann Harris nursed into being for Harper & Row, "The Thorn Birds," is nested solidly at the top of the best-seller list.

Among the guests is Bob Schakne, Ann's brother, whom I first met when he was covering the Korean War for CBS, where of course he still works. Bob was one of a host of reporters on that tense Asian scene in the winter of 1951, and for a while he and I were both attached—had attached ourselves, rather—to the headquarters of the 25th Infantry Division, where we all lived and labored together in a pyramidal tent except when the tent had to be pulled down and hastily moved because the Chinese and North Koreans were forcing our outfit to retreat to a new base. I was working hard as a war correspondent—trying to turn out a long fact piece for *The New Yorker* every week—and the one I liked the best, in retrospect, was written in that press tent under circumstances that fell somewhat short of being ideal. It was an article about the harrowing experiences of a British battalion, troops of the Gloucestershire Regiment, whose survivors I was lucky enough to encounter immediately after the Glosters' epic ordeal.

I had to produce the piece fast, in one sitting, to make a deadline; and the only place to write it was in the press tent, which contained a dozen or so correspondents who had all finished their day's stints and sensibly, not knowing what the morrow might bring (more Chinese, probably), were drinking up everything within reach. One of the more active imbibers was a young wire-service correspondent who felt there was something inherently wrong in one person's trying to work while everyone else was relaxing. So he kept drifting over to the corner where I was huddled over my typewriter and attempting as best as he could to detach me from it. That was the only time in my life—broken-finger times excluded—that I composed most of an article one-handed; I had to keep the other hand free to put out the fires he started by applying the flame of his cigarette lighter to the sheet of paper I was writing on. The arsonist later became a top editor of the *Saturday Evening Post*. The *Saturday Evening Post* soon thereafter folded. *C'est la guerre.*

August 3

The *Times* has a story about the C.I.A.'s once allegedly having paid the late magician John Mulholland three thousand dollars "to write a 'manual' on sleight of hand, or, as the agency referred to it, 'prestidigitation.' " I am on the subscription list of the in-house *Times* publication, *Winners and Sinners*, which Theodore M. Bernstein gets out about once a month; and I wonder if in his chiding of the paper's staff for grammatical and other sins Ted will bring up the quotation marks around "prestidigitation." It is not just the C.I.A. that refers to sleight of hand as that, after all; everybody does, including even some people who cannot spell the heavy-handed word.

Not long ago, Lexy, who prestidigitates at younger kids' birthday parties—for which he receives a robust twenty-dollar fee, although he generously gives a quarter of that to whichever schoolmate he grants the privilege of carrying his equipment to the scene—came home one evening and announced excitedly that he had just met John Mulholland's widow. It will be hard ever to close the generation gap as long as parents persist in playing upmanship against their own children: On this sordid occasion, for instance, I could not resist telling the boy that when I was his age my parents were acquainted with the great Mulholland himself and that I was once or twice privileged to sit at the eminent magician's feet and try to figure out with my bulging eyes what he was doing with his hands.

In contrition, I promise Lexy for the tenth or twentieth time that I will rummage through my office files and try to extract for him a genuine autograph of the late Joseph Dunninger, about whom I did a *New Yorker* Profile in 1940. The magazine did not then hold pieces for publication as long as it often does today, but there were sometimes considerable lacunae between the acceptance of a piece and its publication. In Dunninger's case, some six months elapsed before the finished Profile was scheduled, and I thought I had better call him and find out what he had been up to lately, inasmuch as I hadn't had any contact at all with him over that stretch. So I dialled his home number, listened to a couple of rings, and then heard the magician's voice say, unhesitatingly, "Mr. Kahn! How are you!" I was dumbfounded, and still am. There was no way he could have known I was going to phone him, and no way—no way ascertainable to me, at least—that he could have known I was on the other end of the line. Could he have been answering every incoming phone call in that fashion for six solid months? That was the only explanation that made sense to me, and it was an insane one. Lexy can't figure out how his fellow magician pulled that one off, either. I for my part can't figure out where to begin to look for Dunninger's autograph, assuming that I ever had it in the first place. My files are in hopeless disarray, and I would not want to serve as my own executor.

320

Ellie is going to Hyannis to buy a new typewriter, and I offer to accompany her. It seems the sporting thing to do, inasmuch as it was I who dropped the machine yesterday. At least the old one can be fixed, so now she will have two electric typewriters, which means I can go around dropping them with comparative impunity. We arrive back home to adjudicate a tennis-court dispute that might sorely have tried Solomon. It seems that yesterday I told Jerry Cohen he could bring Derek Bok over to play this morning, forgetting that David had a lesson scheduled with Mike Hooven. Well, Mike was working on David's backhand when Jerry and Derek arrived, and the associate dean of the Harvard Law School and his boss proceeded, innocently enough, to usurp the court. Had I been present, I would have explained to them that they would have to wait, because family has precedence, even though the paterfamilias may have bungled the time schedule. But I am in no position to be censorious toward Jerry. I still owe him a clam pie. For all I know, he may have promised the Boks a taste of it this weekend.

August 4

I am glad I left New York when I did. Apparently everybody had to be evacuated from *The New Yorker*'s offices yesterday because of a bomb scare attributed to the F.A.L.N., the Puerto Rican terrorist group. When they blew up the Fraunces Tavern downtown a few years ago, I was having lunch a block or so away at the India House. At the sound of the explosion, my companion said to me, "What in the world do you suppose that was?" and I said, "Oh, probably just a bomb," which was indicative of more savoir-faire than in truth I have.

Terry brings some Provincetown friends over for tennis, among them a man who tells me that his wife, during my incumbency as chairman of its board of trustees, was flunked out of the Scarborough School. It had not previously occurred to me that we ever dropped a student there for mere academic remissness; I am all at once—retroactively, of course—sorry that we lost some money (her tuition the following year, that is) and proud that we had standards high enough to permit the jettisoning of an income-producing body for that reason.

Poker again tonight, at Dick Miller's. I lose again, but not much, and only because in the very last hand David Lind has a full house to my flush. I am the only non-smoker around the table. It has been five days now since I joined that select fraternity. My breath may be purer, but I reek of smugness.

August 5

The *Times* has an item on its editorial page about the amendment of St. Wapniacl, its acronym for the country's cabinet departments, in their chronological order. I learned it in elementary school—and once wrote a *New Yorker* piece about that—as St. Wapniac Lake. (State—War—Attorney General—Postmaster General—Navy—Interior—Agriculture—Commerce—Labor.) The *Times* brings this up now because Congress has added Energy to the roster, but with War and Navy engulfed by Defense, and with Health, Education and Welfare; Housing and Urban Development; and Transportation also to be reckoned with, the configuration of St. Wapniac Lake is now well-nigh unrecognizable; the newspaper's up-to-date acronym is the cumbersome "ST. DAgIACL HeHoTE." The difference between that long typographical mess and the calm surface of my old pond may be more illustrative than we realize of the difference between federal government these days and half a century ago.

I cannot believe that what has happened to Sidney Simon could have occurred even as recently as ten years ago. Some teenager ran into his station wagon the other day. Sidney got an estimate that the damage could be repaired for two hundred dollars. But because the car is a 1963 model, the insurance company involved insists that it has to be declared totalled, and further insists on sending Sidney *four* hundred dollars. The only unresolved question now is whether or not Sidney has the right to keep a vehicle—of which he is quite fond, and which runs perfectly—that has been officially declared extinct.

Sidney also has an ailing shoulder, which he claims he got from running into a woman on my court, and he has suggested that I take this up with my insurance company. I point out to him that I shall do so only if he will declare himself dead, which might be awkward inasmuch as the woman he hit was his own wife. This is the time of year, a little more than halfway through the summer, when tennis tends to exact its inevitable toll. Joey has a sore hand, but I do not count that, because it resulted from his trying out his son Jaime's skateboard. How foolish for one generation to attempt to keep pace with the next! My own left shoulder is hurting, too, but this has to be put down as a non-competitive disability, being the outcome, in my measured judgment, of excessive straining for blueberries above my head to permit the dog to gobble up those within easier reach.

August 6

To the Robert Jay Liftons' for dinner. They are celebrating the anniversary of the dropping of the bomb on Hiroshima, which to Bob is an occasion as hallowed as Easter or Yom Kippur. He has become so hooked on his professional specialty that he sometimes seems to resemble a press agent with Death as a client. The Gerry Holtons are among the guests. They have just returned from a seminar at Aspen, and Nina says that she heard at the institute there that I am doing a Profile on its incumbent leader, Robert O. Anderson. How on earth can she have learned that? It is true that I am thinking of doing such a piece, at some time or other, but I haven't yet let Anderson himself know about it. This is almost like Dunninger all over again. Another guest is a man who wants to know where I was in 1945 on Hiroshima Day. I was in New York City, I tell him, and ask politely where *he* was. "I was in Buchenwald, or Dachau," he says. The answer is, of course, sobering, but on reflection also puzzling. Can he really not recall which of the two it was?

I visited both Hiroshima and Nagasaki in 1961, when I spent ten weeks in Japan doing research for a *New Yorker* series that became the book "The Stragglers." The year before, I had seen a tiny item in the *Times* to the effect that two Japanese soldiers had been flushed from the jungles of Guam after hiding out there ever since the end of the war, for fifteen long miserable years. I thought it might be interesting to write about them, and about other ex-soldiers who'd had similar experiences. Shawn concurred.

Nobody in Washington—at the State Department, or at Defense, or at the Japanese Embassy—seemed to have any information about these diehard men, many of whom, it would develop, knew that the war was over but had hidden out nonetheless, out of fear or stupidity or determination to die fighting for their emperor, no matter how long that might take, rather than surrender. The embassy, however, did give me an address in Tokyo to which I could write a letter of inquiry. I did, and within a few weeks had all but forgotten the subject.

Months later, I received a letter at *The New Yorker*, in Japanese. Donald Keene, up at Columbia University, translated it for me. It was from the Repatriation Aid Bureau of the Ministry of Health and Welfare, and it didn't say much—merely that if I came to Tokyo, the bureau would be happy to be of what assistance it could be. Inasmuch as Shawn had already approved the idea, I saw no point in wasting his time by discussing it with him again. If he changed his mind, I would be deprived of a trip to Japan. So I flew to Tokyo, and immediately on arriving phoned the Repatriation Bureau. A voice answered, in Japanese. I tried to explain who I was, in English. Both parties soon hung up.

Bob Trumbull was then the New York *Times'* bureau chief in Tokyo, and his wife, Jean, was teaching English to Japanese college students. One of her more advanced pupils, Yuzo Saita, was about to start his vacation from Waseda University, and I hired him as an interpreter. Yuzo phoned the Repatriation Bureau, and we were invited to stop by. The agency occupied an old cavalry stable, mainly unheated, but there was an ever-present mama-san who plied us with cups of hot green tea. We were given a desk in a corner of the stable, and on it was swiftly piled a huge stack of documents, all in Japanese. It took Yuzo fifteen minutes to peruse the top sheet, and as I sat mute next to him, awaiting a translation, I calculated that at this rate I'd be trapped in a Japanese stable longer than any straggler had ever burrowed in anywhere. And at least jungles were warm.

Eventually, Yuzo accelerated, and in a couple of weeks we worked our way through the heap of paper. By then, I had decided arbitrarily to confine my research to men who had remained holed up for a minimum of five years. There turned out to be forty or so of these of whom there was any record. (Some of the records were ten years old.) I dictated letters for Yuzo to write to each survivor, explaining my mission and enclosing a stamped envelope addressed to me at the Imperial Hotel, where I myself had holed up, exceedingly comfortably.

Soon the answers began drifting in. A few were from relatives of ex-soldiers who by now had died civilian deaths. When there seemed to be little likelihood of any more replies, Yuzo and I plotted on a map of Japan the location of all the men I'd heard from. Most of them now lived south of Tokyo, and there appeared to be enough variety among them—they had lain low in the Philippines, on New Guinea, and in the Caroline Islands, as well as on Guam—to provide me with as much material I would need.

So we wrote to those south of us again (the two men from Guam who had aroused my interest in the first place were in Tokyo, and readily accessible), saying we planned to visit them, and soon Yuzo and I were off. We ventured as far south as Nagasaki, with many way stops in between. We spent a whole long night, in Kobe, listening to the eerie saga of a former member of His Imperial Majesty's Forces who'd been hiding on New Guinea, and had been driven, near-starving, to cannibalism. His memories were quite detailed.

At almost every stop, Yuzo, who interpreted his interpreter's role broadly, solicitously undertook to protect me from the advances of dance-hall hostesses. They would approach our table, whenever I could cajole him into accompanying me to one of those dens of diversion, and he would utter a few curt words in Japanese, and they would shrug and disappear. It was some time before I could prevail on Yuzo to tell me what he was telling them. "I said 'He does not dance,' " Yuzo said.

On my way home, I stopped at Guam to talk to the captors of the two men who'd been discovered there. While at Guam, I spent an informative evening with a couple of Americans who were working for the Trust Territory of the Pacific Islands, which had not yet moved its headquarters to Saipan. They urged me to come back sometime and write at length about Micronesia. I proposed that to Shawn when I reached New York, and he said sure, sounded like a good idea.

Three years later, when I was en route to Tokyo again, this time to cover the 1964 Olympics, I told Bill perhaps I ought to stop off in Micronesia for two or three months and do the story he'd approved.

"I *did?*"

I have never known Bill to renege on a pledge he has made, even one he may have forgotten. I am not sure he knew at that moment where or what Micronesia was, but he bade me Godspeed, and so after leaving the Asian mainland after the games I went to the islands and remained there long enough, courtesy of *The New Yorker*, to get a book out of it.

August 7

Both my shoulders hurt. Can this be a psychosomatic reaction to having dinner last night at a psychiatrist's home? Or is it a belated reaction to the time, six or seven years ago, when Bob Lifton and I were playing singles at New Haven, and he suggested that because *he* had an ailing shoulder it would be best if I served when it was my turn to serve and also when it was his. It took me several weeks to recover from that.

Being unable to wield a racquet, I go to Provincetown to watch Terry and Joey team up in the finals of a men's doubles tournament. They had beaten Ray Elman and his partner in the semis, partly because Ray thought, erroneously, that I put a triple whammy on him in the third set, which his side lost, 6–0. My sons, whom I naturally do not even attempt to hex, nonetheless rarely do well when I am present. Today, in my dire ominous proximity, they almost blow the first set after leading 5–1, 40–15; they do lose the second set; and they are down 1–3 in the third; but they finally pull out the match and are appropriately rewarded. There is no breeder's trophy.

During the finals, a woman comes up to me and says, "You don't know who I am. Tell me my name." One would think she would know it herself. When I give up, having no clear recollection of ever having laid eyes on her before, let alone memorized her identity, she says her name is Jane Something. I at once dismiss her surname from my retention, on the theory that the next time she accosts me I will simply say, if I can remember who she is, "Me Tarzan, you Jane."

August 8

Joey leaves for Kansas City, to do some research for a magazine piece, and Hillary for Philadelphia, to do some toward her Ph.D. I am left more or less in charge of Jaime, and since it is very hot and low tide comes at noon, I take my grandson to the beach—first time I've been there before lunch since his father was his age. I am amazed to find the sand strewn with other children, among them my other grandson. I had hoped no one I knew would espy me in such glaring defection from my regular morning routine.

We are going to Provincetown this evening to dine at Diana Michaelis', and before that she brings her house guest, Tom Farmer, around for tennis. Farmer, who apparently used to have something important to do with foreign aid during the Kennedy administration, has lately been appointed chairman by President Carter of a three-man committee that is supposed to oversee the operations of the C.I.A. and other intelligence agencies. But when Tom tells me his watchdog committee has a staff of one, I wonder how effective it can be. He hasn't even been informed, it develops when I raise the subject, that the current *New Yorker* contains an article by Dick Harris about crimes committed by the F.B.I. I would be happier if I knew that the F.B.I. and the C.I.A. were being scrutinized by someone with more robust manpower resources and, come to think of it, a more reliable backhand.

August 10

The Reverend James E. Thomas arrives for a stay with his dog named, since Jet is as much philosopher as Southern Baptist preacher, Hegel. Jet is the Marryin' Sam of our family, having officiated first for Ellie and me and then for Joey and Marian. He tells me my old dishwasher is working fine, at his farm in Maine. I didn't know he had an old dishwasher of mine. The New Hampshire firewood man who turns up in our driveway once or twice a summer to try to sell me a cord of dirt-cheap logs said the other day that my old stove was working fine. I didn't know he had an old stove of mine. I seem to have been exceedingly generous in my time.

At cocktails, with the Holtons in Wellfleet, the local intellectual set is out in heavy force—the Bob Liftons, the Stanley Hoffmanns, the Noam Chomskys, the Harry Levins. Harry's daughter, whom I have never met before, tells me that her father has long been shy about conversing with me. Professor Levin shy about me! He was a learned teaching fellow at Harvard when I was a sophomore, and I have felt shy about talking to him ever since he became a full professor there, although when I was a member of the overseers' committee to visit the English department in Cambridge I possessed a status that, at least on the day of our annual visit, compared creditably with his.

I sidle over toward Harry and engage him in chitchat, to put us both at ease for future confrontations. The diffident professor, warming up (or am I simply imagining this?), confides to me fraternally that he doubts whether Leon Edel could have written about Henry James the way he did had not Edel had a journalistic background. This is the kind of heady talk that journalists like to hear from tenured English professors at Harvard who are recognized experts on Shakespeare. I wonder if it would ever have been possible for me to prattle so insouciantly with George Lyman Kittredge. Kittredge always used to insist that those of us taking his celebrated course on the Bard spell it "Shakspere," but the orthographic gospel he espoused was never much embraced.

August 11

Having a bona-fide ordained minister under our roof is a tonic experience for David, who, being now more than one-third of the way into his seventeenth year, feels an urgent need to decide before too much more time goes by whether he is an atheist or merely an agnostic. He and Jet gnawed at that bone of contention last night long after the rest of the household had retired, without, so far as I know, getting to the marrow. The theme of tonight's dinner-table conversation is: "What is a fact?" That Rainbow is slurping up water from her dog's dish can be considered a fact, Jet argues from his philosopher's seat, only in the context of the moment. I sometimes call myself "a fact writer"—a term often used around *The New Yorker* to characterize individuals who do not write fiction or verse— but it is hard for me, in the context of either office or home, to define what a fact is. I do know for a fact that one should always be skeptical of the second half of any sentence the first half of which begins with "The fact is . . ."

August 12

The papers are full of the arrest of one David Berkowitz, A/K/A "Son of Sam." At tennis, Leo Salzman says he diagnosed that hitherto unknown killer as a schizophrenic from the outset. As a result of less vicarious psychoanalytical research, Leo has a book coming out, he says, on a Navy captain who some years back had a compulsion—never carried out—to kill his wife. Leo is worried about the book, because even though the husband concerned has signed a release, the doctor thinks that the wife might recognize herself and might cause trouble. Dr. Salzman flatteringly invites my analysis of his dilemma. I say that if the woman chooses to identify herself as his character, that is her problem—though, I add hastily, to cover myself, I am of course not a libel lawyer. I am not imprudent, either: the person I have herein called a Navy captain is not really a Navy captain.

Rainbow and I pick some blueberries. This is one time I have really missed smoking; cigarette smoke helps repel mosquitoes. At exactly nine-thirty tomorrow night, if I make it, it will have been two weeks without a puff.

August 13

Tony picks me up at dawn, we two to represent the family at a memorial service at Ballston Beach for Bob Lof, who died, quite young and suddenly, after learning that he had a brain tumor. I suppose half the people in Truro knew him, either through his having married a Worthington or because he was their plumber; and there must be at least one hundred of us assembled at the edge of the ocean—the early hour was picked, I suppose, to preclude weekend vacationers from interrupting—to pay our last respects. There are a few elderly people among the mourners who I suspect haven't been to the beach in a decade. We form a huge circle on the sand, town squires and hippies all together, and one of Bob's ex-stepchildren reads D. H. Lawrence's "Gladness of Death," and the Reverend Dick Aiken, Truro's finest home-bred shortstop, leads us in reciting the 23rd Psalm; and then somebody throws a wreath into the ocean, which the tide tugs back and forth while the older folk—most of us are barefoot—shake the sand out of their shoes; and eventually we all go home saddened to breakfast.

Perry Miller Adato, who is producing some TV shows that are supposed to tie in with Ellie's book on woman artists, arrives for the weekend with husband Neil, and they move into Jet Thomas' hot bed. One cannot get through August on the Cape without house guests. One is lucky if one can limit one's hospitality to guests one has actually invited. So far, we have had no surprises, but there are many leaves of the calendar to be flipped over before Labor Day comes to our rescue.

I take Neil and Perry up to Lee Falk's for his Herman Badillo fund-raiser. Herman says that the trouble with all the looting during the blackout was that there are ten thousand New York cops who don't live in the city; he also says that the municipal police force and he know how to handle rioters, whereas the National Guard does not. One big mistake, Herman goes on, was Con Edison's decision to restore power to Riverdale, when it was able to do so anywhere, ahead of the South Bronx—the first his residential area, the second his congressional district. Perhaps; but as long as our electric power is entrusted to a private utility, cannot an argument be made for giving priority to a neighborhood where most people probably pay their bills on time over one where many probably don't? No matter; I tell Irma Badillo that it is only a short walk from our apartment to Gracie Mansion, so that after Herman gets elected mayor, Ellie and I will be readily available for dinner there. Irma responds, as I knew she would, with a hearty invitation to break bread, when and if, at the mayoral manse.

We are entertaining at dinner tonight ourselves for the Adatos, and I am the chef. Clam pie as a first course, and then a butterfly lamb on the charcoal grill. I earn my keep. The big question is, Will the Motherwells arrive? We dropped an invitation at their home in Provincetown the other evening, but neither Bob or Renate replied, and it took two follow-up calls from Ellie to elicit word that they might come for cocktails and clam pie but that that would be all. Still, there are compensations when they do finally show up: Renate has brought her camera and asks me to step outside and let her take my picture, which, if it turns out like other Ponsold portraits I have seen, should be worth having. I already have some nice pictures of myself that Jill Krementz snapped in Cornwall a couple of years ago when she and Kurt Vonnegut came for lunch; I am in the happy position of having no need for Karsh or Bachrach.

During dinner, after Bob and Renate have taken their preordained leave, Gerry Holton reveals that Stanley Hoffmann and he were both on the selection committee set up by Harvard to pick a new president to succeed Nathan Pusey, and that when they dined one night with Nate he told them, "The first requirement for any president of Harvard is that he has to believe in God." People are always picking on Pusey. I, on the other hand, have always found him thoroughly agreeable, and unstuffy, and I have never been persuaded that in the turbulent sixties anybody else could have coped with the Harvard constituency much better than he did. Gerry also thinks that places like Harvard are admitting too many kids who appear to be geniuses, when in fact they know a lot of scientific and mathematical esoterica simply because they are social misfits who, while other youngsters were out having fun, were forced, for want of any alternative, to pore over their books. Professor Holton is, we learn, more of an all-around boy. Before he left Vienna, in the winter of 1938, he was an ice-hockey goalie, and an All-Star Austrian one to boot. But then a Canadian team came along and beat his team, 21–0. No goalie could be blamed, after an experience as traumatic as that, for deciding to become a physicist instead of a jock.

There is a clam pie left over tonight, mainly because the Motherwells departed early. At long last I can make good on my pledge to the Cohens.

August 14

There is nothing worse in life than to have weekend country house guests on a rainy Sunday. Well, yes, there could be something worse—to have them and not also have the Sunday *Times*.

August 15

A letter from Lexy, at camp: His magic tricks have been stolen from his bunk. These are principally the tricks we bought to replace those his mugger lifted off him on the steps of the Metropolitan Museum. City boys are supposed to go to the country to see cows, not to have their urban nightmares reenacted. Do the New Milford, Connecticut, police, like their compères in Manhattan, have a file of mug shots? A letter, too, from Helena Joshee, my former writing student at Columbia, who is hoping that Ellie and I can join her in New York for dinner with the only democratically elected prime minister (now alas deposed) in the history of Nepal. I miss teaching. Another member of that class was a young woman who was a devotee of Anaïs Nin, and who had had a good deal of personal contact with the elusive diarist. I suggested to that student that she write a diary about herself and Nin, and I thought what she turned out was promising, but she never managed to sell it anywhere. Now that Nin's long forgotten exercise in pornography has resurfaced and is climbing up the best-seller lists, I hope my student can somehow cash in on the boom.

Still another letter is from Bob Trumbull, the veteran *Times* foreign correspondent, who has a book coming out on the South Pacific, and who wonders if I can help him get it a review in *The New Yorker*. I know I cannot; I have not managed to get several of my own books mentioned there. I did once derive much personal satisfaction by reviewing a volume of military history for the magazine, which gave me a chance to get in a few words of praise for my old Army general, Forrest Harding, and at the same time get in a few licks against General Douglas MacArthur. But I feel that I should try to do something for Bob Trumbull, inasmuch as he most handsomely reviewed my "China Hands" for the daily *Times*. But if I did, would this not be exactly the kind of mutual backscratching that detractors of the liberal eastern establishment press so often (and often rightly) accuse it of indulging in?

This afternoon there is a meeting up at Lee Falk's, to make arrangements for the forthcoming annual Truro invitational tennis tournaments. Lee and I are the only males present. I am there because my court will be used for some of the early rounds. There seems to be a tradition that women can best schedule things. Lee wants to hold the elimination matches on a Friday. I demur. If that were the case, it would mean that Palmer Williams, who is commuting to the Cape these days, wouldn't have a chance to take part. I declare mulishly that if Palmer can't play, my court will be unavailable. The ladies demand to know whether it is my position that everybody else's plans should be altered to suit Palmer's convenience. That is precisely it, I rejoin; Palmer is the only person around who regularly volunteers to help me keep my court in shape, and if he can't play, the court will be ruled, by me, unplayable. To my astonishment, I win the argument.

August 16

According to Joey, who had dinner with Diana Thomson last night, Jim T. and Jerry Cohen were summoned—the word grates—to Hyannisport the night before last to help Ted Kennedy draft a speech on United States relations with China. (Interesting that the senator picked the two China experts who have been largely ignored in the policy-making activities of the Carter administration.) Today's Boston *Globe* has a lead story on the Kennedy speech, which quotes Jim Thomson to the effect that the senator made "an important statement." If I didn't consider myself a member of the eastern liberal establishment I might think that this was a bit much.

A call from a Princeton friend who wants me to recommend a lawyer to help get her mother, now living in Provincetown, into a nursing home. There is one attorney I can recommend highly; he once got two of my sons out of a jam when they were arrested for growing marijuana in my Truro kitchen. I believe he established that the cops involved had entered the premises without a search warrant. Ellie and I once planted some pot in a field beyond the lawn of our place in Cornwall, but by the time we got around to trying to harvest our furtive crop the weeds surrounding it had grown to such Olympian heights we couldn't find the damn stuff.

August 17

We get up early to go sea-clamming, and find not a one—the first time I've come back empty-handed in at least twenty-five years. Maybe the clams have meteorological insights beyond human comprehension, for we have scarcely returned to the house when the worst rainfall of the year assaults us. My study floor is flooded, and the roof of Ellie's work shack in the locust grove springs previously unsuspected leaks. She is worried about her new electric typewriter being damaged by the downpour, and David rushes bravely out to carry it to shelter. But an umbrella in one hand and a large typewriter in the other are more than he can manage. He drops the

331

typewriter on our kitchen-porch flagstones. That's two in two weeks. Who can blame me for taking a couple of drags on a cigarette?

August 18

Some day I must keep track of all the morning interruptions when I am trying to work. Today, attempting to write a piece for *Newsday* about the Panama Canal, nobody phones *me*, but I receive calls for David, Joey, Terry, and three people who are on the tennis court. There are calls also from the typewriter store (No. 1 will soon be healthy again but No. 2 is a very sick machine), from the watch-repair store, and from Joan Colebrook, who calls twice to "affirm" some future dinner. Joan Cohen calls to say she expects us for dinner tonight at seven-thirty, which is awkward, because the thrust of Juliet Waters' ensuing call is that we are expected *there* to sup at seven. Why is it so much easier to keep an orderly social calendar in the winter than the summer? By the time Diana Thomson calls to wonder if we happen to have any old spare Easter-egg food coloring lying around, I am snappish to the point of rudeness, and immediately after my churlish dismissal of her I am mortified with guilt, remembering that weeks ago I borrowed some Knox gelatin from her and never got around to replacing it.

We resolve our dilemma by going to the Waterses' to drink and the Cohens' to eat, which does not work out particularly well in either case, since in our effort to keep everybody happy we arrive at the first stop too early and at the second too late. The Kirk Wilkinsons are at the Waterses', and want to know if we would like to buy their art gallery, which they are getting tired of running. I cannot visualize E. and me presiding over a momma-poppa operation, even of a lofty cultural sort, though I suppose a gallery would be less taxing than a candy store. Kirk and Caps, until they find a buyer, have made a joint resolution that could rock the art world: They are going to stop serving drinks at their openings, on the not unreasonable ground that it is high time someone drew the line between free-loading and patronage of the arts.

August 19

The *Times* suggests that something fishy is going on in connection with a million-dollar backgammon tournament that has been announced, with much fanfare, to take place in Las Vegas in December. I had been tempted to enter, and am glad now that I ignored that dark side of my nature.

In the mail, a letter from my dentist: Four out of seven thirty-five-dollar checks that Jules Leaf deposited in May, he reports (I am glad to learn that I am charged his standard prophylactic rate), were mechanically destroyed by his bank, and if I have my cancelled check back would I please send it to him? I don't have it, but I assure him that this doesn't mean that the Chase Manhattan never got it from his bank; the Chase has the same carefree attitude toward random bits of paper as the participants in a ticker-tape parade. Just the other day, I received a copy of a deposit slip, in the amount of $1,209.65, that belonged to Eric or Lee S. Langbaum. Ordinarily, I would have returned it to the Chase, but I hesitated to do so, out of fear that the sum would at once be switched from my account (assuming there is that much in it) to that of the unfortunate Langbaums.

And here is a postcard from a fellow journalist who I had thought was editing a magazine. His typewriter and he, the missive archly reports, have established an office together, "where the crafts of word-spinning and deadline-racing will be more effectively performed." I can read between those lines. He is out of a job, poor fellow, and is going to try to make a go of it, God help him, freelancing. At least he has a typewriter, I deduce, that does not wander around falling out of people's arms and running up huge surgical bills.

Jinny has been around Truro this month. There is absolutely no reason why she shouldn't be. Her children and grandchildren, after all, are on the scene, and it stands to reason that she would want to see as much of them as she can. Still and all, it can be awkward to have both a wife and an ex-wife roaming around one's premises. This afternoon, for instance, John and Mary Bunker, who hadn't been in Truro for a couple of years, came by the house to see if there was any tennis, and the first person they spotted, playing badminton in our backyard with Jaime, was Jinny. Then Joey borrowed our car to go to Wellfleet on some errand, and when it came back and Ellie went out to meet it, Jinny was at the wheel. All I need now is for N. to saunter down the driveway looking for some mixed doubles.

At a beach picnic tonight, over at Corn Hill, someone has brought along a house guest who is introduced as a backgammon hustler, and has a portable board. I am apparently his blind date. I don't have any money with me—I never carry money in Truro—but I play him three games and win eleven dollars, which is all he seems to have on him. A conservative hustler, I should judge.

How did I ever get to be a compulsive gambler? Certainly not through my mother, who never played games of chance, even for fun. My father did, a bit, but not seriously: He devoted the last thirty years of his life to canasta, for God's sake. I suppose my maternal grandfather was as much responsible as anybody else. Grandpa used to bet on horse races (but only when at the track), and play bridge for money (but only for a tenth of a cent a point). I learned how to play bridge by kibitzing, from the age of ten or so on, while my father and grandparents and their friends played, as they did incessantly. The older folks were really dreadful at the game, and it is not untruthful, I believe, to say that in time I profited from their mistakes. I inherited a singular trait from my grandfather. I sometimes sneeze, as he was wont to do, seven times in a row. Never six, never eight; always seven on, so to speak, the nose. When Grandpa began his no less unvarying sequence, we grandchildren would always count his sneezes aloud, and he never failed to stop after the seventh one. So it goes with me, too, though I sneeze unaccompanied. My septimal sneezing occurs exclusively when I have had too much to drink. It had never occurred to me, as a child, that there might be any similar cause-and-effect situation with respect to my grandfather, but in view of my having evidently acquired his other reprobate characteristic, I wonder now what may have motivated all those "*Gesundheits!*" that used to resound through the family halls.

August 21

Yesterday, the tennis tournaments began, and there were the usual nasty scenes. Stuart Miller was an hour and a half late for his doubles match, with David Lind, against Dave Walker and me. Stuart's excuse was that he had clutch trouble, though considering the length of his legs he could have loped to our house in about the length of time it would take me to drive over from his place. Lind was furious because Walker and I wouldn't allow Miller any warmup time. During the matches up at Falk's court, word filters down, Cy Post broke Lee's net strap while measuring the height of the net to make sure it wasn't a millimeter off, and then suggested to Lee that some woman—Lee's Elizabeth was the only one around—drop whatever she might be doing and sew it back together again. By the time this tournament is over there will be several people, you can be sure, who will not be on speaking terms with one another. The only saving grace is that by the time next summer rolls around, we will have forgotten who it is we swore never to talk to again.

I have to drive to Providence today to pick up Lexy, who is being ferried that far by a child psychiatrist who has a kid at the same Connecticut camp and is meeting me halfway. The psychiatrist has no face. Well, he has a face, but it is almost literally covered, except for his eyes and nose, with a mat of uncombed hair. I wonder what a disturbed child must think on first being ushered into his presence.

On returning, I go alone to Provincetown for the opening of a Sidney Simon sculpture show (the gallery owners serve white wine, but only Almaden), inasmuch as Ellie is working, and writing with pen and ink is slow going for her. Jinny turns up at the show, and that is bound to start tongues wagging.

August 22

Ellie receives a report—diagnosis more than prognosis—from the type-writer store that is trying to save the newer of her two machines. They found a mouse nest inside the typewriter, with one baby still inside it. (Some mice once built a nest inside the radiator of an automobile of mine. But a typewriter!) The baby mouse was dead. They cannot say for certain whether the mouse perished when the typewriter was dropped or had earlier been killed by, say, the automatic carriage shift.

A ladies' tennis tournament on our court is interrupted by another savage rainstorm. Molly Kipnis turns out to have left her keys inside her locked car. A window is slightly ajar, and I, having watched enough television to know how to handle this crisis, spend half an hour in the drenching rain trying to open up the car with a coat hanger. Finally I admit defeat, whereupon Lexy takes the coat hanger from me and goes outside and has the car unlocked in an instant. I should have reminded myself, before I risked pneumonia, that he is a prestidigitator.

August 23

The typewriter store calls again. They have found two more dead mice in E.'s machine. I had no idea the interiors of typewriters were so com-modious.

Today would have been my maternal grandfather's one hundred and eighteenth birthday. My paternal grandfather died when I was not yet two, and I have no recollection of him, but Grandpa barely missed making it to ninety, and thus became acquainted with the older two of my three sons. Joey was an infant when he died, though, and Terry only two, and they have no recollection of *him*. So it goes with families; it is largely a matter of chance which progenitors live in memory and which in limbo.

The Pamet Harbor Yacht Club is soliciting contributions for a flagpole and flag honoring the memory of charter member Joseph F. Flanagan. I have no recollection of ever even having heard of him. The first house we rented in Truro had a big flagpole out front, and a flag, which the little boys and I would ceremoniously raise and lower every clear day, marching out in an approximation of proper military formation and standing at attention while the colors fluttered up and down. I had only been out of the Army four years then, after more than four years in it, and was still apparently in some transitional phase of my life, finding old ingrained habits hard to shuck. If there hadn't been a flagpole on the premises, though, I doubt that I would have gone out and got one.

August 24

Today's papers carry pictures of Secretary of State Vance in Peking, wielding chopsticks as he dines with Huang Hua, now the foreign minister of the P.R.C. When Huang was Chinese ambassador to the United Nations, Ellie and I wielded chopsticks with him one night at his residence in New York. He had invited us—along with the Teddy Whites—because my "China Hands" had recently been published. The Chinese Embassy had taken over an old West Side motel, and had fitted it out with exactly the same kind of heavy furniture that we had seen in every hotel we'd stayed at in the People's Republic. And the dinner was a duplicate of those in Shanghai, Nanking, and elsewhere—everyone sitting around sipping hot tea instead of cocktails, and then at the table, as accoutrements to the endless splendid parade of dishes, three glasses: a small one for *mai tai*, a larger one for wine, and a big one for beer or orange juice. It was a warm evening, and Teddy and I were glad to follow our host's lead and doff our suit coats, while we solemnly discussed, as if somehow our words could matter (Huang's probably could) ways and means of ameliorating relations between the two nations. When Mao Tse-tung died, I wrote Huang Hua a note of condolence, on behalf of Ellie and myself; but the only response we got, weeks later, was a mimeographed propaganda tract extolling the Chairman's great virtues and itemizing some of the worst vices of the imperialist Western world.

Joey and Jaime are back from a visit to Martha's Vineyard. At six, Jaime, raised in Tucson, had never been on a boat before, nor to an island, although I suppose one could claim that ever since the Cape Cod Canal was constructed we have been on an island of sorts. The last time I left Martha's Vineyard by water I was aboard a motor yacht that a friend of mine had chartered for a northeast cruise, and because he rammed into and splintered a dock at Edgartown, and then did not bother to wait around and assess the damage, we departed in a roar of spume as a hit-and-run craft, with stentorian island voices screaming after us that they were going to put the Coast Guard on our trail. We never were pursued, though I was braced for a salvo across our bow.

I have bad luck, generally, with friends' boats. A college classmate once hove to in Provincetown harbor, and invited Jinny and me out to his anchored yawl, or sloop, or whatever it was, for dinner. We got out there all right in his dinghy, or gig, or rowboat, or whatever *that* was; but as we headed in it back to shore at midnight, our host tipped over the frail tender and I ended up, fully clad, beneath it. I prefer larger, steadier vessels, of a minimum gross tonnage of around fifty thousand.

August 25

I have never heard Rainbow bark so alarmingly, and when I rush to the door to see what has agitated her I find standing outside a truly wild-looking man, unshaven, unkempt, a derelict who looks as though he had taken a monumentally wrong turn while heading for the Bowery. Before Rainbow can sink her teeth into this wretch, I recognize him, fortunately, as the only fellow I have ever known well who has been an official of the Federal Reserve Board. LeRoy Morgan, after the dog calms down, has an interesting yarn to spin about Provincetown and its recent troubles with the gay set. (One establishment has just had its liquor license revoked for flagrant fellatio.) It seems, our disguised banker reports, that a schoolteacher of his acquaintance—who is resolutely straight—has just had to pay five hundred dollars to a local lawyer to defend him against an assault charge stemming from a summer job. The teacher delivers ice to Provincetown restaurants and bars, and carries it in on one shoulder, using both hands to steady his load. Well, LeRoy says, patrons of these establishments kept pawing at his legs and groin as he walked through, and finally in exasperation he dropped a huge cake of ice on a would-be lover's head, and got sued as a result. The poor teacher had been further irritated because when, off-duty, he had taken his wife dancing in one of these joints, a number of patrons had tried insistently to cut in—on him.

Joan Wulsin asked me not long ago how I make clam pie, and she was so pleased, after following my directions, that she wrote a note to *Gourmet* magazine, flatteringly extolling the dish and saying that if the editors were interested in obtaining the recipe she was sure they could persuade me to let them have it. She sent along my name and address. I have not heard from *Gourmet*, but Joan has: She received a postcard today that said, "Dear Reader, Unfortunately, we are unable to send you the recipe you request. We are sorry to have to disappoint you, but the company that markets this product is unwilling to divulge its secrets. We hope we will have an opportunity to be more helpful to you in the future."

We dine at the Martin Tolchins with, *inter alios*, a couple who rented our Truro house for one month a few summers back. I don't mind meeting *ex*-tenants, but I have found it best, year in and out, to have as little as possible to do with incumbent or future ones. There is always the danger that one might grow fond of them and thus condone their breakage.

August 28

This week's *Phoenix*, one of Boston's two alternative weeklies—Terry was until recently acting managing editor of its rival, *The Real Paper*—has one of those feature stories that some paper or other seems to run nearly every summer. It is about the Outer Cape and its psychiatrists and tennis players. I wrote one such myself for the *Times* a few years ago. The current version cites Bob Lifton as the dean of local living psychiatrists, and comes up with another novel twist: It mentions a Tennis Mafia, consisting of Lee Falk, Kirk Wilkinson, and myself. People are supposed to covet opportunities to play on our three private courts.

I have almost never read a piece of journalism anywhere that dealt with any subject I knew anything about that did not contain mistakes. I suppose people familiar with the subjects I report on have the same reaction; in spite of *The New Yorker*'s redoubtable checkers, it is nearly impossible to get a long fact piece into that magazine without a single error of some sort, and books that do not enjoy the benefit of the magazine's scrupulous scrutiny are larded with inadvertent misinformation, my own books lamentably among them. One is most likely to go astray when one is so certain something is correct that one doesn't bother to verify it. Writers understand this. Readers don't. As a reader, I am bemused by the *Phoenix*'s suggestion that there is a Tennis Mafia and that to be in its good graces is something worth fighting for. In truth, there are so many private tennis courts in our summer community now that we proprietors often have to spend a good deal of time on the telephone trying to cajole Bob Lifton or some lesser personage to make up a fourth for doubles.

August 29

Sea-clamming again this morning, with low tide at 6 A.M., an ideal hour for this arcane sport. I cannot find any adults eager, or even willing, to accompany me, but do manage to recruit David, Lexy, and Jaime. Rainbow needs no urging; there is nothing she likes to do more than to race along the Bay flats, chasing seagulls. She has never come close to catching one, but certainly deserves credit for trying. We are lucky this time, and catch a full bucket with hardly any effort. When the rest of the household eventually arises, Ellie announces that for a change she wants to forgo pies and instead to make a *ceviche* from the clams' thick juicy muscles. I yield, but then she adds some canned tuna to my fresh clams, of which, no matter how the editors of *Gourmet* might feel, I take a dim view.

A non-tennis-playing pediatric shrink comes by for cocktails. I am always interested in learning about other people's work habits, and today my curiosity is amply rewarded when the psychiatrist says that he suffers from a massive occupational handicap. He cannot engage in his practice sitting down. He has to pace. What effect this may have on his sedentary, or supine, patients he does not disclose. He also says that by 5 P.M. he is so restless that when that hour's child turns up for an appointment, the doctor says at once, "Let's go out and have an ice cream cone." If the kid says, "But I just *had* an ice cream cone," the doctor replies, "Well, you're going to have another one." Or so our guest tells the story on himself; how he might describe this behavorial pattern to his own analyst is, of course, something else again.

August 30

Terry and Rose are moving their furniture into our garage, having decided for the moment not to live in Provincetown, for reasons unclear to me. My son says he will discuss his situation later. O.K., I say, but what does he plan to *do*? He is going to have a shot at freelance writing, he replies. I venture the opinion that he may not have the temperament for this kind of demanding, chancy, self-disciplined line of work. He blows up and says this is no time for a lecture, so I shrug and help him unload his furniture, which is the least a father can do when his first-born is apparently in some kind of trouble.

Anyway, Terry has a much more important family matter to discuss than his own immediate future. He was talking to an acquaintance of his in Boston the other day, a man in his mid-forties, and the fellow told Ter that he thought he was my brother. Half-brother, actually; my father's illegitimate son. His name—he uses his mother's surname—rings a bell. I am reminded, for the first time in more than forty years, of a then young woman who worked for a while in my father's office. That would have been in the mid-nineteen thirties, and yes, it all seems likely enough. My father would then have been about fifty, and he and my mother were not on speaking terms, and a man that age—how well I know!—needs loving.

A brother! Until today, I only had two sisters. Terry says that my brother, if it is my brother, was supported for a while by my father, which certainly lends credence to the probability; but that they broke off communication when the Boston man wrote Ely a letter saying he was ill and it was answered by my then stepmother, who accused him and his mother of trying to blackmail my father. So Beatrice knew about this. Who else? Never in his lifetime, nor in his will, did my father ever hint to me of the existence of any such son. Did he have Beatrice write the blackmail letter, or did she intercept his mail and do that on her own? Did any of all this ever actually happen? The mother of the man in question is apparently still alive, somewhere. I must get in touch with her son. My brother.

August 31

I had wild sibling dreams last night, and fraternal speculations while I lay awake. I could not recall whether or not I had ever seen my father's inamorata at our house or at his office. But at five o'clock in the morning her first name suddenly shot into my mind. I had forgotten that I had ever known it.

I charter a fishing boat out of Wellfleet and take Joey, Jaime, David, and Lexy out into the bay. We haul in fourteen bluefish, the largest about a sixteen-pounder, not bad at all for a morning's outing. The only time I caught a big striped bass from a boat was about twenty years or so ago when I found myself spang in the middle of a school of stripers, churning and leaping from the water and grabbing at bare hooks as fast as we could drop them over the side. I have a photograph to prove it. (Today, Lexy forgets to bring his camera along.) Our skipper remembers the incident, too. The boat we are on is the very same one; on my bonanza day, he was its mate, and its captain was his grandfather. Everybody seems to be related to somebody else. Toward the end of our charter, we come upon an outboard occupied by three elderly anglers—by "elderly" I now mean discernibly over seventy—who signal us that they are in distress. Their engine has conked out. One of them shouts to us with mingled defiance and embarrassment that he just had a brand new magneto installed. Our captain noncommittally has his teenage mate throw the old men a line, and we tow them into port, the mate observing sarcastically that perhaps they ought to throw away the magneto and buy themselves an entire new engine. And then he disembowels our fourteen sleek blues and tosses their entrails directly into the path of the little boat we are towing—a terrible indignity, inasmuch as there is no evidence that they caught even a mackerel before their breakdown.

September 1

Summer is nearly over. The nights are getting cooler, the days shorter. There are other ways of judging seasonal variations on the Cape: Our beach plums were ready for picking yesterday. Diana Thomson came by for a bucket. We have more than we know what to do with (including some rare yellow ones), and I am happy to have friends help themselves, though I am less pleased when strangers park their cars at the head of the driveway and without a by-your-leave strip our bushes. Diana will no doubt make a batch of beachplum jelly and, as is her considerate wont, bestow on us a couple of jars; I prefer beachplum brandy, which is easier to concoct, looks prettier, lasts longer, and tastes better. Of course, you can't serve it with meat or on toast.

The Bunkers come by for tennis. Dr. John brings along a medical book he has written, in exchange for which I give him a bluefish. Our version of the barter society. I ask John to inscribe his tome to David, who at the age of ten said he was going to be a physician and, unlike all the kids whose future careers as firemen prove illusory, has in the ensuing six years grown increasingly set in his determination. David takes the book to his room, explaining to his mother and me—perhaps with the sort of truth that is supposed to emerge from the mouths of babes—that it is something we couldn't possibly understand. I recruit David Kerr to be my partner against the Bunkers, who are as formidable a pair as they were twenty years ago: Mary's unique style—she hardly ever seems to move, and yet gets to everything and hits whistling drives with a flick of her wrist—has long terrorized opponents of both sexes.

Tennis is a strange game. Today, for instance, the Bunkers are ahead of us, 5–3, 40–30, Mary serving for game and first set, when Dave hits a nice shot down the middle of the court. Both Bunkers go after it, nearly collide, and miss the ball. That single gaffe brings on total collapse. We win that game and the following nine in a row. Score 7–5, 6–0, in favor of the home team. The Bunkers look as stunned as their fish.

September 2

David goes to Hyannis today to take his driving test for a license. Terry accompanies him to the scene. We have heard from various year-rounders that the Cape Cod examiners are tough, and I am worried for David's sake, because he has a 2 P.M. appointment, and if he draws an inspector who has had a trying morning and a poor lunch David could be in trouble. But the man he gets turns out to be a fellow who once arrested Tony for some infraction or other, and he is so eager to gossip with Terry about that and about Provincetown and regional journalism that he hardly pays any attention to David, who at one point asks his examiner, "What am I supposed to do now?" and receives the reply, "How should I know? *You're* driving the car." So David passes with ease. A big day in the life of any teenager—receiving one's first driver's license. Comparable to what? Getting into college? Losing virginity? It certainly rates up there somewhere.

September 3

I am amazed that David doesn't arise early to go to Truro Center and fetch the mail and the newspapers. It would have been his first chance to drive without a chaperon. So I make the morning run myself, and as soon as I return home, feeling most peculiar, I take to my bed. My temperature is 102. We were supposed to go en famille to the Holtons' for dinner and then to a dance at the Liftons', but by mid-afternoon I am still feverish and know I won't be going anywhere today. At dusk, I send Ellie and the boys off bearing my regrets. At about 11 P.M., I have my first chill, a real bone-breaker. What the hell is going on? I have had fevers before, but never anything like this, at least not since 1943, in Brisbane, Australia. When E. returns home, danced out, at 1:30 A.M., my temperature is 105. I cannot recall—I am perfectly lucid, though afire—at exactly what number of degrees it is that an adult's brains are supposed to boil. E. manages to get a sleepy doctor on the phone, who suggests aspirin. She has a better idea: I must instantly take an ice-cold shower, which is not easy to force oneself to do in such circumstances. I stand shivering naked wet for as long as I can manage, totter back to bed, and eventually fall into a fitful sleep.

September 4

I have another wracking chill soon after I awake, and E. insists that I see a doctor at AIM—the Wellfleet clinic that is our neighborhood outpost of the Cape Cod Hospital, in Hyannis. She talks to Dr. Bardwell at AIM, who says he will arrange for the Truro rescue squad to transport me to Wellfleet; but this is the Labor Day weekend, and what with automobile accidents and drownings, the squad will be busy enough as it is, and I am confident that I can make it down the stairs and into our car. I do, shakily, dragging a blanket with me, like a child taking his security blanket along to his first day of kindergarten. Dr. Bardwell checks me over, clearly puzzled, and asks what whatever I have feels like. I say that it feels like the malaria I had thirty-four years ago in Brisbane. He seems much relieved. He has no facilities at AIM to test for malaria, he says. I will have to go on to Hyannis for that. He will arrange everything at once. He is considerate, and helpful, but delighted, I sense, to get me off his hands and his premises. I am to report to the emergency room of the hospital, he informs me in a minute, and to ask for Dr. Farrish.

Dr. Farrish takes over as soon as my blanket and I reach Hyannis, and very thoroughly. Chest X-ray. An EKG. A good deal of blood extracted for random smears and other tests. A number of questions about my life style. Will I suffer from withdrawal symptoms, for instance, if I have to go without alcohol? I wonder if *he* can be delirious. But then I realize that he asked me earlier how much I drank a day, on the average, and I said I wasn't sure, exactly, and he said, well, would a pint be about it?, and I said that sounded reasonable. I guess he thinks that is unreasonable. I assure him that he need not concern himself about withdrawal symptoms.

Everybody in the emergency room is most attentive, and soon I am hitched up to an intravenous device from which a trickle of liquid (phosphates, vitamins, dextrose, salt, I don't know what all else, but the combination is a hideous yellow color) flows into a hole carved neatly into my wrist. I may get out of bed "as tolerated," the doctor informs me, which means that I may go to the bathroom provided that I have strength enough and that I haul my IV machine along with me. That is the best news I've had in twenty-four hours: I can tolerate urinals, but I can't abide bedpans.

The hospital is crowded. There are no empty beds in private rooms, nor in semi-privates. I am wheeled, till something better opens up, into the solarium, and dropped into a bed, my IV looming over me, with a band around my wrist that reads, "Ely J. Kahn, Jewish." That should solve the problem of which chaplain assigned to this hospital officiates at my rites. My last previous hospital institutionalization was exactly thirty years ago, when a doctor put me in one overnight simply to have some tests made during a routine checkup. My first visitor was a rabbi, who addressed me in murmuring tones I had thought were usually reserved for the doomed. My second caller was the house doctor, a young Indian or Pakistani who, though I was not his patient and not sick, asked me all kinds of questions, including again how much I drank and whether or not I smoked. He shook his head disapprovingly during my forthright replies and declared that I wouldn't live another five years. Whatever may happen this week, I fooled *him*. I also threw him out of my room and told him not to return without written permission from my own physician.

Ellie has the impression from my wrist band that my stay in the solarium is going to set me back (or, technically, the insurance company that handles *The New Yorker*'s group policy) an even hundred dollars a day. She says the band has "$100" written on it. While she is talking to a nurse, I scrutinize it myself and am relieved to see it says "S100," the "S" standing, I deduce, for "Solarium." I forgive Ellie; she has had little sleep, and has been ministering to me so unflaggingly she left her reading glasses at home. The only other patient in the solarium is a fastidious young man who has elegant pajamas, robe, and slippers (I brought only my blanket, and that seems to have vanished), and is forever folding and refolding a towel. He tells me when we are left alone that he is going to lose his mind unless he can get hold of some decent hair pomade. As he unfolds for me his curriculum vitae, I learn that he is a bachelor, living with a sister, and was employed as a cook until he had to quit because his health would not permit him to lift heavy pans. He has had two heart attacks, and is suffering at the moment further from kidney stones and bad headaches. When a doctor comes to look at him, it is a psychiatrist. I learn further, from observation, what unemployed cooks do with their time. They watch old movies on television. This guy would watch them nonstop around the clock if he had his way.

More blood is drained out of me for more tests. A laboratory technician also scans my body for spots. "Could you have been bitten by a tick?" I reply as helpfully as I can that while I thought the tick season was over, I certainly could have fallen prey to one: Rainbow has brought many into the house, and they have crawled across me in bed more than once. She shudders—less, I believe, at the substance of my answer than at its graphic presentation. The cook is still glued to the room's TV set when I lose track of things.

September 5

Last night was the worst ever. Practically no sleep. My temperature climbed up to 105.6, and the doctors elected to try the cold-towel treatment, wrapping me literally from chin to toe in wet shrouds (a tiny warm face cloth, though, for my prick), and replacing towels whenever a batch lost its iciness. But with each hateful change my fever dropped a few tenths of a point. And so the nurses tenderly shepherded me through the night.

At daybreak, I have a fresh attack of the cursed chills, which by now I know heralds yet another rise in temperature. While I am trying to contort my body into a position where the leg cramps that also afflict me will be the least painful, the cook walks over, creasing his towel, and says, "You know what you look like? You look like Sonny Tufts." I have no idea what Sonny Tufts looks like. I had thought he was just a radio joke, but maybe he turned up last night in an old movie. Does Sonny Tufts resemble Norman Mailer? Or Max Lerner? Or Art Buchwald—whom I was taken for not long ago by an airport redcap? I must write down that I look like Sonny Tufts before I drift off into oblivion.

I was delivered some breakfast this morning, of which I could not touch a morsel, and also a menu. If there is anything I do not want to read right now it is a menu. But the menu is made of paper, and I borrow a pen from a hovering nurse's aide and laboriously scribble "Sonny *Tufts!*" A moment later, a sour-faced woman who looks like a hospital dietician materializes at my bedside. She turns out to be a hospital dietician, and she wonders why I have not checked off any items on my menu so her people will know what to bring me next. I say I am not hungry. She sees that I have written

344

something on the menu nonetheless, grabs it, and attempts to read my words. I say they are personal and try to grab it back from her. We have a brief tug of war which, I am glad to perceive, I win despite my debilitation. She glares at me, and in a towering rage stalks away. I suppose I will not be fed again here ever. No matter; the nurses keep replenishing the contents of my trusty old IV machine, and I have no appetite anyway.

I am visited by Dr. Farrish's associate, Dr. Rimso, who says that so far I have proved to be negative for every kind of malaria they ever heard of. He wants to know if I have recently been to Nantucket. The questions these people ask! I haven't been to Nantucket in ten years. He asks about ticks again. It seems unfair, just because these experts cannot diagnose my malaise, to keep trying to blame it on a dog. Next they will be mumbling about rabies. Ellie arrives with today's Boston *Globe*, which has a story about an American Army officer who was once imprisoned for allegedly having collaborated with the enemy while a prisoner of war in Korea, after a "trial for something 'akin to treason.' "

During the Second World War, an American Army enlisted man was convicted of a comparable charge and imprisoned at Fort Leavenworth, after being first sentenced to death. He was a Harvard graduate, a formidable linguist, who had helped some German prisoners of war escape from a stockade at Camp Hale, Colorado, and had got them across the Mexican border before he was caught. In 1949, his lawyer got in touch with me, while the soldier was still in jail, and wondered if I would be interested in writing some articles about what the attorney then believed was a miscarriage of justice.

The case had had practically no publicity, but the lawyer furnished me with a transcript of the court-martial proceedings, which had "Top Secret" stamped all over them. That classification didn't deter me, with the war long over, but what worried me, after doing months of research, was that there hadn't *been* any miscarriage of justice. I told the lawyer that I wanted to write up the story, but could hardly do so along the lines he had had in mind when he approached me. He told me to go ahead anyway, and I did, in four *New Yorker* parts. I was tempted to have them published, some time afterward, in book form, but by then I had read in the *Harvard Alumni Bulletin* that the chief protagonist in this curious drama was out of prison and serving as an executive vice-president of a bank in California, so I decided that enough was enough.

My ailing Escoffier is escorted from our solarium by his psychiatrist, immediately following which a priest enters, looks at a slip of paper in his hand, approaches my bed, and says, "Good day, Mr. Antonelli."

"No, I'm Kahn," I say.

"Con what?" he asks.

I haven't the heart to tell him that the person he is apparently seeking has been shanghaied by a shrink. I reflect as I await a new onslaught of chills that if I ever get out of this place I will be able to say that I lost my summer tan in a solarium.

September 6

Last night was sweat night. The fever was breaking. My bed was so soaked that my sheets had to be changed three times. At 6 A.M. my temperature was subnormal. If this illness, whatever it is, were a poker game, I could go high-low and clean up. But I have barely stopped congratulating myself on my recovery when the chills start up again, and I know the thermometer will rise *en suite*. This time, though, it gets up only to 102, which by now feels to me like normal.

The population of the solarium was augmented, in the midst of the perspiring night, by the arrival of a bearded young man who had been hurt in a motorcycle accident. He and a buddy were both evidently tailgating a truck when it stopped suddenly. Our new patient is just badly bruised, but it seems his companion had some trouble with his helmet and at last report was undergoing brain surgery. Now, at dawn, three females and a male arrive to visit the bearded man—grandmother, mother, girl friend, and kid brother, I surmise. One of them leans over his bed and asks, "How's Danny?"

There is a horrible scream from the pillow. "He's *dead*!"

The cook, whose bed is directly alongside that of the newcomer, gets up and switches off the TV set. The grandmother bursts into hysterics and has to be led out of the room. The mother sobs more reservedly. The girl friend and the kid brother sit stunned. The priest enters our room in the middle of this, goes over to Cook Antonelli to give him communion, and then, oblivious to all the pain and suffering two feet away from him, nods pleasantly to the bearded man and his loved ones and walks away. I guess he doesn't yet have the new patient's name on any list.

Dr. Farrish comes by and wants to know more about my quondam malaria. I tell him how I suffered through it in a private home in Brisbane because I was a soldier trying to avoid living with the Army and how I was treated by a psychiatrist because otherwise he would have had to eat with the Army; and I sense that Dr. Farrish does not believe a word of this outlandish tale. I hope he does not propose a consultation about me with the resident psychiatrist, who went off again this morning with my foppish cook. Cookie returns from this session bearing a tale that that doctor supposedly told him—about a man just brought into our hospital who stuck the hilt of a knife in a wall and then backed swiftly into the blade, to punish himself for all the people he himself had stabbed in the back. Literally or figuratively? I inquire. Cookie does not say, conceivably because he does not know. Anyway, he goes on, he has problems more major than that on his mind. He is trying to get his head together so he can pass a kidney stone, and he hasn't yet found any suitable pomade. He also seems to think, incidentally, that I am off my rocker, because instead of watching television I have been reading a book—Anne Bernays' reviewer's copy of "Members of the Tribe."

At lunch, which I gather I receive because it is my scrappy dietician's day off, the cook declares that the meat loaf is poisonous, and that he ought to know what he is talking about. An attendant nurse concurs. This is too bad, because I had taken a few bites of it and hugely enjoyed it—the first solid food I have ingested in three days.

I have two callers—ladies from the patients-accounts department, who want to know whom they should get in touch with about their bill. I refer them to *The New Yorker*'s insurance-accounts department, and they thank me and depart. This is the first and last mention to me in the hospital of paying my way. They are quickly followed by Dr. Rimso, who brings up leukemia, as casually as Walt Frazier might bring up rim shots. The doctor says my white corpuscle count has taken a leftward drift, and that if it hasn't stabilized tomorrow they are contemplating a bone-marrow biopsy. Well, I never.

September 7

Sometime last evening, Patient Kahn was moved into a conventional hospital room, also occupied by one fellow with a broken leg (non-fatal auto accident) and another who had run an electric screwdriver clean through his hand. Patient K. had a somewhat better night, but not much. His temperature never got beyond 102, and reached that modest height only once. However, there was some trouble around 11 P.M., when a post-op patient (hernia) was trundled in to fill the fourth bed in the room. Patient Hernia was clearly a gentleman: He was chiefly concerned with getting his false teeth reinstalled. He was also in considerable distress, so it seemed unfair for Patient K. to complain about his lower left arm, which was hurting fiercely at and around the spot where the IV tube was attached.

At midnight, K. decided he wouldn't be able to sleep at all unless something was done, and he was about to summon a nurse when he glanced toward the foot of his bed and standing there—hallucination? deus ex machina?—*no*, this was *real*—was Dr. Rimso. In New York City at that hour most doctors would be in their beds, wearing earplugs. Dr. Rimso at once ordered the tube moved from K.'s left arm, which was swollen and sore, to his right one. In between removal and reinsertion, the patient, detached from his contraption and given free use of both arms, skipped blithely down the hall into the bathroom to shave—first depilation in five days. Patient K. looked infinitely better afterward.

First thing this morning, an emissary comes around to collect more of my blood. I am surprised that I still have any to yield up. This is preliminary to a solemn visitation from Dr. Farrish, who arrives with a rather large retinue, has a screen erected around my bed, and with a new supersharp Japanese knife which he cannot praise highly enough extracts some bone marrow, and a bit of bone, too, from my lower back. Dr. Farrish says he specializes in this operation. He went to Nantucket yesterday, he tells me—Nantucket again!—for another bone-marrow job. When Ellie arrives soon afterward and asks me if it hurts, I say, "It probably would have hurt more without the novocaine." I nominate that as a serious contender for Understatement of the Year.

I am being moved again, this afternoon, to a private room, because my case has become so baffling that there appears to be some fear that whatever I have might be contagious. I say to the nurse who tells me of the new shift, "You mean to the room they just took the corpse out of?" She gasps. How, she wonders, did I know *that*? Elementary, my dear Miss Watson: I make a point of keeping my eyes on the corridor, through the open door, and did I not see a man in a dark suit and white shirt and tie go by, head high, eyes directly in front of him, marching in undertaker's stride, wheeling an empty stretcher fifteen minutes ago, and did I not see him just return, even more solemn of mien, with a shrouded body in his custody?

Nurse says I guessed right, but there is no need for me to be worried; the fellow died of a heart attack and can not have left any fatal germs behind him. I assure her that I am not bothered. One can hardly expect to be in a hospital and be far removed from death. In each of my three assigned rooms, I have been in close proximity to someone whose ceaseless groans have had a sadly terminal ring.

September 8

This morning, for the first time since I can remember, I feel genuinely hungry, but my insomniac doctors have issued orders that I am to be permitted no breakfast. Not even a glass of water. It seems that, having exhausted all other avenues of exploration, they are going to have my kidneys X-rayed: They are checking out some sort of rare fever-producing entity that does not manifest itself in mere urine. In any event, my temperature has been normal for twenty-four hours now—I could tolerate the fever, all right, but those chills were something else again—and this afternoon I am to go back home. There is no point in my staying in the hospital any longer, the doctors have concluded; they can't treat me for anything, because they still haven't diagnosed my condition. It is reassuring, though, to know, as they are by now convinced, that I am not suffering from malaria, leukemia, or Rocky Mountain spotted fever.

After the kidney X-rays, I request a cup of coffee, but when the nursing station on my floor phones to the food department, it is told, "But we've already wasted one breakfast on him." I suspect that the dietician with whom I had the wrestling match is back on duty. When Ellie and Lexy come to pick me up, the nurses attending me insist that I be taken by wheelchair to our car. Drs. Farrish and Rimso both stop by to bid me farewell, still mystified; they promise to send me a complete report on all they've done, so Louis Bishop can append it to my medical history. What a weird chapter this one has been!

September 10

I spent most of yesterday resting, but I still feel weak. The neighbors are being gratifyingly solicitous. Joan Cohen stops by, also Jim Thomson and Sidney Simon. Bess Schuyler brings some homemade chicken soup. It is what she had left over when she was cooking a meal for her dogs. The soup tastes delicious, and I feel like a heel not sharing at least some of it with Rainbow.

September 11

A Sunday, and our last day on the Cape this season. I assure Ellie that I will be fit to travel tomorrow, though it is nice to have an excuse not to help clean up and pack up. The *Times* has a flattering feature story, *cum* picture, about Palmer Williams, whom it acclaims as the unsung hero of "60 Minutes." That show got such good ratings this year that Palmer, who has been talking about taking early retirement from CBS, may be stymied by his own success. The *Globe* has a strange feature story about a pop singer named Emmylou Harris. "To allay her nervousness," it says, "she is accompanied by a bizarre, advice-giving character, James E. Thomas, known as 'Jet' from his initials. In his late 30s, he is a Baptist minister and professor of theology at Marlboro University in Vermont." Marlboro, where Joey was also employed for a couple of years, is only a college, not a university, and a very small college at that, but I am nit-picking. The *Globe* piece goes on to quote Emmylou on the subject of Jet: " 'He is my master and always calls me up and asks me if I'm taking care of myself. His ministry is among the nomads of our nation.' " I decide not to show this story to Ellie; she might not appreciate thus having been characterized as a gypsy or drifter.

The book section of the *Times* has a review of Gerald Jonas' "Stuttering," a sixty-eight-page volume consisting of a reprint of a one-part *New Yorker* piece. I often wonder how these slim books do. I have never yet had a book published that did not originate as at least a *two*-part *New Yorker* piece. I think I may hold the record when it comes to articles that have appeared in the magazine and have not been reincarnated in hard covers. Setting this record required little effort on my part. It was simply a matter of no publisher's suggesting that the articles in question merited immortalization. I could easily have been persuaded that they did.

September 13

I took the wheel for much of the trip to New York yesterday—a long one, because we went via Concord, New Hampshire, so we could drop off David's gear—on the ground that piloting is less exhausting than navigating. On reaching the city, I found in the accumulated mail a note from Louis Engel, reporting that Harry is dead. Harry was the conductor on the Hudson Division afternoon train of the New York Central that Louis and I regularly rode on the homeward leg of our daily commute from Westchester. I sometimes play backgammon at the Harvard Club these days with a fellow who is said to be important in administering the receivership of the bankrupt Penn Central. If they had put Harry Nestle in charge of the railroad it might not have foundered. He was a courtly soul who administered the 5:33 P.M. local-express with verve and style, and nonstop concern for the welfare of the bodies chronically in his custody. He would always see to it, for instance, that his wards who wished to play backgammon or gin rummy aboard his flagship obtained facing seats; and collecting tickets was to him a matter of far less significance than inquiring about his fares' health, morale, prospects or, in the case of gin-rummy players, luck.

I don't know how old Harry was, but I am dismayed to learn, reading of Robert Lowell's death in today's *Times*, that he was sixty. I had no idea we were the same age. Leopold Stokowski died yesterday, too, but he was ninety-five and older than my father would have been; Stokowski's passing, though, may give pause to people like Cyrus Eaton, who will be ninety-four in December. I learn at the office when I go there that my Eaton Profile is now No. 14 on a roster that is periodically issued at *The New Yorker* of long fact pieces on the bank, and that theoretically at least lists them in the order in which they can be expected to run. One of the most notable aspects of this itemization of priorities is its total meaninglessness. What runs in the magazine and what doesn't is determined solely by an unwritten list that Bill Shawn keeps in his head. My piece on Ocean Grove—that odd New Jersey enclave with its strict Sunday blue laws—must have been way up on the printed list a couple of weeks ago. Now, Pat Crow tells me, it ranks a humble forty-first. It has about as much chance of ever getting into the magazine as anybody does of getting on an airplane after the waiting list has been closed.

One gets more sensitive about numbers and priorities as one grows older. Sheila McGrath, who has long been in charge of office housekeeping and who is to many of us staff writers the most indispensable individual—Shawn, naturally, excepted—at the magazine, comes in to present me with a new kind of press card. We *New Yorker* reporters have cards issued annually by the city's police department, but these are not regular working-press credentials and do not seem to impress anybody. Whenever I have been asked by a department store to furnish some identification and have proudly flourished my police card, I have more often than not been asked further to show something better, like an expired driver's license.

Now we are still to receive police cards, but to supplement these, *The New Yorker* is issuing its own credentials. Sheila ceremoniously hands me mine. It is Number 142. I am outraged. I had thought I would surely rate higher than *that*. Sheila says that when she had the cards made up she anticipated precisely the idiotic vain reaction I have just exhibited, so she began with No. 100 and gave that one to E. B. White, figuring that no one else would object to his being thus signally honored. I certainly don't. But I feel constrained to point out to her that if she proceeded in orderly sequence from her starting point, there are still forty-two people ahead of me on *that* list. Sheila says that most of them don't also get police cards, and to divert me hastily presents me with one of those, which she insists as usual that I fill out in her presence—height, weight, color of eyes, color of hair, and so on. "No more 'brown,' " she says sternly. "Your hair is grey." Can this otherwise estimable woman be color-blind? She is mouthing the same nonsense that my children have lately been ragging me with.

September 14

How extraordinarily feeble I am! If maple trees could talk, I am sure they would say they feel this way after their sap is tapped. I had a strange dream last night. I dreamt that I was back in my old Scarborough house, except that I was sharing it not with my first family but my present one. David and Lexy had fixed over the downstairs playroom, which looked extremely attractive. It had eight fireplaces. I counted them. I spent an hour (in the dream) reminding myself how nice that house was and how lucky I was to own it. Then (still in the dream) I remembered that I no longer owned it after all. I told Ellie (still in dreamland) how pleasant my reverie had been until the hard truth dawned on me.

On awaking, I wondered if the dream had been spurred by *Time*'s current cover story, about the high prices homes are fetching nowadays—the Scarborough place is probably worth three times what we got for it a decade ago—or perhaps by Jinny's having informed me last week that she is planning to sell her co-op in New York, which was bought with the proceeds of the Scarborough sale. E. thinks rather that it stemmed from the mere fact of our having moved back from the country to the city, though she holds out as another hypothesis to be reckoned with the possibility that I am suffering from a delayed attack of delirium.

In any event, I am so short of sap that I stay home all day today. I watched the first game of a crucial series between the Red Sox and the Yankees on television last night, and I begin watching the second one tonight; but E., who is touchingly worried about my convalescence, suggests that perhaps I would recover more quickly if I stopped comporting myself like Archie Bunker. So I turn off the set and crawl into bed. Too bad; a scoreless tie prevails when I quit, and I have to leave it up to the Red Sox in uniform to try to beat the Yanks all by themselves without my help.

In bed, I pick up the latest issue of *The Real Paper*, which features a piece on Living Together. It isn't by Terry, though; he abandoned participation in *that* project because he was temporarily unliving together. That meant that the weekly could not use my little sidebar, which was to have featured a pro-marriage quotation from Yeats that Ellie had kindly given me: "How else but in custom and ceremony are innocence and beauty born?" I haven't looked it up to check it, but I have total confidence in E.'s recall of poetry. I envy her that. My memory is like a sieve. Not only do I not remember poetry, but when men get together and swap dirty jokes, my larder is as bare of ribaldry as of Robert Frost.

September 15

The Red Sox lost, 2–0. *Mea culpa.*

I treat myself to a taxi ride to the office, to conserve my still minimal strength. A fever of 105.6 may not have poached my brain, but it certainly made itself emphatically known to the rest of my body. Sheila McGrath stops by again and tries considerately to distract me from self-pity by making me think about somebody who is worse off—specifically, a young cousin of hers who came to the office recently as a part-time carpenter. He was making some bookcases the other day for a nineteenth-floor editorial office and cut his arm badly with a power saw. (My mind at once inconsiderately leaps to my stricken roommate at the Hyannis Hospital who ran a screwdriver through his palm, and from him to *his* stricken roommate, me.) The young carpenter was bleeding profusely, but he had been around *The New Yorker* long enough to learn what was truly important there and what was not. Thus, his first thought on gashing himself was to stagger upstairs off the nineteenth floor and to urge somebody to get the blood cleaned up below, lest otherwise Mr. Shawn come by and see it and be upset. And Sheila herself, with a keen appreciation of priorities, had left the young man bleeding (he ultimately required eight stitches), and rushed down to mop up the gore just in time.

I will be well enough to travel soon. I draft a letter for Shawn to send to the government of the Republic of South Africa, stating how important it is to *The New Yorker*—I am not at all sure Bill thinks so—for its Mr. Kahn to be granted a visa as soon as possible. But Steve Biko has just died in a Johannesburg prison, as the result—according to the minister of justice in Pretoria—of a hunger strike, and twelve hundred black students were arrested yesterday at Fort Hare for demonstrating in sympathy, and I cannot believe that these sorrowful developments will expedite my being welcomed over there.

Ellie is going to New Mexico next week to interview Georgia O'Keeffe for her book. To assist me in running the household during her absence, she has engaged a young Portuguese woman who speaks no English. However, she is supposed to be fluent in French. It could have been worse. I could have ended up with a young Ukrainian woman who is fluent in Uzbek.

September 16

In the mail, a bill from the Viking Press for the copies of "The China Hands" I ordered, at the bargain price of fifty cents apiece, when the book was remaindered. Being able to buy one's own work at prices lower even than those of a cut-rate secondhand shop is the only advantage I know of that the painful process of remaindering confers. Viking's invoice is addressed to "E. G. Kohn, Jr." That is a variation on my name that only a publisher could come up with. To have one's book removed from circulation is bad enough; to have one's byline concurrently destroyed is scraping the paint off the lily. I send the bill over to Alan Williams at Viking, saying I hope he can arrange to have it settled, since it is clearly not meant for me.

The mail contains also something more soothing to a writer's bruised vanity—a note from Phinizy Spalding, in Athens, Georgia, asking me to review a history of the mint julep for his *Georgia Historical Quarterly*. Whatever the medical staff of the Cape Cod Hospital may believe about my habits, I have never been partial to mint juleps; but although Phinizy says he naturally does not pay for contributions, I leap to accept his invitation. I mean, after all, how often does one get a chance to be able to add an academic journal like that to one's list of credits? The next time somebody asks me to enumerate the various publications I have written for, I can put the *Georgia Historical Quarterly* down right alongside *Playboy*. It should add tone to my curriculum vitae.

September 17

A stay-at-home Saturday. I am half tempted to test my stamina by going up to Baker Field to watch the Harvard-Columbia football game, but Lexy isn't interested. So I look at the Red Sox trying to stay alive against the Orioles, but when the score gets to 11–0 against Boston it is too painful to stay with them, so I switch to Channel 13, where the public-service network has Bert Lance trying to stay alive against a Senate committee that is interrogating him. Senator Charles Percy is his inquisitor when I tune in, and the Illinoisan seems to have a loose grasp of down-South geography. Lance is being quizzed about his personal use of his bank's private plane, and has been talking about flying from Sea Island—he uses the St. Simons Island airport next door, naturally—due south to Jacksonville, Florida. Percy tries, for no discernible reason, to compare that course to one from *Atlanta* to Jacksonville, which seems cartographically irrelevant. And then it develops that Percy is under the impression that Warm Springs is not in Georgia but in Virginia. That Senate committee ought to borrow somebody from *The New Yorker*'s checking department to help it with its research.

September 18

We make love tonight for the first time since my illness. I had begun to wonder if whatever I had might have rendered me impotent, and E. had been talking, not unreasonably, of taking a lover. Now, happily, she won't have to scout around for one.

September 19

The Democratic party run-offs in the city elections are being held today. I vote for Ed Koch over Mario Cuomo and for Carol Bellamy over Paul O'Dwyer. It is the first time that I recall ever having bet on a winning political parlay. I picked Koch because both Frank Sinatra and Jackie Onassis were for Cuomo, and Bellamy because she is the kind of girl wearing glasses who if she were interested in having passes made at her would surely attract them. Also, I have just about had it with Paul O'Dwyer and his eyebrows. Cuomo's defeat is a blow to Governor Carey's prestige, and to all the oldtime Democratic liberals like Averell Harriman and Arthur Schlesinger, who are forever putting their money (and that of the contributors they invite to fund-raising parties) on wrong horses like Mo Udall. I suppose Koch's triumph could benefit Herman Badillo, who was the first of the vanquished aspirants for the nomination to throw him his support. It is in any event an election campaign that has not generated much excitement. The polls are open till 9 P.M. tonight. When Ellie goes over to vote at eight (she doesn't especially want to, but I urge her to set a good civic example to her children), there are no other voters on the scene.

We vote in a school around the corner, named after Robert F. Kennedy. There is a large photomural of him in the lobby. One cannot get to one's secret booth without passing it. Were I a neighborhood Republican, I would argue that the mural ought to be covered up on Election Day or the district ballots cast somewhere else. If billboard advertising can be said to have any effect, then surely the Kennedy face is bound to have an impact—actual or subliminal—on at least one undecided exerciser of his or her franchise, and that would be unfair in a city full of warnings from the board of elections on days like this that electioneering within one hundred feet of the polls is against the law.

September 20

To Dr. Leaf's for a routine dental checkup. Jules says that I have a healing sore inside my mouth, which he attributes to my recent fever. I hadn't even been aware of this added symptom. We talk, as we often do, of his other patient Irwin Shaw, and Jules is astonished to hear that I have never seen a single installment of "Rich Man, Poor Man" on television. I almost do not dare admit that I have also never seen any part of "Roots" or "Mary Hartman, Mary Hartman"; Jules might tell me to find a new practitioner. As I lie back in my chair, trying not to look like a cultural ignoramus, I remember Ellie's chiding me yesterday for wasting so much of my life on TV. I don't know what she was talking about. I only watched part of a tennis match, part of a baseball game, and two football games—hardly six hours in all.

At the office after lunch, Bill Knapp informs me that Shawn has suddenly scheduled the Eaton Profile. My hunch is that he was motivated to do so by a postscript I appended to a note I sent him last week about South Africa— to the effect that the old man would be ninety-four in December, and perhaps in view of that the piece about him shouldn't lie around too long. Unfortunately, Knapp won't be able to guide it to press. His doctor has told him that his blood pressure is too high and that he should avoid stress. So Bill K. is going to skip the tensions of getting other people's pieces into print and instead devote himself for six months exclusively to something that his doctor and he seem to feel is decidedly less stressful—writing long fact pieces of his own. I am no medical expert, not even after my recent absorption in bone-marrow biopsies, but it would never have occurred to me that the proper cure for the strains of editing articles is to write them.

September 21

Ellie takes off for New Mexico.

I find on trying to give instructions to our new household staff that my French is lamentably rusty.

I fill out a new visa application and send it over to the South African Consulate General.

Lunch with Bob Bingham, who joins Shawn nowadays for weekly meetings with an editorial employees' committee that was set up last year to avert a planned unionization of *The New Yorker* salaried staff. Bob says that Shawn and he are surprised to see how concerned the younger checkers at the magazine, men and women still in their twenties, are about pensions. They seem to plan to be checkers until they retire. In the old days, the checking department was usually considered a stepping-stone, for those who were lucky, toward something better and higher at *The New Yorker*—writing, perhaps, or even editing.

Now that Bingham has brought up the subject, more or less, I lodge an informal complaint about a checking mistake in the Talk department of the current issue. There is a piece in it about E. M. Frimbo, the imaginary railroad buff who is of course our own retired editor Rogers Whitaker (Whitaker writes about himself in collaboration with Tony Hiss), in which Frimbo says flatly that Raymond Loewy invented the Coca-Cola bottle. That didn't sound right to me, so I looked up what I had said about the bottle in my *New Yorker* series about the Coca-Cola Company. I had said— this was substantiated at the time, naturally, by the checking department— that the celebrated receptacle was "invented by two employees of the Root Glass Company, of Terre Haute, Indiana," and that "Raymond Loewy once hailed the Coca-Cola bottle as 'the most perfectly designed package in use today.'" If *The New Yorker* was the source for *The New Yorker*'s misapprehension, then *The New Yorker* cannot even read itself correctly.

We dine at my sister Joan's, and I tell her and Olivia about learning from Terry last month that they might have yet another brother. They had both heard about this earlier, I learn to my surprise, and had dismissed it as preposterous. Now, Joan, predictably, waxes both hot and cold: On the one hand, she wants to welcome her new brother to our increasingly extended family; on the other hand, she demands documentation. Joan proceeds to extend the family to an extent I had never dreamed of. She maintains (without furnishing documentation) that my father's father had eleven brothers. I had never before heard of even one. I had always declared that inasmuch as my father's father and my father and I were all only sons, we had no male Kahn relatives on earth until my own sons came along. If Joan knows what she is talking about, there may be hundreds of male Kahns around who are kin. I do not find the prospect electrifying.

Joan is angry, too, that nobody told her I had a piece in *Newsday* about the Panama Canal. It came out when I was in the hospital, and I had other things on my mind then—paramount among them keeping Joan from knowing I was in a hospital. My room, or my corner of the room, would have been so filled with flowers and fruit and unreadable books that it might have been declared a fire hazard. I promise to try to find her a copy of *Newsday*. That would have been easy a decade or so ago, when Dick Clurman left Time, Inc. to become executive editor, or some such exalted rank, of the Long Island daily. Dick was kind enough to enter a complimentary subscription in my name. I went off to Truro for the summer and forgot to leave any forwarding instructions about the paper at the Scarborough post office. When I got back there, I found three months' worth of the paper awaiting me—ninety rolled-up *Newsdays*. It is a profitable journal, thick with advertising; we burned it in lieu of firewood throughout the ensuing winter.

September 22

I have barely arrived at the office when there is a phone call from Evan Cornog, in checking. A Talk piece I did about Dr. Alexander Kwapong, the Ghanaian who is now vice-rector of the United Nations University, in Tokyo, is scheduled to go to press, and how can Evan check it? I did the piece nearly a year ago, and had assumed it was dead. I do not even know if Dr. Kwapong is alive. I suggest to Evan that he call Japan Air Lines and book himself a seat. Last year, I was responsible for his getting a free ten-day trip to London. For *The New Yorker*'s Fourth of July issue in 1976, I had written a long bicentennial article consisting mainly of quotations from English newspapers of 1776 on the progress of the war against the Colonies. I had enjoyed the research immensely. I spent a couple of weeks in London, staying at the Ritz, since the magazine was footing the bill, and spending my days in the North Reading Room of the British Library, which is tucked inside the massive British Museum, on Great Russell Street. Every morning I would go over there and read two-hundred-year-old daily papers—not on microfilm, not photostated, but the venerable rag-paper originals themselves. It was a heady experience. I would have lunch each day at one of the numerous pubs in the neighborhood—bangers or steak-and-kidney pie, washed down by a pint of bitter—and then return to my precious bound volumes of the *Morning Chronicle and London Advertiser*, and the *Gazetteer and New Daily Advertiser* until my eyes gave out.

There seemed to be no way for *The New Yorker* to check the piece—and like all pieces it needed checking; nobody's note-taking is infallible, least of all toward the end of a long day poring over fine print—except to have an emissary return to the British Library. Evan had been assigned the article to check, so he got the trip. I don't know of any other checker's ever being sent abroad. But Evan and I are both aware that he is not going to be dispatched to Tokyo to authenticate a mere Talk story. He will have to do the best he can, anticlimactically, by phone.

September 23

Ellie is back from Santa Fe. She says that Georgia O'Keeffe, now nearing ninety, told her, *inter alia*, that she writes letters to dogs, both dead and alive. I say I hope E. plans to use this in her book, but suspect she does not intend to. I certainly would if I were writing about the artist.

September 24

The House of Representatives has passed a bill raising the mandatory retirement age from sixty-five to seventy. Coincidentally, I receive, today, a dues-renewal notice from the American Association of Retired Persons. I joined the A.A.R.P. a year ago because I thought then that I was going to write a book about the so-called senior citizens of our nation, and I wanted to receive its publications. Now that I have abandoned that project I propose to let my membership lapse, and to become an ex-retired person.

It has been announced that President Carter is going to visit eight countries in November, among them Nigeria. If he goes, he will be the first president to set foot in Africa while in office since Franklin Roosevelt went to Liberia in 1943. Ellie and I and David and Lexy got to both Liberia and Nigeria late in 1970. We spent Christmas that year up north in Nigeria, at Kaduna, where there was evidence both of that country's colonial past (plum pudding on the hotel menu) and of its African lushness (the colorful poinsettia plants visible from our dinner table were not potted but growing out of doors). We had driven to Nigeria—to Lagos, the coastal capital—from Accra, Ghana, stopping off along the way in both Togo and Dahomey, which has since changed its name, in the Ceylonese fashion, to Benin. It was an instructive experience in decolonialization—going from a former British enclave to a part-German one to a French one and then another British one.

The drive along the shore of the Gulf of Guinea had been easy enough, except that the Accra travel agency through which we'd hired a chauffeured car neglected to ascertain whether or not our Ghanaian driver had a visa for

Nigeria. He did not. Nigerians were not then on especially amicable terms with Ghanaians, and the border officials were so seemingly offended by our shepherd's lack of papers that we feared none of us, though we Americans had bona-fide credentials, might be admitted. We did not then realize, being new to Nigeria, that the gratuity we pressed into the palm of the chief keeper of that one of its portals was too small to earn us instant entry. By the time we left the country, though, we had learned some of the ropes, and when a Nigerian customs official demanded a suitable reward for letting us depart, I already had a five-pound note tucked into my hand. I might otherwise have achieved the distinction of being refused both entry into and exit from the selfsame nation within a single fortnight.

We had flown to Kaduna via Nigeria Airways, planning to spend the whole holiday season up north. Before leaving Lagos, I had spent the better part of a day making appointments, for January 2nd, with a half dozen government officials I was eager to talk to. Then I discovered that the airline, out of a no doubt laudable determination to let its employees also spend Christmas and New Year's with their families, simply did not have any flights at all until January 3rd. The thought of having to cancel all those appointments and to try—in Africa, it is not easy—to set up new ones was too much for me, so in Kaduna I got the United States consul (he was a polo player from Yale, and knew how to arrange things) to engage another car and driver to take me back to Lagos overland. It was only a seven-hundred-and-fifty-mile drive, but noteworthy for its potholes. I saw little hope of the battered old vehicle I had hired making the trip intact (it didn't; but it got me as far as Ibadan, where I caught a bus), and after one of a number of breakdowns my driver said that he guessed we'd had it for good this time, because he had run out of bits of wire with which to tie various parts of his engine together. Fortunately, I had a wire coat hanger in my suitcase, and that got us under way again. I half expected after that that the driver would slip me a tip, or at least knock something off the exorbitant fee he was charging me for interrupting his holidays, but it turned out that before he would release my luggage (minus the coat hanger) from his trunk he had quite contrary expectations of his own.

September 25

Today's *Times* has a story about a mysterious new, malaria-like disease—only twenty-seven known cases on earth so far. A few cases have been fatal. The symptoms are fever, chills, muscle pains, lethargy, and sometimes dark urine. Yes, I had them all. The disease, formally known as babesiosis and informally as Nantucket fever (of eighteen cases detected in the United States since 1970, thirteen were traced to Nantucket), is transmitted to humans from the bite of a tick that has earlier feasted on an infected mouse.

Tony told me by phone a couple of days ago that he found two dead mice in our Truro kitchen. Can that be what the doctors were looking for all along, and, if so, did they find it? They never mentioned babesiosis to me. I fish out a clinical resumé that they prepared for me to deliver to Dr. Bishop in New York: "Mr. Kahn is a 60-year-old white man who is admitted after three episodes of high fever associated with shaking chills in the last two days. He does have a history of having had malaria in 1942 [sic] without subsequent problems. Outside of a recent, slight head cold and using alcohol to excess, a pint per day, he had no other complaints [I never complained about the alcohol; *they* did] and had generally been in good health and took no medications. He denied any allergies. [I am not and have never been an allergic.]"

I read on, fascinated. I am unlikely ever again to learn so much about myself. At admission to the hospital, "His temperature was 144 rectally." This I take to be a typographical mistake, I hope. "Pertinent lab and blood cultures were drawn. . . . Intermediate chest PPD was planted. . . . IV fluids were started. He was maintained on Thiamin because of his alcohol abuse. . . . HEENT: Essentially negative. Neck: Supple, no cervical adenopathy. Carotids were 2+ and without bruits. [Now, how many laymen know *that* about themselves?]. . . . No axillary or inguinal adenopathy; no clubbing, cyanosis, or edema of his extremities. Peripheral pulses were full. . . . He was admitted with a diagnosis of fever of undetermined etiology."

Now for the laboratory data:

Admission CBC revealed a HCT of 41, HGB 13.8 WBC 9,800 with 52 segs, 39 bands, 4 lymphs. Platelets were adequate. Sed. rate was 8. Malaria smears X3 were all negative. His urinalysis revealed 1+ Protein, no Glucose or ketones or blood. He had 5-7 WBC's, 5-8 RBC's, 6-100 hyaline casts, no bacteria. Mono spot was negative. Febrile agglutinins revealed Brucella abortis—negative. Typhoid O and Typhoid H [I'm glad they never mentioned typhoid to me at the time], 1-160 on the rapid scale. Paratyphoid B 1-20 on the rapid scale. Proteus ox 19, 1-160 on the rapid scale. Proteus ox 2, negative. Proteus ox K-140. Acute serum was sent for viral studies. His Glucose was 160, BUN 10, Na 133, K 4.4, Cl 95, CO_2 26, SGOT was initially 26—later fell to 20. Uric acid was 6.5, Alk, p'tase 56, Bili. 0.4, Amylase 42, Total Protein 5.9 with an AG ration of 1.3, Ca 8.3, Protein electrophoresis was normal. His urine culture showed no growth. Chest X-ray was completely normal. His IVP was normal except for some prostatic calcifications. EKG except for sinus tachycardia was within normal limits. A bone marrow biopsy is normal.

And the discharge diagnosis:

(1) Fever of undetermined etiology probably secondary to viral infection.

(2) History of malaria.

(3) Alcohol excess.

But what puzzles me, after all those questions about visits to Nantucket and exposure to ticks, is that nowhere in this admirably detailed exploration of my astonishing body does the word "babesiosis" appear, negative or positive. I do not want to pursue this lacuna any further, because it pleases me to believe, now that my teeth have stopped chattering, that I may rate a footnote in some medical history as the first victim of Nantucket fever in the long and colorful history of neighboring Cape Cod.

September 26

It was announced last night that Los Angeles had beaten out New York as the American candidate to be the host city for the 1984 Summer Olympics. I was rooting for neither of them, hoping Iran would be picked, because I have never been to Iran. (The 1980 Games will, of course, be held in the Soviet Union, chiefly in Moscow, which I have been in favor of all along, not having been there since 1957 and being eager to see how much or how little the atmosphere there has changed.) But Los Angeles will be better than New York. I wouldn't especially want to cover the Olympics from my hometown. It would be tantamount to attending a school as a day student while nearly everyone else is a boarder.

Last night, too, we watched a television program about popular songs. Doris Day sang "Ten Cents a Dance." I sang along, word for word. Ellie was flabbergasted; she had never heard of the song. I was flabbergasted that she had not, nor, it developed as I further probed her difficulty, of Ruth Etting, whose number, of course, it originally was. I once actually met Ruth Etting, at a time when I was so passionately in love with her that at the sight of her I nearly swooned. (She did not, to my chagrin, visibly reciprocate.) I must have been about fourteen at that memorable time—Lexy's age today. I wonder how often he has fallen in love to date. My own first such tumble was aboard an ocean liner—either the *Aquitania* or *Berengaria*, I forget which. In that setting so conducive to romance, I was helplessly smitten by a girl whom I followed around from deck to deck like a puppy, which she may have thought I was. She was sweet sixteen, and I was ten.

September 26

A cheerful postcard today from Warren Munsell, who has arrived in France by ship and, at eighty-eight, is romantically touring bygone Normandy battlefields. Warren and Jean Munsell were the last people I said goodbye to when I went off into the Army in the summer of 1941. (Not long afterward, he joined up himself for his second world war.) It seemed only proper that they should be the ones of whom I took my final leave, for they had served me lovingly, and belovedly, in loco parentis. I drove to their farm in New Jersey, and after maudlin farewells headed my car down their narrow humped dirt road, off into the sunset. My eyes were so filled with tears (when it comes to self-pity I can lick any man in the house) that I couldn't see well, and I ran my car inextricably into a ditch. I had to return to their house for another round of goodbyes while they fetched me a tow truck.

Larry Adler is in town from London. He is beginning to make a comeback in the United States after being so long blacklisted from remunerative work. To eke out what he has been able to earn from his harmonica, he has taken up writing in recent years. He turned out a tart review of the English edition of Gill's "Here at *The New Yorker*" for some journal over there, and he wants to show me an abusive note he received shortly afterward on *New Yorker* stationery, signed only with two scribbled initials that Larry cannot make out. The envelope it came in was marked "18th floor," which is mine, but not Brendan's. I cannot decipher the initials, either, and am just as happy not to be able to.

Larry also writes up restaurants for a London magazine, and he is involved in a lawsuit with some establishment which he described, without considering the possible implications, as a "ripoff." He thinks he has a good chance of winning because he has corralled two eminent lexicographers who are prepared to testify on his behalf—much as other litigants have recruited psychiatrists, I am sorry to have to reflect, to bolster their shaky defenses—that "ripoff" does not necessarily mean what everybody else on earth assumes it normally to mean.

September 27

There have been many thefts recently from *The New Yorker*'s eighteenth-floor offices. (That may account for someone's having maligned Adler on our letterhead.) I have twice had rolls of postage stamps lifted from my desk drawer, and with first-class mail up to thirteen cents, this is no trivial matter. Our door to the elevator landing is henceforth to be kept locked. Delivery men from luncheonettes will have to leave their sandwich bags at the receptionist's desk. Because I generally get to the office before Jan Groth arrives, at 10 A.M., to preside over that desk, Carmine Graziano, the boss of our in-house messengers, gives me a key to the newly locked door. It is characteristic of how *The New Yorker* functions that I have no sooner finished thanking Carmine for his considerateness than I discover that the key doesn't work. Pat Crow, who rarely comes in before ten, learns about my key when I cannot resist bragging about it, and argues—editors are forever thinking that writers enjoy special privileges denied to them—that he should have a key himself. I promise to have an exact duplicate of mine made for him.

A call from a public relations woman at the Cooper-Hewitt Museum. They are doing a show on subways, and they want somebody to write an article on the New York City subway system for their catalogue. Do I know anybody who might be interested? They will pay one hundred dollars for two thousand words. Museums thrive on philanthropy, but I do not know of any writer with so broad a streak of generosity. But I take up the matter with Bruce Bliven, knowing that his son Fred is a longtime subway buff. Bruce says that he himself is not interested, and that while Fred would assuredly be, he cannot spell. But Bruce tells me of a literary service I had never before heard of. It seems that the Society of Magazine Writers has a Dial-a-Writer program. If you want something written about something, you can call a certain number and can be put in touch with somebody with certified knowledgeability in that field. Bruce and I agree that the freelance-writing business is at so low an ebb that there is probably someone somewhere who will tackle the local subways for a nickel a word.

I have never joined the Society of Magazine Writers, though I suppose I am eligible (and will be all the more after the *Georgia Historical Quarterly* comes out), but I am a member in good standing of the Authors Guild and of P.E.N., on the governing boards of both of which I have at one time or another served. I have never regarded myself as an effective servitor—in part, I think, because I don't especially like to hear myself talk. But I admire the individuals in our field who are willing to take huge amounts of time off from their writing (or non-writing, which occupies a great deal of any writer's waking hours and is on the whole far more wearying than his productive spells) to meet and discuss and resolve and amend and otherwise try to improve the occupational lot of us all.

Sheila McGrath stops by with the sad tidings that Geoffrey Hellman died last night, at seventy. He had been ill, cancer, but had nonetheless been planning ahead, and Sheila, the Thomas Cook of *The New Yorker*, had just completed arrangements for him to spend part of the summer at a dude ranch out west. It was engagingly typical of Geoffrey, she says, that he had been pleased to learn that the cabin he was going to occupy had, years ago, housed Alice Roosevelt Longworth. Sheila and I go down the hall to the editorial library to ascertain, from Helen Stark, just when Hellman began writing for the magazine. In 1929. His career at *The New Yorker*, though considerably longer than mine, had similarities. He wrote Talk pieces, long fact pieces, and casuals. He covered court games for a bit, and so did I. But he had a specialty or two—rich German-Jewish families (Warburgs, Schiffs, that crowd) for one, and high-class institutions (the Museum of Natural History, the Smithsonian) for another. I have never had a specialty, unless you could count quadrennial coverage, since 1964, of the Olympics, and I sometimes regret being what for want of any better word has to be called a generalist. It would be nice to be recognized as an expert—if recognized only at *The New Yorker*—on something of continuing interest, like, say, Christmas cards or jury-tampering.

September 28

Geoffrey's obit is the lead one in the *Times* today, with a photograph taken in his twentieth-floor office; Alden Whitman has come out of retirement to write it. It's a deservedly commendatory memorial tribute, and contains a nice quote from Bill Shawn about the humor in Geoffrey's fact-writing. Alva Johnston, St. Clair McKelway, Wolcott Gibbs, Joe Mitchell, and Joe Liebling, among others, also had that gifted touch; and I have always tried to follow their lead, feeling that the injection of humor is, or should be, or could be, one thing that sets fact-writing in *The New Yorker* apart from that in most other periodicals. But there are not many *New Yorker* writers left who seem to care about perpetuating that tradition.

Whitman says in the obit, to my surprise, that Hellman and Gill had a falling out after Geoffrey made a speech at the Grolier Society—I didn't hear it, but later Geoffrey let me read it—taking issue with Brendan's characterization of Harold Ross in his *New Yorker* book. I have no idea what their relationship was—the eighteenth floor is too far away from the twentieth for reverberations to stretch—but I made a speech at the Century along much the same dissenting lines, and Brendan and I are still on speaking terms. Of course, he wasn't in the audience that night, and may not even yet have heard of my apostasy.

Bob Shaplen writes, from Hong Kong: "I forget if I told you that I had run into the South African information minister here, who told me that you wouldn't be returning to Joburg. He didn't seem to feel you were very friendly. I told him I was friendly with everyone, and he said they might let me in." This last sentence is, of course, an attempt of Bob's to inject humor into fact-writing, but that is not his forte to begin with, and in any event I do not find my exclusion from Johannesburg a mirthful topic. But what in the world was Herr Doktor C. P. ("Connie") Mulder, the minister of information and my personal South African *bête noire* (I had better make clear that he is a white Afrikaner) doing in Hong Kong in the first place? My guess is that he was on his way to or from mainland China, where he was hoping to make a deal with Peking to man the barricades alongside Pretoria should the Soviet attack that the South African government has for so long been scaring its subjects about ever actually come to pass.

September 29

Colonel George W. Hinman, Jr., has died, at eighty-five. I am surprised to learn from his obituary that he stayed in the Army until 1953, and after retiring became secretary, librarian, and historian of the Washington Army and Navy Club. I should have thought that job would have gone to a West Pointer. Colonel Hinman was not even a Regular Army officer. He was a one-time Hearst correspondent, and it was probably because of his journalistic background that he got the wartime job he was holding when I first met him. He was in charge of the public relations section of Second Service Command Headquarters, a part of the Army Service Forces, downtown at 90 Church Street, and 1st Lieutenant Virginia Rice, Women's Army Corps, was one of his underlings. I feel a certain sense of retribution in realizing from the obit that Hinman never made brigadier general. That may have been Jinny's involuntary doing; there was never any question in my mind that he was the reason she never made captain.

The public relations offices of the Second Service Command, early in 1945, were on the same floor, at 90 Church, as those of Army Ground Forces, where I was assigned. Jinny and I had begun dating, and when not engaged in pressing duties (our duties were rarely pressing, save for one day when she was basely charged with having lost an entire band somewhere in New England), we would visit one another's chambers. Colonel Hinman took a paternalistic view of our commuting. Indeed, when it seemed for a moment that Jinny's father might not make it down from New Hampshire for our wedding, he offered to give the bride away. General Joseph W. Stilwell, whom Chiang Kai-shek had finally succeeded in dislodging from China, had been put in command of Army Ground Forces. I knew Stilwell only slightly, but he had one trait that I deemed superlative: Unlike a couple of his predecessors, Generals Ben Lear and Jacob Devers, for whom I had been tapped to ghostwrite speeches, Stilwell insisted on writing his own.

I don't know whether Colonel Hinman knew Stilwell at all, but he disliked Vinegar Joe intensely, as I suppose any loyal old Hearst operative in that era naturally would have; and one day, in Jinny's hearing, her colonel made a statement about Stilwell so outrageous and scurrilous that on her next visit down the hall she repeated it to me and to my colonel, Edward Hope Coffey. Well, one thing led to another. Hope passed the story on to our headquarters in Washington, and it quickly moved up through channels to the pinnacle of the Pentagon. In due course, Colonel—never-alas-to-become-General—Hinman was severely dressed down by his superiors, who may very well have agreed with his opinion of Stilwell but, now that General Marshall had been apprised of the conflict between two of the three main branches of his forces (the Army Air Forces, as far as I know, never got into this act), had to make a show of maintaining order in the ranks. Colonel Hinman's response to his own reprimand was predictable: He not only took out his resentment on Jinny, but he also had her desk and chair and phone taken out of her office. Her hopes of promotion vanished with her furniture. Moreover, she was informed that while on duty, however vilely she might elect to comport herself after office hours, she was under no circumstances to communicate in any manner, form, or shape with any New York representatives of the Army Ground Forces, even though she might, as was by then indeed the case, be married to one of them. It is a tribute to the resourcefulness and sheer guts of our fighting men that we won the war despite all this kind of carryings-on at home.

September 30

Our car has been acting up again. It seems to fill up all the time with exhaust fumes, and neither Ellie nor I, to the best of my knowledge, is feeling the least bit suicidal. I take the ailing wagon over to Skipper first thing this morning and tell him, before he can make his own expert diagnosis, that my hunch is that there's a crack in my exhaust pipe. Skipper—who may be in the throes of an identity crisis; he has taken to calling *me* "Doctor"—puts the car up on a rack. I don't have any exhaust pipe. Skipper says that he doesn't want to sell me anything, but that the muffler the exhaust pipe would be attached to if there were one is a terribly sick muffler, and that he would advise its being replaced before all hope is lost. Meaning no disrespect to the doctors who attended me so tenderly at Hyannis, I suspect Skipper would readily have determined what was wrong with me over Labor Day, and wouldn't have charged as much, either. Of course, it might be hard for *The New Yorker* to get reimbursed under its medical coverage for the ministrations of a professional whose principal institutional affiliation is Mobil.

Jerry Mason sends me a copy of a book he's about to publish—John Hammond's memoirs. It has been thirty-seven years since a Profile I wrote on John appeared in the magazine, but although I've seen him from time to time in between, his book provides the first enlightenment I've had since 1940 about a couple of small points. I had mentioned in the Profile how John had roguishly invited to a jazz concert at his mother's elegant town house (she was a Vanderbilt scion) some of his musical friends and some of his stately relatives, notable among the latter his aunt, the dowager Mrs. W. Murray Crane; and how while they were all seated on frail gilded chairs Mrs. Crane's had collapsed and the singer Mildred Bailey, a woman of girth, had turned to her and chortled, "How'm I doin'?" In the autobiography, John now says that "like all subjects of Profiles I was not shown Jack's piece until it was published" (that was true), and that when the article came out

Mrs. Crane had phoned him and was furious. It could have been worse; she could have phoned *me*. John also reveals that as a result of the piece his then employer gave him a fifty-dollar-a-week raise—not bad for 1940—which was more than I got out of it.

The second part of my Eaton Profile is going to press. (He was fifty-seven in 1940, a young man in the prime of life.) Gardner Botsford has assumed the editing of the piece. While I am in his office going over queries, a messenger brings in a proof of an obit on Geoffrey Hellman that Gardner has written for next week's *New Yorker*. He lets me read it. The obit, a touching one, says that Geoffrey wrote more pieces for the magazine than, it is safe to say, anybody else ever will. That, in a magazine devoted to understatement, doesn't sound to me safe to say at all. I do not expect, like Cyrus Eaton, to hit ninety-four, but there are writers hanging around the magazine who are still in their twenties, and I ask Gardner how he can be certain that none of them will ever be old enough or prolific enough to outmatch Geoffrey's splendid output. I do not add that I am not sure I have not already outmatched it. Oh well, this is a checking problem, and the statement will no doubt be appropriately qualified before the piece gets into print.

October 1

I have promised Ellie to escort her on an art gallery safari this afternoon. We begin with the works of Eleanor Antin, the young Californian whose oeuvre includes a series of photographs of herself in the nude, and of hundreds of pairs of empty shoes. Eleanor A.'s offering today is composed of a two-hour television program she devised, having to do with an Israeli commando attack somewhere in Egypt, with herself playing all the parts; and also of a bunch of large cutouts, among them the cross section of an airplane. My Eleanor says this stuff is experimental, not commercial, but Antin tells me that anybody who would like to buy her airplane is welcome to; she will be glad to create a plastic bubble to enclose it. When I ask her how much she wants for the object, she turns coy and says I will have to discuss that with the gallery owner. It would be too big for our apartment in any event.

We press on. At one brand-new gallery I am offered an antique New England chandelier, now electrified, at the bargain price of $15,000. The proprietor also has a fine collection of modern paintings—Stella, Truitt, Gottlieb, and so forth. E. inquires after their provenance. "All on loan," says the proprietor. On loan from whom or where?, E. wants to know. "Well, they're actually mine," says the proprietor. I will never really get to comprehend the workings of the art world.

Ellie and I are heading back to the Cape tomorrow. Her mother is going to stay with Lexy; we are going to spend this Indian-summer month—experimentally, but also, if our work goes well, commercially—in Truro. Joan and Olivia come over for a farewell dinner, Joan characteristically toting a reticule laden with food for us to nibble at en route—candy, soybean nuts, Life Savers, God knows what all. She seems to be under the impression that without her Care package we might starve to death in Rhode Island. As usual, she is furious at her employers. Harper & Row, she announces, have given Clare Boothe Luce a fifty-thousand-dollar advance for her memoirs, and isn't that dreadful? I say that it sounds like a reasonable sum to me.

Joan says that nobody around these days has ever heard of Clare Boothe Luce. I say that in this era of fragmentary education, nobody has heard of anybody. (Dan Lang has a piece in the current *New Yorker*, for instance, revealing that a lot of German teenagers are no more familiar with Hitler than with Charlemagne.) To bolster my argument, I ask Lexy if he has ever heard of George C. Marshall. Negative. Joan says it is unfair thus to quiz a fourteen-year-old, and soon all present are sore at me, as though I had given Lexy a hotfoot or, worse still, a failing grade in History IIIB. Lexy isn't mad, though, because before the meal is over we agree to skip a recital at the 92nd Street Y by a Uruguayan guitarist whom I have never heard of and, instead, to watch "The African Queen" on television. Lexy has heard of that all right.

October 3

I did once before spend a couple of post-season months in Truro. But I was alone, not even a dog to share the premises with, and although I made several off-Cape jaunts to visit N., I was thoroughly miserable most of the time, revelling in self-pity as only a person can who has no one truly to blame for his predicament but himself. This time I will have both Ellie and Rainbow with me, and I am euphoric as we get under way. We leave Joan's goodies with Lexy, as a goodbye present.

At Stamford, we make a detour to take in an exhibit (no elevators) of the art of Reuben Nakian, nearly all of whose works on display are steeped in mythological sex—Leda and the swan, Europa and the bull, a nymph and a goat. I am surprised to see among all these satyric offerings a sculptured bust of Harry Hopkins, and when I call this to E.'s attention, she says, "Now who was Harry Hopkins?" Clare Boothe Luce and George Catlett Marshall knew who Harry Hopkins was. But at the time that FDR won his third term, Ellie was only twelve.

Early in 1945, while General Marshall was chief of staff, Jinny and I once inadvertently delayed this nation's prosecution of the war effort for a few seconds. She went out to Governors Island one day to confer with an aide de camp to a three-star general. While there, she suddenly remembered she had to phone me about something, and asked the aide if there was an unoccupied office nearby that she could call from. He said his boss wasn't around, and waved her into the general's office, where she was confronted by a battery of phones. She picked one up at random, but instead of getting an operator, she got the brisk, self-identifying voice of a man onto whose emergency line she had innocently stumbled. "Marshall," the voice said. Jinny set the phone gently into its cradle and tiptoed out to tell the aide what had happened. When we saw him a month or so afterward, he was still trembling.

Today's *Times* has an interesting article about the state of the United States Military Academy. The Pentagon, of all places, has accused West Point of being too solemn an institution, and academically inadequate to boot. I did a piece on West Point years ago for the old *Holiday* magazine, and not long afterward Lieutenant General Leslie Groves, who had been in charge of the Manhattan Project when the atom bomb was built, came around to *The New Yorker* to thank me. But the receptionist on duty had apparently never heard of him—has anyone ever heard of *anybody?*—and gave him short shrift. The general took his rebuff more graciously than I would have. Indeed, a few years later, after I had written a *New Yorker* Profile on General Lucius Clay, Groves sent me a letter in which he said, "I always enjoy reading your articles dealing with military men and experiences. In my opinion, you stand at the peak of all our writers in portraying the true spirit of the American soldier, both on and off the battlefield." If I had had a fan club, I would have appointed General Groves commander-in-chief of it.

The most spectacular fan I had was a fellow I met at a cocktail party, who, on hearing my name, proceeded to quote at great—and, near as I could make out, accurate—length from half a dozen pieces I had written, some of them decades earlier. I was enchanted. I had never come across anybody with such stunning literary taste and such selective powers of retention. I could not drag myself away from him, as he went on reciting whole paragraphs. I invited him to dinner the following week. It was only later that I learned he was a notorious *idiot savant*, who remembered everything he had ever read by anybody.

After we stop for lunch, Ellie takes the wheel and asks me to read aloud to her, to keep her alert. All we have with us is the *Partisan Review*, which I fear, if this is a typical issue, will have precisely the opposite effect. I try a short story, but it starts putting me to sleep. E. says parenthetically that when her father's eyesight began to fail, her mother would often read aloud to him, and claimed she could drowse while doing so; she got in some good slumber while ploughing through Gibbon's "Decline and Fall." I switch to some book reviews, one of which concludes with the statement that "the book manages to stand very erect on its own two feet." E. says sensibly that if the *Partisan Review* and I can't come up with anything better than that we might as well listen to the radio.

At Hyannis, we detour again, to have a typewriter repair man take a look at the sicker of her two machines. While I am waiting and walking Rainbow, a woman stops to admire our large mongrel, and asks what breed she is. I lie; I say she is a Belgian shepherd, which she is only half of. The woman then says, in dead seriousness, "You know, a dog is man's best friend." She ought to submit her collected thoughts to the *Partisan Review*.

October 5

Everybody in Truro is astonished that we are back. Tony comes by in his van, which breaks down on arrival, or at any rate won't start up again. I hope its malfunction isn't permanent. A friend of Terry's left a crippled Volkswagen van at our house a few years back, and we bought it, for twenty-five dollars, as a toy for David and Lexy, who had great fun playing house in it and, without being subjected to parental remonstrance, smashing all its glass. But by the time they outgrew it, its tires had vanished, and we couldn't figure out how to dispose of the battered hulk. Tony found the solution; he discovered that you can break a Volkswagen into small, transportable pieces with a sledgehammer.

October 6

Humankind can, fundamentally, be divided into two groups: people who save things and people who don't. When I am doing research for a book or a long magazine piece, I am profoundly grateful to subjects who keep scrapbooks and correspondence files and random memorabilia. Perversely, I save practically nothing myself; the souvenirs I have attempted to retain from my travels have not fared especially well. There was the lovely coiled stuffed cobra that Ellie and I brought home, not without difficulty, from Taipeh. We had bought it at a sidewalk bazaar, in that part of the city where, late at night, if you wish to eat snake, you select the one that appeals to you from a writhing cage-full and have it cooked on the spot. There was the lovely zebra skin we lugged back home from Tanzania, and proudly hung in our Manhattan stairwell. (We had a teenage girl travelling with us in Africa, to look after David and Lexy while E. and I were working. The girl was a forthright ecologist and objected strenuously to our buying the skin. She said we were contributing to the destruction of wild life. We pointed our to her that the night before, with unabashed relish, she had dined on zebra steak.) Rainbow ate the zebra skin. She also ate the cobra. It is a tribute to my patience and my love of tamed wild life that I did not propose eating her. In Taiwan, that would have been quite acceptable. A Taipeh taxi I was riding in once barely missed hitting a plump black dog—one not unlike Rainbow in color and size. The cab driver could not comprehend my agitation. He said if he *had* hit the dog, it would simply have been eaten that night, instead of the following month.

I rarely, moreover, keep copies of my own letters. There never seems to be a sheet of carbon paper handy when I need it. This sloppy habit is certainly not congenital. My sister Joan saves everything. She is a nonpareil accumulator. If her cluttered apartment somehow found itself adrift at sea, all she would need to survive comfortably for a couple of years would be a can opener. Last week, I learn today on receipt from her of a batch of yellowed old letters, she had to let some electricians enter one of her closets. To enable them to squirm in, she was obliged to remove some old cardboard boxes, in one of which whe was agreeably surprised to discover some old letters of mine, written to various members of the family as long ago as 1938. Here, for instance, is a July, 1942, V-mail letter from a soldier in Australia to his mother—a technician fourth class who seemed oddly detached from military life:

> It looks at the moment as if I'll continue to serve as the General's secretary and in addition (1) be a *Yank* correspondent and (2) be a *New Yorker* correspondent and (3) put out a newspaper for the local troops.

To show what gung-ho jungle fighters we were going to be when we reached New Guinea, we called the journal—a mimeographed weekly with a captive-audience readership of fifteen thousand—*The Stalker*. Our mail, of course, was censored. We couldn't say exactly where the division was stationed, and when we headed north toward Port Moresby, I tried to convey this information guardedly by writing home, "The last issue of *The Stalker* came out on Friday. We hope to resume publication some time again, circumstances permitting." We never did. I had travelled by train from Adelaide to Melbourne, where General MacArthur then had his headquarters, to receive official permission to send pieces back to *The New Yorker*, and had returned bearing an authorization signed personally by MacArthur—a precious document that, alas, I neglected to save.

The letter goes on:

> . . . I sent Shawn a collect cable last night, which amounted to a minor kind of triumph. I had made tentative arrangements when I went up to GHQ for sending collect service (non-press) messages, but thought nothing would come of them. Last night I went to the Post Office in town (telephone, telegraph, etc., are all handled by the government post office, as in England), wrote out a cable, handed it through the teller's gate and said to the teller amiably that I thought he

might have my name on a list of people who were authorized to send collect cables to one specific address in the U.S. "No," he said sourly, "we don't have your name." I became indignant then and pointed out to him that he couldn't very well tell since I hadn't yet told him what my name was. That argument broke him down, and he consented to look at a card file, where, to his surprise and mine, he found my name. Just to spite him, I proceeded to add ten more words to the cable.

It is now time for me to go to supper, play a nightly fiercely waged game of Monopoly, and, I am afraid, clean a rifle.

Here along with my return address is my serial number: 32160924. How can I have forgotten it? I swore to the corporal who presided over my early days of basic training that I would commit it permanently and ineradicably to memory. I wonder if he ever made sergeant. Remembering *him* well, I hope not. When I was anointed a warrant officer, I shed my old enlisted man's identification and acquired a new number, which I swore to myself I would always remember. W211 - - -. Well, no matter; it was a long time ago.

Here is a letter written that same month to my mother by Jerome Weidman, who was editing my very first book, "The Army Life," for Simon and Schuster. I must have been complaining, as even authors of more than one book sometimes do, that my publishers were paying insufficient attention to my opus, for Jerry was instructing my mother to advise me, "The mighty moguls of the Inner Sanctum know about General MacArthur's interest in the book and are determined to exploit it to the hilt, which, if you know the Inner Sanctum, is something." Then "See Here, Private Hargrove" began to climb up the best-seller lists, and the Inner Sanctum moguls stuck their sword back in its scabbard.

My mother was a writer, too, though she was only once published—a short story in *Story* magazine. When she died, in 1952, she left behind the manuscript of a novel, touchingly autobiographical, for which my sisters and I unavailingly tried to find a publisher. I'm sure Joan has it somewhere, and I'm glad she has saved it.

Here is a wartime letter from me to my sister Olivia, who had written me that she might be going to work for *Newsweek*, which was then owned by Vincent Astor. I am dropping names, mentioning all the people I know at that magazine, and I conclude, "and Mary Cushing Astor once served me tea on the Nourmahal, though I have no doubt she has totally forgotten the incident." So, in 1977, have I.

The weather has been beautifully clear all day, as Indian a summer as anyone could ask for, but Tony predicts frost for tonight. Ellie and I rush down to David's garden, and in the fading light try to harvest his remaining crops. We garner a big mess of peppers and two fat pumpkins, but his watermelons haven't ripened yet, so we leave them to their gelid fate.

October 8

More relics of the past have emerged from my sister's capacious closet. In the latest batch of snippets is a letter I wrote to my sister Olivia in 1938, when she was at college and I was a veteran *New Yorker* reporter, with a whole year's service racked up. "Yesterday afternoon I wandered up to the Polo Grounds to do a piece on Tom Thorp, a big football referee," I reported fraternally. "Since I'd never seen a pro game before, I asked him if I could hang around, and he said sure. So when the game began and the officials walked out on the field, I walked right out with them and planted myself on the Giants' bench. It was all pretty dull and I left after the first half."

Having no independent recollection, naturally, of this experience, I telephone *The New Yorker* office and ask Helen Stark, our knowledgeable librarian, to see what, if anything, the magazine carried about my front-line seat. Helen checks and says that we never ran a word about it. I probably should have hung around for the second half.

Six tennis players materialize today! It seems almost like real summer. I play four sets altogether—my most violent exertion since I left the hospital. Afterward, Ellie and I drive to Provincetown for dinner with the Palmer Williamses, taking along Barbara W.'s dog, a German shepherd which she picked up in a park, and which she says she can't leave alone in their house because it chews everything up. While we are eating, the dog is left alone in their car, a good deal of the upholstery of which, we find on our return to it, the voracious beast has consumed.

October 9

Gale warnings have been posted, or whatever it is that one does with them. It rains hard all day, at the end of which—there is more off-season social life in Truro than I'd anticipated—we go to dinner at the Herman Badillos'. Herman is exceedingly discouraged about New York City, and while as everybody knows he is supporting Ed Koch's candidacy, it is clear that he regards himself as the superior of the two. When he and Koch wander around courting voters, it is Herman, he says, who is the more often recognized—to the extent even that men kiss his hand and women fling themselves upon him. How untidy a politician's life must be!

Herman also believes that there are important distinctions to be made among various categories of wrongdoing. He thinks, if I follow him correctly, that criminal acts politically motivated should be given special consideration—that, for instance, people who blow up airplanes should be judged less harshly than those who hold up candy stores. I am not altogether won over to this point of view.

October 10

The skies have cleared, the air is washed and pure again. The day is so nice that when Tony and Judy stop by with young Ian he can run around without any clothes on. I notice for the first time that my grandson hasn't been circumcized. I thought most doctors did that now to most male babies, for hygienic reasons, but it has been a long time since I have been directly involved in such affairs. Tony has a job, pumping gas at a Mobil station. He hopes this apprenticeship will facilitate his obtaining a semi-annual inspection sticker for his rickety van. When I take my own car in to be inspected, I learn that there is a crack in the new muffler-exhaust-pipe combination I paid eighty-eight dollars to have installed in New York, and also that I have a leak in my radiator and am in need of a freeze plug, whatever that may be.

Amnesty International has won the Nobel Prize for Peace. The papers speak of how little known the organization has heretofore been and how well known it will now become. It was *really* little known when I first heard about it, back in 1969, and went to its headquarters in London to gather material for a *New Yorker* Profile on the organization. If Amnesty was indeed uncelebrated until yesterday's kudos, that does not speak too well for the magazine or for me.

I am telephoned by a young woman who works for *More* magazine. My Eaton Profile is running in *The New Yorker*, and *More* has spotted a mistake in the second part. I happened to mention Gay Talese's book about the New York *Times*, "The Kingdom and the Power," but I called it "The Power and the Glory." The young woman thinks this is the most appalling gaffe she has ever heard of, and demands to know who was responsible for it. I was, of course, though that is the sort of thing our sharp-eyed checkers are supposed to catch and correct. This kind of mistake, actually, is the easiest to make; I was so sure I had the right title that I never bothered to look it up, and it sounded correct to the checkers, too. The root responsibility for the goof-up, I reflect after *More* hangs up, gloatingly, probably belongs to all the pious folk on earth who cajole their fellow men and women into mouthing the words of the Lord's Prayer so often that these become mere rote, with no particular meaning. Someday some *New Yorker* writer, having occasion to allude to the Pledge of Allegiance, will throw in the words "one nation individual" and this will slip by a checker and *More*, if it is still around, will get to gloat again.

October 12

Rain again. This Indian-summer weather I've heard so much about over the years is transitory.

We are visited by Martha Hamer, who cleaned for us last summer. She is looking for her grandmother's prayer mat. Martha says she knelt on it while doing floors. I wonder if her grandmother could get the title of Gay Talese's book straight. Martha, who is twenty-four, is leaving this week with a girl friend for Colorado, or maybe New Mexico or Arizona, they don't quite know which. Both have just split with their boy friends, and are free to travel; the only major non-territorial decision they have to make is which of their beat-up Volkswagens they should gamble on to get them wherever they are going. I am envious of the carefree attitude so characteristic of so many of their contemporaries. But don't these young people ever feel insecure?

While I was working this afternoon, sitting at the kitchen table, a couple of feet from our picture window, a large brown rabbit hopped across the brick terrace outside it and pressed its nose against the glass. I had happened to spot it approaching, and kept perfectly still. Up against the glass wall, the rabbit looked inside and saw me, and it apparently had never seen such a sight in its life before, because it fled in panic. The dog slept through the whole encounter.

At dinner, *à deux*, Ellie and I jointly lament our inability ever to pick up a page of our own writing, no matter how often we may have gone over it, without finding still something else that seems to warrant changing. Is this true too of *haiku* poets? I suggest, to make E. feel better, that any writer worth his or her salt knows there is no such thing as perfection; and that if he gazed upon his own output and didn't alter it, he would be saying, in effect, foolishly and arrogantly, that it was perfect.

October 14

The Boston *Globe* has a story on babesiosis. It is fatal only to people who've had their spleen removed before they contract it. Nobody at the hospital, to the best of my recollection, ever asked whether or not I was spleenless. (For whatever it may be worth to me—my life, conceivably—I still have my spleen.) Two new babesiotic symptoms are cited in this latest account of the scourge: anemia and lethargy. I certainly had both of *them*.

Very high winds and heavy rains all day today. At 10:30 P.M., after Ellie and I have gone to bed, Rainbow barks. I go downstairs to see what has got her worked up, and can find nothing. I go outside. There is a strange, eerie roar, not pulsating, no ups or downs, but steady and scary. It is the ocean. In thirty years I have never heard it growl like this before. The combination of new moon, high tide, and near-hurricane-force winds has made the sea get as agitated as a startled rabbit. Ellie and I throw some clothes on, grab a flashlight, and drive down to the beach. I park the car facing the road, so that if we have to make a quick getaway, we can save a couple of seconds. (My volunteer-fireman background is making its presence known.) We can't see much—no stars, no moon, but the roar is there, all right, though, curiously, not as terrifying, close to the water, as it seemed in our front yard. On the way home, we somehow get into a debate as to whether the Atlantic or the Pacific is the more awesome ocean. We concur finally that discussing such a difference is as pointless as arguing about the degree of killing power of various nuclear weapons.

October 15

The Boston *Globe*, our morning staple for news on the Cape, is a refreshing alternative to the *Times*, but occasionally it upsets me. Yesterday, for instance, one of its sports columnists sent in a piece from Los Angeles, about ten great moments in the history of the World Series. The ninth alluded to the deciding game of the 1926 encounter between the Yankees and the Cardinals. "Grover Cleveland Alexander, 39 years old and worn out," the item went, "is dragged from a barroom to pitch to Tony Lazzeri with the bases loaded, two outs and the Cards ahead, 3–2, in the seventh. He strikes Lazzeri out." Yes, he did, but who was there who can forget that Push 'Em Up Tony first lashed a screaming line drive into the left-field seats, foul by, in my memory, mere inches, that could have made him an all-time hero? Anyway, it is grossly unfair to the hallowed memory of Lazzeri to intimate that he was fanned by a drunk. Baseball was strictly an afternoon pastime back then, and the *Globe* man has the approach of a night-game sportswriter. Ellie didn't grasp what I was muttering about while I read the column. Why should she have? She wasn't alive in 1926.

Tony and Judy are working tonight, guitar and voice, at the Duck Creek Inn in Wellfleet, and Ellie and I are supposed to help pad the house, inasmuch as they are being paid a percentage of the take—one-fifth of all drink sales. We can think of nobody around in the off season to bring along except Joan Colebrook and Bob Lifton, who are ideologically poles apart; perhaps it is the role of the liberal in contemporary society to bridge such gaps to the strains of "Lazy Bones," "Stop Breaking Down," and "Respect Yourself." The kids strike me—I am unabashedly biased—as having great stage presence. The management reports to them at the end of the evening that bar sales have totalled one hundred and twenty dollars, which isn't bad, considering that there were no waiters or waitresses on the scene and you could have sat there all night for nothing.

October 16

Today's Sunday *Times* magazine says *The New Yorker*'s business side is inviting two hundred writers and editors to the Algonquin this week to celebrate the hotel's seventy-fifth anniversary. I wonder how it will be decided which members of the editorial side are to be asked. Shawn, certainly; Bill's photograph is used, along with Harold Ross', to illustrate the *Times* piece. I am not on the list, although—unknown to the hotel's incumbent proprietors—it may be that, owing to my mother's attachment to the establishment, I have been patronizing it longer than any other person now connected with the magazine. Following her hospitable lead, I used to take my own children there when they were quite young, as Frank Sullivan once reminded me in a letter from Saratoga Springs—"I trust your scion got back that balloon that went ceiling-ward in the Algonquin when you were having a family lunch there." Terry didn't, but although the Algonquin hasn't changed much over the years, the balloon has been removed.

Ellie and I forgot to bring a hi-fi to Truro this month, so she has been taping FM radio music broadcasts in the morning and playing them back at dinner. The radio is only a few feet from where I work, and as a result there is a good deal of extra percussion on our tapes—my typewriter keys clicking away in the background. My ear tells me that I have an excellent sense of stenographic rhythm, and that I am adding considerable zest to the works of Bach, Handel, and the rest of the captured gang. I don't want to sound immodest, but while listening to the tapes I believe I play the typewriter better than, back in the pre-war days on East Fourth Street, I played the drums.

October 17

The *Times* ran an interview yesterday with Harry Oppenheimer, who is in New York. I get a letter from him today, written in London. He says he is glad to hear that I have reapplied for a visa to South Africa and that he hopes to see me when I get there. Am I correct in reading between the lines that he is going to do something to expedite my admittance?

Harriet Walden calls from *The New Yorker*. She has been conferring with our circulation people about Tony's subscription, which he told me he hadn't been receiving. The circulation people have told Harriet that their computer says the magazine has been going to Tony at South Pamet Road, which they regard as the key part of his address. We all have post office boxes, and it is totally irrelevant, as far as the receipt of anything is concerned, on what road one does or does not reside. But of course one cannot hope to explain this to a computer or to anybody who puts his trust in one.

We dine tonight in Provincetown with the Jim Thomsons. Diana has just finished knitting a sweater for my grandson Jaime, and throughout the meal is working away admirably at another one, for my son Joey. It would be nice to think that she is planning to continue right up along the generational line. The last person who knitted a sweater for me was N., but I sense disapproval on Ellie's part whenever I wear that one.

It is cool tonight, so E. and I decide to sleep downstairs. Our regular bedroom is upstairs. With the house otherwise empty, we have plenty of options. We are like people with two homes, a summer one and a winter one, except that both of ours happen to be under the same roof. Peter Shenk came by yesterday, incidentally, to give me an estimate on reshingling half the roof, since we can't afford a complete job at the moment. For an additional mere five hundred dollars, he is going to put insulation under the half he attends to. He couched this proposal in such sacrificial terms that I felt on accepting it I was getting away with murder.

October 18

The sun is out this morning, for a change. It looks very handsome.

We go to Ding Watson's for dinner and get back to the house just in time to watch Reggie Jackson hit his third home run in the sixth and deciding game of the Series. Then comes, inevitably, all that silly business about pouring champagne over people's heads. I suspect that this tradition sets the champagne industry back millions of dollars every year. Who would want to serve at a wedding reception or other similarly elegant affair the same stuff that sweating athletes throw all over one another in locker rooms? I saw a television interview with Jackson the other day, and he came across as a softspoken, reflective, exceedingly interesting person—the antithesis of what I would have thought he'd be like. I am sorry he wasn't asked to express his views on the idiocy of sloshing around champagne.

October 19

The November issue of *Ms.* magazine arrives, in it the piece Ellie did, after our Alaska trip, on Kay Fanning and her troubles with the Anchorage *Daily News*. The only illustration on the page containing Ellie's piece is a photo of a woman who murdered her husband because he kept beating her up. The cover of this *Ms.* is obviously aimed at newsstand sales, and is nearly on a par with the covers of, say, *Gallery* or *Saga*, featuring, as it does, a picture of a male hand inside a female bosom, and such come-on titles as Sexual Harassment on the Job and How to Stop It, A Lover's Guide to Living Together, The Loneliness of a Teenage Feminist, The Uncensored Poet, and Woody Allen: Schlemiel as Sex Maniac. And even for a piece with no sexual connotations *Ms.* has found a gamey title: Is Money a Social Disease? I should have thought that this sexist approach to editorial content was directly opposed to everything the women's-lib movement is supposed to be all about. Probably the root trouble at *Ms.* is that the magazine, from its outset, has had a lot of editors but, unlike *The New Yorker,* and other successful magazines that aim at the mind instead of the crotch, no Editor.

My bills arrive from the Cape Cod Hospital. Not including physicians' charges or the twenty-seven dollars for my brief stopover at the AIM clinic, they come to more than a thousand dollars, for a four-day confinement. Most of this, fortunately, will be covered by *The New Yorker*'s group insurance policy. But how in the world do poor people cope with illness?

October 20

South Africa has imprisoned seventy black leaders and shut down three black newspapers. This latest repressive act has impelled even *Die Transvaler,* a staunch pro-government Afrikaans daily, to protest. Helen Suzman is quoted as saying that the jailing of moderate blacks has left a vacuum for "wild men" of Soweto to fill. I wonder how long Prime Minister Vorster can keep the lid on his simmering pot. Longer, I daresay, than much of the rest of the world would like to hope. If I were over there, maybe I could make a more educated guess. But with all the recent turmoil in that country, Ellie now doesn't *want* me to go there. I would go nonetheless if they would have me.

October 22

We took off yesterday for Concord, New Hampshire, to participate in Parents' Day festivities at St. Paul's. Concord is the hometown of Franklin Pierce, New Hampshire's only president. There is a college named after him at Rindge, which was Jinny's hometown, and which she and I used to visit frequently when we were married. Driving to New Hampshire, I got to thinking about my first father-in-law, Harold Rice, who, while a selectman of Rindge and one of that small community's leading citizens, never really seemed to have any professional or occupational calling. He mostly puttered around, doing odd jobs, much the same sort of life Tony is now leading on Cape Cod. I am strictly urban. Can my son's attachment to and activities on the Cape stem from his maternal genes?

I wish I had a Spike Adriance at St. Paul's. Spike had an administrative job at Andover when Terry, Joey, and Tony were students there; I don't recall what his official title was, but he seemed to spend a lot of his time handing out drinks to alumni and others who turned up for campus rites. We have no such genial connections yet at St. Paul's; one of *its* administrators once did urge me, when David got admitted, to be sure to stop by someday for a drink, but he has not followe up on the invitation, and it would probably be infra dig to remind him of it. Ellie is worried because she didn't pack any parents'-weekend clothes when we returned to Truro from New York. All the other mothers, she concluded almost the instant we reached Concord, are outfitted straight out of Peck & Peck. She is in jeans. At least I have my old tweed jacket from my London tailor. If E. can generalize about the women's costumes on the St. Paul's scene, so can I about the men's: At St. Paul's parents' gatherings, then, the men whose pants match their jackets—tweeds and some plaids excepted—are the fathers of scholarship students.

Among the parents we meet during a coffee break in our morning program today (the carefully selected student speakers include a black girl, a Japanese, and—here is a true minority-group representative—a white scholarship boy from Montana) are John McPhee's brother's law partner; Angier Biddle Duke, on whom I did a *New Yorker* Profile when he was chief of protocol in Washington; a retired foreign-service officer who had us to dinner in Abidjan when he was ambassador to the Ivory Coast; a woman we met at Sea Island, Georgia, last spring; and a Harvard classmate of mine who wonders if his daughter should apply there. I hadn't thought he cared much about the old place; though he has ample means, he never even answered me when I wrote him a few months back urging him to contribute to our class' fortieth-reunion gift. I get even with him. I urge him to send his child to Yale. During the coffee break, E. goes to the ladies', and is mortified soon after her return because she left her fly open and is sure everybody else noticed it. I didn't. Anyway, I had always thought that kind of mortification was a male prerogative.

Parents' Days—which when one has children in school one should always humbly capitalize—are a sort of charade, or perhaps a dance the steps of which have been carefully defined, and refined, over many years. The offspring of parents don't mind them; at worst, they know they'll get a meal at a fancy restaurant; at best, a new chair for their room. (E. is appalled at one photograph displayed in David's chamber; it is as if she has never seen the centerfold of any masculine counterpart of *Ms.*) As for the schools involved, although it must be a terrible nuisance for them to put up with all of us for a weekend, the inconvenience is more likely than not to be compensated for by an increase in the gifts we will be counted on to make—out of gratitude, guilt, or whatever—when the next fund-raising drive gets under way.

There is much talk of student initiative in the morning program, and how beneficial this initiative has been to the student radio station, WSPS. Poor Tony! He ran a disc-jockey program for a while on the Andover radio station. One evening, when something went wrong in the studio, on his own unbridled initiative he exclaimed, "Oh, shit!", and as luck had it, the word went out over the air. As worse luck had it, the radio station's faculty advisor happened to be tuned in. The era of permissive language had long since dawned, but Tony was nonetheless put on probation for his coarse language, and one thing led to another, and presently he walked out of the school for good and all. I wonder what a schoolboy could get away with now on the air. Off the air, as we all know, he can get away with practically anything. So can a school. The faculty member in charge of David's all-boy dormitory, in this once high Episcopal academy, is an ordained Episcopal minister—a young, unmarried, female one. No institution I can think of would think of assigning a young unmarried male to take charge of an all-girls' dorm; here is discrimination of the rankest sort, and I am tempted to suggest a piece about the sordid situation to the editors of *Ms.*

At 11:50 A.M., ten minutes before all we parents are supposed to adjourn for a school-furnished lunch, the headmaster announces that owing to a mix-up in negotiations with a caterer, the twelve hundred and fifty lunches that were supposed to have been delivered for consumption today were scheduled instead for next Saturday. So we are to have a pickup meal. Incredibly, one materializes. St. Paul's would be a good place to be marooned during an emergency.

After lunch, come the teachers' conferences, ten minutes or so for each set of parents with each pertinent member of the faculty. David's English tutor says that a paper the boy wrote about gardening reminded him of Thoreau, but David tells us later he got only a High Pass for that lofty effort. What would the teacher have given Henry David? To console the lad, we take him to dinner at a fancy rural restaurant. Half the school population seems to be there, which is just as well; until the caterer turns up, rations will surely be short back on campus.

October 23

After breakfast and chapel, we drive David to Boston and at the Ritz treat him to an elegant lunch, though it is emphatically outclassed by the feast in which a young man and woman, this Sunday, are indulging themselves at the next table—cocktails, a fish course, asparagus, roast lamb, champagne, cherries flambés for dessert (seven dollars a portion, according to my menu), and on top of all that French 75's. I just hope they don't fall asleep before they get to wherever their afternoon rendezvous was supposed to take place.

October 24

A real frost last night, back at Truro. But, wonder of wonders, the rose bush outside our kitchen door chose nonetheless to throw out a single lovely red blossom.

No mail today. It is being celebrated as Veterans Day. For a couple of years, just after the end of the Second World War, I was an active veteran, a member of the governing board of the fledgling American Veterans Committee, which was set up as an antidote to the American Legion and the Veterans of Foreign Wars. Thus its motto, "Citizens First, Veterans Second." The A.V.C. had some remarkable leaders in its heyday (a short-lived heyday): Bill Mauldin; Michael Straight and Gilbert Harrison, both later editors of the *New Republic;* Soapy Williams, who became governor of Michigan; Frank Williams, who became ambassador to Ghana; Dick Bolling, now a congressman heavy with seniority; Merle Miller, Harry Truman's biographer; and others shrouded in my private limbo. But the organization foundered on the reefs of ideology; dangerously rent by a battle for its control between the pro-Communist left and the non-Communist left, it patched itself up, more or less, but never managed to regain its vitality or to attain much of a constituency.

October 26

Joey arrived at noon yesterday, in time to play tennis, and reported that his mother has sold her New York apartment. When Jinny moves out, I guess I will have to collect some belongings of mine that have been at her place for the last nine years because I have been too lazy to go around and get them.

Ellie has been anxiously waiting for a phone call from editor Robert Manning, of the *Atlantic,* who has a piece of hers; and I no less anxiously for a call from editor Shawn. Finally this morning the phone rings and there is an editor on the line wishing a word with a writer Kahn, but it is an editor looking for Joey, who hasn't been waiting around at all but has cavalierly gone out clamming. The watched pot never boils.

October 27

A Provincetown fishing boat sank with all hands a year ago, and in today's

Provincetown *Advocate* there's a personal ad that I have gone back and reread three times: "In Memoriam—For 'Mott' Joseph of the Patricia Marie—You weren't the easiest person to live with and love but you were a man, my man. You told me I couldn't get along without you. You were right. It's been difficult and lonely. As long as there are the waves, winds and aromas of the sea I'll remember. Shalom."

I went out once on one of these small boats, to do an article on the Provincetown fleet for the Sunday *Times* magazine, a sixteen-hour working day that began at 1 A.M. I was only along for the ride, but was exhausted by the time we returned, without mishap, to our pier, and was glad I didn't have to make the trip again. The fishermen, who had to haul in their nets and cull their catch, while I merely watched, would be going out once more in the dark middle of the following night. They were durable and admirable men.

Drinks next door with Joe and Perry Anthony, who have settled in year round, Joe having retired from directing plays. We reminisce sentimentally about Frank Loesser, whose "Most Happy Fella" Joe staged on Broadway. The Anthonys have just seen Truro neighbor Bill Gibson's "Golda" in Boston, on its way to New York, and fear the show is in trouble. Malcolm and Mary Alice Preston join us. Their four-year-old grandson is staying with them, and Malcolm says that when they had dinner company the other night they offered Josh his choice of eating alone in the kitchen or with their guests at the table—provided, that was, he would promise not to crawl underneath it. The boy pondered for a moment, and then said, "I am going to eat with you at the table, crawl under it, and say 'Shit.' " The advantage of being a grandparent is that one can always blame that sort of thing, if it is deemed censurable, on the little tyke's parents, on the part of whom, when they were young, one would never, of course, have tolerated such behavior.

October 28

Today's *Globe* has more than a whole page of news about South Africa, and the *Times* has two men there. Where am I? One of the *Globe*'s items is a story about Donald Woods, the editor of the East London *Daily Dispatch*, who has been banned. Donald took me to his club for lunch when I passed through East London in 1966, and told me about his childhood, growing up in what is now the Transkei in the care of an African nurse who was also a witch doctor, and would sometimes drift off into diverting trances. Now—by South African criteria—he is an outspoken liberal, but he was a late-bloomer: When he entered college, he was so conservative that on being asked if he had any solution for his country's race problem, he replied, "Shoot every kaffir in the country and you won't have a problem." One white South African who was arrested recently for treason or subversion or whatever they are arresting people for these troubled days was under a banning order when I was over there, but I arranged to meet him at a mutual friend's house, and we had a long and illuminating talk. Like Woods, he was a mild person who spoke not of revolution but merely of human rights and human dignity.

One of the most unexpected tennis experiences I ever had occurred in the Transkei—at Umtata, its capital. I was driving across South Africa, and at Port Elizabeth met a chap who, on learning I was fond of the sport, said he'd undertake to arrange a game for me at my next stop. Soon after checking in at my Umtata hotel, I received a phone call from a major. We had a mutual acquaintance, the major said, who had dropped him a note about me and tennis, and when would I like to play? We made a date for the following afternoon. When the major, dressed in whites, came around to pick me up, I noticed a few raised eyebrows among the bellhops. They were used to seeing him in his working clothes—the uniform of the South African Police.

The major took me around to the Police Officers' Club, where we had an enjoyable three sets with another police officer and, as our fourth, the local magistrate. The court surface was a South African variation of clay—ant-heap mixed with salt. Some builders of ant-heap courts, my host told me, also folded in molasses, but the club's recreation budget was too skimpy for that. Afterwards, we all repaired to the clubhouse for a beer. The major and his compatriots began chatting in Afrikaans. I was naturally curious—how often, after all, does one get to socialize with the South African Police—and asked what they were discussing. "All these blokes ever talk about is fishing," the major said.

I have played tennis elsewhere in Africa—in Kinshasa, for instance, on a cement court, barefoot, until I had to quit because the lines were marked in red and my blood was beginning to make it difficult properly to call ins and outs—but never yet behind the Iron Curtain. Tennis did once figure importantly, though, in a minor Russian drama in which I played a major role. Jinny and I were going to the Soviet Union in 1957, and Bud Benjamin asked me if I'd do a favor for Dan Schorr, his colleague at CBS. It seemed that Schorr had had to leave Russia rather hurriedly, and had been unable to take his racquet with him. Would I be willing to fetch it and bring it back?

When I consented, I was directed to present myself to another Western television correspondent who was still in Moscow. Before we got there, though, we stopped off in Leningrad. Late one evening, while we were having supper at the Astoria Hotel, we became aware that two Westerners at the next table were conversing knowledgeably about television. On a hunch that one of them was my contact, I introduced myself and alluded to my Moscow mission. The man looked around the dining room warily, then said he knew all about me, and directed me to get in touch with him when I reached the capital. He scribbled a phone number and passed it across. No further communication was encouraged.

In Moscow, I phoned the designated number. I was instructed to meet the fellow who'd given it to me in the lobby of a certain hotel at a certain hour. He was at the spot when I arrived, holding as beat-up a tennis racquet as I'd ever seen. It had a warped frame and two broken strings. I couldn't conceive of anybody's caring enough about a racquet in that condition to aspire to having it conveyed across Central Park. While I was gazing at it, with astonishment, its bearer said he'd be back in a moment. "I forgot to give you the package," he said.

He disappeared into an elevator, while I sat in the lobby trying to affect the guise of a casual tourist who normally carried around junked tennis racquets. Ten minutes later, he returned with a wrapped parcel. He thrust it into my free hand, wordlessly, and glided away.

Several days later, as Jinny and I were packing preparatory to heading home, she was about to stick the package into one of our suitcases when she paused. "What if Customs asks us what's in it?" she said. "It could be hashish, for all we know."

I agreed. Gingerly, I unwrapped the package. Its contents were innocent enough, but somewhat confusing. They consisted of a bedraggled pair of sneakers, an unprepossessing and unlaundered tennis shirt, and a pair of dirty socks. I have thrown away better stuff that's been left at my Truro court. I never did find out why Dan Schorr was so anxious to retrieve his pitiful possessions; but an addiction to tennis can, as everybody knows, lead people to all sorts of irrational behavior.

The cost of social security is going up: By the 1980s, people with annual incomes of $20,000 or some such may be paying $3,000 a year in social-security taxes alone. How lucky some of us are to be already old! I will be eligible to receive social security, I calculate, at just about the time that I would cease being able to afford to pay for it.

Way back in Section D of the *Times* is an interesting story datelined New Orleans. Something called the Newspaper Readership Council has conducted a poll and has concluded that on any given day sixty-nine percent of all Americans get their news not from radio or television but from newspapers. All is not lost. On the other hand, the survey may have suffered from a touch of bias: It was commissioned by the Newspaper Advertising Bureau and the American Newspaper Publishers Association.

October 29

James M. Cain died yesterday, at eighty-five. He worked for the old New York *World* before he turned to fiction, and we had a lengthy and, for me, most productive correspondence when I was gathering material for my biography of Herbert Bayard Swope, the postman ringing with delightful Cain letters not once or twice but half a dozen informative times. I read Cain's obit just before going to Wellfleet to a memorial service for Donald Slesinger, our Truro neighbor who switched in mid-career from psychology to psychoanalysis. The service, on the unheated premises, this chilly fall day, of the Church of St. James the Fisherman, is a high Episcopal one, with hymns and scripture readings and prayers, but nary a word is said by anyone about the late deceased. Is this the way for a lay analyst to go?

We dine with Jerry and Joan Cohen. He is going to China next month with Ted Kennedy, and will be the only member of the party who speaks Chinese. I tell Jerry to give my regards, when and if they meet, to Foreign Minister Huang Hua. Jerry says that he and Huang, alas, are not on particularly good terms: The last time the two of them met, Huang called him a running dog of capitalism. Could Huang Hua get a visa to South Africa? Maybe one of the things they have in my Pretoria dossier is that the Communist foreign minister, in the traditional gesture made by a Chinese host to an honored guest, once offered my wife a tidbit with his own chopsticks.

October 30

A furniture-repair man I heard about last week, a fellow based in Plymouth, comes around with his van and hauls away our Victorian couch and three antique Windsor chairs, all in sore need of rehabilitation. I am very proud of having discovered him and persuaded him to stop by, and am preening myself, after he departs, when Ellie asks how much he is going to charge us, and I realize that I forgot to ask him.*

We go to a pre-Halloween housewarming that Tony and Judy are holding in the North Truro cottage they've rented for the winter. I am made to feel very much the older generation. People keep offering me a chair, until another old coot arrives who is clearly in greater need of one, his cup of gin swaying gently in his self-created breeze. Judy has dressed herself up as Wonder Woman, and Tony is Batman. He confesses that ever since he was

---

* He charged fifty dollars for everything. What a shrewd bargainer I am!

a little boy he has wanted to be Batman. But I remember him clearly as Superman. Or was that one of his brothers? While I am trying to straighten out the details of my child-raising (at least Tony didn't say "Shit" publicly till he was seventeen), a guest walks in with a real pumpkin over his head, resting on his shoulders. He stays for fifteen minutes, not saying a word, and then leaves, presumably to buy some shampoo. Nobody has any idea after he's gone who he was.

October 31

Halloween. Ellie says no trick-or-treaters will come by this evening, out here in the country. I know better. I carve one of David's pumpkins, set a candle inside it, buy some cookies and raisins, and sit back and wait. No one materializes. Ellie knows better.

Tony and Judy wonder if they can leave Ian with us while they go out to a party. Of course; what else are grandparents for? When they bring him over, they assure E. and me that the young man will quickly go to sleep and has been double-diapered. As soon as they lay him down, he leaps up. They give him some water and coo at him and lie alongside him, and when he slumps down again they make a hasty exit, immediately following which he is bolt upright. Ian's vocabulary is still small—mostly "Mama" and "Dada." I am not sure he knows exactly who I am. While I am trying to imitate a parental coo, he uses his two words alternately and incessantly. I pick him up and take him into my lap, in front of the fire, assuring him that Mama and Dada will be back soon, though five hours was their own estimate of their probable absence. To my astonishment, he soon falls asleep in my arms and is never heard from again.

Before he conks out I learn something: The temptation for a grandparent to call the number that parents have left to be reached at in an emergency is powerfully strong, but it is resistible.

November 1

We have callers this morning—two unknown women rapping at our kitchen door. I guess at a glance that they are Jehovah's Witnesses. Whether it is the way they knock or their manner of dress that identifies them I do not know; but these visitors are *sui generis*, and, especially when they interrupt one at work, a nuisance. The women introduce themselves not as Witnesses but as "neighbors from Eastham." Fifteen miles is a long stretch for neighborliness. If they had come twelve hours sooner, I could have given them some trick-or-treat goodies, but it seems they have something they want to give *me*. I accept two proffered tracts and attempt to bid them good day, which I have learned, from previous such encounters, is not easy. They say after some prolonged palaver that they generally receive a nickel a tract for their words of guidance and revelation. I hand them their literature, explaining stuffily that I only respond to requests for charitable contributions that I receive in the mails. The women are stunned and retreat in confusion.

Why do I feel guilty? They were uninvited trespassers and beggars to boot. I am mad at myself for feeling guilty, mad at the two women for making me feel guilty, mad at the dog for not having scared them off before I felt guilty, mad at Ellie for not working in the kitchen so she could have received the visitors and spared me from feeling guilty—mad, indeed, at just about everybody save Jehovah, who, if he has been witnessing this morning's events, has surely put them all in omniscient perspective.

We work uninterruptedly for the rest of the day, and then drive to the other side of the Pamet River Valley to dine with Nick and Sarah Pileggi, who are surely the only other husband-and-wife writing team in Truro residence this month. I know many of Sarah's associates at *Sports Illustrated*, but have had few acquaintances, at *New York*, under either its old or new management, and I ask Nick whom he works with there. With Elizabeth Crow, he tells me—married to Pat Crow, whom *I* work with, of course, at *The New Yorker*. I didn't know Pat had a wife at *New York*, and that we thus have a spy in, so to speak, the enemy camp. Or maybe they think they have one in ours. The fact is (I am mindful of my expressed distrustfulness of all sentences that begin with "The fact is") that *New York* and *The New Yorker* are really not competitive at all, except titularly: I cannot visualize anyone's taking *New York* seriously aside from its commendable reprinting of crossword puzzles from the London Sunday *Times*.

November 2

Ellie says she had a dream last night about Bill Shawn. She cannot remember any of the details, but he was unquestionably the star performer in her nocturnal drama. But Shawn is *my* dream. How dare she invade my turf? Or can it be that the subject matter of dreams may become, as an offshoot of marriage, community property? I did not dream about Bill last night, come to think of it. Conceivably at some point in the unconscious night I conferred on E. sole ownership of this elusive asset.

E. wants to change her pen name from "Eleanor Munro" to something else. She has her mother's mother's maiden name in mind—LeClerc, pronounced "LeClaire." I suggest that instead of calling herself, professionally, "Eleanor LeClerc," she consider "Claire LeClerc," or better yet, "Clerc LeClerc." Ellie says it is all very well and good to joke about these matters, if that is the sort of thing I find amusing, but the right name can be terribly important to an author, and can anyone really think Francine Gray would have got far in the field without that star-studded "Du Plessix" embedded in the middle of her byline? If Jane Du Plessix Austen had written "Emma Du Plessix," I wonder, would it have made any difference? In any event, E. and I agree that she may one day change her literary identity, and we run through a gamut of possibilities. My own favorite is "Fifi Du Plessix Guinzburg."

Holmes Brown calls from Senator Haskell's office. Brown has been talking about my visa to the South African Consulate in New York, where he was referred to a Mr. Labuschagne. Do I know him? *Do* I! I say with profound understatement that I am somewhat familiar with the name. The senator's man says that Labuschagne sounded a bit "acid" to him on the phone. No doubt, but he may just have been carrying out acidulous instructions from Pretoria.

November 3

We are returning to New York today and shutting down the Truro house for the winter. One would think that 7:30 A.M. on house-closing day would hardly be an appropriate moment to summon a plumber, but that is what we have to do when everything suddenly backs up into the house. Bruce Cagwin, Tony's friend, graciously comes by with his electric snake, and reports after preliminary probing that some locust-tree roots seem to have worked their way through our underground sewage-disposal system. Given a break in the weather, Bruce hopes to have this straightened out by spring.

Driving down to New York, we stop somewhere in Connecticut for lunch, which we can barely pay for, inasmuch as the establishment will not honor a traveller's check Ellie tenders in good faith. The establishment insists, however, on receiving ten cents in cash for a paper cup of water for our dog. If John Kenneth Galbraith were also riding with us, I have no doubt he could extrapolate from this incident some pertinent and pithy comment on the hopeless state of the American economy and how it deserves whatever happens to it.

Farther along in Connecticut, E. asks me what I think about when I am at the wheel. "Generally, nothing," I say, quite truthfully. But her question is posed—her womanly instinct working at fever pitch again?—just as we are passing Exit 41 on the Merritt Parkway, and whenever I go by there, I cannot help thinking of all the times I used to turn off there, to visit N. But, generally speaking, I actually don't think much when I'm driving—except about the driving itself. I commend this approach to all the drivers on the road whom I also think, and worry, about.

We reach New York in time for me to change and go down to the Century for the Members' Dinner, which is, I guess, the club's major annual social event. Henry Cooper has put together a table of *New Yorker* people—Bill Knapp, Ved Mehta, Brendan Gill—to welcome new member Pete Spelman, one of the few individuals on the magazine's business staff to join our fellowship. How nice a way to return to the city in the fall! For at this function one is bound to bump into dozens of acquaintances. Here is Bob Manning, for instance, who does not say whether he has yet read a manuscript E. sent to the *Atlantic* quite a while ago; and there is Alan Williams, who makes no mention of a manuscript of mine that he and I both know is lying around somewhere at the Viking Press premises. Can it be that Bob and Alan are both too polite to let business intrude into a social occasion? If so, that would represent a revolutionary new development in the publishing world.

Here to welcome me back to the city are Harvard classmates Pete Ahrens and Gerry Piel; there is Nathan Pusey, who tells me he has a book coming out himself next spring—from, not illogically, the Harvard University Press. Nate says that Harvard alumni keep stopping him on the street and saying, consolingly, that it was too bad he had to be president of the university during its toughest years; but that he doesn't feel that way at all and will say as much in his forthcoming volume. And over there is Harrison Salisbury, just returned from another trip to China, with some book news of interest to me: Harrison says he saw copies of the hardcover edition of my "The China Hands" in two private libraries in Peking.

Francis Plimpton is the chief after-dinner speaker, and he quotes Mr. Justice Holmes: "No gentleman needs to know Greek. He needs only to have forgotten it." I don't know how Nathan Pusey, whose root discipline was the classics, may feel about that, but it makes me feel enormously better about all the Greek that years ago passed into and clean out of my mind. As I am leaving the Century, our faithful club secretary, Dick Dana, stops me in the lobby and laments that none of the members ever looks at anything on the bulletin board aside from obituaries. In an attempt to make Dick feel better, too, I study the board for a few moments, and learn for the first time that on these considerate premises we can buy an umbrella for $4.50, a black bow tie for $2.50, a handkerchief for fifty-five cents, a pocket comb for a quarter, and a pair of shoelaces for two thin dimes. Very gentlemanly, and reasonable, too. I'll bet the Century would give Rainbow a cup of water on the house.

November 4

I retrieved Shawn last night, in dreamland, though disturbingly. I dreamt I was in Panama, covering a story for *The New Yorker*—as indeed I actually was more than a year ago—and while there picked up a copy of the New York *Times* saying that the famous editor who had been mysteriously and suspiciously stricken with food poisoning had died. Ellie's interpretation (she stuck to her own repertory of dreams last night) is that Bill has become my surrogate father, and that my reverie relates to my real father's having died while I was covering the Olympics in Munich for *The New Yorker*. This strikes me as being too pat an explanation, but I am grateful for it, inasmuch as it eliminates the possibility that I was anticipating something dire happening to Bill.

When I get to the office and inquire hastily about the state of our leader's health, I am informed that he is fine, but will be unavailable for at least a week, during which he and Mary McCarthy are apparently preparing for publication some posthumous works of Hannah Arendt. I am impatient to see Shawn, and to confer with him about my work agenda for the next nine or ten months, but when he declares himself incommunicado there is little anyone can do about it, save in genuine emergencies; I shall have to bide my time and reflect that in this instance, at least, the quick have been sorely bested by the dead.

The office was supposed to have forwarded all my first-class mail to Truro, this past month, so what I find on my desk is largely junk. But buried among the solicitations of gold-stock promoters and French-tickler purveyors I find two first-class letters from South Africa. One, written way back on 22 September, is from the private secretary to Foreign Minister Botha (who evidently cannot bring himself to convey the sad tidings personally), to the effect that the minister "has now been informed that after careful reconsideration of your case, the relevant authorities have concluded that the previous decision to refuse a visa to you cannot be rescinded." The other letter, written a month afterward, is from Helen Suzman: "I have just heard word from the minister of the interior that he has re-examined your file (at my request) and that he is unable to see his way clear to change his decision about your visa. . . . God knows what these people have against you." I certainly don't.

E. and I meet Lexy and her brother Don outside the Paris Theatre, where Truffaut's "The Man Who Loved Women" is playing. Ellie and Don don't much like it, but Lex and I do—I especially because it is all about a man trying to write his memoirs and about the complications, via flashbacks, that his life has got him into. Also, the protagonist finds himself blissfully in bed with his publisher, something that even in my wildest midnight fantasies has never crossed my mind.

November 5

A Saturday, and Ellie and I spend most of the day at home, rearranging pictures. When I last visited David Rockefeller at his Pocantico Hills home, he and his wife were knee-deep in pictures they were rearranging. So as we hold paintings up against the wall, sometimes cursing, and resolve whatever we do to have the new display keep old nail holes and plaster cracks out of view, I feel an agreeable kinship with the rich.

Cynthia Lindsay is in town from California, and is giving a party tonight, with Jo Loesser, at Jo's town house. We have to go out to dinner first, so it is after midnight before we get to Jo's, who has split with her croquet-playing husband and has no further interest in *that* sport. Among the other guests is a girl—well, former girl—whom I haven't seen in a long time and who now tells me that in twenty-two years of marriage I was the only man she ever strayed with. We never strayed beyond having lunch. She says it was a pity we didn't sleep together at the time. Women are certainly getting emancipated.

Cynnie Lindsay has something to say anent *that*. Her daughter brought a demure-looking girl friend to their Malibu house for dinner not long ago, and afterward Cynnie asked her guest politely what she did. "I fuck on camera," the young woman said. When Cynnie started to fall off one side of her chair, the guest realized that she had startled her hostess, so she added that it hadn't occurred to her that Cynnie didn't know she acted in porn flicks. But how could she have known? Cynnie wondered. "Your daughter writes my scripts," the starlet replied. Whereupon, according to Cynnie's account, she fell off the other side of her chair.

November 6

Lexy listens to the radio news in the morning before I have a chance to look at the *Times*. It is thus he, coming down to breakfast, who bears the tidings that Guy Lombardo is dead. When I did a Profile on Lombardo for *The New Yorker*, the *raison d'être* was his Royal Canadians' durability. It seemed then to both Shawn and me that this thoroughly justified my tackling the subject, and so I did. Why, the Lombardo band had been going about its smooth business for an astonishing thirty or so years! That was in 1957, and now twenty more years have passed, and until yesterday, at least, Lombardo was still languidly waving his violin bow. Today, Shawn and I are both older, and neither of us (Bill came to *The New Yorker* in 1933) would be particularly impressed by anybody's having done any one thing for a mere three decades. Of course, a piece about a man who had been a bandleader for *fifty* years or more would be something else again—very interesting, very good idea; a half century plus is a long time to stick to any kind of last.

With mayoral elections two days in the offing, we get a call at home from a woman representing Roy Goodman, the Republican candidate. We must be sure to vote. According to our importuner, we are E. Kahn and Nancy Kahn, registered Republicans. No, I tell her, we are Democrats, and anyway my wife's name is not Nancy. Ellie no more likes being thought of as a Nancy than I do as a Republican.

November 7

When I go to pick up the car at the garage to take it to Skipper—something went wrong with the muffler on our trip down from the Cape—I find that the battery is dead. Why do cars always collapse in their home garage, like an infant in its crib? E. thinks the reason is that I don't tip the garage men enough at Christmas time. I had always thought my generosity to them was not incompatible with that I've habitually shown to my own small children. Perhaps I have been niggardly all around.

Bob Saudek phones, to invite me to a party this afternoon to celebrate the first anniversary of his Museum of Broadcasting. There might be a Talk story in this, but there is no way of getting to Shawn, so I decide to cover the event without consulting him, potential conflict of interest notwithstanding. The conflict lies in the fact that Bob has long been Bill's summer landlord. Naturally, I wouldn't allude to this in Talk, but Shawn might have qualms about putting into print the very same name that he writes out checks to. (A *New Yorker* checker would pounce on me right here: How do I know Shawn writes out checks to Saudek? Maybe Cecille Shawn writes them out. Maybe they pay in cash, or barter. I would be sorry before the checker was through with me that I had ever brought the subject up.) I go to the museum without Shawn's authorization, half reporter, half imposter, and the first person I run into, Martin Segal, the city's commissioner of cultural affairs, reminds me jovially that the last time he and I met was at a lunch Brendan Gill gave for some actor. I have never been at any such gathering, but to avoid an unnecessary refutation profess to remember it with pleasure. Segal thereupon introduces me to my neighbor Mikhail Baryshnikov, who is surrounded by cameramen. The dancer and I are photographed shaking hands, and I make a mental note to obtain a print of this historic embrace, if possible, for Ellie, then remember too late that should I get one I will have to crop it carefully, for there is a lighted cigarette in my other hand and, as E. well knows, I do not smoke.

Host Saudek takes me aside to reminisce about the early days of television, when Bob produced "Omnibus" and I wrote a script for him on the court-martial of Billy Mitchell. I remember that clearly. Obscurely clearly, rather: The transcript of the trial proceedings that Saudek gave me to work from was so poorly reproduced that I feared for a while I might not have enough vision left to view the finished program.

When Bud Benjamin was the producer of "Twentieth Century" for CBS, I did a number of scripts for him. I still get a check every year for something like six dollars and forty-two cents through the Writers Guild of America, of which I am perforce a member, representing my residual payment for some "Twentieth Century" show or other that has recently been televised in, say, Indonesia.

By the time I was assigned to write those scripts, the relevant film footage had already been assembled and spliced. I would be furnished with a shot list, which indicated exactly how much prose I could write for each depicted sequence. In the early days of the space program, Bud produced a show about the moon, which he invited me to write, probably because he knew that I knew absolutely nothing about astronomy or any other science and thus couldn't cause any technical trouble. I accepted, and in due course received my shot list, which contained the stark admonition: "Explain the origin of the solar system in no more than thirty-two words." How could anybody possibly reduce so complex an evolutionary process to a couple of sparse sentences? I wrestled with that for a couple of days, poring over heavy scientific tomes and getting nowhere, and then suddenly was struck with inspiration. I looked up "solar system" in a dictionary. I found a sixteen-word definition. I was able to expand this capsule analysis to double its length.

November 9

We dined at the George Labalmes' last night and later watched the election returns, until we quit out of boredom. Roy Goodman got slaughtered by Ed Koch; the Republicans' last-ditch telephone campaign must have gone totally awry.

Joey is in town and, full of guilt about treating my children as shabbily as garage attendants, I take him to lunch and urge him to stuff himself. Joey says he was looking something up in "Webster's Third New International Dictionary" the other day when my name jumped out of the page at him. It was contained in an example of the use of the word "froggy." ("His gruff, froggy voice—E. J. Kahn.") But where did this come from? "Webster's" does not say, and I certainly do not know. From my book on Frank Sinatra, maybe, but can that be how I described the satiny singer at the time?

Afterward, Joey accompanies me to the "21" Club, where I have volunteered to do a Talk story on a backgammon game between Paul Magriel and George Plimpton. They are announcing the resumption of the ill-fated "million-dollar" tournament that was scheduled for December in Las Vegas, and was subsequently cancelled. Today, Paul will be playing George blindfolded. Oswald Jacoby is present for the clash—he and Magriel are officially co-sponsors of the Vegas competition. Ozzie tells me, flatteringly, as he does every time our paths cross (I do not object to this sort of repetition), that a piece I did for *The New Yorker* thirty-six years ago is the funniest thing ever written about contract bridge. It was published before Magriel was born.

Following much more desultory chitchat—Magriel and I tentatively agree to stage a team backgammon competition, Harvard Club vs. Princeton Club, with Paul to be captain of the Princetonians and my side to be led by Howard Reiling, who is much older even than Jacoby—it is time for the match of the day to get under way. Plimpton cries *"Au table!"* At once *The New Yorker's* crack backgammon correspondent faces a crisis. Do I quote this fellow accurately, or do I correct his French? I decide to quote him accurately, and to let *les chips* fall where they may.* At the table, Paul defeats George despite his handicap. Then they vacate their board, which Joey and I commandeer for a friendly father-and-son tussle. I win a single game from Joe, but his battered pride is soon restored when Magriel returns to the spot, takes my seat, and, unblindfolded, goes down to quick, emphatic defeat. True, Paul has long been saying that in any single game of backgammon any fair player has a forty-five per cent chance of beating an expert like himself; but even so, I am tempted on the basis of this afternoon's performances to enter the Vegas tournament myself.

November 10

I ride downtown this morning on a Lexington Avenue bus whose driver greets everybody with a cheerful "Good morning" and who announces all stops in advance and as he approaches Fifty-ninth Street even calls out "Bloomingdale's!" and "Alexander's!" He puts his passengers into such an amiable frame of mind that they begin smiling and chatting with one another. At one point he even stops his vehicle, when it has already started up, to oblige a woman who is running after it. An extraordinary urban experience. Our newly elected Mayor Koch should relieve this fellow of all his other duties and put him in charge of municipal transportation.

A farewell visit to Dr. Bishop, who will be retiring from practice seven weeks hence. Without a designated successor to take over from him, he has been trying to distribute his regular patients among various physicians who he thinks will be right for them; he has persuaded Dr. George Gorham, who doesn't *want* any more patients, to agree to squeeze me onto his roster. Dr. Bishop—who says he feels sort of like a dying man, dividing up his

* The magazine's checkers routinely changed this to *"À la table."* But a reader who identified himself as an expert on idiomatic linguistics later informed me sternly that the *really* correct conversational usage is *"À table."*

possessions among his heirs—thinks Dr. Gorham will be ideal for me, and I hope I can justify this trust.

I show Louis my Cape Cod doctors' comprehensive account of my illness. He says that they appear to have done a thorough job of exploration, though he is amused by their stress on alcohol. He has never heard of babesiosis. In my presence, his ever-gentle nurse, Laura Klinger, looks it up for her boss in the latest issue of Merck's medical dictionary, which theoretically lists every disease there is, along with its symptoms and cure. Louis says that Laura could practice out of Merck's, or I or anybody else, with one big *caveat:* You have to make the correct diagnosis. Babesiosis has not yet been admitted to *that* dictionary: My brain has attained a measure of lexicographical immortality ahead of the rest of my body.

Louis Bishop asks what I have been up to lately. I mention that, *inter alia,* I have been keeping a daily journal, and he says he keeps one too, a handwritten diary. He pulls out yesterday's entry and reads it aloud. He mentioned the day's heavy rains (I neglected to include them in mine) and that he had a pork chop for dinner that tasted bad and made him feel sick. My diagnosis is incipient trichinosis. Also, he paid a call on his first cousin, the painter Isabel Bishop. It all goes to show what a small world this is, its coincidences known only to diarists: Ellie not long ago paid a call herself on Miss Bishop, who is going to be one of the artists featured in her book. Louis says that one of the commendable things about Dr. Gorham is that he is a family practitioner, and now that he has agreed to take me on, Ellie and the kids have themselves a good new doctor, too. Also, Dr. Gorham makes house calls. This is something to put into one's diary in capital letters, underlined. But what did I have for dinner last night?

Charles and Pam Towill, in from Alaska, come for dinner. They had a moose in their backyard the other day. The Fred Rosens join us. Jane R., hearing of my difficulties with the Ministry of the Interior in Pretoria, says from what she has gleaned from lurking around the United Nations it might be worth my while talking to the South Africans there, but I don't see quite how any South African abroad is likely to be able to countermand a decision made by one of his superiors at home.

Jane thinks, or thought until tonight, that Ellie was my third wife. She is flabbergasted to learn that I have had only two wives. She has been certain for the last forty years or so that I was once married to Peggy Schwarz. Peggy would no doubt be flabbergasted by this, too; she was about sixteen when we stopped seeing each other.

November 11

I get a haircut, from a woman barber. She takes twice as long at it as her *confrères* do, but does what I deem to be a first-rate job until I get home and

Ellie cries "Butchery!" I blame my shame on equal opportunity. The barber asked me if I had ever had a woman do me before. Yes, I said, but not in the United States. She said that's what they all tell her. The other time was in Peking, with results about the same. E. didn't complain that time, probably because she had lesser expectations.

Today is yet another Veterans Day, so Lexy has no school. I am the veteran in the household, but I get no holiday, unless you can count waiting around Skipper's Mobil station to have a muffler installed as falling into that category.

At a memorial evening honoring Alexander Calder, in a huge nineteen-twentyish theatre over on Broadway at Seventy-fourth Street, I encounter my old Columbia writing student, Frank Brady, who, since I taught my non-fiction class, has had biographies published of both Hugh Hefner and Aristotle Onassis. Now, Frank tells me, he is collaborating with another member of the class, Joann Lawless, on a history of famous bookstores. I have put a writing team together! And what an inspired notion for a book! What bookstore on earth could fail to give prominent display to a book about bookstores?

November 12

I resolve at the last moment to go to the Harvard-Yale football game on the bus that Tom and Jill Stix hire every other year—the year The Game is played in New Haven—to transport their guests to the Yale Bowl. Ellie begs off. If I hadn't made this decision, this would have been the first season in fifty years—the war period excepted—in which I hadn't seen at least one Ivy League game. I started off at the Yale Bowl, as a kid, being taken there for several seasons running by a bachelor friend of my parents, Dudley Sicher, who became a family court judge in New York and who, largely because we didn't know anybody else who was qualified, officiated when Jinny and I were married in 1945. Dudley took me to some memorable games, involving gridiron heroes like Yale's Albie Booth, Army's Chris Cagle, Harvard's Barry Wood. There was one game in which an Army player broke his neck and died—my first encounter with death, I guess—and another in which Yale and Dartmouth played to a 33–33 tie. None of these, of course, could compare to the 1968 Yale-Harvard game, the 29–29 tie to which I escorted Ellie when I was courting her.

Today, Harvard needs to beat Yale to tie for the Ivy League championship. Harvard rarely wins these big ones while I am watching. In 1957, I dragged the whole family to the Yale Bowl in a snowstorm to watch Harvard strut its stuff. Harvard lost, 54–0. Never having been on one of the Stixes' expeditions, I do not know their ropes, so I bring along some lunch and some Bloody Marys. Tom and Jill have already laid in an ample supply of both. I am pleased to find the Maurice Lazaruses among the guests, so I will not be the only Harvard rooter in this nest of Elis. (Indeed, classmate Mogie, now a Harvard overseer, has brought along some tickets on the Harvard side of the field.) The Walter Cronkites are in our party, too, and I tell Walter that I am not going to South Africa. He tells me that Bud Benjamin and he can beat John Chancellor and Jimmy Greenfield at tennis any time I would like to bet on it. I admire sporting men.

When we reach New Haven, we find picket lines outside the Bowl portals. Yale's dining-hall employees have been on strike, and we are handed literature got up by a Student Strike Support Committee, which, while certainly less strident in tone than it might have been a decade ago, says in conclusion, "Only when the administration retreats from its intransigent position can the University once again function as a unified, cooperative community of faculty, students, workers, and administration." I note that alumni and alumnae have been omitted from this "unified" academic community. There isn't a private university in this nation, except for a few odd ones like Bob Jones and Oral Roberts, that can function satisfactorily without the sturdy support of its former students.

As we stride past the pickets, Cronkite makes a joke. When Walter Cronkite jests one should take note. Walter tells me that he has heard that the difference between a Harvard man and a Yale man is that at Yale they say, "Everybody hold their own ticket."

Yale wins. I forget the score. Harvard often forgets the score when Yale wins. After one Yale touchdown, the fellow who scores it triumphantly flings the ball into the stands. His team is forthwith penalized fifteen yards for unsportsmanlike conduct, which is the first clearcut evidence I've had of what the pigskins used in Ivy League competition are considered to be worth. Sitting in the Harvard stands, courtesy of the board of overseers, I invite Annabelle Prager—whose husband, like Ellie, has elected to skip the Stixes' foray into school busing—to join me there. I wave to a couple of classmates I spot nearby, and they return my greetings guardedly. They saw Ellie with me at our reunion in June. Now rumors about my being thrice married will no doubt begin to emanate from a new source. I wish my friends were sitting close enough so that I could explain that Ellie and David Prager are going to join Annabelle and me at the Stixes' when we are bused back to our starting point.

November 13

Sister Joan is giving a cocktail party at Sardi's for one of her Harper authors, Arnold Wesker, whose play, "The Merchant," is opening in New York. The usual bunch of literary and theatre people converge, among them Emily Hahn, of whom I inquire, en passant, how many books she has written. Somewhere between forty and fifty, she says—she cannot remember exactly. Many writers can practically cite you the number of words they have turned out. What a remarkable career she has had—a half century of workmanlike productivity. She is over seventy now, but when I get to *The New Yorker* office in the morning—and I get there well ahead of most of the staff writers—she is almost always at her desk just off the elevator landing, already into her day's stint. Even if I never went to bed, I would be hard pressed to match her formidable output.

I leave the party with Edith Oliver and Marian Seldes, who is playing in "The Merchant." Edith is almost a member of our family—Joan's oldest friend—and for a change this evening has no show to review for *The New Yorker*. I offer both of them a lift uptown, and we naturally talk about the theatre. Our eavesdropping cab driver hands us a printed résumé over his shoulder. He is a singer, he says, needs ten thousand dollars for some professional venture or other, has half of it raised, and wonders if we would be good enough to provide him with the other half. I tip generously, but not that much.

"Would like to be able to perform before Frank Sinatra or his representatives," the résumé says, "due to my material being mostly his songs and his style although I do not mimic him. I have been favorably compared to Mr. Sinatra and feel like I would be ideal to play his role in any upcoming movie of his life story." On television the other night, "60 Minutes" had a sequence about a singer who got into trouble because he sounded too much like Bing Crosby. I do not tell this to our charioteer (if he knew I had written a book about Sinatra he would probably run us into a lamppost), but I have a hunch his prototype might not regard him as the ideal screen impersonator.

November 14

Finally, I get to see Shawn. He approves a number of ideas I throw at him—among them, to my surprise and delight, a Sporting Scene piece on the big backgammon tournament at Vegas in January. But Bill thinks it would probably be better if I didn't enter the lists myself. I concur. That sort of participatory involvement in a story may work with *Sports Illustrated*, but *New Yorker* reporters are supposed to exhibit a certain degree of detachment toward their subject matter. Besides, if I won a couple of hundred thousand dollars in the tournament I might end up in an unmanageable tax bracket.

Among the ideas I have hatched on which Bill has bestowed his blessing are two Profiles—one on a scientist who, while searching for a rare old drawing of a herring, helped ascertain the long-unknown whereabouts of some of the world's rarest old musical manuscripts; the other on a retired major general who has become an academic, and whose specialty is terrorism. What makes the subjects especially appealing to me is that both the fish man and the terrorism man are in England. My choice of them to write about is not, I suppose, entirely without ulterior motive. I love to travel, especially at a magazine's expense; given the option of writing about someone in Passaic or in Paris, I could decide without a flicker of hesitation.

Shawn and I briefly discuss my failure to get into South Africa. I would like to raise a stink about it. He points out, with his usual calming approach to excited writers, that *The New Yorker* can't really complain hard about being denied reportorial representation over there: South Africa may have a justified grievance against us, because of our policy of refusing advertising space to the country's airline and its tourist agencies. That wasn't his doing, Bill informs me; it was a policy decision made by others, and may have been a mistake. But the damage—mainly to my chances of getting into the country—has been done, and we must live with it.

So I have swapped Johannesburg for Las Vegas. Not a bad trade, assuming that I don't lose my shirt.

November 15

On the CBS evening news, Walter Cronkite says that the leader of the Spanish Communist party crossed a picket line at Yale today, after Senator George McGovern and others concurrently in New Haven had refused to. Walter does not bother to mention that he himself ignored the pickets there on Saturday. He is not a participatory journalist.

November 16

The New York Public Library has a new fund-raising gimmick. The library is collecting old gold, and giving the donors credit for a contribution at its appraised value. The institution's board chairman, Richard Salomon, apparently got the notion when he was wondering what to do with a single old gold cuff link. Now, finally, *I* have something to do with a single link of my own. I lost its mate in Cornwall a couple of years ago when it slipped out of my hand while I was dressing, rolled along the floor, and disappeared through a crack. There was no way of retrieving it short of tearing the house apart, and we were only subletting.

My sister Joan, who must be having real electrical problems, has retrieved some more of my old letters from a crack in her closet. On January 10, 1939, one of these reminds me, I had just been in Philadelphia with John Hammond, while I was writing my Profile on him. (On some assignments, one cannot expect to travel to exotic destinations, but Philadelphia is probably preferable to Passaic.) We had spent most of a day in Count Basie's dressing room at Nixon's Grand Theatre. "The dressing room at Nixon's Grand Theatre was populated with a lot of strange colored musicians," I wrote, "some of them drunk and some of them sober, but all talking in a strange, unknown language—strange and unknown at least to me."

Toward the end of May, 1940, I am herewith reminded by my own yellowing typescript, I accompanied Bill and Cecille Shawn and Janet Flanner to see Larry Adler in "Keep Off the Grass" (Janet was one of his great fans, and Bill, of course, had often played with Larry in our Bowery band), and then went out with the Wolcott Gibbses to a party (my letter does not indicate where I picked them up or what happened to the Shawns and Flanner or whose party it was), and then proceeded to Fefé's Monte Carlo, one of the nightclubs on my beat (no indication of what happened to the Gibbses), and stayed there until it closed at 4 A.M. I was really living it up back then.

This afternoon, a reporter from the *National Enquirer* stops by my office. He is writing a piece about Coca-Cola, and wants me to tell him all I know about its secret formula. He will not talk to me until he sets up and turns on a tape recorder; apparently reporters for the *Enquirer* are forbidden—conceivably by their lawyers—to interview anybody without one. If at *The New Yorker* we were to receive similar instructions, mutiny might ensue. I have never used one, though I take careful and copious notes. Not long after I wrote my Profile on Al Capp, he was a modest shareholder in a company that was trying to obtain a television franchise in Boston. An opposing group argued before the Federal Communications Commission that Capp and his associates should be turned down because some of his comic strips were salacious, and when Capp took the stand their lawyers asked him—but let *Time* magazine take over here—

about a *New Yorker* profile by E. J. Kahn, Jr., in which Capp was quoted as admitting that when "I was just a kid from the country . . . I became an expert on pornography." The profile also said that Capp's cartoons have "bits of Rabelaisian humor, often . . . adroitly covered up." Unruffled, Capp answered that both he and *New Yorker* Writer Kahn were professional "humorists" who used "exaggerated humor." The "method of *The New Yorker*," he added, "is different from other magazines. Mr. Kahn simply listens; he does not take notes." (Replies Kahn: "Of course I took notes, and I still have them.")

I still have them, and I could show them to the *Enquirer* man today, but he is interested in chemical formulae, not Rabelaisiana. I explain to him that I know absolutely nothing about the basic constituents of Coca-Cola beyond what I put in print, and I offer to lend him a copy of "The Big Drink." No, that will not do. He has to get it on his tape recorder. He proposes that I read aloud, from the book he will not peruse, into his machine. I do, and he seems enormously pleased. Could it be that he is illiterate?

November 17

Today's *Times*, along with a story from South Africa about the inquest into the death of Stephen Biko (the Biko family's lawyer, the liberal Sydney W. Kentridge, once spent an evening at my home, but a word from him would be unlikely to improve my chances of getting a visa), carries a correction of an article that appeared in its home section—one of the many new uses the paper's editors have found for surplus newsprint—way back on August 25th. The item in question referred to a Boston coterie called the Saturday Evening Girls as "young immigrant prostitutes." This morning's addendum: "The Saturday Evening Girls were not prostitutes. The group, founded in 1899, met on Saturday nights to discuss the social, ethical and economic problems of the day, to share books and to practice dance and theater. They are best known for the Paul Revere Pottery, which they operated from 1908 to 1942. The organization's members included children of new Americans. Their supporters were Boston socialites. The *Times* regrets the error."

What wouldn't one give for a peek at the exchange of correspondence there must have been from August 25th until yesterday between the *Times* and Boston, until the aggrieved parties and the embarrassed ones could agree on the wording of this retraction!

I have a drink this afternoon, by coincidence, with, among others, Abe Rosenthal and Artie Gelb, the incumbent power, if not the kingdom, at the *Times*. But before I can bring up the Saturday Evening Girls somebody mentions backgammon, and I mention to Abe and Artie that I am planning to go to Vegas to cover the tournament their columnist Magriel is co-sponsoring. *What* tournament? Artie asks sharply. Why, I say, the one announced at that press conference at "21" the other day. Artie says he has heard nothing about this dubious extracurricular activity of Magriel's and that he is going to fire him tomorrow, on grounds of conflict of interest; and Abe, who I suppose would have the final say in any such drastic action, appears to concur. I feel singularly catalytic: Having proposed Magriel's name to the paper as a backgammon columnist, I now appear to have been also the agent of his undoing.

Somebody who does not seem to care about backgammon changes the subject and asks who anyone present thinks is the greatest living American writer. Abe picks Ruth Prawer Jhabvala. (A long-shot, and maybe ineligible for this race in any event: Ruth is Polish, married to an Indian.) I bet on an entry: E. B. White and John McPhee. Others speak up for Bellow, Cheever, Updike. There is one vote for Red Smith. That cheers Abe and Artie up;

nobody is going to catch *Red* promoting a tag-team wrestling match or roller derby.

November 18

George Gianis stops by the office, shyly, wondering if I would be good enough to look over the text of an obituary he has prepared for the *Times* about his mother-in-law, who has just died, at ninety, and who, heretofore unknown to me, was many years ago a child-prodigy pianist. She married her first husband when she was forty—George's brief account of what must have been an extraordinary life reveals—because she didn't want to change her surname and he happened to have the identical one; she married her second husband because when she saw him at a party she thought he looked like Chopin. I tell George the obit looks splendid just as he has written it, and send him over to the *Times* with it.*

November 19

Anwar Sadat arrives in Israel, unprecedentedly, today, and the Arab world is furious; one segment of it has already attacked the Egyptian Embassy in Athens. The Israelis, by contrast, are treating Sadat like a hero. This convinces me, if one may generalize from particulars, that Jews are more peace-loving than Arabs, which is what I have believed all along.

The latest former C.I.A. man to Tell All is one Frank Snepp, who has accused the United States of abandoning its friends when South Vietnam collapsed. Now it seems that after he had written the book he promised Admiral Stansfield Turner—orally, not in writing—that he would show his manuscript to the agency before publication. But then he welshed and decided not to keep his word, on the ground that the C.I.A. didn't always keep *its* word. But is this two-wrongs-make-a-right performance good for other writers? When I give my word to someone I am writing about that I will or won't include such and such an incident, will my pledge no longer be acceptable on the ground that it has been demonstrated in the Snepp case that you can't trust writers any more? I am afraid some people could react like this. The saving grace may be that he is not a professional writer, and is thus no more bound by our code of ethics than we need be by his.

I wonder if I met Snepp when Ellie and I spent a day in Saigon, in 1970, en route from Hong Kong to Bangkok, when we were introduced to a few C.I.A. types. It was my only visit to Vietnam. There was little chance of

* The *Times* never ran it. Too bad.

my getting to write about the war there for *The New Yorker:* Bob Shaplen was in Southeast Asia permanently, domiciled in Hong Kong, and Jonathan Schell and Frances FitzGerald moved in and out on special assignments. Bob was in Saigon when we turned up, and arranged for Ellie and me to take a ride in a South Vietnamese helicopter, with General Ky's own pilot at the controls. One side door of the 'copter remained open, as it did, the pilot told us, when it was used for less peaceful purposes: People who were to be interrogated were now and then taken up in the vehicle, and if they balked at answering questions, with no door they could easily be pushed out.

Helen Frankenthaler has a show opening today at the Emmerich Gallery, and all the people one expects to find at such occasions—Augie Heckscher, John Sargent, F. duPlessix G., that sort—are out in full bloom. Helen, who professes to have ambivalent feelings about me (I do something peculiar to her vibes) says this time that like all the men she's kissed at her opening I smell good; she attributes that to our using perfumes and colognes. But I haven't applied either. The device I have long been searching for to make me rich overnight might prove to be my own musk.

I thought it was my turn to pick a movie to see on our way home. Ellie always picks foreign-language films; we hardly ever go together to a picture that I can understand without subtitles. I choose "Semi-Tough." We end up at something called "One Sings, the Other Doesn't," which is a translation of its original title; it was made in French. It has a women's-lib theme, more or less, and is not without its comical moments, though I might have found "Semi-Tough" more amusing, and certainly easier to follow. Afterward, E. says that she is not fundamentally interested in sports or politics or, when it comes to that, Sadat's journey to Jerusalem, because these matters are, like wars, simply the playthings of men.

November 20

It is a Sunday, and Lexy and I get in the car to drive downtown and play squash at the Harvard Club. Incredibly, there are no places to park—on Sunday!—on the street, and all the garages I know about, because it's Sunday, are shuttered. The reason seems to be that this is the last day of the close-out sale at Abercrombie & Fitch. I refuse to go to the sale, because it has been announced that Abercrombie credit cards will not be honored. At least I can now lighten the load in my wallet.

I used to shop a lot at Abercrombie's. Once I bought N. a gold cigarette lighter there. Very extravagant. I liked shopping at that store especially when *The New Yorker* was sending me somewhere cold and I knew I would be reimbursed for Abercrombie's attempts to keep me from freezing. I still have my Korea underwear and my Alaska coat. The coat was a duck-hunter's; the salesman who unloaded it on me said, as I recall, that it was guaranteed to keep a body snug and warm in an underwater blind just before the ice formed on a lake. I have put on a little weight since I returned, unfrozen, from Alaska, and the coat is now Ellie's. The underwear was pure cashmere. I bought two sets, at sixty dollars each (1951 dollars, what's more) because I felt that even during a war one should change one's underwear. I can't remember how I got the cashmere underwear washed in Korea (or, more likely, did I never take the first set off?), but in peacetime some idiot put both sets in a washing machine. Although I still have them, I can't button them up. If Abercrombie had had more expense-account patrons like me, it might never have had to shut its doors.

So that Lexy can salvage something from our excursion, I take him to "Oh, God!", a movie I enjoy hugely not so much because it has George Burns as the Deity as because it has no subtitles. We have scarcely got back home when the phone rings. It is a Harvard classmate I never heard of, calling—on a Sunday afternoon—to ask if I wouldn't like to invest some capital in some scheme of his. Perhaps I should be flattered at his apparent belief that I have capital available, but at first I am amazed at his gall. Then, after he hangs up, I feel pity for him. To what forlorn depths must he have sunk, to be driven to phoning his way through a class album on a Sunday afternoon!

This evening, Ellie and I go to the Budd Hopkinses, who are holding a U.F.O. soirée. Their featured guest is a fellow named Hynek who is director of something called a Center for U.F.O. Studies at Northwestern, and who was a consultant for "Close Encounters of the Third Kind," which, when it is next my turn to pick a movie, I have every intention of taking into consideration. Most of the other guests are confirmed believers in U.F.O.s; one, indeed, is a woman who claimed to have been kidnapped by "aliens" in 1961 and has evidently been dining out on the experience ever since. There is much talk of various sightings of unidentified flying objects. The kidnap victim says that the evidence of the best sighting of all has been destroyed. She says that six years ago practically the entire crew of an American aircraft carrier took photographs of a hovering spacecraft, but that the Navy, on orders from higher-ups, exposed all their film, confiscated all their cameras, and even submitted all hands to strip searches to make certain nobody had stashed a shot away.

The nosy, skeptical reporter in me has a brief struggle with me the polite guest. The reporter wins. I ask the woman whether, in view of the obvious importance of this episode, and in view of the obvious eagerness of some of us to pursue the strange hushed-up matter further, she would favor us with the name of the aircraft carrier.

She says she cannot remember it.

Everybody else in the room glowers at me.

I revert to the role of guest.

November 21

Now that Shawn has approved my trip to Europe, I phone my terrorism expert, Major-General Richard Lewis Clutterbuck, at the University of Exeter, in Devon. He will be available in a fortnight. Next I phone the South African Consulate General and inform Mr. Labuschagne's secretary that for once he is not to have the pleasure of notifying me that I am to be turned down, that I am withdrawing my request for a visa, and will he please return my passport, which I sent along with my application?

November 22

A memorable date. To the public, it is the date on which John Kennedy was assassinated. To me, it is also the date both of my mother's birth and her death. She was sixty when she died, which is what I am now. When I look up Clutterbuck in the British "Who's Who," I find that he was born exactly sixty years ago today.

The public library credits me with ten dollars and eighty-two cents for my odd cuff link.

November 23

A young woman phones who is writing a thesis on Frank Sinatra. She called Harper & Row, which (as Harper & Bros.) published the book, but whoever she spoke to had never heard either of the book or of me.

Joey phones from Philadelphia. He wants to take me to a pro football game—Giants vs. Cardinals—on my birthday. But I will be in England. Still, it is the thought that counts. Joey wonders if I saw the item the *Times* ran about the Plimpton-Magriel backgammon match and the announcement of the Las Vegas tournament. No, I missed it, as, evidently, did Rosenthal and Gelb. This is the first evidence I've had that these editorial titans don't read every word in their own newspaper.

November 24

It is Thanksgiving Day, which means it is Thursday, which further means that, when I pick up the *Times*, I defer looking at the obit page until I have scanned the index to see if Magriel's backgammon column is in the paper. It is. He didn't get fired after all. My conscience is clear. Let us give thanks.

This will be the first Thanksgiving in quite a while that I have not celebrated on Cape Cod. It is always appropriate to spend this particular holiday in Truro, which is, of course, Pilgrim territory. But inasmuch as Ellie and I have just left Truro, we don't feel like driving back again. Also, I am not sure we could muster enough relatively able-bodied participants for the touch-football game that for many years was as much a part of our traditional Thanksgiving Day observance as was cranberry sauce. (The current issue of the *Saturday Review* contains something that the editors of *The New Yorker* would never condone—a big Thanksgiving feature article about cranberries, wrapped around a two-page color advertisement for Ocean Spray Cranberries, Inc.) We go instead to Lilo's for a New York Thanksgiving dinner, taking along a jug of our homemade Cape Cod beach-plum brandy, to remind us of our territorial links to Pilgrim history.

November 26

I went Christmas shopping yesterday, because I am not sure how long I will stay in England. It was the ideal time—plenty of merchandise on display, stores not yet overly crowded, a chance for me to reflect leisurely about what I wanted to buy. Usually, I do my shopping so late that I can't have anything delivered and have to lug it around with me—like as not, in a blizzard. Yesterday, the weather was acceptable, and the city was full of sales clerks practically begging to let them wait on me. What a heady experience! Unfortunately, because I was under no calendar pressure, I fell victim to irresolution and ended up by not making a single purchase. But I retain a secret weapon against the demands of that holiday—the duty-free shops that await me at the airports that lie ahead.

A long letter from Chase Peterson, Harvard's vice-president in charge of alumni affairs and development, asking me to write something about the university's specialness. "Would you then help us discover what it is we are about?" he says. Chase, an endrocrinologist from Utah, was dean of admissions at Harvard when I was working on my book about the institution, and thanks to him I was accorded the rare privilege of sitting in on an early-spring session when he and his colleagues in admissions were deciding who would or would not be admitted to Harvard College the following fall. It was an illuminating experience, and I was bound only by my promise not to reveal the identities of any of the candidates whose virtues or lack thereof were so candidly and conscientiously appraised.

Chase spent a few summers at Truro, where to keep up with his profession he practiced medicine at our local clinic. He was also a formidable tennis player, and he would have had no trouble disposing of most of us even if those of us who had children who were thinking of applying for admission to Harvard could not bring ourselves to try especially hard to pass him at the net or drop a lob over his head.

But I do not know how to answer his letter. Having written a whole book about what I thought Harvard was about, I find my mind blank.

After taking in a couple of other art openings, E. and I end up at Jon Schueler's show, and then repair to his new loft for a crowded buffet. Phil Hamburger is there. He is taking over Geoffrey Hellman's old office, at Shawn's invitation, but has qualms about moving into it so soon. I tell him that he shouldn't have any. Geoffrey acquired his corner office, as I acquired mine, by virtue of seniority; and now Phil has got to be one of our most senior one-window-cell prisoners and should deservedly (as Shawn no doubt reckoned when he made the offer) move up into a double-exposure cubicle and thus become, in the *New Yorker* scheme of things, a sort of trusty.

November 27

In the *Times* this Sunday, John McPhee's "Coming into the Country" has the page-one spot in the book review. There's an accompanying interview, in the course of which John is asked, "Do you see yourself as expanding or even creating a new genre of writing—one that began with the Profile?" John starts off his reply with "Not really," then gives proper credit to Bill Shawn for the evolution of *New Yorker* fact-writing, then says, "But the Lieblings, the Alva Johnstons, the Jack Kahns came along much earlier than I." I do not know whether or not to be flattered. Joe Liebling has been dead for thirteen years, and Johnston for more than twice that long. I know McPhee means this as a compliment, and I take it as such and appreciate it, but also I feel prematurely buried.

Quite apart from the publication of John's book, Alaska has been much in the news. There was a report in the papers the other day about Kay Fanning's legal struggles—which have now apparently got into the courts—to keep her *Daily News* going in Anchorage. And now comes word that Lieutenant Governor Lowell Thomas, Jr., just back from a trip to South Africa, first said publicly that the blacks in that country weren't yet ready to enjoy the vote, and then when confronted with that statement by the Black Caucus of Alaska (I didn't know the state had one) compounded the gaffe by saying that he didn't believe—and this in a place full of sensitive Eskimos!— in interracial marriage. He will probably back off, of course; politicians always do. He will say he was misquoted or misunderstood. But maybe the next time I apply for a visa to South Africa, I should try to get a letter of recommendation from this Doubting Thomas.

November 28

Ellie and I call on our new family physician. Nothing wrong with us; it just seemed to make sense to become acquainted with Dr. Gorham while we could talk about something other than what ailed us. He confirms that he makes house calls. What pleases E. about him as much as anything else is that he has a ground-floor office, and that on top of whatever other worries might next take her to his presence she won't have to fret about self-service elevators.

Mr. Labuschagne phones. He apparently is determined to have the last word. So in spite of the fact that I have already notified him that I am withdrawing my visa application, he now wants to inform me officially that the application was "unsuccessful." I accept his statement with the gravity it warrants.

I take the British Airways night flight to London.

November 29

At Heathrow, and in my taxi, there seem to be more signs in Arabic than I recall from my last visit to England, a year ago. At the Hilton Hotel newsstand, the *International Herald Tribune* has a whole section devoted to Arabs, and next to it on display is *El-Arab*, published in Arabic in London. The hotel is aswarm with Arabs, which may be one reason why everybody is frisked on entering the place. But the Hilton has not been taken over, I hear, to the extent of the Dorchester up the street, which is now owned by Arabs and is now colloquially called the Desert Inn.

I drive out to a northwest residential enclave of London to dine with Larry Adler and Selina Hastings. Selina is taking a police training course in connection with a magazine piece she's writing. "I could throw you over my shoulder," she says. But I have already enjoyed this experience, or at any rate have had it. Years ago, when the New York City Police Department began recruiting women for its uniformed ranks, I did a Talk of the Town story on one of them. She came to my office to be interviewed, and when I asked her something about *her* training she stood up and invited me to make a pass at her. I approached her, and she grabbed one of my arms and threw me over her shoulder. Unfortunately, just as we were executing this *pas de deux* one of our senior editors happened to look in my office, and it was some time after that before any suggestion of mine about doing a piece on any young female was favorably entertained.

I was, however, judged to be up to dealing with people who were—well—odd. This stemmed in part, I guess, from my having survived a reportorial weekend, on Long Island, in the company of a group that called itself the Royal Fraternity of Master Metaphysicians. The fraternity had bought a hundred-and-ten-room mansion once the property of William K. Vanderbilt, and in this large gilded cage was preparing to raise, unto immortality, a five-month-old girl who had been entrusted to its care.

Not long after my fraternization with that curious child-guidance center, I was sitting in my *New Yorker* office, minding my own business, when a receptionist, who had apparently been tipped off that I did well with freaks, ushered into my cubicle a man who had with him a small live animal that he was sure we would want to write up in our pages. It was a fitch—a variety of polecat. He deposited the fitch on my desk, and some secretary spotted it scampering about there, and called another secretary to have a look at the cute little thing, and in short order most of the women on the premises came by to view and cuddle it, and to admire its strange musky scent.

Finally Janet Flanner, who was in New York at the time (the Nazis had her Paris) materialized. Inasmuch as her pen name was "Genet"—civet cat— it seemed especially fit for her to be introduced to the visiting polecat, and she, too, buried her nose in its fur. She said the odor reminded her of the base of good French perfumes. The oohing and aahing of the women who had commandeered all the space around my desk effectively drowned out the voice of the fitch's owner, who was trying to explain to me that fitches, for all their lovability, were untidy creatures, one of whose less beguiling habits was to roll in their own urine.

Secretaries aside, Ross had never had many women working for him. Janet was one notable exception, of course, and there were memorable others—Katharine White in her fiction department, Mollie Panter-Downes in London, Dorothy Parker, Helen Hokinson, Phyllis McGinley, Lois Long, and Margaret Case Harriman (who was sort of family, since her father owned the Algonquin). Otherwise Ross, who before he started *The New Yorker* had edited the *American Legion Monthly*, seemed to feel that the role of women in important enterprises should be largely an auxiliary one. When the Second World War came along and so many of his male contributors and editors were whisked away from his premises, he was pleasantly surprised to discover that women—Andy Logan, for instance, Lillian Ross—were every bit as capable of acceptable work as men.

November 30

As some people go to Evian or Vichy, or even Bath, for the waters, so do I go to London for the crossword puzzles. My passion for them is nearly orgiastic, assuming there can be a one-person orgy. Crossword puzzles are less costly and complicating than most orgies, too, although the London

Times is up to fifteen pence, putting it—at a $1.84-to-the-pound exchange rate—in a price bracket slightly above that of its New York counterpart.

Those marvelous letters that the London *Times* runs are still much in evidence. Today's paper carries one headed Modernization of the Lord's Prayer and another headed Safeguarding the Otter.

In midafternoon I decide it is time to get to work. I was not sent to London to do a socioeconomic survey on the impact of Arabs on what remains of the British Empire. So I betake myself to the British Museum of Natural History, on Cromwell Road—I have often driven by this huge old pile, but have never entered it—to call on Peter Whitehead, one of my two reasons for being here. Dr. Whitehead, who my sources have informed me is one of the foremost herring-and-anchovy experts on earth, suggests that we go out to dinner after he has given me a brief guided tour of his shop. The shop is stocked mostly with jars of pickled fish. He also takes me, as it were, backstage—to the underground caverns where the museum, large as it is, keeps all the specimens it hasn't room to put on public display. In that connection, my escort, whose formal title is head of the Fish Section of the Department of Zoology, confesses harboring some disappointment about his colleagues' attitude toward his field of inquiry: He used to have a lovely fish gallery in one of the exhibition halls, he says, but now—he shakes his head wonderingly at the absurdity of the whole business—it has been taken away from him and converted into a display devoted to, of all things, the biology of man.

When we move along to a restaurant, I take note that my ichthyologically oriented companion orders neither herrings nor anchovies, nor any other kind of seafood. "I do like anchovies, actually," he tells me, "but whenever I eat them I feel a bit of a cannibal. I spend so much of my days admiring their beautiful structure, you know, and then to eat them seems a bit much. I don't mind anchovy paste. That softens the blow." He orders beef.

I admire Dr. Whitehead's necktie, which is clearly a club tie, and I ask him which club it symbolizes. I rather hope the answer will be something like "the Royal Engrauloid Society." He seems surprised, knowing I hail from midtown New York, that I do not recognize the four-in-hand. It is that of the New York Yacht Club—an institution, it turns out further, through whose portals the wearer has never yet passed. Whitehead got the tie from a bona fide member who is his mother's brother-in-law. Sensing that I may have embarrassed him by accusing him, however innocently and indirectly, of sporting false colors, I attempt to cheer him up by saying that I have never been inside the yacht club either, even though it is a mere one hundred feet from my office.

That is a white lie, but barely. I once spent twenty minutes inside that club. I had an appointment to interview a member there at 11:30 one morning. At 11:50, he phoned me at the club, and explained that he had got himself unexpectedly tied up. Would I mind meeting him instead at an upper-east-side apartment? I knew he lived on Long Island. He was doing me a favor by letting me pick his brains, so, though considerably inconvenienced both by the delay and the change of venue, I proceeded uptown. He was tying his necktie—a run-of-the-mill foulard—when I arrived, and there was other evidence on the scene that, until not very long before my arrival, it had also been occupied by someone else. I still don't know much about the yacht club, but I am prepared to uphold the negative in any future debate having to do with whether or not its members are universally faithful.

December 1

At Paddington Station, I board a 10:30 express to the southwest, which leaves exactly on time. I have bought a first-class ticket—nothing is too good for one of Shawn's emissaries embarking on a research expedition to far-off Devon—but after peering into a coach, admiring its elegance, and happily settling into one of its clean, comfortable seats, I find when the ticket-taker comes along that this is only second class. I am too cozy to move. I reflect en route to the University of Exeter and my first confrontation with Major General, now Doctor, Clutterbuck, that I have something of a problem facing me when it comes to writing about him and terrorism: Shawn, on approving the idea a couple weeks ago, said that there was another *New Yorker* piece in the works—he naturally did not identify the writer; that is not our way of doing things—about the relationship between terrorism and the media, so will I please not go into *that*. But how in the television era can one write anything sensible about terrorism and ignore television? Well, I shall try; it's a pity, though, to be constrained from the outset to avoid describing the day that I, and hundreds of other media people, stood outside the Olympic Village at Munich in 1972, watching the Arab terrorists who had murderously invaded the Israeli quarters, and watching West German snipers, camouflaged as athletes, try to sneak around and get Arabs in their sights, while on all sides television cameras ground away for the rest of the world to witness our collective anguish.

Clutterbuck, when I arrive, is hospitable and, more to my point, articulate. I mention the tight security at the Hilton in London, and he says he regards that as sensible, because the I.R.A. has already set off one bomb in that hotel and everybody expects a repeat performance. Also, he says the watchfulness is useful because there are so many people who stay at the Hilton who are eminently kidnappable. (I hope he is referring to the Arabs, though it would be interesting to learn how much ransom Shawn thinks I am worth.) I am to spend this night in downtown Exeter at the White Hart Inn, where Clutterbuck has booked me a room. It is a funny old hostelry, and there is no frisking in the lobby. The main danger is not being able to find one's room. The inn—reminiscent in this respect alone of Frank Lloyd Wright's Imperial Hotel in Tokyo—has so many interior twists and turns and levels that despite its modest size one can get quite lost.* Clutterbuck has to work this evening, but his research assistant, Louise Perry, graciously consents to keep me company at dinner. I feel especially secure in her presence; she used to be a cop. We conclude our meal with Stilton and port. I have a birthday coming up momentarily, and the main surprise I will receive on it is, probably, an attack of gout.

December 2

I don't have gout this morning, but I do have a port hangover, which may have been partly caused by my having preceded the cocktail hour by joining Clutterbuck and trying to match him down a pint and a half of strong draught ale. One could hardly blame him: His alternative was to go straight home and tackle the galley proofs of a book.

The terrorist expert and I reconvene in the morning and spend a good part of this day, like yesterday, talking, until it is time for me to catch a train back to London. I buy a first-class ticket, again, mainly out of curiosity. First class is first class, all right, but not markedly better than second class. The British may have their problems (their firemen and elevator mainte-nance men are on strike at the moment), but in some respects they have their former colonies thoroughly beaten.

I get back to London in time to dine with Tom Whiteside, who is en route to Italy to work on a *New Yorker* piece and who knew I was abroad, too. We elect to go to Wheeler's, on Old Compton Street, one of my favorite London restaurants. I have not been working with Dr. Whitehead long enough yet to have any compunctions about eating fish. Tom and I reflect that this is a rare occasion indeed—two *New Yorker* writers travelling abroad on assign-ments for the magazine, two expense accounts, and only one meal. How do we handle so unusual a situation? Very simple: We flip a coin. I lose. I urge Tom to eat heartily. Over oysters, he wonders what has brought me to this part of the world, and I start talking about terrorism. A funny look comes over Tom's face. It shortly develops that the piece on terrorism and the media Shawn alluded to is *his* piece. Bill, in his conscientious fashion, had told Tom about *my* piece before giving me the go ahead, but in his cautious fashion hadn't identified me as the writer involved. Over Dover sole, and a moderate-priced Chablis (we *New Yorker* writers do not believe in taking

* It is not until checkout time the following morning that I learn my way around with confidence; when and if I next return to the White Hart, I will no doubt have to start the educational process all over again.

undue advantage of our generous patron), Tom and I agree to steer as clear as possible of one another's turf, and we agree further not to disclose to Shawn that one of his secrets has accidentally been exposed; we would not wish to be the unwitting cause of the subversion of his arcane system of governance.

I once came close to finding out how Shawn copes with words other than those over which he has total control. It occurred in the sixties, when the Sunday magazine section of the New York *Herald Tribune* ran Tom Wolfe's nasty attack on *The New Yorker* and on Bill personally. The Wolfe opus was in two parts, and after the first snide part came out, somebody at *The New Yorker* thought it might be possible to stop publication of the second. There was only one person at the *Tribune* with the authority to do that—its owner and publisher, John Hay Whitney.

It happened, by chance, that Whitney's secretary at the paper had earlier worked for *The New Yorker*, but even so nobody at our magazine could get through to him on the phone. There was only one person at *The New Yorker* who had Jock Whitney's unlisted home phone number—me. I had done a two-part (non-snide) Profile on Jock back in 1951, and he and I were, though by no means close friends, on friendly terms.

I was attending a Parents' Day at Andover when I got an urgent call from *The New Yorker*. Mr. Shawn wanted to sit down face-to-face, as soon as possible, with Mr. Whitney. Could I—would I—set this up? I called Jock at his home. He was understandably reluctant to agree to such a confrontation. I beseeched him. He yielded, but with one stipulation: Inasmuch as he knew me but did not know Shawn, I had to accompany my editor to the meeting. I called back *The New Yorker*, triumphantly: I had an appointment set up for the following day, such and such a place, such and such a time. There was, however, this one condition: Bill would have to take me along.

The date was never kept. I never learned why, nor did I deem it my business to try to find out. The second part of the Wolfe piece was published on schedule. It probably would have been in any event.

December 3

I spend the morning alternately reading various items of literature that Dr. Whitehead and Dr. Clutterbuck have kindly pressed upon me. Can there be any connection between terrorism and fish? Of course there is; if only I had addressed myself to this question sooner, I could have written "Jaws" and retired. After lunch, to clear my head of such disturbing thoughts, I take a stroll around London. The papers are full of stories about the distressing state of the local economy (notwithstanding the pound's recently increasing strength vis-à-vis the dollar), but in the West End—the part of London that visiting Arabs and I tend mostly to frequent—one would never guess it. The streets practically throb with affluence.

Larry and Selina have invited me to accompany them to a West End cocktail party, and thence to a dinner party at Hampstead Heath or some such outlying oasis. They evidently want to leave the dinner party early and return to the cocktail party, so I am instructed to say at dinner that I have to catch a plane, whereupon they will offer to drive me to the airport, whereupon we can all return to Party No. 1. I point out to them that should somebody else at the dinner chance to be catching a plane and propose that I accompany him I will be in a hell of a fix; a round trip to Heathrow is not my idea of Saturday-night fun and games. Larry says I worry too much.

Our first hostess (and, in due course, also our third) has affluence spilling all over her triplex. I am told that in bygone days she used to preside over Sunday-afternoon literary gatherings, but then she switched her salon hour to Saturday night. Not, however, wishing to lose touch entirely with the Sabbath, she expects her Saturday guests to stay until 6 A.M. Sunday morning. Among them, this weekend, I am pleased to find the new editor of *Punch*, Alan Coren, who invites me to lunch next week if I am still around. I accept, and say that if I have left by then he should lunch with me in New York, and I boldly propose, inasmuch as Coren says he has never met Shawn, to bring the editor of *The New Yorker* along. *In vino*, bravado. Among the other writers on the scene is Hella Pick, of the *Guardian*, who says she would invite me for dinner tomorrow if she had enough food, but since she doesn't won't I come in—Larry is included—for dessert? I have a lot of reading still to do, so I leave the marathon bash well before dawn, thus regrettably missing an opportunity to chat at more than superficial length with a woman who says her mission in life for the next couple of years is going to be to rescue the dirigible from oblivion.

December 4

My birthday, and how different from last year's, when Ellie threw me the big party and I was blissfully awash in ego-building sentimentality! Ginger and Don Reiman brought a family tree they made, bearing so many of the names that have figured importantly in my life—Larry Adler, Nathan Pusey, Tommy Kane, my Truro neighbor; Minagawa, one of the Japanese stragglers I wrote about; my dog Barge; and *Ursus Americanus*, a bear that may or may not have sniffed around my suburban garbage shed. A sixty-first birthday warrants no such gala rites, but it is a nice one notwithstanding, carrying with it heartening connotations that nine long years will yet pass before another milestone anniversary materializes.

It is Sunday, and—conceivably because of the research I am engaged in—the papers seem unusually full of stories that have to do with terrorists.

They are rampant in Rhodesia. There is so much unrest in Bermuda that Britain is flying troops in. The Queen's Gallantry Award is being bestowed, posthumously, on a tube-train driver who was shot by the I.R.A. during a bombing nineteen months ago. There are no stories about herrings or anchovies.

Parts of *The New Yorker*—it all has to do, I gather, with color advertising pages taking more time to print than monochromatic ones—go to press at different times. This is also true, of course, of many Sunday newspapers: The New York *Times'* weekly book section is usually available five days before the Sunday date it bears. (The New York *News* used to have a complete Sunday paper—front page, sports section, the works—that one could find in small New England towns several days before the Sunday in question; the news and sports sections, it goes without saying, contained mostly feature stories.) Today's Sunday *Telegraph* graphically illustrates the dangers inherent in *seriatim* printing. In the feature section there is an interview with an English actress who begins her day, according to the story, by drinking champagne at three in the afternoon. " 'Go on—carve me up!' " the story has the actress telling the interviewer. " 'Everyone else has.' " The interviewer does go on to say that the actress had not long ago been dropped from a play because she couldn't remember her lines. It is by and large a sympathetic interview. But elsewhere in the same paper, in an up-to-the-minute news section, there is an item to the effect that the same actress has been fined one hundred and seventy-five pounds and disqualified from driving for twelve months because when the police stopped her car she wouldn't give her name and address and wouldn't take a breath test.

London is a tense city. People are really worried about terrorists and their destructiveness. Along with theatrical posters, one sees in the Underground stations warnings not to pick up unattended bags.

Larry Adler and I, killing time before we repair to Hella Pick's for dessert, have a leisurely dinner at the splendidly ornate Café Royale. I cannot imagine when Hella's dessert hour will begin; our restaurant is nearly empty at seven-thirty and does not begin to fill up till nine. I mention to Larry having read somewhere not long ago that Artur Rubinstein, old as he is, still practices the piano six hours a day, and I wonder if harmonica virtuosos have any comparable discipline. Not exactly, Larry says. Well, I press on, what would his average daily stint of practicing amount to? "I *never* practice," he says. That has got to be virtuosity unparalleled.

At Hella's (where at ten o'clock the dinner guests are still in mid-entrée), we find a couple of diplomats, one English, one American. The American one, now a full-fledged ambassador in western Europe, looks startled when I enter. It develops that, hearing I was en route, he had told some nasty stories about me, but had been thinking about somebody else. He will not confess who it was he calumniated, but in any event he would hardly seem to have behaved diplomatically. The ambassador attempts to divert attention from himself by asking what I am up to, and when I mention terrorism, he says that the State Department, because of the threats of violence that have been lately levelled against personages like himself, has furnished him with an armored limousine. The only hitch is that the limousine is so long it can't turn into the narrow street where his office is situated, so his chauffeur-bodyguard has to let him out at a corner, a block from his destination, and he walks unescorted the rest of the way.

I feel I should make some recognition of my natal anniversary. When dessert is finally over and everybody leaves the table, I blow out the candles on it.

December 5

The Hilton thinks we are all Arabs, or at any rate Moslems. I sent some laundry out yesterday morning as "Kahn" and got it back last night as "Khan." At least I got it back. Prime Minister Begin of Israel, who is also in town, has been less fortunate. He has come down with a stomach disorder that the local newspapers bluntly describe—terrorism or mere botulism?—as having been caused by food poisoning.

Whenever I am in England, I make a point of having kippers for breakfast—except, I suddenly realize, when I am writing about herrings. I spend all day today at the Nathismus, which is the cable address of Dr. Whitehead's institution and is what I have taken familiarly to calling it in my notes. (People sometimes ask how I can possibly take notes accurately in view of my unfamiliarity with shorthand. The answer is that, like most other reporters, I have developed my own personal kind of speedwriting, marked by excessive use of initials and abbreviations. "HBS," for instance, stands for either "Herbert Bayard Swope" or "Harvard Business School," unless, of course, I happen to be writing an article about the producer of "High Button Shoes.") It is sort of fun to be shifting gears like this between two reportorial ventures so utterly dissimilar. I don't often attempt to gobble up research on one piece—let alone two—so voraciously, but I don't like travelling alone, and am already tentatively planning to leave Araby on Wednesday.

At the end of a long day at the museum, Peter Whitehead and I repair to a pub near Oxford Circus, where he wants me to meet a young friend of his— a fellow who does freelance pieces for newspapers. The young man says he likes my wrinkles, a compliment about which I have mixed feelings. I seek to compliment *him* by congratulating him on having begun to make his mark

417

as a journalist. He replies rather stuffily that he is not a journalist but a writer. By the time he gets to be thirty, he will probably settle for nothing less than "author." His bones are probably impervious to sticks and stones. People may call me anything they like, provided only that they pay me enough for what I produce to preclude my having to attempt to learn a trade.

December 6

David Bruce is dead, at seventy-nine. Whoever goes next—Averell Harriman or Ellsworth Bunker—the survivor will unarguably be the most Nestorian diplomat of our time. I have had dealings of a sort with the entire venerable triumvirate—Harriman when I wrote a *New Yorker* Profile about him, Bunker when he was negotiating the Panama Canal treaties and I was heading toward the canal, Bruce when he was running the American liaison office in Peking. I played hookey from both of the options offered to our tour group in China one morning—a visit either to a university or a primary school—to call on the ambassador for a comradely chat. He had been in China only briefly, but told me with pleasure how Madame Mao Tse-tung, who was then still untainted with gangsterism, had done him the unusual honor of joining him to watch a friendly basketball game between their respective nations. When Mr. Bruce, who as ambassador to London had presided over a staff of eight hundred, and who as ambassador to Bonn over a staff of three thousand, remarked that in Peking he had only two dozen assistants, I suggested jokingly that his retinue might be nearly as small as that attached to the American ambassador to Lomé, Togo. "Probably smaller," he replied, unflappably. But he did not seem overworked. I spent the better part of the morning at the liaison office and never once heard a phone ring.

When I returned to our hotel, I learned that our group was having lunch at the Summer Palace. One of the cars assigned to us was still around, and drove me out into the Western Hills to join Ellie and the rest of our leftist gang of sixteen. A member of our party who had already begun harboring suspicions that I was a reactionary asked me where I had been all morning, and when it came out that I had been playing footsie with Ambassador Bruce, eyebrows were raised all around. A few minutes later, I heard one of the women among us, perhaps inspired by my defection from her orthodoxy, say to a Chinese sitting next to her that *all* professors specializing in Far Eastern studies at *all* American universities, from John K. Fairbank on up or down, were "pawns of the imperialist State Department." I was tempted to interject that as long as ten years after the death of Senator Joe McCarthy that department had been loath to let Fairbank cross its threshold, because he was thought to be too radical, but I held my tongue; it was early in our tour of the People's Republic and I was trying to mend my political fences, or at the least keep them from becoming irreparably unravelled.

I head back to Exeter, second class. I do not mind squandering Shawn's money on oysters for Whiteside, but why should I pamper myself? Today I am to audit a couple of Clutterbuck's seminars, so I can observe him in pedagogical action. When he pauses for a coffee break in midmorning, his students all conscientiously drop coins into a coffee can—coffee tin, I should say, remembering where I am. On being proffered a mug, I ask a young woman what the tab is. She says twopence. In my haste to make myself part of the gang, I drop two coppers into the can, realizing an instant later that each was a twopenny piece. It would be undignified to fish one of them out again (see, I am thinking of fish), so I let this pass. Rather than look like a profligate when I submit my expense account, however, I resolve not to request any reimbursement at all for this particular outlay. That is the kind of small favor we *New Yorker* ambassadors are forever doing for the magazine and for which, since we do not bring them up ourselves in our dispatches, we receive far too little credit.

Dr. Clutterbuck drives me out to his home, in the suburban village of Thorverton, for a thumping lunch, which makes me drowsy; I am glad I shall not have to take an examination on what I gleaned in class this afternoon. By the time I am ready to return to London, I realize I'll be having dinner on the train, so I switch back to first class, where the menu is presumably more in keeping with the standards that have been set for me at noon. My table companion is a ship's engineer, who boarded the train at some seaport or other, having just brought in a vessel—more or less singlehanded, judging from his account of the voyage—from Spain.

"You know much about engines?" he asks.

If I say "Yes," he will want to discuss ships' engines with me, and if I say "No," he will explain them to me. I compromise with a "Not much," whereupon I am treated to a half-hour recapitulation of how my companion removed a cylinder head in a Force Nine gale, with tools flying into the bilge in every which direction.

Then he asks what I do, and I say I write. This is a mistake. A writer! *His* life story would make a spectacular book, he tells me, and perhaps I could help him with it. Or, failing that, a book about his son, who designs jewelry, might be equally absorbing. I say, trying to abort this collaboration before it gets out of hand, that I write only on international politics, which would startle Shawn if he and my engineer ever met up on the teetering brink of the same bilge.

Then my messmate, who has been consuming gins and tonic as if to compensate for a slow-boat-to-China abstinence, proposes that we guess one another's age. He will go first. He guesses that I am not yet fifty. I am beginning to like this chap enormously. It is my turn. I figure him for about sixty-seven or sixty-eight, but to flatter him I say, "Sixty-three."

He says I am a year off.

"Sixty-four?"

No, he will be sixty-two, next year, and what about me?

My God, we are virtually chronological twins. How did I ever get into this tactless mess? I mutter that I am closer to his age than he believes, and, because a young woman is providentially walking past our table, he does not pursue his line of interrogation. "A woman is as old as she looks," he says instead, "and a man is old when he stops looking at a woman's legs." He does not stop until he espies the dining-car steward and orders another drink.

Today is his wife's birthday, the engineer goes on when his glass is refilled, and he is going to celebrate with a real booze-up. He bought his wife a leather bag in Spain for only twenty quid, and himself a pair of shoes, presumably also leather, for another fifteen quid. He shows me both bargain purchases. He would also have bought a pair of handsome porcelain doves, for ten pounds, but he ran out of quid, having spent more than he had anticipated on some brandy and some wine, which he consumed while waiting for our train. I must say that he holds it all rather well, for a man our age.

December 7

I decide I have enough material for my articles and on impulse fly back to New York. The airport bookstall features a couple of recent paperbacks entitled "Dubai" and "Oil Sheik," and also sells the "Arabic Guide to London." Rushing through the duty-free shop, I grab, among other Christmas gifts, a box of Havana cigars for my brother-in-law, who I know will be charmed with this fragrant contraband.* When I reach New York, it is midafternoon—though, of course, six hours later according to the time at which I arose in London—so I go to the office and discover that Shawn has approved a Talk idea I suggested: the opening this very day of a Cooper-Hewitt Museum exhibit about subways, in a subway station. I wander over there, notebook in hand, but am too laden with jet lag to take coherent cognizance of the proceedings. I excuse my failure by reminding myself that Shawn has a Talk story of mine in type about an earlier Cooper-Hewitt show that he hasn't run yet.

Ellie is out when I arrive home, but her East German typewriter, the one

---

* The careful shopper takes his time. When on December 25th Patrick Smith unwraps his treasure, the cigars turn out to have been made in the Philippines.

that got dropped during the Truro rainstorm, is on the floor next to the front door. I know what that means. Her "i" key, which suffered the worst harm in the accident, must have stopped functioning again. It will not budge. At least we have found a solution to this problem: It is to take the typewriter for a ride in the car and jiggle it. I bought E. some duty-free perfume (L'Heure Bleu, naturally; I can never remember her shoe size but I know *that*), but now I will give her a real surprise. I call the garage, get the car out, and drive her typewriter restoratively around Central Park. When I return, the "i" key leaps at a finger's touch from its bed.

December 8

I am tricked this morning, maybe because I am still on a European time schedule. My office phone rings, and when I pick it up a woman's voice says, "Hello, sweetheart."

I pause. The voice is certainly familiar.

"Do you know who this is?" the voice goes on.

How can I pretend I do not? "N.," I say.

"Who is N.?" the voice asks.

I am not only tricked but trapped. The voice turns out to be that of the wife of a friend from abroad whom I haven't talked to in ages. Nor have I to N. But I never thought I would fail to recognize her voice.

Barbara Solonche, one of whose jobs at *The New Yorker* is to handle illustrations for long fact pieces, pops into my office. My Georgia Profile, a two-parter, has been tentatively scheduled to run early next year (practically tomorrow, by our timetable), and for one part Mr. Shawn wants a photograph of an urban scene—but not Savannah—for her to give to the artist who will do the job, and for the other part Mr. Shawn wants a photograph of a rural scene, perhaps a pecan grove—but emphatically *not* peanuts. My office couch is piled from one end to the other with printed materials about Georgia, and I begin to rummage through them. The best I can come up with is an ad in a copy of *Atlanta* magazine containing an attractive depiction of a landscape, but when I present it triumphantly to Barbara she perceives on closer inspection that the area portrayed is upstate New York. So much research, and none of it suitable to the purpose at hand! Let us hope that the magazine won't decide to assign photographers to its writers, for that is a prospect that any writer would naturally dread.

At home, Lexy, who is going on fifteen, calls my attention to a color ad in *The New Yorker* showing, in profile, the upper torso of a naked woman, with her left nipple clearly in view. It had never previously occurred to me that the lad was interested in the products of Princess Marcella Borghese. People sometimes accuse *The New Yorker* of being stodgy, but Lexy's discovery is proof, if any were needed, that we march with the times. A generation ago, we were squeamish about accepting bra-and-panty ads. It wouldn't surprise me if a generation hence we reached the stage of two nipples, full front.

December 9

I made it back from Europe in time for the lunch that a few of my Harvard classmates have been attending annually for the last several years at the Bowery Savings Bank, ever since Rusty Crawford became the chairman of its board. Of the regular crowd, Fag Goodhue, Paul Killiam, Dick Lewisohn, Walter Page, and Charlie Thieriot are present today, and Rusty has invited Pete Ahrens to join us. Rusty reminds us that a year ago we all bet on who would be the next mayor of New York, and to put our money where our mouths were, we each gave Rusty a dollar. It turns out that Lewisohn was the only one among us who favored Ed Koch, so Dick is now presented with the pool, which Rusty has thoughtfully invested in the Bowery at six per cent.

Pete Ahrens talks revealingly about the research he has been doing at Rockefeller University on cholesterol. He says, *inter alia*, that it is his professional surmise, as a physician, that smoking may be all right for some people. I doubt that I am among them. (Back at the magazine, Pat Crow is drawing up an agreement for him and me about who can stop smoking first; he wants to start the competition on January 3, so we can both inhale freely over the holiday weekend.) Dr. Ahrens invites all of us at lunch to come to Rockefeller any time as patients; there will be no charge. He adds hastily that at the moment we all look to him, from perfunctory observation, to be in great shape. When cake is passed around, I notice that Pete doesn't take any, so I skip it, too.

Most banks don't serve drinks at lunch, even in private dining rooms like Chairman Crawford's, but we have not gathered for banking business. Along with toasting one another for still being alive and with reasonable prospects of reconvening one year hence (when Rusty retires, as he will soon, we will have to come up with an alternate plan, conceivably one involving treating *him* to lunch), we drink a special toast to Walter Page, who is about to become chairman of the board of J. P. Morgan. Walter says on departing that somebody mentioned to him en passant that his Morgan Guaranty has just borrowed a million dollars from Rusty's Bowery. Rusty says nobody has mentioned it to him. To both of them, the amount is clearly a bagatelle.

What a day for longevity this one has turned into! I want to interview Guy Bolton, who at ninety-five has just finished a new play, and when I call him at his Long Island home he comes to the phone and in a sturdy voice invites me out to lunch one day soon; I share a cab, heading uptown, with Howard Reiling, who will be celebrating his eighty-eighth birthday this weekend; and we are to dine at the Blivens' with Bruce's mother, Rosie, who is just now turning eighty-nine.

Rosie Bliven, who has known me since I was three, asks me how old my nurse Bertha is, or would be if she were still alive. My sisters and I lost track of her not long after she, although a naturalized American, rather injudiciously elected to return to her native Germany just before the outbreak of the Second World War. (Until just before the onset of my second birthday, my mother once told me, I spoke more German than English.) Let's see, Bertha joined our household in 1917, sixty years ago, so if by any wild chance she were still alive she would be just about Rosie's age today.

Bruce and Naomi have a belated birthday gift for me—two giant jars of Zabar's dill pickles. Now, there is a present a person can *use*.

December 12

Ellie and I spent all day yesterday, Sunday, at home. There was a cocktail party for a women's cause and an evening affair for a children's cause, for both of which we had duly purchased benefit tickets. Having thus fulfilled our obligations to our consciences, we felt under no obligation to go.

At tennis this morning, there is no heat inside the bubble, and predictably, I catch a cold. In an exhaustive questionnaire I filled out yesterday to oblige our new doctor, who I must say is inquisitive, I answered "No" to the question "Do you often have colds?" I certainly have them occasionally, like right now. What does "often" mean, clinically?

Conscience-driven, I go to a meeting of the newly reconstituted guiding body of the African Student Aid Fund, of which I have been a less than exemplary director for several years. We have a new leader, who invites all of us—and our spouses—to a buffet afterward. He explains that his wife and he have been abroad, on business, for ten years, and that they have no friends in New York: *We* are to be his friends. At dinner, Ellie loses a friend—a woman of whom E. sharply asks in a heated discussion about some intellectual point or other (this is turning out to be a big week for personal questions) whether she ever went to college. Turns out the respondent has a Ph.D. During the preprandial meeting of the Student Aid Fund, people kept using the word "interface." I shall never be able to make a go of it at institutional gatherings until I learn how to use that word in a sentence. Others seem to employ it blithely both as a verb and a noun. I have no idea what it means in either guise, and suspect it came into being in the first place as a result of a lisp on the part of somebody in an interfaith movement.

December 13

In a television chat between Eric Sevareid and Charles Kuralt, both of them tieless to symbolize their retirement from CBS, Sevareid says, while I silently applaud, "You can't take the picture of an idea. You have to use words." Having thrown that tasty bone to us purveyors of print, he then defends television by saying that less of its time is devoted to advertisements than is space in newspapers and magazines. True enough, perhaps, statistically, but it is easier to skip the ads in our media than in his. I rarely look at the ads in *The New Yorker*, which is an heretical thing to say since they support me, and perhaps even worse to confess this very week when we are mourning the death of Joe Russell, who for so many years presided over the magazine's business affairs.

Contrarily, however, there are many people (I run into them all the time) who seem to enjoy *The New Yorker* principally *because* of its ads, and who may not even be aware that we have just finished running Hannah Arendt's enormous three-part treatise on Thinking, possibly the greatest compendium of ideas that do not lend themselves to graphic illustration in our history. I know of at least one senior *New Yorker* editor who could not get through the first page of the first part of the Arendt opus. I proposed to Ellie when they came out, that, inasmuch as she is the ranking intellectual in our family, she read them for both of us, but even she bogged down somewhere between Orrefors crystal and Dewar's Scotch.

December 14

Sheila McGrath stops by with an expense check. She says we contract writers may be eligible for a *New Yorker* dental plan some time next year and that everybody is waiting for that before going to the dentist. There must be a lot of aching teeth in our halls. Sheila is fit to be tied because somebody on the staff—she does not yet know who the culprit was, but woe betide him or her when she finds out—gave an editorial personnel list to the Hotel Algonquin, which wanted to complement the observation of its seventy-fifth birthday by sending everybody on the staff a Christmas card. The last time this sort of thing happened was when a writer—who not long afterward forfeited his office—gave out such a list to a Ban-the-Bomb group, an indiscretion that infuriated the management not because it was pro-Bomb but because the roster contains some unlisted telephone numbers of editors who would just as soon not be bombarded at home by importunate outside writers who have come up with the definitive response, in seven tight-packed parts, to Hannah Arendt's thoughts on thinking.

Sheila says that one of her jobs as office manager is to escort friends of our advertising department around the editorial premises, since our business-oriented colleagues do not feel comfortable on our supposedly creative floors. George Green, our corporate president, sent one such character to Sheila not long ago, without identification, and she gave him her tongue-in-cheek tour. This includes asking the visitor if he would like to see our complaints department, and then opening a door immediately behind which lies—God knows why—a brick wall. Roger Angell once affixed a sign to that dead-end door reading "Enter here for salary raises," but the management was then having some difficulties with employees who thought they were underpaid, and the jape was unappreciated and hastily removed. Sheila's tourist was not amused either; he turned out to be a large minority shareholder in the magazine, to whom editorial japes were of considerably less concern than full-page color ads.

When Ellie heard about my gold strike at the New York Public Library, she resolved to ascertain whether some old bits of the metal she had lying around would be as handsomely appraised as my odd cuff link. Today she hands me a gnarled hunk of gold and urges me to contribute it to the library. When I ask her what in the world it is, she says it is her first husband's mother's dental plate. That lady, apparently, took proper care of herself; we are forthwith credited with a further charitable contribution in the amount of one hundred and twenty-two dollars and ninety-six cents. I may be the only person on earth who can honestly claim to have held in his very own hand his wife's ex-husband's mother's false teeth.

To dinner at the Kermit Lansners'. Ed Diamond, whom I last saw when we were joustingly promoting books of our own at a Boston store, is there; he is working on a psychohistorical study of Jimmy Carter. Ed says that when he was returning to New York on the Eastern shuttle last week, he asked a stewardess passing out magazines for a *New Yorker*, and she replied, "We dropped it last week, and hundreds of people have been asking for it ever since." That is the sort of intelligence that investors taking Sheila McGrath's guided tour would probably receive with mixed feelings.

December 15

Lunch at the Century with Ned Chase, now in publishing, who says he sends his actor son Chevy, now on the West Coast, regular shipments of East Coast magazines to help alleviate the despair of living out there. Ned spent three years at *The New Yorker*, many years ago, as a checker, and he reminds me that he checked my Profiles both on Frank Sinatra and on Leon M. Birkhead, a feisty clergyman who ran a now long-gone anti-fascist organization called Friends of Democracy. Birkhead, a conspicuously non-Elmer Gantry–like minister, was a friend of Sinclair Lewis, and I drove up to Williamstown, Massachusetts, to talk to the author about him. Lewis had me to lunch and, while he got very drunk, was also very helpful. (After that one was published, I received some feisty letters from people like the long-gone Gerald L. K. Smith.) Ned recalls no particular difficulties with either of those pieces, but he tells me of his worst checking experience ever. He had had a tennis date one day, was in a hurry to get his whites from a dry cleaner, leapt over a counter there, caught his eye on a hook, ripped his eyelid, went to a hospital to have it stitched, arrived at *The New Yorker* with a patch over the eye, and was at once instructed to check a book review by Hamilton Basso that was being rushed to press.

With only one eye, and pressed for time, Ned didn't bother to authenticate either the name of the book, "Raintree County," or of the author, Ross Lockridge. He just assumed that the copy had *them* right. But what the review had was "Raintree Coun*try*," by Ross Lock*wood*. And thus the magazine went to press. Shortly afterward, Ross Lockridge committed suicide, and Walter Winchell, who had had no love for *The New Yorker* ever since St. Clair McKelway had torn him apart in a Profile, insinuated that it was the magazine's mistakes that had brought about the tragedy. The mistakes were of the sort that would normally make Harold Ross scratch his own eyes out, but in this instance all Ross did, Ned recalls admiringly, was to write a letter to one of Winchell's bosses denouncing the columnist for his allegation and, while he was at it, defending his checking department.

Ned wonders how the magazine operates these days and why certain writers have contributed to it over the years and certain others have not. His guess is that the main difference between *New Yorker* writers and other writers is that the former are characterized by irony and wit. True enough, I guess, but there have been times when I wished more of the people who contribute to us now had more of these two ingredients in their creative make-up.

Back at the office, I receive a phone call from an editor at *Chicago* magazine, who wants me to write a piece for him—witty, ironic—on the political intrigues as a result of which Hannah Gray, the president *pro tem* of Yale, has been appointed the full-time president not of that academy but of the University of Chicago. I am puzzled, and say that I have some acquaintance with shenanigans and other affairs at Harvard, but that I really know very little about what transpires up at New Haven. "But you did that piece not long ago on Yale alumni," he says.

"That was Princeton."

He retreats in confusion. At least I am firmly associated in Midwest editorial circles with the Ivy League.

December 16

Ned Chase asked me yesterday how many Profiles I had written for *The New Yorker*, and I answered, with airiness no checker would tolerate, "Oh, somewhere over a hundred, I suppose." Out of curiosity, I stop in at our editorial library this morning to check that out with Helen Stark, and she informs me, deflatingly, that I have done only fifty-four Profiles, in ninety-three parts. I thought it was more than one hundred *people*. I do not expect to live long enough—quick trips to England notwithstanding—to make my own grossly swollen estimate of my productivity come true.

Pat Crow, holding a page proof, accosts me in an eighteenth-floor corridor. I assume he wants to discuss details of our non-smoking wager. Not at all. He wants to know whether or not in my opinion the "s" in "summer" preceding "Olympics" should be upper-case or lower-case. I have no opinion in the matter, though I must have used the phrase. (I never read my pieces in the magazine; too much chance of finding an error it is too late to change.) I suggest that Pat ask Weekes. Hobey Weekes has retired as our preceptor in charge of such matters, but he still comes by occasionally, because he is working on a revision of *The New Yorker*'s definitive style book. Our styles have changed over the years. We used to insist on an extra "s" after the apostrophe in s-ending words—i.e., "Harold Ross's magazine"— but lately we tolerate phrases like "Hobey Weekes' style book." We are one of the few publications I know of, though, that has steadfastly clung to the insertion of a comma between the penultimate and ultimate words of a series—i.e., "Winken comma Blinken *comma* and Nod."

But Weekes is evidently not around today, and Crow has to put a piece— he does not tell me what one—to press. Pat accosts me again after lunch. We have gone to press. He brings up the Olympics again. Now, suddenly, I wonder who is horning in on my territory, and demand elucidation. Pat says I have nothing to worry about; he has merely been editing an Andy Logan political piece in which she leads off by alluding to Los Angeles' having beaten out New York as the host city for the 1980 Olympic Games scheduled to take place between spring and fall. But that isn't so, I say. Pat blanches. It is true, I tell him, that New York has lost, but L. A. hasn't won: The International Olympic Committee has not yet even met to decide on the city's application. Pat demands to know why I didn't bring that up this morning. I point out that the only matter *he* brought up was the capitalization of a single word. He decides not to stop the presses or rip open the forms or whatever would have to be done to qualify Andy's assertion, and says that anyway she assured him that Los Angeles was a shoo-in. Maybe so, but it would be more in keeping with *The New Yorker*'s traditional editorial cautiousness to wait for confirmation from Lord Killanin.

Should we turn out to be wrong, will *More* magazine jump us for this one? If it does, I should be a shoo-in to win my non-smoking competition with Pat Crow. Of course, should he feel obliged to commit hara kiri over the incident, I suppose all bets would be off.

At the Harvard Club, it is an unwritten rule that one does not play backgammon for more than a dollar a point during lunch, but that after that there is no limit. When I stop by on my way home, nickel-a-point players (a "nickel," of course, being five dollars), are in bloodthirsty session. One of them has just returned from Paris on a Concorde, and says that the nicest thing about supersonic travel is that the airline takes your hat and coat at your departure airport, and you don't have to worry about them again until you reach your destination. But if like me you never wear a hat, half this deluxe service doesn't matter much at the outset, and if like me, further, you have a topcoat so old and dirty your wife is forever threatening to throw it away, having it returned to you might be not measurably an improvement over losing it.

We go to the Lee Falks' for dinner. Lee is euphoric, because of all the publicity there has been about one of his comic-strip characters, The Phantom, getting married after all these years. I am in a testy mood (largely, I suspect, because Ellie told me that my failure to be harshly critical of a chapter of her book, which I liked, was unhusbandly), so I suggest to Lee that maybe he should devise a really spectacular marriage for his other strip—have Mandrake the Magician, that is, wed his servant Lothar, and thus achieve a crosscultural, interracial, homosexual union that would stand *sui generis*, at least in comic strips, for a long time to come.

Lee has a new dog, which he has named Mandrake. Thank God he is naming animals after himself. His last dog, though not named after me directly, was called Jacques, and used to try to bite me whenever I came within range.

Abe Burrows is at the Falks'. He and Carin have sold their house in Provincetown, because, he says, they never seemed to go there enough. Abe is writing his memoirs. He reminds me of the time he drove through my tomato patch after a cocktail party at my Truro place. He has an all-embracing memory that will sharply differentiate his memoirs from mine. (Also, he has my Profile of him to draw on.) He could easily have avoided the tomato patch, moreover, if he had looked where he was going. There is much talk, at dinner, naturally, about Outer Cape Cod, and, because all present knew him, of Mark Rothko, whose works have lately been the subject of considerable litigation.

I met Mark the same summer I met Ellie, and she had us both to dinner. Mark was zonked. I brought along some Truro oysters. That was back in the days when one could find oysters, not to mention mussels and steamers, in Truro in abundance. Now we are mainly reduced to sea clams. Mark was painting a mural for Harvard University at the time, and, on hearing that I was writing a book about the institution, favored me with an anecdote that I requote: "After working in Cambridge for a few days and going to all those horrible Faculty Club lunches, I found the air shuttle to New York didn't give me time enough to regain my composure. So I took to going back by train. I'd get on the sleeper with a bottle of Scotch and by the next morning I would just about have recovered from Harvard." I didn't learn until long after my book "Harvard" was published that Nathan Pusey, to whose conservative tastes one might have thought Rothko's work might not have appealed, had actually insisted—over the demurrers of some *really* conservative members of the Harvard establishment—that the painter be given a free hand to execute his commission in any way that appealed to *him*. Maybe I should tell Chase Peterson that this sort of thing is what Harvard is all about.

December 17

People who do not know my dog turn apprehensive within ten feet of her, but actually Rainbow has never bitten anyone but me. That was excusable: I had my hand in her mouth, and she sneezed. She has excellent teeth; went right through to the bone. Walking her on Eighty-eighth Street this morning, I notice in the gutter (it was not there yesterday) a discarded Christmas tree—rather, the mere trunk of one, with not a single pine needle left on it. There is surely only one conclusion to arrive at from this phenomenon: That there are people in New York City who do not throw out one year's tree until they have obtained its successor.

December 18

Jimmy Carter visited me in a dream last night. (So did George C. Marshall, but that is less uncommon, and besides he was still only a four-star general when he dropped in.) The president had come to Truro—a special rail line was opened, or rehabilitated—to look into the possibility of starting up a large new urban community in an undeveloped section (on the ocean side, our side) of the Cape Cod National Seashore. Mr. Carter took me aside to solicit my views on the venture. I told the president to be wary of new urban developments, because, frankly, the cores of many existing ones had shown themselves to be susceptible to rot. He was surprised; he hadn't heard about that. I urged him to look into it, and he said he certainly would before he proceeded any further. I had read in the papers that he was looking tired, after nearly a year in office, but I must say that he appeared extremely fit.

Terry, Joey, and Tony are all in town this holiday week, and Jinny is giving a party at her apartment, to which Ellie and I have been invited. E. cannot go, because *we* are giving a dinner for Joan Mitchell, just in from Paris and one of the featured characters in E.'s forthcoming book, so I go over to Jinny's alone, and feel strange, surrounded by so much of my past life—my furniture, my books, my sons, my sisters, just about everything except for my old friends from Scarborough (who would be present if it were not sleeting) and my dog Barge.

I can't stay long in any event, with guests due at home, among them the Patrick Smiths and the Harold Rosenbergs. There is much drinking before and during dinner, and at the table one lady present calls another lady present "a fucking liar," whereupon the addressee retreats to our bedroom to lick her wounds, and, conceivably, to devise an appropriate retort. Patrick says when order has been more or less restored that Andrew Porter is paid seven hundred and fifty dollars for each music department he writes for *The New Yorker*. Harold and I do not blink. I have no idea whether or not this statement is true, but in any event it is the first time in forty years that I have heard from any source what any contributor to the magazine gets paid for anything.* I know the terms of my own remuneration, and obviously Harold knows his, but this is not the sort of information that we contributors exchange among one another, in or out of the office. Now that we are on the subject of *The New Yorker*, Harold says, to my surprise, that *he* hasn't been able to read the Hannah Arendt series, either. It is his contention that Bill Shawn heard her give a lecture on the subject of Thinking, and asked her to put her views in print; Miss Arendt, Harold goes on, said that she couldn't believe the magazine's readers would be interested but Mr. Shawn said that didn't matter, it would be good for them.

December 19

To dinner, down Park Avenue, at the apartment of Sidney Gluck and Bel Kaufman. They have a Chinese cook, a woman who comes in a couple of times a week. After the meal, the cook is ushered into the dining room and we must all clap hands. The same adulatory practice is observed at the Henry Hydes', who have a full-time male Chinese cook. In my experience, this never happens with non-Chinese cooks. Can it be written into the

---

* It is probably safe for me to disclose now that in 1942, when I was in the Army and my mother was handling my finances, Bill Shawn wrote to her, while passing along checks for three of my Army Life pieces, "Jack is rich." Each check was for $150.00. Coming across an old letter like that makes one more conscious of inflation than any number of reports issued by the Federal Reserve Board.

employment contracts of Chinese ones that they are entitled to applause after every repast?

The last time we were at the Glucks, Sidney drew me aside after dinner and asked in muted tones if I would like a glimpse of his special books. I girded myself expectantly for a diverting pornographic interlude, and was a bit let down to find that he specializes in Marxist literature.

Lester and Barbara Tuchman are present, and Barbara asks me considerately how "The China Hands" is doing. I reply that it has been remaindered; one of my sons saw it on sale for a dollar the other day. I ask Barbara if any of *her* books has ever been remaindered, and she says yes, but that was merely the English edition of one of them. She is working on a history of the fourteenth century, which will no doubt make that hitherto unsung era hugely fashionable.

The Arnold Newmans are also members of the cook's latest claque. Arnold reminds me that we first met, ten years ago, at the King David Hotel in Jerusalem, in the euphoric aftermath of the Six Day War; he was taking photographs to illustrate a piece of mine on Israel for *Holiday*. I liberated a brand-new pair of Syrian Army pants from the Golan Heights, but they were too big for me. *New Yorker* pieces occasionally produce lucrative spinoffs, but in this instance the reverse proved true. I interviewed three Israelis whose experiences didn't seem to fit into a travel story—Chaim Herzog, the general whose radio broadcasts during the Six Day War did for his country what Ed Murrow had done for his during the Second World War; Dan Ben-Amotz, the Art Buchwald of Tel Aviv; and Abie Nathan, the inveterate crusader for Mid-East peace—and sold *The New Yorker* an article about them. It never ran, but that was only a decade ago, and Shawn has held pieces longer than that.

The Glucks have one of those compressed-paper logs blazing in their fireplace, and when I say that we use them ourselves, and how different they are (though much more manageable) from the real wood I used to burn when I lived in the suburbs, Bel says that my remark is indicative of my Jewish guilt, which stumps me. I don't feel any guilt of any sort, except perhaps for having once wrongly suspected Sidney of collecting dirty books.

December 20

Christmas cards are coming in. We receive two weirdos this morning. One from a couple who wish all their friends copulation for 1978, another from a couple whose card bears a photograph of two naked women climbing into an ancient automobile, in pursuit of what vehicular thrills one hesitates to speculate. Eleanor Harding, my wartime general's widow, who is represented by a much more seasonable card, says on it that at the age of eighty-seven she is feeling fine, but has reached a stage of life at which she finds she cannot enjoy the company of her grandchildren—she has six—when she encounters them en masse.

Back in the days when first-class postage was more of a bargain, we scarcely had room, at Christmas time, to display all the cards we got. For a number of years, I received holiday remembrances each December from Mabel Dodge Luhan, about whom I once wrote a Talk story; from Meyer Davis, whose band I once mentioned in a piece; and from Frank Erickson, although to the best of my knowledge the bookmaker and I had never had any dealings, professional or social. Jinny and I, in turn, would send out several hundred cards annually, some of them to people the spelling of whose names we weren't quite certain of when, on December 21st or 22nd, we rushed bundles of greetings to the post office. The comparatively few Christmas cards that Ellie and I are sending out now bear photographs of David, standing alongside a wheelbarrow laden with vegetables from his Truro garden. The photographs are in full color. By the time we have paid for them, the cost of each tomato he harvested this year will have risen to approximately one dollar and thirty-seven cents.

December 22

I had a cab driver yesterday who said it took him forty minutes to traverse a single midtown block, during which stretch he had three fares, the first two of which gave up—though not, of course, without paying their tariff—in despair. "In this business, you win some and lose some," he said. "At the end of the year it all evens out." Spoken like a true philosopher—and one, moreover, who has learned how to get rich while idling.

Ellie is working so hard that she isn't doing much celebrating this holiday season, but she does take an hour off to accompany me to Barbara Kerr's cocktail party, among the last remaining social functions at which one can be fairly certain of bumping into practically everybody one has ever met. Here are Daphne Hellman and Arthur Schlesinger, there are Jack Bingham and Nora Sayre, farther along, fighting like everyone else for standing room, are Elizabeth Janeway and Francis Plimpton. I fall into conversation with these last—both trustees of Barnard—about all the fuss there has lately been about who will or will not be the new president of Yale. Plimpton (who went to Amherst but whose many honorary degrees include an LL.D from Yale in 1972) predicts trouble for the new Yale president, whoever it may be, from Yale's alumni: He says they tend to be so stuffy that at Antigua, where many of them frolic on vacations, they even snubbed Kingman Brewster. It is hard for me to conceive that many Harvard alumni, no matter how hidebound, would be deliberately rude to a Harvard president. Of course, no Harvard president has harbored William Sloane Coffin as his chaplain.

I have a call today from a man associated with the Hoover Institution at

Stanford University. He wants to know if I would be interested in turning over my papers to its Far East archives. What papers? Well, I was in the Foreign Service, wasn't I? No. But I have spent much time in China, haven't I? Not exactly—twenty-three days, in the spring of 1973. Well, I have written a book about China, and often a manuscript is much longer than the published version, and perhaps the unpublished parts of my manuscript might have some permanent historical value.

This guy doesn't give up easily, is a real fighter, perhaps should be considered for the presidency of Yale. I say that, unfortunately, there was nothing of consequence in my manuscript that didn't appear in the book. (I refrain from adding that a couple of sentences in the hardcover edition had to be deleted from the paperback, to avoid a threatened libel suit.) My caller is rattled, but not routed. He says he will write me a letter and explain in greater detail what he wants.

After he hangs up, I suddenly remember that I have an entire un-published manuscript about my 1973 trip to China. Maybe the Stanford University Press would like to bring it out.

December 23

Christmas makes itself manifest in various ways. To those of us who live in Dumas territory, for whom Christmas without a Bûche de Noël would be unthinkable, we know the grim day is drawing near when a Hertz rental truck takes up its station outside the bakery's door. The shop doesn't have enough floor space to handle its seasonal volume of traffic in creamed logs. I stay home today, to "help" with Christmas. I attempt to mediate a no-holds-barred battle between David and Lexy, over the question of whether Rainbow's Christmas present should be wrapped with or without a ribbon. But my observation that the dog not only may not care one way or the other but may not even care about Christmas (or, when it comes to that, Hanukah, either) is drowned out.

Ellie feels we should have a shared cultural experience with the boys before the holiday season slips by. Luckily, she cannot obtain tickets to some ballet she thinks would be just right. Searching for a suitable alternative, I find that the Rangers and the Cleveland Barons are playing at the Garden tonight. What could be more fitting than a hockey game! After all, the boys' grandparents lived in Cleveland. The Patrick Smiths go with us. During the game, Patrick tells us about two friends of his, childless, who have a stuffed monkey that they take with them everywhere, including the opera; the husband has special oversized pockets sewn in his suits, to tote the monkey around in, and they send out Christmas cards in the monkey's name. Our own eccentricities, like giving presents to our dog, seem suddenly mild.

The Rangers are leading 5–4, with two minutes yet to go, when we depart, hoping thereby to retrieve our car from a parking garage before the crush starts. I wonder whatever happened to the bright-red set of hockey goals that Bob Wolf made for our pond in Scarborough. We used to have pick-up hockey games there every winter weekend (weather, obviously, permitting), with men, women, children, and dogs all participating. Goals scored by dogs did not count. One game was highlighted by a touching display of filial devotion. A neighbor and I were scrambling for a loose puck, and he checked me rather more savagely than was our custom. Not long after I had picked myself up and returned to the fray, there was a melée in front of one of the goals, and when it was untangled we discovered my assailant at the bottom of the heap, bleeding slightly, with all three of my sons on top of him.

December 24

According to Robin Herman's account of the Rangers game in this morning's *Times*, nothing much happened in the final two minutes. Ellie is amazed to hear that Robin Herman is a woman. It turns out E. has never heard, further, about Ms. Herman's efforts to gain admission to locker rooms, for post-game interviews, on an equal footing with her male counterparts. Maybe the trouble with women's lib is that some of its advocates are too preoccupied with theory to keep up with practice.

Ellie has a special place where she stows things to worry about. I find there a Christmas card signed "Helen," saying she still hopes to see me "here." It is from Helen Suzman, and the "here" means South Africa. E. had thought it was from Helen Frankenthaler and had put it in her worry pile because she couldn't comprehend what Helen F. meant.

Christmas Eve dinner, chez nous, with members from all sides of the family (my stepmother's sister, for instance), and a few special non-related guests, like Warren Munsell, who is as sprightly as ever, and at peace with death. He has already set up a trip to Burgundy for next summer, when he will be eighty-nine, and says that he is looking forward to it, provided, of course, that he is still alive. Ellie and I get far the better of our annual exchange of gifts with Warren. We always give him one bottle of rye, and he always gives us two bottles of champagne. My sister Joan is of the opinion that there are too few gifts on hand for my grandson Ian. But for heaven's sake, he is not even two; he is quite content, like any normal kid of his age, to play with ashtrays.

December 25

Three dishwasher loads of glassware to cope with this morning, plus further exchanges of gifts. I seem to have got E. the wrong kind of cape and the wrong kind of luggage. She gives me a sleepcoat, which is great, because all the buttons have disappeared from my only other nightwear. E. wants to go to a church and hear some music, so we hie ourselves over to Heavenly Rest. The officiating clergypersons seem to be largely black and female, though this bastion of High Episcopalianism has not yet, so far as I can perceive, got itself a black woman minister. We arrive too late for the sermon, which is a break for us, and just in time for the collection, which is a break for the Church of the Heavenly Rest.

We pay our annual Christmas call on the Henry Hydes, and bring them some beach-plum brandy, which I decant from our large jug into an unlabelled jar. Lisa thanks us profusely and sets the jar down with a big batch of gifts; when she next comes upon it she will have forgotten what it is and take it for somebody's travel-kit Lavoris. We drank some of the home brew ourselves after dinner last night, and then after everybody else had left, David and two of his teenage friends finished up all the undrained brandy glasses. David seems all right today. I got drunk for the first time ever, at about his age, on apricot brandy, during Prohibition, at the home of a fellow editor of our high-school paper. His parents were out. We had just put that week's issue to bed. The apricot brandy put me to bed, and I couldn't get out of it the following morning. The two boys I swigged with that watershed night both died young. Probably no connection, but that apricot brandy certainly was lethal.

December 26

The *Times* carries a report that charcoal cooking may be carcinogenic. Cigarettes, bacon, now this. Cancer research is inexorably depriving us of—or at any rate making us apprehensive about indulging in—all our pleasures. The day may not be far off when the surgeon general will be warning against sex.

A tennis day, Terry joining our group this Monday, and afterward he and Jonathan Baumbach come back to the apartment for oysters (Ter brought us a batch from the Cape, for Christmas) and Bloody Marys. If Bloody Marys can give you cancer, we are all doomed. The *Times* has been running a series of articles about the involvement of journalists with the C.I.A., and my son wants to know if I have ever worked for that agency. Negative. But I have no doubt that I have often been briefed by C.I.A. men attached to foreign embassies, and while they may have fed me some propaganda, the knowledgeability they also shared with me has always been most welcome. Terry, incidentally, not long ago ran into a C.I.A. man who spent nineteen years in a Communist Chinese prison. The only mail he was allowed to receive was from his mother, who along with letters sent him three authorized publications from the United States— the *National Guardian*, the *Worker*, and *The New Yorker*. In due course, the prisoner was denied access to the *Guardian*, because it was in favor of legalizing the use of marijuana. Next the *Worker* was taken away, because its editors seemed to prefer Russia to China. He was left solely dependent, for enlightenment about his native land, on *The New Yorker*. The ideal reader.

Walking on Park Avenue, I spot a newspaper reporter I know hailing a cab. He lives down in the Village; what is he doing here on a holiday afternoon? He may have been attending services at the Church of the Heavenly Rest, or spying for the C.I.A., but it is more likely that he has been visiting his mistress, a Madison Avenue resident. Just as he is about to get into a taxi, I play a dirty trick on him. I hail him and wish him a Merry Christmas. To cap his bad luck, there is a fire one block away. He could easily be the first reporter on the scene, but how would he ever be able to explain how he happened to be in the neighborhood to begin with? He drives off, after wishing me a Merry Christmas singularly low on mirth.

December 27

Prime Minister Begin has left Egypt, and, to give Ellie a chance to work uninterruptedly for a week, I leave for West Cornwall, taking David, Lexy, and Rainbow along. The boys are going to be skiing, and E. suggests that rather than drive back and forth to the slopes to deliver and fetch them, I take my research with me and work at a table in the lodge. She says Francine Gray used to do this while her kids skied. (Is *that* how Francine was inspired to write those peculiar sex scenes in "Lovers and Tyrants"?) I tell E. I would rather commit myself to the additional driving, but, come to think of it, a ski slope might not be a bad spot at which to reflect seriously on terrorism.

December 28

Eight A.M. temperature: five degrees. I am gladder than ever that I have given up skiing.

For some years now—ever since that nasty leg break that converted me into an incurable coward—I have been preaching the virtues of non-skiing to anybody who will listen to me. I think of myself as a reformed sinner working the evangelical hustings. But as sometimes lamentably happens to evangelists whose families simply will not quit cussing, my family dotes on skiing. Nearly every spring, accordingly, when school holidays come along, and when paterfamiliases luckier than I am trek with their loved ones to

Aruba or Guadeloupe, I find myself shivering in lonely daytime meditation at some Vermont or New Hampshire or Colorado pseudo-chalet, waiting for après-ski time, when, if I and they are blessed, my wife and children will return to me intact. It has been a heavy cross for me to bear, but I have managed. I am not, after all, an *anti*-skier. That would be atheism. I am merely an agnostic.

A couple of years ago, when I had hoped to celebrate Easter in Jamaica or Nassau, Ellie and the boys resolved by near-unanimous vote—there was one abstention—that what we needed was a Swissair package trip to the Alps, and specifically to Lech, in Austria. Lech, which rhymes with "ech," is part of the Arlberg, practically the birthplace of modern skiing, whence Satan dispatched Hannes Schneider to the American shores some forty years ago to debouch and enslave millions. I had abstained, instead of voting in the negative, because it seemed important to me then to betake myself to the scene of the origin of the whole business and to Make a Statement—the non-skier's variant, so to speak, of streaking. If Billy Graham could go to places like Las Vegas to spread *his* word, I had reasoned, why should I shun the Tyrol?

We spent a pleasant enough two weeks at Lech, in 1974. David, then thirteen, set what has got to be a world's skiing record: For fourteen straight days, he had the same kind of chocolate cake for lunch. I myself preferred the *bratwurst-und-sauerkraut*. The chocolate-cake king always complains at home that we don't serve enough sauerkraut. In Lech, where they all but give the stuff away, he wouldn't touch it. That is indicative of how skiing can skew one's sense of values.

Ellie, for her part, normally as scared of self-service elevators as I am of T-bars or Poma lifts, shrugged off her apprehensions in the Tyrol and blithely entrusted herself to cable cars so frail that I could not believe a hawk would board one without a parachute. When at the end of a long Alpine day my frau would miraculously descend to my level, she would tell me about butterflies she'd seen above the timberline. "Yellow butterflies," she would say. "It's unbelievable."

To a non-skier, nothing connected with skiing is unbelievable. What taxes his credulity is that so many people can voluntarily devote so many of their waking hours to such pagan rites. E. would also occasionally complain in Austria, après ski, that she was too stiff to schottische. A non-skier is never stiff. That is one of the beauties of the non-sport. One can indulge in it at any time under any weather conditions. Also, the cash savings—no skis, no poles, no boots, no parkas, no lift tickets, no orthopedists' bills—can be enormous. The only person who saved more at Lech than I did was a teenage waitress at our pension who said that our outrageous demands upon her kept her too busy to ski, and who on top of that got tips.

I was one of the few non-skiers at Lech that spring. I do not include in this category, of course, very old people with canes. They are *can't*-skiers, and I had no idea what the handful of them I bumped into at the Arlberg were doing on that scene. Maybe they had got on the wrong bus at the Zurich airport. I could not legitimately count them as converts to my cause, of whom, to tell the honest truth, I made precious few during that revival meeting.

I thought I had one woman leaning my way after I described to her, at graphic length, my leg fractures and their intricate surgical aftermath. But after letting me think I was making some real progress she said devilishly that she had not long before broken her *back* skiing and, following six months in a body cast, had returned without hesitation to the slopes. When, similarly, at a cocktail party our middle-aged host asked me which local runs I liked best, perhaps, *nur*, overland to Zurs? and I explained that I had abandoned skiing because of my shattered tibia and fibula, he said that his mother had broken both her legs skiing at the age of seventy-two, and now, at eighty, would be late for this soirée because she was on a twilight schuss. I got so discouraged that I would now and then try to keep out of conversational hot water by dissembling, and by discoursing with lepidopteral deceit about saffron butterflies of my recent acquaintance. It is easier sometimes to tell a soaring lie than to face up to the mundane truth.

By not skiing, I get more work done today—driving or no driving—than in the two previous weeks altogether.

December 29

The *Times* carries a full-page ad for one of its subsidiaries, the Arno Press. The headline, a big, bold one, reads, "We Are Not the University of Arno." The point of this is supposed to be that the press boasts so many celebrated books and authors that it is just about as good as a real university. But is the copywriter responsible for the headline aware of the double entendre he has concocted? Out in the Marshall Islands there is a lovely atoll called Arno. The legend is that for many years young Marshallese women were there taught the arts of love. Their training area was known as the University of Arno. Reportorial conscientiousness made me take a boat over to Arno from Majuro, to seek out the fabled finishing school. But I never did find it, and nobody at Arno would direct me to it. Perhaps it didn't exist. Perhaps I asked the wrong kinds of questions. I am tempted to propose to the Arno Press that I write a book about it.

December 30

Lexy thinks he broke his thumb skiing yesterday, the same one he broke playing ball last spring. So I spend much of this morning taking him over to Sharon to be X-rayed and examined. (Should I write to Chase Peterson, at Harvard, that my faith and trust in the thitherto unknown orthopedist who receives us is immensely enhanced when I perceive on his office wall two diplomas signed by Nathan Pusey?) There is no fracture, merely a sprain or bruise or some such. We get this good clinical news in time for me to drive up into Massachusetts to pick up David, who has gone skiing there with a friend. I take Rainbow along, and as we are returning to West Cornwall in the early-evening dark, she blows the opportunity of a dog's lifetime. She is lying down on the front seat with her head on my lap, and thus misses a chance to bark at three deer that loom up at roadside. It was almost exactly one year ago, in this same setting, that I last saw any deer. Nineteen seventy-seven, in terms of dramatic unity, has been absolutely Aristotelian.

December 31

New Year's Eve Day. We have no plans. We have no invitations for tonight. That is just as well, for if I work straight through to midnight I can probably finish up Clutterbuck. A tidy way, all things considered, to wrap up a year.

I have already framed a tentative agenda for next year. I am going to stop smoking, stop taking bad doubles at backgammon, get myself into South Africa, and seek out my brother.

Index